VISUAL C#™ .NET DEVELOPER'S HANDBOOK™

JOHN PAUL MUELLER

ISBN: 0-7821-4047-5   672 pages   US $59.99

Now that you've learned the essentials of C#, it's time to start using the power of the language to develop complex enterprise applications. *Visual C# .NET Developer's Handbook* details C#'s strengths and gets you started building real-world projects. Author John Mueller also details what C# doesn't do well, to help you through difficult programming situations and provide you with solutions for your own applications. As you'll discover, C# combines the ease of Visual Basic with the power required to tap into both the .NET Framework and the Windows API. You'll master standard application development with C#, including creating controls and components, working with threads and Active Directory, and programming security. You'll also master C#'s database connectivity capabilities through ADO.NET and its support for distributed development. You'll be able to build flexible applications that can connect desktops over a LAN or that work over the web with XML and SOAP, or even provide wireless access to mobile devices.

.NET FRAMEWORK
IN SEARCH OF THE

JOHN PAUL MUELLER

ISBN: 0-7821-4134-X   592

D1319951

If you've begun programming using Microsoft's .NET Framework, you've discovered a lot of new and improved functionality. But, more than likely, you've also discovered a lot of missing functionality. Indeed, a third of the functions supported by the old Win32 API are not yet supported by .NET. Although you may not at first notice the loss of Win32 API functionality in .NET, the more you program, the more you'll realize how essential it is. As a programmer, you will not want to do without these solutions. *.NET Framework Solutions: In Search of the Lost Win32 API* is a complete guide to your options for dealing with the functionality missing from .NET. As you'll learn, some functions are handily situated within Visual Basic or C#. In most cases, however, you'll need to access the old Win32 API from the .NET Framework. This is demanding work, but this book makes it easy, walking you through every step and paying special attention to the work of managing memory manually—the most error-prone part of the process. The topics covered inside are as varied as the missing functionality: direct hardware access, low-level security control, certain aspects of OS access, support for multimedia and utilities, and DirectX. You also get hard-to-find information on COM access, plus a collection of examples—dealing with DirectX and the MMC Snap-ins—that unite COM and Win32 access in especially illuminating ways. Over time, you can expect to see the .NET Framework expanded to include much of what it now lacks. But your programming tasks can't wait, and *.NET Framework Solutions* makes you productive—today.

MASTERING™ C#™ DATABASE PROGRAMMING

JASON PRICE

ISBN: 0-7821-4183-8   800 pages   US $59.99

Any programmer creating web applications needs to understand database programming. *Mastering C# Database Programming* helps you attain this valuable skill with Microsoft's hot new object-oriented programming language, specifically designed for the .NET platform. With coverage of advanced topics not discussed in any other C# database programming titles, this book is your logical next step after *Mastering Visual C# .NET* or *Visual C# .NET Programming*. While it provides focused coverage of ADO and how it relates to C#, it also tackles other complex topics including transactions, Windows forms, Web Forms, XML, and Web Services. This book is ideal for veteran C# programmers who want to learn database programming, as well as Visual C++ and VB programmers who are learning C#.

C# COMPLETE

C# Complete

SYBEX®

SAN FRANCISCO ► LONDON

Associate Publisher: Joel Fugazzotto

Acquisitions Editor: Denise Santoro Lincoln

Developmental Editor: Carol Henry

Compilation Editor: Matt Tagliaferri

Production Editor: Kelly Winquist

Copyeditor: Rebecca Rider

Compositor: Rozi Harris, Interactive Composition Corporation

Proofreaders: Nancy Riddiough, Yariv Rabinovitch, Emily Hsuan, Leslie Higbee Light, Laurie O'Connell, Monique Vandenberg

Indexer: Nancy Guenther

Book Designer: Maureen Forys, Happenstance Type-O-Rama

Cover Designer: Design Site

Cover Illustrator: Suza Scalora, PhotoDisc

Copyright © 2003 SYBEX Inc., 1151 Marina Village Parkway, Alameda, CA 94501. World rights reserved. No part of this publication may be stored in a retrieval system, transmitted, or reproduced in any way, including but not limited to photocopy, photograph, magnetic, or other record, without the prior agreement and written permission of the publisher.

Library of Congress Card Number: 2002115481

ISBN: 0-7821-4203-6

SYBEX and the SYBEX logo are either registered trademarks or trademarks of SYBEX Inc. in the United States and/or other countries.

Screen reproductions produced with FullShot 99. FullShot 99 © 1991–1999 Inbit Incorporated. All rights reserved.
FullShot is a trademark of Inbit Incorporated.

Screen reproductions produced with Collage Complete.
Collage Complete is a trademark of Inner Media Inc.

Netscape Communications, the Netscape Communications logo, Netscape, and Netscape Navigator are trademarks of Netscape Communications Corporation.

Netscape Communications Corporation has not authorized, sponsored, endorsed, or approved this publication and is not responsible for its content. Netscape and the Netscape Communications Corporate Logos are trademarks and trade names of Netscape Communications Corporation. All other product names and/or logos are trademarks of their respective owners.

Internet screen shot(s) using Microsoft Internet Explorer reprinted by permission from Microsoft Corporation.

TRADEMARKS:

SYBEX has attempted throughout this book to distinguish proprietary trademarks from descriptive terms by following the capitalization style used by the manufacturer.

The author and publisher have made their best efforts to prepare this book, and the content is based upon final release software whenever possible. Portions of the manuscript may be based upon pre-release versions supplied by software manufacturer(s). The author and the publisher make no representation or warranties of any kind with regard to the completeness or accuracy of the contents herein and accept no liability of any kind including but not limited to performance, merchantability, fitness for any particular purpose, or any losses or damages of any kind caused or alleged to be caused directly or indirectly from this book.

Manufactured in the United States of America

10 9 8 7 6 5 4 3 2 1

CONTENTS AT A GLANCE

Introduction   *xxiii*

Chapter 1   Introduction to Visual C# and the .NET Framework   1
Adapted from Mastering Visual C# .NET
by Jason Price and Mike Gunderloy
ISBN 0-7821-2911-0

Chapter 2   Zen and Now: The C# Language   23
Adapted from Visual C# .NET Programming
by Harold Davis
ISBN 0-7821-4046-7

Chapter 3   Strings, Dates, Times, and Time Spans   75
Adapted from Mastering Visual C# .NET
by Jason Price and Mike Gunderloy
ISBN 0-7821-2911-0

Chapter 4   Object-Oriented Programming   151
Adapted from Mastering Visual C# .NET
by Jason Price and Mike Gunderloy
ISBN 0-7821-2911-0

Chapter 5   Derived Classes   215
Adapted from Mastering Visual C# .NET
by Jason Price and Mike Gunderloy
ISBN 0-7821-2911-0

Chapter 6   Arrays, Indexers, and Collections   265
Adapted from Visual C# .NET Programming
by Harold Davis
ISBN 0-7821-4046-7

Chapter 7   Reflecting on Classes   305
Adapted from Visual C# .NET Programming
by Harold Davis
ISBN 0-7821-4046-7

Chapter 8   Building a Better Windows Interface   341
Adapted from Visual C# .NET Programming
by Harold Davis
ISBN 0-7821-4046-7

Chapter 9   Building Desktop Applications   385
Adapted from Visual C# .NET Developer's Handbook
by John Paul Mueller
ISBN 0-7821-4047-5

Chapter 10   Working with Threads   435
Adapted from Visual C# .NET Developer's Handbook
by John Paul Mueller
ISBN 0-7821-4047-5

Chapter 11   Overview of the ADO.NET Classes   475
Adapted from Mastering C# Database Programming
by Jason Price
ISBN 0-7821-4183-8

Chapter 12   ADO.NET Application Development   495
Adapted from Visual C# .NET Developer's Handbook
by John Paul Mueller
ISBN 0-7821-4047-5

Chapter 13   Using *DataSet* Objects to Store Data   539
Adapted from Mastering C# Database Programming
by Jason Price
ISBN 0-7821-4183-8

Chapter 14   Using *DataSet* Objects to Modify Data   601
Adapted from Mastering C# Database Programming
by Jason Price
ISBN 0-7821-4183-8

Chapter 15   Introduction to C# Web Applications   691
Adapted From Mastering ASP.NET with C#
by A. Russell Jones
ISBN 0-7821-2989-7

Chapter 16   Using XML in Web Applications   727
Adapted from Mastering ASP.NET with C#
by A. Russell Jones
ISBN 0-7821-2989-7

Chapter 17   Web Services   769
Adapted from Mastering ASP.NET with C#
by A. Russell Jones
ISBN 0-7821-2989-7

Chapter 18   Building Your Own Web Controls   809
Adapted from Mastering ASP.NET with C#
by A. Russell Jones
ISBN 0-7821-2989-7

Chapter 19   Overcoming Holes in the .NET Framework   845
Adapted from .NET Framework Solutions: In Search
of the Lost Win32 API
by John Paul Mueller
0-7821-4134-X

Chapter 20   Overcoming Security Issues   865
Adapted from .NET Framework Solutions: In Search
of the Lost Win32 API
by John Paul Mueller
ISBN 0-7821-4134-X

Chapter 21   Getting Started with the Mobile Internet Toolkit   911
Adapted from .NET Wireless Programming
by Mark Ridgeway
ISBN 0-7821-2975-7

Contents

Introduction   *xxiii*

**Chapter 1 □ Introduction to Visual C# and the .NET
          Framework**   **1**

Developing Your First C# Program   2
   Understanding the *Main()* Method   4
   Compiling a Program   6
   Introducing the Microsoft Intermediate Language (MSIL)   9
Introducing Visual Studio .NET   9
   Starting Visual Studio .NET and Creating a Project   11
   Compiling and Running the Program   16
Using the .NET Documentation   17
   Accessing the Documentation Using the .NET SDK   17
   Accessing the Documentation Using VS .NET   20
Summary   21
What's Next   21

Chapter 2 □ Zen and Now: The C# Language   **23**

Identifiers   24
Keywords   25
Variables   26
   Definite Assignment   27
   Constants   28
   Enumeration Constants   29
Types   33
   String Variables   35
   C# Is a Strongly Typed Language   36
Type Conversion   39
   Implicit Conversion   40
   Explicit Conversion   41
   The *as* Operator   44
   Conversion Methods   45
Commenting Code   48
   Self-Documenting Code   49
   So, What About Comments?   49

Operators	50
Flow Control Statements	55
Flow to with *goto*	55
while Statements	58
do while Statements	58
Structs	59
Exceptions	61
Understanding Structured Exception Handling	62
Throwing Exceptions	68
Exception Objects	71
Summary	72
What's Next	73

Chapter 3 ◻ Strings, Dates, Times, and Time Spans   75

Using Strings	76
Creating Strings	76
Using *String* Properties and Methods	76
Creating Dynamic Strings	100
Creating *StringBuilder* Objects	101
Using *StringBuilder* Properties and Methods	102
Representing Dates and Times	110
Creating *DateTime* Instances	110
Introducing Time Spans	112
Using *DateTime* Properties and Methods	115
Using Time Spans	136
Creating *TimeSpan* Instances	136
Using *TimeSpan* Properties and Methods	137
Summary	149
What's Next	150

Chapter 4 ◻ Object-Oriented Programming   151

Introducing Classes and Objects	152
Declaring a Class	153
Creating Objects	155
Null Values	157
Default Field Values and Initializers	160
Using Methods	162
Defining Methods	163
Calling Methods	165

Hiding   168
The *this* Object Reference   170
More on Parameters   171
Method Overloading   178
Defining Properties   181
Working with Events   183
Declaring an Event   184
Declaring the Delegate Class Used with an Event   185
Declaring the *Reactor* Class   186
Declaring the *ReactorMonitor* Class   187
Creating and Using a *Reactor* and *ReactorMonitor* Object   188
Using Access Modifiers   192
Creating and Destroying Objects   197
Using Constructors   198
Using Destructors   207
Introducing Structs   208
Summary   212
What's Next   213

Chapter 5 ▫ Derived Classes   **215**

Introducing Inheritance   216
Learning about Polymorphism   221
Specifying Member Accessibility   226
Hiding Members   230
Versioning   234
Using the *System.Object* Class   238
Overriding the *System.Object Class Methods*   241
Boxing and Unboxing   243
Using Abstract Classes and Methods   245
Declaring Sealed Classes and Methods   248
Sealed Classes   248
Sealed Methods   248
Casting Objects   251
Upcasting   252
Downcasting   253
Operator Overloading   257
Overloading the Equal Operator   258
Overloading the Addition Operator   260
Overloading Other Operators   263

Summary   263
What's Next   264

Chapter 6 ▫ Arrays, Indexers, and Collections   265

Arrays   266
   Creating an Array   268
   foreach Statement   271
   Arrays of Structs   272
   n-Dimensional Arrays   275
   Arrays of Arrays   277
   Creating a Non-Zero Lower Bound   280
Indexers   282
Collection Classes   284
   Collection Interfaces   286
   Stacks   287
   Queues   291
   The *ArrayList* Element   295
   Dictionaries   300
Summary   303
What's Next   303

Chapter 7 ▫ Reflecting on Classes   305

Assemblies and Namespaces   306
   The Assembly Manifest   306
   Assembly References   307
   Namespaces   309
.NET Namespaces   313
Reflection   314
Tracking Members with the Class View Window   323
Navigating with the Object Browser   325
   Opening the Object Browser   325
   Using the Object Browser Interface   327
Creating a Class Library   330
   Adding a Field   332
   Adding a Property   333
   Adding a Method   333
   Adding an Event   333
   Invoking the Class Members   336
What's Next   340

Chapter 8 □ Building a Better Windows Interface   341

Round Buttons Dancing   342
   Making a Button Round   342
   Toggling the Round Button   344
   One for All and All for One   344
   Animating the Controls   345
ListBoxes Listing   348
   Adding an Item   348
   Adding an Array   349
   Positioning by Index   350
   Retrieving Selected Text   352
   Retrieving by Index   353
   Retrieving Multiple Checked Items   353
   Clearing an Item   354
   Deleting Items   355
   Retrieving Multiple Selections   355
Menus   359
   The Auto-Generated Menu Code   361
Doing the Common Dialog Thing   368
   Implementing an Edit Menu   370
   The Color Dialog   371
   The Font Dialog   372
   The Save As and Open Dialogs   373
MDI Applications   377
   Setting the Startup Object   379
   Displaying Children   380
   The MDI Window Menu   381
What's Next   384

Chapter 9 □ Building Desktop Applications   385

Desktop Application Types   386
   Console   387
   Standard Windows   388
   Web-Based Applications   392
Writing Console Applications   393
   Simple Example   394
   Script-Based Example for Batch Jobs   397

Resource Essentials   405
    Accelerators and Menus   405
    Accessibility Features   408
    Graphics   410
    Timers   411
    Toolbars   411
Writing Windows Applications   414
    Dialog-Based Example   414
    SDI Example   421
Application Debugging   427
    Using the Debugger   427
    Performing Remote Debugging   429
    Performing Standard Debugging Tasks   431
Summary   434
What's Next   434

Chapter 10 ▫ Working with Threads   **435**

An Overview of Threads   436
    Uses for Threads   437
    Types of Threads   444
Working with Threads   446
    Desktop Application Example   446
    Local DLL Example   456
    Server-Based DLL Example   461
Understanding Critical Sections   470
Understanding Thread Safety   473
Using Your Knowledge   474
What's Next   474

Chapter 11 ▫ Overview of the ADO.NET Classes   **475**

The Managed Provider and Generic Data Set Classes   476
    The Managed Provider Classes   476
    The Generic Data Classes   480
Performing a SQL *SELECT* Statement and Storing the Rows Locally   484
    Outlining the Procedure   484
    Putting It All Together   490
Summary   493
What's Next   494

Chapter 12 □ ADO.NET Application Development   495

Comparing ADO to ADO.NET   496
Using *OleDbDataAdapter* for Data Transfer to ADO.NET   499
Writing a *DataReader* Application   500
    Creating the Application Shell   500
    Adding Some Code   502
    Testing Using NUnit   507
Writing a Dataset Application   513
    Coding the Grid View   513
    Coding the Detail View   525
Importing and Exporting XML Example   529
    Writing the Code   529
    Using the Microsoft XML Notepad   531
Using *StringBuilder* to Improve Performance   534
Summary   537
What's Next   538

Chapter 13 □ Using *DataSet* Objects to Store Data   539

The *SqlDataAdapter* Class   540
    Creating a *SqlDataAdapter* Object   543
The *DataSet* Class   544
    Creating a *DataSet* Object   548
    Populating a *DataSet* Object   549
    Populating a *DataSet* with Multiple *DataTable* Objects   560
    Merging *DataRow*, *DataSet*, and *DataTable* Objects
     into Another *DataSet*   568
Writing and Reading XML Using a *DataSet* Object   572
    Using the *WriteXml()* Method   572
    Using the *WriteXmlSchema()* Method   575
    Using the *ReadXml()* Method   576
Mapping Tables and Columns   580
Reading a Column Value Using Strongly Typed *DataSet* Classes 584
    Creating a Strongly Typed *DataSet* Class   585
    Using a Strongly Typed *DataSet* Class 589
Creating a *DataAdapter* Object Using Visual Studio .NET   591
Creating a *DataSet* Object Using Visual Studio .NET   596
Summary   599
What's Next   599

Chapter 14 □ Using *DataSet* Objects to Modify Data   601

The *DataTable* Class   602
The *DataRow* Class   604
The *DataColumn* Class   606
Adding Restrictions to *DataTable* and *DataColumn* Objects   607
    Adding the Restrictions Yourself   609
    Adding Restrictions by Calling the *DataAdapter* Object's
      FillSchema() Method   622
Finding, Filtering, and Sorting Rows in a *DataTable*   628
    Finding a *DataRow* in a *DataTable*   628
    Filtering and Sorting *DataRow* Objects in a *DataTable*   629
Modifying Rows in a *DataTable*   636
    Setting Up a *DataAdapter* to Push Changes to
      the Database   636
    Adding a *DataRow* to a *DataTable*   641
    Modifying a *DataRow* in a *DataTable*   645
    Removing a *DataRow* from a *DataTable*   648
Retrieving New Identity Column Values   650
Using Stored Procedures to Add, Modify, and Remove
  Rows from the Database   653
    Creating the Stored Procedures in the Database   654
    Setting Up a *DataAdapter* to Call Stored Procedures   658
    Adding a *DataRow* to a *DataTable*   661
    Modifying a *DataRow* in a *DataTable*   663
    Removing a *DataRow* from a *DataTable*   665
Automatically Generating SQL Statements   667
Exploring the *DataAdapter* and *DataTable* Events   669
    The *DataAdapter* Events   669
    The *DataTable* Events   674
Dealing with Update Failures   679
    An Update Failure Scenario   679
    Setting the *ContinueUpdateOnError* Property   680
    Programming a Failed Update Example   681
    Checking for Errors   683
    Fixing the Error   684
Using Transactions with a *DataSet*   685
    Using the *DataAdapter Command* Object's
      Transaction Property   685

Modifying Data Using a Strongly Typed *DataSet*   686
Summary   689
What's Next   690

Chapter 15 □ Introduction to C# Web Applications   691

Applications versus Websites   692
The *web.config* and *machine.config* Files   701
  Is the *web.config* File Required?   701
  The *.config* File Hierarchy   702
Site Hierarchy versus Directory Hierarchy   711
Inside Configuration Files   712
Creating Custom Configuration Sections   714
  Creating a Custom Configuration Handler   719
Configuration File Location and Lock Settings   721
  Location-Specific Tags Override Higher-Level Settings   722
What's Next   725

Chapter 16 □ Using XML in Web Applications   727

Introduction to the *System.Xml* Namespace   730
  What Can You Do with XML?   730
Reading XML Documents   741
  DOM versus SAX   741
  Using *XmlReader* Classes   742
  Querying XML Documents for Data   753
Using the *XmlDataDocument* Class   755
The *XmlException* Classes   759
Performing XSLT Transforms Programmatically   760
What's Next   768

Chapter 17 □ Web Services   769

Introduction to Web Services   770
  Remote Method Calls and XML   770
  Interoperating Across Applications/Platforms   772
  When Should You Use Web Services?   773
  How Does VS.NET Help?   774
Building a Web Service   776
  The Web Service Description Language (WSDL) File   783
  The WSDL Document   783

Consuming a Web Service   789
  Consuming Web Services from IE   789
  Consuming Web Services from a .NET Windows
    Forms Application   794
  Cross-Platform Interface Issues   798
SOAP (Simple Object Access Protocol)   801
  Benefits and Disadvantages of Using SOAP   802
  SOAP Basics   803
  Complex SOAP Messages   805
  Secured Web Services   806
Finding Web Services (UDDI)   807
What's Next   808

Chapter 18 ▫ Building Your Own Web Controls   809

Building a User Control   810
  Loading User Controls at Runtime   819
  Partial Page Caching and User Controls   819
Building a Composite Control   820
  Customizing the Toolbox   828
  Test the LabeledTextBox Composite Control   829
Building a Custom Server Control   830
  Creating the DateTable Custom Control   831
Transferring Data Between ASP.NET Web Forms and Components   842
What's Next   843

Chapter 19 ▫ Overcoming Holes in the .NET Framework   845

Why Access the Win32 API?   846
  A Case of Missing Functionality   847
  Win32 Function Types   849
  Win32 Access Requirements   852
Win32 Access for C# Developers   857
  Understanding the Effects of Unsafe Code   857
  Understanding the Effects of Pointers   859
  Advantages for the C# Developer   860
Win32 Access for Visual Basic Developers   861
  Understanding Visual Basic Limitations   862
  Advantages for the Visual Basic Developer   863
Summary   863
What's Next   864

Chapter 20 □ Overcoming Security Issues   **865**

An Overview of Windows Security   866
   A Detailed View of the Windows Security API   868
   An Overview of the Functions   877
Using the Access Control Editor   883
Using the Security Configuration Editor   885
Understanding How .NET Role-Based Security Differs   888
Looking Up an Account SID Example   892
Using the *GetFileSecurity()* Function Example   897
Working with an ACEs Example   902
Summary   909
What's Next   909

**Chapter 21 □ Getting Started with the Mobile
Internet Toolkit**   **911**

Checking System Requirements   912
Introducing the Microsoft Mobile Internet Toolkit   912
   Obtaining the Toolkit   913
   Toolkit Contents   914
   Toolkit Overview   914
The Openwave SDK   916
Supported Devices   918
Getting Started   919
   The Toolbox   921
   The Mobile Web Form Designer   922
   The Properties Window   923
   Testing the Application with the Emulators   925
Building a Simple Two-Card Deck   927
Using Code Behind   931
Summary   935

INTRODUCTION

C# *Complete* is a one-of-a-kind computer book—valuable both for the breadth of its content and for its low price. This thousand-page compilation of information from some of Sybex's very best books provides comprehensive coverage of the C# programming language. This book, unique in the computer book world, was created with several goals in mind:

- ► To offer a thorough guide covering all the important user-level features of C# at an affordable price

- ► To acquaint you with some of our best authors, their writing styles and teaching skills, and the level of expertise they bring to their books—so that you can easily find a match for your interests and needs as you delve deeper into C#.

Thus *C# Complete* is designed to provide you with all the essential information you'll need to get the most from the C# language and the .NET Framework. At the same time, *C# Complete* will invite you to explore the even greater depth and wider coverage of material in the original books.

If you have read other software development books, you have seen that there are as many different programming styles as there are programmers. The books from which *C# Complete* was compiled represent this range of development styles. From the essential, fundamental examples found in *Visual C# Programming* to the more advanced and detailed work *.NET Framework Solutions: In Search of the Lost Win32 API*, you will be able to choose an approach and a level of expertise that works best for you. You will also see what these books have in common: a commitment to clarity, accuracy, and practicality.

In these pages, you will find ample evidence of the high quality of Sybex's authors. Unlike publishers who produce "books by committee," Sybex authors are encouraged to write in their individual voices, voices which reflect their own experience with the software at hand and with the evolution of today's personal computers, so you know you are getting the benefit of their direct experience. Nearly every book represented here is the work of a single writer or a pair of close collaborators. Similarly, all of the chapters here are based on the individual experience of the authors, their first-hand testing of pre-release software, and their subsequent expertise with the final product.

In adapting the various source materials for inclusion in *C# Complete*, the compilation editor preserved these individual voices and perspectives.

Chapters were edited to minimize duplication, omit coverage of nonessential information, update technological issues, and revise the cross-referencing so you can easily follow a topic across chapters. Some sections may have been edited for length in order to include as much updated, relevant, and important information as possible.

Who Can Benefit from This Book?

C# Complete is designed to meet the needs of a wide range of programmers and developers working with the C# language. C# has some elements that everyone uses, as well as features that may be essential only to some. Therefore, although you could read this book from beginning to end, not all of you will need to read every chapter. The contents and the index will guide you to the subjects you're looking for. You'll find everything from the essentials of C# to the elements of advanced C# development, as well as important help with C#-based application and database development, and excellent coverage of using C# to develop web applications and web services.

Beginners   Even if you have only a little familiarity with programming, this book will start you working with the C# language and the .NET Framework. You'll find step-by-step instructions for the creation of your first "Hello World" program, and will slowly build up to more complex and useful software. You'll want to start at the very beginning of this book and read the first seven chapters that cover the basics.

Intermediate Level   If you have some background in software development, perhaps even some experience in C# or Visual Basic, you'll find most of this book contains useful nuggets of information throughout. The .NET Framework is a vast set of libraries and has been available for only a relatively short time, so it is often useful to see what other developers have uncovered during their mastering of this new language.

Advanced "Bitheads"   The advanced developer will find this book useful in learning all the differences between the .NET languages and the "old ways." For example, ADO.NET represents an entirely new way to connect to a back-end database, and with this new functionality come new tricks and caveats. This is just one of the hundreds of changes since we entered the C# world from previous languages such as C++. Garbage collection, thread use, and XML Web Services represent other new challenges to the experienced developer.

How This Book Is Organized

Here's a look at what *C# Complete* covers:

The first seven chapters of C# Complete introduce you to Visual C# .NET essentials. This includes the C# language, the .NET Framework, and Visual Studio.NET—the tool that Microsoft provides for the creation of your programs. You'll learn how to create applications of various types, and you'll begin to dive into the enormous set of tools and classes found within the .NET Framework. You'll also begin to learn the basic C# syntax.

Starting with Chapter 8, we put the pieces together and show how complete applications are developed. Chapters 8 and 9 explore the various types of applications, including console applications vs. "standard" Windows applications. You'll see examples of where each type can be useful. Chapter 10 gives you important material about the advantages and pitfalls of threads.

Most applications exist to read and write some sort of data, so connectivity to databases is obviously of great importance. The process of database development changes pretty dramatically in .NET languages, and Chapters 11 through 14 will introduce you to all the new ways to pump data in and out of databases like SQL Server.

Next come the four important chapters (15 through 18) on ASP.NET and web services. Web application development takes a huge step forward in C#, giving you much of the object-oriented power found in the Windows side of the development house. XML Web Services represent a new way of connecting to classes on the other side of the world through the basic http protocol, allowing for distributed functionality.

The last three chapters of the book cover advanced topics such as security concerns in the .NET Framework, as well as "dropping back" to the Windows API when the .NET Framework fails to support a function required for your application. You will also learn how to work with the Microsoft Mobile Internet Toolkit.

There's a bonus chapter, too, "Working with Win32 API Data," available at this book's page at www.sybex.com. To use the Win32 API, you have to work with C/C++ libraries. And that means converting data from the Visual Studio .NET managed environment into a form that the library functions will understand. The bonus chapter explores the special handling required in a managed application for the four levels of data manipulated by the Win32 API: variables, data structures, pointers, and enumerations. The chapter also discusses importing resources from the unmanaged environment into the managed application environment.

A Few Typographic Conventions

Within each chapter, the figures, tables, and code listings have all been renumbered to match their new chapter numbers. For example, Chapter 5 in this book was originally Chapter 7 in the book from which it was excerpted, so all of the numbers have been converted to reflect the Chapter 5 numbering (for example, Figure 7.1 is now Figure 5.1). However, if the name of a code element—such as a source filename, class name, or a member name—contains an embedded chapter reference, this reference has *not* been modified. You can see an example in Chapter 5, where class names are Example7_4, Example7_5, and so on. These names were left as is, so that the source code in the book match the code available at www.sybex.com.

This typeface is used to identify code elements, Internet URLs, and filenames and paths. **Boldface** is used to indicate key parts of a code listing, and occasionally keyboard input. *Italic* represents placeholders such as *file* and *object*.

You'll find these types of special notes throughout the book:

TIP

Tips tell you about quicker and smarter ways to accomplish a task. These Tips have been accumulated by the authors after many hours working with C#.

NOTE

Notes usually represent alternate ways of accomplishing a task or some important additional information.

WARNING

Warnings are significant instructions that will save you from disaster. When you see a Warning, do pay attention to it.

YOU'LL ALSO SEE SIDEBAR BOXES LIKE THIS

These sections provide added explanations of special topics that are referred to in the surrounding discussions and that you may want to explore separately in greater detail. They may also provide notes on minor enhancements that were made to a chapter brought over from its original book.

For More Information

Visit the Catalog at the Sybex website, www.sybex.com, to learn more about all the books contributing to *C# Complete*. That's also where you'll find the supporting code for each source book. Look for the Download link on the book's Catalog page. The bonus chapter is available there, too. We hope you enjoy this *C# Complete* collection and find it useful.

Chapter 1

INTRODUCTION TO VISUAL C# AND THE .NET FRAMEWORK

In this chapter, you'll be introduced to the C# language. You'll see a simple example program that displays the words *Hello World!* on your computer's screen, along with the current date and time.

You'll also learn about Microsoft's Rapid Application Development (RAD) tool, Visual Studio .NET. Visual Studio .NET enables you to develop and run programs in an integrated development environment. This environment uses all the great features of Windows, such as the mouse and intuitive menus, and increases your productivity as a programmer.

In the final sections of this chapter, you'll see how to use the extensive documentation from Microsoft that comes with the .NET Software Development Kit (SDK) and Visual Studio .NET. You'll find this documentation invaluable as you become an expert C# programmer.

Adapted from *Mastering Visual C# .NET* by Jason Price and Mike Gunderloy

ISBN 0-7821-2911-0

NOTE

Before you can develop C# programs, you'll need to install the .NET SDK or Visual Studio .NET. You can download the .NET SDK from http://msdn .microsoft.com/downloads. Once you've downloaded the executable file, go ahead and run it. Follow the instructions on the screen to install the .NET SDK on your computer. You can also purchase a copy of Visual Studio .NET from Microsoft at their website.

DEVELOPING YOUR FIRST C# PROGRAM

Learning a new programming language is sometimes a daunting task. To get you started, you'll begin with a variation on the classic "Hello World" program. This program traditionally starts all programming books—and who are we to argue with tradition?

THE ORIGINS OF THE "HELLO WORLD" PROGRAM

As far as we know, the tradition of the "Hello World" program being used to start programming books began in the seminal work *The C Programming Language* by Brian Kernighan and Dennis Ritchie (Prentice Hall PTR, 1988). Incidentally, C is one of the languages that C# owes its development to, along with Java and C++.

The following program displays the words *Hello World!* on your computer's screen. The program will also display the current date and time retrieved from your computer. This program, shown in Listing 1.1, illustrates a few simple tenets of the C# language.

Listing 1.1: The "Hello World" Program

```
/*
    Example1_1.cs: a variation on the classic "Hello World!" program.
    This program displays the words "Hello World!" on the screen,
    along with the current date and time.
*/
```

```
class Example1_1
{

  public static void Main()
  {

    // display "Hello World!" on the screen.
    System.Console.WriteLine("Hello World!");

    // display the current date and time
    System.Console.WriteLine("The current date and time is " +
      System.DateTime.Now);
  }


}
```

This program is contained in a text file named Example1_1.cs. This file is known as a *program source file*, or simply a *source file*, because it contains the lines that make up the program. You use a compiler to translate a source file into an executable file that a computer can run; you'll learn more about this later in the "Compiling a Program" section.

NOTE

You can download all the source files for the programs featured in this chapter from the Sybex website at http://www.sybex.com. Search for this chapter's source book by its ISBN number, 2911, or its title, *Mastering Visual C# .NET*. Look for the Download link on the right. Once you've downloaded the files, you can follow along with the examples without having to type in the program listings.

You'll notice that the extension for the Example1_1.cs file is .cs—this is the recommended extension for C# source files. Because the file is a text file, you can open and view the Example1_1.cs file using a text editor such as Notepad. Go ahead and open the file if you want.

TIP

You can also edit and save source files using Notepad, although as you develop more complex programs you'll find that Visual Studio .NET is a much more efficient tool to use. You'll learn about Visual Studio .NET later in this chapter.

Let's go through the lines in Example1_1.cs. The first four lines are as follows:

```
/*
Example1_1.cs: a variation on the classic "Hello World!" program.
This program displays the words "Hello World!" on the screen,
along with the current date and time.
*/
```

The compiler ignores anything placed between the /* and */ characters. They denote comments that we've used to inform you of what the program does. Later, you'll see the use of single-line comments that start with two forward slash characters (//).

The next two lines start a class using the class keyword:

```
class Example1_1
{
```

The open curly brace ({) marks the beginning of the Example1_1 class. Similarly, the close curly brace (}), shown at the end of Listing 1.1, marks the end of the Example1_1 class. As you'll learn in Chapter 4, "Object-Oriented Programming," you use a *class* to define a template that contains methods and fields—and you can use this template to create objects of that class.

Methods are self-contained units of code that carry out a specific task, and they typically consist of one or more program lines. *Fields* are named storage areas where you can store values. The Example1_1 class doesn't contain any fields, but it does contain a method named Main().

NOTE
Programs typically contain a Main() method. This method is run, or called, automatically when you run your program. The exception is a type library, which requires another program to call its functionality and therefore doesn't require a Main() method.

In the next section, we'll take you through the lines in the Main() method.

Understanding the *Main()* Method

As mentioned, methods typically consist of one or more program lines that carry out the method's task. The program lines that make up a method begin and end with open and close curly braces, respectively. The `Main()` method in the example "Hello World" program is defined as follows:

```csharp
public static void Main()
{

    // display "Hello World!" on the screen
    System.Console.WriteLine("Hello World!");

    // display the current date and time
    System.Console.WriteLine("The current date and time is " +
        System.DateTime.Now);

}
```

The `public` keyword is an access modifier that specifies the level of availability of the method outside of the class; `public` specifies that the `Main()` method is available without restriction and may be called anywhere.

NOTE
You'll learn more about access modifiers in Chapter 4.

The `static` keyword indicates that the `Main()` method belongs to the class, rather than any particular object of the class. If we didn't use the `static` keyword when defining the method, we would have to first create an object of the class and then call the method. Methods can return a value to the statement from which they are called. For example, you might want to perform some kind of calculation in a method and return the result of that calculation. However, you may not always want to return a value, and that's what the `void` keyword does. As you can see in the example program, the `void` keyword indicates that the `Main()` method doesn't return a value.

Let's take a look at the program lines contained within the open and close curly brackets; these lines carry out the tasks for the method and are run when the `Main()` method is called. The first program line is as follows:

```csharp
// display "Hello World!" on the screen
```

This line begins with two forward slash characters (//). These indicate that the line is a comment. As mentioned, the /* and */ characters also mark the beginning and end of comments. The difference between these two ways of marking lines as comments is that the // characters mark a single line as a comment, whereas the /* and */ characters mark multiple lines as comments. You'll learn more about comments in Chapter 2, "Zen and Now: the C# Language."

The second program line in the Main() method is as follows:

```
System.Console.WriteLine("Hello World!");
```

This line calls the WriteLine() method. This method displays a line of output on your computer's screen. In the example program, the call to this method displays a line containing the words *Hello World!*

As you'll learn in Chapter 7, "Reflecting on Classes," *namespaces* separate class declarations, and System is a namespace created by Microsoft. The System namespace contains a number of useful classes you can use in your programs, and you'll see some of them in this book The Console class is one of the classes in the System namespace. The Console class contains methods you can use to display output on a computer's screen.

As you can see from the previous line, a period (.) separates the System namespace, the Console class, and the WriteLine() method. The period is known as the *dot operator*, and it may be used to separate the namespace, class, and method parts of a program line. The third line in the Main() method is another single line comment:

```
// display the current date and time
```

The fourth line in the Main() method displays the current date and time:

```
System.Console.WriteLine("The current date and time is " +
    System.DateTime.Now);
```

As you can see, this line uses System.DateTime.Now to display the current date and time. Now is a *property* of DateTime that returns the current date and time set for the computer on which the program is running. In a nutshell, the Now property reads the current date and time from your computer. Now is a static property, which means you can call it without first creating a DateTime object.

The remaining lines in Example1_1.cs contain close curly braces that end the Main() method and the Example1_1 class.

Compiling a Program

A program source file is written in text that you can read. Unfortunately, a computer cannot directly run the instructions contained in that source file, and you must first *compile* that file using a piece of software known as a *compiler*. The compiler reads your program source file and converts the instructions contained in that file into code that a computer may then run, or *execute*. The file produced by the compiler is known as an *executable file*. Once you've compiled your program, you can then run it.

You can compile a program using either the command-line compiler that comes with the .NET SDK, or you can use Visual Studio .NET. In this section, you'll see how to use the command-line version of the compiler to compile the Example1_1.cs program. Later, in the "Introducing Visual Studio .NET" section, you'll see how to use Visual Studio .NET to compile a program.

You run the command-line version of the compiler by entering csc in the Command Prompt tool, followed by the name of your program source file. For example, to compile Example1_1.cs, you would enter the following command in the Command Prompt tool:

```
csc Example1_1.cs
```

NOTE
You can also enter one or more options that are then passed to the compiler. These options control things like the name of the executable file produced by the compiler. You can view the compiler options by entering csc /help in the Command Prompt tool.

If you want to follow along with the examples, go ahead and start the Command Prompt tool by selecting Start ➢ Programs ➢ Accessories ➢ Command Prompt.

NOTE
If you're using Windows XP rather than Windows 2000, you start the Command Prompt tool by selecting Start ➢ All Programs ➢ Accessories ➢ Command Prompt.

Next, you need to change directories to where you copied the Example1_1.cs file. To do this, you first enter the partition on your hard disk where you saved the file. For example, let's say you saved the file in the C#\programs directory of the C partition of your hard disk. To access the C partition, you enter the following line into the Command Prompt tool, and then you press the Enter key:

```
C:
```

Next, to move to the C#\programs directory, you enter cd followed by C#\programs:

```
cd C#\programs
```

To compile `Example1_1.cs` using `csc`, you enter the following command:

```
csc Example1_1.cs
```

Notice that the name of the program source file follows `csc`—it's `Example1_1.cs` in this case.

WARNING

If you get an error when you are running `csc`, you'll need to add the directory where you installed the SDK to your `Path` environment variable. The `Path` environment variable specifies a list of directories that contain executable programs. Whenever you run a program from the Command Prompt tool, the directories in the `Path` variable are searched for the program you want to run. Your current directory is also searched. To set your `Path` environment variable, select Start ➢ Settings ➢ Control Panel. Then double-click System and select the Advanced tab. Next, click the Environment Variables button and double-click `Path` from the system variables area at the bottom. Finally, add the directory where you installed the SDK to your `Path` environment variable. Click OK to save your change, and then click OK again on the next dialog box. Next, restart the Command Prompt tool so that your change is picked up. You should then be able to run `csc` successfully.

The compiler takes the `Example1_1.cs` file and compiles it into an executable file named `Example1_1.exe`. This file contains instructions that a computer can run—the `.exe` file extension indicates the file is an executable file.

You run an executable file using the Command Prompt tool by entering the name of that executable file. For example, to run `Example1_1.exe`, you enter the following line in the Command Prompt tool and then you press the Enter key:

```
Example1_1
```

NOTE

As you can see, you can omit the `.exe` extension when running a program.

When you run the program, you should see the following text displayed in your Command Prompt window:

```
Hello World!
The current date and time is 8/1/2002 12:22:44 PM
```

Needless to say, your date and time will differ from that shown in the previous line. This date and time is read from your computer when you run the program.

Introducing the Microsoft Intermediate Language (MSIL)

When you compile a program, the .exe file produced by the compiler contains instructions written in Microsoft Intermediate Language (MSIL). MSIL is frequently abbreviated to IL. Now, a computer can only run programs written in their own native tongue: machine code. *Machine code* is a series of binary numbers (zeros and ones) that a computer can understand and run.

IL instructions are not written in machine code—and therefore an additional step is required to convert the IL into machine code before your program is run for the first time. This step is performed automatically by a piece of software known as the Just In Time (JIT) compiler.

When you run your program, the IL instructions in your .exe file are converted by the JIT compiler into machine code that the computer then runs. This is efficient because the JIT compiler detects the type of Central Processing Unit (CPU) in the computer and produces machine code specifically tailored to that CPU. This results in machine code that runs as fast as possible.

NOTE
When you distribute your programs, you can then be sure your program will run as fast as possible, regardless of the CPU used by the computer on which your program runs.

JIT compilation is only performed the first time your program is run, and the resulting machine code is automatically stored. When your program runs again, the stored machine code is reused. That way, the computer doesn't need to keep recompiling the IL instructions into machine code. Of course, when the computer is turned off or rebooted, the JIT will need to recompile your program into IL instructions when it is run again.

INTRODUCING VISUAL STUDIO .NET

Visual Studio .NET (VS .NET) is Microsoft's RAD tool. VS .NET is an integrated development environment that you can use to create many types of .NET programs. VS .NET is a more productive tool than a simple text editor such as Notepad. This is because VS .NET allows you to enter your program, compile it, and run it—all within an easy to use graphical Windows environment.

In the previous section, you saw a program that displayed the words *Hello World!* along with the current date and time on your computer's screen. This type of program is known as a *console application* because it displays output directly on the computer's screen on which the program is running.

You can use VS .NET to create console applications, as well as the following type of applications:

Windows applications   Windows applications are programs that take advantage of the visual controls offered by the Windows operating system, such as menus, buttons, and editable text boxes. Windows Explorer, which you use to navigate the filesystem of your computer, is one example of a Windows application. You'll learn about Windows programming in Chapters 8–10.

ASP.NET applications   ASP.NET applications are programs that run over the Internet. You access an ASP.NET application using a web browser, such as Internet Explorer. Examples of ASP.NET applications would be online banking, stock trading, or auction systems. You'll learn about ASP.NET programming in Chapters 15–18.

ASP.NET web services   ASP.NET web services are also programs that run over the Internet. ASP.NET web services are also known as XML web services. The difference is that you can use them to offer a service that could be used in a distributed system of interconnected services. For example, Microsoft's Passport web service offers identification and authentication of web users you could then use in your own web application. You'll learn about web services in Chapters 15–18.

The previous list is not an exhaustive list of the types of applications you can develop with VS .NET, but it does give you a taste of the broad range of VS .NET's capabilities.

In the rest of this section, you'll see how to develop and run the "Hello World" program using VS .NET. If you've installed VS .NET on your computer, you'll be able to follow along with the example. If you don't have VS .NET, then don't worry—you'll be able to see what's going on from the figures provided.

Starting Visual Studio .NET and Creating a Project

All of your work in VS .NET is organized into *projects*. Projects contain the source and executable files for your program, among other items. If you have VS .NET installed, go ahead and start it by selecting Start ➤ Programs ➤ Microsoft Visual Studio .NET ➤ Microsoft Visual Studio .NET. Once VS .NET has started, you'll see the Start page (see Figure 1.1).

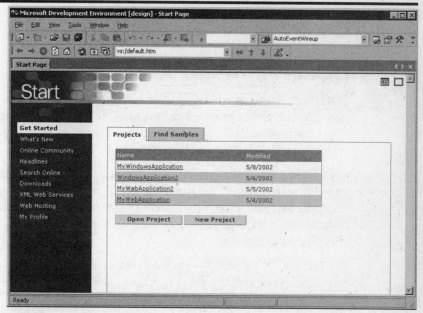

FIGURE 1.1:   The Start page

From the Start page, you can see any existing projects you've created. You can open and create projects using the Open Project and New Project buttons, respectively. You'll create a new project shortly.

Using the VS .NET Links

As you can see from Figure 1.1, VS .NET contains a number of links on the left of the Start page. Some of these links provide access to useful information on the Internet about .NET; the links are as follows:

Get Started   Opens the Start page. You can open and create projects from the Start page, and you saw an example Start page earlier in Figure 1.1.

What's New   Use this link to view any updates for VS .NET or Windows. You can also view upcoming training events and conferences.

Online Community   Get in touch with other members of the .NET community. This includes links to websites and newsgroups.

Headlines   View the latest news on .NET.

Search Online   Use this link to search the MSDN Online Library for technical material such as published articles on .NET.

Downloads   Download trial applications and example programs from the websites featured here.

XML Web Services   Find registered XML web services that you can then use in your own programs. XML web services are also known as ASP.NET web services. You'll learn more about web services in Chapter 17, "Web Services."

Web Hosting   A web hosting company is an organization that can take your program and run it for you. They take care of the computers on which your program runs. You use the Web Hosting link to view companies that provide web hosting services to run your programs.

My Profile   This link allows you to set items such as your required keyboard scheme and window layout.

Go ahead and click these links and explore the information provided. As you'll see, there's a huge amount of information about .NET on the Internet.

Creating a New Project

When you're finished examining the information in the previous links, go ahead and create a new project by clicking the New Project button on the Get Started page.

NOTE
You can also create a new project by selecting File ➤ New ➤ Project or by pressing Ctrl+Shift+N on your keyboard.

When you create a new project, VS .NET displays the New Project dialog box that you use to select the type of project you want to create. You also enter the name and location of your new project; the location is the directory where you want to store the files for your project.

Because you're going to be creating a C# console application, select Visual C# Projects from the Project Types section on the left of the New Project dialog box, and select Console Application from the Templates section on the right. Enter **MyConsoleApplication** in the Name field, and keep the default directory in the Location field. Figure 1.2 shows the completed New Project dialog box with these settings.

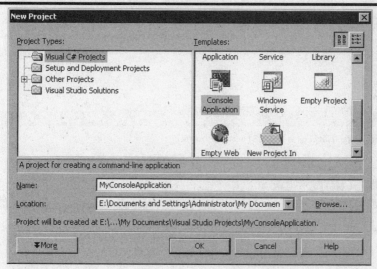

FIGURE 1.2:   The New Project dialog box with the appropriate settings for a
                  C# console application

Click the OK button to create the new project.

Working in the VS .NET Environment

Once your new project has been created, the main development screen is displayed (see Figure 1.3). This screen is the environment in which you'll develop your project. As you can see, VS .NET has already created some starting code for you; this code is a skeleton for your program—you'll see how to modify it shortly. In this section, we'll give you a brief description of the different parts of the VS .NET environment.

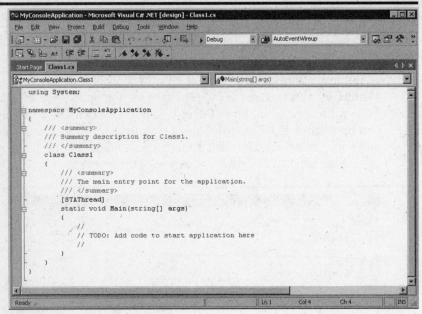

FIGURE 1.3:   The VS .NET environment

NOTE

Depending on your settings for VS .NET, your screen may look slightly different from that shown in Figure 1.3.

The VS .NET menu contains the following items:

File   From the File menu, you can open, close, and save project files.

Edit   From the Edit menu, you can cut, copy, and paste text from the Clipboard. The Clipboard is a temporary storage area.

View   From the View menu, you can hide and show different windows such as the Solution Explorer (which allows you to see the files that make up your project), the Class View (which allows you to see the classes and objects in your project), the Server Explorer (which allows you to explore items such as databases, and the Properties window (which allows you to set the properties of objects, such as the size of a button), among others. You can also use the View menu to select the toolbars you want to display.

Project   From the Project menu, you can add class files to your project and add Windows forms and controls (you'll learn about Windows forms and controls in Chapters 8–10).

Build   From the Build menu, you can compile the source files in your project.

Debug   From the Debug menu, you can start your program with or without debugging. Debugging enables you to step through your program line-by-line looking for errors.

Tools   From the Tools menu, you can connect to a database and customize your settings for VS .NET (for example, you can set the colors used for different parts of your program lines or set the initial page displayed by VS .NET when you start it).

Window   From the Window menu, you can switch between files you've opened and hide windows.

Help   From the Help menu, you can open the documentation on .NET. You'll learn how to use this documentation later in this chapter in the "Using the .NET Documentation" section.

The VS .NET toolbar contains a series of buttons that act as shortcuts to some of the options in the menus. For example, you can save a file or all files, cut and paste text from the Clipboard, and start a program using the debugger.

The code shown in the window (below the toolbar) with the title `Class.1.cs` is code that is automatically generated by VS .NET, and in the next section you'll modify this code.

Modifying the VS .NET–Generated Code

Once VS .NET has created your project, it will display some starting code for the console application with a class name of `Class1.cs`. You can use this code as the beginning for your own program. Figure 1.3–shown earlier–shows the starting code created by VS .NET.

The `Main()` method created by VS .NET is as follows:

```
static void Main(string[] args)
{
  //
  // TODO: Add code to start application here
  //
}
```

As you can see, this code contains comments that indicate where you add your own code. Go ahead and replace the three lines in the Main() method with the lines shown in the following Main() method:

```
static void Main(string[] args)
{
  // display "Hello World!" on the screen
  System.Console.WriteLine("Hello World!");

  // display the current date and time
  System.Console.WriteLine("The current date and time is " +
    System.DateTime.Now);
}
```

Notice that the new lines display the words *Hello World!* on the screen, along with the current date and time. Once you've replaced the code in the Main() method, the next steps are to compile and run your program.

Compiling and Running the Program

As always, you must first compile your program before you can run it. Because programs in VS .NET are organized into projects, you must compile the project—this is also known as *building* the project. To build your project, select Build ➤ Build Solution. This compiles the Class1.cs source file into an executable file.

TIP
You can also press Ctrl+Shift+B on your keyboard to build your project.

You can now run your program. To run your program, select Debug ➤ Start Without Debugging. When you select Start Without Debugging, the program will pause at the end allowing you to view the output.

TIP
You can also press Ctrl+F5 on your keyboard to run your program.

When you run your program, VS .NET will run the program in a new Command Prompt window, as shown in Figure 1.4. Your program is run in a Command Prompt window because it is a console application.

To end the program, go ahead and press any key. This will also close the Command Prompt window.

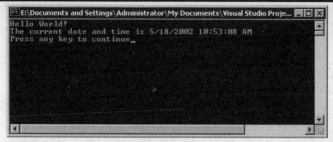

FIGURE 1.4:   The running program

In the next section, you'll learn how to use the extensive documentation that comes with .NET.

USING THE .NET DOCUMENTATION

Both the .NET SDK and VS .NET come with extensive documentation, including the full reference to all the classes in .NET. As you become proficient with C#, you'll find this reference documentation invaluable.

In the following sections, you'll see how to access and search the .NET documentation, and then you'll view some of its contents. Depending on whether you're using the .NET SDK or VS .NET, you access the documentation in a slightly different way. You'll see how to use both of these ways in this section.

NOTE
The documentation that comes with the .NET SDK is a subset of the documentation that comes with VS .NET.

Accessing the Documentation Using the .NET SDK

If you're using the .NET SDK, you access the documentation by selecting Start ➤ Programs ➤ .NET Framework SDK ➤ Overview. Figure 1.5 shows the .NET Framework SDK Documentation home page—this is the starting page for the documentation.

On the left of the page, you can see the various sections that make up the contents of the documentation. You can view the index of the documentation by selecting the Index tab at the bottom of the page.

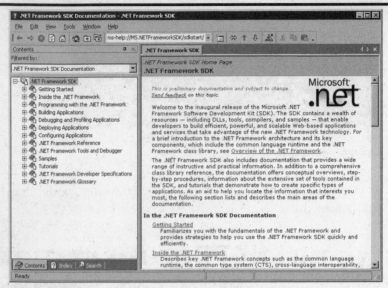

FIGURE 1.5:   The documentation home page

TIP

You can also view the Index window by selecting Help ➢ Index or by pressing Ctrl+Alt+F2 on your keyboard.

You can search the index by entering a word in the Look For field of the Index tab. Figure 1.6 shows the results of searching for *Console*. Figure 1.6 also shows the overview for the Console class on the right. We opened this overview by double-clicking the About Console Class link in the Index window on the left of the screen.

You can also search all pages in the documentation using the Search tab. You display the Search tab by selecting it from the bottom of the screen.

TIP

You can also view the Search window by selecting Help ➢ Search or by pressing Ctrl+Alt+F3 on your keyboard.

You enter the words you want to search for in the Look For field of the Search window. Figure 1.7 shows the Search tab and the search results returned by a search for *WriteLine*. When you run the search, the names of the pages that contain your required words are displayed in the Search Results window that appears at the bottom of the screen (you can see this window in Figure 1.7).

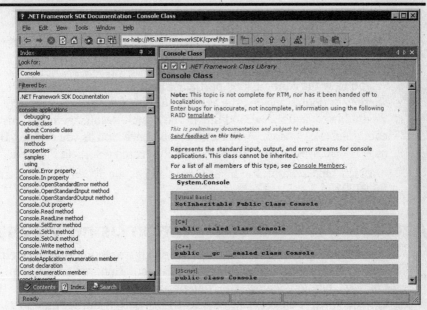

FIGURE 1.6:   Searching the index for the word *Console*

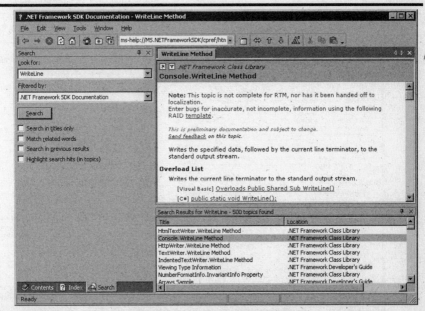

FIGURE 1.7:   Searching all of the documentation for the word *WriteLine*

TIP

You can also view the Search Results window by selecting Help ➢ Search results or by pressing Shift+Alt+F3 on your keyboard.

You view the contents of a particular page shown in the Search Results window by double-clicking the appropriate line. For example, in Figure 1.7, we double-clicked the second line in the Search Results window. This line contained the Console. WriteLine Method page, and as you can see, this page is displayed in the window above the search results in Figure 1.7.

In the next section, you'll see how to access the documentation using VS .NET.

Accessing the Documentation Using VS .NET

If you're using VS .NET, you access the documentation using the Help menu. To access the contents of the documentation, you select Help ➢ Contents. Figure 1.8 shows the contents displayed in VS .NET. Notice that the documentation is displayed directly in VS .NET, rather than in a separate window as is done when viewing documentation with the .NET SDK.

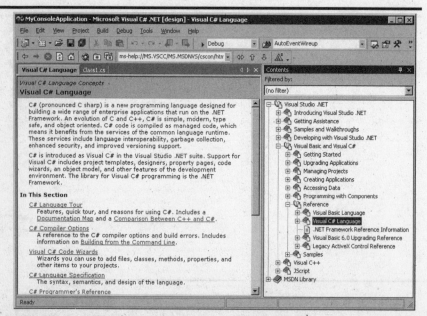

FIGURE 1.8:   The documentation contents viewed in VS .NET

NOTE
The same keyboard shortcuts shown in the previous section also apply to VS .NET.

The Help menu also provides access to similar Index and Search windows as you saw in the previous section.

SUMMARY

In this chapter, you were introduced to the C# language. You saw a simple example program that displayed the words *Hello World!* on your computer's screen, along with the current date and time. You also learned about the compiler.

You also learned about Microsoft's Rapid Application Development (RAD) tool, Visual Studio .NET. Visual Studio .NET allows you to develop, run, and debug programs in an integrated development environment.

In the final sections of this chapter, you saw how to use the extensive documentation from Microsoft that comes with the .NET SDK and Visual Studio .NET. As you become an expert C# programmer, you'll find this documentation invaluable.

WHAT'S NEXT

In the next chapter, you'll learn about the basic structure and form of the C# language.

Chapter 2

Zen and Now: The C# Language

"O, wonder!" exclaims Miranda in Shakespeare's play *The Tempest*. "How many goodly creatures are there here! How beauteous mankind is! O brave new world that has such people in't!"

Our brave new world is, in fact, a brave new language: C#.

It has no "creatures" in it. Nor, for that matter, does it have the pharmacopoeia of Aldous Huxley's famous dystopia, *Brave New World*.

C# does have things like types, operators, variables, and expressions, all of which are glued together using a distinctive syntax. O brave new language! The introduction of a new language is a rare event. Although C# borrows from Java, C++, C, and even Visual Basic and Pascal, it is a truly new language—and, in the opinion of this author, quite wondrous.

Adapted from *Visual C# .NET Programming* by Harold Davis

ISBN 0-7821-4046-7

Since C# is new, and since language and syntax are the blocks on which programs are built, it's especially important to pay attention to the rules of the language. This chapter reviews the nuts and bolts of the C# language.

IDENTIFIERS

Identifiers are names used to denote variables, constants, types, methods, objects, and so on. An identifier begins with a letter or an underscore and ends with the character just before the next white space.

C# identifiers are case sensitive. For example, the three variables *deeFlat*, *DeeFlat*, and *DEEFLAT* are all different, as running this click procedure will show:

```
private void btnClickMe_Click(object sender, System.EventArgs e) {
    string deeFlat = "deeFlat";
    string DeeFlat = "DeeFlat";
    string DEEFLAT = "DEEFLAT";
    MessageBox.Show(deeFlat + " " + DeeFlat + " " + DEEFLAT,
        "Hello, Variables!", MessageBoxButtons.OK);
}
```

Microsoft suggests using "camel notation" for identifiers used as names of variables. Camel notation means an initial lowercase letter followed by uppercase letters ("internal caps") for initial letters of subsequent words in the identifier—for example, deeFlat.

Pascal notation—an initial uppercase letter, with internal caps as needed—is supposed to be used for identifiers that represent method names and most other non-variable objects. In addition, an identifier used for a method should use a verb-noun combination to describe the purpose of the method—for example, GetColorValues.

For more on Microsoft's suggested identifier naming conventions, look up "Naming Guidelines" using the Search feature in online help.

NOTE

It's always good programming practice to use identifiers that clearly communicate the contents and/or nature of the variable or other object identified. Code that uses clear identifiers may be almost self-documenting. For more suggestions of this kind, see the "Self-Documenting Code" section later in this chapter.

It is not legal to use an identifier that is also a C# keyword. (You'll find a list of C# reserved keywords in the next section.) If, for some really perverse reason, you must use a keyword as an identifier, you can preface the keyword with the @ symbol. For example, if cannot be used as an identifier (because it is a keyword), but @if can; this code snippet shows it employed as a string variable:

```
string @if = "@if";
MessageBox.Show(@if, "Hello, Variables!",
    MessageBoxButtons.OK);
```

For that matter, if you were really bound and determined to create an identifier like a keyword, you could simply vary the case. So If is a perfectly legal identifier—albeit an idiotic choice because it is similar to a keyword and so potentially confusing—because the keyword if is all lowercase.

TIP

Visual Basic programmers, who are used to case insensitivity, may find that C#'s case sensitivity regarding identifiers leads to the introduction of bugs. Fortunately, these kinds of bugs are found pretty easily once you are on the watch for them, and you will find that paying attention to the case of identifiers will become second nature shortly.

KEYWORDS

Another way to think of a keyword is as a predefined reserved identifier. Table 2.1 shows the complete list of C# keywords.

TABLE 2.1: C# Keywords (Reserved Identifiers)

abstract	do	in	protected	true
as	double	int	public	try
base	else	interface	readonly	typeof
bool	enum	internal	ref	uint
break	event	is	return	ulong
byte	explicit	lock	sbyte	unchecked
case	extern	long	sealed	unsafe
catch	false	namespace	short	ushort
char	finally	new	sizeof	using
checked	fixed	null	stackalloc	virtual
class	float	object	static	void
const	for	operator	string	volatile
continue	foreach	out	struct	while
decimal	goto	override	switch	
default	if	params	this	
delegate	implicit	private	throw	

You can find this list of C# keywords by looking up "keyword, C#" using the online help's Index facility. The online help topic is then hyperlinked to the definition of each keyword.

VARIABLES

A *variable* combines a type with a way to store a value of the specified type. (I discuss types later in this chapter, but you are certainly already familiar with some of the C# types, such as int [integer] and string.) The value of a variable can be assigned, and that value can also be changed programmatically at any point.

A variable is created in C# by declaring its type and then giving it an identifier. For example,

```
int theInt;
string deeFlat;
```

The variable can be initialized, meaning given an initial value, at the time it is declared—although this is not required. Here are the same variables declared *and* initialized:

```
int theInt = 42;
string deeFlat = "This is a string!";
```

Alternatively, of course, with the same effect, you could declare the variables and later assign them values:

```
int theInt;
string deeFlat;
...
theInt = 42;
deeFlat = "This is a string!";
```

To digress for a second here: you may not know that even simple value types such as int inherit from object. This implies that you could declare an int (or other value type) variable using the new constructor. So

```
int i = new int();
```

is equivalent to the standard int declaration:

```
int i;
```

Definite Assignment

One thing you should know is that C# requires that variables be assigned a value—either through initialization or programmatic assignment—before they are used. This is known as *definite assignment* and codifies what is good practice in any case. As they say, an uninitialized variable is like an unmade bed—you never know what you'll find in it.

For example,

```
string unMadeBed;
MessageBox.Show(unMadeBed, "Hello, Variables!",
    MessageBoxButtons.OK);
```

produces a syntax error and will not compile because of the attempted use of an unassigned variable.

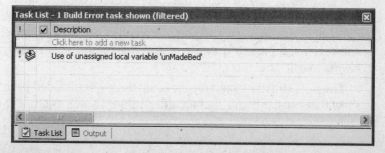

Constants

A *constant* is an identifier used in place of a value. (You can think of a constant as a variable whose value cannot be changed.) Constants should be used for fixed values that occur many places in your code. They should also be used in place of a value whose purpose is not immediately clear from the value.

Constants used in this way—also called *symbolic constants*—are declared in C# using the const keyword followed by the constant's type, an identifier, and the assignment of value. A constant must be initialized when it is declared, and once it has been initialized the value cannot be changed.

For example, here are the declarations for three notional constants:

```
const int maxSearchRecords = 41928;
const decimal interestRate = 6.75M;
const string companyMotto = "Best of the Best of the Best!";
```

The first of these, maxSearchRecords, might represent the maximum number of records in a search routine. Even if you use this value only once, using an identifier in this manner makes what it represents much clearer than would be the case if the value itself was used.

NOTE
For constants that you may need to change, it is also a good idea to put them in a place where you can find them—at the top of a procedure, or in their own class module, as appropriate.

The second constant, interestRate, might be used in a financial application. The M following the value tells the compiler that the value is of type decimal rather than double. Assigning 6.75, which alone would be a literal of type double, to a decimal-type constant would produce a conversion error. (The trailing letter here can be upper- or lowercase: m or M.)

If the interestRate value is used repeatedly in the program, it's certainly easier—and a better practice—to only change it once, when the constant value is assigned, rather than throughout the application. (Of course, in the real world you'd probably want to do this technique one better and provide a way to change the interest rate used without having to edit—and recompile—code.)

The final constant example, companyMotto, is included primarily to show that constants can contain string values, as well as other data types.

Here's companyMotto used with a MessageBox.Show method:

```
MessageBox.Show(companyMotto, "Sir!", MessageBoxButtons.OK);
```

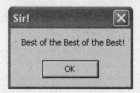

The same reasons for using constants rather than literal values apply to string types, and perhaps companyMotto is an example of this: You don't have to retype the string in numerous places in your application, and if the company changes its motto, you only have to change it in one place.

NOTE
Dynamic properties, found at the top of the Properties window, allow you to load properties from an external configuration file. These values, which can easily be changed without the need for recompiling a project, can be used in the place of constants in an application. For more information, look up "Introduction to Dynamic Properties" in online help.

Enumeration Constants

Enumerations are lists of named constants—called *enumeration constants*—of the same type. (The list of constants within an enumeration is also called the *enumerator list*.)

Built-In Enumerations

You've almost certainly used the enumeration constants that are part of the .NET Framework's pre-built types. One often-used example is MessageBox enumeration constants, which define the buttons and graphics shown in a message box.

The fourth MessageBox.Show method argument represents the icon that will be displayed in the message box. This icon is selected by choosing from a list of enumeration constants, each a member of the MessageBoxIcon enumeration. You'll see the list of constants for the enumeration supplied by the auto-completion feature of the Code Editor when you type in a MessageBox.Show (Figure 2.1).

```
string ii = ii ;
MessageBox.Show        Asterisk
    "Hello, Vari        Error        eBoxButtons.OK);
string unMadeBe        Exclamation
MessageBox.Show        Hand
    "Hello, Vari        Information    eBoxButtons.OK);*/
const int maxSe        None          1928;
const decimal c        Question      = 6.75M;
const string co        Stop          Best of the Best of the Best!";
MessageBox.Show        Warning        "Sir!", MessageBoxButtons.OK,
    MessageBoxIcon.);
```

1 of 12 System.Windows.Forms.DialogResult **MessageBox.Show** (System.Windows.Forms.IWin32Window owner, string text)
Displays a message box in front of the specified object and with the specified text.

FIGURE 2.1: The auto-completion feature of the Code Editor supplies the members of an enumerator list.

You can also find member information for an enumerator list in the Object Browser, as shown in Figure 2.2.

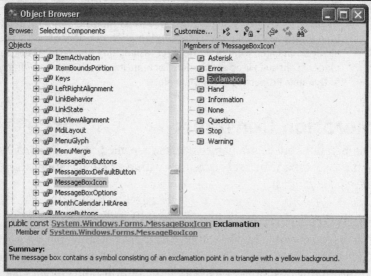

FIGURE 2.2: The members of an enumeration constant list are shown in the Object Browser.

The icon that represents the choice made by the selection of the enumeration constant from the list of MessageBoxIcon members will be displayed when the message box is displayed:

```
const string companyMotto = "Best of the Best of the Best!";
MessageBox.Show(companyMotto, "Sir!", MessageBoxButtons.OK,
    MessageBoxIcon.Exclamation);
```

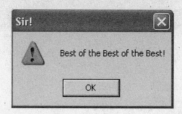

Custom Enumerations

Enumerations are too good to just use with types provided by .NET—you'll want to use your own enumerations, using the enum keyword, in situations where related items form a natural list of possibilities.

An enumeration has a *base* type, which is the underlying C# intrinsic type for items in the enumeration. If the base type of an enumeration is not specified, it defaults to int. In addition, you needn't assign a value to each enumeration constant (but you can if you wish). In the default case, the first item in the enumerator list has a value of zero, and each successive enumerator is increased by one. For example, if you created an enumeration named *toys* with three items

```
enum toys {train, dinosaur, truck};
```

the items would have values as follows:

Enumerator	Value
toys.train	0
toys.dinosaur	1
toys.truck	2

Now, when you attempt to use this enumeration, the members appear alphabetically in the Code Editor's auto-completion list, just like a built-in enumeration.

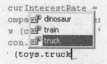

The members of the *toys* enumeration will also appear in the Object Browser.

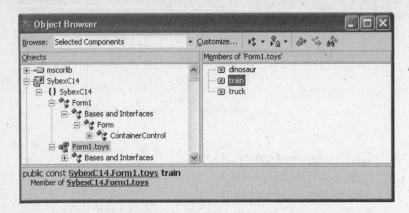

By the way, if you attempted to display the value of toys.truck using a statement along the lines of

```
MessageBox.Show(toys.truck.ToString());
```

you'd get the string "truck" rather than the underlying value.

To access the underlying value of the enumeration constant, you would have to cast it to integer type. For example, under this scenario,

```
int x = (int) toys.truck;
```

the variable *x* now has a value of 2. For more about casting, see "Type Conversion" later in this chapter.

NOTE   The enum declaration should appear as part of a class definition, rather than inside a method, because placing one inside a method causes compilation errors.

If you wish to explicitly assign values to the enumeration items, you can do so in the enum declaration. For example,

```
enum toys {train = 12, dinosaur = 35, truck = 42};
```

You can also start an enumeration list at whatever value you'd like and only assign values to some items—in which case, the default is to increment by 1. So, if the *toys* enumeration were modified as follows:

```
enum toys {train = 12,
    dinosaur,
    excavator = 41,
    truck
};
```

then `toys.dinosaur` would have a value of 13 and `toys.truck` a value of 42.

TYPES

Everything in C# is a type—which is why the topic of types has already come up numerous times in this discussion of basic C# syntax. So we had better get C# and types under our belt right away to put an end to the continuing possibility of circular definitions.

So far in this chapter I've used a few types—`int`, `string`, and `decimal`— to provide examples of constants, variables, and enumerations. Table 2.2 shows the complete list of C# predefined, or intrinsic, types (also sometimes called *primitive* types). These predefined types are declared using a keyword that functions as an alias or shorthand for the type provided by the system. For example, the keyword `int` refers to the `System.Int32` type, and the keyword `string` refers to the `System.String` type. (Stylistically, you should use the keyword rather than the fully qualified name of the underlying type to refer to the type.)

TABLE 2.2: Predefined C# Types

Keyword	.NET Type	Bytes Reserved in Memory	Description
byte	System.Byte	1	Unsigned 8-bit integer value (0 to 255).
char	System.Char	1	Unicode character.
bool	System.Boolean	1	Boolean type: either true or false. Visual Basic users should note that the bool type can contain only true or false, and not an integer value of 0, 1, or –1 as in some versions of VB.
sbyte	System.Sbyte	1	Signed 8-bit integer value (–128 to 127).

TABLE 2.2 continued: Predefined C# Types

KEYWORD	.NET TYPE	BYTES RESERVED IN MEMORY	DESCRIPTION
short	System.Int16	2	Signed 16-bit integer value (–32,768 to 32,767).
ushort	System.Uint16	2	Unsigned 16-bit integer value (0 to 65,535).
int	System.Int32	4	Signed 32-bit integer value (–2,147,483,647 to 2,147,483,647).
uint	System.Uint32	4	Unsigned 32-bit integer value (0 to 4,294,967,295).
float	System.Single	4	Single-precision floating point number.
double	System.Double	8	Double-precision floating point number.
decimal	System.Decimal	8	Fixed-precision number up to 28 digits and the position of the decimal place. Used in financial calculations. Requires an m or M appended (see example in the "Constants" section earlier in this chapter).
long	System.Int64	8	Signed 64-bit integer.
ulong	System.Uint64	8	Unsigned 64-bit integer.
object	System.Object	N/A	All data types, predefined and user-defined, inherit from the System.Object class, aliased as object.
string	System.String	N/A	A sequence of Unicode characters. See the next section, and Chapter 3, "Strings, Dates, Times, and Time Spans."

In Table 2.2, object and string are *reference* types, meaning that a pointer to the data is stored rather than the data itself, while the other types in the table are *value* types (meaning that the actual value of the type is stored in memory).

In addition to the predefined types, you can use C# to create custom reference types. As you'll probably gather as you continue to read this book, the heart of programming in C# is creating your own types by designing classes (which are reference types) that serve as a blueprint for objects. Besides classes, other important reference types include arrays, delegates, and interface types.

String Variables

As you probably know, you can't build much of a program without using strings. (Strings are so important that we've devoted a whole chapter—Chapter 3—to some of C#'s sophisticated ways of working with them.)

Placing double quotes around a string of alphanumeric characters creates a string literal. For example,

```
"I am a string!"
```

NOTE

Obviously, within string literals, white space does have a meaning—as opposed to everywhere else in C# where it does not. So the string literal `"I am a string!"` is not the equivalent of `"Iamastring!"`.

String variables are declared using the keyword `string`. You'll see many examples of string variables in this book, and here's another that declares a string variable and assigns a literal string value to it:

```
string sloganOfTheDay = "Today is the first day of the rest
    of your life.";
```

As usual, you can declare an uninitialized variable of type `string` and later assign a value to it programmatically. However, definite assignment requires that you never actually use an unassigned variable, string or otherwise.

UNICODE CHARACTER ENCODING SYSTEM

As I noted in Table 2.2, strings in .NET are made up of Unicode characters—actually, characters encoded using UTF-16 (Unicode transformation format, 16-bit encoding).

The Unicode formats provide a unique number for every character, no matter what the platform, no matter what the program, and no matter what the language.

You can find out more information about Unicode at `http://www.unicode.org`.

As I mentioned before, the keyword `string` is actually a kind of alias to the `System.String` class, so by declaring a variable of type `string`, you are creating an instance of a `System.String` object. You'll find out more about working with `System.String` objects in Chapter 3, but for now, you might want to have a look at the members of the `System.String` class using the Object Browser (Figure 2.3).

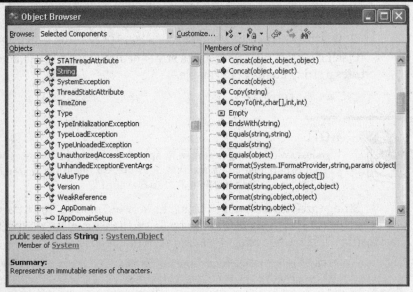

FIGURE 2.3:   You can learn how to work with string variables, which are actually objects based on the `System.String` class, using the Object Browser.

NOTE

To view the `System.String` type—and the other predefined C# types—in the Object Browser, first expand the `mscorlib` assembly node, and then expand the `System` namespace node.

C# Is a Strongly Typed Language

You've probably already heard the phrase "C# is a strongly typed language"—and may, indeed, already know what it means (in which case, you can skip this section with "type safety"). However, this whole area of strong typing and type conversions is one of the most frustrating things for programmers coming to C# from a weakly typed environment such as Visual Basic—so this and the next section are especially for those of you in that boat.

In a strongly typed language, all variables have a type that must be declared. In addition, the compiler verifies the type consistency of expressions (and expressions are always of a type defined by the C# language, or are user-defined types).

TIP

To make VB .NET strongly typed in much the way that C# .NET is, you'd run VB .NET with the compiler option `Strict` set to On, accomplished either in the IDE Options dialog box, or by adding the statement `Option Strict On` at the beginning of each code module. Note that VB6 and earlier versions of Visual Basic had no way to enforce strong typing—and were, by definition, weak type environments.

As a practical matter, working in a strongly typed language means that you need to be very clear about the type of information that will be stored in a variable. Strong typing enforces programming discipline and clarity about the contents of variables. It also prevents possible program errors that can occur in weakly typed environments when the compiler finds the wrong kind of value in a type. Another way of thinking of this is that weak typing allows a programmer to be lazy—in a possibly dubious type conversion, the compiler "guesses" what the programmer most likely meant (which can occasionally introduce errors).

The trade-off for the benefits of strong typing is more work up front. For one thing, you must explicitly declare the type of all variables (which is good programming practice even in weakly typed environments, where it may not be required). For another, you must pay close attention in your code every time a value of one type is converted to another. Much of the time, you must provide explicit guidance to the compiler using casting or a conversion method about the type conversion you'd like (see the "Explicit Conversion" section later for information about how to do this).

Type conversion can get pretty convoluted, and can involve multiple conversions within a single statement. For example, the following statement

```
mbb = (MessageBoxButtons) Convert.ToInt16(rb.Tag.ToString());
```

involves three conversions that had to be specified by the programmer:

- ▶ A cast to type `MessageBoxButtons`

- ▶ A conversion to type `short` using the `ToInt16` method of the `System.Convert` object

- ▶ A conversion to type `string` using the `ToString` method inherited by all objects from `System.Object`

A simple example is probably the best way to get a feel for the difference between working in a weakly and strongly typed environment.

If you run the following code in VB .NET (with `Option Strict` disengaged),

```
Dim theFloat As Double = 3.5
Dim X As Integer = 2
X = X + theFloat
MessageBox.Show(X)
```

the program will run without syntax errors. The value of *theFloat* will be rounded up and off to 4 when it is added and assigned to the integer *X*.

Next, in the message box statement, the integer argument *X* is automatically converted to a string type, and the value 6 is displayed.

TIP

This is convenient if it is what you want to have happen, but it is also the possible source of the introduction of errors in more complex programs if you are not counting on the round-up. Adding 3.5 and 2 and getting 6 as the integer result is not unreasonable. However, adding 2.5, 3.5, and 2 and getting 9—which is what would happen in VB—is pretty weird (8 would be a better result).

The comparable code in C#,

```
double theFloat = 3.5;
int X = 2;
X = X + theFloat;
MessageBox.Show(X);
```

simply will not compile due to several conversion-related syntax errors.

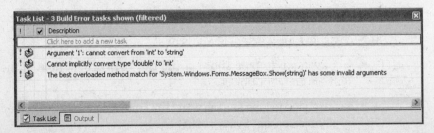

You can correct the C# code snippet by casting the double-type variable *theFloat* to int and using the ToString method to display the contents of the variable *X* in the message box:

```
double theFloat = 3.5;
int X = 2;
X = X + (int) theFloat;
MessageBox.Show(X.ToString());
```

This code compiles and runs just fine without any syntax errors, but—interestingly—it produces different results than the VB code, truncating *theFloat* to 3 and displaying 5 as the result. The (int) cast has simply taken the whole-number portion of *theFloat* variable. To perform the round-off operation that you'd normally expect when converting 3.5 to an integer value (e.g., 4), you need to use the explicit Convert.ToInt16 method:

```
double theFloat = 3.5;
int X = 2;
X = X + Convert.ToInt16(theFloat);
MessageBox.Show(X.ToString());
```

Type Conversion

All this leads us to the topic of type conversion. It isn't rocket science, and if you pay attention to it in the beginning, you will save yourself a great deal of grief. It's your job as a programmer in C# to stage-manage conversions from one type to another. As the example at the end of the previous section shows, there can be subtle differences between various ways of converting. (The example showed that casting a double to integer produced a different round-off result than using an explicit conversion function on the double.)

There are three general ways to convert from one type to another:

- Implicit conversion

- Explicit conversion via casting

- Use of a conversion method

NOTE

You can define implicit and explicit conversions for types you create. For more information, look up "User-Defined Conversions Tutorial" in online help.

I hope I haven't implied that all conversions must be explicit in C#—because that's not the case. Provided that there is no way that the conversion will lose information, C# will implicitly convert for you without any special syntax. Implicit conversions must be guaranteed to succeed and not lose information, while explicit conversions are needed if either:

▶ run-time exigencies determine whether the conversion will succeed;

▶ or, some data might be lost during conversion.

In other words, if you explicitly convert using casting, you are responsible for making sure that the results are what you anticipate and don't lead to any unexpected run-time errors.

Implicit Conversion

Table 2.3 shows the implicit conversions that are available for simple types.

TABLE 2.3:   Implicit Conversions for Simple C# Types

TYPE (CONVERSION FROM)	LEGAL IMPLICIT CONVERSION TO
Sbyte	short, int, long, float, double, or decimal
Byte	short, ushort, int, uint, long, ulong, float, double, or decimal
Short	int, long, float, double, or decimal
ushort	int, uint, long, ulong, float, double, or decimal
Int	long, float, double, or decimal
Uint	long, ulong, float, double, or decimal
Long	float, double, or decimal
Char	ushort, int, uint, long, ulong, float, double, or decimal
Float	double
Ulong	float, double, or decimal

In addition:

▶ There are no allowable implicit conversions from the bool, double, or decimal types.

▶ There are no implicit conversions allowed *to* the char type.

▶ There are no implicit conversions allowed between the floating-point types and the `decimal` type.

As its name implies, no special syntax is required to perform implicit conversion, which can take place in several situations, including assignment statements and method invocations. For example,

```
double F;
int X = 2;
F = X; // implicit conversion
```

implicitly (and successfully) converts an `int` value to type `double`.

Here's another example that implicitly converts an `int` to a `long` in a method invocation (the method takes a `long` as its argument):

```
long doubleIt(long inNum) {
    return inNum * 2;
}
...
int X = 2;
MessageBox.Show(doubleIt(X).ToString()); // displays 4
```

NOTE

For a discussion of the `ToString` method, which converts the integral return value of the `doubleIt` method to a string so that it can be displayed by the `MessageBox.Show` method, see the "Conversion Methods" section later in this chapter.

Implicit conversions are also possible for more complex reference types. Generally, when you eyeball two reference types to see whether you can do an implicit conversion, you should be asking the same question as with simple type conversions: Can I guarantee the success of the operation without data loss?

In addition, some rules do apply to reference-type implicit conversions. For example, any reference type can be implicitly converted to `object`. And, any derived class can be implicitly converted to the class it was derived from.

For more information about implicit reference conversions, search for the topic "Implicit Reference Conversions" in online help.

Explicit Conversion

In the preceding example, I showed you that an `int` value could be implicitly converted to a `long` value implicitly without any additional

C# syntax. As you'd probably suppose, and as you can see in Table 2.3, the reverse is not true: a long value cannot be implicitly converted to type int. It is easy to see why this should be the case. longs have a much larger range of possible values than ints, and there is no way the compiler can know that a long-to-int conversion won't occur when the long stores a bigger value than the int can store, causing a run-time error. In other words, the conversion isn't guaranteed safe.

If you change the code in the example around, to attempt to cause an implicit conversion,

```
int doubleIt(int inNum) {
    return inNum * 2;
}
...
long X = 2;
MessageBox.Show(doubleIt(X).ToString());
```

it won't compile, and you'll get a syntax error.

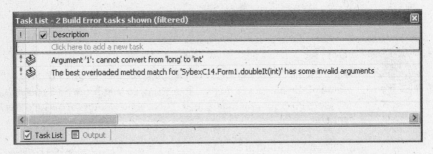

However, it might be perfectly reasonable on the part of you, the all-knowing programmer, to want to convert the long value to an int. You might know perfectly well that the variable holding the long value in the program will never hold a big enough number at the point it is converted to int to cause a problem.

In this case, you'd use an explicit conversion by placing a cast operator in front of the expression to be converted. A *cast operator* is the name of the type being converted to inside parentheses. For example, to convert the long variable *X* to an integer variable *Y*:

```
int Y = (int) X;
```

If we use this cast in the example that gave us a syntax error, it will compile and run fine now:

```
int doubleIt(int inNum) {
    return inNum * 2;
```

```
    }
    ...
    long X = 2;
    int Y = (int) X; // cast the long value to an int
    MessageBox.Show(doubleIt(Y).ToString()); // now it displays 4
```

Note that you don't really need a separate statement for the performance of the cast; it can be done at the same time as the method invocation. The doubleIt method, which expects an int argument, receives it in the form of a cast from long to int:

```
    ...
    long X = 2;
    MessageBox.Show(doubleIt((int)X).ToString());
```

Table 2.4 shows the explicit numeric conversions that you can do using casting.

TABLE 2.4: Permissible Explicit Numeric Conversions

Type (Conversion From)	Legal Explicit Conversion To
Sbyte	byte, ushort, uint, ulong, or char
Byte	sbyte or char
Short	sbyte, byte, ushort, uint, ulong, or char
ushort	sbyte, byte, short, or char
int	sbyte, byte, short, ushort, uint, ulong, or char
uint	sbyte, byte, short, ushort, int, or char
long	sbyte, byte, short, ushort, int, uint, ulong, or char
ulong	sbyte, byte, short, ushort, int, uint, long, or char
char	sbyte, byte, or short
float	sbyte, byte, short, ushort, int, uint, long, ulong, char, or decimal
double	sbyte, byte, short, ushort, int, uint, long, ulong, char, float, or decimal
decimal	sbyte, byte, short, ushort, int, uint, long, ulong, char, float, or double

NOTE

You can explicitly cast one type to another even if the conversion could be handled by implicit conversion (for example, int to long).

Casts can be done between more complex reference types as well as simple numeric types. Of course, some rules do apply. For example, object can be cast to any reference type, and a base class can be explicitly converted to a derived class.

For example, the *sender* parameter of an event procedure is cast here to the type Control:

```
Control ctrl = (Control) sender;
```

This cast will not fail, because each object stored in the *sender* parameter had to be a control and derived from the Control class.

In actual practice, you may have to test these conversions on a case-by-case basis. If an explicit reference conversion fails, a System .InvalidCastException is thrown. (For more information about exceptions, see the "Exceptions" section toward the end of this chapter.)

The *as* Operator

Operators aren't really discussed until later in this chapter. However, I've already used several of them in this book—for example, the simple assignment operator (=). Casts, which we've just discussed, are operators. You probably have a pretty good notion of what most of the operators in C# are likely to be (for more information, see the "Operators" section later in this chapter).

So it seems appropriate to discuss the as operator here. The as operator works like a cast, except that if it can't perform the indicated conversion, it returns null rather than throwing an exception.

NOTE
The null keyword represents a null reference, one that does not refer to any object.

For example, the following code snippet will store a null reference in the variable *str* (with the resulting display that "i is not a string"):

```
object i = 42;
string str = i as string;
if (str == null){
    MessageBox.Show("i is not a string");
}
else {
    MessageBox.Show(str);
}
```

Had the variable *i* contained string data, such as

```
object i = "hello";
```

then the string data "hello" would have been displayed in the message box after the object type *i* was converted to the string type *str*.

Conversion Methods

The shared public members of the System.Convert class can be used to convert a base data type to another base data type. For example, somewhat trivially, the Convert.ToBoolean method converts the string "False" to the bool value false:

```
if (Convert.ToBoolean("False") == false){
    MessageBox.Show("False");
}
else {
    MessageBox.Show("True");
}
```

If you run this code snippet, you can use it to display yet another "False" string!

In theory, a Convert class method exists to convert every base type to every other base type, and you'll probably find yourself using these methods quite a bit. For example, in Chapter 8, "Building a Better Windows Interface," you'll see how to retrieve an item's text from a ListBox by index. As part of that demonstration, the user enters the index to be retrieved as a text string. That string, for example "4", will require conversion to an integral value so that the item's text can be displayed:

```
MessageBox.Show
    (checkedListBox1.Items [Convert.ToInt16(txtIndex.Text)]
        .ToString(),
```

```
    "Here is your text", MessageBoxButtons.OK,
        MessageBoxIcon.Information);
```

If you look up the System.Convert class in the Object Browser, as shown in Figure 2.4, you'll see that there are really a huge number of these conversion methods.

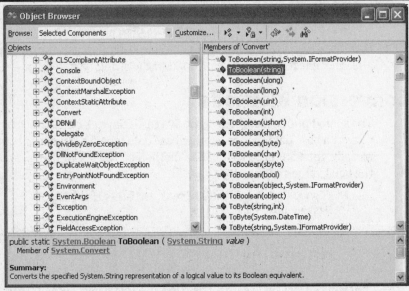

FIGURE 2.4:   If you look in the Object Browser, you'll see that the Convert class has a great many conversion methods.

You should know that the Convert methods throw an exception (and don't do any conversion) when meaningful results cannot be obtained. For example, calling any of the methods that convert the reference type System.DateTime to or from anything other than string always produces an exception (and no conversion takes place).

NOTE

If a method always throws an exception when invoked, this is noted in the summary in the Descriptions pane of the Object Browser. Why include these methods, such as ToDateTime(long), which throw an exception whenever invoked and *never* convert anything? Beats the heck out of me...

In addition, an overflow exception is thrown (and no conversion takes place) if you try to stuff too large a value into a type that cannot store it.

The *ToString* Method

Another very useful conversion method is System.Object.ToString. I've already used this method several times in this chapter, but here is another example. In the following code lines, the ToString method is used to display method information about methods of a class obtained via reflection:

```
foreach (MethodInfo method in theMethods){
    lstMethods.Items.Add(method.ToString());
```

The good news about the ToString method is that since it is a member of the object type, all other types inherit it. Whatever your object is, it has a ToString method that delivers a string.

One thing that ToString is always good for is converting numbers to their string representation—a common task in displaying numbers, among other things. For example, you can use the ToString method to display the first four places of the expansion of Π:

```
double theNumber = 3.1415;
MessageBox.Show(theNumber.ToString());
```

A moment ago, I told you that the good news is that the ToString of any object will always deliver a string. The bad news is that it may not always be the string you want or need. By definition, the ToString method of an object returns a string that represents the object. The problem is that it is up to the implementer of a class to decide what is returned by objects based on the class. Most of the time, ToString is implemented so that it returns something reasonably useful, but you won't know until you try.

For example, if you invoke a form's ToString method, you'll get the fully qualified form name, followed by the literal ", Text:", followed by the contents of the form's Text property (its caption), as shown in Figure 2.5.

Now, most likely what you really wanted was the unqualified name of the form—and it is true that you could parse this out of the string returned by the ToString method—but the point stands that with complex objects, you need to be careful about exactly what ToString returns.

FIGURE 2.5:   The `ToString` method of a form provides quite a bit of information.

NOTE

When it comes time to create your own classes, you should understand that you are responsible for implementing the `ToString` method in a way that returns a useful value.

COMMENTING CODE

I described the mechanisms for commenting, or annotating, C# code early in this book, in Chapter 1, "Introduction to Visual C# and the .NET Framework"—but commenting is such an important part of producing good code that it is worth reminding you about them.

Two forward slash marks (//) designate a comment in the so-called C++ style. Everything on the line following the two forward slash marks is considered a comment and is ignored by the compiler. Here are two examples:

```
// I am a comment!
double theNumber = 3.1415; // This is another comment...
```

C# also supports comments that begin with /* and end with */. (This is called C-style commenting.) Everything within these delimiters is a comment, which can span multiple lines. For example:

```
/* I am a comment! */
/* I
   am
   another
   comment! */
```

Self-Documenting Code

The content of a comment is, of course, more important than its form. Comments should be used in the context of code that is crafted for clarity. Clear code is largely self-documenting.

Self-documenting code

- ▶ Pays attention to the structural and conceptual design of a program and the objects used in it.

- ▶ Uses expressions and statements that are written for clarity of purpose.

- ▶ Makes sure that flow control statements clearly express what they are doing.

- ▶ Uses white space and statement layout to promote clarity of intention.

- ▶ Uses identifiers intelligently.

- ▶ Uses variable and constant identifiers that express the nature of the variable or value being stored.

- ▶ Makes sure that method identifiers express what the method does.

- ▶ Uses method parameters that clearly convey expected inputs and outputs.

- ▶ Uses class identifiers to convey the nature of objects that can be instantiated based on the class.

- ▶ Doesn't try to make objects (or methods) serve multiple purposes.

So, What About Comments?

So if the code is clearly written and it's so gosh darn self-documenting, when should comments be used?

Comments should be used to clarify anything that is not otherwise obvious—for example, the expected value range of a method argument. In another example, if you have a complicated double or triple cast and conversion, you might want to add a comment to the code explaining what it is doing (so that you don't have to figure it out again next time you look at the code).

It is also a good general practice to add a comment at the beginning of each type—such as a class—indicating the author, date, revision history, and purpose of the type, with notes about anything unusual or not likely to be clear on casual inspection.

XML DOCUMENTATION

C# lines beginning with three slashes (///) are called XML documentation, a special form of commenting. *XML documentation* is information contained between tags that can be used to automatically create a set of documentation for a program. This documentation can be used online in a special viewer provided by Visual Studio or to create a separate documentation file.

The great advantage of using XML documentation is that it is easy to document projects while you work—but harder if someone has to come back later and do it. (The sad truth, most of the time, is that if you don't document it while you do it, a project most likely never gets documented.)

For a complete list of the XML tags that can be used with the documentation facility, see the "Tags for Documentation Comments" topic in online help.

OPERATORS

As you'd expect, C# has a full complement of operators in various categories, most of which are shown in Table 2.5. You should also know that many operators can be *overloaded* in user-defined types—in other words, the meaning of the operators can be customized when user-defined types, such as classes, are involved in operations (for more on overloading, see Chapter 5, "Derived Classes").

TABLE 2.5:   C# Operators

OPERATOR ARITHMETIC	MEANING
+	Addition.
–	Subtraction.
*	Multiplication.

TABLE 2.5 continued: C# Operators

Operator Arithmetic	Meaning
/	Division.
%	Modulus.
Logical (Boolean and Bitwise)	
&	AND.
|	OR.
^	Exclusive OR.
!	NOT.
~	Bitwise complement.
&&	Conditional AND—only evaluates its second operand if necessary.
||	Conditional OR—only evaluates its second operand if necessary.
String Concatenation	
+	Concatenates two strings.
Increment, Decrement	
++	Increments operand by 1 (see following text).
--	Decrements operand by 1 (see following text).
Comparison	
==	Equality. Note that this operator, which compares two operands, should not be confused with the assignment operator (=).
!=	Inequality.
<	Less than.
>	Greater than.
<=	Less than or equal.
>=	Greater than or equal.
Assignment	
=	Assigns the value of the right operand to the left operand. Not to be confused with the equality comparison operator (==).
+=	Addition assignment.
-=	Subtraction assignment.

TABLE 2.5 continued: C# Operators

OPERATOR ARITHMETIC	MEANING
Assignment	
*=	Multiplication assignment.
/=	Division assignment.
%=	Modulus assignment.
&=	AND assignment.
|=	OR assignment.
^=	Exclusive OR assignment.
Member Access	
.	The member access operator, also called the dot operator; used to access members of a type. For example, Form1.Text can be used to get or set the Text property of Form1.
Indexing	
[ ]	Array indexing (square brackets are also used to specify attributes). For more about indexing, see Chapter 6, "Arrays, Indexers, and Collections."
Casting	
( )	See "Explicit Conversion" earlier in this chapter.
as	See "The *as* Operator" earlier in this chapter.
Conditional	
?:	Conditional operator (see following text).
Delegate Addition and Removal	
+	Adds a delegate. (Delegates are pointers to methods such as events. See the "Adding an Event" section in Chapter 7, "Reflecting on Classes," for an example of how to use a delegate.)
-	Removes a delegate.
Object Creation	
new	Creates an instance of an object.
Type Information	
is	Type comparison (see following text).
sizeof	Returns the size, in bytes, of a value type.
typeof	Returns the type of an object as a System.Type object.

When the increment operator is placed before the operand (a prefix increment operator), the result of the operation is the value of the operand after it has been incremented. When placed after the operand (a postfix increment operator), the result of the operation is the value of the operand before it has been incremented. The decrement operator works in similar fashion.

The conditional operator (?:), also called the ternary operator, returns one of two values depending on the value of a conditional expression. For example, the variable *whichOne* in the expression

```
string whichOne = (1 == 0) ? "Condition True" : "Condition False";
```

is assigned the string value "Condition False" because the expression 1 == 0 always evaluates to false, thus causing the second choice to be selected.

The is operator checks to see whether the run-time type of an object is of a given type. A little more precisely, it evaluates true if the test expression, which must be a reference type, can be cast to the specified type without throwing an exception.

TIP

VB programmers are used to one operator symbol (=) performing both assignment and comparison. In contrast, C# uses different symbols for the two different operators: == for comparison, and = for assignment. This can be a little confusing until you get used to it, but it probably is a better way of doing things in the long run because using a single operator for a single purpose has less potential for confusion.

SHORT-CIRCUIT EVALUATION

The conditional AND and OR operators (&& and ||) perform what is sometimes called *short-circuit evaluation*. This means that they do not evaluate the second part of an expression if there is no need to. For example, if you have the expression a && b, and *a* has evaluated to false, *b* will not be evaluated. Obviously, there is some performance benefit to not having to look at the second operand.

However, this contains the seeds of a hidden pitfall if the evaluation of an expression contained in *b* is required for successful execution. (In the classic example, *b* is a function that performs other tasks

CONTINUED ➡

before returning its Boolean result.) Since *b* never gets evaluated, the program will fail. So be cautious when you are using short-circuit evaluation to make sure that you aren't introducing an unexpected side effect by not evaluating an operand.

As a matter of good programming practice, I'd hate to see you writing code that uses evaluations performed in a logical operation to perform some other action needed for program success. This kind of tricky code can be fun to write, but it violates the precepts of writing clear code and keeping objects and methods from doing more than one thing. If you don't try to get too fancy for your own good, you shouldn't have problems with short-circuit evaluations.

NOTE

The indirection and address operators (*, ->, [ ], and &) are used to declare, reference, and deference pointers, and obtain memory addresses, all within "unsafe" code—that is, code within a context, such as a method, that has been marked with the unsafe keyword. Although you should know that they exist, it is unlikely that you will want to use them. Code using them cannot be run as "safe" by the .NET Common Language Runtime (CLR), and it's obvious why they are unsafe. If you have direct access to memory, and can control pointers to memory, corruption can always occur. Generally, you should not have any use for these operators—except in certain specialized situations, such as interoperating with COM objects.

Table 2.6 shows operator *precedence,* or the order in which a series of operators are evaluated, in C#. When an operand occurs between two operators of equal precedence, operations are performed from left to right (except in the case of the assignment and conditional operators, which are evaluated right to left).

TABLE 2.6: Operator Precedence (in Descending Order of Category Precedence)

CATEGORY	OPERATORS
Primary	Member access operator (.), order indicated by parentheses, indexing, x++, x--, new, typeof
Unary	Cast operator, +, -, !, ~, ++x, --x

TABLE 2.6 continued: Operator Precedence (in Descending Order of Category Precedence)

CATEGORY	OPERATORS
Multiplicative	*, /, %
Additive	+, –
Relational and type testing	<, >, <=, >=, is, as
Equality	==, !=
Logical AND	&
Logical exclusive OR	^
Logical OR	|
Conditional AND	&&
Conditional OR	||
Conditional	?:
Assignment	=, *=, /=, %=, +=, –=, <<=, >>=, &=, ^=, |=

As a matter of good programming practice and to make code clearer to read, you should not rely on the order of operator precedence if this might be confusing—instead, use parentheses to make the evaluation order explicit and clear. Order indicated by parentheses takes precedence over operator-driven order, except that of the member access operator.

FLOW CONTROL STATEMENTS

Almost every programming language contains the basic flow control statements such as if else, for, foreach, and switch (or a variant thereof). I'll assume that you know how to work with these basic flow control statements—which are fairly straightforward in any case—and use this section to explain some other C# flow control statements.

Flow to with *goto*

The lowly goto statement is alive and well in C#. goto statements are easy to use and direct; however, as is well known, over-reliance on them leads to unmanageable "spaghetti" code. In C#, goto statements are useful in a special situation—with `switch` statements. So it's worth having a look at the ancient, decrepit granddaddy of all flow control statements, one that surely gets no respect, the `goto`.

A `goto` statement causes an immediate, unconditional jump to a label, which is an identifier followed by a colon. For example,

```
IamAlabel:
```

To put this in the context of a short program, suppose the user gets to input a favorite member of the Beatles musical group in a TextBox named *txtBeatle*. The following code in a Button click event procedure uses `goto` statements and labels to display an appropriate message box if the user enters "John" or "Ringo," as shown in Figure 2.6, and otherwise, it displays no message:

```csharp
private void btnClickMe_Click(object sender, System.EventArgs e) {
    string msg = "";
    if (txtBeatle.Text == "John")
        goto john;
    if (txtBeatle.Text == "Ringo")
        goto ringo;
    goto done;
    john:
        msg = "I like John best, too!";
        goto done;
    ringo:
        msg = "Are you a drummer?";
        goto done;
    done:
        if (msg != "")
            MessageBox.Show(msg, "Beatle choice",
                MessageBoxButtons.OK);
}
```

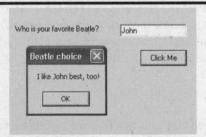

FIGURE 2.6:   Flow control can be achieved using `goto` statements and labels.

A couple of things are worth noting about the code snippet just shown. First, even in this simple example, one can see why using goto statements produces fragmented, confusing code.

Second, the if statements in this example are in the simplest form possible, namely the expression to be evaluated followed by a single statement. Curly braces following the evaluation expression in the if statement can also be used, which allows you to include a *statement block*—as many statements as you'd like—even when this wasn't strictly necessary because I only had one statement to execute.

Using *goto* in a *switch*

Of course, you can easily simplify this code by using a switch statement rather than goto statements and labels:

```
string msg = "";
switch (txtBeatle.Text) {
    case "John":
        msg = "I like John best, too!";
        break;
    case "Ringo":
        msg = "Are you a drummer?";
        break;
}
if (msg != "")
    MessageBox.Show(msg,"Beatle choice", MessageBoxButtons.OK);
```

Let's say you want to add another possibility to this switch statement, for people who enter "Mick" but really mean they like John. For this situation, a goto case statement—to the "John" case—can be added at the end of the "Mick" case. Users who enter "Mick" will be told they really like John and then they will be redirected so that they also get the "John" message:

```
switch (txtBeatle.Text) {
    case "John":
        msg = "I like John best, too!";
        break;
    case "Mick":
        MessageBox.Show("People who like Mick really like John.",
            "Beatle choice", MessageBoxButtons.OK);
        goto case "John";
    case "Ringo":
        msg = "Are you a drummer?";
        break;
}
```

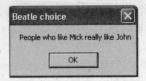

while Statements

Looping is an important flow control element of most programs. As in most other languages that have a while statement, the code within a while statement block is executed as long as the Boolean test at the beginning of the statement evaluates to true. As soon as the test evaluates to false, execution jumps to the statement immediately following the while statement block.

For example, the following while loop displays the integers from 1 to 9 in the title bar of a form:

```
int i = 1;
string caption = "While";
while (i < 10){
    caption = caption + " + " + i.ToString();
    i++;
}
this.Text = caption;
```

do while Statements

The do while statement works like the while statement, except that the evaluation takes place at the end of the loop. Statements in a do while loop will get executed at least once—even if the condition evaluates to false at the end. In contrast, if the condition is false, the statements in a while loop never get executed at all because the condition is evaluated at the start. Most of the time, the same results can be accomplished using either loop syntax, but there are some times when one works better than the other.

NOTE

For example, if you are reading and operating on data and don't know whether there is any data, you might want use a while statement to test for the existence of the data—perhaps testing for an end of file marker—so that if the data doesn't exist, no statements get executed.

Here's a do while statement that displays the first 9 numbers in the Fibonacci series in the title bar of a form:

```
int A = 1; int B = 1; int C;
string caption = "Fibonacci: ";
do {
    caption = caption + A.ToString() + " ";
    C = A + B;
    A = B;
    B = C;
} while (A < 50);
this.Text = caption;
```

NOTE

If the condition in this loop were impossible, for instance, if A < 0, it would still print the first number in the series, which would not be the case in a while loop with the condition at the top.

Fibonacci: 1 1 2 3 5 8 13 21 34

STRUCTS

A struct is a simple user-defined type, a poor person's lightweight alternative to a class. Like classes, structs can contain properties, methods, and fields. Unlike classes, structs do not support inheritance. More precisely, structs derive from System.Object, like all types in C#, but they cannot inherit from any other class (or struct), and no class or struct can derive from a struct.

NOTE

A class can also be marked so that it cannot be inherited from, by using the sealed keyword, as I'll explain in Chapter 5.

Structs are value types, not reference types, and—like simple value types—they can be used without the new keyword.

MEMORY, VALUE-TYPE VARIABLES, AND REFERENCE-TYPE VARIABLES

Value-type variables hold their values, or data, within their own memory allocation. Technically, these values are stored in memory allocated for the value-type variable within a structure known as the program's *stack*, and they can be accessed from within the program as long as they are within scope.

In contrast, reference-type variables—such as classes and strings—are implemented using a global memory structure called the *run-time heap*. Reference-type variables contain instances of classes, which are "pointers" to objects stored in memory on the heap.

Here's a simple example of a struct that might be used to store information about an employee:

```
public struct Employee {
    public string fullName, rank;
    public long SSN;
    public Employee (string fullName, string rank, long SSN){
        this.fullName = fullName;
        this.rank = rank;
        this.SSN = SSN;
    }
}
```

NOTE
You can create properties, using get and set accessors, within structs.

Here's one way the Employee struct might be declared, initialized, and used:

```
// Declare an instance
Employee HopperK;

// Initialize
HopperK.fullName = "Ken Hopper";
HopperK.rank = "Master Sergeant";
HopperK.SSN = 000112222;

// Display it
string str = HopperK.fullName + " has the rank of " +
    HopperK.rank + "!";
```

```
MessageBox.Show(str, "Structs Forever!",MessageBoxButtons.OK,
    MessageBoxIcon.Information);
```

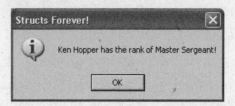

Alternatively, you could create the instance of the struct by invoking its constructor, and then you can initialize it in one fell swoop:

```
Employee DavisJ = new Employee("Julian Davis", "City Hall",
    123456789);
```

EXCEPTIONS

An *exception* is an unexpected condition in a program. For example, an exception may occur if you attempt to connect to the database but can't, because the database server is down. The C# Exception object is used to store information about errors and abnormal events.

In real-world practice, industrial-strength programs must anticipate run-time errors. For example, a network resource might not be available because the network is down. Or a file can't be written to disk because the disk drive is full. With the best code in the world, these things happen. In the release version of a program, these and other errors must be handled, which in C# is done with exceptions.

What does it mean to "handle" an exception (or error)? These are the basics:

▶ Your program should not crash under any circumstances.

▶ If the situation can be recovered from, and the program can continue execution, it should.

- ▶ If execution cannot continue, a reasonably comprehensible message should explain that the program is terminating, and if appropriate, explain why.

- ▶ Data should not be lost due to an unplanned failure.

- ▶ The program should shut down gently.

- ▶ In any case, information necessary for debugging the problem should be saved, either to a file or the system event log. (It's easy to simultaneously send the user a message and write to the system log with MessageBox.Show.)

Understanding Structured Exception Handling

Structured exception handling is recognized as the best way for a programming language to deal with common errors.

Using *try...catch...finally* Statements

When an exception does occur, you can use try catch finally statements to handle it.

The program statements in the try block are the body of the program that is being monitored for errors. Statements in a catch block are executed in response to a particular exception being thrown, as indicated in the catch statement's argument—or, if without an argument, the statement will catch any kind of exception, in which case it is referred to as a *general catch clause*.

As you would expect, code in the optional finally block is executed, whether an error has been caught or not.

NOTE

Not only is finally optional, so is catch. In other words, you can have a try without a finally and also a try finally construction with no catch block Valid exception handling constructs include try...catch, try...finally, and try..catch..finally.

For example, if you have a form with a TextBox control and a Button control, you could add the following code in the button's Click event to catch different kinds of problems:

```
private void btnExceptions_Click(object sender,
    System.EventArgs e) {
    int i; double d;
```

```
try {
    i = Convert.ToInt16(txtIn.Text);
    d = 42 / i;
}
catch (DivideByZeroException){
    MessageBox.Show("You are naughty to even think of
        dividing by zero!",
        "Exceptions", MessageBoxButtons.OK,
            MessageBoxIcon.Error);
}
catch (FormatException){
    MessageBox.Show("Please enter a number!", "Exceptions",
        MessageBoxButtons.OK, MessageBoxIcon.Error);
}
}
```

In this example, `catch` deals with the situation if the user enters zero—which would cause a division by zero—as shown in Figure 2.7.

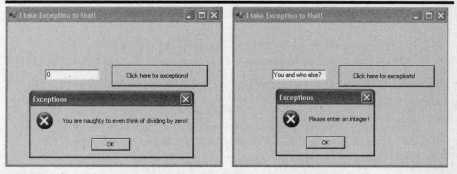

FIGURE 2.7: The `DivideByZeroException` (left) and the `FormatException` (right) are caught.

As you can also see in the figure, a `FormatException` catch block can be used to handle the exception that occurs when the user enters something that can't be converted to integer by `Convert.ToInt16`.

It's possible to have the first `catch` filter without any conditions:

```
catch
    statement block
```

You could also just catch the general `Exception` type:

```
catch (Exception excep)
```

In these cases, the `catch` filter will catch all errors. In some situations, you can use this as a centralized error-processing mechanism along the lines of "if any error happens, go here and take care of it." Often, however, it is a better idea to use specific catch clauses to handle certain types of exceptions. A final, generic catch clause could deal with all exceptions that don't need special handling—or that you didn't think of when you wrote the code.

Listing 2.1 shows the exception example with an added, general catch clause at the end.

Listing 2.1: Handling Exceptions with try catch

```
private void btnExceptions_Click(object sender,
    System.EventArgs e) {
    int i; double d;
    try {
        i = Convert.ToInt16 (txtIn.Text);
        d = 42 / i;
    }
    catch (DivideByZeroException){
        MessageBox.Show("You are naughty to even think of
            dividing by zero!",
            "Exceptions", MessageBoxButtons.OK,
                MessageBoxIcon.Error);
    }
    catch (FormatException){
        MessageBox.Show("Please enter a number!", "Exceptions",
            MessageBoxButtons.OK, MessageBoxIcon.Error);
    }
    catch (Exception excep) {
        MessageBox.Show(excep.Message);
    }
}
```

WARNING

If you reverse the order shown in Listing 2.1 and put the general catch clause before the specific catch exceptions, then the specific exception blocks are never processed.

If you run the code shown in Listing 2.1, you can trigger an error that is not handled by one of the specific catch handlers—for example, you can cause an overflow exception if the user enters a number larger than will fit in the data type, as shown in Figure 2.8.

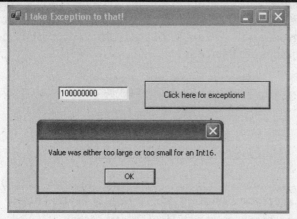

FIGURE 2.8:   Since the OverflowException is not handled by a specific catch clause, it is handled by the general catch clause at the end of the catch blocks.

By the way, instead of displaying the Message property of the Exception object, you could make use of its ToString method, which contains a great deal of information, including the procedure, method, and line number that threw the exception. If you changed the final catch clause in Listing 2.1 to show the information returned by the ToString method to this

```
catch (Exception excep) {
    MessageBox.Show(excep.ToString());
}
```

it would appear as shown in Figure 2.9.

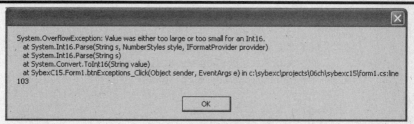

FIGURE 2.9:   The ToString method of the Exception object contains a great deal of information about a thrown exception.

Boy, is that finally clause out of its mind, or what? You can't stop it from being executed, regardless of whether exceptions are thrown or, if thrown, handled or unhandled. This makes the finally clause the place to put clean-up code that you want executed no matter what happens.

Listing 2.2 shows the exception handling demonstration with a finally clause added. When you run the program, you'll see that the message box invoked in the finally clause is always displayed whether or not the exceptions are handled.

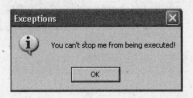

Listing 2.2: Exception Handling with a *finally* Block Added

```
private void btnExceptions_Click(object sender,
   System.EventArgs e) {
   int i; double d;
   try {
      i = Convert.ToInt16(txtIn.Text);
      d = 42 / i;
   }
   catch (DivideByZeroException){
      MessageBox.Show("You are naughty to even think of
         dividing by zero!",
         "Exceptions", MessageBoxButtons.OK,
            MessageBoxIcon.Error);
   }
   catch (FormatException){
      MessageBox.Show("Please enter an integer!", "Exceptions",
         MessageBoxButtons.OK, MessageBoxIcon.Error);
   }
   catch (Exception excep) {
      MessageBox.Show(excep.Message);
      MessageBox.Show(excep.ToString());
   }
   finally {
      MessageBox.Show("You can't stop me from being
         executed!", "Exceptions",
         MessageBoxButtons.OK, MessageBoxIcon.Information);
   }
}
```

NOTE

In the real world, you'll want to use `finally` blocks to close open files and database connections, and generally to make sure that all resources used by a program are released.

What happens if you leave off the `catch` blocks—resulting in a `try finally` statement? We can find out by modifying the code shown in Listing 2.2 to remove the `catch` blocks:

```
private void btnExceptions_Click(object sender,
    System.EventArgs e) {

    int i; double d;

    try {
        i = Convert.ToInt16(txtIn.Text);
        d = 42 / i;
    }
    finally {
        MessageBox.Show("You can't stop me from being
            executed!", "Exceptions",
            MessageBoxButtons.OK, MessageBoxIcon.Information);
    }
}
```

If the click event procedure runs without generating exceptions, the code in the `finally` block executes as you'd expect and the message box displays.

What happens next depends on whether you are running in debug mode in the development environment or whether the compiled executable was launched. Within the development environment, a Visual Studio exception message is displayed.

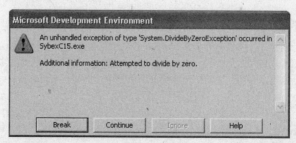

If Break is clicked, the program terminates. If Continue is clicked, the code in the `finally` clause is executed, the message box is displayed, and then the application shuts down.

Of somewhat more interest is the behavior of the stand-alone executable (because exception handling is meant to deal with problems that occur in the run-time environment, not at design time).

If you run the stand-alone executable, the `finally` block code executes. Then, if an exception had been thrown, the .NET Framework dialog shown in Figure 2.10 is displayed.

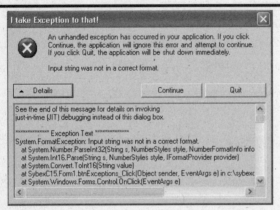

FIGURE 2.10:   When run outside the development environment, if an exception is thrown, the `finally` block executes, and then this dialog is displayed.

Not bad, really, as a user interface for all unhandled exceptions—and the `finally` code did execute before it was displayed, so in the real world, you could have saved data, closed open files, and so forth!

If the user clicks Continue in the dialog shown in Figure 2.10, the application reopens.

Throwing Exceptions

Throwing an exception means creating your own exception under certain conditions. Throwing custom exceptions should not be done to facilitate normal program communication, but it may make sense as part of a scheme for dealing with *logical errors,* which occur when a program works properly but produces wrong results. Throwing an exception is what your application should do in many circumstances if it asked to do something impossible.

To throw an exception, use the throw keyword with a new instantiation of the Exception class or one of the classes derived from Exception (the Exception object and classes are described in the next section). ApplicationException is the subclass of Exception used for exceptions thrown by an application, so it's a good one to throw.

NOTE

As a good programming practice, your application should throw only ApplicationException objects, or those that inherit ApplicationException. It's not good practice to throw instances of System.Exception.

In the real world, you may want to subclass ApplicationException to add functionality to the exception thrown.

A string representing the Exception.Message property is used to instantiate the new exception, which can then be used to catch it, as in this example:

```
throw(new ApplicationException("AttilaTheHun"));
```

This exception would probably be caught within a catch (Exception excep) block using a conditional:

```
catch (Exception excep) {
    if (excep.Message == "AttilaTheHun"){
...
```

Let's look at an example of throwing and catching an exception in practice.

There is something in business—and software development—known as the "cockroach" theory: if one problem becomes apparent, there are probably more problems lurking (like roaches).

Suppose, in the example I've used so far to show you exceptions, that the user types the phrase "cockroaches" in the TextBox. We take it that this means there are more roaches in the system and decide to throw an exception. Here's how to throw a "roaches" exception:

```
if (txtIn.Text == "cockroaches"){
    throw(new ApplicationException("roaches"));
}
```

The next step is to catch the exception to handle the situation and make sure the roaches check in but don't check out:

```
catch (Exception excep) {
    if (excep.Message == "roaches"){
```

```
        MessageBox.Show("You have roaches in your program!",
            "Exceptions",
            MessageBoxButtons.OK, MessageBoxIcon.Error);
    }
    else {
    ...
```

Listing 2.3 shows the complete code for the example, including throwing and catching the exception related to cockroaches.

Listing 2.3: Throwing and Catching an Exception

```
    private void btnExceptions_Click(object sender,
        System.EventArgs e) {
        int i; double d;
        try {
            if (txtIn.Text == "cockroaches") {
                throw(new ApplicationException("roaches"));
            }
            i = Convert.ToInt16(txtIn.Text);
            d = 42 / i;
        }
        catch (DivideByZeroException) {
            MessageBox.Show("You are naughty to even think of
                dividing by zero!",
                "Exceptions", MessageBoxButtons.OK,
                    MessageBoxIcon.Error);
        }
        catch (FormatException) {
            MessageBox.Show("Please enter an integer!", "Exceptions",
                MessageBoxButtons.OK, MessageBoxIcon.Error);
        }
        catch (Exception excep) {
            if (excep.Message == "roaches") {
            MessageBox.Show("You have roaches in your program!",
                "Exceptions",
                MessageBoxButtons.OK, MessageBoxIcon.Error);
            }
            else {
                MessageBox.Show(excep.Message);
                MessageBox.Show(excep.ToString());
            }
        }
```

```
finally {
    MessageBox.Show("You can't stop me from being
        executed!", "Exceptions",
        MessageBoxButtons.OK, MessageBoxIcon.Information);
    }
}
```

When the program is run, "cockroaches" is entered in the TextBox, and the button is clicked, the exception is thrown, and the bad news is out (Figure 2.11)!

FIGURE 2.11: This "cockroach" exception illustrates that you can throw and catch custom exceptions.

Exception Objects

So far in this discussion, exceptions have been used only as *sentinels*—the presence of the exception signals the error like a canary falling ill in a mine. It's worth thinking a little about the nature of an exception object, because they can be used for more than this.

The first thing you should know about the Exception object and the classes that inherit from it is that (for the most part) the subclasses do not vary from Exception by implementing additional members or functionality. This means that—by and large—the only difference between the parent and child classes is the name of the class. (An important exception to this is SqlException, which is thrown when SQL Server returns a rather specific warning or error.) The implication is that if you have a compelling reason to add additional information to the exception class, you certainly can, but it should still make sense to deal with your exception as a generic exception (meaning, no matter how much information you add, you should still implement a meaningful "message" property so that programmers can throw and catch it in the normal fashion).

Table 2.7 shows some of the commonly used properties and methods of the Exception object.

TABLE 2.7: Commonly Used Properties and Methods of the Exception Object

PROPERTY OR METHOD	PURPOSE
HelpLink	A link to the help file associated with the exception
Message	A message that describes the current exception
StackTrace	A string that contains the stack trace immediately before the exception was thrown
TargetSite	The method that threw the current exception
ToString	A string that contains the name of the exception and a great deal of other information, such as the error message and the stack trace

In general, the Exception class has two subclasses: Application-Exception and SystemException. In theory, ApplicationExceptions are created by your application, and SystemExceptions are created by the run-time (CLR) and operating environment.

As you would expect, there are a great many subclasses of System-Exceptions, some of which you've seen in the examples earlier in this section (for example, FormatException). Most of these exception classes are the members of the System namespace, but others are located further down the namespace tree (for example, IOException is a member of System.IO rather than System directly).

The best place to learn about individual exceptions and their class relationships is the Object Browser (details of which are explained in Chapter 7).

SUMMARY

This chapter has covered a lot of ground and explained a good deal of the syntax that you need to successfully program in C#. Great flights of fancy and soundly engineered heroic structures cannot be created without solid foundations; with this material under your belt, you can build wonderful things!

I started this chapter with Miranda's wonder at the "goodly creatures" in her "brave new world." Of course, the joke in *The Tempest* is that she had seen few people of any kind. One wonders whether they soon became commonplace to her. Perhaps she picked up the magic book belonging to Prospero and began to create new worlds and visions... which is my hope for what you will do with the rudiments of C# syntax presented in this chapter.

WHAT'S NEXT

In the next chapter, you'll learn more about some of the more commonly used types in C#—strings, dates, times, and time spans—and you'll see usage examples of each.

Chapter 3

STRINGS, DATES, TIMES, AND TIME SPANS

You've already seen examples of strings in earlier chapters. In this chapter, you'll delve deeper into the use of strings and how you manipulate them in your programs. You'll also see how you can create dynamic strings, which have efficient manipulation methods.

In addition to strings and the other built-in types, you can also represent dates and times in your programs. Examples of using a date and time would include storing a person's birth date and recording when a financial transaction took place.

You can also represent time intervals in your programs—these are known as *time spans*. An example of a time span is 4 days, 12 minutes, and 10 seconds.

Adapted from *Mastering Visual C# .NET* by Jason Price and Mike Gunderloy

ISBN 0-7821-2911-0

Using Strings

You often need to store a series of characters in your programs. For this purpose, you use a string to represent characters, which are stored as *Unicode*. Unicode is the standard for encoding most of the world's written languages, and it uses 16 bits to represent each letter. Although you've already seen examples of creating strings in previous chapters, you'll see more examples in this section to formalize their treatment. Later, you'll see the various methods you can use to manipulate strings.

Creating Strings

The following example creates a string named myString:

```
string myString = "To be or not to be";
```

You can embed escape characters in your strings. For example, the following string contains a tab character, which is specified using the \t escape character:

```
string myString2 = "...\t that is the question";
```

When this string is displayed, a tab character will appear after the ellipsis:

```
...    that is the question
```

You can also create *verbatim* strings, meaning that your string's characters are to be treated "as is." In a verbatim string, characters that make up an escape character are treated as regular characters. Verbatim strings may also be split over multiple lines. You indicate that your string is to be treated verbatim by placing an at sign (@) at the start of the string. In the following example, the verbatim string contains \t and is split across multiple lines:

```
string myString3 = @"\t Friends, Romans, countrymen,
lend me your ears";
```

When this string is displayed, it will appear as follows:

```
\t Friends, Romans, countrymen,
lend me your ears
```

Using *String* Properties and Methods

Strings are actually objects of the System.String class; this class contains properties and a rich set of methods you can use in your programs to manipulate strings.

NOTE

In fact, all the built-in types are represented using classes or structs, and they therefore have properties and methods you can use. For example, the `int` type is represented using the `System.Int32` struct, the `double` type is represented using the `System.Double` struct, and `bool` is represented using the `System.Boolean` struct. You can view the properties and methods for all the types in the .NET reference documentation.

Table 3.1 lists the `Length` public property of the `String` class.

TABLE 3.1:   String Length Property

PROPERTY	TYPE	DESCRIPTION
Length	int	Gets the number of characters in the string

The `String` class also contains a number of public methods, as shown in Table 3.2.

TABLE 3.2:   String Methods

METHOD	RETURN TYPE	DESCRIPTION
Compare()(static)	int	Overloaded. Compares the characters stored in two strings, taking into account the national language or culture.
CompareOrdinal() (static)	int	Overloaded. Compares the characters stored in two strings, without taking into account the national language or culture.
Concat()(static)	string	Overloaded. Returns the result of concatenating one or more strings. The returned string is built up by adding each string to the end of the previous string. The overloaded addition operator (+) also concatenates strings.
Copy()(static)	string	Returns a new string that is a copy of the supplied string. The overloaded assignment operator (=) also copies a string.
Equals()(static and instance versions)	bool	Overloaded. Returns a bool that specifies whether two strings are equal. The overloaded equal to operator (==) also checks whether two strings are equal.
Format()(static)	string	Overloaded. Returns a string formatted according to a supplied format.

TABLE 3.2 continued: String Methods

METHOD	RETURN TYPE	DESCRIPTION
Intern()(static)	string	Returns a system reference to the supplied string.
IsInterned()(static)	string	Returns a reference to the supplied string.
Join()(static)	string	Overloaded. Returns a string that is built up by taking the elements from an array of strings, along with a separator string. The separator is inserted between each string element in the returned string. Chapter 6, "Arrays, Indexers, and Collections," covers arrays.
Clone()	Object	Returns a reference to the string.
CompareTo()	int	Overloaded. Compares the string with a supplied string.
CopyTo()	void	Copies a specified number of characters from the string to a specified position in an array of characters.
EndsWith()	bool	Returns a bool indicating whether the string has a supplied string at the end.
GetEnumerator()	CharEnumerator	Returns an enumerator that can iterate through the characters stored in the string. Enumerators are covered in Chapter 6.
GetHashCode()	int	Returns a hash code for the string.
GetType()(inherited from Object)	Type	Returns the type of the current instance.
GetTypeCode()	TypeCode	Returns the type code for the string.
IndexOf()	int	Overloaded. Returns the index of the first occurrence of a specified substring or characters within the string. A *substring* is a portion of the original string. Indexes start at zero.
IndexOfAny()	int	Overloaded. Returns the index of the first occurrence of any character in a supplied array of characters.
Insert()	string	Inserts a supplied string into the string at a specified index.
LastIndexOf()	int	Overloaded. Returns the index of the last occurrence of a supplied substring or character in the string.

TABLE 3.2 continued: String Methods

Method	Return Type	Description
LastIndexOfAny()	int	Overloaded. Returns the index of the last occurrence of any character in a supplied array of characters.
PadLeft()	string	Overloaded. Right-aligns the characters in the string, padding to the left with spaces or a specified character for a specified total length for the new string.
PadRight()	string	Overloaded. Left-aligns the characters in the string, padding to the right with spaces or a specified character for a specified total length for the new string.
Remove()	string	Removes a specified number of characters from the string, starting at a specified index in the string.
Replace()	string	Overloaded. Replaces all occurrences of a supplied substring or character with another substring or character.
Split()	string[]	Overloaded. Splits up the string into an array of strings using a supplied separator. The array of strings is then returned.
StartsWith()	bool	Returns a bool indicating whether the string has a supplied string at the start.
Substring()	string	Overloaded. Returns a substring from the string.
ToCharArray()	char[]	Overloaded. Copies the characters from the string to a supplied character array.
ToLower()	string	Overloaded. Returns a copy of the string with all the characters converted to lowercase.
ToString()	string	Overloaded. Returns the value of the string.
ToUpper()	string	Overloaded. Returns a copy of the string with all the characters converted to uppercase.
Trim()	string	Overloaded. Removes spaces or specified characters from the beginning and end of the string.
TrimEnd()	string	Removes the specified characters (or spaces) from the end of the string.
TrimStart()	string	Removes the specified characters (or spaces) from the beginning of the string.

The following sections illustrate the Length property and some of the methods shown in Table 3.2.

Reading Individual Characters from a String Using the *Length* Property

You can use the Length property to get the number of characters in a string. The Length property returns an int value. In the following example, myString.Length is displayed:

```
Console.WriteLine(myString.Length);
```

This example displays the following:

```
18
```

This result is the total number of characters in myString, which is set to "To be or not to be".

You can read the individual characters from your string by specifying the position index of the character in the string (the first character has an index of zero). For example, myString is set to "To be or not to be", and myString[0] is T.

You can use the Length property in a for loop to read all the characters in a string. For example, the following for loop displays all the characters in myString:

```
for (int count = 0; count < myString.Length; count++)
{
  Console.WriteLine("myString[" + count + "] = " +
    myString[count]);
}
```

This example displays the following:

```
myString[0] = T
myString[1] = o
myString[2] =
myString[3] = b
myString[4] = e
myString[5] =
myString[6] = o
myString[7] = r
myString[8] =
myString[9] = n
myString[10] = o
myString[11] = t
myString[12] =
```

```
myString[13] = t
myString[14] = o
myString[15] =
myString[16] = b
myString[17] = e
```

Comparing Two Strings Using the *Compare()* Method

You can use the Compare() method to compare the characters stored in two strings, taking into account the national language or culture. The Compare() method returns an int that specifies whether the first string is greater than, equal to, or less than the second string.

The comparison is performed alphabetically on letters and numerically on any numbers that appear in the strings. The Compare() method uses the following rules to determine the int value returned:

▶ If the first string is greater than the second string, then 1 is returned.

▶ If the first string is equal to the second string, then 0 is returned.

▶ If the first string is less than the second string, then −1 is returned.

The Compare() method is overloaded and therefore contains several versions you can call, each with different parameters (method overloading will be covered in Chapter 4, "Object-Oriented Programming"). Also, because the Compare() method is static, this method belongs to the String class; therefore, you call the Compare() method using the String class, rather than an actual string object. The simplest version of Compare() accepts two string parameters and uses the following syntax:

```
String.Compare(string1, string2)
```

where *string1* and *string2* are the strings you want to compare.

The following example shows the use of this version of Compare():

```
int result = String.Compare("bbc", "abc");
```

Because "bbc" is alphabetically greater than "abc", Compare() returns 1, which is then stored in the int variable result.

In the next example, the two strings are switched in the call to Compare() and therefore Compare() returns −1:

```
result = String.Compare("abc", "bbc");
```

Next, two identical strings are compared—therefore `Compare()` returns 0:

```
result = String.Compare("bbc", "bbc");
```

Using the Case of Strings in the Comparison   Another version of `Compare()` accepts a `bool` parameter that specifies whether you want to also use the case of the two supplied strings in the comparison. This version of `Compare()` uses the following syntax:

```
String.Compare(string1, string2, ignoreCase)
```

where *ignoreCase* is a `bool` that specifies whether you want to use the case of *string1* and *string2* in the comparison. If you set *ignoreCase* to `true`, then the case of the two strings is not considered in the comparison (this is the default). If you set *ignoreCase* to `false`, then the case of the strings is considered in the comparison.

In the following example, `Compare()` returns 0 because case is ignored when comparing `"bbc"` and `"BBC"`:

```
result = String.Compare("bbc", "BBC", true);
```

But `Compare()` returns −1 in the next example because `"bbc"` is less than `"BBC"` when case isn't ignored:

```
result = String.Compare("bbc", "BBC", false);
```

Comparing Parts of Strings   You can also compare parts of strings, known as *substrings*, by specifying the indexes to start comparison and the maximum number of characters to compare in each string passed to `Compare()`. This version of `Compare()` uses the following syntax:

```
String.Compare(string1, index1, string2, index2,
    numberOfChars)
```

where *index1* and *index2* are `int` parameters that specify the indexes to start at in *string1* and *string2*, respectively, and *numberOfChars* is an `int` parameter that specifies the maximum number of characters to compare in each string.

In the following example, the `"World"` parts of two strings are compared, and `Compare()` returns 0 because both parts of the strings are equal:

```
result = String.Compare("Hello World",
    6, "Goodbye World", 8, 5);
```

Other overloaded versions of `Compare()` enable you to use a `System.Globalization.CultureInfo` object in the comparison. The `CultureInfo` class represents information about a specific culture, such as the language, the writing system, and the calendar used by a culture.

Concatenating Strings Using the *Concat()* Method

You can use the static Concat() method to concatenate strings. The Concat() method returns a new string that is built up by adding each supplied string to the end of the previous one. Concat() is overloaded, and the simplest version accepts two strings using the following syntax:

```
String.Concat(string1, string2)
```

where *string1* and *string2* are the strings you want to concatenate.

The following example uses this version of Concat() to concatenate two strings, "Friends," " " and "Romans", storing the returned string in myString4:

```
string myString4 = String.Concat("Friends, "", "Romans");
```

The string "Friends, Romans" will be stored in myString4.

You can pass any number of strings to Concat(), and the following example passes three strings to Concat():

```
string myString5 = String.Concat
    ("Friends, "", "Romans, ", "and countrymen");
```

The string "Friends, Romans, and countrymen" will be stored in myString5.

NOTE

As you'll see later in the "Creating Dynamic Strings" section, the String-Builder class is more efficient when you have to concatenate a lot of strings.

Concatenating Strings Using the Overloaded Addition Operator

You can also use the overloaded addition operator (+) to concatenate strings. For example,

```
string myString6 = "To be, "" + "or not to be";
```

The string "To be, or not to be" will be stored in myString6.

Copying Strings Using the *Copy()* Method

You can use the static Copy() method to copy a specified string. The Copy() method uses the following syntax:

```
String.Copy(string1)
```

where *string1* is the string you want to copy.

The following example shows the use of the Copy() method to copy myString4 to myString7:

```
string myString7 = String.Copy(myString4);
```

Copying Strings Using the Overloaded Assignment Operator

You can also copy strings using the overloaded assignment operator (=) to copy one string to another. For example,

```
myString7 = myString4;
```

Checking If Two Strings Are Equal Using the *Equals()* Method

You can use the Equals() method to check whether two strings are equal. The Equals() method returns a bool and has a static version as well as an instance version. You call the static version of Equals() through the String class, and it accepts two string parameters that are checked to see if they are the same. The syntax for the static version of Equals() is

```
String.Equals(string1, string2)
```

where *string1* and *string2* are the two strings you want to compare.

In the following example, Equals() returns true because the two strings are equal:

```
bool boolResult = String.Equals("bbc", "bbc");
```

You call the instance version of Equals() using an actual string, and it compares that string to the supplied string parameter. The syntax for this version of Equals() is

```
string1.Equals(string2)
```

where *string1* and *string2* are the two strings you want to compare.

In the following example, Equals() returns false because the contents of myString and myString2 are different:

```
boolResult = myString.Equals(myString2);
```

Checking If Two Strings Are Equal Using the Overloaded Equal to Operator

You can also use the overloaded equal to operator (==) to check if two strings are equal. In the following example, boolResult is set to false because the contents of myString and myString2 are different:

```
boolResult = myString == myString2;
```

Formatting Strings Using the *Format()* Method

You can use the overloaded static Format() method to return a string formatted according to a specified format. One use for the Format() method is to format a string containing a floating-point number, as shown in the following example:

```
float myFloat = 1234.56789f;
string myString8 = String.Format("{0, 10:f3}", myFloat);
```

The format is "{0, 10:f3}", meaning that the string containing myFloat is to be formatted with a width of 10, and myFloat is to be rounded to 3 decimal places; myString8 will be set to " 1234.568" (with two spaces in front).

Joining Multiple Strings Together Using the *Join()* Method

You can use the static Join() method to build up a new string by joining the elements from an array of strings, along with a separator string. The separator is inserted between each string element in the new string.

Although the details of arrays are covered in Chapter 6, the basics are easy to understand. The following example creates an array of strings:

```
string[] myStrings = {"To", "be", "or",
    "not", "to", "be"};
```

There are six string elements in myStrings, with myStrings[0] set to "To", myStrings[1] set to "be", and so on up to myStrings[5], which is also set to "be".

The Join() method is overloaded, and its simplest version accepts a string containing your separator and an array of strings using the following syntax:

```
String.Join(separator, stringArray)
```

where *separator* is the string used to separate the strings contained in *stringArray*.

In the following example, Join() returns a string containing all the strings in myStrings, with each string separated by a period (.):

```
string myString9 = String.Join(".", myStrings);
```

After this statement is run, myString9 will contain "To.be.or.not.to.be".

Splitting Strings Using the *Split()* Method

You can use the Split() method to split up a string into an array of strings, using a separator to identify where your original string is to be split. The array of strings is then returned by Split(). The Split() method is overloaded, and its simplest version uses the following syntax:

```
originalString.Split(separator)
```

where *separator* is the string used to separate the strings contained in *originalString*.

In the following example, the Split() method splits myString9 up into an array of strings using a period (.) as the separator:

```
myStrings = myString9.Split('.');
```

You can then use the following foreach loop to display the strings in the myStrings array:

```
foreach (string mySplitString in myStrings)
{
  Console.WriteLine("mySplitString = " + mySplitString);
}
```

This displays the following:

```
mySplitString = To
mySplitString = be
mySplitString = or
mySplitString = not
mySplitString = to
mySplitString = be
```

Checking the Start and End of a String Using the *StartsWith()* and *EndsWith()* Methods

You can use the StartsWith() and EndsWith() methods to check whether a string contains a specified substring at its start or end. The StartsWith() and EndsWith() methods both return a bool. The syntax for these methods is

```
string1.StartsWith(substring)
string1.EndsWith(substring)
```

where *substring* is the string to search for in *string1*.

Let's consider an example. Earlier, myString was set to "To be or not to be", and the following examples use StartsWith() and EndsWith()

to check if myString starts with "To" and ends with "be":

```
if (myString.StartsWith("To"))
{
   Console.WriteLine("myString starts with \"To\"");
}
if (myString.EndsWith("be"))
{
   Console.WriteLine("myString ends with \"be\"");
}
```

Because myString does start with "To" and end with "be", the StartsWith() and EndsWith() methods both return true.

TIP

To add quotes within a string, you put a backslash (\) in front of the quotes. That way, the string contains the actual quotes, rather than using them to terminate the string. You can see this in the previous example that displays strings with quotes. You can also use the backslash character to specify escape characters.

Finding Substrings and Characters in a String Using the *IndexOf()* and *LastIndexOf()* Methods

You can use IndexOf() and LastIndexOf() methods to get the index of a supplied substring or a character within a string. The IndexOf() method finds the first occurrence of the substring or character, and LastIndexOf() finds the last occurrence. Both methods return an int index, starting at 0. If the substring or character isn't found in the string, then the methods return −1.

The IndexOf() and LastIndexOf() methods are overloaded, and the simplest versions accept a substring or character value using the following syntax:

```
string1.IndexOf(value)
string1.LastIndexOf(value)
```

where *value* is the substring or character for which to search *string1*.

The following examples show these versions of IndexOf() and LastIndexOf() to search for "be" in myString:

```
int index1 = myString.IndexOf("be");
int index2 = myString.LastIndexOf("be");
```

Because myString contains "To be or not to be", index1 is set to 3 because "be" first occurs at index 3 (remember that indexes start at 0). Similarly, index2 is set to 16 because "be" last occurs at index 16.

The following examples use IndexOf() and LastIndexOf() to search for 'b' in myString:

```
index1 = myString.IndexOf('b');
index2 = myString.LastIndexOf('b');
```

Because 'b' first occurs at index 3 and last occurs at index 16, index1 and index2 are set to 3 and 16, respectively.

Another version of IndexOf() and LastIndexOf() allows you to start searching at a specified index of a string:

```
string1.IndexOf(value, startIndex)
string1.LastIndexOf(value, startIndex)
```

where startIndex is the index to start searching string1 for value.

You can also specify the number of characters in the string to search using the following syntax:

```
string1.IndexOf(value, startIndex, numberOfChars)
string1.LastIndexOf(value, startIndex numberOfChars)
```

where numberOfChars is the number of characters in string1 to search for value, starting at startIndex of string1.

Finding Characters Using the *IndexOfAny()* and *LastIndexOfAny()* Methods

You can use the IndexOfAny() and LastIndexOfAny() methods to get the index of the first and last occurrence of any character in a supplied array of characters. Both methods are overloaded and return an int index.

The simplest versions of IndexOfAny() and LastIndexOfAny() use the following syntax:

```
string1.IndexOfAny(charArray)
string1.LastIndexOfAny(charArray)
```

where charArray is an array of characters to search for in string1.

The following example shows this version of IndexOf() and LastIndexOf():

```
char[] myChars = {'b', 'e'};
int index1 = myString.IndexOfAny(myChars);
int index2 = myString.LastIndexOfAny(myChars);
```

Because myString contains "To be or not to be", index1 is set to 3 because 'b' first occurs at index 3. Similarly, index2 is set to 17 because 'b' last occurs at index 17.

Another version of `IndexOfAny()` and `LastIndexOfAny()` allows you to start searching from a specified index of a string; this version of these methods uses the following syntax:

```
string1.IndexOfAny(charArray, startIndex)
string1.LastIndexOfAny(charArray, startIndex)
```

where *startIndex* is the index to start searching *string1* for the characters in *charArray*.

You can also specify the number of characters in the string to search using the following syntax:

```
string1.IndexOfAny(charArray, startIndex, numberOfChars)
string1.LastIndexOfAny(charArray, startIndex numberOfChars)
```

where *numberOfChars* is the number of characters in *string1* to search for the characters in *charArray*, starting at *startIndex* of *string1*.

Inserting a Substring into a String Using the *Insert()* Method

You can use the `Insert()` method to insert a supplied substring into a string at a specified index. The `Insert()` method returns a new string and uses the following syntax:

```
string1.Insert(index, substring)
```

where *substring* is the string to be inserted into *string1*, and *index* is the position in *string1* to insert *substring*.

The following example shows the use of the `Insert()` method:

```
string myString10 = myString.Insert(6, "friends, ");
```

Because `myString` contains `"To be or not to be"`, `myString10` is set to `"To be friends, or not to be"`. Notice that the substring `"friends"` is inserted at index 6.

Removing Characters from a String Using the *Remove()* Method

You can use the `Remove()` method to remove a specified number of characters from a string starting at specified index. This method returns a new string and has the following syntax:

```
string1.Remove(startIndex, numberOfChars)
```

where *startIndex* is the index in *string1* to start removing characters, and *numberOfChars* is the number of characters to remove.

The following example shows the use of the Remove() method:

```
string myString11 = myString10.Remove(14, 7);
```

Now, myString10 contains "To be friends, or not to be"; and so myString11 is set to "To be friends, to be". Notice that " or not" has been removed (these are the seven characters that start at index 14).

Replacing Characters in a String Using the *Replace()* Method

You can use the Replace() method to replace all occurrences of a supplied substring or character with another substring or character. The Replace() method returns a new string and is overloaded. When replacing characters, the syntax of the Replace() method is

```
string1.Replace(oldChar, newChar)
```

where *string1* is the string to be modified, and *oldChar* is the character to be replaced by *newChar*.

The following example uses this version of the Replace() method to replace any commas (,) in myString11 with question marks (?):

```
string myString12 = myString11.Replace(',', '?');
```

Because myString11 contains "To be friends, to be", and the comma is replaced by a question mark, myString12 is set to "To be friends? to be". Notice the comma has been replaced by a question mark.

The other version of Replace() replaces one substring with another and uses the following syntax:

```
string1.Replace(oldSubstring, newSubstring)
```

where *string1* is the string to be modified, and *oldSubstring* is the substring to be replaced by *newSubstring*.

The following example uses this version of the Replace() method to replace "to be" in myString12 with "Or not to be friends":

```
string myString13 = myString12.Replace
    ("to be", "Or not to be friends");
```

Because myString12 contains "To be friends? to be", myString13 is set to "To be friends? Or not to be friends".

Right-Aligning Strings Using the *PadLeft()* Method

You can use the PadLeft() method to right-align the characters in a string, padding the string with specified characters or spaces on the left. The PadLeft() method returns a new string, and this method is overloaded.

The simplest version of PadLeft() pads a string with spaces for a specified total length and uses the following syntax:

```
string1.PadLeft(length)
```

where *string1* is the string to be padded with spaces, and *length* is an int that specifies the total length for the returned string.

The following example uses PadLeft() to right-align myString with spaces for a total length of 20 characters:

```
string myString14 = '(' + myString.PadLeft(20) + ')';
```

Because myString contains "To be or not to be", myString14 is set to "(To be or not to be)" (with two spaces after the open parenthesis).

The other version of PadLeft() pads a string with specified characters for a total length and uses the following syntax:

```
string1.PadLeft(length, padChar)
```

where *string1* is the string to be padded with *padChar* characters, and *length* is an int that specifies the total length for the returned string.

The following example uses this version of PadLeft() to right-align myString with periods for a total length of 20 characters:

```
string myString15 = '(' + myString.PadLeft(20, '.') + ')';
```

Because myString contains "To be or not to be", myString15 is set to "(..To be or not to be)".

Left-Aligning Strings Using the *PadRight()* Method

The PadRight() method works in the opposite manner to PadLeft(), and you use it to left-align the characters in a string. Like PadLeft(), PadRight() also has two versions, and the following examples illustrate their use:

```
string myString16 = '(' + myString.PadRight(20) + ')';
string myString17 = '(' +
  myString.PadRight(20, '.') + ')';
```

This results in myString16 and myString17 being set to the following respective strings:

```
"(To be or not to be  )"
"(To be or not to be..)"
```

Trimming the Start and End of a String Using the *Trim()* Method

You can use the Trim() method to remove spaces or specified characters from the beginning and end of a string. This method returns a string and is overloaded. The simplest version of Trim() removes spaces from the string and uses the following syntax:

```
string1.Trim()
```

where `string1` is the string to be trimmed.

The following example uses this version of Trim() to remove spaces from a string:

```
string myString18 = '(' + "  Whitespace  ".Trim() + ')';
```

In this example, myString18 is set to "(Whitespace)".

Trimming the Start of a String Using the *TrimStart()* Method

The TrimStart() method operates in the same manner as Trim(), except that it removes characters or spaces from the start of a string. For example,

```
string myString19 = '(' +
    "  Whitespace  ".TrimStart() + ')';
```

Here, myString19 is set to "(Whitespace)".

Trimming the End of a String Using the *TrimEnd()* Method

The TrimEnd() method removes characters or spaces from the end of a string. For example:

```
string myString20 = '(' + "  Whitespace  ".TrimEnd() + ')';
```

Here, myString20 is set to "(Whitespace)".

Retrieving Substrings from a String Using the *Substring()* Method

You can use the Substring() method to retrieve a substring from a string. The Substring() method returns a string and is overloaded. The simplest version of Substring() returns the substring starting at a specified index and uses the following syntax:

```
string1.Substring(index)
```

where `index` is an int that specifies the character position to start reading from `string1`.

The following example uses this version of Substring() to retrieve a substring from myString, starting at index 3:

```
string myString21 = myString.Substring(3);
```

Because myString is set to "To be or not to be", myString21 is set to "be or not to be".

The other version of Substring() uses a second int parameter to specify the number of characters to read and uses the following syntax:

```
string1.Substring(index, numberOfChars)
```

The following example uses this version of Substring():

```
string myString22 = myString.Substring(3, 2);
```

Here, myString22 is set to "be".

Converting the Case of a String Using the *ToUpper()* and *ToLower()* Methods

You can use the ToUpper() and ToLower() methods to convert the case of a string. ToUpper() returns the string's characters in uppercase, and ToLower() returns the string's characters in lowercase. Both methods return a new string and are overloaded. The simplest versions of these methods use the following syntax:

```
string1.ToUpper();
string1.ToLower();
```

The following examples use the ToUpper() and ToLower() methods:

```
string myString23 = myString.ToUpper();
string myString24 = myString.ToLower();
```

This results in myString23 and myString24 being set to the following respective strings:

```
"TO BE OR NOT TO BE"
"to be or not to be"
```

Listing 3.1 illustrates the use of strings.

Listing 3.1: Strings

```
using System;

class Example9_1
{

    public static void Main()
    {

        // create some strings
        string myString = "To be or not to be";
```

```
    string myString2 = "...\t that is the question";
    string myString3 = @"\t Friends, Romans, countrymen,
lend me your ears";

    // display the strings and their Length properties
    Console.WriteLine("myString = " + myString);
    Console.WriteLine("myString.Length = "
      + myString.Length);
    Console.WriteLine("myString2 = " + myString2);
    Console.WriteLine
      ("myString2.Length = " + myString2.Length);
    Console.WriteLine("myString3 = " + myString3);
    Console.WriteLine
      ("myString3.Length = " + myString3.Length);

    // display all the characters in myString using
    // a for loop
    for (int count = 0; count < myString.Length; count++)
    {
      Console.WriteLine
        ("myString[" + count + "] = " + myString[count]);
    }

    // use the Compare() method to compare strings
    int result;
    result = String.Compare("bbc", "abc");
    Console.WriteLine
      ("String.Compare(\"bbc\", \"abc\") = " + result);
    result = String.Compare("abc", "bbc");
    Console.WriteLine
      ("String.Compare(\"abc\", \"bbc\") = " + result);
    result = String.Compare("bbc", "bbc");
    Console.WriteLine
      ("String.Compare(\"bbc\", \"bbc\") = " + result);
    result = String.Compare("bbc", "BBC", true);
    Console.WriteLine
      ("String.Compare(\"bbc\", \"BBC\", true) = " + result);
    result = String.Compare("bbc", "BBC", false);
    Console.WriteLine
      ("String.Compare(\"bbc\", \"BBC\", false) = " + result);
    result = String.Compare
      ("Hello World", 6, "Goodbye World", 8, 5);
```

```
Console.WriteLine
  ("String.Compare(\"Hello World\", 6, " +
  "\"Goodbye World\", 8, 5) = " + result);

// use the Concat() method to concatenate strings
string myString4 = String.Concat("Friends, ", "Romans");
Console.WriteLine
  ("String.Concat(\"Friends, \", \"Romans\") = "
  + myString4);
string myString5 = String.Concat
  ("Friends, ", "Romans, ", "and countrymen");
Console.WriteLine
  ("String.Concat(\"Friends, \", \"Romans, \", " +
  "\"and countrymen\") = " + myString5);

// use the addition operator (+) to concatenate strings
string myString6 = "To be, " + "or not to be";
Console.WriteLine
  ("\"To be, \" + \"or not to be\" = " + myString6);

// use the Copy() method to copy a string
Console.WriteLine("myString4 = " + myString4);
Console.WriteLine
  ("Copying myString4 to myString7 using Copy()");
string myString7 = String.Copy(myString4);
Console.WriteLine("myString7 = " + myString7);

// use the Equals() method and equality operator
// to check if two strings are equal
bool boolResult;
boolResult = String.Equals("bbc", "bbc");
Console.WriteLine
  ("String.Equals(\"bbc\", \"bbc\") is " + boolResult);
boolResult = myString.Equals(myString2);
Console.WriteLine
  ("myString.Equals(myString2) is " + boolResult);
boolResult = myString == myString2;
Console.WriteLine
  ("myString == myString2 is " + boolResult);

// use the Format() method to format a string
float myFloat = 1234.56789f;
```

```
string myString8 = String.Format("{0, 10:f3}", myFloat);
Console.WriteLine
  ("String.Format(\"{0, 10:f3}\", myFloat) = " +
  myString8);

// use the Join() method to join strings
string[] myStrings = {"To", "be", "or", "not",
  "to", "be"};
string myString9 = String.Join(".", myStrings);
Console.WriteLine("myString9 = " + myString9);

// use the Split() method to split strings
myStrings = myString9.Split('.');
foreach (string mySplitString in myStrings)
{
  Console.WriteLine("mySplitString = " + mySplitString);
}

// use the StartsWith() and EndsWith() methods
// to check if a string contains a specified
// substring at the start and end
Console.WriteLine("myString = " + myString);
if (myString.StartsWith("To"))
{
  Console.WriteLine("myString starts with \"To\"");
}
if (myString.EndsWith("be"))
{
  Console.WriteLine("myString ends with \"be\"");
}

// use the IndexOf() and LastIndexOf() methods to search
// for substrings and characters;
// IndexOf() returns the first occurrence
// of a substring or character, and LastIndexOf()
// returns the last occurrence of a
// substring or character
int index = myString.IndexOf("be");
Console.WriteLine("\"be\" first occurs at index "
  + index + " of myString");
index = myString.LastIndexOf("be");
Console.WriteLine("\"be\" last occurs at index "
  + index + " of myString");
```

```
index = myString.IndexOf('b');
Console.WriteLine("'b' first occurs at index "
  + index + " of myString");
index = myString.LastIndexOf('b');
Console.WriteLine("'b' last occurs at index "
  + index + " of myString");

// use the IndexOfAny() and LastIndexOfAny() methods
// to search for character arrays in a string
char[] myChars = {'b', 'e'};
index = myString.IndexOfAny(myChars);
Console.WriteLine("'b' and 'e' occur at index "
  + index + " of myString");
index = myString.LastIndexOfAny(myChars);
Console.WriteLine("'b' and 'e' last occur at index "
  + index + " of myString");

// use the Insert(), Remove(), and Replace()
// methods to modify strings
string myString10 = myString.Insert(6, "friends, ");
Console.WriteLine("myString.Insert(6,
  \"friends, \") = " + myString10);
string myString11 = myString10.Remove(14, 7);
Console.WriteLine("myString10.Remove(14, 7) = " +
  myString11);
string myString12 = myString11.Replace(',', '?');
Console.WriteLine("myString11.Replace(',', '?') = " +
  myString12);
string myString13 =
  myString12.Replace("to be", "Or not to be friends");
Console.WriteLine(
  "myString12.Replace(\"to be\",
  \"Or not to be friends\") = " + myString13);

// use the PadLeft() and PadRight()
// methods to align strings
string myString14 = '(' + myString.PadLeft(20) + ')';
Console.WriteLine("'(' + myString.PadLeft(20)
+ ')' = " + myString14);
string myString15 = '(' + myString.PadLeft(20, '.')
+ ')';
Console.WriteLine("'(' + myString.PadLeft(20, '.') =
 " + myString15);
```

```
string myString16 = '(' + myString.PadRight(20)
+ ')';
Console.WriteLine("'(' + myString.PadRight(20) + ')' =
" + myString16);
string myString17 = '(' +
myString.PadRight(20, '.') + ')';
Console.WriteLine("'(' +
myString.PadRight(20, '.') + ')' = " + myString17);

// use the Trim(), TrimStart(), and TrimEnd() methods to
// trim strings
string myString18 = '(' +
"  Whitespace  ".Trim() + ')';
Console.WriteLine("'(' +
\"  Whitespace  \".Trim() + ')' = " + myString18);
string myString19 = '(' + "  Whitespace  ".TrimStart() + ')';
Console.WriteLine("'(' +
\"  Whitespace  \".TrimStart() + ')' = " + myString19);
string myString20 =
'(' + "  Whitespace  ".TrimEnd() + ')';
Console.WriteLine("'(' +
\"  Whitespace  \".TrimEnd() + ')' = " + myString20);

// use the Substring() method to retrieve substrings
string myString21 = myString.Substring(3);
Console.WriteLine("myString.Substring(3) = "
+ myString21);
string myString22 = myString.Substring(3, 2);
Console.WriteLine("myString.Substring(3, 2) = "
+ myString22);

// use the ToUpper() and ToLower() methods
// to convert the case of a string
string myString23 = myString.ToUpper();
Console.WriteLine("myString.ToUpper() = "
+ myString23);
string myString24 = myString.ToLower();
Console.WriteLine("myString.ToLower() = "
+ myString24);

}

}
```

The output from this program is as follows:

```
myString = To be or not to be
myString.Length = 18
myString2 = ...  that is the question
myString2.Length = 25
myString3 = \t Friends, Romans, countrymen,
lend me your ears
myString3.Length = 50
myString[0] = T
myString[1] = o
myString[2] =
myString[3] = b
myString[4] = e
myString[5] =
myString[6] = o
myString[7] = r
myString[8] =
myString[9] = n
myString[10] = o
myString[11] = t
myString[12] =
myString[13] = t
myString[14] = o
myString[15] =
myString[16] = b
myString[17] = e
String.Compare("bbc", "abc") = 1
String.Compare("abc", "bbc") = -1
String.Compare("bbc", "bbc") = 0
String.Compare("bbc", "BBC", true) = 0
String.Compare("bbc", "BBC", false) = -1
String.Compare("Hello World", 6,
"Goodbye World", 8, 5) = 0
String.Concat("Friends, ", "Romans") = Friends, Romans
String.Concat("Friends, ", "Romans, ",
"and countrymen") =
 Friends, Romans, and countrymen
"To be, " + "or not to be" = To be, or not to be
myString4 = Friends, Romans
Copying myString4 to myString7 using Copy()
myString7 = Friends, Romans
String.Equals("bbc", "bbc") is True
myString.Equals(myString2) is False
myString == myString2 is False
String.Format("{0, 10:f3}", myFloat) =   1234.568
myString9 = To.be.or.not.to.be
```

```
mySplitString = To
mySplitString = be
mySplitString = or
mySplitString = not
mySplitString = to
mySplitString = be
myString = To be or not to be
myString starts with "To"
myString ends with "be"
"be" first occurs at index 3 of myString
"be" last occurs at index 16 of myString
'b' first occurs at index 3 of myString
'b' last occurs at index 16 of myString
'b' and 'e' occur at index 3 of myString
'b' and 'e' last occur at index 17 of myString
myString.Insert(6, "friends, ") = To be friends,
or not to be
myString10.Remove(14, 7) = To be friends, to be
myString11.Replace(',', '?') = To be friends? to be
myString12.Replace("to be", "Or not to be friends") =
 To be friends? Or not to be friends
'(' + myString.PadLeft(20) + ')' = (  To be or not to be)
'(' + myString.PadLeft(20, '.') = (..To be or not to be)
'(' + myString.PadRight(20) + ')' =
(To be or not to be  )
'(' + myString.PadRight(20, '.') + ')' =
(To be or not to be..)
'(' + "  Whitespace  ".Trim() + ')' = (Whitespace)
'(' + "  Whitespace  ".TrimStart() + ')' = (Whitespace  )
'(' + "  Whitespace  ".TrimEnd() + ')' = (  Whitespace)
myString.Substring(3) = be or not to be
myString.Substring(3, 2) = be
myString.ToUpper() = TO BE OR NOT TO BE
myString.ToLower() = to be or not to be
```

CREATING DYNAMIC STRINGS

The System.Text.StringBuilder class allows you to create *dynamic strings*. Unlike a regular string of the String class, a dynamic string's characters may be modified directly; with a regular string, you always modify a copy of the string. In addition, the StringBuilder methods are fast and provide efficient string manipulation capabilities.

However, as you'll see, the methods provided by the StringBuilder class are not as comprehensive as those provided by the String class. The

StringBuilder class does provide a ToString() method that converts a StringBuilder object to a string, and you can use this method if you need to use the additional String methods.

In this section, you'll learn how to create StringBuilder objects, and then you'll see the various StringBuilder properties and methods.

TIP

If speed is your priority, then you should use the StringBuilder class to create and manipulate strings because the StringBuilder manipulation methods are faster. This is because when you manipulate a regular string, a whole new string has to be created and this takes time, whereas when you manipulate a StringBuilder object, no new object is created.

Creating *StringBuilder* Objects

The StringBuilder constructor is overloaded, and you can therefore create a StringBuilder object using a variety of techniques. The following example creates a StringBuilder object named myStringBuilder:

```
StringBuilder myStringBuilder = new StringBuilder();
```

NOTE

This section's examples assume that the System.Text class is imported with the using System.Text statement. You can also use the fully qualified name-space and class name when creating a StringBuilder object.

By default a StringBuilder object can initially store up to 16 characters, but as you add to the object, its capacity will automatically increase. You can also specify the initial capacity of a StringBuilder object by supplying an int parameter to the constructor. For example,

```
int capacity = 50;
StringBuilder myStringBuilder2 =
    new StringBuilder(capacity);
```

You can set the maximum capacity for a StringBuilder object by passing a second int parameter to the constructor. For example,

```
int maxCapacity = 100;
StringBuilder myStringBuilder3 =
    new StringBuilder(capacity, maxCapacity);
```

The maximum capacity for a `StringBuilder` object is 2147483647 (this is also the default capacity for `StringBuilder` objects).

You can also set the initial string stored in a `StringBuilder` object by passing a string to its constructor:

```
string myString = "To be or not to be";
StringBuilder myStringBuilder4 =
    new StringBuilder(myString);
```

Lastly, you can pass a string, the index of the string to start copying from, the number of characters to copy from the string, and the capacity to the `StringBuilder` constructor:

```
int startIndex = 0;
int stringLength = myString.Length;
StringBuilder myStringBuilder5 =
    new StringBuilder(myString, startIndex,
    stringLength, capacity);
```

In the next section, you'll see some of the `StringBuilder` properties and methods.

Using *StringBuilder* Properties and Methods

The `StringBuilder` class provides a number of properties and methods you can use in your programs. Table 3.3 lists some of the public properties of the `StringBuilder` class.

TABLE 3.3: StringBuilder Properties

PROPERTY	TYPE	DESCRIPTION
Capacity	int	Gets or sets the maximum number of characters that can be stored in the `StringBuilder` object
Length	int	Gets or sets the number of characters in the `StringBuilder` object
MaxCapacity	int	Gets the maximum capacity of the `StringBuilder` object

Table 3.4 shows the `StringBuilder` public methods.

TABLE 3.4: StringBuilder Methods

Method	Return Type	Description
Append()	StringBuilder	Overloaded. Appends the string representation of a specified object to the end of the StringBuilder object.
AppendFormat()	StringBuilder	Overloaded. Appends a formatted string to the end of the StringBuilder object.
EnsureCapacity()	int	Ensures that the current capacity of the StringBuilder object is at least equal to a specified value and returns an int containing the current capacity of the StringBuilder object.
Equals()	bool	Overloaded. Returns a bool that specifies whether the StringBuilder object is equal to a specified object.
GetHashCode()	int	Returns an int hash code for the type.
GetType() (inherited from Object)	Type	Returns the type of the current object.
Insert()	StringBuilder	Overloaded. Inserts the string representation of a specified object into the StringBuilder object at a specified index.
Remove()	StringBuilder	Removes a specified number of characters from the StringBuilder object, starting at a specified index.
Replace()	StringBuilder	Overloaded. Replaces all occurrences of a specified string or character with another string or character in the StringBuilder object.
ToString()	string	Overloaded. Converts the StringBuilder object to a string.

As you can see, there are fewer methods for manipulating a dynamic string than for regular strings (the string methods were shown earlier in Table 3.2). The following sections illustrate some of the StringBuilder methods.

Appending to a *StringBuilder* Object Using the *Append()* and *AppendFormat()* Methods

You can use the Append() method to append the string representation of a specified object to the end of a StringBuilder object. The Append() method, like many of the other StringBuilder methods, modifies the StringBuilder object directly.

The Append() method is overloaded, allowing you to pass a variable or object of the various built-in types, each of which is converted to a string and then appended to the StringBuilder object. The simplest version of Append() uses the following syntax:

```
stringBuilder.Append(value)
```

where *stringBuilder* is the StringBuilder object, and *value* is the item to be appended to *stringBuilder*.

The following example uses the Append() method to append two strings, an int and a bool, to myStringBuilder (which was created in the previous section):

```
string myString = "To be or not to be";
myStringBuilder.Append(myString);
myStringBuilder.Append(", that is the question ... ");
int myInt = 1234;
myStringBuilder.Append(myInt);
bool myBool = true;
myStringBuilder.Append(myBool);
```

Another version of Append() enables you to repeatedly append a character to a StringBuilder object. This version of Append() uses the following syntax:

```
stringBuilder.Append(appendChar, repeat)
```

where *appendChar* is the character to append to *stringBuilder*, and *repeat* is the number of times to perform the append.

The following example appends 'z' fives times to myStringBuilder:

```
myStringBuilder.Append('z', 5);
```

You can also append a substring to a StringBuilder object using the following syntax:

```
stringBuilder.Append(appendString, startIndex, numberOfChars)
```

where *appendString* is a string, *startIndex* is the index from which to start reading from *appendString*, and *numberOfChars* is the number of characters to read from *appendString*.

In the following example, the substring "Here" is appended to myStringBuilder:

```
myStringBuilder.Append("Here's another string", 0, 4);
```

At this point, myStringBuilder contains the following:

```
To be or not to be, that is the question ...
   1234TruezzzzzHere
```

You can use the AppendFormat() method to append a formatted string to a StringBuilder object. For example,

```
float myFloat = 1234.56789f;
myStringBuilder.AppendFormat("{0, 10:f3}", myFloat);
```

Now myStringBuilder contains the following:

```
To be or not to be, that is the question ...
   1234TruezzzzzHere   1234.568
```

Inserting a String into a *StringBuilder* Object Using the *Insert()* Method

You can use the Insert() method to append the string representation of a specified object into a StringBuilder object at a specified index. Like the Append() method, Insert() is also overloaded, allowing you to pass a variable or object of the various built-in types to this method.

The simplest version of Insert() uses the following syntax:

```
stringBuilder.Insert(index, value)
```

where *index* is the index at which the string representation of *value* is to be inserted into *stringBuilder*.

The following example uses the Insert() method to insert the string "friends, " at index 6 of myStringBuilder:

```
myStringBuilder.Insert(6, "friends, ");
```

You can also insert multiple copies of a string into a StringBuilder object using the following syntax:

```
stringBuilder.Insert(index, string, repeat)
```

The following example inserts three copies of the string "Romans, " at index 22 of myStringBuilder:

```
myStringBuilder.Insert(22, "Romans, ", 3);
```

Removing Characters from a *StringBuilder* Object Using the *Remove()* Method

You can use the Remove() method to remove a specified number of characters from a StringBuilder object, starting at a specified index. The Remove() method uses the following syntax:

```
stringBuilder.Remove(index, numberOfChars)
```

where *index* is the index at which the removal is to start, and *number-OfChars* is the number of characters to remove from *stringBuilder*.

The following example uses the Remove() method to remove seven characters from myStringBuilder, starting at index 14:

```
myStringBuilder.Remove(14, 7);
```

Replacing Characters in a *StringBuilder* Object Using the *Replace()* Method

You can use the Replace() method to replace all occurrences of a specified string or character with another string or character in a StringBuilder object. The Replace() method uses the following syntax:

```
stringBuilder.Replace(oldValue, newValue)
```

where *oldValue* is the string or character to replace, and *newValue* is the string or character to replace *oldValue* with in *stringBuilder*.

The following example uses the Replace() method to replace all occurrences of commas (,) with question marks (?) in myStringBuilder:

```
myStringBuilder.Replace(',', '?');
```

Converting a *StringBuilder* Object to a String Using the *ToString()* Method

You can use the ToString() method to convert a StringBuilder object to a string. The ToString() method uses the following syntax:

```
stringBuilder.ToString()
```

where *stringBuilder* is the StringBuilder object to convert to a string.

The following example uses the ToString() method to convert myStringBuilder to a string, storing the returned string in myString2:

```
string myString2 = myStringBuilder.ToString();
```

Listing 3.2 illustrates the use of StringBuilder objects.

Listing 3.2: StringBuilder **Objects**

```
using System;
using System.Text;

class Example9_2
{

  public static void DisplayProperties(
    string name,
    StringBuilder myStringBuilder
  )
  {

    // display the properties for the StringBuilder object
    Console.WriteLine(name + ".Length = " +
      myStringBuilder.Length);
    Console.WriteLine(name + ".Capacity = " +
      myStringBuilder.Capacity);
    Console.WriteLine(name + ".MaxCapacity = " +
      myStringBuilder.MaxCapacity);

  }


  public static void Main()
  {

    // create some StringBuilder objects
    StringBuilder myStringBuilder = new StringBuilder();
    int capacity = 50;
    StringBuilder myStringBuilder2 =
        new StringBuilder(capacity);
    int maxCapacity = 100;
    StringBuilder myStringBuilder3 =
      new StringBuilder(capacity, maxCapacity);
    string myString = "To be or not to be";
    StringBuilder myStringBuilder4 =
        new StringBuilder(myString);
    int startIndex = 0;
    int stringLength = myString.Length;
```

```
StringBuilder myStringBuilder5 =
  new StringBuilder(myString, startIndex, stringLength,
    capacity);

// display the StringBuilder objects' properties
DisplayProperties("myStringBuilder", myStringBuilder);
DisplayProperties("myStringBuilder2", myStringBuilder2);
DisplayProperties("myStringBuilder3", myStringBuilder3);
DisplayProperties("myStringBuilder4", myStringBuilder4);
DisplayProperties("myStringBuilder5", myStringBuilder5);

// use the Append() method to append two strings,
// an int, and a bool to myStringBuilder
myStringBuilder.Append(myString);
myStringBuilder.Append(", that is the question ... ");
int myInt = 1234;
myStringBuilder.Append(myInt);
bool myBool = true;
myStringBuilder.Append(myBool);

// use the Append() method to append
// a character to myStringBuilder
myStringBuilder.Append('z', 5);

// use the Append() method to append
// a substring to myStringBuilder
myStringBuilder.Append("Here's another string", 0, 4);

// display the contents of myStringBuilder
Console.WriteLine("myStringBuilder = "
+ myStringBuilder);

// use the AppendFormat() method to add a formatted
// string containing a floating point
// number to myStringBuilder
float myFloat = 1234.56789f;
myStringBuilder.AppendFormat("{0, 10:f3}", myFloat);
Console.WriteLine("myStringBuilder = "
+ myStringBuilder);

// use the Insert() method to insert strings
// into myStringBuilder
myStringBuilder.Insert(6, "friends, ");
```

```
        myStringBuilder.Insert(22, "Romans, ", 3);
        Console.WriteLine("myStringBuilder = "
        + myStringBuilder);

        // use the Remove() method to remove
        // part of myStringBuilder
        myStringBuilder.Remove(14, 7);
        Console.WriteLine("myStringBuilder = "
        + myStringBuilder);

        // use the Replace() method to replace
        // part of myStringBuilder
        myStringBuilder.Replace(',', '?');
        Console.WriteLine("myStringBuilder = "
        + myStringBuilder);

        // use the ToString() method to convert myStringBuilder
        // to a string
        string myString2 = myStringBuilder.ToString();
        Console.WriteLine("myString2 = " + myString2);

    }


}
```

The output from this program is as follows:

```
myStringBuilder.Length = 0
myStringBuilder.Capacity = 16
myStringBuilder.MaxCapacity = 2147483647
myStringBuilder2.Length = 0
myStringBuilder2.Capacity = 50
myStringBuilder2.MaxCapacity = 2147483647
myStringBuilder3.Length = 0
myStringBuilder3.Capacity = 50
myStringBuilder3.MaxCapacity = 100
myStringBuilder4.Length = 18
myStringBuilder4.Capacity = 32
myStringBuilder4.MaxCapacity = 2147483647
myStringBuilder5.Length = 18
myStringBuilder5.Capacity = 50
myStringBuilder5.MaxCapacity = 2147483647
myStringBuilder = To be or not to be,
that is the question ... 1234TruezzzzzHere
```

```
myStringBuilder = To be or not to be,
that is the question ... 1234TruezzzzHere  1234.568
myStringBuilder = To be friends, or not Romans, Romans,
Romans, to be, that is the question ...
1234TruezzzzHere  1234.568
myStringBuilder = To be friends,
Romans, Romans, Romans, to
 be, that is the question ... 1234TruezzzzHere  1234.568
myStringBuilder = To be friends? Romans?
 Romans? Romans? To be? that is the question ...
 1234TruezzzzHere  1234.568
myString2 = To be friends? Romans? Romans? Romans? to be?
 that is the question ... 1234TruezzzzHere  1234.568
```

REPRESENTING DATES AND TIMES

In addition to strings and the other built-in types, you can also represent dates and times in your programs. Examples of using a date and time would be to store a person's birth date or to record when a financial transaction took place. You can represent dates and times in your programs using the System.DateTime struct.

In this section, you'll learn how to create DateTime instances and use the various DateTime properties and methods. You'll also be introduced to time spans, which represent time intervals.

NOTE

As mentioned in Chapter 2, "Zen and Now: The C# Language," a *struct* is a value type and is typically used as a lightweight alternative to a class.

Creating *DateTime* Instances

The constructor for the DateTime struct is overloaded, and therefore there are several ways to create an instance of a DateTime. For example, you can create a DateTime instance with a specified year, month, and day, passing these int values to the DateTime constructor:

```
int year = 2002;
int month = 12;
int day = 25;
DateTime myDateTime = new DateTime(year, month, day);
```

You can also supply the hour (in 24-hour format), minute, second, and optional millisecond when creating a DateTime instance. For example,

```
int hour = 23;
int minute = 30;
int second = 12;
int millisecond = 5;
DateTime myDateTime2 =
    new DateTime(year, month, day, hour,
    minute, second, millisecond);
```

You can also supply an object of the System.Globalization.Calendar class as the last parameter to the DateTime constructor. The Calendar class represents time in divisions, such as weeks, months, and years. There are a number of classes that implement the Calendar class, including GregorianCalendar (the default for the United States), HebrewCalendar, HijriCalendar, JapaneseCalendar, and JulianCalendar. The following example specifies the year, month, and day, along with a JulianCalendar object:

```
System.Globalization.JulianCalendar myCalendar =
    new System.Globalization.JulianCalendar();
DateTime myDateTime3 =
    new DateTime(year, month, day, myCalendar);
```

Finally, you can supply a long value to the DateTime constructor; this value is the number of *ticks*, measured in 100-nanosecond intervals after January 1 of the year 1 at 12 A.M. For example,

```
DateTime myDateTime4 = new DateTime(0);
```

You can view the date and time settings for a DateTime instance using the Year, Month, Day, Hour, Minute, Second, Millisecond, and Ticks properties. For example,

```
Console.WriteLine(myDateTime.Year);
Console.WriteLine(myDateTime.Month);
Console.WriteLine(myDateTime.Day);
Console.WriteLine(myDateTime.Hour);
Console.WriteLine(myDateTime.Minute);
Console.WriteLine(myDateTime.Second);
Console.WriteLine(myDateTime.Millisecond);
Console.WriteLine(myDateTime.Ticks);
```

You'll learn more about the other properties and the methods in the DateTime struct shortly; but before doing that, you'll look at time spans.

Introducing Time Spans

In addition to representing dates and times, you can also represent time intervals in your programs—these are known as *time spans*. An example of a time span is 4 hours, 12 minutes, and 10 seconds. You use the System.TimeSpan class to represent a time span. The following example creates a TimeSpan instance that represents an interval of 4 hours, 12 minutes, and 10 seconds:

```
TimeSpan myTimeSpan = new TimeSpan(4, 12, 10);
```

You can add a TimeSpan to a DateTime. The following example adds myTimeSpan to myDateTime4:

```
myDateTime4 += myTimeSpan;
```

Before this statement is run, the time part of myDateTime4 is set to 12:00:00 A.M., and after, it is set to 4:12:10 A.M. You'll learn more about the TimeSpan class shortly in the section "Using Time Spans."

Listing 3.3 shows a complete program that uses DateTime and TimeSpan instances.

Listing 3.3: DateTime and TimeSpan Instances

```
using System;

class Example9_3
{

  public static void DisplayDateTime(
    string name, DateTime myDateTime
  )
  {

    Console.WriteLine(name + " = " + myDateTime);

    // display the DateTime's properties
    Console.WriteLine(name + ".Year = " + myDateTime.Year);
    Console.WriteLine(name + ".Month = "
    + myDateTime.Month);
    Console.WriteLine(name + ".Day = " + myDateTime.Day);
    Console.WriteLine(name + ".Hour = " + myDateTime.Hour);
    Console.WriteLine(name + ".Minute = "
    + myDateTime.Minute);
```

```
      Console.WriteLine(name + ".Second = "
      + myDateTime.Second);
      Console.WriteLine(name + ".Millisecond = " +
        myDateTime.Millisecond);
      Console.WriteLine(name + ".Ticks = " +
        myDateTime.Ticks);

}


public static void Main()
{

    // create a DateTime instance, specifying the year,
    // month, and day
    int year = 2002;
    int month = 12;
    int day = 25;
    DateTime myDateTime = new DateTime(year, month, day);

    // create a DateTime instance, specifying the year,
    // month, day, hour, minute, second, and millisecond
    int hour = 23;
    int minute = 30;
    int second = 12;
    int millisecond = 5;
    DateTime myDateTime2 =
      new DateTime(year, month, day, hour,
      minute, second, millisecond);

    // create a DateTime instance, specifying the year,
    // month, day, and JulianCalendar object
    System.Globalization.JulianCalendar myCalendar =
      new System.Globalization.JulianCalendar();
    DateTime myDateTime3 =
      new DateTime(year, month, day, myCalendar);

    // create a DateTime instance, specifying
    // the number of ticks
    DateTime myDateTime4 = new DateTime(0);
```

```
        // display the various DateTime instances
        DisplayDateTime("myDateTime", myDateTime);
        DisplayDateTime("myDateTime2", myDateTime2);
        DisplayDateTime("myDateTime3", myDateTime3);
        DisplayDateTime("myDateTime4", myDateTime4);

        // create a TimeSpan instance, and add it to myDateTime4
        TimeSpan myTimeSpan = new TimeSpan(4, 12, 10);
        myDateTime4 += myTimeSpan;
        DisplayDateTime("myDateTime4", myDateTime4);

    }


}
```

The output from this program is as follows:

```
myDateTime = 12/25/2002 12:00:00 AM
myDateTime.Year = 2002
myDateTime.Month = 12
myDateTime.Day = 25
myDateTime.Hour = 0
myDateTime.Minute = 0
myDateTime.Second = 0
myDateTime.Millisecond = 0
myDateTime.Ticks = 631763712000000000
myDateTime2 = 12/25/2002 11:30:12 PM
myDateTime2.Year = 2002
myDateTime2.Month = 12
myDateTime2.Day = 25
myDateTime2.Hour = 23
myDateTime2.Minute = 30
myDateTime2.Second = 12
myDateTime2.Millisecond = 5
myDateTime2.Ticks = 631764558120050000
myDateTime3 = 1/7/2003 12:00:00 AM
myDateTime3.Year = 2003
myDateTime3.Month = 1
myDateTime3.Day = 7
myDateTime3.Hour = 0
myDateTime3.Minute = 0
myDateTime3.Second = 0
myDateTime3.Millisecond = 0
myDateTime3.Ticks = 631774944000000000
myDateTime4 = 1/1/0001 12:00:00 AM
myDateTime4.Year = 1
```

```
myDateTime4.Month = 1
myDateTime4.Day = 1
myDateTime4.Hour = 0
myDateTime4.Minute = 0
myDateTime4.Second = 0
myDateTime4.Millisecond = 0
myDateTime4.Ticks = 0
myDateTime4 = 1/1/0001 4:12:10 AM
myDateTime4.Year = 1
myDateTime4.Month = 1
myDateTime4.Day = 1
myDateTime4.Hour = 4
myDateTime4.Minute = 12
myDateTime4.Second = 10
myDateTime4.Millisecond = 0
myDateTime4.Ticks = 151300000000
```

Using *DateTime* Properties and Methods

Now that you've been introduced to DateTime and TimeSpans, you can
learn the various properties and methods offered by the DateTime struct.
Table 3.5 lists the public properties of the DateTime struct.

TABLE 3.5: DateTime Properties

Property	Type	Description
Now (static)	DateTime	Gets the current date and time from the computer.
Today (static)	DateTime	Gets the current date from the computer, with the time set to 12 A.M. (12:00:00).
UtcNow (static)	DateTime	Gets the current date and time from the computer expressed as *Universal Coordinated Time (UTC)*. It is abbreviated UTC, rather than UCT, because the initials are based on the French words. UTC used to be known as *Greenwich Mean Time (GMT)* and is based on the time zone in Greenwich, England. UTC is 8 hours ahead of *Pacific Standard Time (PST)*.
Date	DateTime	Gets the date part of the DateTime, with the time set to 12 A.M.
Day	int	Gets the day part of the DateTime. This value is between 1 and 31.
DayOfWeek	DayOfWeek	Gets the day of the week of the DateTime. This value is between 0 (Sunday) and 6 (Saturday).

TABLE 3.5 continued: DateTime Properties

PROPERTY	TYPE	DESCRIPTION
DayOfYear	int	Gets the day of the year of the DateTime. This value is between 1 and 366.
Hour	int	Gets the hour part of the DateTime. This value is between 0 and 23.
Millisecond	int	Gets the millisecond part of the DateTime. This value is between 0 and 999.
Minute	int	Gets the minute part of the DateTime. This value is between 0 and 59.
Month	int	Gets the month part of the DateTime. This value is between 1 and 12.
Second	int	Gets the second part of the DateTime. This value is between 0 and 59.
Ticks	long	Gets the number of ticks (100-nanosecond intervals) for the DateTime that have elapsed since 12 A.M. on January 1, 0001 (1/1/0001 12:00:00).
TimeOfDay	TimeSpan	Gets the time of day of the DateTime. This value is a TimeSpan that contains the time interval that has elapsed since 12 A.M. of that day.
Year	int	Gets the year part of the DateTime. This value is between 1 and 9999.

Table 3.6 shows the DateTime public methods.

TABLE 3.6:   DateTime Methods

METHOD	RETURN TYPE	DESCRIPTION
Compare() (static)	int	Compares two DateTime instances and returns an indication of their relative values.
DaysInMonth() (static)	int	Returns the number of days in the specified month and year.
Equals() (static and instance versions)	bool	Overloaded. Returns a bool that indicates whether two DateTime instances are equal. The overloaded equal to operator (==) also does this.

TABLE 3.6 continued: DateTime Methods

METHOD	RETURN TYPE	DESCRIPTION
FromFileTime() (static)	DateTime	Returns a DateTime equivalent to the specified operating system file time-stamp, passed as a long parameter.
FromOADate() (static)	DateTime	Returns a DateTime equivalent to the specified OLE Automation date, passed as a double parameter. OLE stands for *Object Linking and Embedding*.
IsLeapYear() (static)	bool	Indicates whether the specified year is a leap year.
Parse() (static)	DateTime	Overloaded. Converts the specified string representation of a date and time to its equivalent DateTime.
ParseExact() (static)	DateTime	Overloaded. Converts the specified string representation of a date and time to an equivalent DateTime. The format of the string must match the specified format exactly.
Add()	DateTime	Adds the specified TimeSpan to the DateTime. The overloaded addition operator (+) also does this.
AddDays()	DateTime	Adds the specified number of days to the DateTime.
AddHours()	DateTime	Adds the specified number of hours to the DateTime.
AddMilliseconds()	DateTime	Adds the specified number of milli-seconds to the DateTime.
AddMinutes()	DateTime	Adds the specified number of minutes to the DateTime.
AddMonths()	DateTime	Adds the specified number of months to the DateTime.
AddSeconds()	DateTime	Adds the specified number of seconds to the DateTime.
AddTicks()	DateTime	Adds the specified number of ticks to the DateTime.
AddYears()	DateTime	Adds the specified number of years to the DateTime.

TABLE 3.6 continued: DateTime Methods

METHOD	RETURN TYPE	DESCRIPTION
CompareTo()	int	Compares the DateTime to a specified object and returns an indication of their relative values.
GetDateTimeFormats()	string[]	Overloaded. Converts the value of the DateTime to an array of strings containing all the formats supported by DateTime.
GetHashCode()	int	Returns the hash code for the DateTime.
GetType() (inherited from Object)	Type	Returns the type of the current instance.
Subtract()	TimeSpan	Overloaded. Subtracts the specified DateTime or TimeSpan from the DateTime. You can also use the overloaded subtraction operator (–) for this purpose.
ToFileTime()	long	Converts the value of the DateTime to an operating system file timestamp.
ToLocalTime()	DateTime	Converts the current UTC to local time.
ToLongDateString()	string	Converts the date part of the DateTime to the equivalent long date string. For example: "Thursday, January 15, 2004".
ToLongTimeString()	string	Converts the time part of the DateTime to the equivalent long time string. For example, "11:02:05 PM".
ToOADate()	double	Converts the DateTime to the equivalent OLE Automation date.
ToShortDateString()	string	Converts the DateTime to the equivalent short date string representation. For example, "1/15/2004".
ToShortTimeString()	string	Converts the DateTime to the equivalent short time string representation. For example, "11:02 PM".
ToString()	string	Overloaded. Converts the DateTime to the equivalent string representation.
ToUniversalTime()	DateTime	Converts the current local time to UTC.

The following sections illustrate some of these properties and methods.

Now and UtcNow Properties

You use the static Now property to get the current date and time from your computer. Similarly, you use the static UtcNow property to get the current date and time in UTC. Because both the Now and UtcNow properties are static, you access them using the DateTime struct. For example,

```
DateTime myDateTime = DateTime.Now;
DateTime myDateTime2 = DateTime.UtcNow;
```

Assuming the computer is in California (or, uses PST), myDateTime and myDateTime2 will be set to something like this:

```
myDateTime = 3/24/2002 10:40:28 AM
myDateTime2 = 3/24/2002 6:40:28 PM
```

Notice that myDateTime2 is 8 hours behind myDateTime. This is because UtcNow was used to set myDateTime2, and UtcNow is 8 hours behind PST.

Date Property

You use the Date property to get the date part of a DateTime instance (the time will be returned as 12 A.M.). For example,

```
Console.WriteLine("myDateTime.Date = " + myDateTime.Date);
```

Because myDateTime is set to 3/34/2002 10:40:28 A.M., this example displays the following:

```
myDateTime.Date = 3/24/2002 12:00:00 AM
```

Day Property

You use the Day property to get the numeric day of the month of a DateTime instance. For example,

```
Console.WriteLine("myDateTime.Day = " + myDateTime.Day);
```

This example displays the following:

```
myDateTime.Day = 24
```

DayOfWeek Property

You use the DayOfWeek property to get the day of the week of a DateTime instance. For example,

```
Console.WriteLine("myDateTime.DayOfWeek = "
+ myDateTime.DayOfWeek);
```

This example displays the following:

```
myDateTime.DayOfWeek = Sunday
```

DayOfYear **Property**

You use the DayOfYear property to get the numeric day of the year of a DateTime instance. For example,

```
Console.WriteLine("myDateTime.DayOfYear = "
+ myDateTime.DayOfYear);
```

Because 3/34/2002 is the 83rd day of the year, this example displays the following:

```
myDateTime.DayOfYear = 83
```

Ticks **Property**

You use the Ticks property to get the number of ticks (100-nanosecond intervals) for a DateTime instance that have elapsed since 12 A.M. on January 1, 0001. For example,

```
Console.WriteLine("myDateTime.Ticks = "
    + myDateTime.Ticks);
```

This example displays the following:

```
myDateTime.Ticks = 631526496292475040
```

TimeOfDay **Property**

You use the TimeOfDay property to get the time of day of a DateTime instance. This value is a TimeSpan that contains the time interval that has elapsed since 12 A.M. of that day. For example,

```
Console.WriteLine("myDateTime.TimeOfDay = "
    + myDateTime.TimeOfDay);
```

This example displays the following:

```
myDateTime.TimeOfDay = 10:40:29.2475040
```

Comparing Two *DateTime* Instances Using the *Compare()* Method

You can use the static Compare() method to compare two DateTime instances. This method returns an int, which is determined using the following rules:

▶ If the first DateTime is greater than the second DateTime, then 1 is returned.

▶ If the first DateTime is equal to the second DateTime, then 0 is returned.

▶ If the first DateTime is less than the second DateTime, then −1 is returned.

Because the Compare() method is static, you call it using the DateTime struct. The Compare() method uses the following syntax:

```
DateTime.Compare(dateTime1, dateTime2)
```

where *dateTime1* and *dateTime2* are the two DateTime instances you want to compare.

The following example creates two DateTime instances and compares them using the Compare() method:

```
DateTime myDateTime3 = new DateTime(2004, 1, 13);
DateTime myDateTime4 = new DateTime(2004, 1, 14);
int intResult = DateTime.Compare(myDateTime3, myDateTime4);
```

Because myDateTime3 is less than myDateTime4, Compare() returns −1, which is stored in intResult.

Comparing *DateTime* Instances Using Overloaded Operators

You can also use the following overloaded operators to compare the following DateTime instances: greater than (>), greater than or equal to (>=), less than (<), less than or equal to (<=), equal to (==), and not equal to (!=). For example,

```
bool boolResult = myDateTime3 < myDateTime4;
```

Because myDateTime3 is less than myDateTime4, boolResult is set to true.

Checking If Two *DateTime* Instances Are Equal Using the *Equals()* Method

You can use the Equals() method to check if two DateTime instances are equal. This method returns a bool and has a static version and an instance version. The static version is called using the DateTime struct and accepts two DateTime instances as parameters. It uses the following syntax:

```
DateTime.Equals(dateTime1, dateTime2)
```

where *dateTime1* and *dateTime2* are the two DateTime instances you want to compare.

In the following example, `Equals()` returns `false` because `myDateTime3` and `myDateTime4` are different; this result is stored in `boolResult`:

```
bool boolResult = DateTime.Equals(myDateTime3,
    myDateTime4);
```

The instance version of `Equals()` is called using a `DateTime` instance and uses the following syntax:

```
dateTime1.Equals(dateTime2)
```

where *dateTime1* and *dateTime2* are once again the two `DateTime` instances you want to compare.

In the following example, `Equals()` returns `false` because `myDateTime3` and `myDateTime4` are different:

```
boolResult = myDateTime3.Equals(myDateTime4);
```

Obtaining the Number of Days in a Month Using the *DaysInMonth()* Method

You use the static `DaysInMonth()` method to obtain the number of days in a particular month and year. This method returns an `int` and its syntax is

```
DateTime.DaysInMonth(year, month)
```

where *year* and *month* are the year and month for which you want to find the number of days.

The following example uses the `DaysInMonth()` method to get the number of days in January 2004:

```
int days = DateTime.DaysInMonth(2004, 1);
```

Because there are 31 days in January, `DaysInMonth()` returns 31, which is stored in `days`.

Determining If a Year Is a Leap Year Using the *IsLeapYear()* Method

You can use the static `IsLeapYear()` method to determine if a year is a leap year. This method returns a `bool` and uses the following syntax:

```
DateTime.IsLeapYear(year)
```

The following example uses the `IsLeapYear()` method to determine if 2004 is a leap year:

```
boolResult = DateTime.IsLeapYear(2004);
```

Because 2004 is a leap year, `IsLeapYear()` returns `true`, which is stored in `boolResult`.

Converting a String to a *DateTime* Instance Using the *Parse()* Method

You can use the static `Parse()` method to convert a specified string representing a date and time to an equivalent `DateTime` instance. The `Parse()` method is overloaded and returns a `DateTime`. The simplest version of `Parse()` accepts a string parameter and uses the following syntax:

```
DateTime.Parse(string1)
```

where *string1* is the string you want to convert to a `DateTime`.

The date part of the string passed to `Parse()` may be formatted as MM/dd/yyyy, where MM is the month, dd is the day, and yyyy is the year. The time part, if you supply one, may be formatted as HH:mm:ss, where HH is the hour (from 0 to 23), mm is the minute (from 0 to 59), and ss is the second (from 0 to 59). For example,

```
DateTime myDateTime5 = DateTime.Parse("1/13/2004");
DateTime myDateTime6 =
    DateTime.Parse("1/13/2004 23:10:30");
```

By default, when these `DateTime` instances are displayed, they appear as follows:

```
myDateTime5 = 1/13/2004 12:00:00 AM
myDateTime6 = 1/13/2004 11:10:30 PM
```

You'll see how to display `DateTime` instances in different formats shortly.

Other versions of `Parse()` allow you to specify a culture-specific format when parsing the supplied string.

Adding to and Subtracting from *DateTime* Instances Using the *Add()* and *Subtract()* Methods

You can use the `Add()` method to add a `TimeSpan` to a `DateTime`. Similarly, you can use the `Subtract()` method to subtract a `TimeSpan` from a `DateTime`. Both of these methods return a new `DateTime` and use the following syntax:

```
dateTime.Add(timeSpan)
dateTime.Subtract(timeSpan)
```

where *dateTime* is the `DateTime` you want to add to or subtract from, and *timeSpan* is the `TimeSpan` to be added or subtracted.

The following example creates a TimeSpan of 1 day, 2 hours, 4 minutes, and 10 seconds and adds this TimeSpan to myDateTime6 using the Add() method:

```
TimeSpan myTimeSpan = new TimeSpan(1, 2, 4, 10);
DateTime myDateTime7 = myDateTime6.Add(myTimeSpan);
```

This sets myDateTime7 to the following:

```
1/15/2004 1:14:40 AM
```

The next example subtracts myTimeSpan from myDateTime6 using the Subtract() method:

```
myDateTime7 = myDateTime6.Subtract(myTimeSpan);
```

This sets myDateTime7 to the following:

```
1/12/2004 9:06:20 PM
```

Using the Overloaded Addition and Subtraction Operators with *DateTime* and *TimeSpan* Instances

You can also add or subtract a TimeSpan from a DateTime using the overloaded addition and subtraction operators (+ and -). For example,

```
DateTime myDateTime8 = myDateTime6 + myTimeSpan;
myDateTime8 = myDateTime6 - myTimeSpan;
```

Adding Periods to a *DateTime* Using the *AddYears()*, *AddMonths()*, *AddDays()*, *AddHours()*, and *AddMinutes()* Methods

You can add different periods to a DateTime using the AddYears(), AddMonths(), AddDays(), AddHours(), and AddMinutes() methods. Each of these methods accepts a double parameter, which specifies a whole or fractional period. For example,

```
DateTime myDateTime9 = new DateTime(2004, 1, 1);
myDateTime9 = myDateTime9.AddYears(1);
myDateTime9 = myDateTime9.AddMonths(5);
myDateTime9 = myDateTime9.AddDays(3);
myDateTime9 = myDateTime9.AddMinutes(30);
myDateTime9 = myDateTime9.AddSeconds(15);
```

The initial and final settings of myDateTime9 are as follows:

```
1/1/2004 12:00:00 AM
6/4/2005 12:30:15 AM
```

NOTE

You can also pass a negative number to each method, in which case the period is subtracted from the DateTime.

Converting *DateTime* Instances to and from Timestamps Using the *ToFileTime()* and *FromFileTime()* Methods

You can use the ToFileTime() method to convert the value of a DateTime to an operating system file *timestamp*. A timestamp is a long value containing the number of 100-nanosecond intervals between 12 A.M. on January 1, 1601 and the DateTime used with the ToFileTime() method.

The syntax for the ToFileTime() method is as follows:

```
dateTime.ToFileTime()
```

where *dateTime* is the DateTime to be converted to a timestamp.

The following example creates a DateTime and converts it to a timestamp using the ToFileTime() method:

```
DateTime myDateTime10 =
    new DateTime(2004, 1, 15, 23, 2, 5);
long myFileTime = myDateTime10.ToFileTime();
```

This sets myFileTime to 127187101250000000, which is the number of 100-nanosecond intervals between 12 A.M. on January 1, 1601 and myDateTime10.

Similarly, the static FromFileTime() method converts a long value to a DateTime and has the following syntax:

```
DateTime.FromFileTime(fileTime)
```

where *fileTime* is the long value to be converted to a DateTime.

The following example converts myFileTime to a DateTime using the FromFileTime() method:

```
DateTime myDateTime11 = DateTime.FromFileTime(myFileTime);
```

This sets myDateTime11 to the following:

```
1/15/2004 11:02:05 PM
```

Notice that this is the same as myDateTime10, which was used earlier when generating myFileTime.

Converting Dates to Long and Short Strings Using the *ToLongDateString()* and *ToShortDateString()* Methods

You can use the ToLongDateString() method to convert the date part of a DateTime to the equivalent long date string. This string contains the name of the day and month, along with the numerical year.

In the following example, the ToLongDateString() method is called using myDateTime11 (created in the previous section):

```
Console.WriteLine(myDateTime11.ToLongDateString());
```

This example displays the following:

```
Thursday, January 15, 2004
```

Similarly, you use the ToShortDateString() method to convert the date part of DateTime to the equivalent short date string. This string contains the numerical month, day, and year. For example,

```
Console.WriteLine(myDateTime11.ToShortDateString());
```

This example displays the following:

```
1/15/2004
```

Converting Times to Long and Short Strings Using the *ToLongTimeString()* and *ToShortTimeString()* Methods

You can use the ToLongTimeString() method to convert the time part of a DateTime to the equivalent long time string. This string contains the numerical hour, minute, and second, along with an A.M./P.M. indicator. For example,

```
Console.WriteLine(myDateTime11.ToLongTimeString());
```

This example displays the following:

```
11:02:05 PM
```

Similarly, you use the ToShortTimeString() method to convert the time part of DateTime to the equivalent short time string. This string contains the numerical hour and minute, along with an A.M./P.M. indicator. For example,

```
Console.WriteLine(myDateTime11.ToShortTimeString());
```

This example displays the following:

```
11:02 PM
```

Converting a *DateTime* to a String Using the *ToString()* Method

You can use the overloaded ToString() method to convert a DateTime to an equivalent string. The simplest version of the ToString() method accepts zero parameters, as shown in the following example:

```
DateTime myDateTime12 =
    new DateTime(2004, 1, 12, 22, 2, 10);
Console.WriteLine(myDateTime12.ToString());
```

This example displays the following:

```
01/12/2004 10:02:10 PM
```

You can also pass a string to ToString(), which specifies the format for the converted DateTime. This version of ToString() uses the following syntax:

```
dateTime.ToString(format)
```

where *dateTime* is the DateTime to convert, and *format* is the string containing the format for the conversion.

You'll be pleased to know you can use a variety of formats for the conversion. Before getting into some of the formats you can use, you need to understand the components that make up a format. Table 3.7 shows the various format components, along with a description and an example.

TABLE 3.7: Date and Time Format Components

FORMAT COMPONENT	EXAMPLE	DESCRIPTION
d	2	The day of the month, *without* a leading zero for single-digit days.
dd	02	The day of the month, *with* a leading zero for single-digit days.
ddd	Mon	The abbreviated name for the day of the week.
dddd	Monday	The full name for the day of the week.
f	2	The fraction of a second with a precision of one digit. You can use up to seven f characters to increase the precision up to seven digits. Any remaining digits are truncated.
M	1	The month number, *without* a leading zero for single-digit months.

TABLE 3.7 continued: Date and Time Format Components

FORMAT COMPONENT	EXAMPLE	DESCRIPTION
MM	01	The month number, *with* a leading zero for single-digit months.
MMM	Jan	The abbreviated name of the month.
MMMM	January	The full name of the month.
y	4	The year without the century. Values less than 10 are displayed *without* a leading zero.
yy	04	The year without the century. Values less than 10 are displayed *with* a leading zero.
yyyy	2004	The full four-digit year.
gg	A.D.	The period or era. This is ignored if the date doesn't have a period or era.
H	5	The hour in 12-hour format, *without* a leading zero for single-digit hours.
Hh	05	The hour in 12-hour format, *with* a leading zero for single-digit hours.
H	9	The hour in 24-hour format, *without* a leading zero for single-digit hours.
HH	09	The hour in 24-hour format, *with* a leading zero for single-digit hours.
m	7	The minute, *without* a leading zero for single-digit minutes.
mm	07	The minute, *with* a leading zero for single-digit minutes.
s	9	The second, *without* a leading zero for single-digit seconds.
ss	09	The minute, *with* a leading zero for single-digit minutes.
t	AM	The first character in the A.M./P.M. designator.
tt	A	The A.M./P.M. designator.
z	−8	The time zone offset for the hour, *without* a leading zero for single-digit hours.
zz	−08	The time zone offset for the hour, *with* a leading zero for single-digit hours.
zzz	−08:00	The full time zone offset including the hour and minutes, *with* leading zeros for single-digit hours and minutes.

You can use the format components shown in Table 3.7 to build up your own format. For example,

```
Console.WriteLine(myDateTime12.ToString("MMMM dd, yyyy"));
```

This example displays the following:

```
January 12, 2004
```

In addition, the format characters are also used in various built-in formats that you can pass to the ToString() method. For example, if you pass "f" to ToString(), your DateTime is formatted as dddd, MMMM dd, yyyy HH:mm:ss:

```
Console.WriteLine(myDateTime12.ToString("f"));
```

This example displays the following:

```
Monday, January 12, 2004 10:02 PM
```

Of course, "f" is only one of the built-in formats you can use. Table 3.8 shows the other characters and the format they represent. This table also shows example output from ToString() when the format is applied to a DateTime.

TABLE 3.8:   Built-In Date and Time Formats

CHARACTER	FORMAT	EXAMPLE
d	MM/dd/yyyy	01/12/2004
D	dddd, MMMM dd, yyyy	Monday, January 12, 2004
f	dddd, MMMM dd, yyyy HH:mm	Monday, January 12, 2004 10:02 PM
F	dddd, MMMM dd, yyyy HH:mm:ss	Monday, January 12, 2004 10:02:10 PM
g	MM/dd/yyyy HH:mm	01/12/2004 10:02 PM
G	MM/dd/yyyy HH:mm:ss	01/12/2004 10:02:10 PM
m, M	MMMM dd	January 12
r, R	ddd, dd MMM yyyy HH':'mm':'ss 'GMT'	Mon, 12 Jan 2004 22:02:10 GMT
s	yyyy'-'MM'-'dd'T'HH':'mm':'ss	2004-01-12T22:02:10
t	HH:mm	10:02 PM
T	HH:mm:ss	10:02:10 PM
U	yyyy'-'MM'-'dd HH':'mm':'ss'Z'	2004-01-12 22:02:10Z

TABLE 3.8 continued: Built-In Date and Time Formats

CHARACTER	FORMAT	EXAMPLE
U	dddd, MMMM dd, yyyy HH:mm:ss	Tuesday, January 13, 2004 06:02:10 AM
y, Y	yyyy, MMMM	January, 2004

Listing 3.4 shows the various DateTime properties and methods described in this section, including some of the formats described in Table 3.8.

Listing 3.4: DateTime Properties and Methods

```
using System;

class Example9_4
{

  public static void Main()
  {

    // use the Now and UtcNow properties to get the currrent
    // date and time
    Console.WriteLine("DateTime.Now = " + DateTime.Now);
    Console.WriteLine("DateTime.UtcNow = "
        + DateTime.UtcNow);
    DateTime myDateTime = DateTime.Now;
    Console.WriteLine("myDateTime = " + myDateTime);
    DateTime myDateTime2 = DateTime.UtcNow;
    Console.WriteLine("myDateTime = " + myDateTime);

    // display the Date, Day, DayOfWeek, DayOfYear,
    // Ticks, and TimeOfDayProperties of myDateTime
    Console.WriteLine("myDateTime.Date = "
        + myDateTime.Date);
    Console.WriteLine("myDateTime.Day = "
        + myDateTime.Day);
    Console.WriteLine("myDateTime.DayOfWeek = "
        + myDateTime.DayOfWeek);
    Console.WriteLine("myDateTime.DayOfYear = "
        + myDateTime.DayOfYear);
```

```
Console.WriteLine("myDateTime.Ticks = "
  + myDateTime.Ticks);
Console.WriteLine("myDateTime.TimeOfDay = "
  + myDateTime.TimeOfDay);

// use the Compare() method to compare
// DateTime instances
DateTime myDateTime3 = new DateTime(2004, 1, 13);
DateTime myDateTime4 = new DateTime(2004, 1, 14);
Console.WriteLine("myDateTime3 = " + myDateTime3);
Console.WriteLine("myDateTime4 = " + myDateTime4);
int intResult = DateTime.Compare(myDateTime3,
    myDateTime4);
Console.WriteLine("DateTime.Compare(myDateTime3,
  myDateTime4) = " + DateTime.Compare(myDateTime,
  myDateTime2));

// use the overloaded less than
// operator (<) to compare two
// DateTime instances
bool boolResult = myDateTime3 < myDateTime4;
Console.WriteLine("myDateTime3 < myDateTime4 is " +
  boolResult);

// use the Equals() method to compare DateTime instances
boolResult = DateTime.Equals(myDateTime3, myDateTime4);
Console.WriteLine("DateTime.Equals(myDateTime3,
    myDateTime4) = " + boolResult);
boolResult = myDateTime3.Equals(myDateTime4);
Console.WriteLine(
    "myDateTime3.Equals(myDateTime4) is " + boolResult);

// use the DaysInMonth() method to
// retrieve the number of days in a
// particular month and year
int days = DateTime.DaysInMonth(2004, 1);
Console.WriteLine("DateTime.DaysInMonth(2004, 1) = " +
  days);

// use the IsLeapYear() method
// to determine if a particular
// year is a leap year
```

```
boolResult = DateTime.IsLeapYear(2004);
Console.WriteLine("DateTime.IsLeapYear(2004) = " +
  boolResult);

// use the Parse() method to convert
// strings to DateTime instances
DateTime myDateTime5 = DateTime.Parse("1/13/2004");
DateTime myDateTime6 =
  DateTime.Parse("1/13/2004 23:10:30");
Console.WriteLine("myDateTime5 = " + myDateTime5);
Console.WriteLine("myDateTime6 = " + myDateTime6);

// use the Add() method to add a TimeSpan to a DateTime
TimeSpan myTimeSpan = new TimeSpan(1, 2, 4, 10);
DateTime myDateTime7 = myDateTime6.Add(myTimeSpan);
Console.WriteLine("myTimeSpan = " + myTimeSpan);
Console.WriteLine("myDateTime6.Add(myTimeSpan) = " +
  myDateTime7);

// use the Subtract() method to subtract
// a TimeSpan from a DateTime
myDateTime7 = myDateTime6.Subtract(myTimeSpan);
Console.WriteLine(
  "myDateTime6.Subtract(myTimeSpan) = " +
   myDateTime7);

// use the overloaded addition operator (+)
// to add a TimeSpan to a DateTime
DateTime myDateTime8 = myDateTime6 + myTimeSpan;
Console.WriteLine
  ("myDateTime6 + myTimeSpan = " + myDateTime8);

// use the overloaded subtraction operator (-)
// to subtract a TimeSpan from a DateTime
myDateTime8 = myDateTime6 - myTimeSpan;
Console.WriteLine(
  "myDateTime6 - myTimeSpan = " + myDateTime8);

// use the AddYears(), AddMonths(), AddDays(),
// AddMinutes(), and AddSeconds() methods to
// add periods to a DateTime
DateTime myDateTime9 = new DateTime(2004, 1, 1);
```

```
Console.WriteLine(
  "Initial myDateTime9 = " + myDateTime9);
myDateTime9 = myDateTime9.AddYears(1);
myDateTime9 = myDateTime9.AddMonths(5);
myDateTime9 = myDateTime9.AddDays(3);
myDateTime9 = myDateTime9.AddMinutes(30);
myDateTime9 = myDateTime9.AddSeconds(15);
Console.WriteLine(
    "Final myDateTime9 = " + myDateTime9);

// use the ToFileTime() method to convert a DateTime to
// an operating system file timestamp
DateTime myDateTime10 =
  new DateTime(2004, 1, 15, 23, 2, 5);
long myFileTime = myDateTime10.ToFileTime();
Console.WriteLine("myDateTime10.ToFileTime() = " +
  myDateTime10.ToFileTime());

// use the FromFileTime() method to convert
// an operating system file timestamp to a DateTime
DateTime myDateTime11 =
  DateTime.FromFileTime(myFileTime);
Console.WriteLine("DateTime.FromFileTime() = " +
  myDateTime11);

// use the ToLongDateString() and
// ToShortDateString() methods to convert the
// date parts of a DateTime to long and short
// date strings
Console.WriteLine("myDateTime11 = " + myDateTime11);
Console.WriteLine(
    "myDateTime11.ToLongDateString() = " +
  myDateTime11.ToLongDateString());
Console.WriteLine(
    "myDateTime11.ToShortDateString() = " +
  myDateTime11.ToShortDateString());

// use the ToLongTimeString() and
// ToShortTimeString() methods
// to convert the time parts of a DateTime
// to long and short time strings
```

```
Console.WriteLine(
  "myDateTime11.ToLongTimeString() = " +
  myDateTime11.ToLongTimeString());
Console.WriteLine("
  myDateTime11.ToShortTimeString() = " +
  myDateTime11.ToShortTimeString());

// use the ToString() method to convert a DateTime
// to a string
DateTime myDateTime12 =
  new DateTime(2004, 1, 12, 22, 2, 10);
Console.WriteLine("myDateTime12.ToString() = " +
  myDateTime12.ToString());
Console.WriteLine(
  "myDateTime12.ToString(\"MMMM dd, yyyy\") = " +
  myDateTime12.ToString("MMMM dd, yyyy"));
Console.WriteLine("myDateTime12.ToString(\"d\") = " +
  myDateTime12.ToString("d"));
Console.WriteLine("myDateTime12.ToString(\"D\") = " +
  myDateTime12.ToString("D"));
Console.WriteLine("myDateTime12.ToString(\"f\") = " +
  myDateTime12.ToString("f"));
Console.WriteLine("myDateTime12.ToString(\"F\") = " +
  myDateTime12.ToString("F"));
Console.WriteLine("myDateTime12.ToString(\"g\") = " +
  myDateTime12.ToString("g"));
Console.WriteLine("myDateTime12.ToString(\"G\") = " +
  myDateTime12.ToString("G"));
Console.WriteLine("myDateTime12.ToString(\"m\") = " +
  myDateTime12.ToString("m"));
Console.WriteLine("myDateTime12.ToString(\"r\") = " +
  myDateTime12.ToString("r"));
Console.WriteLine("myDateTime12.ToString(\"s\") = " +
  myDateTime12.ToString("s"));
Console.WriteLine("myDateTime12.ToString(\"t\") = " +
  myDateTime12.ToString("t"));
Console.WriteLine("myDateTime12.ToString(\"T\") = " +
  myDateTime12.ToString("T"));
Console.WriteLine("myDateTime12.ToString(\"u\") = " +
  myDateTime12.ToString("u"));
Console.WriteLine("myDateTime12.ToString(\"U\") = " +
  myDateTime12.ToString("U"));
```

```
            Console.WriteLine("myDateTime12.ToString(\"y\") = " +
               myDateTime12.ToString("y"));


        }


    }
```

The output from this program is as follows:

```
DateTime.Now = 3/31/2002 4:34:12 PM
DateTime.UtcNow = 4/1/2002 12:34:12 AM
myDateTime = 3/31/2002 4:34:12 PM
myDateTime = 3/31/2002 4:34:12 PM
myDateTime.Date = 3/31/2002 12:00:00 AM
myDateTime.Day = 31
myDateTime.DayOfWeek = Sunday
myDateTime.DayOfYear = 90
myDateTime.Ticks = 631531892524029264
myDateTime.TimeOfDay = 16:34:12.4029264
myDateTime3 = 1/13/2004 12:00:00 AM
myDateTime4 = 1/14/2004 12:00:00 AM
DateTime.Compare(myDateTime3, myDateTime4) = -1
myDateTime3 < myDateTime4 is True
DateTime.Equals(myDateTime3, myDateTime4) = False
myDateTime3.Equals(myDateTime4) is False
DateTime.DaysInMonth(2004, 1) = 31
DateTime.IsLeapYear(2004) = True
myDateTime5 = 1/13/2004 12:00:00 AM
myDateTime6 = 1/13/2004 11:10:30 PM
myTimeSpan = 1.02:04:10
myDateTime6.Add(myTimeSpan) = 1/15/2004 1:14:40 AM
myDateTime6.Subtract(myTimeSpan) = 1/12/2004 9:06:20 PM
myDateTime6 + myTimeSpan = 1/15/2004 1:14:40 AM
myDateTime6 - myTimeSpan = 1/12/2004 9:06:20 PM
Initial myDateTime9 = 1/1/2004 12:00:00 AM
Final myDateTime9 = 6/4/2005 12:30:15 AM
myDateTime10.ToFileTime() = 127187101250000000
DateTime.FromFileTime() = 1/15/2004 11:02:05 PM
myDateTime11 = 1/15/2004 11:02:05 PM
myDateTime11.ToLongDateString() = Thursday, January 15, 2004
myDateTime11.ToShortDateString() = 1/15/2004
myDateTime11.ToLongTimeString() = 11:02:05 PM
myDateTime11.ToShortTimeString() = 11:02 PM
myDateTime12.ToString() = 1/12/2004 10:02:10 PM
myDateTime12.ToString("MMMM dd, yyyy") = January 12, 2004
```

```
myDateTime12.ToString("d") = 1/12/2004
myDateTime12.ToString("D") = Monday, January 12, 2004
myDateTime12.ToString("f") =
  Monday, January 12, 2004 10:02 PM
myDateTime12.ToString("F") =
  Monday, January 12, 2004 10:02:10 PM
myDateTime12.ToString("g") = 1/12/2004 10:02 PM
myDateTime12.ToString("G") = 1/12/2004 10:02:10 PM
myDateTime12.ToString("m") = January 12
myDateTime12.ToString("r") = Mon, 12 Jan 2004 22:02:10 GMT
myDateTime12.ToString("s") = 2004-01-12T22:02:10
myDateTime12.ToString("t") = 10:02 PM
myDateTime12.ToString("T") = 10:02:10 PM
myDateTime12.ToString("u") = 2004-01-12 22:02:10Z
myDateTime12.ToString("U") =
  Tuesday, January 13, 2004 6:02:10 AM
myDateTime12.ToString("y") = January, 2004
```

USING TIME SPANS

As you saw earlier, a TimeSpan instance represents an interval of time—
4 days, 12 minutes, and 10 seconds, for example. This section will go deeper
into the details of how to create TimeSpan instance, and you'll see the
various properties and methods of the TimeSpan class.

Creating *TimeSpan* Instances

The constructor for the TimeSpan class is overloaded, and there are several
ways you can create a TimeSpan instance. You can create a TimeSpan
instance with a specified number of hours, minutes, and seconds, passing
these int values to the TimeSpan constructor. For example,

```
int hours = 4;
int minutes = 12;
int seconds = 10;
TimeSpan myTimeSpan =
  new TimeSpan(hours, minutes, seconds);
```

You can also create a TimeSpan instance with a specified number of days:

```
int days = 1;
TimeSpan myTimeSpan2 =
  new TimeSpan(days, hours, minutes, seconds);
```

You can also supply the number of milliseconds when creating a TimeSpan instance:

```
int milliseconds = 20;
TimeSpan myTimeSpan3 =
    new TimeSpan(days, hours, minutes, seconds, milliseconds);
```

Finally, you can also create a TimeSpan instance with a specified number of ticks:

```
long ticks = 300;
TimeSpan myTimeSpan4 = new TimeSpan(ticks);
```

In the next section, you'll see the various TimeSpan properties and methods.

Using *TimeSpan* Properties and Methods

The TimeSpan class provides a number of properties and methods you can use in your programs. Table 3.9 lists the public properties of the TimeSpan class.

TABLE 3.9:   TimeSpan Properties

PROPERTY	TYPE	DESCRIPTION
Days	int	Gets the number of days from the TimeSpan
Hours	int	Gets the number of hours from the TimeSpan
Milliseconds	int	Gets the number of milliseconds from the TimeSpan
Minutes	int	Gets the number of minutes from the TimeSpan
Seconds	int	Gets the number of seconds from the TimeSpan
Ticks	long	Gets the value of the TimeSpan in ticks
TotalDays	double	Gets the value the TimeSpan as days
TotalHours	double	Gets the value the TimeSpan as hours
TotalMilliseconds	double	Gets the value the TimeSpan as milliseconds
TotalMinutes	double	Gets the value the TimeSpan as minutes
TotalSeconds	double	Gets the value the TimeSpan as seconds

Table 3.10 shows the TimeSpan public methods.

TABLE 3.10:   TimeSpan Methods

Method	Return Type	Description
Compare() (static)	int	Compares two TimeSpan instances and returns an indication of their relative values.
Equals() (static and instance versions)	bool	Overloaded. Returns a bool that indicates whether DateTimeSpan instances are equal. The overloaded equal to operator (==) also does this.
FromDays() (static)	TimeSpan	Returns a TimeSpan containing the specified number of days.
FromHours() (static)	TimeSpan	Returns a TimeSpan containing the specified number of hours (a double value).
FromMilliseconds() (static)	TimeSpan	Returns a TimeSpan containing the specified number of milliseconds (a double value).
FromMinutes() (static)	TimeSpan	Returns a TimeSpan containing the specified number of minutes (a double value).
FromSeconds() (static)	TimeSpan	Returns a TimeSpan containing the specified number of seconds (a double value).
FromTicks() (static)	TimeSpan	Returns a TimeSpan containing the specified number of ticks (a long value).
Parse() (static)	TimeSpan	Converts the specified string representation of a time period to the equivalent TimeSpan.
Add()	TimeSpan	Adds the specified TimeSpan to the current TimeSpan. The overloaded addition operator (+) also does this.
CompareTo()	int	Compares two TimeSpan instances and returns an indication of their relative values.
Duration()	TimeSpan	Returns a TimeSpan whose value is the absolute value of this instance.
GetHashCode()	int	Returns the hash code for the TimeSpan.

TABLE 3.10 continued: TimeSpan Methods

Method	Return Type	Description
GetType() (inherited from Object)	Type	Returns the type of the current instance.
Negate()	TimeSpan	Returns a TimeSpan whose value is the negative value of the current TimeSpan.
Subtract()	TimeSpan	Subtracts the specified TimeSpan from the current TimeSpan. You can also use the overloaded subtraction operator (–) for this purpose.
ToString()	string	Converts the TimeSpan to the equivalent string representation.

The following sections illustrate some of these properties and methods.

Days, Hours, Minutes, Seconds, and Milliseconds Properties

You get the various parts of a TimeSpan using the Days, Hours, Minutes, Seconds, and Milliseconds properties. These properties all return int values. The following example shows the use of these properties:

```
Console.WriteLine("myTimeSpan.Days = " + myTimeSpan.Days);
Console.WriteLine("myTimeSpan.Hours = "
  + myTimeSpan.Hours);
Console.WriteLine("myTimeSpan.Minutes = "
  + myTimeSpan.Minutes);
Console.WriteLine("myTimeSpan.Seconds = "
  + myTimeSpan.Seconds);
Console.WriteLine("myTimeSpan.Milliseconds = "
  + myTimeSpan.Milliseconds);
```

Because myTimeSpan was created earlier as a period of 4 hours, 12 minutes, and 10 seconds, the previous examples display the following:

```
myTimeSpan.Days = 0
myTimeSpan.Hours = 4
myTimeSpan.Minutes = 12
myTimeSpan.Seconds = 10
myTimeSpan.Milliseconds = 0
```

Notice that Days and Milliseconds are zero. This is because myTimeSpan didn't have settings for these parts.

Ticks Property

You get the value of a TimeSpan in ticks using the Ticks property, which returns a long value. As mentioned earlier, a tick is a 100-nanosecond interval. The following example shows the use of the Ticks property:

```
Console.WriteLine("myTimeSpan.Ticks = "  + myTimeSpan.Ticks);
```

This example displays the following:

```
myTimeSpan.Ticks = 151300000000
```

TotalDays, TotalHours, TotalMinutes, TotalSeconds, and TotalMilliseconds Properties

You can get the total length of a TimeSpan in different periods using the TotalDays, TotalHours, TotalMinutes, TotalSeconds, and TotalMilliseconds properties. Each of these properties returns a double value. For example, TotalDays returns the value of a TimeSpan in days, TotalHours returns the value in hours, and so on.

If the values created earlier for myTimeSpan are assumed (a period of 4 hours, 12 minutes, and 10 seconds), the following example shows the use of these properties of myTimeSpan:

```
Console.WriteLine("myTimeSpan.TotalDays = " +
   myTimeSpan.TotalDays);
Console.WriteLine("myTimeSpan.TotalHours = " +
   myTimeSpan.TotalHours);
Console.WriteLine("myTimeSpan.TotalMinutes = " +
   myTimeSpan.TotalMinutes);
Console.WriteLine("myTimeSpan.TotalSeconds = " +
   myTimeSpan.TotalSeconds);
Console.WriteLine("myTimeSpan.TotalMilliseconds = " +
   myTimeSpan.TotalMilliseconds);
```

These examples display the following:

```
myTimeSpan.TotalDays = 0.175115740740741
myTimeSpan.TotalHours = 4.20277777777778
myTimeSpan.TotalMinutes = 252.166666666667
myTimeSpan.TotalSeconds = 15130
myTimeSpan.TotalMilliseconds = 15130000
```

Creating *TimeSpan* Instances Using the *FromDays()*, *FromHours()*, *FromMinutes()*, *FromSeconds()*, and *FromMilliseconds()* Methods

You can create new TimeSpan instances using the static FromDays(), FromHours(), FromMinutes(), FromSeconds(), and FromMilliseconds() methods. Each of these methods accepts a double parameter that specifies the period (days, hours, and so on) and return a new TimeSpan instance for that period.

For example, passing 5 to FromDays() returns a TimeSpan of 5 days. Similarly, passing 10 to FromHours() returns a TimeSpan of 10 hours. Because each method accepts a double value, you can pass fractional periods to each method. For example, passing 2.5 to FromDays() returns a TimeSpan of 2.5 days.

The following examples show the various methods in action:

```
TimeSpan myTimeSpan5 = TimeSpan.FromDays(5);
TimeSpan myTimeSpan6 = TimeSpan.FromHours(10);
TimeSpan myTimeSpan7 = TimeSpan.FromMinutes(30);
TimeSpan myTimeSpan8 = TimeSpan.FromSeconds(15);
TimeSpan myTimeSpan9 = TimeSpan.FromMilliseconds(200);
```

Creating *TimeSpan* Instances Using the *FromTicks()* Method

You can also create TimeSpan instances using the static FromTicks() method. This method accepts a long value that specifies the number of ticks and returns a new TimeSpan instance. For example,

```
TimeSpan myTimeSpan10 = TimeSpan.FromTicks(500);
```

Converting Strings to *TimeSpan* Instances Using the *Parse()* Method

You can use the Parse() method to convert a specified string representation of a time period to the equivalent TimeSpan. The string passed to Parse() uses the following format:

```
[ws][-][d.]hh:mm:ss[.ff][ws]
```

Table 3.11 describes all of these elements.

NOTE

The elements in the square brackets ([and]) are optional.

TABLE 3.11: Parse Format Elements

ELEMENT	DESCRIPTION
ws	Optional white space
-	Optional sign that indicates the time interval is negative
D	Optional days
hh	The hours in 24-hour format
mm	The minutes
ss	The seconds
ff	Optional fraction of a second specified using one to seven digits

The following example uses the Parse() method to create a new TimeSpan of 8 hours, 10 minutes, and 30 seconds:

```
TimeSpan myTimeSpan11 = TimeSpan.Parse("8:10:30");
```

The next example creates a new TimeSpan of 1 day, 8 hours, 10 minutes, and 30.1234567 seconds:

```
TimeSpan myTimeSpan12 = TimeSpan.Parse("1.8:10:30.1234567");
```

Adding to and Subtracting from a *TimeSpan* Instance Using the *Add()* and *Subtract()* Methods

You can use the Add() method to add a TimeSpan to the current TimeSpan. Similarly, you can use the Subtract() method to subtract a TimeSpan from the current TimeSpan. These methods both return a new TimeSpan instance.

The following example creates two TimeSpan instances named myTimeSpan13 and myTimeSpan14, and then uses the Add() method to add myTimeSpan14 to myTimeSpan13, assigning the returned result to myTimeSpan15:

```
TimeSpan myTimeSpan13 = new TimeSpan(1, 10, 13);
TimeSpan myTimeSpan14 = new TimeSpan(2, 6, 10);
TimeSpan myTimeSpan15 = myTimeSpan13.Add(myTimeSpan14);
```

The result assigned to myTimeSpan15 is 3 hours, 16 minutes, and 23 seconds, which is the sum of the components of myTimeSpan13 and myTimeSpan14.

The next example subtracts myTimeSpan14 from myTimeSpan13, assigning the result to myTimeSpan15:

```
myTimeSpan15 = myTimeSpan13.Subtract(myTimeSpan14);
```

The result assigned to myTime15 is a period of –55 minutes and –57 seconds, which is a negative period. The following example displays myTimeSpan15:

```
Console.WriteLine(myTimeSpan15);
```

This example displays the following:

```
-00:55:57
```

NOTE

It is perfectly legal to assign a negative period to a TimeSpan.

Obtaining the Absolute Value of a *TimeSpan* Instance Using the *Duration()* Method

You can use the Duration() method to get the absolute value of a TimeSpan instance. In the case when you have a negative period stored in a TimeSpan, Duration() will return the positive value.

For example, myTimeSpan15 was set to –55 minutes and –57 seconds in the previous example, and myTimeSpan15.Duration() returns a TimeSpan of 55 minutes and 57 seconds—a positive value:

```
Console.WriteLine(myTimeSpan15.Duration());
```

This example displays the following:

```
00:55:57
```

Negating a *TimeSpan* Instance Using the *Negate()* Method

You can use the Negate() method to return a TimeSpan whose value is the negative of the current TimeSpan. Components of a TimeSpan that are negative are returned as positive, and vice versa.

For example, myTimeSpan15.Negate() returns a positive TimeSpan of 55 minutes and 57 seconds:

```
Console.WriteLine(myTimeSpan15.Negate());
```

This example displays the following:

```
00:55:57
```

Now, myTimeSpan14 was set to 2 hours, 6 minutes, and 10 seconds earlier, so myTimeSpan14.Negate() returns a negative TimeSpan of −2 hours, −6 minutes, and −10 seconds. For example:

```
Console.WriteLine(myTimeSpan14.Negate());
```

This example displays the following:

```
-02:06:10
```

Listing 3.5 shows the use of the various TimeSpan properties and methods described in this section.

Listing 3.5: TimeSpan Properties and Methods

```
using System;

class Example9_5
{

  public static void DisplayTimeSpan(
    string name, TimeSpan myTimeSpan
  )
  {

    Console.WriteLine(name + " = " + myTimeSpan);

    // display the TimeSpan's properties
    Console.WriteLine(name + ".Days = " + myTimeSpan.Days);
    Console.WriteLine(name + ".Hours = "
      + myTimeSpan.Hours);
    Console.WriteLine(name + ".Minutes = "
      + myTimeSpan.Minutes);
    Console.WriteLine(name + ".Seconds = "
      + myTimeSpan.Seconds);
    Console.WriteLine(name + ".Milliseconds = "
      + myTimeSpan.Milliseconds);
```

```
      Console.WriteLine(name + ".Ticks = "
        + myTimeSpan.Ticks);

}


public static void Main()
{

  // create a TimeSpan instance, specifying
  // the hours, minutes, and seconds
  int hours = 4;
  int minutes = 12;
  int seconds = 10;
  TimeSpan myTimeSpan =
    new TimeSpan(hours, minutes, seconds);
  Console.WriteLine("myTimeSpan = " + myTimeSpan);

  // create a TimeSpan instance, specifying the days,
  // hours, minutes, and seconds
  int days = 1;
  TimeSpan myTimeSpan2 =
    new TimeSpan(days, hours, minutes, seconds);
  Console.WriteLine("myTimeSpan2 = " + myTimeSpan2);

  // create a TimeSpan instance, specifying the days,
  // hours, minutes, seconds, and milliseconds
  int milliseconds = 20;
  TimeSpan myTimeSpan3 =
    new TimeSpan(days, hours, minutes,
    seconds, milliseconds);
  Console.WriteLine("myTimeSpan3 = " + myTimeSpan3);

  // create a TimeSpan instance, specifying the
  // number of ticks
  long ticks = 300;
  TimeSpan myTimeSpan4 = new TimeSpan(ticks);
  Console.WriteLine("myTimeSpan4 = " + myTimeSpan4);

  // display the properties for myTimeSpan
  Console.WriteLine("myTimeSpan.Days = " +
    myTimeSpan.Days);
```

```
Console.WriteLine("myTimeSpan.Hours = " +
  myTimeSpan.Hours);
Console.WriteLine("myTimeSpan.Minutes = " +
  myTimeSpan.Minutes);
Console.WriteLine("myTimeSpan.Seconds = " +
  myTimeSpan.Seconds);
Console.WriteLine("myTimeSpan.Milliseconds = " +
  myTimeSpan.Milliseconds);
Console.WriteLine("myTimeSpan.Ticks = " +
  myTimeSpan.Ticks);
Console.WriteLine("myTimeSpan.TotalDays = " +
  myTimeSpan.TotalDays);
Console.WriteLine("myTimeSpan.TotalHours = " +
  myTimeSpan.TotalHours);
Console.WriteLine("myTimeSpan.TotalMinutes = " +
  myTimeSpan.TotalMinutes);
Console.WriteLine("myTimeSpan.TotalSeconds = " +
  myTimeSpan.TotalSeconds);
Console.WriteLine("myTimeSpan.TotalMilliseconds = " +
  myTimeSpan.TotalMilliseconds);

// use the FromDays(), FromHours(),
// FromMinutes(), FromSeconds(), FromMilliseconds(),
// and FromTicks() methods to create new
// TimeSpan instances
TimeSpan myTimeSpan5 = TimeSpan.FromDays(5);
Console.WriteLine("TimeSpan.FromDays(5) = " +
  myTimeSpan5);
TimeSpan myTimeSpan6 = TimeSpan.FromHours(10);
Console.WriteLine("TimeSpan.FromHours(10) = " +
  myTimeSpan6);
TimeSpan myTimeSpan7 = TimeSpan.FromMinutes(30);
Console.WriteLine("TimeSpan.FromMinutes(30) = " +
  myTimeSpan7);
TimeSpan myTimeSpan8 = TimeSpan.FromSeconds(15);
Console.WriteLine("TimeSpan.FromSeconds(15) = " +
  myTimeSpan8);
TimeSpan myTimeSpan9 = TimeSpan.FromMilliseconds(200);
Console.WriteLine("TimeSpan.FromMilliseconds(200) = " +
  myTimeSpan9);
TimeSpan myTimeSpan10 = TimeSpan.FromTicks(500);
Console.WriteLine("TimeSpan.FromTicks(500) = " +
  myTimeSpan10);
```

```
// use the Parse() method to convert
// strings to TimeSpan instances
TimeSpan myTimeSpan11 = TimeSpan.Parse("8:10:30");
Console.WriteLine("TimeSpan.Parse(\"8:10:30\") = " +
  myTimeSpan11);
TimeSpan myTimeSpan12 =
  TimeSpan.Parse("1.8:10:30.1234567");

Console.WriteLine(
  "TimeSpan.Parse(\"1.8:10:30.1234567\") = " +
  myTimeSpan12);

// use the Add() method to add a
// TimeSpan instance to another
TimeSpan myTimeSpan13 = new TimeSpan(1, 10, 13);
TimeSpan myTimeSpan14 = new TimeSpan(2, 6, 10);
TimeSpan myTimeSpan15 = myTimeSpan13.Add(myTimeSpan14);
Console.WriteLine("myTimeSpan13 = " + myTimeSpan13);
Console.WriteLine("myTimeSpan14 = " + myTimeSpan14);
Console.WriteLine("myTimeSpan15 = " + myTimeSpan15);

// use the Subtract() method to subtract
// a TimeSpan instance from another
myTimeSpan15 = myTimeSpan13.Subtract(myTimeSpan14);
Console.WriteLine("myTimeSpan15 = " + myTimeSpan15);

// use the Duration() method to add
// two TimeSpan instances
Console.WriteLine("myTimeSpan15.Duration() = " +
  myTimeSpan15.Duration());

// use the Negate() method to add two TimeSpan instances
Console.WriteLine("myTimeSpan15.Negate() = " +
  myTimeSpan15.Negate());
Console.WriteLine("myTimeSpan14.Negate() = " +
  myTimeSpan14.Negate());

  }

}
```

The output from this program is as follows:

```
myTimeSpan = 04:12:10
myTimeSpan2 = 1.04:12:10
```

```
myTimeSpan3 = 1.04:12:10.0200000
myTimeSpan4 = 00:00:00.0000300
myTimeSpan.Days = 0
myTimeSpan.Hours = 4
myTimeSpan.Minutes = 12
myTimeSpan.Seconds = 10
myTimeSpan.Milliseconds = 0
myTimeSpan.Ticks = 151300000000
myTimeSpan.TotalDays = 0.175115740740741
myTimeSpan.TotalHours = 4.20277777777778
myTimeSpan.TotalMinutes = 252.166666666667
myTimeSpan.TotalSeconds = 15130
myTimeSpan.TotalMilliseconds = 15130000
TimeSpan.FromDays(5) = 5.00:00:00
TimeSpan.FromHours(10) = 10:00:00
TimeSpan.FromMinutes(30) = 00:30:00
TimeSpan.FromSeconds(15) = 00:00:15
TimeSpan.FromMilliseconds(200) = 00:00:00.2000000
TimeSpan.FromTicks(500) = 00:00:00.0000500
TimeSpan.Parse("8:10:30") = 08:10:30
TimeSpan.Parse("1.8:10:30.1234567") = 1.08:10:30.1234567
myTimeSpan13 = 01:10:13
myTimeSpan14 = 02:06:10
myTimeSpan15 = 03:16:23
myTimeSpan15 = -00:55:57
myTimeSpan15.Duration() = 00:55:57
myTimeSpan15.Negate() = 00:55:57
myTimeSpan14.Negate() = -02:06:10
```

Listing 3.6 shows another program, which measures the time taken to add some numbers.

Listing 3.6: Measuring the Time Taken to Add Some Numbers

```
using System;

class Example9_6
{

  public static void Main()
  {

    // create a DateTime object and set it to the
    // current date and time
    DateTime start = DateTime.Now;
```

```
// add numbers using a for loop
long total = 0;
for (int count = 0; count < 1000000; count++)
{
  total += count;
}

// subtract the current date and time from the start,
// storing the difference in a TimeSpan
TimeSpan timeTaken = DateTime.Now - start;

// display the number of milliseconds taken
// to add the numbers
Console.WriteLine(
  "Milliseconds = " + timeTaken.Milliseconds);

// display the total of the added numbers
Console.WriteLine("total = " + total);

    }


  }
```

The output from this program is as follows:

```
Milliseconds = 10
total = 499999500000
```

SUMMARY

In this chapter, you learned about strings, dates, times, and time spans. Specifically, you use a string to represent a series of characters, which is stored as Unicode. Strings are actually objects of the System.String class. This class contains properties and a rich set of methods you can use in your programs to manipulate strings.

The System.Text.StringBuilder class allows you to create *dynamic strings*. Unlike a regular string of the String class, a dynamic string's characters may be modified directly; with a regular string, you always modify a copy of the string. In addition, the StringBuilder methods are fast and provide you with efficient string manipulation capabilities.

In addition to strings and the other built-in types, you can also represent dates and times in your programs. Examples of using a date and time would be to store a person's date-of-birth, or to record when a financial transaction took place. You can represent dates and times in your programs using the System.DateTime struct. The DateTime struct contains many properties and methods that allow you manipulate dates and times.

Finally, you also learned that you can represent time intervals in your programs—these are known as *time spans*. An example of a time span is 4 days, 12 minutes, and 10 seconds. You use the System.TimeSpan class to represent a time span. The TimeSpan class contains many properties and methods that allow you manipulate time periods.

WHAT'S NEXT

In the next chapter, you'll learn about the nature of object-oriented programming, the difference between a class and an object, and the components that make up a class.

Chapter 4

OBJECT-ORIENTED PROGRAMMING

I n Chapter 2, "Zen and Now: The C# Language," you learned about the various C# built-in types and how to declare variables using those types. In this chapter, you'll learn how to define your own types using classes and structs, and how to put those types to work in your programs. You'll also see how you can create objects from classes. In addition, you'll see how you can use classes and objects to model things that exist in the real world and how they can simplify the task of writing programs to solve complex problems.

Adapted from *Mastering Visual C# .NET* by Jason Price and Mike Gunderloy

ISBN 0-7821-2911-0

Introducing Classes and Objects

Our world is filled with objects. My car is an object, my bike is an object, and my house is an object—in fact, any tangible item is an object. Similar objects may be grouped together into a *class*. For example, my car is similar to other cars on the road: It has an engine and four wheels, and it's operated with pedals and a steering wheel. So, my car can be grouped into a generic class of cars, all of which have similar characteristics and behaviors. An object can also represent more abstract things—such as an electronic order, for example.

A class specifies the characteristics and behaviors shared by all members of that class. For example, all cars have the following characteristics: make, model, color, and year they were built. All cars also have the following behaviors: the ability to start, stop, and run at different speeds.

NOTE
You can think of a class as a blueprint from which individual objects are created.

An object has *individual* characteristics. For example, my car's make is Toyota, its model is MR2, its color is black, and it was built in 1995; my neighbor's car's make is Buick, its model is Century, its color is silver, and it was built in 1992—the point is that both cars have their own characteristics. Of course, some characteristics are common to both our cars—they both have four wheels, for example. In addition, some of the behaviors of our cars are common—for example, both our cars can be started and stopped.

NOTE
An object has its own individual characteristics, but it has the same behaviors as other objects.

Classes and objects can be modeled using a computer program. The ability to model classes and objects using a programming language is not new to C#—the idea was developed back in the 1970s at Xerox PARC, and many earlier programming languages have been able to model classes and objects, including Smalltalk, Eiffel, Object Pascal, C++, and more recently, Java. These languages are known as *object-oriented programming (OOP)* languages.

Object-oriented programming is a powerful way of solving complex problems. The advantage of using classes and objects in a program is that you can use them to model objects in the real world, which can help reduce the complexity involved in creating a program to solve difficult problems. You can *encapsulate*, or group together, the characteristics and behaviors of a real object in a class and develop your program from those simple building blocks. For example, imagine writing a program to simulate a nuclear reactor—a complex piece of machinery—by using objects to model features such as the fuel rods, sensors, pumps, boilers, and heat exchangers. In other words, you can break the problem up into smaller components that mirror the real system you're trying to simulate.

DECLARING A CLASS

A class defines the characteristics and behaviors for objects—you can think of a class as a template from which objects are created. In C#, the characteristics are stored in variables known as *fields*, and the behaviors are modeled by *methods*—which are groups of statements that perform a specific task and may return a value. Together, the fields and methods of a class are known as *class members*.

NOTE

You've already seen an example of one method in Chapter 3: Main(). Main() is a special method that acts as a starting point for a program. In all the programs you've seen so far, the Main() method has performed all the actions of the program. When you ran these programs, Main() was run—or called—automatically.

You declare a class using the class keyword, which uses the following simplified syntax:

```
[access-modifier] class class-name {class-body}
```

The syntax elements are as follows:

access-modifier   The degree to which your class is available to the outside world.

class-name   The name you assign to your class.

class-body   The body of your class.

Classes are usually declared using the public access modifier, meaning that the class is available without restriction—you'll learn more about access modifiers later in this chapter (see "Using Access Modifiers"). The previous syntax has been simplified because we don't want to overload you with too much information at this stage. Don't worry, though, you'll see examples that use the full class syntax as this book progresses.

We talked a little bit about cars earlier in this chapter, so we'll continue with cars in the code examples. For instance, the following example declares a class named Car—you'll use this class to create objects later:

```
public class Car
{

  // declare the fields
  public string make;
  public string model;
  public string color;
  public int yearBuilt;

  // define the methods
  public void Start()
  {
    System.Console.WriteLine(model + " started");
  }

  public void Stop()
  {
    System.Console.WriteLine(model + " stopped");
  }

}
```

As you can see, the Car class declares four fields: make, model, color, and yearBuilt. The make, model, and color fields are strings that store the make, model, and color of a car, respectively; the yearBuilt field is an integer variable that stores the year a car was built. Each field also has an access modifier, and the four fields of this class are declared using the public access modifier—indicating that the fields are accessible without restriction.

The Car class also defines two methods—Start() and Stop()—that simulate the action of starting and stopping a car. When the Start() method is called, it displays a string containing the value for the model field followed by the word *started*; similarly, the Stop() method displays the model field followed by the word *stopped*. You'll notice that these methods are also public, indicating they can be called without restriction. These methods also use the void keyword—this indicates that the methods don't return a value. You'll learn more about methods, and how they may be used to return values, later in this chapter.

CREATING OBJECTS

As you now know, a class defines a template for creating objects. Once you've declared a class, you can then create objects of that class.

The following statements create a Car object:

```
Car myCar;
myCar = new Car();
```

The first statement declares a *reference* to a Car object, named myCar, and it is used to hold the memory location of an actual Car object. The second statement actually creates a Car object in the computer's memory. The new operator allocates the memory for the Car object, and the Car() method creates the object—the Car() method is known as a *constructor*, and you'll learn more about them later in this chapter. The memory location of the newly created Car object is assigned to myCar, and myCar is a reference through which you can access the actual Car object.

NOTE

The new operator and the constructor are used to create an object. You access an object through an object reference, which holds the location of the actual object in memory.

To access the fields and methods for an object, you use the *dot operator* (.) with an object reference. You can assign values to the fields of the new Car object through the myCar reference, as shown in the following statements:

```
myCar.make = "Toyota";
myCar.model = "MR2";
myCar.color = "black";
myCar.yearBuilt = 1995;
```

In these examples, the make, model, color, and yearBuilt fields for the Car object are set to "Toyota", "MR2", "black", and 1995, respectively. The following statement displays the value of the model field:

```
System.Console.WriteLine("myCar is an " + myCar.model);
```

This statement displays the following line of output:

```
myCar is an MR2
```

To call the methods, you also use the dot operator. The following statement calls the `Start()` method for the `Car` object using the `myCar` reference:

```
myCar.Start()
```

This runs the statements contained in the `Start()` method and displays the following line of output:

```
MR2 started
```

Similarly, calling the `myCar.Stop()` method displays the following line:

```
MR2 stopped
```

The following statement creates another `Car` object:

```
Car redPorsche = new Car();
```

Notice that the declaration of the object reference and the creation of the new object are combined into one statement. The `redPorsche` reference is used to access this new `Car` object.

NOTE
Creating an object is also called *instantiating* an object, with the object being known as an instance of the class.

Each `Car` object has its own copy of the fields declared in the class, and the following statements set its fields using `redPorsche`:

```
redPorsche.make = "Porsche";
redPorsche.model = "Boxster";
redPorsche.color = "red";
redPorsche.yearBuilt = 2000;
```

Because an object reference contains a location of an object in memory, you can change the object actually referenced. For example, let's say I traded in my MR2 for a Porsche (I wish!); then I could record this programmatically using the following statement:

```
myCar = redPorsche;
```

Now `myCar` references the same object referenced by `redPorsche`. This may be verified using the following statement:

```
System.Console.WriteLine("myCar is a " + myCar.model);
```

This statement displays the following line:

```
myCar is a Porsche
```

Null Values

When you declare an object reference, it is initially set to null—you can think of null as meaning "no reference." When you declare an object reference, it doesn't initially reference an actual object in memory. For example, the following statement declares an object reference named myOtherCar:

```
Car myOtherCar;
```

Here, myOtherCar is initially set to null, and it doesn't reference an actual object. Because myOtherCar doesn't yet reference an object (or, is not assigned), the following line will not compile:

```
System.Console.WriteLine(myOtherCar.model);
   // causes compilation error
```

Attempting to compile this line causes the following compilation error:

```
error CS0165: Use of unassigned local variable 'myOtherCar'
```

WARNING

Before you attempt to access an object's fields or methods though an object reference, the object reference must reference an object. This is another example of definite assignment, described earlier in Chapter 2.

You can also assign null to an object reference. For example,

```
myCar = null;
```

This means that myCar no longer references an object. Unless the Car object previously referenced by myCar is referenced elsewhere, then that Car object is no longer available to the program—as you'll see later, the object will be scheduled for removal from memory in a process known as *garbage collection*.

Listing 4.1 illustrates the Car class and objects.

Listing 4.1: A Simple Class and Objects

```
// declare the Car class
public class Car
{

   // declare the fields
   public string make;
   public string model;
```

```
      public string color;
      public int yearBuilt;

      // define the methods
      public void Start()
      {
        System.Console.WriteLine(model + " started");
      }

      public void Stop()
      {
        System.Console.WriteLine(model + " stopped");
      }

    }


  class Example5_1
  {

    public static void Main()
    {

      // declare a Car object reference named myCar
      Car myCar;

      // create a Car object, and assign its address to myCar
      System.Console.WriteLine(
        "Creating a Car object and assigning " +
        "its memory location to myCar");
      myCar = new Car();

      // assign values to the Car object's fields using myCar
      myCar.make = "Toyota";
      myCar.model = "MR2";
      myCar.color = "black";
      myCar.yearBuilt = 1995;

      // display the field values using myCar
      System.Console.WriteLine("myCar details:");
      System.Console.WriteLine("myCar.make = " + myCar.make);
```

```
System.Console.WriteLine("myCar.model = " + myCar.model);
System.Console.WriteLine("myCar.color = " + myCar.color);
System.Console.WriteLine(
  "myCar.yearBuilt = " + myCar.yearBuilt);

// call the methods using myCar
myCar.Start();
myCar.Stop();

// declare another Car object reference and
// create another Car object
System.Console.WriteLine(
  "Creating another Car object and " +
  "assigning its memory location to redPorsche");
Car redPorsche = new Car();
redPorsche.make = "Porsche";
redPorsche.model = "Boxster";
redPorsche.color = "red";
redPorsche.yearBuilt = 2000;
System.Console.WriteLine(
  "redPorsche is a " + redPorsche.model);

// change the object referenced by
// the myCar object reference
// to the object referenced by redPorsche
System.Console.WriteLine("Assigning redPorsche to myCar");
myCar = redPorsche;
System.Console.WriteLine("myCar details:");
System.Console.WriteLine("myCar.make = " + myCar.make);
System.Console.WriteLine("myCar.model = " + myCar.model);
System.Console.WriteLine("myCar.color = " + myCar.color);
System.Console.WriteLine(
  "myCar.yearBuilt = " + myCar.yearBuilt);

// assign null to myCar (myCar will no longer reference
  an object)
myCar = null;

  }


}
```

The output from this program is as follows:

```
Creating a Car object and assigning
    its memory location to myCar
myCar details:
myCar.make = Toyota
myCar.model = MR2
myCar.color = black
myCar.yearBuilt = 1995
MR2 started
MR2 stopped
Creating another Car object and assigning
    its memory location to redPorsche
redPorsche is a Boxster
Assigning redPorsche to myCar
myCar details:
myCar.make = Porsche
myCar.model = Boxster
myCar.color = red
myCar.yearBuilt = 2000
```

Default Field Values and Initializers

When an object is created from a class, the object will get its own copy of the fields declared in the class. Table 4.1 shows the default values taken by fields of various types.

TABLE 4.1: Default Field Values

Type	Default Value
All numeric types	0
bool	false
char	'\0'
string	null

You can set the default value for a field in a class using an *initializer*. Using an initializer is just like assigning a value to a variable, except that it is placed in the class declaration and it specifies a default value for a field.

The following Car class uses initializers to set default values for the make, model, and yearBuilt fields (we've not supplied an initializer for the color field, so it keeps its default of null because color is a string):

```
public class Car
{

  // declare the fields
  public string make = "Ford";
  public string model = "T";
  public string color;  // default value of null
  public int yearBuilt = 1910;

  // define the methods
  ...
}
```

When a Car object is created, its make, model, color, and yearBuilt fields have the default values of "Ford", "T", null, and 1910 respectively.

TIP

You should only use initializers when an object can be assumed to have certain characteristics.

Listing 4.2 illustrates how to assign default values to fields using initializers.

Listing 4.2: Using Initializers

```
// declare the Car class
public class Car
{

  // declare the fields
  public string make = "Ford";
  public string model = "T";
  public string color;  // default value of null
  public int yearBuilt = 1910;

  // define the methods
  public void Start()
  {
    System.Console.WriteLine(model + " started");
  }
```

```
    public void Stop()
    {
      System.Console.WriteLine(model + " stopped");
    }

}


class Example5_2
{

  public static void Main()
  {

    // create a Car object
    Car myCar = new Car();

    // display the default values for the Car object fields
    System.Console.WriteLine("myCar.make = " + myCar.make);
    System.Console.WriteLine("myCar.model = " + myCar.model);
    if (myCar.color == null)
    {
      System.Console.WriteLine("myCar.color is null");
    }
    System.Console.WriteLine(
      "myCar.yearBuilt = " + myCar.yearBuilt);

  }

}
```

The output from this program is as follows:

```
myCar.make = Ford
myCar.model = T
myCar.color is null
myCar.yearBuilt = 1910
```

USING METHODS

A *method* is a group of declarations and other statements that perform a specific task—a method may be called repeatedly to perform that task. In the previous section, the Car class defined two simple methods, Start()

and Stop(). These methods contained a single statement that displayed a line of output. When those methods were called using an object, the statement contained in the methods was run. In this section, you'll delve deeper into the details of methods.

Defining Methods

A method may return a value to the statement that called it, and a method may also accept values from the calling statement—these values are known as *parameters*. The simplified syntax for defining a method is as follows:

```
[access-modifier] return-type method-name(
[parameter-type parameter-name[, ...]]
) {method-body}
```

The syntax elements are as follows:

access-modifier Determines the degree to which your method is accessible by other classes.

return-type The type of the variable returned by the method (a method can also return an object of a specified class). Your method must return a value using the return keyword, and it must return a value that matches *return-type*.

method-name The name you assign to your method.

parameter-type The type of the parameter passed to your method (a method can also accept objects of a specified class).

parameter-name The name of the parameter passed to your method.

The following Car class defines two methods, named Age() and Distance(), along with a new field named maximumSpeed. The Age() method calculates and returns the age of the car in years, and the Distance() method calculates and returns the distance traveled by the car in miles. The maximumSpeed field stores the maximum speed of the car in miles per hour:

```
public class Car
{

    public int yearBuilt;
    public double maximumSpeed;
```

```
// the Age() method calculates and returns the
// age of the car in years
public int Age(int currentYear)
{
  int age = currentYear - yearBuilt;
  return age;
}

// the Distance() method calculates and returns the
// distance traveled by the car, given its initial speed,
// maximum speed, and time for the journey
// (assuming constant acceleration of the car)
public double Distance(double initialSpeed, double time)
{
  return (initialSpeed + maximumSpeed) / 2 * time;
}

}
```

The Age() method calculates and returns the age of the car in years. This method returns an int and accepts an int parameter named currentYear. The age of a car is calculated by subtracting the year the car was built (stored in the yearBuilt field) from the current year (passed as the current-Year parameter)—the result of this calculation is stored in an int variable named age. The return keyword is used to return the value stored in age to the statement that calls the method.

The Distance() method calculates and returns the distance traveled by the car in miles. This distance is calculated using the following formula (assuming constant acceleration for the car and that the car travels in a straight line):

```
(initial speed + maximum speed) / 2 * time
```

The initial speed of the car is passed to the Distance() method as the initialSpeed parameter; the maximum speed of a car is stored in the maximumSpeed field; and the time for the journey is also passed to the method as the time parameter. The speeds are specified in miles per hour, and the time is specified in hours. The double value returned by Distance() is the total distance traveled by the car in miles.

Returning a Value from a Method

Methods that return a value use the return keyword, followed by an expression. That expression may be just a literal value, it may be a variable, or it may even be a complete calculation. In fact, it can be any expression that evaluates to a matching return type for the method. For example, a method that returns an `int` could return the following literal value:

```
return 3;
```

The method could also return an `int` variable:

```
int intValue = 2;
return intValue;
```

The method could also evaluate and then return the result of a calculation:

```
return intValue * 4;
```

When a `return` statement is run, the expression is evaluated and the result is returned to the statement that called the method.

NOTE

A method with a return type of `void` doesn't return a value and therefore doesn't require a return statement.

Local Variables

The scope of a variable is the section of code where that variable exists. When a variable is declared in a method, then that variable only exists in that particular method, and its scope is limited to that method. These are known as *local variables* because their scope is local to the method.

In the `Age()` method shown earlier, age is a local variable and its scope is limited to that method. Therefore, the age variable may only be used within that method. Similarly, the parameter `current-Year` is also local to the `Age()` method. We'll talk more about parameters shortly.

Calling Methods

Let's take a look at examples of calling the `Age()` and `Distance()` methods defined in the previous section. First, the following statements create a `Car` object, store a reference to that object in `redPorsche`, and assign values to the object's fields:

```
Car redPorsche = new Car();
redPorsche.yearBuilt = 2000;
redPorsche.maximumSpeed = 150;
```

You call a method using an object reference and the name of the method, along with any values for the parameters. The following statement calls the Age() method using the redPorsche object reference and passes the value 2001 as the current year:

```
int age = redPorsche.Age(2001);
```

The Age() method calculates the age of the car by subtracting the value in the yearBuilt field for this Car object (2000) and by subtracting the currentYear parameter passed to it (2001)—therefore the value returned by the Age() method is 1.

Second, the following statement calls the Distance() method, which calculates and returns the distance traveled by the Car object; notice that the double value returned by this method is displayed directly in a call to the System.Console.WriteLine() method:

```
System.Console.WriteLine("redPorsche travels " +
    redPorsche.Distance(31, .25) + " miles.");
```

The first parameter passed to the Distance() method specifies the initial speed of the car in miles per hour (31), and the second parameter specifies the total time of the journey in hours (.25, or a quarter of an hour).

Listing 4.3 shows how the Age() and Distance() methods return values and accept parameters.

Listing 4.3: Methods That Return a Value and Accept Parameters

```
// declare the Car class
public class Car
{

    public int yearBuilt;
    public double maximumSpeed;

    // the Age() method calculates and returns the
    // age of the car in years
    public int Age(int currentYear)
    {
        int age = currentYear - yearBuilt;
        return age;
    }

    // the Distance() method calculates and returns the
    // distance traveled by the car, given its initial speed,
```

```
      // maximum speed, and time for the journey
      // (assuming constant acceleration of the car)
      public double Distance(double initialSpeed, double time)
      {
        return (initialSpeed + maximumSpeed) / 2 * time;
      }

    }


    class Example5_3
    {

      public static void Main()
      {

        // declare a Car object reference and
        // create a Car object
        System.Console.WriteLine("Creating a Car object and " +
          "assigning its memory location to redPorsche");
        Car redPorsche = new Car();

        // assign values to the fields
        redPorsche.yearBuilt = 2000;
        redPorsche.maximumSpeed = 150;

        // call the methods
        int age = redPorsche.Age(2001);
        System.Console.WriteLine(
          "redPorsche is " + age + " year old.");
        System.Console.WriteLine("redPorsche travels " +
          redPorsche.Distance(31, .25) + " miles.");

      }

    }
```

The output from this program is as follows:

```
Creating a Car object and
  assigning its memory location to redPorsche
redPorsche is 1 year old.
redPorsche travels 22.625 miles.
```

Hiding

If you declare a local variable in a method that has the same name as a field, then the local variable *hides* the field. The following class illustrates this point, with the maximumSpeed field being hidden in the Age() method by a variable of the same name:

```
public class Car
{

  ...
  public double maximumSpeed;

  public int Age(int currentYear)
  {
    int maximumSpeed = 100;  // hides the field
    System.Console.WriteLine("In Age(): maximumSpeed = " +
      maximumSpeed);
    ...
  }

  public double Distance(double initialSpeed, double time)
  {
    System.Console.WriteLine(
      "In Distance(): maximumSpeed = " +maximumSpeed);
    ...
  }

}
```

In this Car class, the Age() method declares its own local maximum-Speed variable, and sets it to 100. This maximumSpeed variable hides the maximumSpeed field of the class. Thus, when maximumSpeed is displayed in the Age() method, the value displayed is 100—the value assigned to the variable in the Age() method.

Now, in the Distance() method, the maximumSpeed field is not hidden, and when this field is displayed in the Distance() method, the value displayed is whatever the field was set to for the particular Car object for which the method was called.

Listing 4.4 illustrates hiding.

Listing 4.4: Hiding

```
// declare the Car class
public class Car
{
```

```
public int yearBuilt;
public double maximumSpeed;

public int Age(int currentYear)
{
  int maximumSpeed = 100;   // hides the field
  System.Console.WriteLine("In Age(): maximumSpeed = " +
    maximumSpeed);
  int age = currentYear - yearBuilt;
  return age;
}

public double Distance(double initialSpeed, double time)
{
  System.Console.WriteLine(
    "In Distance(): maximumSpeed = " + maximumSpeed);
  return (initialSpeed + maximumSpeed) / 2 * time;
}

}


class Example5_4
{

  public static void Main()
  {

    // create a Car object
    Car redPorsche = new Car();
    redPorsche.yearBuilt = 2000;
    redPorsche.maximumSpeed = 150;

    int age = redPorsche.Age(2001);
    System.Console.WriteLine(
      "redPorsche is " + age + " year old.");
    System.Console.WriteLine("redPorsche travels " +
      redPorsche.Distance(31, .25) + " miles.");

  }

}
```

The output from this program is as follows:

```
In Age(): maximumSpeed = 100
redPorsche is 1 year old.
In Distance(): maximumSpeed = 150
redPorsche travels 22.625 miles.
```

The *this* Object Reference

The this keyword is an object reference, and it references the *current* object in use. The this object reference is useful when you want to set the value for a field in a method but the field is hidden by a parameter. In the following class, the yearBuilt field is hidden in the SetYearBuilt() method:

```
public class Car
{

  public int yearBuilt;

  public void SetYearBuilt(int yearBuilt)
  {
    // the yearBuilt parameter hides the
    // the yearBuilt field
    this.yearBuilt = yearBuilt;
  }

}
```

The SetYearBuilt() method sets the yearBuilt field to a value supplied in the yearBuilt parameter. Because the yearBuilt parameter is a local variable in this method, it hides the yearBuilt field. To get around this problem, the method uses the this object reference to access the current object, and this.yearBuilt refers to the yearBuilt field of the current object. Thus, the method can successfully use a parameter and field of the same name.

You're probably asking why we didn't simply use different names for the parameter and the field. Well, we could have done that, but then the names become a little contorted—for example, we might use builtYear or yearOfManufacture for the parameter name, but those names aren't very elegant. Using the this object reference is a much neater solution, and you'll see its use again later in the "Using Constructors" section.

Listing 4.5 illustrates the this object reference.

Listing 4.5: Using the this Object Reference

```
// declare the Car class
public class Car
{

  public int yearBuilt;

  public void SetYearBuilt(int yearBuilt)
  {
    // the yearBuilt parameter hides the
    // the yearBuilt field
    this.yearBuilt = yearBuilt;
  }

}


class Example5_5
{

  public static void Main()
  {

    // create a Car object
    Car myCar = new Car();

    myCar.SetYearBuilt(2000);
    System.Console.WriteLine(
      "myCar.yearBuilt = " + myCar.yearBuilt);

  }

}
```

The output from this program is as follows:

```
myCar.yearBuilt = 2000
```

More on Parameters

You were introduced to method parameters earlier in the chapter. In this section, you'll learn about what happens when parameters are passed to a method.

Passing Parameters by Value

In the methods you've seen so far, the parameters act as local variables to the method. Because of this, when you pass a variable to a method from a calling statement, the method makes a *copy* of the variable. Then, any changes made to the parameter inside the method are made to that copy—and not the actual variable in the calling statement. This is known as passing a parameter by *value*.

NOTE

If you pass an object reference as a parameter to a method, no copy of the referenced object is made. You can modify the object directly in the method using the object reference parameter. The information in this section therefore applies only to value types—such as `int` parameters, for example.

Passing parameters by value is best understood by looking at an example, as shown in Listing 4.6.

Listing 4.6: Passing Parameters by Value

```
// declare the Swapper class
public class Swapper
{

    // the Swap() method swaps parameters passed by value
    public void Swap(int x, int y)
    {

        // display the initial values
        System.Console.WriteLine("In Swap(): initial x = " + x +
            ", y = " + y);

        // swap x and y
        int temp = x;
        x = y;
        y = temp;

        // display the final values
        System.Console.WriteLine("In Swap(): final  x = " + x +
            ", y = " + y);
    }

}
```

```
class Example5_6
{

  public static void Main()
  {

    // declare x and y (the variables whose values
    // are to be swapped)
    int x = 2;
    int y = 5;

    // display the initial values
    System.Console.WriteLine("In Main(): initial x = " + x +
      ", y = " + y);

    // create a Swapper object
    Swapper mySwapper = new Swapper();

    // swap the values in x and y
    mySwapper.Swap(x, y);

    // display the final values
    System.Console.WriteLine("In Main(): final   x = " + x +
      ", y = " + y);


  }


}
```

The output from this program is as follows:

```
In Main(): initial x = 2, y = 5
In Swap(): initial x = 2, y = 5
In Swap(): final   x = 5, y = 2
In Main(): final   x = 2, y = 5
```

As you can see, the x and y variables are initially set to 2 and 5 (respectively) in the Main() method, which also displays the initial x and y values:

```
In Main(): initial x = 2, y = 5
```

The x and y variables are then passed as parameters to the Swap() method. Swap() then makes local copies of these variables and displays the initial values of the copies:

```
In Swap(): initial x = 2, y = 5
```

Next, Swap() swaps the values, but because *copies* of the variables were made, the values swapped are the copies–not the actual variables originally passed. The final values of these copies are displayed by Swap():

```
In Swap(): final    x = 5, y = 2
```

Program control returns to the calling statement in Main(), where the final values for x and y are displayed:

```
In Main(): final    x = 2, y = 5
```

Notice that the variables still have their original values. This is as expected because the values in x and y were *copied* and then swapped; the actual x and y variables that were passed as parameters remain unaffected.

Passing Parameters by Reference

If you want to change the value for a variable passed as a parameter, you must pass a reference to that variable–that way, the method will change the actual variable, not a copy of it. This is known as passing a parameter by *reference*.

WARNING

Only modify referenced parameters in your methods when you absolutely must. This practice is generally frowned upon because it can easily cause logical errors in your programs.

To pass a parameter by reference, you use the ref keyword–this is placed in front of the parameter type in the method definition. The following example shows the use of the ref keyword to indicate that the x and y parameters are passed by reference:

```
public class Swapper
{

    public void Swap(ref int x, ref int y)
    {
        ...
    }
}
```

You also need to use the ref keyword in the calling statement. For example,

```
int x = 2;
int y = 5;
mySwapper.Swap(ref x, ref y);
```

This time, when the Swap() method is called, references to the x and y variables are passed. When the x and y parameters are changed by the method, then the underlying variables to which they refer are changed—not copies of them.

NOTE

When passing parameters by value or by reference, the variables that are passed as parameters must be assigned a value before the method is called. This is another example of definite assignment, described in Chapter 2.

Listing 4.7 illustrates passing parameters by reference.

Listing 4.7: Passing Parameters by Reference

```
// declare the Swapper class
public class Swapper
{

    // the Swap() method swaps parameters passed by reference
    public void Swap(ref int x, ref int y)
    {

        // display the initial values
        System.Console.WriteLine("In Swap(): initial x = " + x +
            ", y = " + y);

        // swap x and y
        int temp = x;
        x = y;
        y = temp;

        // display the final values
        System.Console.WriteLine("In Swap(): final   x = " + x +
            ", y = " + y);
    }

}


class Example5_7
{
```

```
public static void Main()
{

    // declare x and y (the variables whose values
    // are to be swapped)
    int x = 2;
    int y = 5;

    // display the initial values
    System.Console.WriteLine("In Main(): initial x = " + x +
        ", y = " + y);

    // create a Swapper object
    Swapper mySwapper = new Swapper();

    // swap the values, passing a reference to the Swap()
        method
    mySwapper.Swap(ref x, ref y);

    // display the final values
    System.Console.WriteLine("In Main(): final   x = " + x +
        ", y = " + y);


}


}
```

The output from this program is as follows:

```
In Main(): initial x = 2, y = 5
In Swap(): initial x = 2, y = 5
In Swap(): final   x = 5, y = 2
In Main(): final   x = 5, y = 2
```

Notice that x and y are swapped.

Out Parameters

Methods can only return one value using a return statement. Sometimes you might need to return more than one value, and out parameters are useful for this purpose. An *out parameter* acts like a reference to a variable, except that you don't assign a value to the variable before passing it to the method—an out parameter is assigned a value inside the method. You can use more than one out parameter in a method.

WARNING

Typically, your methods should return only one value. This works for 90 percent or more of your programming needs, and it provides a good level of abstraction in your programs. Out parameters are useful, but they are an exception, rather than a rule.

Listing 4.8 illustrates passing parameters by reference, and it declares a class that defines a method named SinAndCos(); this method accepts a double parameter that contains an angle (specified in radians) and uses out parameters to return the sine and cosine values for that angle.

Listing 4.8: Using Out Parameters

```
// declare the MyMath class
public class MyMath
{

  // the SinAndCos() method returns the sin
  // and cos values fora given angle (in radians)
  public void SinAndCos(double angle,
    out double sin, out double cos)
  {
    sin = System.Math.Sin(angle);
    cos = System.Math.Cos(angle);
  }

}


class Example5_8
{

  public static void Main()
  {

    // declare and set the angle in radians
    double angle = System.Math.PI / 2;

    // declare the variables that will
    // be used as out paramters
    double sin;
    double cos;
```

```
    // create a MyMath object
    MyMath myMath = new MyMath();

    // get the sin and cos values from
    // the SinAndCos() method
    myMath.SinAndCos(angle, out sin, out cos);

    // display sin and cos
    System.Console.WriteLine(
      "sin = " + sin + ", cos = " + cos);


  }


}
```

You'll notice that this program uses the System.Math class—this class contains many mathematical methods and constants that you can use in your programs. In this program, the System.Math.Sin() and System .Math.Cos() methods get the sine and cosine values for an angle, and the System.Math.PI constant represents the value of the mathematical constant pi.

The output from this program is as follows:

```
sin = 1, cos = 6.12303176911189E-17
```

Method Overloading

With *method overloading*, you can define methods in a class that have the same name but use different parameters. An overloaded method may have a different number of parameters or the parameters may have different types. For example,

```
int DoComputation(int value1, int value2);
int DoComputation(int value1);
int DoComputation(int value1, float value2);
```

You can assume the DoComputation() method performs some kind of calculation and returns an int value. This method is overloaded and has three different lists of parameters—the first has two int parameters, the second has one int parameter, and the third has one int and one float parameter. When the method is called with a given list of parameters, the method with the matching list of parameters will be run.

WARNING

If you attempt to compile a program with a method call that doesn't match any of the methods, then the compiler will generate an error and your program won't compile. Also, if your overloaded method has different return types, but the list of parameters for those methods are the same, then your program won't compile. In addition, you cannot have a method that has the same parameter list but different output types.

Let's consider an example. Earlier, you saw the Swap() method defined in the Swapper class—that method accepted two references to int parameters and swapped them. You might want to also swap float parameters using the same name of Swap() for the method.

Listing 4.9 illustrates a class that overloads the Swap() method to swap both int and float parameters.

Listing 4.9: Method Overloading

```
// declare the Swapper class
public class Swapper
{

  // this Swap() method swaps two int parameters
  public void Swap(ref int x, ref int y)
  {
    int temp = x;
    x = y;
    y = temp;
  }

  // this Swap() method swaps two float parameters
  public void Swap(ref float x, ref float y)
  {
    float temp = x;
    x = y;
    y = temp;
  }

}


class Example5_9
{
```

```csharp
public static void Main()
{

    // create a Swapper object
    Swapper mySwapper = new Swapper();

    // declare two int variables
    int intValue1 = 2;
    int intValue2 = 5;
    System.Console.WriteLine(
      "initial intValue1 = " + intValue1 +
      ", intValue2 = " + intValue2);

    // swap the two float two int variables
    // (uses the Swap() method that accepts int parameters)
    mySwapper.Swap(ref intValue1, ref intValue2);

    // display the final values
    System.Console.WriteLine(
      "final   intValue1 = " + intValue1 +
      ", intValue2 = " + intValue2);

    // declare two float variables
    float floatValue1 = 2f;
    float floatValue2 = 5f;
    System.Console.WriteLine(
      "initial floatValue1 = " + floatValue1 +
      ", floatValue2 = " + floatValue2);

    // swap the two float variables
    // (uses the Swap() method that accepts float parameters)
    mySwapper.Swap(ref floatValue1, ref floatValue2);

    // display the final values
    System.Console.WriteLine(
      "final   floatValue1 = " + floatValue1 +
      ", floatValue2 = " + floatValue2);
    mySwapper.Swap(ref floatValue1, ref floatValue2);

}

}
```

Based on the parameters to the Swap() method, the appropriate method is called. The output from this program is as follows:

```
initial intValue1 = 2, intValue2 = 5
final   intValue1 = 5, intValue2 = 2
initial floatValue1 = 2, floatValue2 = 5
final   floatValue1 = 5, floatValue2 = 2
```

DEFINING PROPERTIES

Properties allow you to set and get fields using methods. Properties are a valuable feature of C# because they enable you to hide fields from your class users by making the fields private, while still giving users an easy way to get at those fields. You can think of a property as a wrapper around a private field, through which the field is accessed.

TIP

Private fields and properties promote encapsulation. You should always try to use private fields and provide access to those fields using properties, rather than using public fields. For brevity, this book doesn't always follow this rule, but you should do so in your own programs.

A property can define two methods: get and set (brackets are omitted from these method definitions). The get method returns the value of the field, and the set method sets the value of the field. The following class declares a private field named make and a property named Make; notice the get method that returns the value for the make field, and the set method that assigns a value to the make field:

```
public class Car {

  // declare a private field
  private string make;

  // declare a property
  public string Make {
    get {
      return make;
    }
    set {
      make = value;
    }
  }

}
```

The `value` keyword in the `set` method is an implicit parameter supplied to this method, and it contains the value to be assigned to the field. Instead of accessing the field directly, you use the property; depending on the context, either the `get` or `set` method will be used to actually access the underlying field.

Let's look at an example. The following statement creates a `Car` object:

```
Car myCar = new Car();
```

To set the value for the make field, you assign a value to the Make property. The following statement assigns the value of `"Porsche"` to `myCar.Make`:

```
myCar.Make = "Porshe";
```

Here, the context is an assignment and therefore the `set` method assigns the value to the make field. The `value` implicit parameter is set to `"Porsche"`, and therefore the make field is set to `"Porsche"`.

The following statement displays the value of `myCar.Make`:

```
System.Console.WriteLine("myCar.Make = " + myCar.Make);
```

This time, because the context is retrieval, the `get` method of the Make property is called, which returns the value of the make field.

NOTE

You don't have to provide both a `get` and `set` method. If you just provide a `get` method, then you can only read from the property. If you just provide a `set` method, then you can only write to the property.

Listing 4.10 illustrates a property.

Listing 4.10: Using a Property

```
// declare the Car class
public class Car {

  // declare a private field
  private string make;

  // declare a property
  public string Make {
    get {
      return make;
    }
```

```
      set {
        make = value;
      }
    }

  }


  class Example6_4 {

    public static void Main() {

      // create a Car object
      System.Console.WriteLine("Creating a Car object");
      Car myCar = new Car();

      // set the Car Make
      System.Console.WriteLine("Setting the Car object's Make
          property to Porsche");
      myCar.Make = "Porsche";

      System.Console.WriteLine("myCar.Make = " + myCar.Make);

    }

  }
```

The output from this program is as follows:

```
Creating a Car object
Setting the Car object's Make property to Porsche
myCar.Make = Porsche
```

WORKING WITH EVENTS

Events allow one object to notify another object that something has
occurred. For example, when you click a mouse button in a Windows
application, an event occurs, or is *raised*. Depending on which button you
clicked and in what position in the application you clicked it, the application takes a particular action when handling the event. The piece of code
that handles the event is known as an *event handler*. For example, if you

clicked the right mouse button in an application, the application might handle the event by displaying a pop-up context-sensitive menu; if you clicked the left mouse button on the application's minimize button, the application will handle the event by minimizing the application. Just moving the mouse raises many events that Windows handles by moving the pointer on the screen.

NOTE

Events are a special kind of *delegate*. A delegate acts like a pointer to a function. You can read more about delegates in Chapter 12 of *Mastering Visual C# .NET* by Jason Price and Mike Gunderloy (Sybex, 2002).

In the next section, you'll see an example of a simple nuclear reactor simulator. The reactor will raise an event when the reactor core temperature is set too high and the core melts down. The event handler will display a message stating that a reactor meltdown is in progress. You'll also see how to create an object to monitor the reactor for the meltdown event.

Declaring an Event

You declare an event using the event keyword, which uses the following simplified syntax:

```
[access-modifier] event delegate-class-name event-name;
```

The syntax elements are as follows:

access-modifier   The degree to which your event is available to the outside world. This can be public, protected, and so on.

delegate-class-name   The delegate class to use with your event. This delegate class represents the method that handles the event—this method is called when the event is raised.

event-name   The name you want to assign to your event. By convention, event names begin with the word *On*—OnClick, OnDisplay, OnMeltdown, for example.

The following example declares an event named OnMeltdown that uses the MeltdownHandler delegate class:

```
public event MeltdownHandler OnMeltdown;
```

This event will be raised when the temperature of the nuclear reactor core is set too high. You'll learn about the `MeltdownHandler` delegate class in the next section.

Declaring the Delegate Class Used with an Event

You must declare the delegate class used with your event. In the previous example, the `OnMeltdown` event uses a delegate class named `Meltdown-Handler`. This class represents the method that is called when the `OnMeltdown` event is raised. The `MeltdownHandler` delegate class is declared as follows:

```
public delegate void MeltdownHandler(
   object reactor,
   MeltdownEventArgs myMEA
);
```

All event handler delegates must return `void` and accept two parameters. The first parameter is an `object`, and it represents the object that raises the event—in the example, this is a reactor that may melt down. The second parameter is an object of a class that is derived from the `System.EventArgs` class. The `EventArgs` class is the base class for event data and represents the details of the event. In the example, the second parameter is of the class `MeltdownEventArgs`, which is declared as follows:

```
public class MeltdownEventArgs : EventArgs
{

   // declare a private field named message
   private string message;

   // define a constructor
   public MeltdownEventArgs(string message)
   {
      this.message = message;
   }

   // define a property to get the message
   public string Message
   {
      get
      {
```

```
            return message;
        }
    }

    }
```

The MeltdownEventArgs class declares a private field named message that stores a message describing that a reactor meltdown is in progress, as you'll see shortly. The message field is set using the constructor for the MeltdownEventArgs class and can be read using the Message property that defines a get method.

Declaring the *Reactor* Class

The next step is to declare a class to represent a reactor—we'll name this class Reactor. The Reactor class will contain the declaration for the OnMeltdown event and the MeltdownHandler delegate class shown in the preceding section. The Reactor class is declared as follows:

```
public class Reactor
{

  // declare a private field named temperature
  private int temperature;

  // declare a delegate class named MeltdownHandler
  public delegate void MeltdownHandler(
    object reactor,
    MeltdownEventArgs myMEA
  );

  // declare an event named OnMeltdown
  public event MeltdownHandler OnMeltdown;

  // define a property to set the temperature
  public int Temperature
  {
    set
    {
      temperature = value;

      // if the temperature is too high, the reactor melts down
      if (temperature > 1000)
      {
        MeltdownEventArgs myMEA =
          new MeltdownEventArgs("Reactor meltdown in progress!");
```

```
                OnMeltdown(this, myMEA);
            }
        }
    }

}
```

As you can see, the `Reactor` class declares a private field named `temperature`, which is set using the `set` method of the `Temperature` property. If the setting for `temperature` is too high (greater than 1,000 degrees Centigrade), then a reactor meltdown occurs. Let's take a closer look at the `if` statement that checks `temperature`:

```
if (temperature > 1000)
{
  MeltdownEventArgs myMEA =
    new MeltdownEventArgs("Reactor meltdown in progress!");
    OnMeltdown(this, myMEA);
}
```

The first line after the `if` creates a `MeltdownEventArgs` object named myMEA, passing the string `"Reactor meltdown in progress!"` to the constructor. This sets the `message` field of myMEA to that string. The second line raises the `OnMeltdown` event, passing the current `Reactor` object (using the `this` object reference), and myMEA as parameters to `OnMeltdown`.

Declaring the *ReactorMonitor* Class

The `OnMeltdown` event can be monitored by another object, and for this purpose, we'll declare a `ReactorMonitor` class that will be used to create an object to monitor a `Reactor` object. The `ReactorMonitor` class is declared as follows:

```
public class ReactorMonitor
{

  // define a constructor
  public ReactorMonitor(Reactor myReactor)
  {
    myReactor.OnMeltdown +=
      new Reactor.MeltdownHandler(DisplayMessage);
  }

  // define the DisplayMessage() method
  public void DisplayMessage(
    object myReactor, MeltdownEventArgs myMEA
```

```
)
{
    Console.WriteLine(myMEA.Message);
}

}
```

The constructor for ReactorMonitor accepts a Reactor parameter named myReactor and monitors that object for the OnMeltdown event. You do this using the following statement; notice the use of the shortcut addition operator (+=):

```
myReactor.OnMeltdown +=
    new Reactor.MeltdownHandler(DisplayMessage);
```

This statement indicates that when myReactor raises the OnMeltdown event, the DisplayMessage() method is called to handle the event. Earlier, you saw that MeltdownHandler is a delegate that may be set to a method that returns void and accepts two parameters: an object and a MeltdownEventArgs object. This is exactly the method signature for DisplayMessage().

DisplayMessage() simply displays the Message property for the Reactor object. Therefore, when the Reactor object raises the OnMeltdown event, the string "Reactor meltdown in progress!" is displayed. You'll see an example of this in the next section.

Creating and Using a *Reactor* and *ReactorMonitor* Object

We're now ready to create and use the Reactor and ReactorMonitor objects. The examples shown in this section could be placed in the Main() method of a program.

The following example creates a Reactor object and a ReactorMonitor object, passing the Reactor object to the ReactorMonitor constructor:

```
Reactor myReactor = new Reactor();
ReactorMonitor myReactorMonitor =
    new ReactorMonitor(myReactor);
```

Next, the Temperature property of myReactor is set to 100 degrees Centigrade—well within the safety limit of 1,000:

```
myReactor.Temperature = 100;
```

Finally, the Temperature property is set to 2,000 degrees Centigrade—this causes myReactor to meltdown, and therefore myReactor raises the OnMeltdown event:

```
myReactor.Temperature = 2000;
```

When myReactor raises the OnMeltdown event, myReactorMonitor notices the event and calls DisplayMessage(), which displays this:

```
Reactor meltdown in progress!
```

Listing 4.11 illustrates this example event.

Listing 4.11: An Event

```
using System;


// declare the MeltdownEventArgs class (implements EventArgs)
public class MeltdownEventArgs : EventArgs
{

  // declare a private field named message
  private string message;

  // define a constructor
  public MeltdownEventArgs(string message) {
    this.message = message;
  }

  // define a property to get the message
  public string Message
  {
    get
    {
      return message;
    }
  }

}


// declare the Reactor class
public class Reactor
{
```

```
// declare a private field named temperature
private int temperature;

// declare a delegate class named MeltdownHandler
public delegate void MeltdownHandler(
  object reactor,
  MeltdownEventArgs myMEA
);

// declare an event named OnMeltdown
public event MeltdownHandler OnMeltdown;

// define a property to set the temperature
public int Temperature
{
  set
  {
    temperature = value;

    // if the temperature is too high, the reactor melts down
    if (temperature > 1000)
    {
      MeltdownEventArgs myMEA =
        new MeltdownEventArgs("Reactor meltdown in progress!");
      OnMeltdown(this, myMEA);
    }
  }
}

}


// declare the ReactorMonitor class
public class ReactorMonitor
{

  // define a constructor
  public ReactorMonitor(Reactor myReactor)
  {
    myReactor.OnMeltdown +=
      new Reactor.MeltdownHandler(DisplayMessage);
  }
```

```csharp
    // define the DisplayMessage() method
    public void DisplayMessage(
      object myReactor, MeltdownEventArgs myMEA
    )
    {
      Console.WriteLine(myMEA.Message);
    }

}


class Example12_4
{

  public static void Main()
  {

    // create a Reactor object
    Reactor myReactor = new Reactor();

    // create a ReactorMonitor object
    ReactorMonitor myReactorMonitor =
      new ReactorMonitor(myReactor);

    // set myReactor.Temperature to 100 degrees Centigrade
    Console.WriteLine("Setting reactor temperature to
      100 degrees Centigrade");
    myReactor.Temperature = 100;

    // set myReactor.Temperature to 500 degrees Centigrade
    Console.WriteLine("Setting reactor temperature to
      500 degrees Centigrade");
    myReactor.Temperature = 500;

    // set myReactor.Temperature to 2000 degrees Centigrade
    // (this causes the reactor to meltdown)
    Console.WriteLine("Setting reactor temperature to
      2000 degrees Centigrade");
    myReactor.Temperature = 2000;


  }


}
```

The output from this program is as follows:

```
Setting reactor temperature to 100 degrees Centigrade
Setting reactor temperature to 500 degrees Centigrade
Setting reactor temperature to 2000 degrees Centigrade
Reactor meltdown in progress!
```

Using Access Modifiers

Access modifiers enable you to specify the degree to which a class member is available outside of the class. You can also use an access modifier to specify the degree to which the class itself is available—although as mentioned, you'll usually declare your classes as being public.

Table 4.2 shows the access modifiers in decreasing order of availability: public is the most accessible, and private is the least accessible. Some of the access modifiers mention *derived classes* and *assemblies*—derived classes are covered in Chapter 5, "Derived Classes," and assemblies are covered in Chapter 7, "Reflecting on Classes."

TABLE 4.2:   Access Modifiers

Access Modifier	Accessibility
public	Member accessible without restriction.
protected internal	Member only accessible within the class, a derived class, or class in the same program (or assembly).
internal	Member only accessible within the class or class in the same program (or assembly).
protected	Member only accessible within the class or derived classes.
private	Member only accessible within the class. This is the default.

So far, you've only seen examples of members that use the public access modifier. The following Car class illustrates the use of the various access modifiers for the class members:

```
public class Car
{

  // declare the fields
  public              string make;
  protected internal  string model;
  internal            string color;
```

```
protected          int horsepower = 150;
private            int yearBuilt;

// define the methods
public void SetYearBuilt(int yearBuilt)
{
  this.yearBuilt = yearBuilt;
}

public int GetYearBuilt()
{
  return yearBuilt;
}

public void Start()
{
  System.Console.WriteLine("Starting car ...");
  TurnStarterMotor();
  System.Console.WriteLine("Car started");
}

private void TurnStarterMotor()
{
  System.Console.WriteLine("Turning starter motor ...");
}

}
```

TIP

You should include the access modifier when declaring class members, even for your private members (the `private` access modifier is the default). This is just good programming practice, and by including the access modifiers, your classes will be easier to read.

Because the make, model, and color fields respectively use the access modifiers public, protected internal, and internal, they are available to other classes in the same program. However, the horsepower and yearBuilt fields respectively use the protected and private access modifiers and are therefore not available to other classes in the same program (unless there is a derived class, in which case the protected members would be accessible within that class—you'll learn about derived classes in Chapter 5). The horsepower field uses an initializer to set it to 150.

The value for the yearBuilt field is set using the public SetYearBuilt() method, and its value is retrieved using the public GetYearBuilt() method.

The public Start() method calls the private method TurnStarter-Motor(); this closely models a real car, which uses a starter motor to start the car's engine. Think of a real car: As a driver, you don't directly use your car's starter motor to start your car—you just use your ignition key. Going back to the Car class that models a car, when the Start() method is called, it calls the TurnStarterMotor() method for you. You can't call the TurnStarterMotor() method directly—just as in the real world, you don't directly use your car's starter motor to start your car.

TIP

This illustrates an important part of object-oriented programming: You should hide the internal details of how your class works from the outside world by using private members as much as possible. The act of hiding details in this way is called encapsulation.

Let's take a look at some examples of accessing the members of this Car class. The following statement creates a Car object:

```
Car myCar = new Car();
```

You can access the make, model, and color fields of this Car object without any restriction, and the following statements assign values to these fields using the myCar object reference:

```
myCar.make = "Toyota";
myCar.model = "MR2";
myCar.color = "black";
```

You cannot access the horsepower or yearBuilt fields directly because these fields use the protected and private access modifiers respectively and are therefore only available within the code contained in the Car class itself. The horsepower field is set to 150 by an initializer in the Car class, and the yearBuilt field may be set using the SetYearBuilt() method—the following statement uses this method to set the yearBuilt field to 1995:

```
myCar.SetYearBuilt(1995);
```

To get the value for the yearBuilt field, you use the GetYearBuilt() method, as shown in the following statement:

```
System.Console.WriteLine(
    "myCar.GetYearBuilt() = "
    + myCar.GetYearBuilt());
```

The following statement calls the Start() method, which then calls the private TurnStarterMotor() method:

```
myCar.Start();
```

Listing 4.12 illustrates the Car class and how the access modifiers affect accessibility to class members.

Listing 4.12: Using Access Modifiers

```
// declare the Car class
public class Car
{

  // declare the fields
  public              string make;
  protected internal  string model;
  internal            string color;
  protected           int horsepower = 150;
  private             int yearBuilt;

  // define the methods
  public void SetYearBuilt(int yearBuilt)
  {
    this.yearBuilt = yearBuilt;
  }

  public int GetYearBuilt()
  {
    return yearBuilt;
  }

  public void Start()
  {
    System.Console.WriteLine("Starting car ...");
    TurnStarterMotor();
    System.Console.WriteLine("Car started");
  }

  private void TurnStarterMotor()
  {
    System.Console.WriteLine("Turning starter motor ...");
  }
```

```
    }


    class Example5_10
    {

      public static void Main()
      {

        // create a Car object
        Car myCar = new Car();

        // assign values to the Car object fields
        myCar.make = "Toyota";
        myCar.model = "MR2";
        myCar.color = "black";

        // protected field not accessible
        // myCar.horsepower = 200;
        // private field not accessible
        // myCar.yearBuilt = 1995;
        // call the SetYearBuilt() method to
        // set the private yearBuilt field
        myCar.SetYearBuilt(1995);

        // display the values for the Car object fields
        System.Console.WriteLine("myCar.make = " + myCar.make);
        System.Console.WriteLine("myCar.model = " + myCar.model);
        System.Console.WriteLine("myCar.color = " + myCar.color);

        // call the GetYearBuilt() method to get
        // the private yearBuilt field
        System.Console.WriteLine(
        "myCar.GetYearBuilt() = " + myCar.GetYearBuilt());

        // call the Start() method
        myCar.Start();

        // private method not accessible
        // myCar.TurnStarterMotor();
      }


    }
```

The output from this program is as follows:

```
myCar.make = Toyota
myCar.model = MR2
myCar.color = black
myCar.GetYearBuilt() = 1995
Starting car ...
Turning starter motor ...
Car started
```

CREATING AND DESTROYING OBJECTS

You've already seen examples of creating objects in C#. A *constructor* is a method that has the same name as the class. As you will see in this section, you can define your own constructors so that you can do things such as initialize fields using parameters. You can also define overloaded constructors that accept different parameters, and you can even define constructors that allow you to copy the fields from one object to another.

One thing you haven't seen until this point is how C# manages objects and variables stored in the computer's memory. In Chapter 2, you saw that variables are declared using value types—int, float, and char, for example. Variables are stored in an area of memory known as the *stack*. You can think of the stack as a pile of dish plates—variables are *pushed* onto the stack to store them and *popped* off of the stack to remove them. The reference types—objects and strings—are stored in a different area of memory known as the *heap*.

The stack is program-specific memory, and each program has its own stack. The heap, however, is universally accessible memory. Because value types are generally small, storing them on the stack is good. With objects, however, it's better to store them on the heap and create an object reference to them on the stack.

Variables, objects, and strings are removed from memory—or *destroyed*—by a process known as *garbage collection*. The object that does the garbage collection is known as the *garbage collector*. The garbage collector periodically cleans up the data stored in memory that is no longer used. When a variable goes out of scope, it is scheduled for destruction by the garbage collector. An example of this is when a local variable is declared by a method: When the method is called, the local variable is pushed onto the stack, and when the method ends, the local variable goes out of scope and is scheduled for destruction—when the variable is destroyed it is popped off the stack. Similarly, when all references to an object are gone, then that object is scheduled for removal by the garbage collector.

Normally, you don't have to concern yourself with memory cleanup—you can just let the garbage collector take care of it. There are cases, however, when you might want to do some cleaning up of your own. For example, if you have an object that opens a file, then you might want to close that file gracefully before destroying your object. You can use *destructors* to do this, which you'll learn about shortly. Now, you'll learn about constructors.

Using Constructors

In the previous examples, you saw Car objects being created using statements similar to the following one:

```
Car myCar = new Car();
```

We mentioned earlier that the Car() method is a constructor, and it is used in conjunction with the new operator to create an object.

NOTE
A constructor has the same name as the class.

You can define a constructor in your class, or you can use the default constructor that is always available; the default constructor doesn't take any parameters. The default constructor creates a new object for you, but it doesn't do anything else.

If you want to do something in addition to just creating a new object, then you must define your own constructor. The most common reason for defining your own constructor is to initialize the fields of the new object—passing the values for those fields as parameters to your constructor. The following class defines a constructor:

```
public class Car
{

    // declare the fields
    private string make;
    private string model;
    private string color;
    private int yearBuilt;
```

```
// define the constructor
public Car(string make, string model,
   string color, int yearBuilt)
{
   System.Console.WriteLine("In Car() constructor");
   this.make = make;
   this.model = model;
   this.color = color;
   this.yearBuilt = yearBuilt;
}

   ...

}
```

Notice that the constructor accepts four parameters (one for each field) and sets the fields of the new object to the values provided using the parameters. You can see the usefulness of the `this` object reference in the constructor—as you saw earlier, `this` refers to the current object.

NOTE

You cannot use a constructor to return a value.

The following statement creates a `Car` object, passing parameter values to the constructor:

```
Car myCar = new Car("Toyota", "MR2", "black", 1995);
```

The constructor sets the `make`, `model`, `color`, and `yearBuilt` fields to `"Toyota"`, `"MR2"`, `"black"`, and 1995 respectively.

Listing 4.13 illustrates the use of the constructor shown in this section.

Listing 4.13: Defining a Constructor

```
// declare the Car class
public class Car
{

   // declare the fields
   private string make;
   private string model;
   private string color;
   private int yearBuilt;
```

```
// define the constructor
public Car(string make, string model,
  string color, int yearBuilt)
{
  System.Console.WriteLine("In Car() constructor");
  this.make = make;
  this.model = model;
  this.color = color;
  this.yearBuilt = yearBuilt;
}

// define a method to display the fields
public void Display()
{
  System.Console.WriteLine("Car details:");
  System.Console.WriteLine("make = " + make);
  System.Console.WriteLine("model = " + model);
  System.Console.WriteLine("color = " + color);
  System.Console.WriteLine("yearBuilt = " + yearBuilt);
}

}


class Example5_11
{

  public static void Main()
  {

    // create a Car object using the constructor
    // defined in the class
    Car myCar = new Car("Toyota", "MR2", "black", 1995);

    // display the values for the Car object fields
    myCar.Display();

  }

}
```

The output from this program is as follows:

```
In Car() constructor
Car details:
make = Toyota
model = MR2
color = black
yearBuilt = 1995
```

Overloaded Constructors

Earlier, you saw how multiple methods can be overloaded—overloaded methods all have the same name as each other but a different list of parameters. Because a constructor is a method, you can overload it.

Now, with the Car class shown in the previous listing, you *cannot* create Car objects using the following statements:

```
Car myCar2 = new Car();  // causes compilation error
```

```
// causes compilation error
Car myCar3 = new Car("Chevrolet");When you define a constructor
    that accepts parameters, you should also define a default
    constructor with no parameters.
```

The reason why these statements cause compilation errors is that there is no matching constructor in the Car class. Notice that there isn't even a default constructor. You must provide a constructor with a matching list of parameters using method overloading to get the two previous statements to compile. The following class shows the additional constructors required to handle the two previous statements:

```
public class Car
{

    ...

    // define the overloaded constructors
    public Car()
    {
      this.make = "Ford";
      this.model = "Mustang";
      this.color = "red";
      this.yearBuilt = 1970;
    }
```

```
public Car(string make)
{
  this.make = make;
  this.model = "Corvette";
  this.color = "silver";
  this.yearBuilt = 1969;
}

  ...

}
```

Notice that initializers assign values to the fields whose values are not supplied using a parameter—we didn't have to do this, we could have just left those fields as the default, but we wanted to explicitly set them just to make the example more complete.

With this class, the two statements shown earlier will now compile:

```
Car myCar2 = new Car();
Car myCar3 = new Car("Chevrolet");
```

So, myCar2.make is "Ford", and myCar3.make is "Chevrolet". The rest of the fields are set to the other values shown in the class.

Listing 4.14 illustrates overloaded constructors.

Listing 4.14: Overloaded Constructors

```
// declare the Car class
public class Car
{

  // declare the fields
  private string make;
  private string model;
  private string color;
  private int yearBuilt;

  // define the overloaded constructors
  public Car()
  {
    this.make = "Ford";
    this.model = "Mustang";
    this.color = "red";
    this.yearBuilt = 1970;
  }
```

```csharp
    public Car(string make)
    {
      this.make = make;
      this.model = "Corvette";
      this.color = "silver";
      this.yearBuilt = 1969;
    }

    public Car(string make, string model,
      string color, int yearBuilt)
    {
      this.make = make;
      this.model = model;
      this.color = color;
      this.yearBuilt = yearBuilt;
    }

    // define method to display the fields
    public void Display()
    {
      System.Console.WriteLine("make = " + make);
      System.Console.WriteLine("model = " + model);
      System.Console.WriteLine("color = " + color);
      System.Console.WriteLine("yearBuilt = " + yearBuilt);
    }

}


class Example5_12
{

  public static void Main()
  {

    // create three Car objects using the constructors
    // defined in the class
    Car myCar = new Car("Toyota", "MR2", "black", 1995);
    Car myCar2 = new Car();
    Car myCar3 = new Car("Chevrolet");

    // display the values for the Car object's fields
    System.Console.WriteLine("myCar details:");
```

```
    myCar.Display();
    System.Console.WriteLine("myCar2 details:");
    myCar2.Display();
    System.Console.WriteLine("myCar3 details:");
    myCar3.Display();


  }


}
```

The output from this program is as follows:

```
myCar details:
make = Toyota
model = MR2
color = black
yearBuilt = 1995
myCar2 details:
make = Ford
model = Mustang
color = red
yearBuilt = 1970
myCar3 details:
make = Chevrolet
model = Corvette
color = silver
yearBuilt = 1969
```

Copy Constructors

C# doesn't provide a default way for you to copy one object's fields to another. To do this, you must write your own copy constructor. The following class shows a copy constructor—the constructor accepts a Car object reference as a parameter and copies the fields from the referenced object to the newly created Car object:

```
public class Car
{

  ...

  // define the copy constructor
  public Car(Car car)
  {
    this.make = car.make;
    this.model = car.model;
```

```
      this.color = car.color;
      this.yearBuilt = car.yearBuilt;
   }

   ...

}
```

The following statement creates a Car object:

```
Car myCar = new Car("Toyota", "MR2", "black", 1995);
```

In the next statement, the myCar object reference is then passed to the copy constructor, which copies the field values of the previous Car object to the new object:

```
Car carCopy = new Car(myCar);
```

This Car object also has the same field values as the previous one: "Toyota", "MR2", "black", and 1995.

Listing 4.15 illustrates a copy constructor.

Listing 4.15: A Copy Constructor

```
// declare the Car class
public class Car
{

   // declare the fields
   private string make;
   private string model;
   private string color;
   private int yearBuilt;

   // define the copy constructor
   public Car(Car car)
   {
      this.make = car.make;
      this.model = car.model;
      this.color = car.color;
      this.yearBuilt = car.yearBuilt;
   }

   public Car(string make, string model,
      string color, int yearBuilt)
   {
```

```
      this.make = make;
      this.model = model;
      this.color = color;
      this.yearBuilt = yearBuilt;
   }

   // define method to display the fields
   public void Display()
   {
      System.Console.WriteLine("make = " + make);
      System.Console.WriteLine("model = " + model);
      System.Console.WriteLine("color = " + color);
      System.Console.WriteLine("yearBuilt = " + yearBuilt);
   }

}


class Example5_13
{

   public static void Main()
   {

      // create a Car object
      Car myCar = new Car("Toyota", "MR2", "black", 1995);

      // create a copy of this Car object
      Car carCopy = new Car(myCar);

      // display the values for the Car object's fields
      System.Console.WriteLine("myCar details:");
      myCar.Display();
      System.Console.WriteLine("carCopy details:");
      carCopy.Display();

   }

}
```

The output from this program is as follows:

```
myCar details:
make = Toyota
model = MR2
```

```
color = black
yearBuilt = 1995
carCopy details:
make = Toyota
model = MR2
color = black
yearBuilt = 1995
```

Using Destructors

You can use a *destructor* to clean up after your objects before they're removed from memory by the garbage collector. You might want to use a destructor to close a file.

Like a constructor, a destructor has the same name as the class, but it is preceded by a tilde (~). Destructors don't accept parameters and can't return a value. The following class shows a destructor:

```
public class Car
{

    ...


    // define the destructor
    ~Car()
    {
        // do any cleaning up here
        ...
    }

    ...


}
```

NOTE

Prior to an object being destroyed by the garbage collector, the destructor is called and any code contained within it is run.

Listing 4.16 illustrates a simple destructor for the Car class.

Listing 4.16: A Destructor

```
// declare the Car class
public class Car
{
```

```
    // define the destructor
    ~Car()
    {
      System.Console.WriteLine("In ~Car() destructor");
      // do any cleaning up here
    }

}


class Example5_14
{

  public static void Main()
  {

    // create a Car object
    Car myCar = new Car();

    System.Console.WriteLine("At the end of Main()");

  }

}
```

The output from this program is as follows:

```
At the end of Main()
In ~Car() destructor
```

Notice that the ~Car() destructor is run at the end of the program.

NOTE

The memory of C# (and all .NET Framework languages) is managed by the .NET Framework garbage collector. This means that you cannot directly control when the destructors of your objects are called, so putting resource-cleanup code in a destructor may not be a good idea. Please refer to the .NET Framework online help for more information on garbage collection and resource management.

INTRODUCING STRUCTS

Structs are similar to classes, but they offer a somewhat "lighter" alternative to classes. Structs are treated as value types and are therefore stored on the stack—which means that when an instance of a struct goes out of scope, it is immediately removed from memory. This is a fundamental difference of structs when compared to objects: Objects are stored on the heap and are only removed from memory when the garbage collector runs; structs look like classes, but they are implemented differently.

TIP

Structs are intended to be small. Consider using them when you have a few fields and methods.

Just like classes, structs can have fields, methods, and constructors, but structs have some limitations when compared to classes:

▶ Structs don't support inheritance (you'll learn about inheritance in Chapter 5).

▶ You cannot define the default constructor for a struct.

▶ You cannot define a destructor for a struct.

▶ You cannot use an initializer to set a field to a value.

You declare structs using the `struct` keyword, and their declarations are similar to classes; the following example declares a struct named `Rectangle`, which represents a rectangular shape:

```
public struct Rectangle
{

  // declare the fields
  public int Width;
  public int Height;

  // define a constructor
  public Rectangle(int Width, int Height)
  {
    this.Width = Width;
    this.Height = Height;
  }

  // define the Area() method
  public int Area() {
    return Width * Height;
  }

}
```

Notice that this struct declares two fields, named Width and Height, which are used to store the width and height of a given rectangle. A constructor is provided to set these fields to values provided as parameters—a constructor isn't actually required because a default constructor is always supplied. The Area() method returns the area of the rectangle (this is calculated by multiplying the Width field by the Height field).

To create an instance of a struct, you should use the new keyword followed by a constructor. The following example creates an instance of the Rectangle struct named myRectangle:

```
Rectangle myRectangle = new Rectangle(2, 3);
```

Notice that the previous example uses the constructor defined in the Rectangle struct. C# also supplies a default constructor for a struct that you cannot redefine. The following example uses this default constructor to create another Rectangle instance and assigns values to its Width and Height fields:

```
Rectangle myRectangle2 = new Rectangle();
myRectangle2.Width = 3;
myRectangle2.Height = 4;
```

When you use the new keyword to create an instance of a struct using the default constructor, the fields will be assigned to default values for the field type—int fields will be set to 0, for example. So, in the previous example, if the last statement that assigned the value of 4 to Height was left out, then Height would have a default value of 0.

Because structs are value types, you don't even need to use new to create an instance—although we recommend you always do use new. The following example shows an example that doesn't use new:

```
Rectangle myRectangle3;
myRectangle3.Width = 1;
myRectangle3.Height = 2;
```

NOTE

If you don't use new when creating an instance of a struct, then its fields will be unassigned—they won't even be set to a default value. You therefore need to assign a value to a field before using it. We recommend you always use new.

You can also copy one struct to another. For example,

```
Rectangle myRectangle4 = myRectangle3;
```

This copies the field values from myRectangle3 to myRectangle4. Listing 4.17 illustrates a struct.

Listing 4.17: A Struct

```
// declare the Rectangle struct
public struct Rectangle
{

  // declare the fields
  public int Width;
  public int Height;

  // define a constructor
  public Rectangle(int Width, int Height)
  {
    this.Width = Width;
    this.Height = Height;
  }

  // define the Area() method
  public int Area()
  {
    return Width * Height;
  }

}


class Example5_15
{

  public static void Main()
  {

    // create an instance of a Rectangle
    System.Console.WriteLine(
      "Creating a Rectangle instance");
    Rectangle myRectangle = new Rectangle(2, 3);

    // display the values for the Rectangle instance
    System.Console.WriteLine(
      "myRectangle.Width = " + myRectangle.Width);
```

```
     System.Console.WriteLine(
       "myRectangle.Height = " + myRectangle.Height);

     // call the Area() method of the Rectangle instance
     System.Console.WriteLine(
       "myRectangle.Area() = " + myRectangle.Area());

   }


 }
```

The output from this program is as follows:

```
Creating a Rectangle instance
myRectangle.Width = 2
myRectangle.Height = 3
myRectangle.Area() = 6
```

SUMMARY

In this chapter, you learned that you can use classes and objects to model the real world. In fact, they can help simplify the task of writing programs to solve complex problems. C# builds on the seminal research work done by Xerox PARC in the 1970s and the other object-oriented languages developed since then.

A *class* is a template from which individual *objects* are created. A class contains fields and methods. A *field* is a variable or object, and a *method* is a group of declarations and other statements that perform a specific task. Fields and methods are collectively known as *members*.

A method may return a value to the statement that called it, and a method may also accept *parameters* from the calling statement. *Overloaded methods* have the same name but have different parameters. An *access modifier* allows you to specify the degree to which a class member is available outside of the class. The default access modifier is `private`.

An object is created from the class and has its own copy of the fields declared in the class. The `this` keyword accesses the current object.

A *constructor* method is called when an object is created. You can define your own constructors, through which you can do things such as initialize an object's fields using parameters. You can use a *destructor* to clean up after your objects before they're removed from memory by the *garbage collector*.

Structs are similar to classes, but they offer a "lighter" alternative to classes. Structs are treated as value types and are therefore stored on the *stack*, unlike objects that are stored on the *heap*. Structs are intended to be small, and you should consider using them when you have a few fields and methods.

WHAT'S NEXT

In the next chapter, you'll learn about two of the primary tenets of object-oriented programming: inheritance and polymorphism. You'll also learn the difference between a public class member and a private one, and the levels in between the two. Also covered is an introduction to System.Object, the great-great ancestor of all other objects in the .NET Framework.

Chapter 5

DERIVED CLASSES

In Chapter 4, "Object-Oriented Programming," you learned how to define classes and create objects from those classes. Here in this chapter, you'll learn how a class can be *derived* from another class. You'll also learn how you can overload an operator to perform your own code when a particular operator is used rather than using the default provided by C#.

Adapted from *Mastering Visual C# .NET* by Jason Price and Mike Gunderloy

ISBN 0-7821-2911-0

INTRODUCING INHERITANCE

The examples in the previous chapter featured a class named `Car`. Cars aren't the only type of motor vehicle—there are also motorcycles, trucks, and sports-utility vehicles on the road today. All of these forms of transportation are kinds of motor vehicles, and you can use the *"is a"* relationship to model this. For example, a car "is a" motor vehicle, a motorcycle "is a" motor vehicle, and so on. The "is a" relationship is different from the "has a" relationship described in the previous chapter.

TIP

By building a hierarchy of classes, you can potentially simplify the task of modeling complex systems by creating a tree of classes.

You model the "is a" relationship in C# using *inheritance*. With inheritance, one class is the parent of another class. The parent class is the *base class*, and the child class is the *derived class*. Derived classes inherit the members of their base class.

Going back to the vehicle example, the class that represents motor vehicles would be the base class, and the classes that represent cars and motorcycles would then be derived classes. Let's take a look at some code to clarify these ideas. The following class, named `MotorVehicle`, represents motor vehicles:

```
public class MotorVehicle
{

  // declare the fields
  public string make;
  public string model;

  // define a constructor
  public MotorVehicle(string make, string model)
  {
    this.make = make;
    this.model = model;
  }

  // define a method
  public void Start()
  {
    Console.WriteLine(model + " started");
  }

}
```

The MotorVehicle class declares two public fields: make and model. This class defines a constructor to set the make and model fields, and it also defines a method named Start(). Both the constructor and the Start() method are public.

To derive a class from a base class, you place a colon (:) after the derived class name, followed by the name of the base class. For example, the following Car class is derived from the previous MotorVehicle class:

```
public class Car : MotorVehicle
{

  // declare an additional field
  public bool convertible;

  // define a constructor
  public Car(string make, string model, bool convertible) :
  base(make, model)  // calls the base class constructor
  {
    this.convertible = convertible;
  }

}
```

Now, a derived class inherits the members of its base class; because the Car class is derived from the MotorVehicle class, the Car class inherits the members of the MotorVehicle class. This means that the Car class inherits the make and model fields, along with the Start() method of the MotorVehicle class.

The Car class also declares an additional field named convertible; this field indicates if a car's roof may be put down. When a Car object is created from this class, it will have three fields: make, model, and convertible.

NOTE
Derived classes do not inherit base class constructors. If you define a constructor in your base class, then you must also define a constructor in your derived class. If you want to call the base class constructor, your derived class constructor must explicitly call it.

The Car class defines a constructor that accepts three parameters: make, model, and convertible. The make and model fields are passed to the constructor of the MotorVehicle class using the base keyword. The base keyword refers to the base class, and whenever C# sees this keyword, it will search the base class for the specified member. In the constructor defined in the Car class, base(make, model) refers to the constructor in the MotorVehicle class. You'll notice that the base(make, model) call goes after a colon (:).

The following statement creates a Car object:

```
Car myCar = new Car("Toyota", "MR2", true);
```

This example calls the Car constructor, which in turn calls the MotorVehicle constructor to set the make and model fields to "Toyota" and "MR2", respectively. The Car constructor then sets the convertible field of the new Car object to true.

Of course, you can derive more than one class from the same base class. The following code defines a class named Motorcycle that is also derived from the MotorVehicle class:

```
public class Motorcycle : MotorVehicle
{

  // declare an additional field
  public bool sidecar;

  // define a constructor
  public Motorcycle(string make, string model,
    bool sidecar) :
  base(make, model)  // calls the base class constructor
  {
    this.sidecar = sidecar;
  }

  // define an additional method
  public void PullWheelie()
  {
    Console.WriteLine(model + " pulling a wheelie!");
  }

}
```

The Motorcycle class declares an additional field named sidecar, which represents whether the motorcycle has an attached sidecar for passengers. Motorcycle objects will therefore get three fields: make, model, and sidecar.

The Motorcycle class also defines an additional method named PullWheelie(). For those of you who are unfamiliar with motorcycles, a motorcyclist "pulls a wheelie" when the front wheel of their motorcycle leaves the ground.

Listing 5.1 shows these classes and illustrates inheritance.

NOTE   You can download all the source files for the programs featured in this chapter from the Sybex website at http://www.sybex.com. Search for this chapter's source book by its ISBN number, 2911, or its title, *Mastering Visual C# .NET*, and look for the Download link on the right. Once you've downloaded the files, you can follow along with the examples without having to type in the program listings.

Listing 5.1: Inheritance

```csharp
using System;


// declare the MotorVehicle class (the base class)
public class MotorVehicle
{

  // declare the fields
  public string make;
  public string model;

  // define a constructor
  public MotorVehicle(string make, string model)
  {
    this.make = make;
    this.model = model;
  }

  // define a method
  public void Start()
  {
    Console.WriteLine(model + " started");
  }

}


// declare the Car class (derived from
// the MotorVehicle base class)
public class Car : MotorVehicle
{

  // declare an additional field
  public bool convertible;
```

```csharp
    // define a constructor
    public Car(string make, string model, bool convertible) :
    base(make, model)  // calls the base class constructor
    {
      this.convertible = convertible;
    }

  }


  // declare the Motorcycle class (derived
  // from the MotorVehicle base class)
  public class Motorcycle : MotorVehicle
  {

    // declare an additional field
    public bool sidecar;

    // define a constructor
    public Motorcycle(string make,
      string model, bool sidecar) :
    base(make, model)  // calls the base class constructor
    {
      this.sidecar = sidecar;
    }

    // define an additional method
    public void PullWheelie()
    {
      Console.WriteLine(model + " pulling a wheelie!");
    }

  }


  class Example7_1
  {

    public static void Main()
    {

      // declare a Car object, display the
      // object's fields, and call the
      // Start() method
      Car myCar = new Car("Toyota", "MR2", true);
```

```
    Console.WriteLine("myCar.make = " + myCar.make);
    Console.WriteLine("myCar.model = " + myCar.model);
    Console.WriteLine(
        "myCar.convertible = " + myCar.convertible);
    myCar.Start();

    // declare a Motorcycle object,
    // display the object's fields, and call the Start() method
    Motorcycle myMotorcycle =
        new Motorcycle("Harley-Davidson", "V-Rod", false);
    Console.WriteLine(
        "myMotorcycle.make = " + myMotorcycle.make);
    Console.WriteLine(
        "myMotorcycle.model = " + myMotorcycle.model);
    Console.WriteLine(
        "myMotorcycle.sidecar = " + myMotorcycle.sidecar);
    myMotorcycle.Start();
    myMotorcycle.PullWheelie();

  }


}
```

The output from this program is as follows:

```
myCar.make = Toyota
myCar.model = MR2
myCar.convertible = True
MR2 started
myMotorcycle.make = Harley-Davidson
myMotorcycle.model = V-Rod
myMotorcycle.sidecar = False
V-Rod started
V-Rod pulling a wheelie!
```

LEARNING ABOUT POLYMORPHISM

Polymorphism comes from the Greek words *poly*, meaning many, and *morph*, meaning form. Therefore, *polymorphism* means many forms. In an object-oriented programming language, polymorphism refers to the fact that a method in a derived class may contain a different set of statements from the method in the base class; the method in the derived class is said to *override* the method in the base class.

To best understand polymorphism, let's return to the vehicle example. Now, to accelerate a car you must push the gas pedal, but to accelerate a motorcycle you must twist the throttle. The actual mechanism involved in acceleration isn't of much interest to you; you simply want the vehicle to move faster.

Polymorphism allows you to take account of the different ways that a car and a motorcycle accelerate. The MotorVehicle class should have a method—let's call it Accelerate()—which should contain the actions common to all accelerating motor vehicles. This Accelerate() method should be overridden in the derived Car and Motorcycle classes to account for the differences between accelerating cars and motorcycles.

To allow a method to be overridden, you use the virtual keyword in the method definition contained in the base class. For example, the following MotorVehicle class uses the virtual keyword in the Accelerate() method definition:

```
public class MotorVehicle
{

  ...

  // define the Accelerate() method (may be overridden in a
  // derived class)
  public virtual void Accelerate()
  {
    Console.WriteLine(model + " accelerating");
  }

}
```

The virtual keyword indicates that the Accelerate() method may be overridden in a derived class. This Accelerate() method displays a single line of text, indicating that a particular MotorVehicle object is accelerating.

Next, to override a base method in a derived class, you use the override keyword in the method definition contained in the derived class. The following Car class overrides the previous Accelerate() method defined in the MotorVehicle class:

```
public class Car : MotorVehicle
{

  ...

  // override the base class Accelerate() method
  public override void Accelerate()
```

```
    {
      Console.WriteLine("Pushing gas pedal of " + model);
      // calls the base class Accelerate() method
      base.Accelerate();      }

  }
```

This time, the `Accelerate()` method displays a line of text indicating that a particular `Car` object's gas pedal is being pushed and then calls the `base.Accelerate()` method—which calls the `Accelerate()` method in the `MotorVehicle` class.

NOTE

When you override a method, the method in the derived class must contain the same parameter list as the method in the base class.

Now, in the case of a motorcycle, the throttle is twisted to accelerate it. This is modeled in the following `Motorcycle` class, which also overrides the `Accelerate()` method previously defined in the `MotorVehicle` class:

```
public class Motorcycle : MotorVehicle
{

  ...

  // override the base class Accelerate() method
  public override void Accelerate()
  {
    Console.WriteLine("Twisting throttle of " + model);
    // calls the Accelerate() method in the base class
    base.Accelerate();
  }

}
```

Listing 5.2 shows these classes and illustrates polymorphism.

Listing 5.2: Polymorphism

```
using System;


// declare the MotorVehicle class
public class MotorVehicle
{
```

```csharp
    // declare the fields
    public string make;
    public string model;

    // define a constructor
    public MotorVehicle(string make, string model)
    {
      this.make = make;
      this.model = model;
    }

    // define the Accelerate() method
    // (may be overridden in a derived class)
    public virtual void Accelerate()
    {
      Console.WriteLine(model + " accelerating");
    }

}


// declare the Car class (derived from MotorVehicle)
public class Car : MotorVehicle
{

  // define a constructor
  public Car(string make, string model) :
  base(make, model)
  {
    // do nothing
  }

  // override the base class Accelerate() method
  public override void Accelerate()
  {
    Console.WriteLine("Pushing gas pedal of " + model);
    // calls the Accelerate() method in the base class
    base.Accelerate();  }

}


// declare the Motorcycle class
// (derived from MotorVehicle)
```

```
public class Motorcycle : MotorVehicle
{

  // define a constructor
  public Motorcycle(string make, string model) :
  base(make, model)
  {
    // do nothing
  }

  // override the base class Accelerate() method
  public override void Accelerate()
  {
    Console.WriteLine("Twisting throttle of " + model);
    // calls the Accelerate() method in the base class
    base.Accelerate();     }

}


class Example7_2
{

  public static void Main()
  {

    // create a Car object and call
    // the object's Accelerate() method
    Car myCar = new Car("Toyota", "MR2");
    myCar.Accelerate();

    // create a Motorcycle object and
    // call the object's Accelerate() method
    Motorcycle myMotorcycle =
      new Motorcycle("Harley-Davidson", "V-Rod");
    myMotorcycle.Accelerate();

  }

}
```

Notice that the Car and Motorcycle classes don't add any fields to the base class, and therefore the Car and Motorcycle constructors just call the base class constructor.

The output from this program is as follows:

```
Pushing gas pedal of MR2
MR2 accelerating
Twisting throttle of V-Rod
V-Rod accelerating
```

SPECIFYING MEMBER ACCESSIBILITY

In the previous chapter, you saw how the various access modifiers—such as public and private—specify the degree to which a class member is available outside of the class (in Chapter 4, Table 4.2 lists the access modifiers). In this section, you'll see how the access modifiers affect member accessibility in derived classes.

The following MotorVehicle class uses the public, private, and protected access modifiers:

```
public class MotorVehicle
{

  // declare the fields
  private   string make;
  protected string model;

  // define a constructor
  public MotorVehicle(string make, string model)
  {
    this.make = make;
    this.model = model;
  }

  // define the Start() method (may be overridden in a
  // derived class)
  public virtual void Start()
  {
    TurnStarterMotor();
    System.Console.WriteLine("Vehicle started");
  }

  // define the TurnStarterMotor() method
  private void TurnStarterMotor()
  {
    System.Console.WriteLine("Turning starter motor...");
  }

}
```

The make field is private and is therefore only accessible within the MotorVehicle class. The model field is protected, meaning it is accessible within the MotorVehicle class and any derived classes. The constructor and the Start() method are public and are therefore accessible without restriction. The Start() method may be overridden in a derived class; this method calls the TurnStarterMotor() method, which is private and therefore only accessible within the MotorVehicle class.

Next, the following Car class is derived from this MotorVehicle class:

```csharp
public class Car : MotorVehicle
{

  // define a constructor
  public Car(string make, string model) :
  base(make, model)
  {
    // do nothing
  }

  // override the base class Start() method
  public override void Start()
  {
    // model accessible
    Console.WriteLine("Starting " + model);
    // calls the Start() method in the base class
    base.Start();
    // make is not accessible
    // Console.WriteLine("make = " + make);  }

}
```

The Car constructor calls the base class constructor. The Start() method overrides the base class Start() method and displays a string containing the model field; because the model field is protected, this field is accessible within the Car class. The make field is not accessible because it is private to the MotorVehicle class, and therefore the statement that attempts to access the make field is commented out so that the code will compile.

Listing 5.3 uses these classes and illustrates member accessibility.

Listing 5.3: Member Accessibility

```csharp
using System;


// declare the MotorVehicle class
```

```csharp
public class MotorVehicle
{

  // declare the fields
  private   string make;
  protected string model;

  // define a constructor
  public MotorVehicle(string make, string model)
  {
    this.make = make;
    this.model = model;
  }

  // define the Start() method (may be overridden in a
  // derived class)
  public virtual void Start()
  {
    TurnStarterMotor();
    System.Console.WriteLine("Vehicle started");
  }

  // define the TurnStarterMotor() method
  private void TurnStarterMotor()
  {
    System.Console.WriteLine("Turning starter motor...");
  }

}


// declare the Car class (derived from MotorVehicle)
public class Car : MotorVehicle
{

  // define a constructor
  public Car(string make, string model) :
  base(make, model)
  {
    // do nothing
  }

  // override the base class Start() method
  public override void Start()
```

```
    {
        // model accessible
        Console.WriteLine("Starting " + model);
        // calls the Start() method in the base class
        base.Start();
        // make is not accessible
        // Console.WriteLine("make = " + make);
    }

}


class Example7_3
{

    public static void Main()
    {

        // create a Car object and call
        // the object's Accelerate() method
        Car myCar = new Car("Toyota", "MR2");
        myCar.Start();

        // make and model are not accessible,
        // so the following two lines are commented out
        // Console.WriteLine("myCar.make = " + myCar.make);
        // Console.WriteLine("myCar.model = " + myCar.model);

    }

}
```

Notice that neither the make nor the model field is accessible to the Example7_3 class, and therefore the statements that attempt to access these fields are commented out so that the code will compile. The make field is not accessible because this field is private to the MotorVehicle class and the field is therefore only available within that class. The model field is not accessible because this field is protected and is therefore only available within the MotorVehicle and Car classes.

The output from this program is as follows:

```
Starting MR2
Turning starter motor...
Vehicle started
```

HIDING MEMBERS

Members of a derived class may *hide* members of a base class using the new keyword, which defines a new member in the derived class, separate from the member in the base class. Because the member in the derived class has the same name as the member in the base class, the member in the base class is hidden by the derived class. This might seem like a useless feature, but you'll see how using the new keyword to hide a method can be useful (see the "Versioning" section).

NOTE

By using the new keyword, you're telling the compiler that you've intentionally used the same name for the method.

Let's take a look at some examples that make member hiding clearer. The following MotorVehicle class declares two public fields named make and model, along with a constructor that sets these fields and a DisplayModel() method to display the value of the model field:

```
public class MotorVehicle
{

  // declare the fields
  public string make;
  public string model;

  // define a constructor
  public MotorVehicle(string make, string model)
  {
    Console.WriteLine("In MotorVehicle constructor");
    this.make = make;
    this.model = model;
    Console.WriteLine("this.make = " + this.make);
    Console.WriteLine("this.model = " + this.model);
  }

  // define the DisplayModel() method
  public void DisplayModel()
  {
    Console.WriteLine(
      "In MotorVehicle DisplayModel() method");
    Console.WriteLine("model = " + model);
  }

}
```

Next, the following Car class hides the model field and the Display-Model() method, which was previously defined in the MotorVehicle class, by defining new members of the same name (notice that the constructor in this class calls the base constructor with a dummy value of "Test" for the model field—you'll see why this is important shortly)

```
public class Car : MotorVehicle
{

  // hide the base class model field
  public new string model;

  // define a constructor
  public Car(string make, string model) :
  base(make, "Test")
  {
    Console.WriteLine("In Car constructor");
    this.model = model;
    Console.WriteLine("this.model = " + this.model);
  }

  // hide the base class DisplayModel() method
  public new void DisplayModel()
  {
    Console.WriteLine("In Car DisplayModel() method");
    Console.WriteLine("model = " + model);
    // calls the DisplayModel() method in the base class
    base.DisplayModel();      }

}
```

Because the new keyword defines new model and DisplayModel() members in this Car class, these members hide the member of the same name previously defined in the base class. Let's consider what happens when a Car object is created, as shown in the following statement:

```
Car myCar = new Car("Toyota", "MR2");
```

The Car constructor is called with the make and model parameters being set to "Toyota" and "MR2", respectively. The Car constructor then calls the MotorVehicle base class constructor with this setting for the make parameter ("Toyota"), but with the model parameter set to "Test". So, in the MotorVehicle constructor, the make field is set to "Toyota" and the model field is set to "Test"—these settings are confirmed in the MotorVehicle constructor by displaying the values of the make and model fields for the current object. After the MotorVehicle constructor has displayed the field values, program control returns to the Car constructor. In this constructor, the model field (which hides the base model field) is set to "MR2"—this is the original value set in the statement that created the Car object.

Next, the following statement calls the Car object's DisplayModel() method:

```
myCar.DisplayModel();
```

The DisplayModel() method in the Car class displays a string containing the model field value—this is set to "MR2" for the current Car object. The DisplayModel() method in the Car class then calls the base DisplayModel() method that displays the hidden model field, whose value is "Test".

Listing 5.4 shows these classes and illustrates member hiding.

Listing 5.4: Member Hiding

```
using System;


// declare the MotorVehicle class
public class MotorVehicle
{

  // declare the fields
  public string make;
  public string model;

  // define a constructor
  public MotorVehicle(string make, string model)
  {
    Console.WriteLine("In MotorVehicle constructor");
    this.make = make;
    this.model = model;
    Console.WriteLine("this.make = " + this.make);
    Console.WriteLine("this.model = " + this.model);
  }

  // define the DisplayModel() method
  public void DisplayModel()
  {
```

```
      Console.WriteLine(
        "In MotorVehicle DisplayModel() method");
      Console.WriteLine("model = " + model);
    }

}


// declare the Car class (derived from MotorVehicle)
public class Car : MotorVehicle
{

  // hide the base class model field
  public new string model;

  // define a constructor
  public Car(string make, string model) :
  base(make, "Test")
  {
    Console.WriteLine("In Car constructor");
    this.model = model;
    Console.WriteLine("this.model = " + this.model);
  }

  // hide the base class DisplayModel() method
  public new void DisplayModel()
  {
    Console.WriteLine("In Car DisplayModel() method");
    Console.WriteLine("model = " + model);
    // calls DisplayModel() in the base class
    base.DisplayModel();    }

}


class Example7_4
{

  public static void Main()
  {

    // create a Car object
    Console.WriteLine("Creating a Car object");
```

```
Car myCar = new Car("Toyota", "MR2");

Console.WriteLine("Back in Main() method");
Console.WriteLine("myCar.make = " + myCar.make);
Console.WriteLine("myCar.model = " + myCar.model);

// call the Car object's DisplayModel() method
Console.WriteLine("Calling myCar.DisplayModel()");
myCar.DisplayModel();

    }

}
```

The output from this program is as follows:

```
Creating a Car object
In MotorVehicle constructor
this.make = Toyota
this.model = Test
In Car constructor
this.model = MR2
Back in Main() method
myCar.make = Toyota
myCar.model = MR2
Calling myCar.DisplayModel()
In Car DisplayModel() method
model = MR2
In MotorVehicle DisplayModel() method
model = Test
```

VERSIONING

At first glance, you may think that method hiding doesn't appear particularly useful. There is a situation where you might need to use it, however. Let's say you want to use a class named MotorVehicle that was written by another programmer, and you want to use this class to derive your own class. Further, let's also assume you want to define an Accelerate() method like the following in your derived class:

```
public class Car : MotorVehicle
{

    ...
```

```
    // define the Accelerate() method
    public void Accelerate()
    {
      Console.WriteLine("In Car Accelerate() method");
      Console.WriteLine(model + " accelerating");
    }


}
```

Next, let's suppose that the other programmer later modifies the MotorVehicle class and decides to add their own virtual Accelerate() method:

```
public class MotorVehicle
{

  ...

    // define the Accelerate() method
    public virtual void Accelerate()
    {
      Console.WriteLine(
        "In MotorVehicle Accelerate() method");
      Console.WriteLine(model + " accelerating");
    }


}
```

The addition of this Accelerate() method by the other programmer causes a problem: The Accelerate() method in your Car class hides the inherited Accelerate() method now defined in their MotorVehicle class. Later, when you come to compile your Car class, it isn't clear to the compiler whether you actually intended your method to hide the inherited method. Because of this, the compiler reports the following warning when you try to compile your Car class:

```
warning CS0114: 'Car.Accelerate()' hides inherited member
'MotorVehicle.Accelerate()'. To make the current
member override that implementation, add the override
keyword. Otherwise add the new keyword.
```

By adding the new keyword to your Accelerate() method definition, you make it clear to the compiler that you intend your method to hide the inherited method (see Listing 5.5).

NOTE

The important difference between new and overrides is the ability to call the parent method. When you use overrides, you are stuck with the new implementation, with no way to call the base class method. There are exceptions, of course, but generally this is true.

Listing 5.5: Versioning

```csharp
using System;


// declare the MotorVehicle class
public class MotorVehicle
{

  // declare the fields
  public string make;
  public string model;

  // define a constructor
  public MotorVehicle(string make, string model)
  {
    this.make = make;
    this.model = model;
  }

  // define the Accelerate() method
  public virtual void Accelerate()
  {
    Console.WriteLine(
      "In MotorVehicle Accelerate() method");
    Console.WriteLine(model + " accelerating");
  }

}


// declare the Car class (derived from MotorVehicle)
public class Car : MotorVehicle
{
```

```
    // define a constructor
    public Car(string make, string model) :
    base(make, model)
    {
       // do nothing
    }

    // define the Accelerate() method (uses the new keyword to
    // tell the compiler a new method is to be defined)
    public new void Accelerate()
    {
       Console.WriteLine("In Car Accelerate() method");
       Console.WriteLine(model + " accelerating");
    }

}


class Example7_5
{

  public static void Main()
  {

    // create a Car object
    Console.WriteLine("Creating a Car object");
    Car myCar = new Car("Toyota", "MR2");

    // call the Car object's Accelerate() method
    Console.WriteLine("Calling myCar.Accelerate()");
    myCar.Accelerate();

  }

}
```

The output from this program is as follows:

```
Creating a Car object
Calling myCar.DisplayModel()
In Car Accelerate() method
MR2 accelerating
```

USING THE *SYSTEM.OBJECT* CLASS

The System.Object class acts as the base class for all classes; in other words, all classes are ultimately derived from the System.Object class. This derivation of classes from the System.Object class is implicit—C# does it behind the scenes. Because this derivation is implicit, you don't explicitly indicate that your classes are derived from the System.Object class.

The System.Object class provides a number of useful methods, shown in Table 5.1.

TABLE 5.1:   System.Object Class Methods

METHOD	DESCRIPTION
public virtual string ToString()	Returns a string that is, by default, equal to the name of the object's class.
public virtual int GetHashCode()	Returns a hash value for a particular type; suitable for use in hashing algorithms and data structures such as hash tables.
public virtual bool Equals(*object*)	Returns true if two objects are equal; this method is an instance method and is overloaded with the Equals() class method described in the following line.
public static bool Equals (*object, object*)	Returns true if two objects are equal. This method is a class method and is overloaded with the Equals() instance method described in the previous line.
public static bool ReferenceEquals(*object, object*)	Returns true if two object references are equal—in other words, they reference the same object.
public Type GetType()	Returns the class (or type) of the object (or variable).
protected virtual void Finalize()	Allows an object to perform any cleaning up before the garbage collector removes the object from memory. The Finalize() method is basically the same as a destructor (described in Chapter 4).
protected object MemberwiseClone()	Creates a copy of the object.

Because all classes are derived from the System.Object class, any object may use these methods. Listing 5.6 declares a Car class and creates two Car objects; these objects then use some of the System.Object methods.

Listing 5.6: Object Class Methods

```
using System;


// declare the Car class
public class Car
{

  // declare the fields
  public string make;
  public string model;

  // define a constructor
  public Car(string make, string model)
  {
    this.make = make;
    this.model = model;
  }

  // define the Display() method
  public void Display()
  {
    Console.WriteLine("make = " + make);
    Console.WriteLine("model = " + model);
  }

  // define the Copy() method
  public static Car Copy(Car car)
  {
    // perform memberwise clone
    return (Car) car.MemberwiseClone();
  }

}


class Example7_6
{

  public static void Main()
  {
```

```
// create Car objects
Console.WriteLine("Creating Car objects");
Car myCar = new Car("Toyota", "MR2");
Car myOtherCar = new Car("Porsche", "Boxter");
Console.WriteLine("myCar details:");
myCar.Display();
Console.WriteLine("myOtherCar details:");
myOtherCar.Display();

// call some of the methods inherited from the
   System.Object class
Console.WriteLine(
  "myCar.ToString() = " + myCar.ToString());
Console.WriteLine(
  "myCar.GetType() = " + myCar.GetType());
Console.WriteLine(
  "myCar.GetHashCode() = " + myCar.GetHashCode());
Console.WriteLine("Car.Equals(myCar, myOtherCar) = " +
  Car.Equals(myCar, myOtherCar));
Console.WriteLine(
  "Car.ReferenceEquals(myCar, myOtherCar) = " +
  Car.ReferenceEquals(myCar, myOtherCar));

// set the myCar object reference equal to myOtherCar
Console.WriteLine("Setting myCar equal to myOtherCar");
myCar = myOtherCar;

// check for equality
Console.WriteLine("Car.Equals(myCar, myOtherCar) = " +
  Car.Equals(myCar, myOtherCar));
Console.WriteLine(
  "Car.ReferenceEquals(myCar, myOtherCar) = " +
  Car.ReferenceEquals(myCar, myOtherCar));

// perform a memberwise clone of myCar
// using the Car.Copy() method
Console.WriteLine(
  "Performing a memberwise clone of myCar to myOldCar");
Car myOldCar = Car.Copy(myCar);
Console.WriteLine("myOldCar details:");
myOldCar.Display();
```

}

}

Notice that the Car class defines a static method named Copy(); this method uses the Memberwise-Clone() method to perform a copy of the Car object passed to it.

The output from this program is as follows:

```
Creating Car objects
myCar details:
make = Toyota
model = MR2
myOtherCar details:
make = Porsche
model = Boxter
myCar.ToString() = Car
myCar.GetType() = Car
myCar.GetHashCode() = 65
Car.Equals(myCar, myOtherCar) = False
Car.ReferenceEquals(myCar, myOtherCar) = False
Setting myCar equal to myOtherCar
Car.Equals(myCar, myOtherCar) = True
Car.ReferenceEquals(myCar, myOtherCar) = True
Performing a memberwise clone of myCar to myOldCar
myOldCar details:
make = Porsche
model = Boxter
```

Overriding the *System.Object* Class *Methods*

The virtual methods of the System.Object class may be overridden in any of your classes. A common method to override in your classes is the ToString() method. As you saw in the previous example, the ToString() method returns the name of the class by default—which isn't particularly useful (but depends on the object, of course).

In this section, you'll see a program that causes the ToString() method to return a string containing the make and model fields of a Car object (see Listing 5.7). In the "Operator Overloading" section later in this chapter, you'll see a program that overrides the Equals() method.

Listing 5.7: Overriding the *ToString()* Method

```csharp
using System;


// declare the Car class
public class Car
{

  // declare the fields
  public string make;
  public string model;

  // define a constructor
  public Car(string make, string model)
  {
    this.make = make;
    this.model = model;
  }

  // override the ToString() method
  public override string ToString()
  {
    return make + " " + model;
  }

}


class Example7_7
{

  public static void Main()
  {

    // create Car objects
    Console.WriteLine("Creating Car objects");
    Car myCar = new Car("Toyota", "MR2");
    Car myOtherCar = new Car("Porsche", "Boxter");
```

```
        // call the ToString() method for the Car objects
        Console.WriteLine("myCar.ToString() = " +
          myCar.ToString());
        Console.WriteLine("myOtherCar.ToString() = " +
          myOtherCar.ToString());

    }


}
```

The output from this program is as follows:

```
Creating Car objects
myCar.ToString() = Toyota MR2
myOtherCar.ToString() = Porsche Boxter
```

Boxing and Unboxing

You've now seen that all classes are derived from the System.Object class. In fact, even value types such as int and char are derived from the System.Object type and may therefore use the methods defined in the System.Object class. For example, the following statements declare an int variable and then call the ToString() and GetType() methods using this int variable:

```
int myInt1 = 10;
Console.WriteLine("myInt1.ToString() = " +
  myInt1.ToString());
Console.WriteLine("myInt1.GetType() = " +
  myInt1.GetType());
```

The last two statements display the following:

```
myInt1.ToString() = 10
myInt1.GetType() = System.Int32
```

This is, at first glance, a somewhat surprising result: How can a variable act like an object? The answer is that at runtime, the variable is first implicitly converted to an object of the System.Object class—this process is known as *boxing*.

In the following example, an int variable is explicitly assigned to a System.Object object:

```
int myInt2 = 10;
object myObject = myInt2;  // myInt2 is boxed
```

Here, myInt2 is first boxed and then assigned to myObject.

NOTE

System.Object and object mean the same thing: They both refer to Sys-tem.Object. Therefore, in the example, myObject is an object of the System .Object class.

On the other side of the coin, an object of the System.Object class may be converted to a value type—this process is known as *unboxing*. In the following example, myObject is unboxed to an int variable:

```
int myInt3 = (int) myObject;  // myObject is unboxed
```

Notice that myObject is cast to an int.

Listing 5.8 illustrates boxing and unboxing.

Listing 5.8: Boxing and Unboxing

```
using System;

class Example7_8
{

  public static void Main()
  {

    // implicit boxing of an int
    int myInt1 = 10;
    Console.WriteLine(
      "myInt1.ToString() = " + myInt1.ToString());
    Console.WriteLine(
      "myInt1.GetType() = " + myInt1.GetType());

    // explicit boxing of an int to an object
    int myInt2 = 10;
    object myObject = myInt2;  // myInt2 is boxed
    Console.WriteLine("myInt2 = " + myInt2);
    Console.WriteLine("myObject = " + myObject);

    // explicit unboxing of an object to an int
    int myInt3 = (int) myObject;  // myObject is unboxed
    Console.WriteLine("myInt3 = " + myInt3);

  }

}
```

The output from this program is as follows:

```
myInt1.ToString() = 10
myInt1.GetType() = System.Int32
myInt2 = 10
myObject = 10
myInt3 = 10
```

USING ABSTRACT CLASSES AND METHODS

Abstract classes enable you to define classes that represent abstract concepts. For example, you can consider a motor vehicle an abstract concept, and you could define an abstract MotorVehicle class to represent the concept of a motor vehicle. You could then use the MotorVehicle class to derive a Car class to represent actual cars—you'll see an example of this shortly. You use the abstract keyword to specify that a class is abstract.

You can also declare *abstract methods* using the abstract keyword, which specifies that the method must be overridden in a derived class. An abstract method may not contain any code; the code for the method must be implemented in the derived class.

You can declare the following MotorVehicle class as abstract using the abstract keyword; this class also declares an abstract Accelerate() method:

```
abstract public class MotorVehicle
{

    ...

    // declare the abstract Accelerate() method (no code)
    abstract public void Accelerate();

}
```

Notice that the abstract Accelerate() method doesn't contain any code; the code must be implemented in the derived class.

There are a few points to note about abstract classes and methods:

▸ You *cannot* create objects of an abstract class.

▸ You *cannot* mark a constructor as abstract.

▶ You may use an abstract class to derive other classes, including other abstract classes.

▶ You must override any abstract methods in a base class with methods that contain code in a derived class.

You derive classes from an abstract base class using the usual colon (:) between the base and derived class names. The following Car class is derived from the MotorVehicle class, and it overrides the Accelerate() method with a method containing code:

```
public class Car : MotorVehicle
{

  ...

  // override the Accelerate() method (contains code)
  public override void Accelerate()
  {
    Console.WriteLine("In Car Accelerate() method");
    Console.WriteLine(model + " accelerating");
  }

}
```

Listing 5.9 shows abstract classes and methods.

Listing 5.9: Abstract Classes and Methods

```
using System;


// declare the abstract MotorVehicle class
abstract public class MotorVehicle
{

  // declare the fields
  public string make;
  public string model;

  // define a constructor
  public MotorVehicle(string make, string model)
  {
    this.make = make;
    this.model = model;
  }
```

```csharp
  // declare the abstract Accelerate() method (no code)
  abstract public void Accelerate();

}


// declare the Car class (derived from MotorVehicle)
public class Car : MotorVehicle
{

  // define a constructor
  public Car(string make, string model) :
  base(make, model)
  {
    // do nothing
  }

  // override the Accelerate() method (contains code)
  public override void Accelerate()
  {
    Console.WriteLine("In Car Accelerate() method");
    Console.WriteLine(model + " accelerating");
  }

}


class Example7_9
{

  public static void Main()
  {

    // create a Car object
    Console.WriteLine("Creating a Car object");
    Car myCar = new Car("Toyota", "MR2");

    // call the Car object's Accelerate() method
    Console.WriteLine("Calling myCar.Accelerate()");
    myCar.Accelerate();

  }

}
```

The output from this program is as follows:

```
Creating a Car object
Calling myCar.Accelerate()
In Car Accelerate() method
MR2 accelerating
```

DECLARING SEALED CLASSES AND METHODS

Sealed classes and methods restrict inheritance and polymorphism. You might want to use sealed classes and methods in code that you are going to sell when you don't want someone attempting to alter your code.

Sealed Classes

You cannot use a sealed class to derive a class. You mark a class or method as sealed using the `sealed` keyword. The following example declares a sealed class:

```
sealed public class MotorVehicle
{
  ...
}
```

You cannot derive a class from this sealed `MotorVehicle` class.

Sealed Methods

You cannot override a sealed method in a derived class. You may declare a sealed method in a non-sealed class, but that sealed method cannot be overridden in a derived class. The following example declares a non-sealed `MotorVehicle` class that defines a virtual `Accelerate()` method:

```
public class MotorVehicle
{

  ...

  // define the Accelerate() method
  public virtual void Accelerate()
  {
    Console.WriteLine("In MotorVehicle Accelerate() method");
    Console.WriteLine(model + " accelerating");
```

```
      }

   }
```

Next, the following Car class (derived from the MotorVehicle class) overrides the Accelerate() method with a sealed method:

```
public class Car : MotorVehicle
{

   ...

   // override the Accelerate() method (sealed)
   sealed public override void Accelerate()
   {
      Console.WriteLine("In Car Accelerate() method");
      Console.WriteLine(model + " accelerating");
   }

}
```

Because this Accelerate() method is sealed, any classes derived from the Car class cannot override this method.

Listing 5.10 shows these classes and illustrates sealed methods.

Listing 5.10: Sealed Methods

```
using System;


// declare the MotorVehicle class
public class MotorVehicle
{

   // declare the fields
   public string make;
   public string model;

   // define a constructor
   public MotorVehicle(string make, string model)
   {
      this.make = make;
      this.model = model;
   }

   // define the Accelerate() method
   public virtual void Accelerate()
```

```csharp
    {
      Console.WriteLine("In MotorVehicle Accelerate() method");
      Console.WriteLine(model + " accelerating");
    }

  }


  // declare the Car class (derived from MotorVehicle)
  public class Car : MotorVehicle
  {

    // define a constructor
    public Car(string make, string model) :
    base(make, model)
    {
      // do nothing
    }

    // override the Accelerate() method (sealed)
    sealed public override void Accelerate()
    {
      Console.WriteLine("In Car Accelerate() method");
      Console.WriteLine(model + " accelerating");
    }

  }


  class Example7_10
  {

    public static void Main()
    {

      // create a Car object
      Console.WriteLine("Creating a Car object");
      Car myCar = new Car("Toyota", "MR2");

      // call the Car object's Accelerate() method
      Console.WriteLine("Calling myCar.Accelerate()");
      myCar.Accelerate();

    }

  }
```

The output from this program is as follows:

```
Creating a Car object
Calling myCar.Accelerate()
In Car Accelerate() method
MR2 accelerating
```

CASTING OBJECTS

You can cast an object of a derived class to the base class (known as an *upcast*) and vice versa (known as a *downcast*). Because all classes are derived from the System.Object class, you can always upcast an object to this class.

You can only cast an object to a class when that class is compatible with the object's class. What do we mean by *compatible*? A derived class is compatible with its base class. For example, say class C was derived from class B, and class B was derived from class A; then C is compatible with B and A. You can therefore cast objects between A, B, and C. When you cast an object to a class, you only have access to the members of that class (you'll see an example of this shortly).

A class that is not derived from another class is not compatible. For example, say class B1 is derived from A, and B2 is also derived from A; then B1 and B2 are not compatible. Therefore, you cannot cast objects between B1 and B2.

The examples in the rest of this section use three classes, named MotorVehicle, Car, and Motorcycle. The Car and Motorcycle classes are both derived from a MotorVehicle class. The MotorVehicle class is as follows:

```
public class MotorVehicle
{

  public string model;

  public MotorVehicle(string model)
  {
    this.model = model;
  }

  public void Start()
  {
    Console.WriteLine(model + " started");
  }

}
```

The Car class is as follows:

```
public class Car : MotorVehicle
{

  public bool convertible;

  public Car(string model, bool convertible) :
  base(model)
  {
    this.convertible = convertible;
  }


}
```

The Motorcycle class is as follows:

```
public class Motorcycle : MotorVehicle
{

  public bool sidecar;

  // define a constructor
  public Motorcycle(string model, bool sidecar) :
  base(model)
  {
    this.sidecar = sidecar;
  }

  public void PullWheelie()
  {
    Console.WriteLine(model + " pulling a wheelie!");
  }

}
```

The following sections describe upcasts and downcasts using these classes.

Upcasting

An upcast occurs when an object of a derived class is cast to its base class. For example, an object of either the Car or Motorcycle class could be upcast to the `MotorVehicle` class. The following statement creates a `Car` object:

```
Car myCar = new Car("MR2", true);
```

Next, the following statement performs an upcast of this object to the `MotorVehicle` class:

```
MotorVehicle myMotorVehicle = (MotorVehicle) myCar;
```

Now, because the `MotorVehicle` class only contains the `model` field and the `Start()` method, `myMotorVehicle` only has access to these members; `myMotorVehicle` doesn't have access to the additional member defined in the `Car` class, so it cannot access the `convertible` field (attempting to access this field will cause a compilation error).

Similarly, the following statements create a `Motorcycle` object and then cast that object to the `MotorVehicle` class:

```
Motorcycle myMotorcycle = new Motorcycle("V-Rod", true);
MotorVehicle myMotorVehicle2 = (MotorVehicle) myMotorcycle;
```

Now, `myMotorVehicle2` only has access to the members of the `MotorVehicle` class and cannot access the `sidecar` field or `PullWheelie()` method.

Downcasting

A downcast occurs when an object of the base class is cast to a derived class. The following statement downcasts `myMotorVehicle2` (created in the previous section) to the `Motorcycle` class:

```
Motorcycle myMotorcycle2 = (Motorcycle) myMotorVehicle2;
```

Because `myMotorcycle2` is of the `Motorcycle` class, it now has access to all the members of the `Motorcycle` class, and therefore the `sidecar` field and `PullWheelie()` methods are also now available.

One thing you cannot do is downcast `myMotorVehicle2` to the `Car` class. This is because `myMotor-Vehicle2` was obtained (in the previous section) by upcasting `myMotorcycle` (a `Motorcycle` object), and you cannot cast a `Motorcycle` object to a `Car` object because the `Motorcycle` and `Car` classes are incompatible.

Listing 5.11 illustrates casting objects.

Listing 5.11: Casting Objects

```csharp
using System;


// declare the MotorVehicle class (the base class)
public class MotorVehicle
{

  public string model;

  public MotorVehicle(string model)
  {
    this.model = model;
  }

  public void Start()
  {
    Console.WriteLine(model + " started");
  }

}


// declare the Car class
public class Car : MotorVehicle
{

  public bool convertible;

  public Car(string model, bool convertible) :
  base(model)
  {
    this.convertible = convertible;
  }

}


// declare the Motorcycle class
public class Motorcycle : MotorVehicle
{

  public bool sidecar;
```

```
   // define a constructor
   public Motorcycle(string model, bool sidecar) :
   base(model)
   {
     this.sidecar = sidecar;
   }

   public void PullWheelie()
   {
     Console.WriteLine(model + " pulling a wheelie!");
   }

}


class Example7_11
{

   public static void Main()
   {

     // create a Car object
     Car myCar = new Car("MR2", true);

     // cast myCar to MotorVehicle (upcast)
     MotorVehicle myMotorVehicle = (MotorVehicle) myCar;

     // myMotorVehicle only has a model
     // field and Start() method
     // (no convertible field)
     Console.WriteLine("
       myMotorVehicle.model = " + myMotorVehicle.model);
     myMotorVehicle.Start();
     // Console.WriteLine("myMotorVehicle.convertible = " +
     //   myMotorVehicle.convertible);

     // create a Motorcycle object
     Motorcycle myMotorcycle = new Motorcycle("V-Rod", true);

     // cast myMotorcycle to MotorVehicle (upcast)
     MotorVehicle myMotorVehicle2 =
       (MotorVehicle) myMotorcycle;
```

```
                  // myMotorVehicle only has a
                  // model field and Start() method
                  // (no sidecar field or PullWheelie() method)
                  Console.WriteLine(
                    "myMotorVehicle2.model =
                   " +   myMotorVehicle2.model);
                  myMotorVehicle2.Start();
                  // Console.WriteLine("myMotorVehicle2.sidecar = " +
                  //   myMotorVehicle2.sidecar);
                  // myMotorVehicle2.PullWheelie();

                  // cast myMotorVehicle2 to Motorcycle (downcast)
                  Motorcycle myMotorcycle2 = (Motorcycle) myMotorVehicle2;

                  // myMotorCycle2 has access to all
                  // members of the Motorcycle class
                  Console.WriteLine(
                    "myMotorcycle2.model = " + myMotorcycle2.model);
                  Console.WriteLine(
                    "myMotorcycle2.sidecar = " + myMotorcycle2.sidecar);
                  myMotorcycle2.Start();
                  myMotorcycle2.PullWheelie();

                  // cannot cast a Motorcyle
                  // object to the Car class because
                  // their classes are not compatible
                  // Car myCar2 = (Car) myMotorVehicle2;

              }


          }
```

The output from this program is as follows:

```
myMotorVehicle.model = MR2
MR2 started
myMotorVehicle2.model = V-Rod
V-Rod started
myMotorcycle2.model = V-Rod
myMotorcycle2.sidecar = True
V-Rod started
V-Rod pulling a wheelie!
```

OPERATOR OVERLOADING

Operator overloading enables you to write your own code to handle the operation performed by an operator, instead of just using the default operation. In Chapter 2, "Zen and Now: The C# Language," you learned that operators perform arithmetic, compare values, and so on. If you have written your own classes, then you might want an operator to do something different from the default operation.

For example, say you have a class named `Rectangle` that declares two fields named `width` and `height`:

```
public class Rectangle
{

  // declare the fields
  public int width;
  public int height;

  // define constructor
  public Rectangle(int width, int height)
  {
    this.width = width;
    this.height = height;
  }

}
```

You also create two `Rectangle` objects with the same values for their `width` and `height` fields:

```
Rectangle myRectangle = new Rectangle(1, 4);
Rectangle myRectangle2 = new Rectangle(1, 4);
```

Next, the following `if` statement uses the equal operator (`==`):

```
if (myRectangle == myRectangle2)
{
  Console.WriteLine("myRectangle is equal to myRectangle2");
}
else
{
  Console.WriteLine(
    "myRectangle is not equal to myRectangle2");
}
```

In this case, the `==` operator compares the object references, and because `myRectangle` and `myRectangle2` reference different objects, this `if` statement always displays the text indicating that myRectangle and myRectangle2 are not equal. You might want to overload the equal operator (==) to compare the width and height of the two rectangles instead; if they are the same, then the two objects are *identical*.

Also, the following statement attempts to use the addition operator (+) to add the two rectangles:

```
Rectangle myRectangle3 = myRectangle + myRectangle2;
```

This statement causes a compilation error because the addition operator (+) expects two numeric values. Therefore, you might also want to overload the addition operator, which would then add the width and height fields of both objects and return a new Rectangle object with these field values.

In the following sections, you'll see how to overload the equal operator and the addition operator. You'll also learn about the other operators you can overload.

Overloading the Equal Operator

You overload an operator using the operator keyword in a method for your class. For example, the following method overloads the equal operator (==); notice that the operator keyword follows the return type of the method (bool), and the operator to be overloaded (==) goes after the operator keyword:

```
public static bool operator ==(Rectangle lhs, Rectangle rhs)
{
  Console.WriteLine("In operator ==");
  if (lhs.width == rhs.width && lhs.height == rhs.height)
  {
    return true;
  }
  else
  {
    return false;
  }
}
```

NOTE
Overloaded operator methods are always static because they belong to the class.

This method accepts two Rectangle parameters named lhs and rhs; these correspond to the two objects on the left and right sides of the == operator. For example, when myRectangle == myRectangle2 is evaluated, myRectangle is passed into the method as the lhs parameter, and myRectangle2 is passed in as the rhs parameter. The method returns true if lhs and rhs have the same values for their width and height fields; otherwise it returns false.

WARNING

If you overload the equal operator, you should also overload the opposite not equal operator (!=); if you don't, then you'll get a compilation warning.

The following method overloads the not equal (!=) operator:

```
public static bool operator !=(Rectangle lhs, Rectangle rhs)
{
  Console.WriteLine("In operator !=");
  return !(lhs==rhs);
}
```

Notice that this simply invokes the equal operator (==) to check if lhs is equal to rhs and returns the logical opposite of this result—this saves you from writing similar code to what you previously wrote for the equal operator.

Finally, because you are overloading the equal operator, you should also override the Equals() method inherited from the System.Object class (described earlier in this chapter in "Using the System.Object Class"):

```
public override bool Equals(object obj)
{
  Console.WriteLine("In Equals()");
  if (!(obj is Rectangle))
  {
    return false;
  }
  else
  {
    return this == (Rectangle) obj;
  }
}
```

If the object is not a Rectangle, then you simply return false. If the object is a Rectangle, then you invoke the equal operator (==) to perform the comparison.

Overloading the Addition Operator

You also want to overload the addition operator (+) for the Rectangle class so that the following statement will work:

```
Rectangle myRectangle3 = myRectangle + myRectangle2;
```

This statement will create a new Rectangle object whose width and height fields are set to the sum of those fields from myRectangle and myRectangle2.

The following method shows the required overload of the addition operator (+):

```
public static Rectangle operator +(Rectangle lhs, Rectangle rhs)
{
  Console.WriteLine("In operator +");
  return new Rectangle(lhs.width + rhs.width,
    lhs.height + rhs.height);
}
```

Listing 5.12 illustrates operator overloading.

Listing 5.12: Operator Overloading

```
using System;


// declare the Rectangle class
public class Rectangle
{

  // declare the fields
  public int width;
  public int height;

  // define constructor
  public Rectangle(int width, int height)
  {
    this.width = width;
    this.height = height;
  }

  // override the ToString() method
  public override string ToString()
  {
    return "width = " + width + ", height = " + height;
  }
```

```csharp
// overload the == operator
public static bool
  operator ==(Rectangle lhs, Rectangle rhs)
{
  Console.WriteLine("In operator ==");
  if (lhs.width == rhs.width && lhs.height == rhs.height)
  {
    return true;
  }
  else
  {
    return false;
  }
}


// overload the != operator
public static bool
  operator !=(Rectangle lhs, Rectangle rhs)
{
  Console.WriteLine("In operator !=");
  return !(lhs==rhs);
}


// override the Equals() method
public override bool Equals(object obj)
{
  Console.WriteLine("In Equals()");
  if (!(obj is Rectangle))
  {
    return false;
  }
  else
  {
    return this == (Rectangle) obj;
  }
}

// overload the + operator
public static Rectangle
  operator +(Rectangle lhs, Rectangle rhs)
{
  Console.WriteLine("In operator +");
```

```
        return new Rectangle(
          lhs.width + rhs.width, lhs.height + rhs.height);
    }

}


class Example7_12
{

  public static void Main()
  {

    // create Rectangle objects
    Rectangle myRectangle = new Rectangle(1, 4);
    Console.WriteLine("myRectangle: " + myRectangle);
    Rectangle myRectangle2 = new Rectangle(1, 4);
    Console.WriteLine("myRectangle2: " + myRectangle2);

    if (myRectangle == myRectangle2)
    {
      Console.WriteLine(
        "myRectangle is equal to myRectangle2");
    }
    else
    {
      Console.WriteLine(
        "myRectangle is not equal to myRectangle2");
    }

    Rectangle myRectangle3 = myRectangle + myRectangle2;
    Console.WriteLine("myRectangle3: " + myRectangle3);

  }

}
```

The output from this program is as follows:

```
myRectangle: width = 1, height = 4
myRectangle2: width = 1, height = 4
In operator ==
myRectangle is equal to myRectangle2
In operator +
myRectangle3: width = 2, height = 8
```

Overloading Other Operators

You can overload many operators, but you should only overload an operator if it makes sense to do so. For example, the previous example overloaded the addition operator, along with the equal and not equal operators—but there was no need to overload the multiplication operator. You shouldn't typically overload every operator you possibly can in your classes, as this may lead to confusing code. Table 5.2 lists the operators that may be overloaded.

TABLE 5.2: Overloadable Operators

OPERATOR CATEGORY	OPERATORS
Unary	+, -, ++, --, !, ~, true, and false
Multiplicative	*, /, and %
Additive	+ and -
Bitwise shifts	<< and >>
Relational	<, >, <=, and >=
Equality	==, and !=
Bitwise AND	&
Bitwise exclusive OR	^
Bitwise OR		

As mentioned earlier, if you overload one of the relational or equality operators, you should also overload the opposite operator. For example, if you overload the equal operator (==), then you should also overload the not equal operator (!=). Similarly, if you overload the less than operator (<), you should also overload the greater than operator (>).

SUMMARY

In this chapter, you learned all about derived classes. Specifically, with *inheritance*, one class is used as the parent of another class. The parent class is known as the *base class*, and the child class is known as the *derived class*. Derived classes inherit the members of their base class. A class is derived from a base class by placing the name of the base class after a colon (:).

In an object-oriented programming language, *polymorphism* means a method in a derived class may contain a different set of statements from the method in the base class; the method in the derived class is said to *override* the method in the base class. A method that may be overridden in a derived class is declared using the `virtual` keyword in the base class and is overridden in the derived class using the `override` keyword.

Depending on the access modifier used with a member in a base class, that member may or may not be accessible to a derived class. In addition, members of a base class may be hidden by members of a derived class using the new keyword. This technique is useful when you want to define your own version of a method that has been previously defined as virtual in the base class.

The `System.Object` class acts as the base class for all classes: All classes are ultimately derived from the `System.Object` class, including the value types such as `int` and `char`. The `System.Object` class provides a number of useful methods, some of which may be overridden in a class—a common method to override is the `ToString()` method. Value types may be implicitly converted to objects of the `System.Object` class using a process known as *boxing*; similarly, objects may be converted to value types using *unboxing*.

You also learned about declaring abstract classes and sealed classes. *Abstract classes* allow you to define classes that represent abstract concepts. *Abstract methods* must be overridden in a derived class, which must also implement the code for the method. You declare a class or method to be abstract using the `abstract` keyword. You use *sealed* classes and methods to restrict inheritance and polymorphism. You might want to use sealed classes and methods in code that you are going to sell, and you don't want someone attempting to add to your code. You declare a class or method as sealed using the `sealed` keyword.

Finally, *operator overloading* allows you to write your own code to handle the operation performed by an operator, instead of just using the default operation.

What's Next

In the next chapter, you'll learn ways to group several instances of the same object (or multiple instances of different objects) together in the form of collections and arrays. You'll also learn about members called indexers that can access multiple objects.

Chapter 6

ARRAYS, INDEXERS, AND COLLECTIONS

In the real world, programming usually involves groups of objects. Arrays are specifically designed to store groups of objects, with the object being retrieved using an index value. Collections—and the structures based on collections in C#, such as queues, ArrayLists, and much more—are an alternative mechanism for grouping and coping with multiple objects.

If you don't know how to deal with multiple items in arrays (and other classes designed for use with multiples, such as those based on the System.Collection classes), then your programs will never scale—nor will it be of much use when you are dealing in an automated fashion with the large amount of data presented by the real world.

It's important to pick the right underlying structure for dealing with groups of objects, and you also need to know how to work with the structure you've selected. This chapter covers both aspects of dealing with arrays, collections, and related classes.

Adapted from *Visual C# .NET Programming*
by Harold Davis
ISBN 0-7821-4046-7

ARRAYS

In C#, an *array* is an object that is used to store objects of the same type and provides access to the objects using an index. You should know that just as the `string` keyword is used to create an object of type `System.String`, the syntax and expressions used to create arrays actually create an object based on the `System.Array` class. This means that you can use the members—methods and properties—provided by the `Array` class when you work with arrays. Most `Array` methods are shown in Table 6.1, and `Array` properties are shown in Table 6.2.

TABLE 6.1:   Array Methods

METHOD	MEANING
BinarySearch	Searches a one-dimensional sorted array.
Clear	Sets a range of elements in an array to 0, to `false`, or to a null reference, depending on the type of the array elements.
Copy	Copies a range of elements from one array to another.
CopyTo	Copies all the elements of a one-dimensional array to another one-dimensional array, starting at the specified destination array index in the new array.
CreateInstance	A static method that explicitly instantiates and initializes a new array instance. Note that this method allows you to specify a lower bound for the array that is non-zero (see the example later in this chapter).
GetLength	Gets the number of elements in a specified dimension of the array.
GetLowerBound	Gets the lower bound of the specified dimension in the array. Note that if the array has been created using normal syntax—in other words, not using `CreateInstance`—the lower bound of each dimension will be 0.
GetUpperBound	Gets the upper bound of the specified dimension in the array.
GetValue	Gets the value of the specified element in the array.
IndexOf	Returns the index of the first occurrence of a value in a one-dimensional array (or in a portion of the array).
Initialize	Initializes every element of a value-type array by calling the default constructor of the value type.
LastIndexOf	Returns the index of the last occurrence of a value in a one-dimensional array (or in a portion of the array).
Reverse	Reverses the order of the elements in a one-dimensional array (or in a portion of the array).

TABLE 6.1 continued: Array Methods

METHOD	MEANING
SetValue	Sets the specified element in the current array to the specified value.
Sort	Sorts the elements in a one-dimensional array.

TABLE 6.2: Array Properties

PROPERTY	RETURNS
IsFixedSize	A Boolean value indicating whether the array has a fixed size
IsReadOnly	A Boolean value indicating whether the array is read-only
IsSynchronized	A Boolean value indicating whether the array is thread-safe
Length	The total number of elements in all the dimensions of an array
Rank	The number of dimensions of an array
SyncRoot	An object that can be used to synchronize access to the array

Arrays in C# are, for the most part, zero-indexed—meaning that the array indices start at 0 (but see the example later in this chapter that shows how to start an array at another index).

One-dimensional arrays can be thought of as a table with one column that can be accessed using an index. Multidimensional arrays use multiple indices to access their values, so a two-dimensional array can be pictured as a table with rows and columns. In a *jagged* array—also called an array of arrays—each "row" in the array is itself an array, with a potentially different size than the arrays making up the other rows.

BOXING AND UNBOXING

You may have observed that types of a class that are derived from a class can be assigned to an array of that class, even though, as I mentioned above, an array is used to store objects of "the same type." Specifically, objects of any type can be stored in an array of *objects* (since all types are derived from the object type).

CONTINUED ➡

For example, the following is legal code, and creates an array of objects that are assigned three different types:

```
int theInt; string theString; Button1 button1;
object [] stuff = new object [3];
stuff [0] = theInt;
stuff [1] = theString;
stuff [2] = button1;
```

What has actually happened is the various types have been implicitly converted to type object. (If you look at the members of each element of the stuff [] array, you'll find the members of an object type.) However, the extended information relating to the derived type has been preserved. This is called *boxing*.

To reverse the process, and *unbox* the types stored as objects, you need to explicitly cast the element of the object array to the original type. For example,

```
int newInt = (int) stuff [0];
string newString = (string) stuff [1];
Button button2 = (Button) stuff [2];
```

Creating an Array

Let's start with one-dimensional arrays. The process of creating an array is a three-step dance (although these steps can be combined, as we'll see in a moment):

- ▶ First, the array must be declared.

- ▶ Next, it is instantiated.

- ▶ Finally, it is initialized with values.

To declare an array, follow a type with square brackets and continue with the array's identifier. For example, you could declare an integer array *numbers* and a string array *names* as follows:

```
int [] numbers; // declares integer array
string [] names; // declares string array
```

To instantiate the array, as you'd expect, the new keyword is used. The statement

```
numbers = new int [3];
```

instantiates a new three-element, zero-based array with the previously declared variable *numbers*. (The elements are *numbers[0]*, *numbers[1]*, and *numbers[2]*.)

The two statements can be combined into one, so that you can instantiate while you declare:

```
int [] numbers = new int[3];
```

At this point, you should know that the three elements of the integer array *numbers* have been initialized to 0. (Arrays of reference-type elements are initialized to a null reference.)

NOTE
You can use a constant or variable rather than a literal to size the dimensions of an array.

As it turns out, you can initialize the array at the same time as you declare and instantiate it, by placing the initial values within curly braces. Here are one-step examples that declare, instantiate, and initialize an integer array and a string array:

```
int [] numbers = new int[3] {3,1,4};
string [] names = new string[3] {"Tom", "Dick", "Harry"};
```

There are a couple of shorthand ways to say the same thing. If you are initializing an array, you can leave off the dimension, in which case it is created with the number of elements specified by the initialization. So these statements create three-element arrays just like the preceding ones:

```
int [] numbers = new int[] {3,1,4};
string [] names = new string[] {"Tom", "Dick", "Harry"};
```

If you really prefer to be terse, you can also leave off the new part of the statement (once again, assuming you've provided initial values). The compiler is smart enough to know that it is implied. So here's the shortest way to declare, instantiate, and initialize these two arrays:

```
int [] numbers = {3,1,4};
string [] names = {"Tom", "Dick", "Harry"}
```

Moving on, let's try a little example of creating and using an array. Let's suppose we want an array to store the first seven numbers in the Fibonacci series, which comes up in art, nature, mathematics, and mysticism. Here's the shorthand way to create that array and stuff the right values into it:

```
int [] fibArray = new int[7] {1,1,2,3,5,8,13};
```

Let's say, instead, that we are fond of iteration. As you probably know, the first two elements of the Fibonacci series are 1; after that, the element n in the series is equal to the sum of the elements $(n - 1)$ and $(n - 2)$.

First, we can declare and instantiate the array with seven zero-based elements:

```
int [] fibArray = new int[7];
```

Next, we can assign the first two values in the series.

```
fibArray[0] = fibArray[1] = 1;
```

Finally, we can use iteration to assign the rest of the values in the array:

```
for (int i = 2; i < 7; ++i)
    fibArray[i] = fibArray[i - 1] + fibArray[i - 2];
```

You can use a message box to display an element of the array to make sure that this has all worked correctly, as shown in Listing 6.1.

Listing 6.1: Creating an Integer Array and Displaying an Element

```
private void btnCreate_Click(
    object sender, System.EventArgs e)
    // int [] fibArray = new int[7] {1,1,2,3,5,8,13};
    int [] fibArray = new int[7];
    fibArray[0] = fibArray[1] = 1;
    for (int i = 2; i < 7; ++i)
        fibArray[i] = fibArray[i - 1] + fibArray[i - 2];
    string fifthFib = fibArray[4].ToString();
    MessageBox.Show(
        "The fifth number in the Fibonacci series is " +
            fifthFib,
        "Arrays", MessageBoxButtons.OK, MessageBoxIcon
            .Information);
}
```

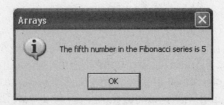

foreach Statement

The foreach statement is a simple way to iterate through the elements of an array. If we continue with our array of Fibonacci numbers, it's easy to use a foreach statement

```
foreach (int fib in fibArray) {
    lstFib.Items.Add(fib.ToString()); }
```

to cycle through the Fibonacci array and, one by one, add the string representation of each element to a ListBox (named *lstFib*).

The complete revised click event procedure that creates the array and then uses foreach to cycle through it, adding the elements to the ListBox, is shown in Listing 6.2. If you run the code and then click the button, the Fibonacci numbers will appear in the ListBox as shown in Figure 6.1.

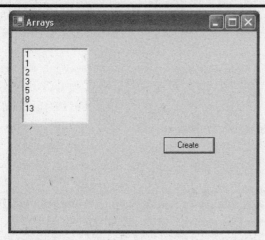

FIGURE 6.1:   The foreach statement can be used to display array elements in a ListBox.

Listing 6.2: Adding the Integer Array to a ListBox

```
private void btnCreate_Click(
    object sender, System.EventArgs e) {
    int [] fibArray = new int[7];
    fibArray[0] = fibArray[1] = 1;
    for (int i = 2; i < 7; ++i)
        fibArray[i] = fibArray[i - 1] + fibArray[i - 2];
    string fifthFib = fibArray[4].ToString();
```

```
foreach (int fib in fibArray) {
    lstFib.Items.Add(fib.ToString());
}
}
```

By the way, if you'd stored the Fibonacci numbers as elements in a string array in the first place (rather than as integers), you could add the elements in the array to the ListBox with a single AddRange method call. Here's the declaration and instantiation of the Fibonacci array as a string:

```
string [] fibArray = new string[7];
```

followed by the assignment of the first two numbers, as strings, of course, in the series:

```
fibArray[0] = fibArray[1] = "1";
```

To pull off the iteration, we have to get a little tricky in our conversions. First, the n - 1 and n - 2 elements are each converted to an integer. The integers are added together, and the result is converted back to string:

```
for (int i = 2; i < 7; ++i) {
    fibArray[i] = (Convert.ToInt16(fibArray[i - 1]) +
        Convert.ToInt16(fibArray[i - 2])).ToString(); }
```

Finally, the payoff—it takes only a single statement to fill the ListBox:

```
lstFib.Items.AddRange (fibArray);
```

Listing 6.3 shows the process of filling a string array with strings representing the Fibonacci series and adding them to a ListBox.

Listing 6.3: Using *AddRange* to Add a String Array to a ListBox

```
string [] fibArray = new string[7];
fibArray[0] = fibArray[1] = "1";
for (int i = 2; i < 7; ++i) {
    fibArray[i] = (Convert.ToInt16(fibArray[i - 1]) +
        Convert.ToInt16(fibArray[i - 2])).ToString();
}
lstFib.Items.AddRange (fibArray);
```

Arrays of Structs

Who says the elements of your array have to be simple value types? Often, it makes sense to define classes or structs that are used as the template for each element of an array.

As an example, let's go back to the *Employee* struct defined in Chapter 2, "Zen and Now: The C# Language":

```
public struct Employee {
    public string fullName, rank;
    public long SSN;
    public Employee(string fullName,
      string rank, long SSN) {
        this.fullName = fullName;
        this.rank = rank;
        this.SSN = SSN;
    }
}
```

It's easy to create instances based on this struct. For example,

```
Employee DavisN =
    new Employee("Nicholas Davis", "Opera Singer", 12345678);
```

Next, we can declare, instantiate, and initialize a three-element array with *Employee* structs for elements (assuming all three struct elements are defined):

```
Employee [] theRoster = {HopperK, DavisN, DavisJ};
```

As I explained earlier in this chapter, this statement is shorthand for the more formal:

```
Employee [] theRoster =
    new Employee [3] {HopperK, DavisN, DavisJ};
```

Next, if you'd like, you can display some of the information stored in a struct element:

```
MessageBox.Show(theRoster[1].fullName +
    " is an " + theRoster[1].rank + ".",
    "Arrays", MessageBoxButtons.OK, MessageBoxIcon .Information);
```

Finally, it's easy to use a foreach statement to iterate through the array of structs and to add specific field information to a ListBox:

```
foreach (Employee emp in theRoster) {
    lstRoster.Items.Add(emp.fullName);
}
```

If you run the code shown in Listing 6.4, the contents of the *fullname* field of each struct in the array will be added to a ListBox (Figure 6.2).

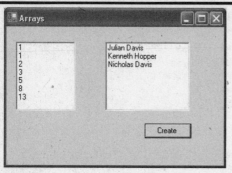

FIGURE 6.2:   You can create arrays of structs and display struct elements.

Listing 6.4: Creating and Displaying an Array of Structs

```
public struct Employee {
    public string fullName, rank;
    public long SSN;
    public Employee (string fullName,
        string rank, long SSN) {
        this.fullName = fullName;
        this.rank = rank;
        this.SSN = SSN;
    }
}

private void btnCreate_Click(object sender,
    System.EventArgs e) {
    Employee DavisJ =
        new Employee("Julian Davis", "City Hall", 12345678);
    Employee DavisN =
        new Employee("Nicholas Davis", "Opera Singer", 12345678);
    Employee HopperK =
        new Employee("Kenneth Hopper", "Proprietor", 12345678);

    Employee [] theRoster = {HopperK, DavisN, DavisJ};

    MessageBox.Show(theRoster[1].fullName + " is an "
        + theRoster[1].rank + ".", "Arrays",
        MessageBoxButtons.OK, MessageBoxIcon.Information);
```

```
    foreach (Employee emp in theRoster) {
        lstRoster.Items.Add(emp.fullName);
    }
}
```

n-Dimensional Arrays

n-Dimensional, or multidimensional, arrays are easy to declare and use. They work just like one-dimensional arrays, except that a comma is placed within the square brackets between the array dimensions.

It's easy to see why you might want to use a two-dimensional array to represent the "board" of a game like checkers or chess. *n*-dimensional arrays become handy when more information is needed to adequately model a situation. For example, a three-dimensional array might be used to store stock prices and volume over time.

Here are the declarations for a two-dimensional integer array and a three-dimensional string array:

```
int [,] numbers;
string [,,] words;
```

Let's have a look at an example. First, declare and instantiate a two-dimensional integer array *the2d*, with five "rows" and three "columns":

```
const int rows = 5;
const int cols = 3;
int [,] the2d = new int [rows, cols];
```

Next, populate the array by assigning as a value to each element its row times its column:

```
for (int i = 0; i < rows; i++) {
    for (int j = 0; j < cols; j++) {
        the2d[i,j] = i * j;
    }
}
```

Next, iterate through both dimensions of the array. For each element, create a string consisting of its coordinates in the array followed by its value, and add it to a ListBox:

```
for (int i = 0; i < rows; i++) {
    for (int j = 0; j < cols; j++) {
        string theItem = "the2d ["
            + i.ToString() + "," + j.ToString() + "] is "
            + the2d[i,j].ToString() + ".";
```

```
            lstMulti.Items.Add(theItem);
        }
    }
```

If you run the code (see Listing 6.5), you'll see that the contents of the array are displayed in the ListBox (Figure 6.3).

FIGURE 6.3:   It's easy to declare and initialize multidimensional arrays.

Listing 6.5: Creating and Displaying a Two-Dimensional Array

```
private void btnMulti_Click(
    object sender, System.EventArgs e) {
    const int rows = 5;
    const int cols = 3;

    // declare 5X3 array
    int [,] the2d = new int [rows, cols];

    // populate the array
    for (int i = 0; i < rows; i++) {
        for (int j = 0; j < cols; j++) {
            the2d[i,j] = i*j;
        }
    }

    // display it
    for (int i = 0; i < rows; i++) {
        for (int j = 0; j < cols; j++) {
```

```
            string theItem = "the2d ["
               + i.ToString() + "," + j.ToString() +
               "] is " + the2d[i,j].ToString() + ".";
            lstMulti.Items.Add(theItem);
        }
    }
}
```

Arrays of Arrays

An *array of arrays* (also called a *jagged* array because of its "unevenness" compared to a standard *n*-dimensional array) is an array where each row is a one-dimensional array. Jagged arrays can be declared and instantiated in a single statement—using side-by-side square braces—but there is no way to initialize the elements of the jagged array in the same statement.

For example, here's how you might declare a two-dimensional jagged string array, with the first dimension having seven rows and the second dimension varying—considerably—in the number of elements:

```
const int rows = 7;
string [] [] jaggedA = new string [rows] [];

jaggedA[0] = new string [2];
jaggedA[1] = new string [3];
jaggedA[2] = new string [1];
jaggedA[3] = new string [4];
jaggedA[4] = new string [40];
jaggedA[5] = new string [2];
jaggedA[6] = new string [86];
```

Next, individual elements could be assigned values. For example,

```
jaggedA [1] [2] = "jagged";
```

Some of the jagged one-dimensional arrays within arrays are filled using iteration:

```
for (int dash = 0; dash < 86; dash++)
    jaggedA [6] [dash] = "-";
```

Next, each "column" can be displayed as a single concatenated item in a ListBox:

```
string column = "";
for (int i = 0; i < 2; i++) {
    column = column + " " + jaggedA [0] [i] + " ";
}
lstMulti.Items.Add(column);
```

Listing 6.6 shows the rather messy code that does this for the entire seven rows (messy because with each "column" array a different size, nested iteration is not easy). If you run the code, a graph depiction of "jaggedness" will appear in the ListBox (Figure 6.4).

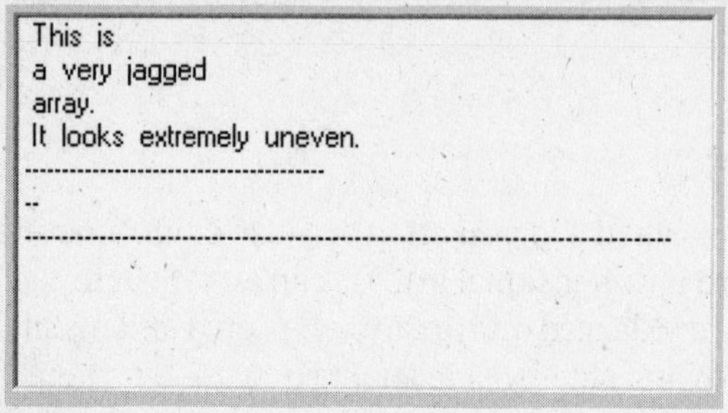

```
This is
a very jagged
array.
It looks extremely uneven.
---------------------------------------
--
---------------------------------------------------------------------------
```

FIGURE 6.4:   When the column elements of a jagged string array are displayed in a ListBox, rows of unequal length are created.

Listing 6.6: Declaring, Populating, and Displaying a Jagged String Array

```
private void btnJagged_Click(
    object sender, System.EventArgs e) {
    // declare a jagged array with 7 rows
    const int rows = 7;
    string [] [] jaggedA = new string [rows] [];

    // give it some column arrays
    jaggedA[0] = new string [2];
    jaggedA[1] = new string [3];
    jaggedA[2] = new string [1];
    jaggedA[3] = new string [4];
    jaggedA[4] = new string [40];
    jaggedA[5] = new string [2];
    jaggedA[6] = new string [86];

    // populate it
    jaggedA [0] [0] = "This";
    jaggedA [0] [1] = "is";

    jaggedA [1] [0] = "a";
    jaggedA [1] [1] = "very";
    jaggedA [1] [2] = "jagged";
```

```
jaggedA [2] [0] = "array.";

jaggedA [3] [0] = "It";
jaggedA [3] [1] = "looks";
jaggedA [3] [2] = "extremely";
jaggedA [3] [3] = "uneven.";

// fill the final three columns with dashes (-)
for (int dash = 0; dash < 40; dash++)
    jaggedA [4] [dash] = "-";
for (int dash = 0; dash < 2; dash++)
    jaggedA [5] [dash] = "-";
for (int dash = 0; dash < 86; dash++)
    jaggedA [6] [dash] = "-";

// display it
string column = "";
for (int i = 0; i < 2; i++) {
    column = column + " " + jaggedA [0] [i] + " ";
}
lstMulti.Items.Add(column);
column = "";
for (int i = 0; i < 3; i++) {
    column = column + " " + jaggedA [1] [i] + " ";
}
lstMulti.Items.Add(column);
column = "";
for (int i = 0; i < 1; i++) {
    column = column + " " + jaggedA [2] [i] + " ";
}
lstMulti.Items.Add(column);
column = "";
for (int i = 0; i < 4; i++) {
    column = column + " " + jaggedA [3] [i] + " ";
}
lstMulti.Items.Add(column);
column = "";
for (int i = 0; i < 40; i++) {
    column = column + jaggedA [4] [i];
}
lstMulti.Items.Add(column);
column = "";
```

```
        for (int i = 0; i < 2; i++) {
            column = column + jaggedA [5] [i];
        }
        lstMulti.Items.Add(column);
        column = "";
        for (int i = 0; i < 86; i++) {
            column = column + jaggedA [6] [i];
        }
        lstMulti.Items.Add(column);
    }
```

Creating a Non-Zero Lower Bound

Toward the beginning of the chapter, I teased you by saying I would show you how to create an array with a non-zero lower bound. Here goes!

WARNING
You probably won't want to use non-zero lower bounds very often in C#, because arrays created in the way and shown in this example do not have many of the conveniences—such as square bracket notation—that we've come to expect when working with arrays.

First, you need to create two integer arrays. The first array is used to store the size of each dimension you wish to create in its elements (the number of elements indicates the number of dimensions). The second array stores the lower bound for each dimension.

In this example, I've used one-dimensional arrays to create an array with six elements where the index of the first element is five—but you could use multidimensional arrays to create an array with different numbers of elements and different lower bounds for different dimensions.

Here are statements that create the two arrays:

```
int [] theLengths = new int [1] {6};
int [] theBounds = new int [1] {5};
```

Next, the CreateInstance method of the System.Array class is used to create a non-zero-lower-bound array in the variable *theArray*. The CreateInstance method is static, indicating that an object of the Array class is not instantiated to use it—as the name of the method implies, it does its own creating of instances.

The first argument of the method is the System.Type of the array to be created, which is derived using the typeof operator—for example, for an integer array, typeof(int). The second and third arguments are the arrays we previously created, which represent the size and lower bound of each dimension:

```
Array theArray =
    Array.CreateInstance(typeof(int), theLengths, theBounds);
```

To test this, let's assign values to each of the putative elements of the array:

```
for (int i = 5; i < 11; i++) {
    theArray.SetValue(i,i);
}
```

We can then use the GetValue method to retrieve and display a value by its index:

```
MessageBox.Show(theArray.GetValue(7).ToString());
```

The GetLowerBound method, used with an argument of 0 to retrieve the first—and, in this case, only—dimension of the array, shows that the lower bound is what it is supposed to be, 5:

```
MessageBox.Show(theArray.GetLowerBound(0).ToString());
```

Finally, if you try to invoke an element using an index that would normally be in-bounds for a six-element array,

```
MessageBox.Show(theArray.GetValue(2).ToString());
```

an out-of-bounds exception is fired.

The code for generating and testing the non-zero-lower-bound array is shown in Listing 6.7.

Listing 6.7: Creating, Populating, and Testing an Array with a Specified (Non-Zero) Lower Bound

```
private void btnNonZero_Click(
  object sender, System.EventArgs e) {
    int [] theLengths = new int [1] {6};
    int [] theBounds = new int [1] {5};
    Array theArray =
      Array.CreateInstance(typeof(int),
      theLengths, theBounds);

    for (int i = 5; i < 11; i++) {
        theArray.SetValue(i,i);
    }
```

```
        MessageBox.Show(theArray.GetValue(7).ToString());
        MessageBox.Show(theArray.GetLowerBound(0).ToString());
        MessageBox.Show(theArray.GetValue(2).ToString());
    }
```

INDEXERS

An indexer is a class member that allows an object to be referenced in the same way as an array using square brackets ([]). Since indexers use the square bracket array notation, they neither need nor have a name.

Listing 6.8 shows a class that contains an indexer. The class encapsulates a 42-element integer array, which is private to the class, and the indexer simply provides a means of saving or retrieving array values, providing that the index passed to the indexer is within the range of the array.

Listing 6.8: Creating a Class with an Indexer

```
class IAmAnIndexerClass {
    private int [] theArray = new int[42];

    //declare the indexer
    public int this [int ndx] {
        get {
            if (ndx < 0 || ndx >= 42)
                return 0;
            else
                return theArray [ndx];
        }
        set {
            if (!(ndx < 0 || ndx >= 42))
                theArray [ndx] = value;
        }
    }
}
```

Here's the indexer declaration:

```
public int this [int ndx] {
    ...
}
```

If you look at Listing 6.8, you'll see `get` and `set` accessors within the indexer—just like in a property statement.

To use the `IAmAnIndexerClass` class, an object of the type of the class must be instantiated:

```
IAmAnIndexerClass iaaio = new IAmAnIndexerClass();
```

As a demonstration, I'll use the `IAmAnIndexerClass` indexer to access *iaaio*—short for "I am an indexer object"—using array syntax. Each "element" in *iaaio* will be examined using a hypothetical web service named `IsPrime`. If the index of the element is a prime, then that prime is saved to the element; otherwise, the value of the element is left at the default, which is 0.

Before invoking the web service, you might want to turn the mouse pointer to an hourglass so that the user knows to expect a delay:

```
this.Cursor = Cursors.WaitCursors;
```

The service needs to be named and instantiated as *theService*:

```
theService.SybexC2Service theService =
    new theService.SybexC2Service();
```

Next, we can easily check whether a given integer is prime, and if it is, we can use the *iaaio* indexer to store the value:

```
for (int i = 0; i < 42 ; i++) {
    if (theService.IsPrime(i,0))
        iaaio [i] = i;
}
```

NOTE
The second argument sent to the `IsPrime` method represents a delay in seconds; this is irrelevant to the current task.

Once the calls to the web service have completed, the mouse pointer should be returned to the normal default:

```
this.Cursor = Cursors.Default;
```

Finally, we can do a bit of displaying to make sure this came out right. Since 23 is a prime and 24 is not, the value of `iaaio[23]` should be 23 and the value of `iaaio[24]` should be 0, as shown here.

The code for instantiating an object based on the class and accessing its members using the indexer is shown in Listing 6.9.

Listing 6.9: Instantiating an Object Based on the Indexer Class and Accessing Its Members Using Index Syntax

```
private void btnIndexer_Click(
  object sender, System.EventArgs e) {
    IAmAnIndexerClass iaaio = new IAmAnIndexerClass();
    this.Cursor = Cursors.WaitCursors;
    theService.SybexC2Service theService = new
      theService.SybexC2Service();
    for (int i = 0; i < 42 ; i++) {
      if (theService.IsPrime(i,0))
        iaaio [i] = i;
    }
    this.Cursor = Cursors.Default;
    MessageBox.Show("iaaio [23] is " +
      iaaio [23].ToString() + " and iaaio [24] is "
      + iaaio [24].ToString(), "Indexers",
      MessageBoxButtons.OK, MessageBoxIcon.Information);
}
```

COLLECTION CLASSES

In quite a few cases, structures that are based on classes other than System.Array will work better to organize groups of items for specific purposes. We'll have a look at working with objects based on some of these classes—ArrayList, Queue, Stack, and SortedList—in the remainder of this chapter. In the meantime, you should know that for the most part these classes appear in the System.Collections namespace (some of the classes that are based on Dictionary structures are located in the System.Collections.Specialized namespace).

As you can see in Figure 6.5, you can find out a great deal about these classes by pointing the Object Browser at System.Collections.

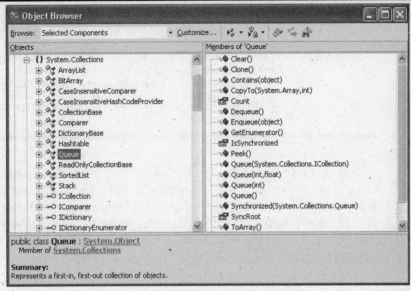

FIGURE 6.5: You can use the Object Browser to inspect the collection classes that are the members of `System.Collections`.

Table 6.3 describes some of the most useful collection classes. You should know that each one of these classes has quite a few members (properties and methods) that you will need to know about to successfully use the class. (Most of these classes have members comparable in extent and utility to the `Array` members shown in Tables 6.1 and 6.2.)

TABLE 6.3: Useful Collection Classes

CLASS	DESCRIPTION
ArrayList	Used to create an array-like structure whose size is dynamically altered as items are added and removed (see example later in this chapter).
CollectionBase	Provides the abstract base class for a collection. This means that the class cannot be instantiated, only inherited, and that it can contain abstract (or nonimplemented) members.
DictionaryBase	Provides the abstract base class for a dictionary-style collection of key/value pairs.
Hashtable	Used to create a collection of key/value pairs that are organized based on the hash code of the key.
Queue	Used to create a first in, first out collection of objects (see example later in this chapter).

TABLE 6.3 continued: Useful Collection Classes

CLASS	DESCRIPTION
SortedList	Used to create a collection of key/value pairs that are sorted by the keys and are accessible by key and by index—so it combines the features of an array with those of a dictionary (see example later in this chapter).
Stack	Used to create a last in, first out collection of objects (see example later in this chapter).

You can find out a lot about collection classes and class members using the Object Browser (and auto-completion in the Code Editor), but if you are programming an object based on one of these classes, you really should review the full list of the (copious) properties and methods by looking up the class name followed by the word *Members* in online help (for example, "ArrayList Members" or "Queue Members").

Collection Interfaces

An interface provides a binding contract with any class that uses the members specified in the interface. In other words, when a class implements an interface, it tells any object that uses the class that it will support the methods, properties, events, and indexers of the named interface.

This means that objects based on classes that implement the interface all work in the same, comfortable, familiar way.

Interfaces in the .NET Framework, by convention, start with a capital I— for example, IEnumerator. Internally, the syntax of an interface looks like the signatures for a bunch of methods, properties, and so on, without the implementation specifics for these members. Table 6.4 shows some of the interfaces implemented by the collection classes. In addition, if you need to implement a custom data structure, you should plan to implement at least some of these interfaces.

TABLE 6.4: Selected Collection Interfaces

INTERFACE	DESCRIPTION
ICollection	Defines size, enumerators, and synchronization methods for all collections
IComparer	Exposes a method that compares two objects

TABLE 6.4 continued: Selected Collection Interfaces

INTERFACE	DESCRIPTION
IDictionary	Represents a collection of key/value pairs
IDictionaryEnumerator	Enumerates the elements of a dictionary
IEnumerable	Exposes the enumerator, which supports a simple iteration over a collection
IEnumerator	Supports a simple iteration over a collection
IHashCodeProvider	Supplies a hash code for an object using a custom hash function
IList	Represents a collection of objects that can be individually accessed by an index

Stacks

A stack is a last in, first out (LIFO) collection of items. The most recent thing to go on the stack (in stack terminology, something that goes on a stack is said to be "pushed") is also the first to come off the stack ("popped").

NOTE

In addition to pushing and popping, stacks (and queues) support "peeking," which returns the object on top of the stack (or queue) without removing it from the stack. I'll show you how this works in the Queue demonstration.

An array can fairly easily be used to simulate a stack (or a queue), but why go to the trouble of doing this if the functionality you need is already built into the Stack class? The essential difference between stacks and queues on the one hand, and arrays and lists on the other, is that when you pop an item off the stack or queue, it goes away. Arrays don't normally work this way.

To demonstrate the System.Collections.Stack class, let's write an application that puts the current form of the mouse pointer (or cursor) on a stack. Here's how it will work: the user will be able to change the mouse pointer to a random pointer (referred to as the "current" mouse pointer). The current mouse pointer can always be pushed on the stack. When the stack is popped, the last pointer placed on it becomes the current mouse pointer.

Before we get started, you should know that the mouse pointer is set using a form's Cursor property, the default mouse pointer being indicated, naturally enough, by the Cursors enumeration value Default (for example, Form1.Cursor = Cursors.Default).

Our application will need

▶ A mechanism for choosing a new mouse pointer. This will be accomplished by randomly choosing a new enumeration value from the Cursors enumeration list.

▶ A way to push the stack to store the current mouse pointer.

▶ A way to pop the stack to make the mouse pointer on the top of the stack the current cursor.

Figure 6.6 shows the interface that will be used to accomplish this, with one button for each task.

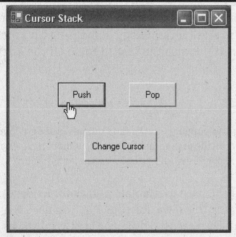

FIGURE 6.6:   The current cursor can be changed, placed on a stack, and
popped off the stack.

First let's look at Listing 6.10, which shows the click event that randomly selects a new cursor and assigns it to the form. This code declares an array of type Cursor named *acursor*, and loads it with all possible values of the Cursors enumeration. Next, a new Random object is created using a default seed value.

WARNING

The System.Random class generates pseudo-random numbers and should not be relied on to return truly random numbers in applications that involve things like cryptography.

With a Random object in place, its Next method is used to generate a random integer between 0 and 27 that is used to select an element (there are 28 members of the Cursors enumeration, so the *acursor* array index goes between 0 and 27). The selected element, which is of type Cursor, is then assigned to the form's current cursor.

Listing 6.10: Changing the Cursor to a Random Cursor

```
private void btnChange_Click(
  object sender, System.EventArgs e) {
    Cursor [] acursor = {
        Cursors.AppStarting, Cursors.Arrow,
        Cursors.Cross,        Cursors.Default,
        Cursors.Hand,         Cursors.Help,
        Cursors.HSplit,       Cursors.IBeam,
        Cursors.No,           Cursors.NoMove2D,
        Cursors.NoMoveHoriz,  Cursors.NoMoveVert,
        Cursors.PanEast,      Cursors.PanNE,
        Cursors.PanNorth,     Cursors.PanNW,
        Cursors.PanSE,        Cursors.PanSouth,
        Cursors.PanSW,        Cursors.PanWest,
        Cursors.SizeAll,      Cursors.SizeNESW,
        Cursors.SizeNS,       Cursors.SizeNWSE,
        Cursors.SizeWE,       Cursors.UpArrow,
        Cursors.VSplit,       Cursors.WaitCursor
    };
    Random rnd = new Random();
    Cursor cur = acursor[rnd.Next(27)];
    this.Cursor = cur;
}
```

It's actually really easy to push a cursor on the stack. First, a new Stack object needs to be instantiated, using the variable *curStack*:

```
Stack curStack = new Stack();
```

Next, this click event code pushes the current form mouse pointer onto the stack:

```
private void btnPush_Click(
    object sender, System.EventArgs e) {
    curStack.Push(this.Cursor);
}
```

Popping the stack is only slightly trickier. You need to make sure that something is actually on the stack—by using the curStack.Count property—before you try to pop:

```
private void btnPop_Click(
    object sender, System.EventArgs e) {
    if (curStack.Count > 0)
        this.Cursor = (Cursor) curStack.Pop();
    else
        MessageBox.Show("Nothing on the stack to pop!",
            "Too tired to pop!",
            MessageBoxButtons.OK, MessageBoxIcon.Exclamation);
}
```

The code for pushing and popping the stack is shown in Listing 6.11. If you run the demonstration application, you'll see that you can change the mouse pointer for a random new selection, place the current mouse pointer on the stack, and assign the mouse pointer on the top of the stack to the form. If you've popped everything off the stack—or there isn't anything on it to begin with—an error message will be displayed.

Listing 6.11: Pushing and Popping a Cursor on a Stack

```
...
Stack curStack = new Stack();

private void btnPush_Click(
    object sender, System.EventArgs e) {
    curStack.Push(this.Cursor);
}
```

```
  private void btnPop_Click(
    object sender, System.EventArgs e) {
    if (curStack.Count > 0)
      this.Cursor = (Cursor) curStack.Pop();
    else
      MessageBox.Show("Nothing on the stack to pop!",
      "Too tired to pop!", MessageBoxButtons.OK,
      MessageBoxIcon.Exclamation);
  }
  ...
```

Queues

Queues are just like stacks, except that the objects collected by them are first in, first out (FIFO). The metaphor is waiting in line or, as the British say, "on queue." The idea is that if you are the first one waiting for the ticket booth to open, you should be the first one able to buy tickets.

The Enqueue method puts an item on the queue. The Dequeue method returns (and removes) the item that is at the front of the queue, and the Peek method looks at the item at the front of the queue (without removing it from the queue).

As an example, let's set up a queue of strings. The user can use TextBoxes and Buttons to put a string on the queue (Enqueue), take the front string off the queue (Dequeue), or just have a quiet look at the front string (Peek).

To make this application a little clearer to follow, I've added a ListBox named *lstQ* and set its Enabled property to False in the Properties window. The contents of the queue are shown in this ListBox, which is updated every time an item is put on or taken off of the queue.

First, a Queue object needs to be declared and instantiated:

```
Queue theQueue = new Queue();
```

Here's the code to enqueue a string:

```
private void btnEnqueue_Click(
  object sender, System.EventArgs e) {
  theQueue.Enqueue(txtIn.Text);
  txtIn.Text = "";
  lstQ.Items.Clear();
  foreach (string s in theQueue) {
    lstQ.Items.Add(s);
  }
}
```

Dequeuing is pretty much the same thing, although (as you'd suspect) a check needs to be added to see that there is actually something on the queue:

```
private void btnDequeue_Click(
    object sender, System.EventArgs e) {
    if (theQueue.Count > 0) {
        txtOut.Text = (string) theQueue.Dequeue();
        lstQ.Items.Clear();
        foreach (string s in theQueue) {
            lstQ.Items.Add(s);
        }
    }
    else
        MessageBox.Show("Nothing on the queue to dequeue!",
            "No more waiting in line!", MessageBoxButtons.OK,
            MessageBoxIcon.Exclamation);
}
```

You should also note that the string value could be enqueued directly, but when it is dequeued, it needs to be cast to `string`, since items on the queue are maintained as type `object`.

TIP
You can implicitly cast from `string` to `object`, but not from `object` to `string`.

Peeking works like dequeuing:

```
private void btnPeek_Click(
    object sender, System.EventArgs e) {
    if (theQueue.Count > 0) {
        string str = (string) theQueue.Peek();
        MessageBox.Show("'"
            + str + "' is at the head of the queue!",
            "You peeked!", MessageBoxButtons.OK,
            MessageBoxIcon.Exclamation);
    }
    else
        MessageBox.Show("Nothing on the queue to peek at!",
            "You peeked!", MessageBoxButtons.OK,
            MessageBoxIcon.Exclamation);
}
```

It's time to compile and run the project. Next, enter a text string word by word in the Text In box—for example, "Able" "Was" "I" "Ere" "I" "Saw" "Elba". After you've entered the last word in your string, you can peek to make sure the first word is at the head of the queue (Figure 6.7).

FIGURE 6.7:   Peeking retrieves the object at the front of the queue without removing it from the queue.

Next, dequeue the first item ("Able"). If you peek now, you'll see that "Was" is now at the front of the queue (Figure 6.8).

Of course, if you keep dequeuing, pretty soon there will be nothing left "in line" to dequeue (Figure 6.9)—all the words must have bought their tickets!

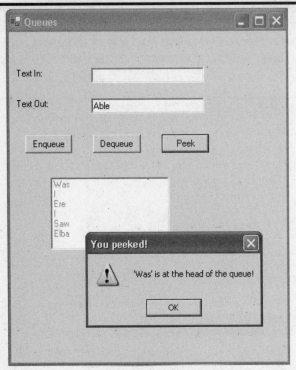

FIGURE 6.8:   With "Able" dequeued, peeking discloses that "Was" is at the front of the queue.

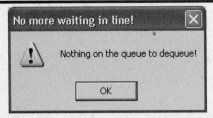

FIGURE 6.9:   It's important to check that something is on the queue before you attempt to dequeue (or peek).

The code for enqueuing, dequeuing, and peeking is shown in Listing 6.12.

Listing 6.12: Enqueuing, Dequeuing, and Peeking

```
...
Queue theQueue = new Queue();
```

```csharp
private void btnEnqueue_Click(
  object sender, System.EventArgs e) {
  theQueue.Enqueue(txtIn.Text);
  txtIn.Text = "";
  lstQ.Items.Clear();
  foreach (string s in theQueue) {
    lstQ.Items.Add(s);
  }
}


private void btnDequeue_Click(
  object sender, System.EventArgs e) {
  if (theQueue.Count > 0)
    txtOut.Text = (string) theQueue.Dequeue();
  else
    MessageBox.Show("Nothing on the queue to dequeue!",
        "No more waiting in line!", MessageBoxButtons.OK,
        MessageBoxIcon.Exclamation);
}


private void btnPeek_Click(
  object sender, System.EventArgs e) {
  if (theQueue.Count > 0) {
    string str = (string) theQueue.Peek();
    MessageBox.Show("'" + str +
      "' is at the head of the queue!",
      "You peeked!", MessageBoxButtons.OK,
      MessageBoxIcon.Exclamation);
  }
  else
    MessageBox.Show(
      "Nothing on the queue to peek at!", "You peeked!",
      MessageBoxButtons.OK, MessageBoxIcon.Exclamation);
}
...
```

The *ArrayList* Element

The ArrayList works like an array, except that it's dynamically resized depending on how many elements are actually stored in it.

TIP

VB6 programmers will welcome this functionality as comparable to the ReDim statement.

The demonstration application in this section shows you how to add and remove objects from an ArrayList, how to display a single element by index, and how to display all ArrayList elements.

Figure 6.10 shows the user interface (in design mode) that we'll use for this purpose.

Note that an ErrorProvider component has been added from the Toolbox to the "tray" at the bottom of the form. This ErrorProvider—in a (hopefully) profitable detour from the main topic of this section—will be used to check that user input in the Index TextBox really is a number.

To set this up, add the code shown in Listing 6.13 to the Validating event of the TextBox to check.

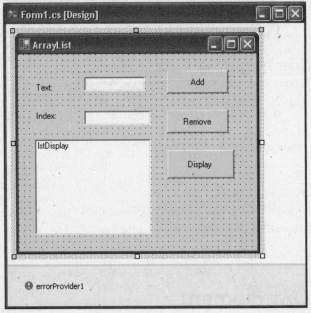

FIGURE 6.10:   In design mode, the ErrorProvider sits on the "tray" at the bottom of a form.

Listing 6.13: Using an *ErrorProvider* to Validate Numeric Input

```
private void txtIndex_Validating(object sender,
    System.ComponentModel.CancelEventArgs e) {
    try {
        int x = Int32.Parse(txtIndex.Text);
        errorProvider1.SetError(txtIndex, "");
    }
    catch {
        errorProvider1.SetError(txtIndex,
          "Requires an integer value!");
        txtIndex.Text = "0";
    }
}
```

If the user tries to enter nonnumeric data in this TextBox and then navigates away from the field, a red warning icon appears, and the error message specified in Listing 6.13 is displayed (see Figure 6.11). Next, the TextBox Text property is set in code to 0, presumably an innocuous value.

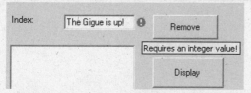

FIGURE 6.11: If the user input in the TextBox fails the validation—because it is a noninteger value—an error message is displayed.

The routine for working with the ArrayList should seem pretty familiar by now. First, an ArrayList object is instantiated:

```
ArrayList al = new ArrayList();
```

You'll find the code for adding a text element to the ArrayList, removing an element by index, displaying an element by index, and displaying all elements along with an ArrayList count, in Listing 6.14.

Listing 6.14: Adding, Removing, and Displaying the Items in an *ArrayList*

```
...
ArrayList al = new ArrayList();
```

```csharp
private void btnAdd_Click(
  object sender, System.EventArgs e) {
  al.Add(txtIn.Text);
  txtIn.Clear();
}

private void btnRemove_Click(object sender, System.EventArgs e) {
  int i;
  if (txtIndex.Text == "")
    i = 0;
  else
    i = Convert.ToInt32(txtIndex.Text);
  if (i >= 0 && i < al.Count) {
    al.RemoveAt(i);
    txtIndex.Clear();
  }
  else
    MessageBox.Show("Please try to keep within range!",
      "ArrayList Demo", MessageBoxButtons.OK,
      MessageBoxIcon.Information);
}

private void btnDisplay_Click(
  object sender, System.EventArgs e) {
  int i;
  if (txtIndex.Text == "")
    i = 0;
  else
    i = Convert.ToInt32(txtIndex.Text);
  if (i >= 0 && i < al.Count) {
    MessageBox.Show("Element " + txtIndex.Text +
      " of the ArrayList is " + al[i].ToString() +
      ".", "ArrayList Demo", MessageBoxButtons.OK,
      MessageBoxIcon.Information);
    txtIndex.Clear();
  }
  else
    MessageBox.Show("Please try to keep within range!",
      "ArrayList Demo", MessageBoxButtons.OK,
      MessageBoxIcon.Information);
}
```

```
private void btnDisAll_Click(
  object sender, System.EventArgs e) {
  for (int i = 0; i < al.Count; i++)
     lstDisplay.Items.Add(al[i]);
  lstDisplay.Items.Add("ARRAY COUNT IS: "
     + al.Count.ToString());
}
...
```

Run the application and play with it to verify that the ArrayList is resizing dynamically (Figure 6.12).

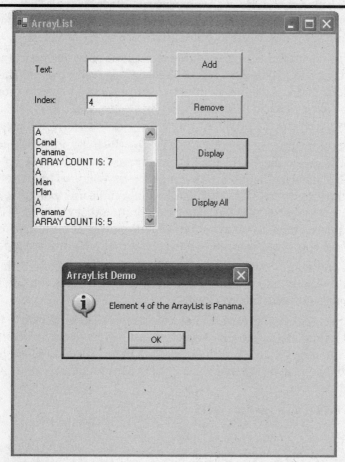

FIGURE 6.12: It's easy to dynamically resize ArrayLists.

Dictionaries

Dictionaries are structures that implement the IDictionary interface, providing for a collection of keys and values—the key is used to access the value. There are several dictionary classes that can be used, such as HashTable and SortedList in the System.Collections namespace; and HybridDictionary, ListDictionary, and StringDictionary in the System.Collections.Specialized namespace.

The *SortedList* Class

One of the more useful classes that implements IDictionary is SortedList. SortedList is actually kind of a crossbreed because it implements both dictionary key/value access and also array-style access by index.

The demonstration example in this section will show you how to save a text string and a color to a SortedList using key/value pairing. The text and color will then be retrieved from the SortedList and used to populate the Text and BackColor properties, respectively, of a form. I'll show you how to retrieve these values using indices as well as key/value pairs.

The user interface consists of a TextBox in which the user can enter the text; a button that opens the Color common dialog box (this dialog box is explained in Chapter 8, "Building a Better Windows Interface") in which the user can select a color; another button the user can use to save the choices to the SortedList; and a third button that will retrieve the values and use them to populate the properties of a new form (this user interface is shown in Figures 6.13 and 6.14 at the end of this section).

As a preliminary step, add a new Form to the project by selecting Project ➤ Add Windows Form, selecting Windows Form in the Add New Item dialog box, and clicking Open.

Next, in the original form and at the form class level, declare a Form variable, then instantiate the new Form, a ColorDialog variable, a Color variable initialized to the quaintly named Color.AliceBlue—which happens to be the first value in the Color enumeration—and the SortedList:

```
Form2 Form2 = new Form2();
private System.Windows.Forms.ColorDialog colorDialog1;
Color theColor = Color.AliceBlue;
SortedList sl = new SortedList();
```

Now implement the Color common dialog box—which also sets the background color of the button that invokes it—as follows:

```
private void btnColor_Click(
  object sender, System.EventArgs e) {
  colorDialog1.AllowFullOpen = true;
  colorDialog1.AnyColor = true;
  colorDialog1.ShowDialog();
  theColor = colorDialog1.Color;
  btnColor.BackColor = theColor;
}
```

Save the keys and values to the SortedList:

```
private void btnSave_Click(
  object sender, System.EventArgs e) {
  sl.Add("Text",txtText.Text);
  sl.Add("BackColor", theColor);
}
```

The only thing remaining for you to do is show the new form, retrieve the values, and use them to set the *Form2* properties. Here's how this would look if you were using the index features of the SortedList:

```
private void btnGet_Click(
  object sender, System.EventArgs e) {
  Form2.Show();
  Form2.BackColor = (Color) sl.GetByIndex(0);
  Form2.Text = sl.GetByIndex(1).ToString();
}
```

Note that the BackColor has to be cast to (Color) since—once again—it has been stored as simply an object. Similarly, the text value that has been saved as an object must be reconverted to a string.

Actually, I think that it's much more fun to use keys and values rather than an index, and anyhow, if you wanted to use an index, you'd have used an array in the first place. Here's how the procedure looks using the dictionary functionality of the SortedList:

```
private void btnGet_Click(
  object sender, System.EventArgs e) {
  Form2.Show();
  Form2.Text = sl["Text"].ToString();
  Form2.BackColor = (Color) sl["BackColor"];
}
```

Note once again that conversion and casting from object to string and Color is required.

Now it is time to run the project. Enter a text string in the TextBox and click the Choose Color button to open the Color dialog box (Figure 6.13).

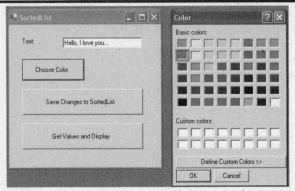

FIGURE 6.13:   The user enters text and a color via the common dialog box; these choices are then saved with appropriate keys to a SortedList.

Next, save the changes to the SortedList. Finally, click the third button to display the new form with the properties retrieved from the SortedList (Figure 6.14). Listing 6.15 illustrates how to use a SortedList to store and retrieve text and a color by key.

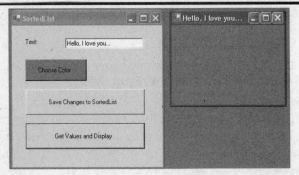

FIGURE 6.14:   User selections are retrieved by key from the SortedList and applied to a new form.

Listing 6.15: Using a *SortedList* to Store and Retrieve Text and a Color by Key

```
...
Form2 Form2 = new Form2();
private System.Windows.Forms.ColorDialog colorDialog1;
```

```
Color theColor = Color.AliceBlue;
SortedList sl = new SortedList();

private void btnColor_Click(
  object sender, System.EventArgs e) {
    colorDialog1.AllowFullOpen = true;
    colorDialog1.AnyColor = true;
    colorDialog1.ShowDialog();
    theColor = colorDialog1.Color;
    btnColor.BackColor = theColor;
}

private void btnSave_Click(
  object sender, System.EventArgs e) {
    sl.Add("Text", txtText.Text);
    sl.Add("BackColor", theColor);
}

private void btnGet_Click(
  object sender, System.EventArgs e) {
    Form2.Show();
    // Form2.Text = sl.GetByIndex(1).ToString();
    Form2.Text = sl["Text"].ToString();
    // Form2.BackColor = (Color) sl.GetByIndex(0);
    Form2.BackColor = (Color) sl["BackColor"];
}
...
```

SUMMARY

This chapter explained how to work with arrays and other structures, such as collections, stacks, and queues, to store groups of objects. This is not the most exciting topic in the universe, but it is very useful. Almost all programs use these structures. Choosing the proper structure to manipulate your data, and implementing it correctly, will go a long way toward assuring the soundness of your projects.

WHAT'S NEXT

Next, Chapter 7 covers the way that classes are organized into class libraries, and it discusses a way to enumerate available classes and their members at runtime using a process known as *reflection*.

Chapter 7
REFLECTING ON CLASSES

"**N**o man is an island," wrote seventeenth-century poet John Donne. This famous epigram equally applies to program code—it runs in a context, after compilation, on an operating system, and quite likely, it invokes run-time libraries of code. Certainly, this is true of C# .NET code, which uses the class libraries of the .NET Framework for functionality and can only run through the grace of the Common Language Runtime (CLR).

So far in this book, C# code has been presented basically as separate and apart—as an island, as it were. It's time to have a look at the connectedness of the C# programs that you write to the class libraries that make up the .NET Framework.

This chapter explores the organization of programs, internally and for deployment. I also explain reflection, which is used to glean information about the types that make up a compiled program; this information can be used dynamically while the program in question is running.

Adapted from *Visual C# .NET Programming* by Harold Davis
ISBN 0-7821-4046-7

How are the classes in the .NET Framework organized? I explain how to use the Object Browser, the best discovery tool for exploring the .NET Framework. When it comes time to deploy your own class libraries, following the design guidelines for .NET classes will help you organize for maximum usability.

ASSEMBLIES AND NAMESPACES

Assemblies are the fundamental unit for deployment, version control, security, and more, for a .NET application. In other words, assemblies are deployable units of code that correspond to stand-alone executable files or DLL libraries. Each compiled C# .NET program has at least one related assembly. Every time you build an executable (EXE) or a library (DLL) file in .NET, you are creating an assembly.

Namespaces are used to organize the classes within assemblies. Assemblies can contain many namespaces, which, in turn, can contain other namespaces. Namespaces are used to make it easier to refer to items, to avoid ambiguity, and to simplify references when large groups of classes are involved.

The Assembly Manifest

When you start a new C# project, it is the basis of an assembly. Within each built assembly is a *manifest,* as part of the executable or library. In C#, some of the general manifest information is contained in a file that is part of the project, named `AssemblyInfo.cs`. Figure 7.1 shows a small project in the Visual Studio Solution Explorer and shows the contents of a sample `AssemblyInfo.cs` file when it is opened with the Visual Studio editor.

The assembly manifest can be thought of as a "table of contents" for an application. It includes the following information:

▶ The assembly's name and version number

▶ A file table, listing and describing the files that make up the assembly

▶ An assembly reference list, which is a catalog of external dependencies

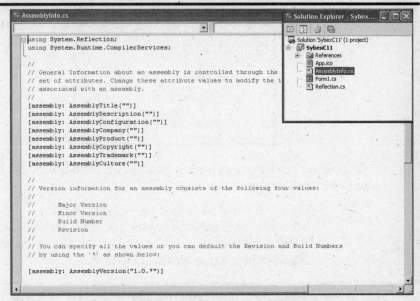

FIGURE 7.1: Each C# .NET project includes a file that forms the basis of the assembly manifest. The manifest carries information about content, version, and dependencies so that C# .NET applications don't depend on Registry values.

The external dependencies in the assembly reference list may be library files created by someone else, and it's likely that some of them are part of the .NET Framework.

Assembly References

To use an assembly, or a class within an assembly, the assembly must be referenced in your project. Depending on the type of project, you'll find that many of the assemblies that are part of the .NET Framework are referenced by default.

Different project types have different default references. The references that come "out of the box" for a Windows forms project are not the same as those for a web forms project, although both do reference certain important .NET assemblies such as System.dll.

You can see which assemblies are already referenced in a project by expanding the References node in the Solution Explorer.

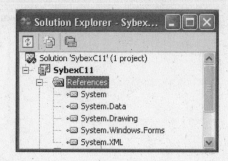

If you need to reference an assembly that is not already included in your project, follow these steps:

1. Select Project ➤ Add Reference. (Alternatively, select the References node in Solution Explorer. Right-click, and select Add Reference from the context menu.) The Add Reference dialog box will open, as shown in Figure 7.2.

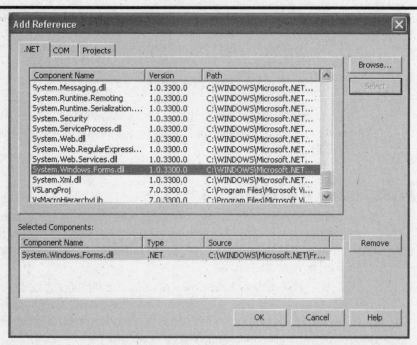

FIGURE 7.2: The Add Reference dialog box is used to add a reference to a project.

2. Select a .NET assembly to add (listed in the Component Name column of the .NET tab).

3. Click the Select button to add the assembly to the Selected Components list (shown at the bottom of Figure 7.2).

4. Click OK to add the reference to the .NET component.

Alternatively, if the assembly you want to add a reference to does not appear on the .NET tab, click the Browse button in the upper-right corner of the Add Reference dialog. The Select Component dialog will open. Locate the assembly to be added and click Open. The assembly will be added to the Selected Components panel of the Add Reference dialog box. Click OK to add the reference to your project.

Namespaces

If you drill down one step below the assembly level, you'll find that the members of a given assembly are namespaces. Another way of putting this is that namespaces are the internal organization of the classes defined in an assembly. For example, Microsoft.CSharp is a namespace that is part of the System assembly. It contains classes that support compilation and code generation using the C# language. (What can get a little confusing is that sometimes a namespace and an assembly can have the same name.)

By default, every executable file you create in C# .NET contains a namespace with the same name as your project, although you can change this default name.

You should also know that namespaces can span multiple assemblies. In other words, if two assemblies both define classes within a namespace myNameSpace, then myNameSpace is treated as a single set of names.

The .NET Framework uses a dot operator (.) syntax to designate hierarchies. Related types are grouped into namespaces, so that they can be more easily found. Reading left to right, the first part of a type, up to the first dot, is the namespace name. The last part of the name, to the right of the final period, is the type name. For example System.Boolean designates a Boolean value-type in the System namespace. System .Windows.Forms.MessageBox designates the MessageBox class within the Forms namespace, which is part of the Windows namespace, that is part of System.

As these examples suggest, the System namespace is the root namespace for all types within the .NET Framework. All base data types used by all applications are included in the System namespace or the Microsoft namespace.

One of the most important types within the System namespace is System.Object, also called the Object class. This class is the root of the .NET type hierarchy and the ultimate parent (or *superclass*) of all classes in the .NET Framework. This implies that the members of the Object class—such as GetType() and ToString()—are contained in all .NET classes.

Namespace Directives

You have several ways of referring to an object based on a class within a namespace once the assembly containing the class you are interested in has been referenced.

The *using* Directive   You can use the *fully qualified* name of the item, as in this variable declaration for *btnClear*:

```
private System.Windows.Forms.Button btnClear;
```

Alternatively, you can place a using *namespace* directive at the beginning of a code module, as shown here:

```
using System.Windows.Forms;
```

After you add a using directive, all of the names in the imported namespace can be used (provided they are unique to your project), like this:

```
private Button btnClear;
```

NOTE
The using System directive will automatically be included in most C# modules. This means that you don't have to explicitly invoke System: Windows .Forms.Button btnClear will mean the same thing as System .Windows.Forms.Button btnClear.

The Alias Directive   An alias namespace directive allows a program to use its own, internally assigned, shorthand name for a namespace (or a namespace plus a type belonging to the namespace). This can save you a great deal of typing of long, qualified namespaces, possibly followed by types—and it can help make your code clearer.

Here's how it works. If you add an identifier and an assignment to the using directive, then the identifier can be used in place of the assigned namespace (and type). For example,

```
using swfb = System.Windows.Forms.Button;
```

Given this directive, a corresponding variable declaration for a variable named *btnClear* of type Button could look like this:

```
private swfb btnClear;
```

Creating Namespaces

It's truly easy to create a namespace. The keyword namespace is followed by an identifier that is the name of the namespace. Curly braces enclose the contents of the namespace—meaning, the members of the namespace (see the following section). Namespaces can be nested within each other.

Listing 7.1 shows an example of namespaces nested three levels deep containing a single class. The class contains a single static method that displays a message box (because the method is static, there's no need to instantiate an object based on the class to use it).

Listing 7.1: Nested Namespaces

```
// Namespaces.cs
using System;
using swf = System.Windows.Forms;
namespace noman {
    namespace isan {
        namespace island {
            public class theClass {
                public theClass() {
                // No constructor code
                }
                public static void bellTolls (string inStr){
                    swf.MessageBox.Show(
                        "The bell tolls for " + inStr + "!",
                        "For thee...", swf.MessageBoxButtons.OK,
                        swf.MessageBoxIcon.Exclamation);
                }
            }
        }
    }
}
```

The static method shown in Listing 7.1 can easily be invoked. For example, from within a form module button's click event, in the same project as the nested namespaces code module, the following will do the trick:

```
private void btnGreeting_Click(
    object sender, System.EventArgs e) {
      noman.isan.island.theClass.bellTolls("Dolly");
}
```

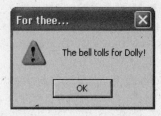

NOTE

If the namespace code is compiled in an assembly external to the code trying to invoke the method, then a reference to the assembly must be added to the calling project.

Namespace Members

Namespaces are at the pinnacle of the tree of C# language elements. Namespaces can encapsulate other namespaces (as shown in Listing 7.1), but no other language element can encapsulate a namespace. So one way of answering the question of what can go in a namespace is, everything. Somewhat more formally, namespace blocks may contain:

- ▶ Other namespaces
- ▶ Classes
- ▶ Delegates
- ▶ Enumerations
- ▶ Interfaces
- ▶ Structs
- ▶ using and alias directives

NOTE

If you've forgotten what some of these constructs are, you can review them in Chapter 2, "Zen and Now: The C# Language."

.NET NAMESPACES

Some of the built-in namespaces that are likely to be most important to C# .NET programmers are described in Table 7.1.

TABLE 7.1:   Important .NET Namespaces

NAMESPACE	DESCRIPTION
Microsoft.CSharp	Supports compilation and code generation using the C# language.
System	Contains fundamental classes that define types, arrays, strings, events, event handlers, exceptions, interfaces, data-type conversion, mathematics, application environment management, and much more.
System.Collections	Includes a set of classes that lets you manage collections of objects, such as lists, queues, arrays, hash tables, and dictionaries.
System.Data	Consists mainly of the classes that compose the ADO.NET architecture.
System.Diagnostics	Provides classes used for debugging, tracing, and interacting with system processes, event logs, and performance counters.
System.Drawing	Contains classes that provide access to GDI+ basic graphics functionality (namespaces that are hierarchically beneath System.Drawing—including System.Drawing.Drawing2D and System.Drawing.Text—provide more advanced and specific GDI+ graphics functionality).
System.IO	Contains types and classes used for reading from and writing to data streams and files, and general input/output (I/O) functionality.
System.Reflection	Contains classes and interfaces that provide type inspection and the ability to dynamically bind objects.
System.Reflection.Emit	Generates assemblies on the fly.
System.Text	Contains classes used for character encoding, converting blocks of characters to and from blocks of bytes, and more.
System.Text.Regular Expressions	Contains classes that provide access to the .NET Framework regular expression engine.

TABLE 7.1 continued: Important .NET Namespaces

NAMESPACE	DESCRIPTION
System.Timer	Provides the Timer component (see the section "Round Buttons Dancing" in Chapter 8, "Building a Better Windows Interface," for an example using the Timer).
System.Web	Contains the classes that are used to facilitate browser-server communication and other web-related functionality.
System.Web.Services	Contains the classes used to build and consume web services.
System.Web.UI	Provides classes and interfaces used in the creation of the user interface of web pages and controls.
System.Windows.Forms	Contains the classes for creating a Windows-based user interface.
System.XML	Provides classes that support processing XML.

REFLECTION

Reflection is the ability to use the metadata provided by a program to gather information about its types. The example in this section will show you how to use reflection to gather type and member information about compiled .NET assemblies. The information you can gather is not as extensive or as convenient to use as that provided by the Object Browser tool that ships with Visual Studio, which is explained later in this chapter. However, with the ability to gather information about the internal program elements of compiled code on the fly, a great deal of advanced functionality becomes possible, including automated and dynamic code and assembly generation, dynamic "late bound" run-time determination of what code needs to be executed, and automated code documenters.

To see how reflection works, let's create a Windows forms application that will open and "inspect" any .NET assembly (.exe or .dll file). The application will provide an Open button. When the user clicks this button, the OpenFileDialog will allow the choice of a file for reflection. Clicking Open in the common dialog box displays the selected file in a TextBox. When the Perform Reflection button is clicked, the types in the selected file are displayed in a Types ListBox. When a type, or class, is selected, and the user clicks the Get Type Info button, the constructors, fields, methods, properties, and events for the type are displayed in respective ListBoxes. This user interface is shown in design mode in Figure 7.3.

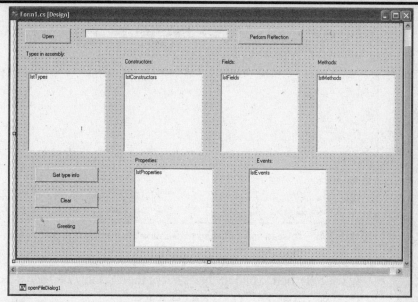

FIGURE 7.3: The form has a ListBox for types in an assembly and separate ListBoxes for each kind of member of a type.

NOTE

Working with ListBoxes and the common dialog box controls will be further explained in Chapter 8.

Here's the code that displays the Open dialog box and loads the user's choice into the TextBox:

```
private void btnOpen_Click(
  object sender, System.EventArgs e) {
    openFileDialog1.InitialDirectory =
      Application.ExecutablePath;
    openFileDialog1.DefaultExt = "exe";
    openFileDialog1.Filter =
      "Executable (*.exe)|*.exe|DLL (*.dll)|*.dll";
    openFileDialog1.ShowDialog();
    txtFileToOpen.Text =openFileDialog1.FileName;
}
```

The user can now select any .NET assembly to examine—including the running file, as shown in the Open dialog box depicted in Figure 7.4.

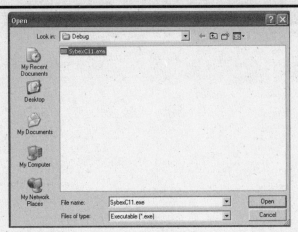

FIGURE 7.4:   You can use reflection to examine the metadata of the program that is running.

To use reflection to pull the types out of the assembly, first add a directive to use the System.Reflection namespace:

```
using System.Reflection;
```

Next, within the form class, declare an array (named *typeArray*) to hold the type information and a variable, *theAssembly*, of type System .Reflection.Assembly:

```
Type[] typeArray;
Assembly theAssembly;
```

When the user clicks Perform Reflection, *theAssembly* is set to the file selected by the user using the Assembly.LoadFrom method, and the Assembly.GetTypes method is used to load the types in the assembly into *typeArray*. The elements of the array are then added to the Type ListBox (see Figure 7.5):

```
private void btnReflect_Click(
    object sender, System.EventArgs e) {
    theAssembly = Assembly.LoadFrom(txtFileToOpen.Text);
    GetTypeInfo(theAssembly);
}
private void GetTypeInfo(Assembly theAssembly){
    typeArray = theAssembly.GetTypes();
    foreach (Type type in typeArray) {
        lstTypes.Items.Add(type.FullName);
    }
}
```

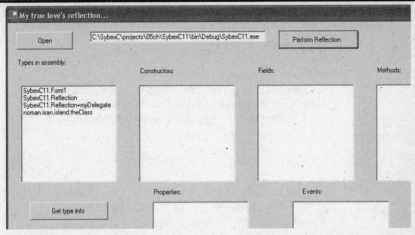

FIGURE 7.5:   The types, or classes, within the assembly are displayed.

So far, this is great! We've used reflection to display the types in an assembly. The next step is to let the user choose a type, by selecting it in the Types ListBox. When the user clicks Get Type Info, the members of the type will be displayed in the appropriate ListBox.

But, before we get started with this, we probably should make sure that the ListBoxes we are going to use are empty so that the type information for only one assembly is displayed. To do this, I've created some code to loop through all the ListBoxes on the form (rather than clearing them by name):

```
private void btnGetTypeInfo_Click(
    object sender, System.EventArgs e) {
    // Clear the ListBoxes except lstTypes
    foreach (object o in this.Controls) {
        if (o is ListBox) {
            ListBox lb = (ListBox) o;
            if (!(lb.Name == "lstTypes"))
                lb.Items.Clear();
        }
    }
    ...
```

Continuing with the reflection, here's the code that checks to see whether a type is selected, uses the System.Reflection.Type[].GetMethods method to retrieve the methods for the type, and then displays them by adding them to the Methods ListBox (I'm showing method reflection here, but if you look below at the complete code for the Get Type Info procedure, you'll see that the other kinds of members are reflected as well):

```
if (lstTypes.Text != ""){
    ...
    MethodInfo[] theMethods =
        typeArray[lstTypes.SelectedIndex].GetMethods();
        foreach (MethodInfo method in theMethods) {
            lstMethods.Items.Add(method.ToString());
        }
    ...
}
else {
    MessageBox.Show("Please select a type for further info!",
        "Nothing Selected!", MessageBoxButtons.OK,
        MessageBoxIcon.Information);
}
```

Listing 7.2 shows the complete code for generating member information—that is, information about constructors, fields, properties, methods, and events—about types in an assembly using reflection. Listing 7.3 shows a class module, SybexC11.Reflection, that I added to the reflection project to simply show a variety of type members. You'll see these members "reflected" in Figure 7.6.

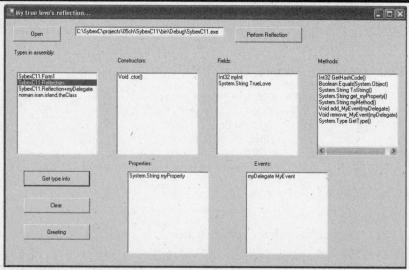

FIGURE 7.6: Member information for a type is displayed.

Listing 7.2: Displaying Types and Members Using Reflection

```csharp
// Form1.cs
...
using System.Reflection;
...
public class Form1 : System.Windows.Forms.Form
{
...
Type[] typeArray;
Assembly theAssembly;
...
    private void btnOpen_Click(
      object sender, System.EventArgs e) {
      openFileDialog1.InitialDirectory =
        Application.ExecutablePath;
      openFileDialog1.DefaultExt = "exe";
      openFileDialog1.Filter =
        "Executable (*.exe)|*.exe|DLL (*.dll)|*.dll";
      openFileDialog1.ShowDialog();
      txtFileToOpen.Text =openFileDialog1.FileName;
    }

    private void btnReflect_Click(
      object sender, System.EventArgs e) {
      theAssembly = Assembly.LoadFrom(txtFileToOpen.Text);
      GetTypeInfo(theAssembly);

    }
    private void GetTypeInfo(Assembly theAssembly){
      typeArray = theAssembly.GetTypes();
      foreach (Type type in typeArray) {
          lstTypes.Items.Add(type.FullName);
      }
    }

    private void btnGetTypeInfo_Click(
      object sender, System.EventArgs e) {
      // Clear the ListBoxes except lstTypes
      foreach (object o in this.Controls) {
          if (o is ListBox) {
```

```
            ListBox lb = (ListBox) o;
            if (!(lb.Name == "lstTypes"))
                lb.Items.Clear();
        }
    }

    if (lstTypes.Text != ""){
        ConstructorInfo[] theConstructors =
            typeArray[
            lstTypes.SelectedIndex].GetConstructors();
        foreach (ConstructorInfo constructor
          in theConstructors){
            lstConstructors.Items.Add(
                constructor.ToString());
        }
        FieldInfo[] theFields =
         typeArray[lstTypes.SelectedIndex].GetFields();
        foreach (FieldInfo field in theFields) {
            lstFields.Items.Add(field.ToString());
        }
        MethodInfo[] theMethods =
            typeArray[lstTypes.SelectedIndex].GetMethods();
        foreach (MethodInfo method in theMethods) {
            lstMethods.Items.Add(method.ToString());
        }
        PropertyInfo[] theProps =
            typeArray[
            lstTypes.SelectedIndex].GetProperties();
        foreach (PropertyInfo prop in theProps) {
            lstProperties.Items.Add(prop.ToString());
        }
        EventInfo[] theEvents =
         typeArray[lstTypes.SelectedIndex].GetEvents();
        foreach (EventInfo anEvent in theEvents) {
            lstEvents.Items.Add(anEvent.ToString());
        }

    }
```

```
        else {
            MessageBox.Show(
                "Please select a type for further info!",
                "Nothing Selected!", MessageBoxButtons.OK,
                MessageBoxIcon.Information);
        }
    }
    ...
}
```

Listing 7.3: A Class with Members to Demonstrate Reflection

```
// Reflection.cs
using System;
namespace SybexC11
{
    public class Reflection
    {
        public int myInt;
        public string TrueLove;
        public Reflection()
        {

        }
        public string myProperty {
            get {
                return "reflection";
            }
        }
        public static string myMethod() {
            return "True love";
        }
        public delegate string myDelegate();

        public event myDelegate MyEvent =
            new myDelegate(myMethod);
    }
}
```

NOTE

The code in Listing 7.3 uses the `ToString()` method to simply display information about each member. You'll find quite a bit of additional programmatic capabilities in the `System.Reflection` namespace.

Of course, you can also turn the reflection spotlight on the form module itself in the project. Before we do, let's add some class-level variable declarations and assignments (these will show up as fields):

```
...
public class Form1 : System.Windows.Forms.Form
{
    ...
    public string myTrueLove = "Phyllis";
    public bool isTheFairest = true;
```

When you run the application now, you'll see these fields as well as the standard form methods, properties, and events (Figure 7.7).

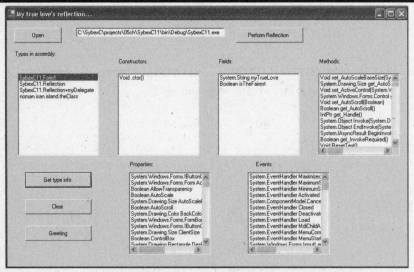

FIGURE 7.7:   Variables declared at the form's class level appear as fields; all form methods, properties, and events are displayed in the appropriate ListBoxes.

The reflection application can be used to inspect the assemblies that are part of the .NET Framework, as shown in Figure 7.8.

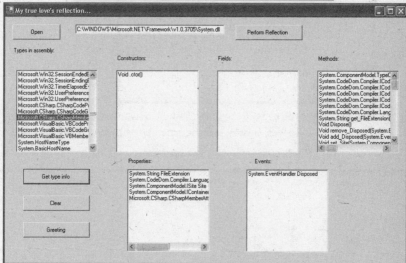

FIGURE 7.8:   Select System.dll, a key class of the .NET Framework (top), and
click Open. All the types in the assembly will be displayed (bottom).

TRACKING MEMBERS WITH THE CLASS VIEW WINDOW

Visual Studio's Class View window (Figure 7.9) is an excellent way to
keep track of namespaces, classes, and class members within a project.

To open the Class View window, select View ➤ Class View. The Class
View window can also be opened by clicking a button on the Visual Studio
toolbar (Figure 7.10).

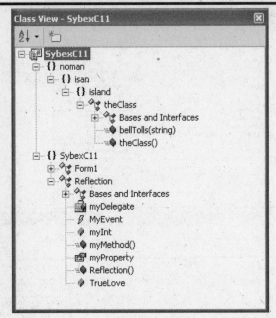

FIGURE 7.9:   You can use the Class View window to understand how namespaces, classes, and their members are structured in a project.

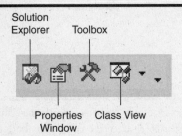

FIGURE 7.10:   The Class View window can be conveniently opened using a
toolbar icon.

With a member of a class selected in the Class View window, if you
right-click, a context menu appears. From this context menu, Go To
Definition takes you to the code that declares the member (opening the
Code Editor if necessary). Go To Reference takes you to the first use of
the member. And Browse Definition opens the Object Browser with the
member loaded (Figure 7.11).

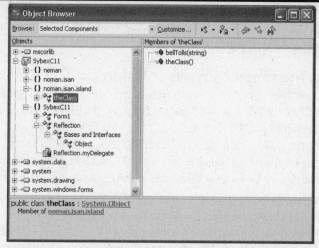

FIGURE 7.11: By choosing Browse Definition with a member selected in the Class View window, the Object Browser will open, displaying the member's definition.

NAVIGATING WITH THE OBJECT BROWSER

The Object Browser lets you determine the members of .NET objects or classes, and the relationships of objects to each other. You can easily use the Object Browser to learn about the objects available for use in your programs.

The Object Browser also teaches about the structure of the .NET Framework. You can use it to discern the hierarchy of classes, members of classes, as well as the properties, events, and methods of each object.

Thus, the Object Browser is a tool of discovery, rather than a tool you use to actually do anything. But it's probably the single most important discovery tool included in the Visual Studio .NET development environment.

Opening the Object Browser

To open the Object Browser, use one of the following methods:

▶ Select View ➤ Other Windows ➤ Object Browser from the Visual Studio menu.

▶ Highlight a member in the Class View window, right-click, and choose Browse Definition.

▶ Press the keyboard shortcut, Ctrl+Alt+J.

▶ In the Code Editor, place the cursor on a .NET object, right-click, and choose Go To Definition.

Opening the Object Browser Using Go To Definition

When you open the Object Browser from the Code Editor (by choosing Go To Definition from a .NET object's context menu), the Object Browser will open with the highlighted object defined. Note that this does not work if the cursor is hovering over a variable or keyword. In the case of a keyword, Go To Definition does nothing. In the case of a variable, method, or procedure or functional call, Go To Definition takes you to the declaration for the object.

For example, suppose you have a component in your project named *openFileDialog1* of type System.Windows.Forms.OpenFileDialog. With the cursor over the statement using *openFileDialog1*, right-click and select Go To Definition. You will be taken to the declaration for *openFileDialog1* at the beginning of the module. Likely, this declaration was generated for you when you added the OpenFileDialog control to your form. It's probably along these lines:

```
private System.Windows.Forms.OpenFileDialog openFileDialog1;
```

If you move the cursor to OpenFileDialog at the end of this declaration statement, and then you select Go To Definition again, the Object Browser will open to the definition of the OpenFileDialog class, as shown in Figure 7.12.

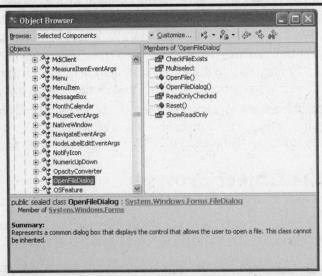

FIGURE 7.12: The class definition of an object is shown in the Object Browser.

Using the Object Browser Interface

The Object Browser interface consists of a toolbar and three panes: the Objects pane, the Members pane, and the Description pane. Figure 7.13 shows the full Object Browser interface, with information for the MessageBox class.

Objects pane   Toolbar

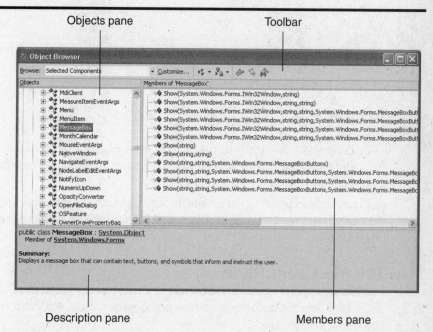

Description pane   Members pane

FIGURE 7.13:   The Members pane shows the members of an object selected in the Objects pane, and the Description pane provides information about the selected object.

The Objects Pane

The Objects pane provides a hierarchical view of the objects (or classes) contained in the namespaces that are within the scope of the Object Browser. Here is an example of the Objects pane with System.Drawing .Color selected and some of the members of Color visible in the Members pane.

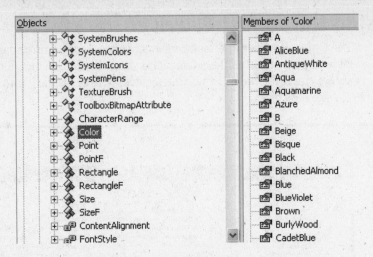

Clicking the + or – icons in the Objects pane expands or contracts the tree view of objects. (Color is a member of System.Drawing, so expanding System.Drawing shows the Color class.)

If you fully expand an object in the Objects pane, a great deal about the object—such as the classes that it is based on—will be displayed in the Objects pane.

The Members Pane

The Members pane shows the members of an object selected in the Objects pane. *Members* means properties, methods, events, variables, constants, and enumeration values.

A different icon indicates each different kind of member. In addition, one other icon, a key, means the member is protected, or only accessible from within its own class (or a derived class).

The Description Pane

The Description pane provides a great deal of information about the object currently selected in the Objects pane. This information isn't the same for all objects, but it usually includes the following:

- ▶ A description of the object
- ▶ The name of the object and its parent object
- ▶ The object syntax
- ▶ Links to related objects and members

NOTE

The links in the Description pane take you to objects that are related to the selected object. They are immensely valuable for quickly gathering information about an object.

The Toolbar

The Object Browser toolbar is used to customize the Object Browser scope, arrange the contents of the Object Browser, navigate, and find identifiers (such as object names, but called *symbols* here).

SETTING THE OBJECT BROWSER SCOPE

When the Object Browser opens, you have a choice regarding the *scope* of the browser (or which objects it will see). The two scope options are available in the Browse drop-down list in the upper-left corner of the Object Browser. Selected Components is the default initial selection. You can customize the objects included in this scope.

The other scope option is Active Project, which includes the active project and its references (for example, System, and, in the case of a form-based application, System.Windows.Forms). The Active Project setting does not allow any customization of the objects that can be browsed. (But you could go back to the project and add or remove a reference in the Solution Explorer.)

To customize the objects included within the Selected Components scope of the Object Browser, click the Customize button to the right of the Browse drop-down list.

Click the Add button in the Selected Components dialog to open the Component Selector dialog. You can use the Component Selector to choose .NET and COM components to add. To add other projects, executables, and other types of files (such as OLB or TLB type libraries or dynamic link libraries), click the Browse button. Components added to the Selected Components box at the bottom of the Component Selector will appear in the Selected Components dialog and, if checked, will be available to browse in the Object Browser.

It's likely that the most useful toolbar button is the Find Symbol (the button with the binoculars icon). When you click the Find Symbol button, the dialog shown in Figure 7.14 opens.

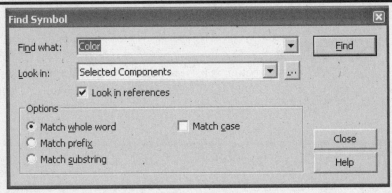

FIGURE 7.14:   The Find Symbol dialog box lets you search for objects using the object's name.

The Find Symbol dialog box allows you to search for objects including namespaces, classes, and structures—and the members of these objects—using the object's name.

NOTE

Obviously, using the Object Browser tools such as the Find Symbol dialog box is the easiest way to locate specific objects within the Object Browser. But pure recreational browsing can teach you a great deal about the way .NET is structured, how to work with it, and even the best way to construct your own object hierarchies (for more on this, see the next section).

CREATING A CLASS LIBRARY

Now that you've seen how to inspect the class libraries that are part of the .NET Framework, let's walk through the process of creating your own class library. The class library will contain a single class, which will, in turn, contain a field, a property, a method, and an event. The point of this is to be very bare bones. These class members will not be fancy.

After I've shown you how to create each of these members, I'll show you how to use them from a Windows forms project.

To start with, use the New Project dialog box to create a Class Library project by selecting Visual C# Projects in the Project Types pane and Class Library in the Templates pane, and giving the project a name (Figure 7.15).

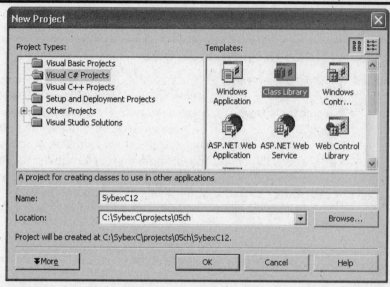

FIGURE 7.15: A new project can be opened to serve as the basis for a class library.

When the project opens, it will have a class code module containing (by default) the project name as the namespace and a class named Class1. Our class will be the template representing a baby, and the objects based on the class will be specific babies.

If we keep the namespace, change the class name to Baby to reflect the kinds of objects that will be created based on the class, and remove the class constructor—since we're not going to be using it—we'll now have a code module that looks like this:

```
using System;

namespace SybexC12
{
    public class Baby
    {

    }
}
```

NOTE

It probably goes without saying, but let's say it anyhow: the order of members within a class does not matter.

THE .NET DESIGN GUIDELINES

Getting familiar with the Class View and Object Browser tools is a very good thing! There's also no doubt that it will pay for you to become familiar with the organization, structure, and way of doing things that goes with the classes in the .NET Framework since successful .NET programming largely involves working with these classes. But the biggest payoff is in improved usability of your own classes and class libraries. To the extent that you pattern these after the .NET structure, you will be doing things in the way that other developers expect—and they will find your work accessible and understandable.

By following the .NET Framework design guidelines, your code libraries will behave in a predictable and familiar way—cutting down on maintenance effort and making it easier for others to use your libraries, even if they don't have access to the source code.

To view the .NET design guidelines, search the online help for "Design Guidelines for Class Library Developers." This document functions as a table of contents for class library design topics, and it touches on many more areas than will be covered in this section. (You should particularly have a look at "Naming Guidelines," which explains the .NET suggested naming conventions for types in class libraries.)

Adding a Field

A field is simply a variable declared at the class level using the `public` keyword. Since each baby object has a name, let's reflect that fact by giving the Baby class a Name field:

```
...
public class Baby
{
    public string Name = "";
    ...
```

Adding a Property

Properties differ from fields, since *accessor* get and set methods serve as a kind of "gatekeeper" for access to the value contained in the property.

Let's add an Age property to the Baby class. The first step is to declare a private variable to hold the property value internally (in the example, it is initialized to 0):

```
private int m_Age = 0;
```

Next, a property procedure is used to provide read—using the get accessor—and write—using the set accessor—access to the property:

```
public int Age {
    get {
        return m_Age;
    }
    set {
        m_Age = value;
    }
}
```

The property is set using the special keyword value. If you want to, you can make the property read-only or write-only by only including a get or set accessor function, respectively. You can also include validation code within the property procedures—or, as you'll see in a moment, raise (meaning "fire" or "trigger") an event when a property value is changed.

Adding a Method

A method is simply a public function belonging to the class. Here's one that returns a sound often made by baby objects:

```
public string GetSound() {
    return "Waaah!";
}
```

Adding an Event

To raise an event in the Baby class, we must first declare a *delegate,* which is a type that defines a method signature—meaning a method's arguments, their types, and the method return type. A delegate instance can hold and invoke a method (or methods) that matches its signature.

In turn, the class declares the event by applying the event keyword to a delegate.

Here are the delegate and event declarations for an OnBirthDay event:

```
public delegate void
    BirthDayEventHandler (object sender, System.EventArgs e);
public event BirthDayEventHandler OnBirthDay;
```

It remains to raise the event, which is done by calling the OnBirthDay method with the arguments indicated in the related delegate's signature.

In our Baby class, let's raise the OnBirthDay method when the Age property changes so that it is greater than it was (since it is an integer field, this presumably means that the baby object is a year older). We can do this from within the Age property set method, as follows:

```
...
set {
    if (value > m_Age) {
        // Raise the event
        if (OnBirthDay != null) {
            System.EventArgs e = new System.EventArgs();
            OnBirthDay(this, e);
        }
    }
    m_Age = value;
}
...
```

The conditional OnBirthDay != null checks to see that something is using, or, in the lingo, *subscribing to* the event—otherwise there is no point in firing it. Assuming that the event has subscribers, it is then raised. By the way, the two lines of code

```
System.EventArgs e = new System.EventArgs();
OnBirthDay(this, e);
```

could be rewritten for compactness (although not for clarity):

```
OnBirthDay(this, new System.EvenetArgs());
```

OK. Let's go ahead and build the class library (Build ➢ Build Solution). The next step will be to open a new Windows forms project with the purpose of instantiating a baby object based on the Baby class and invoking the class methods. In the meantime, Listing 7.4 shows the complete code in the Baby class, with a few comments added for clarity.

Listing 7.4: The *Baby* Class

```csharp
using System;

namespace SybexC12
{
    public class Baby
    {
        // Field
        public string Name = "";

        // Private variable for property
        private int m_Age = 0;

        // Property
        public int Age {
            get {
                return m_Age;
            }
            set {
                if (value > m_Age) {
                    // Raise the event
                    if (OnBirthDay != null) {
                        System.EventArgs e =
                            new System.EventArgs();
                        OnBirthDay(this, e);
                    }
                }
                m_Age = value;
            }
        }

        // Method
        public string GetSound(){
            return "Waaah!";
        }

        // Event declarations
        public delegate void
            BirthDayEventHandler(object sender,
            System.EventArgs e);
        public event BirthDayEventHandler OnBirthDay;
    }
}
```

Invoking the Class Members

Open a new Windows forms project. The first step is to add a reference to the SybexC12 assembly so that we can instantiate an object based on the Baby class contained in that assembly. To do so, as explained earlier in this chapter, open the Add Reference dialog box (Project ➢ Add Reference), and click the Browse button in its upper-right corner. In the Select Component dialog box, shown in Figure 7.16, locate SybexC12 and click Open.

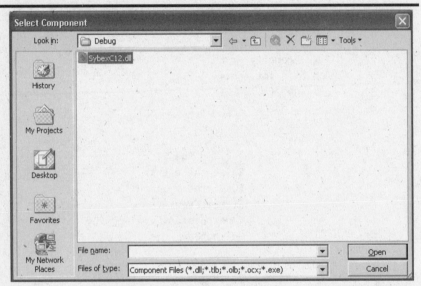

FIGURE 7.16:   The Select Component dialog box, opened from the Add Reference dialog box, is used to locate the assembly containing the class library.

The SybexC12.dll assembly, which contains the Baby class library, now appears in the Selected Components pane of the Add Reference dialog box (Figure 7.17). Click OK to add the reference.

The reference to the SybexC12.Baby class library has now been added to the project. If you open the Object Browser, you'll easily be able to find the Baby class members (Figure 7.18).

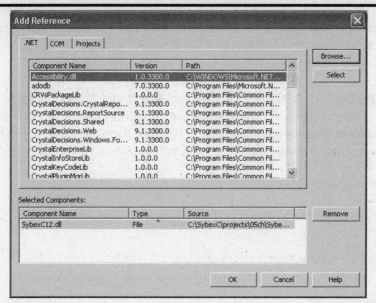

FIGURE 7.17: The assembly containing the class library now appears in the Selected Components pane.

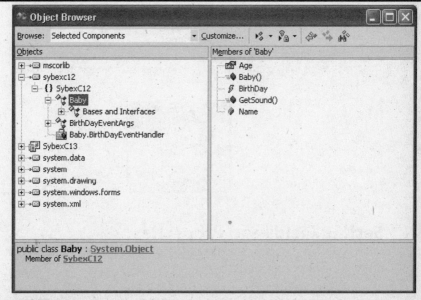

FIGURE 7.18: Once the reference has been added, the class members appear in the Object Browser.

The next step is to add some TextBoxes and Buttons to the form that can be used to invoke the members of the class library. Let's add TextBoxes for the baby name and age, a button to set them, and a Get Sound button to get a representation of the noise often made by the baby object.

Instantiating an Object Based on the Class

Turning to the form code, the first step is to add a using directive that refers to the SybexC12 namespace. Next, we'll instantiate an object, in this case stored in a variable named *myBaby*, based on the Baby class:

```
...
using SybexC12;
...
public class Form1 : System.Windows.Forms.Form
{
    ...
    Baby myBaby = new Baby();
    ...
```

Using a Class Method

It's a simple matter now to invoke the myBaby.GetSound method in the click event of the Get Sound button:

```
private void btnGetSound_Click(
    object sender, System.EventArgs e) {
    string msg = myBaby.GetSound();
    MessageBox.Show(msg, "Hi from my Baby!",
        MessageBoxButtons.OK, MessageBoxIcon.Exclamation);
}
```

Setting Fields and Properties

It's equally simple to set the Name field and Age property in the click event handler of the Set button:

```
private void btnSet_Click(
    object sender, System.EventArgs e) {
```

```
    myBaby.Age = Convert.ToInt16(txtAge.Text);
    myBaby.Name = txtName.Text;
}
```

Wiring the Event

To wire the event, we first need to create a method in the form class with the same signature as the event delegate. This method will be executed when the event is raised. For example, we can simply display a message box in a method named Baby_OnBirthDay whose signature matches the event delegate:

```
private void Baby_OnBirthDay(
  object sender, System.EventArgs e) {
    MessageBox.Show("The Baby.OnBirthDay event was raised!",
      "Happy, Happy Birthday to my baby!",
      MessageBoxButtons.OK, MessageBoxIcon.Exclamation);
}
```

Next, in the form's constructor, the myBaby.OnBirthDay event is wired via the event delegate to the Baby_OnBirthDay method.

```
myBaby.OnBirthDay += new
    Baby.BirthDayEventHandler(this.Baby_OnBirthDay);
```

If you run the project and enter an age for the baby object that will trigger the event (for example, 1, since the initial value for the age is 0), you will see that the OnBirthDay event will be triggered, as shown in Figure 7.19.

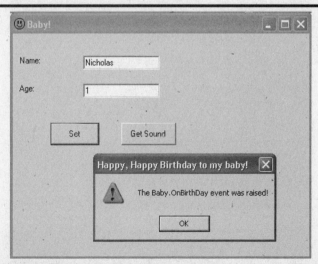

FIGURE 7.19: The OnBirthDay event is raised when the age is changed.

What's Next

Programming with C# and the .NET Framework means programming with classes. This chapter and the ones before have covered a lot of ground and started you down the path of programming well with classes. It's now time to start putting the classes to good work and creating some Windows applications, so let's move on to the next chapter.

Chapter 8

BUILDING A BETTER WINDOWS INTERFACE

Windows, windows, windows! Here's a truism for you: Most Windows applications have user interfaces built around windows. This chapter focuses on building the windowing interface. The first project in this chapter will show you how to make ovoid labels, buttons, and other controls—and then it will use a Timer component to make these controls "dance" across the screen. In a slightly less frivolous vein, this chapter will also show you how to work with ListBoxes, create menus using code, use the common dialog controls, and create an MDI application.

Adapted from *Visual C# .NET Programming*
by Harold Davis
ISBN 0-7821-4046-7

ROUND BUTTONS DANCING

The Region property of a form can be used to set the shape of the form by assigning a GraphicsPath object to the property. (The AddEllipse method was used to make the GraphicsPath oval.)

Region is a member of System.Windows.Forms.Control that sets (or gets) the window region associated with a control. It's therefore a property you can use for all objects that inherit from Control. This includes the Form object, which inherits from Control via Scrollable-Control and ContainerControl. It also includes all controls in the Toolbox that have a visual interface: Buttons, TextBoxes, Labels, and so on.

Making a Button Round

Let's write a general method that we can use to make a control round, using the logic in which the AddEllipse method of a GraphicsPath object is used to make an oval based on the size of the control:

```
public void MakeItRound(Control c) {
    GraphicsPath gp = new GraphicsPath();
    gp.AddEllipse(
        new Rectangle(0, 0, c.Size.Width - 5, c.Size.Height - 5));
    c.Region = new Region(gp);
}
```

NOTE
I've subtracted five pixels off both the width and the height of the oval to eliminate the line produced by the "raised" bevel when you make a button round.

Place a button named button1 on the form. (For the sake of aesthetic harmony, use the Properties window to delete the contents of its Text property and the other controls used later in this example—although, of course, this is a matter of your choice. They can have text if you'd like.)

If you call the MakeItRound method with a control, such as button1, as an argument, the control will become round:

```
private void btnRound_Click(
    object sender, System.EventArgs e) {
    MakeItRound(button1);
}
```

Let's add a panel, docked along the bottom of a form, to act as the control panel for this application (see Figure 8.1). The panel has three buttons whose click events will be used to

▶ Make a single control round, as explained earlier (this will be expanded in a second to toggle back and forth between "roundness" and "squareness"). This button is named btnRound and has the initial text "Round One."

▶ Turn all the controls in the client area of the form—that is, the form excluding the panel that I placed on it—round. This button has the text "Round All."

▶ Animate all controls in the client area, with the text toggling between "Dance" and "Stop."

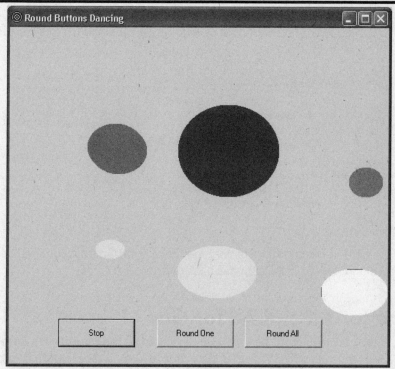

FIGURE 8.1:   Making round controls dance

NOTE
The *client space* of a form is the form background area, exclusive of title bar, toolbars, menus, and border.

Toggling the Round Button

To toggle the single control, we need to store the initial value of its `Region` property in a variable declared outside the click event (so that the value persists). We can do this by declaring a variable named `theRegion` as part of the initial class declaration:

```
public class Form1 : System.Windows.Forms.Form {
    ...
    System.Drawing.Region theRegion;
    ...
```

Next, the click event of `btnRound` can be modified to store the initial control `Region` and restore it when toggled:

```
private void btnRound_Click(
    object sender, System.EventArgs e) {
    if (btnRound.Text == "Round One") {
        theRegion = button1.Region;
        MakeItRound(button1);
        btnRound.Text = "Square One";
    }
    else {
        button1.Region = theRegion;
        btnRound.Text = "Round One";
    }
}
```

Try it! If you run the project and click Round One, `button1` will become round. If you click again, it is back to its normal shape.

One for All and All for One

It's easy to extend the rounding process to all the controls in a form's control collection. To see this in action, add a gaggle of Buttons, Labels, TextBoxes—and any other control you'd like—to the form, making sure that the `Text` property of each is empty (just to keep the aesthetics neat).

With a bunch of controls added to the client area of the form, code can be added to the click event of the Round All button to cycle through the form's control collection, rounding each one in turn:

```
private void btnRoundAll_Click(
  object sender, System.EventArgs e) {
   foreach (Control c in this.Controls) {
      MakeItRound(c);
   }
}
```

Animating the Controls

Now that we have all these nice, round controls, let's use a `Timer` component to animate them. When you drag a `Timer` component from the Toolbox to a form, it sits on the "tray" beneath the form—which is symbolic of the fact that the `Timer` has no run-time visual representation.

Essentially, the `Timer` component is a mechanism for the time-based firing of an event. As you may know, the key `Timer` members are the properties `Enabled` and `Interval`. If `Enabled` is `true`, the Timer's sole event—`Tick`—is repeatedly fired after the `Interval` (expressed in milliseconds).

The object of animating the controls is to move them in the `Tick` property in one direction, and to reset things when they reach the edge of a form. If we let the control pass out of the form's coordinates, it won't be visible.

Use the Properties window to set the `Timer`'s `Enabled` property to `false`, and its `Interval` property to 100 (or one-tenth of a second).

In the click event of the button used to start the animation, toggle the Timer's `Enabled` property:

```
private void btnDance_Click(
  object sender, System.EventArgs e) {
   if (btnDance.Text == "Dance") {
      timer1.Enabled = true;
      btnDance.Text = "Stop";
   }
   else {
      timer1.Enabled = false;
      btnDance.Text = "Dance";
   }
}
```

Next, in the Timer's Tick event, add the code to move each control in the control's collection, sending each one back to the upper-left of the form as it goes off to the lower right:

```
private void timer1_Tick(
   object sender, System.EventArgs e) {
    int xIncrement = 5; int yIncrement = 5;
    foreach (Control c in this.Controls) {
        if (c.Location.X > this.Size.Width - 30) {
            xIncrement = -500;
        }
        if (c.Location.Y > this.Size.Height - 50) {
            yIncrement = -500;
        }
        if (c.Location.X <= 0) {
            xIncrement = 5;
        }
        if (c.Location.Y <= 0) {
            yIncrement = 10;
        }
        c.Location = new Point(c.Location.X + xIncrement,
            c.Location.Y + yIncrement);
    }
}
```

In creating this kind of procedure, it's helpful to use the Debug object to track where objects actually are so that code can be adjusted accordingly, along these lines:

```
using System.Diagnostics;
...
Debug.WriteLine("XLocation: " + c.Location.X.ToString());
Debug.WriteLine("X Increment: " + xIncrement.ToString());
Debug.WriteLine("YLocation: " + c.Location.Y.ToString());
Debug.WriteLine("Y Increment: " + yIncrement.ToString());
```

Save the project (the code is shown in Listing 8.1). If you run it, you'll see that turning controls round and animating them is almost as good as watching a lava lamp!

Listing 8.1: Making Round Controls Dance

```
...
using System.Drawing.Drawing2D;

private void btnRound_Click(
   object sender, System.EventArgs e) {
    if (btnRound.Text == "Round One") {
```

```
            theRegion = button1.Region;
            MakeItRound(button1);
            btnRound.Text = "Square One";
        }
        else {
            button1.Region = theRegion;
            btnRound.Text = "Round One";
        }
    }

    public void MakeItRound(Control c) {
        GraphicsPath gp = new GraphicsPath();
        gp.AddEllipse(
            new Rectangle(
            0, 0, c.Size.Width - 5,c.Size.Height - 5));
        c.Region = new Region (gp);
    }

    private void btnRoundAll_Click(
        object sender, System.EventArgs e) {
        foreach (Control c in this.Controls) {
            MakeItRound(c);
        }
    }

    private void btnDance_Click(
        object sender, System.EventArgs e) {
        if (btnDance.Text == "Dance") {
            timer1.Enabled = true;
            btnDance.Text = "Stop";
        }
        else {
            timer1.Enabled = false;
            btnDance.Text = "Dance";
        }
    }

    private void timer1_Tick(
        object sender, System.EventArgs e) {
        int xIncrement = 5; int yIncrement = 5;
        foreach (Control c in this.Controls) {
            if (c.Location.X > this.Size.Width - 30) {
                xIncrement = -500;
            }
```

```
      if (c.Location.Y > this.Size.Height - 50) {
         yIncrement = -500;
      }
      if (c.Location.X <= 0) {
         xIncrement = 5;
      }
      if (c.Location.Y <= 0) {
         yIncrement = 10;
      }
      c.Location = new Point(c.Location.X + xIncrement,
         c.Location.Y + yIncrement);
   }
}
```

LISTBOXES LISTING

Moving on, ListBoxes in their various varieties provide a visual mechanism for dealing with collections of items. As such, they are an important part of many user interfaces. (For more information about programming the collections of items that lie underneath the ListBox classes, see Chapter 6, "Arrays, Indexers, and Collections.")

The three ListBox controls you'll find on the Toolbox—all inheriting from System.Windows.Forms.ListControl—are ComboBox, ListBox, and CheckedListBox. These controls are all far more alike than they are unalike. The ComboBox combines an editing field with the list of items in a ListBox, which allows the user to select an item from the list or to enter a new item. The CheckedListBox is just like a ListBox, except that it includes a Checked property. In addition, CheckedListBoxes do not support multiple selection. (To enable multiple selection with a ListBox, set its SelectionMode property to MultiSimple or MultiExtended.)

The example in this section primarily works with CheckedListBoxes, because those checks are so much fun, but you could substitute Combo-Boxes or ListBoxes without changing very much.

Adding an Item

The Add method of the CheckedListBox's Items collection will add an item at the bottom of the CheckedListBox, as shown in Figure 8.2:

```
private void btnAdd_Click(
   object sender, System.EventArgs e) {
```

```
            checkedListBox1.Items.Add(txtAdd.Text);
        }
```

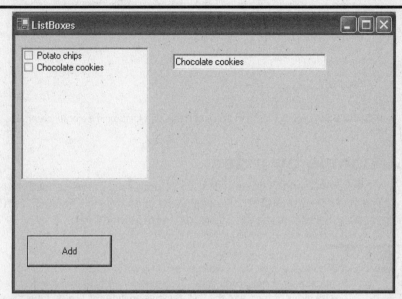

FIGURE 8.2:   It's easy to add items to a ListBox.

Adding an Array

The Items.AddRange method allows you to add an array of items to the Items collection of a ListBox. Here's code to generate an array of items (Item # 1 ... Item # *n*) and add them to a ListBox. Both the specific control and the number of items are passed in to the procedure:

```
    private void AddToList(ListBox lb, int size) {
        string[] myarray = new string [size];
        for (int i = 0; i < size; i++) {
            myarray[i] = "Item # " + (i+1).ToString();
        }
        lb.Items.AddRange(myarray);
    }
```

You can invoke this method with a specific control and the number of elements you want to add, with the results shown in Figure 8.3:

```
    private void btnAddArray_Click(
      object sender, System.EventArgs e) {
      AddToList(checkedListBox1, 10);
    }
```

FIGURE 8.3:   You can add an array of items to a ListBox in a single statement.

Positioning by Index

We've already added an item to the bottom of the Items collection using Items.Add. Alternatively, you can position an item in CheckedListBox's items collection using the Items.Insert method.

TIP

Remember that the Items collection is zero based, so that the first item in it has an index of zero, and the last item has an index of Items.Count - 1.

You could use the Items.Insert method to position an item in the specified place as shown in Figure 8.4 (the first argument is the index position, the second is the text to add):

```
checkedListBox1.Items.Insert(
    Convert.ToInt16(txtIndex.Text), txtAdd.Text);
```

It's probably a good idea, and easy enough, to check that the insertion is within the range of the items in the collection:

```
private void btnInsert_Click(
    object sender, System.EventArgs e) {
    if ((Convert.ToInt16(txtIndex.Text) >= 0) &&
        (Convert.ToInt16(txtIndex.Text) <=
            checkedListBox1.Items.Count)) {
            checkedListBox1.Items.Insert(
                Convert.ToInt16(txtIndex.Text),
                txtAdd.Text);
    }
    else {
        MessageBox.Show("Out of Range", "Please try again",
```

```
                   MessageBoxButtons.OK, MessageBoxIcon.Exclamation);
     }
  }
```

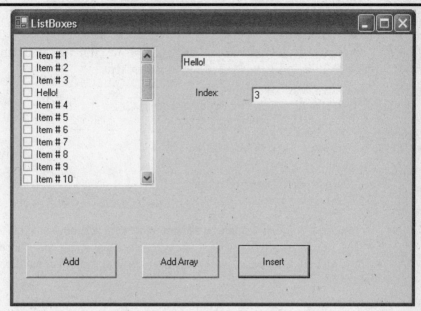

FIGURE 8.4:   You can insert an item anywhere you'd like using an index value.

This way, if the user attempts to enter an index that is out of range, you can display an appropriate message.

WARNING

Generally, the code in this chapter omits exception handling, but this is not a good idea in the real world. For more about exceptions, see Chapter 2, "Zen and Now: The C# Language."

Retrieving Selected Text

It's easy to retrieve the text of a selected item from a CheckedListBox by using its Text property, checkedListBox1.Text. (Alternatively, checkedListBox1.SelectedItem.ToString() amounts to the same thing.)

Before we display the selected item, let's write a function that determines, by item index, whether an item is checked:

```
private bool IsItChecked(
  CheckedListBox clb, int theIndex) {
    if (clb.GetItemChecked(theIndex) == true){
      return true;
    }
    else {
      return false;
    }
}
```

First, we also need to make sure that an item is actually selected by testing the checkedListBox1.Text property. Assuming that there is an item selected, we can display it (Figure 8.5) and display whether it is checked:

```
private void btnSelect_Click(
  object sender, System.EventArgs e) {
    if (checkedListBox1.Text != ""){
      MessageBox.Show("Selected Item Text: " +
        // checkedListBox1.SelectedItem.ToString(),
        checkedListBox1.Text,
          "Here is your text", MessageBoxButtons.OK,
          MessageBoxIcon.Information);
      if (IsItChecked(checkedListBox1,
        checkedListBox1.SelectedIndex)) {
        MessageBox.Show("Checked");
      }
      else {
        MessageBox.Show("Unchecked");
      }
    }
    else {
      MessageBox.Show("Nothing selected!","No text today",
        MessageBoxButtons.OK, MessageBoxIcon.Information);
    }
}
```

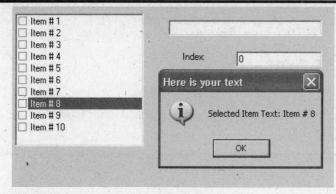

FIGURE 8.5: It's easy to retrieve selected text.

Retrieving by Index

You can also retrieve the text of an item by using its index in the Items collection. For example,

```
private void btnRetrieve_Click(
  object sender, System.EventArgs e) {
  MessageBox.Show(
    checkedListBox1.Items
    [Convert.ToInt16(txtIndex.Text)].ToString(),
    "Here is your text", MessageBoxButtons.OK,
    MessageBoxIcon.Information);
  if (IsItChecked(checkedListBox1,
    Convert.ToInt16(txtIndex.Text))) {
    MessageBox.Show("Checked");
  }
  else {
    MessageBox.Show("Unchecked");
  }
}
```

Retrieving Multiple Checked Items

Sometimes you'd like to get all the checked items in one list (such as a CheckedListBox) and read them into another CheckedListBox. You can do this by iterating through the Items collection of the first CheckedListBox. Each time a checked item is found, the item is added to the new Checked-ListBox (and marked checked):

```
private void btnGetChecked_Click(
  object sender, System.EventArgs e) {
```

```
for (int i = 0; i < checkedListBox1.Items.Count; i++){
    if (IsItChecked(checkedListBox1,i)) {
        clb2.Items.Add(checkedListBox1.Items[i],
            CheckState.Checked);
    }
}
}
```

When the iteration is complete, the checked items have been added to the new box (Figure 8.6).

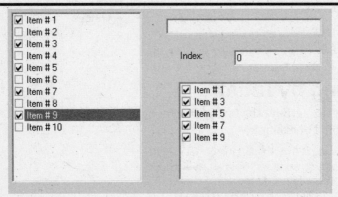

FIGURE 8.6:   You can loop through the CheckedListBox to retrieve all checked items.

This procedure uses the `IsItChecked` function, which you'll recall I first showed you in the section on retrieving text. Here it is again:

```
private bool IsItChecked(
    CheckedListBox clb, int theIndex) {
    if (clb.GetItemChecked(theIndex) == true){
        return true;
    }
    else {
        return false;
    }
}
```

Clearing an Item

It's easy to delete a collection of items using the `Clear` method. For example, here is the code you would need to delete the items in a pair of CheckedListBoxes and a ListBox:

```
private void btnClear_Click(
    object sender, System.EventArgs e) {
```

```
        checkedListBox1.Items.Clear();
        clb2.Items.Clear();
        listBox1.Items.Clear();
    }
```

Deleting Items

You can delete an individual item from a CheckedListBox if it is selected using the Remove method of the Items collection:

```
checkedListBox1.Items.Remove(
    checkedListBox1.SelectedItem);
```

Similarly, if you know the text of the item you want to delete, you can use this:

```
checkedListBox1.Items.Remove(txtAdd.Text);
```

On the other hand, if you want to delete an item from the Items collection by position (index), you will need to use the RemoveAt method. This code checks to see that a given index is within the count of the Items collection and, if it is, it deletes the corresponding item:

```
if ((Convert.ToInt16(txtIndex.Text) >= 0) &&
    (Convert.ToInt16(txtIndex.Text) <=
    checkedListBox1.Items.Count)) {
    checkedListBox1.Items.RemoveAt(
        Convert.ToInt16(txtIndex.Text));
    }
```

Retrieving Multiple Selections

Retrieving multiple selections from a ListBox works in the same way as retrieving multiple checked items from a CheckedListBox (see "Retrieving Multiple Checked Items" earlier in this chapter).

First, we'll need to add a ListBox to the project and set its Selection-Mode property to MultiSimple. We can populate it, using the same procedure used to populate the CheckedListBox:

```
private void btnPopulateLB_Click(
    object sender, System.EventArgs e) {
    AddToList(listBox1,30);
    }
```

In case you don't remember, here's the AddToList method:

```
private void AddToList(ListBox lb, int size) {
    string[] myarray = new string [size];
```

```
        for (int i = 0; i < size; i++) {
            myarray[i] = "Item # " + (i+1).ToString();
        }
        lb.Items.AddRange(myarray);
}
```

Finally, we can iterate through the ListBox, adding items to a "results" CheckedListBox for each selected item in the ListBox:

```
private void btnGetSelect_Click(
    object sender, System.EventArgs e) {
    for (int i = 0; i < listBox1.SelectedItems.Count; i++){
        clb2.Items.Add(listBox1.SelectedItems[i]);
    }
}
```

If you save the project, run it, populate the ListBox, select some items, and click the Get Selected button, the selected items will be displayed in the new CheckedListBox (Figure 8.7).

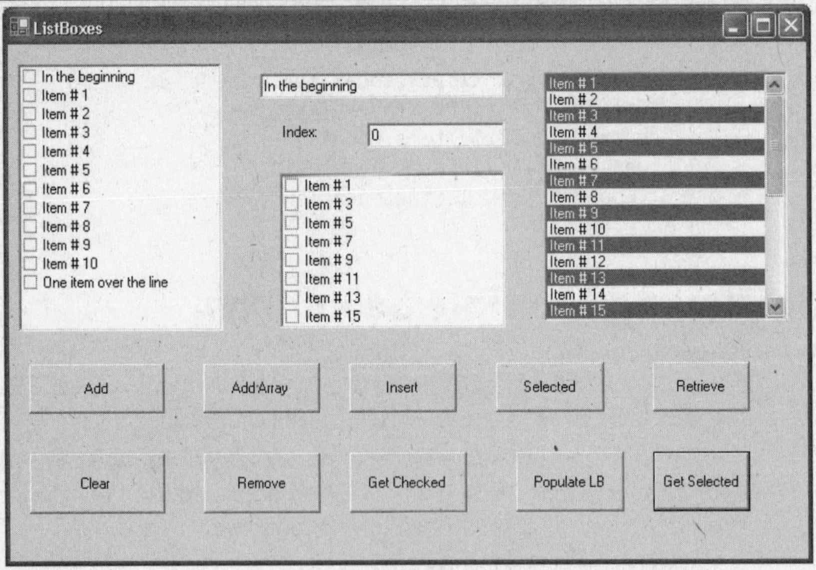

FIGURE 8.7: You can have lots of fun with ListBoxes (retrieving all selected items shown).

I'm sure you'll agree that ListBoxes, CheckedListBoxes, and their respective Items collections are lots of fun—and very useful. The ListBox operations performed in this section are shown in Listing 8.2.

Listing 8.2: Fun and Games with CheckedListBoxes (ListBox Operations)

```csharp
private void btnAdd_Click(
   object sender, System.EventArgs e) {
      checkedListBox1.Items.Add(txtAdd.Text);
}
private void btnAddArray_Click(
   object sender, System.EventArgs e) {
      AddToList(checkedListBox1, 10);
}
private void AddToList(ListBox lb, int size) {
      string[] myarray = new string [size];
      for (int i = 0; i < size; i++) {
         myarray[i] = "Item # " + (i+1).ToString();
      }
      lb.Items.AddRange(myarray);
}
private void btnInsert_Click(
   object sender, System.EventArgs e) {
      if ((Convert.ToInt16(txtIndex.Text) >= 0) &&
         (Convert.ToInt16(txtIndex.Text) <=
         checkedListBox1.Items.Count)) {
         checkedListBox1.Items.Insert(
         Convert.ToInt16(txtIndex.Text),
            txtAdd.Text);
      }
      else {
         MessageBox.Show("Out of Range", "Please try again",
            MessageBoxButtons.OK, MessageBoxIcon.Exclamation);
      }
}
private void btnSelect_Click(
   object sender, System.EventArgs e) {
      if (checkedListBox1.Text != ""){
         MessageBox.Show("Selected Item Text: " +
            // checkedListBox1.SelectedItem.ToString(),
            checkedListBox1.Text, "Here is your text",
               MessageBoxButtons.OK, MessageBoxIcon.Information);
         if (IsItChecked(checkedListBox1,
            checkedListBox1.SelectedIndex)) {
            MessageBox.Show("Checked");
```

```
        }
        else {
            MessageBox.Show("Unchecked");
        }
    }
    else {
        MessageBox.Show("Nothing selected!", "No text today",
            MessageBoxButtons.OK, MessageBoxIcon.Information);
    }
}
private void btnRetrieve_Click(
    object sender, System.EventArgs e) {
    MessageBox.Show(
        checkedListBox1.Items[
        Convert.ToInt16(txtIndex.Text)].ToString(),
        "Here is your text", MessageBoxButtons.OK,
        MessageBoxIcon.Information);
    if (IsItChecked(checkedListBox1,
        Convert.ToInt16(txtIndex.Text))) {
        MessageBox.Show("Checked");
    }
    else {
        MessageBox.Show("Unchecked");
    }
}
private bool IsItChecked(CheckedListBox clb, int theIndex) {
    if (clb.GetItemChecked(theIndex) == true){
        return true;
    }
    else {
        return false;
    }
}
private void btnClear_Click(
    object sender, System.EventArgs e) {
    checkedListBox1.Items.Clear();
    clb2.Items.Clear();
    listBox1.Items.Clear();
}
private void btnRemove_Click(
    object sender, System.EventArgs e) {
    // by index
```

```
//    if ((Convert.ToInt16(txtIndex.Text) >= 0) &&
//        (Convert.ToInt16(txtIndex.Text) <=
//        checkedListBox1.Items.Count)) {
//        checkedListBox1.Items.RemoveAt(
//        Convert.ToInt16(txtIndex.Text));
//    }
// selected
//    checkedListBox1.Items.Remove(
//      checkedListBox1.SelectedItem);

// by text
   checkedListBox1.Items.Remove(txtAdd.Text);
}
private void btnGetChecked_Click(
  object sender, System.EventArgs e) {
    for (int i = 0; i < checkedListBox1.Items.Count; i++){
      if (IsItChecked(checkedListBox1,i)) {
        clb2.Items.Add(checkedListBox1.Items[i],
          CheckState.Checked);
      }
    }
}
private void btnPopulateLB_Click(
  object sender, System.EventArgs e) {
    AddToList(listBox1,30);
}
private void btnGetSelect_Click(
  object sender, System.EventArgs e) {
    for (int i = 0;
      i < listBox1.SelectedItems.Count; i++){
       clb2.Items.Add(listBox1.SelectedItems[i]);
    }
}
```

MENUS

If ever a user interface cried to heaven, "Give me menus," it is the one shown in Figure 8.7 with its 10 clunky buttons. So let's put this user interface out of its misery, and give it a menu already!

To create a menu visually, using the tools supplied by Visual Studio, drag a MainMenu control to your form. Like the Timer, the instance of the control added to the form appears on the tray beneath the form.

With the MainMenu control sitting on the tray, you can go ahead and add menus—that is, the high-level menu items across the top of the form—and menu items, which are the items beneath each menu, by entering the appropriate information in position (Figure 8.8).

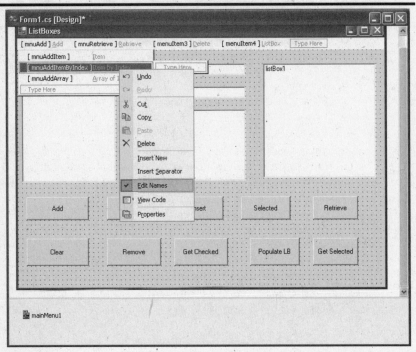

FIGURE 8.8:   When you add a MainMenu control to the tray, you can edit the menu visually (shown here in Edit Names mode).

By right-clicking and selecting Edit Names from the context menu, the menu insertion is performed in Edit Names mode, which allows you to edit in place the internal names of the menu items you are adding.

Let's use the visual interface to add some menus and menu items, and then check out the auto-generated menu code that Visual Studio has created on our behalf. The application will have four menus running along the top of the form: Add, Retrieve, Delete, and ListBox.

To keep things simple, I'll just look at the first menu, the Add menu, which as you can see in Figure 8.8 is in the normal place of a File menu. The menu item names and text are as shown in Table 8.1 (with access keys ignored).

TABLE 8.1: Add (mnuAdd) Menu Item Names and Text

MENU ITEM NAME	TEXT
mnuAdd (parent menu)	Add
MnuAddItem	Item
mnuAddItembyIndex	Item by Index
MnuAddArray	Array of Items

In keeping with the RAD "look, Ma, no code" theme of the menu designer, you should note that the Events tab of the Properties window can be used to assign menu item click events to button click event handlers (Figure 8.9). This means that no new code needs to be written to make these menus functional: mnuAdd's click event handler is assigned to the (already existing) handler for btnAdd's click event, and so on.

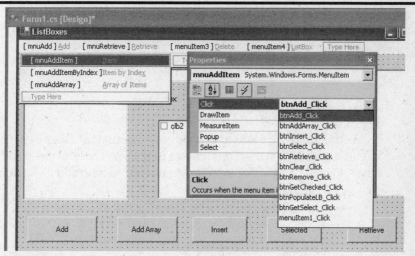

FIGURE 8.9: Menu item events can be assigned to an existing handler using the Events tab of the Properties window.

The Auto-Generated Menu Code

What code has been created for us to implement the menus we've visually added? To start with, a variable of type MainMenu has been declared, along with MenuItem variables for each of the menus and menu items:

```
private System.Windows.Forms.MainMenu mainMenu1;
private System.Windows.Forms.MenuItem mnuAdd;
private System.Windows.Forms.MenuItem mnuAddItem;
...
```

NOTE

Most of the action takes place within the "hidden" region of Windows Form Designer–generated code, so you will have to expand the region to view the action.

Next, the MainMenu and each of the MenuItems are instantiated:

```
this.mainMenu1 = new System.Windows.Forms.MainMenu();
this.mnuAdd = new System.Windows.Forms.MenuItem();
this.mnuAddItem = new System.Windows.Forms.MenuItem();
...
```

Next, the main menu collection of menu items is created, using the collection's AddRange method to add the four top-level menu items (Add, Delete, Retrieve, and ListBox):

```
this.mainMenu1.MenuItems.AddRange(
  new System.Windows.Forms.MenuItem[] {
    this.mnuAdd,
    this.mnuRetrieve,
    this.mnuDelete,
    this.mnuListBox});
```

As promised, we'll look at mnuAdd only, ignoring the other three menus. Here's the code that positions mnuAdd as the first top-level menu and uses the AddRange method of *its* menu items collection to add its contents:

```
this.mnuAdd.Index = 0;
this.mnuAdd.MenuItems.AddRange(
  new System.Windows.Forms.MenuItem[] {
    this.mnuAddItem,
    this.mnuAddItemByIndex,
    this.mnuAddArray});
```

Finally, each menu item *below* mnuAdd is given a position by Index in mnuAdd's collection, and its properties (for example, text and event handlers) fleshed out:

```
this.mnuAddItem.Index = 0;
this.mnuAddItem.Text = "&Item";
this.mnuAddItem.Click +=
  new System.EventHandler(this.btnAdd_Click);
```

As a last, but not least, required step, the whole menu construction is then assigned to the Menu property of the form:

```
this.Menu = this.mainMenu1;
```

Listing 8.3 shows the relevant portions of the auto-generated menu code.

Listing 8.3: Auto-Generated Menu Code (Excerpted)

```
public class Form1 : System.Windows.Forms.Form
{
...

    private System.Windows.Forms.MainMenu mainMenu1;
    private System.Windows.Forms.MenuItem mnuAdd;
    private System.Windows.Forms.MenuItem mnuAddItem;
    ...

    // within Initialize Component,
    // called by Form1 constructor
    this.mainMenu1 = new System.Windows.Forms.MainMenu();
    this.mnuAdd = new System.Windows.Forms.MenuItem();
    this.mnuAddItem = new System.Windows.Forms.MenuItem();
    ...
//
// mainMenu1
//
this.mainMenu1.MenuItems.AddRange(
  new System.Windows.Forms.MenuItem[] {
  this.mnuAdd,
  this.mnuRetrieve,
  this.mnuDelete,
  this.mnuListBox});
//
// mnuAdd
//
this.mnuAdd.Index = 0;
this.mnuAdd.MenuItems.AddRange(
  new System.Windows.Forms.MenuItem[] {
  this.mnuAddItem,
  this.mnuAddItemByIndex,
  this.mnuAddArray});
//
// mnuAddItem
//
```

```
this.mnuAddItem.Index = 0;
this.mnuAddItem.Text = "&Item";
this.mnuAddItem.Click +=
  new System.EventHandler(this.btnAdd_Click);
...

  this.Menu = this.mainMenu1;
...
}
```

Analyzing what the auto-generation does, the general process is:

▶ Declare and instantiate a MainMenu and MenuItems for each menu item.

▶ Use the AddRange method of the MainMenu's menu item collection to add the top-level menus.

▶ For each top-level menu, position it in the collection using the Index property, and then use its collection's AddRange to add its own menu items.

▶ For each menu item, use the collection Index property to assign a location on the menu, and assign properties such as text and handlers.

▶ Assign the whole menu structure to the Menu property of the form.

Based on this, it certainly looks like we could pretty easily construct a menu ourselves in code doing at least as well as the auto-generated one. Ultimately, depending on your preferences, you may find it less work to construct menus in code yourself rather than relying on Visual Studio for auto-generation.

Let's construct a menu in code for a completely new application that will use a RichTextBox control and the common dialog wrappers to build a Notepad-like application. Table 8.2 shows the menus that we need.

TABLE 8.2: "Notepad" Application Menus

FILE	EDIT	FORMAT
Open (mnuFileOpen)	Cut (mnuEditCut)	Font (mnuFormatFont)
Save (mnuFileSave)	Copy (mnuEditCopy)	Color (mnuFormatColor)
- (separator)	Paste (mnuEditPaste)	
Exit (mnuFileExit)		

First, within the form's constructor, create a `MainMenu` instance and assign it to the form's Menu property:

```
Menu = new MainMenu();
```

NOTE

The preceding statement is equivalent to `this.Menu = new MainMenu();`. In other words, the omitted `this` is implied.

Next, declare and instantiate a File menu item, and add it to the main menu's `MenuItems` collection:

```
MenuItem mnu = new MenuItem("&File");
Menu.MenuItems.Add(mnu);
```

The File menu will be referred to as `Menu.MenuItems[0]`. Now, go ahead and add the items to the File menu's menu items collection, starting with the Open menu item:

```
MenuItem mnuFileOpen = new MenuItem("&Open");
mnuFileOpen.Click += new EventHandler(mnuFileOpen_Click);
mnuFileOpen.Shortcut = Shortcut.CtrlO;
Menu.MenuItems[0].MenuItems.Add(mnuFileOpen);
```

In this code, a new menu item, `mnuFileOpen`, is declared and instantiated. A click handler is assigned to it, so you have to create the framework for the event handler:

```
void mnuFileOpen_Click(object sender, EventArgs e){

}
```

A shortcut key is also assigned to `mnuFileOpen`. Finally, the Add method for the File menu collection of items is used to add the item (so, effectively, `mnuFileOpen` is `Menu.MenuItems[0].MenuItems[0]`). The key concept is that a `MenuItems` collection can itself contain a `MenuItems` collection!

Listing 8.4 shows the completely fleshed-out menu. As you can see in Figure 8.10, this is a fully functional menu, up to all factory specifications. The code shown in Listing 8.4 could, perhaps, be improved by substituting variables for the hard-coded index values. This would create the ability to be easily flexible about menu order in the future.

A menu is probably easier to maintain if you create it in code this way than if you auto-generate it. However, the choice is yours; at the least, you should be aware of what the menu designer is doing "under the hood" in case you need to tweak it.

FIGURE 8.10:   You can easily create fully functional menus in code.

Listing 8.4: Coding a Menu by Hand

```
// Form1 constructor
public Form1()
{
    InitializeComponent();

    // Add Menus
    Menu = new MainMenu();

    // File menu
    MenuItem mnu = new MenuItem("&File");
    Menu.MenuItems.Add(mnu);

    // File Open
    MenuItem mnuFileOpen = new MenuItem("&Open");
    mnuFileOpen.Click += new EventHandler(mnuFileOpen_Click);
    mnuFileOpen.Shortcut = Shortcut.CtrlO;
    Menu.MenuItems[0].MenuItems.Add(mnuFileOpen);

    // File Save
    MenuItem mnuFileSave = new MenuItem("&Save");
    mnuFileSave.Click += new EventHandler(mnuFileSave_Click);
    mnuFileSave.Shortcut = Shortcut.CtrlS;
    Menu.MenuItems[0].MenuItems.Add(mnuFileSave);

    // separator
    mnu = new MenuItem("-");
    Menu.MenuItems[0].MenuItems.Add(mnu);
```

```
// File Exit
MenuItem mnuFileExit = new MenuItem("E&xit");
mnuFileExit.Click += new EventHandler(mnuFileExit_Click);
mnuFileExit.Shortcut = Shortcut.AltF4;
Menu.MenuItems[0].MenuItems.Add(mnuFileExit);

// Edit
mnu = new MenuItem("&Edit");
Menu.MenuItems.Add(mnu);

// Edit Cut
MenuItem mnuEditCut = new MenuItem("Cu&t");
mnuEditCut.Click += new EventHandler(mnuEditCut_Click);
mnuEditCut.Shortcut = Shortcut.CtrlX;
Menu.MenuItems[1].MenuItems.Add(mnuEditCut);

// Edit Copy
MenuItem mnuEditCopy = new MenuItem("&Copy");
mnuEditCopy.Click += new EventHandler(mnuEditCopy_Click);
mnuEditCopy.Shortcut = Shortcut.CtrlC;
Menu.MenuItems[1].MenuItems.Add(mnuEditCopy);

// Edit Paste
MenuItem mnuEditPaste = new MenuItem("&Paste");
mnuEditPaste.Click +=
    new EventHandler(mnuEditPaste_Click);
mnuEditPaste.Shortcut = Shortcut.CtrlV;
Menu.MenuItems[1].MenuItems.Add(mnuEditPaste);

// Format
mnu = new MenuItem("&Format");
Menu.MenuItems.Add(mnu);

// Format Font
MenuItem mnuFormatFont = new MenuItem("&Font");
mnuFormatFont.Click +=
    new EventHandler(mnuFormatFont_Click);
mnuFormatFont.Shortcut = Shortcut.CtrlF;
Menu.MenuItems[2].MenuItems.Add(mnuFormatFont);

// Format Color
MenuItem mnuFormatColor = new MenuItem("&Color");
mnuFormatColor.Click +=
    new EventHandler(mnuFormatColor_Click);
```

```
        mnuFormatColor.Shortcut = Shortcut.CtrlShiftC;
        Menu.MenuItems[2].MenuItems.Add(mnuFormatColor);


}
...
void mnuFileOpen_Click(object sender, EventArgs e){
}
void mnuFileSave_Click(object sender, EventArgs e){
}
void mnuFileExit_Click(object sender, EventArgs e){
}
void mnuEditCut_Click(object sender, EventArgs e){
}
void mnuEditCopy_Click(object sender, EventArgs e){
}
void mnuEditPaste_Click(object sender, EventArgs e){
}
void mnuFormatFont_Click(object sender, EventArgs e){
}
void mnuFormatColor_Click(object sender, EventArgs e){
}
...
```

DOING THE COMMON DIALOG THING

Now that we have a menu, created in code, let's build an application around the menu. This will be a Notepad-like application that allows users to open and save rich text files; cut, copy, and paste selected text to and from the clipboard; and change the color and font characteristics of selected text. The primary user interface will be provided by a RichTextBox control. Common dialog controls will provide users with a way to make choices.

Common dialog controls provide a "wrapper" for dialogs that perform commonly needed tasks, which means that they provide easy access to the functionality of standard Windows dialog boxes. For example, the SaveFileDialog control displays the standard Save As dialog for naming and locating a file to be saved—the same dialog as the dialog box you see in Microsoft Word and other applications.

By using the .NET common dialog controls to display these dialogs, the appearance of your applications becomes standardized. Users see dialogs that are similar to dialog boxes that they recognize and already know how to use.

However, although the common dialog controls show dialogs that allow the user to make choices, they don't actually do the work. For example, the SaveFileDialog control doesn't save the contents of a file after the user chooses to save a file. We'll use the methods of the RichTextBox control to do the actual work of changing the characteristics of selected text, working with the Clipboard, and saving and opening files. It's very easy to implement functionality using the methods of the RichTextBox so that we can concentrate on the common dialogs. But you will need to know how to work directly with files. You should also know that the Clipboard can alternatively be programmed using the members of the Clipboard class.

To get the ball rolling, in the same project with the hand-created menu, add a RichTextBox control. Name it rtb and clear its Text property. Set its Dock property to Fill, which means that it will take up the entire client area of the form and change size with the form.

Next, add ColorDialog, FontDialog, OpenFileDialog, and SaveFileDialog controls to the form (these are the common dialog controls the project will implement). Each control appears on the tray beneath the form (Figure 8.11).

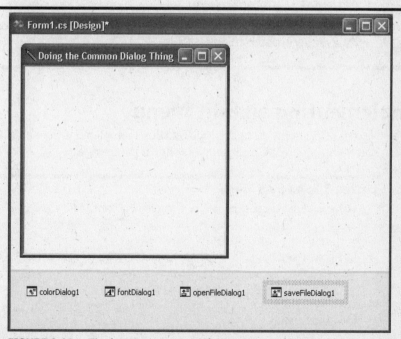

FIGURE 8.11: The form in design mode with common dialog controls in the tray.

FILE ACCESS

The .NET Framework has numerous classes for accessing the computer's file and directory system. For directories, you can use the Directory class or the DirectoryInfo class. Both classes contain the same functionality—the difference being that the former implements all its methods as static methods (meaning you can call them without creating an instance of the Directory class), while the latter implements its methods in a non-static way. Similarly, you can access files using either the File class (containing static methods), or the FileInfo class (containing non-static methods).

Once you find the file you wish to read or write, you will often use some form of *stream* to read or write the data. A stream is an abstract concept representing a stream of bytes. Streams have a source and a destination. The :NET Framework supports several different stream classes, including the FileStream (reading and writing to/from the file system), the MemoryStream (reading and writing to/from memory locations), and the NetworkStream (I/O using low-level network interface).

Please refer to the .NET Framework online help for more information on file access and streams.

Implementing an Edit Menu

Next, use the methods of the RichTextBox to implement the items on the Edit menu—cut, copy, and paste—as shown in Listing 8.5.

Listing 8.5: An Edit Menu

```
void mnuEditCut_Click(object sender, EventArgs e){
    rtb.Cut();
}
void mnuEditCopy_Click(object sender, EventArgs e){
    rtb.Copy();
}
void mnuEditPaste_Click(object sender, EventArgs e){
    rtb.Paste();
}
```

These editing methods are inherited by the RichTextBox class from the TextBoxBase class, which implements the core feature set of text-manipulation controls—so, for example, TextBoxes share most of the same functionality, also via inheritance from TextBoxBase. You'll find that the TextBoxBase class has other useful methods that could be used to extend an Edit menu—for example, Redo and Undo.

The Color Dialog

Within the click handler for the Color menu item, configure the Color dialog:

```
colorDialog1.AllowFullOpen = true;
colorDialog1.AnyColor = true;
```

By setting the AllowFullOpen property of the ColorDialog control to true, the user can use the Color dialog to define custom colors. If the AnyColor property is set to true, the dialog displays all available colors; if not, only solid colors—those with 100 percent opacity—are selectable.

Next, display the dialog (see Figure 8.12):

```
colorDialog1.ShowDialog();
```

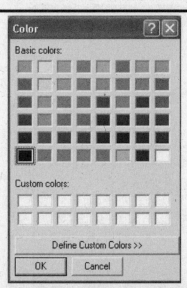

FIGURE 8.12:   The Color common dialog is used to set the color of the selected text.

Finally, set the selected text to the color chosen in the dialog:

```
rtb.SelectionColor = colorDialog1.Color;
```

Note that you might want to store the user selection of color, perhaps to reapply it later to some text. To do this, you could use a variable to capture the user's selection, for example,

```
Color theColor = colorDialog1.Color;
```

The Font Dialog

The Font dialog works in much the same way as the Color dialog. If you'd like, you can set its characteristics before invoking it, or you can just use the default, as in this example:

```
void mnuFormatFont_Click(object sender, EventArgs e){
    fontDialog1.ShowDialog();
    rtb.SelectionFont = fontDialog1.Font;
}
```

When the user selects some text and chooses the Font menu item, the Font dialog is displayed (Figure 8.13). Font choices made in this dialog are applied to the selected text, as in Figure 8.14.

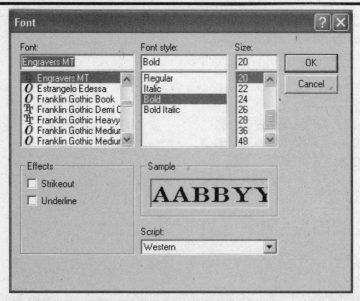

FIGURE 8.13: The Font common dialog is used to set the font and related attributes of the selected text.

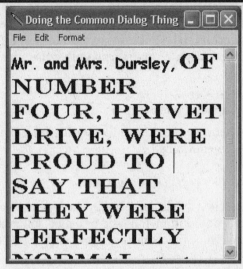

FIGURE 8.14: Changes to the text formatting are displayed in the RichTextBox.

The Save As and Open Dialogs

The SaveFileDialog control allows the user to pick a filename and location for saving a file via the standard Save As dialog box. The OpenFileDialog control lets the user select a file for opening using the Open dialog. To say it once again: designating the file is all these dialogs do; they don't do any of the actual work of saving or loading. We'll let the RichTextBox do the lifting here.

As a first order of business, we'll save the contents of the RichTextBox and then retrieve its contents, formatting and all. Note that the functionality for saving the rich text contents is implemented before the functionality for opening it. It's generally easier to do things in this order rather than looking around for an RTF file (and, even when you find one, you can't be absolutely sure what it should look like).

Saving the Contents of a RichTextBox

It's really very easy to use the SaveFileDialog to implement saving the contents of the RichTextBox. First, set some of the initial characteristics of the Save As dialog.

```
openFileDialog1.InitialDirectory =
    Application.ExecutablePath;
```

This sets the initial directory to the application's executable path (in the case of a C# application running in the development environment, this is the \bin\Debug directory that stores the application's EXE file). Next, set the initial filename to Harold.rtf (a name, other than the suffix, that is dear to my heart!).

```
SaveFileDialog1.DefaultExt = "rtf";
SaveFileDialog1.FileName = "Harold";
```

Finally, set a filter to determine the choices that are available to the user in the Save As Type drop-down list.

```
saveFileDialog1.Filter =
    "Rich Text Files (*.rtf) | *.rtf|All files (*.*) | *.*";
```

The Filter property is a text string delimited by the pipe character (|). Each item consists of a description, followed by a pipe, followed by the file suffix, usually using wildcard characters. Another pipe is used to start the next item.

In the example above, the following is one item:

```
Rich Text Files (*.rtf) | *.rtf
```

It is the description followed by the specification, namely *.rtf.

And here's another item:

```
All Files (*.*) | *.*
```

This has the specification, *.*, displaying files of all types.

WARNING

Be careful not to include extra spaces between the end of one item and the beginning of the next. Otherwise, the filter may not work properly.

Next, show the dialog:

```
SaveFileDialog1.ShowDialog();
```

The contents of the RichTextBox are saved using its SaveFile method, with the filename selected by the user as its argument:

```
rtb.SaveFile(SaveFileDialog1.FileName);
```

To see that this works, run the program and enter some heavily formatted text in the RichTextBox.

Next, choose File ➤ Save. The Save As dialog will open, suggesting a filename, type, and location—Harold.rtf in the \bin\Debug directory.

WARNING

Unless you set the `OverwritePrompt` property of the SaveFileDialog to `true` (either in code or in the Properties window), the user can pick an existing file, possibly resulting in overwriting its contents. Setting `OverwritePrompt` to `true` causes a message with a warning to appear but allows the user to proceed if they still want to.

Accept the filename, type, and location suggestions. Click Save. A file with the rich text contents will be created at the indicated location. To verify this, you can locate the file and open it in Microsoft Word.

Retrieving Rich Text from a File

The next step is to create the code that will load rich text into the RichTextBox in the application. To do this, we will display an Open dialog using the OpenFileDialog control.

You initialize the OpenFileDialog the same way you initialize the SaveFileDialog:

```
openFileDialog1.InitialDirectory =
   Application.ExecutablePath;
openFileDialog1.DefaultExt = "rtf";
openFileDialog1.FileName = "Harold";
openFileDialog1.Filter =
   "Rich Text Files (*.rtf) | *.rtf|All files (*.*) | *.*";
```

NOTE

As you probably know, the `Filter` property works the same way in the OpenFileDialog and the SaveFileDialog.

With the OpenFileDialog's properties set, we then need to show the dialog and use the `LoadFile` method of the RichTextBox to load the contents of the file selected by the user into the control:

```
OpenFileDialog1.ShowDialog();
rtb.LoadFile(OpenFileDialog1.FileName);
```

When the user selects File ➢ Open from the menu, the Open dialog will allow a choice of a file (Figure 8.15). When a file is selected and the Open button is clicked, the file is loaded into the RichTextBox.

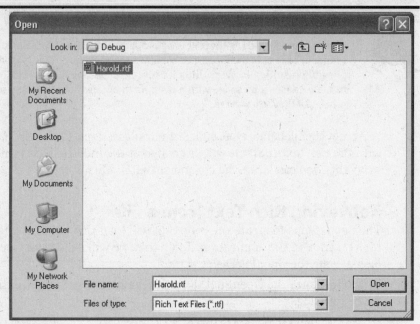

FIGURE 8.15:   The contents of the RichTextBox can be saved and then opened.

The complete code for opening and saving Rich Text files, and for setting the selected text color and font, is shown in Listing 8.6.

Listing 8.6: Opening, Saving, and Setting Font and Color with the Common Dialogs

```
void mnuFileOpen_Click(object sender, EventArgs e){
    openFileDialog1.InitialDirectory =
        Application.ExecutablePath;
    openFileDialog1.DefaultExt = "rtf";
    openFileDialog1.FileName = "Harold";
    openFileDialog1.Filter =
        "Rich Text Files (*.rtf) " +
        "| *.rtf|All files (*.*) | *.*";
    openFileDialog1.ShowDialog();
    rtb.LoadFile(openFileDialog1.FileName);
}

void mnuFileSave_Click(object sender, EventArgs e){
```

```
    saveFileDialog1.InitialDirectory =
        Application.ExecutablePath;
    saveFileDialog1.DefaultExt = "rtf";
    saveFileDialog1.FileName = "Harold";
    saveFileDialog1.Filter =
        "Rich Text Files (*.rtf) | *.rtf|All files (*.*) |
          *.*";
    saveFileDialog1.ShowDialog();
    rtb.SaveFile(saveFileDialog1.FileName);
}

void mnuFormatFont_Click(object sender, EventArgs e){
    fontDialog1.ShowDialog();
    rtb.SelectionFont = fontDialog1.Font;
}

void mnuFormatColor_Click(object sender, EventArgs e){
    colorDialog1.AllowFullOpen = true;
    colorDialog1.AnyColor = true;
    colorDialog1.ShowDialog();
    // Color theColor = colorDialog1.Color;
    rtb.SelectionColor = colorDialog1.Color;
}
```

MDI APPLICATIONS

In Multiple Document Interface (MDI) applications, there is one MDI form, or *parent form*. There are usually many MDI *child forms*. There can be more than one type of MDI child form, but all children, whatever their type, must fit into the client space of the parent MDI window.

It is perhaps the case that MDI applications are no longer very stylish. The thinking is that it probably makes just as much sense to open multiple copies of a single application as to have one application with multiple client windows. Be that as it may, it's easy to rig MDI applications in .NET—and you should know how.

As an example of how to "wire" an MDI application, let's turn the Notepad applet created in the last section into the child form of an MDI application.

The first step is to add a new form (to serve as the parent) to the project. Choose Project ➤ Add Windows Form to open the Add New Item dialog (Figure 8.16).

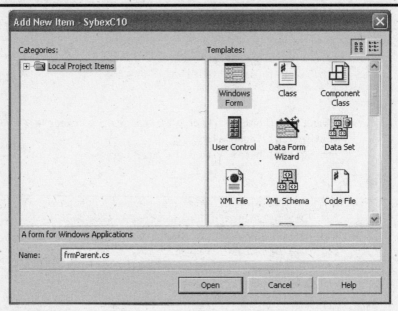

FIGURE 8.16: The Add New Item dialog is used to add a "parent" form to a project.

In the Add New Item dialog, make sure Windows Form is selected, name the form frmParent.cs, and click Open. The new parent form will be added to the project.

Open frmParent in its designer. Add a panel to the bottom of the form, and a button, btnShowChild, to the right side of the panel (the bottom-right of the form). Use the Properties window to set the Anchor property of btnShowChild to Bottom, Right.

Next, use the Properties window to set the IsMDIContainer property of frmParent to true (Figure 8.17).

TIP

When you set IsMDIContainer to true, you'll note that the client area of frmParent shifts in color, becoming a darker shade of gray.

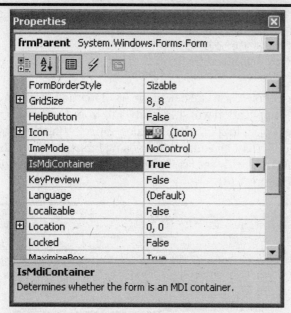

FIGURE 8.17:   Setting the form's `IsMDIContainer` to true means that it can become a parent.

Setting the Startup Object

The next step in helping `frmParent` to become a parent is rejiggering the application to let it start from `frmParent`. In order for a form to be a Startup Object, it needs a `Main` method. Because the original form in the project, `Form1` (the basis for the Notepad applet), had a `Main` method, Visual Studio didn't automatically give `frmParent` a main method. You need to give `frmParent` one now:

```
[STAThread]
static void Main() {
    Application.Run(new frmParent());
}
```

The Run method of the `Application` object is invoked with the constructor method for the `frmParent` class.

NOTE

The [STAThread] attribute tells the CLR that a single-threaded apartment model is being used.

Form1 still has its own `Main` method:

```
[STAThread]
static void Main() {
    Application.Run(new Form1());
}
```

You now have a choice: you can delete the `Main` method from `Form1`, in which case, the application will start by default from `frmParent`; or you can open the project Property Pages dialog—by selecting the project in Solution Explorer, right-clicking, and choosing Properties from the context menu—and explicitly set `frmParent` as the Startup Object using the General tab (Figure 8.18).

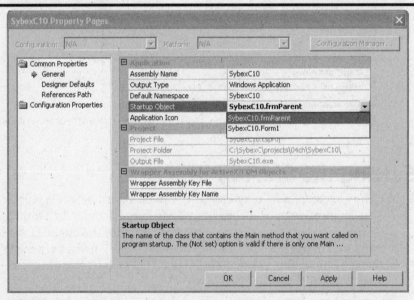

FIGURE 8.18:   If there are multiple modules with entry points—Main methods—then the Startup Object is set using the project's properties pages.

Displaying Children

With the application set to open `frmParent` first off, the mechanism for displaying the child form needs to be created. This goes in the click event handler for `btnShowChild`. First, a variable named *frmChild*, of type `Form1`, is instantiated:

```
Form1 frmChild = new Form1();
```

Next, the MdiParent property of *frmChild* is set to the current form, frmParent:

```
frmChild.MdiParent = this;
```

The child form is given text for its caption bar using a counter variable, *i*, to indicate which child it is:

```
frmChild.Text = "I am child #" + i.ToString();
```

The counter, which was declared at the class level, is iterated:

```
i++;
```

Finally, the new instance of Form1 is shown:

```
frmChild.Show()
```

Listing 8.7 shows the frmParent class declaration, the counter variable, its Main method, and the click event handler for displaying child forms.

Listing 8.7: Adding Child Forms

```
...
public class frmParent : System.Windows.Forms.Form {
    private System.Windows.Forms.Panel panel1;
    private System.Windows.Forms.Button btnShowChild;
    int i = 1;
    ...
    [STAThread]
    static void Main() {
        Application.Run(new frmParent());
    }
    ...
    private void btnShowChild_Click(
      object sender, System.EventArgs e) {
      Form1 frmChild = new Form1();
      frmChild.MdiParent = this;
      frmChild.Text = "I am child #" + i.ToString();
      i++;
      frmChild.Show();
    }
  }
...
```

The MDI Window Menu

A crucial part of the look and feel of an MDI application is a special MDI Window menu. This menu displays a list of all open MDI children and places a check mark next to the currently active child window. It allows the user to navigate between child windows by selecting one from the list on the MDI Window menu. In addition, it's also conventional and convenient to include the ability to arrange the children forms (in several ways) on the MDI Window menu.

The MDI Window is constructed in the MDI container—frmParent, in our example. You can create it by adding a MainMenu control to the form and using the visual menu designer—or by constructing it entirely in code, as shown in Listing 8.8. Note that setting a top-level menu's MdiList property to true

```
mnu.MdiList = true;
```

sets up the MDI list of child windows. It's also worth observing that the menu shown in Listing 8.8 *merges* with the menu belonging to a child form when the child is displayed. Aesthetically, the child menu should come before the Window menu. This is controlled by the MergeOrder property:

```
mnu.MergeOrder = 3;
```

Listing 8.8: An MDI Window Menu

```
Menu = new MainMenu();

// MDI Window menu
MenuItem mnu = new MenuItem("&Window");
mnu.MdiList = true;
mnu.MergeOrder = 3;
Menu.MenuItems.Add(mnu);

// Cascade
MenuItem mnuCascade = new MenuItem("&Cascade");
mnuCascade.Click += new EventHandler(MDImenu_Click);
Menu.MenuItems[0].MenuItems.Add(mnuCascade);

// Tile Horizontal
MenuItem mnuTileH = new MenuItem("&Tile Horizontal");
mnuTileH.Click += new EventHandler(MDImenu_Click);
Menu.MenuItems[0].MenuItems.Add(mnuTileH);

// Tile Vertical
MenuItem mnuTileV = new MenuItem("Tile &Vertical");
```

```
mnuTileV.Click += new EventHandler(MDImenu_Click);
Menu.MenuItems[0].MenuItems.Add(mnuTileV);

// Arrange Icons
MenuItem mnuArrange = new MenuItem("&Arrange Icons");
mnuArrange.Click += new EventHandler(MDImenu_Click);
Menu.MenuItems[0].MenuItems.Add(mnuArrange);
```

Note that the menu shown in Listing 8.8 does not implement functionality in child window arrangements; for each choice, it merely invokes a common event, MDImenu_Click. The MDIMenu_Click event handler, shown in Listing 8.9, has the job of determining which menu item invoked it by casting the *sender* parameter to a MenuItem and then checking its Text property:

```
MenuItem mnu = (MenuItem) sender;
switch (mnu.Text) {
    ...
```

The LayoutMdi method of the parent form is then used with the appropriate argument to arrange the child windows as shown in Listing 8.9.

Listing 8.9: Implementing MDI Window Functionality

```
void MDImenu_Click(object sender, EventArgs e) {
    MenuItem mnu = (MenuItem) sender;
    switch (mnu.Text) {
        case "&Cascade":
            this.LayoutMdi(MdiLayout.Cascade);
            break;
        case "&Tile Horizontal":
            this.LayoutMdi(MdiLayout.TileHorizontal);
            break;
        case "Tile &Vertical":
            this.LayoutMdi(MdiLayout.TileVertical);
            break;
        case "&Arrange Icons":
            this.LayoutMdi(MdiLayout.ArrangeIcons);
            break;
    }
}
```

If you run the application, you'll see that it is fully functional within normal parameters for an MDI application (Figure 8.19).

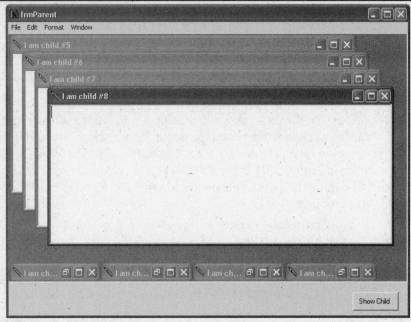

FIGURE 8.19:   It's easy to create MDI applications.

What's Next

This chapter has explored the use of Visual C#, Visual Studio, and the .NET Framework to create functional and exciting user interfaces. Next, in Chapter 9, we'll study more closely the creation of desktop applications.

Chapter 9

BUILDING DESKTOP APPLICATIONS

With all of the emphasis on distributed applications that only appear on the Internet, it's easy to forget that not every application ever created appears on someone's website. While distributed application development is extremely important, the desktop application hasn't gone away and it's unlikely to go away in the near future. The simple fact is that desktop applications serve the needs of many computer users who don't need access to the Internet, much less access to a business partner's network.

You can create a vast assortment of application types with C#, including desktop applications. This chapter is going to build on your knowledge of desktop applications and show you how to create several application types including dialog-based, Single Document Interface (SDI), and Multiple Document Interface (MDI).

Adapted from *Visual C# .NET Developer's Handbook* by John Paul Mueller
ISBN 0-7821-4047-5

DESKTOP APPLICATION TYPES

Desktop applications come in a variety of shapes and sizes. C# is quite capable of creating any application you can imagine (and perhaps a few that you can't). However, there are five application types that exemplify desktop applications as a whole, and that's what we'll concentrate on first.

Console applications   Represent those situations when you don't need a full-fledged interface for the user to work with. Many console applications appear as part of script, task scheduler, or remote machine access applications.

Dialog-based applications   Are normally reserved for utilities or applications that are too small to require complete menuing systems. Many dialog-based applications provide informational displays, and they're known for their small memory footprint.

Single-document applications   Are representative of simple applications that work with their own data, like note takers or small database front ends. These applications also require a menuing system of some type. A single-document application works with one document at a time.

Multiple-document applications   Include full-fledged applications like word processors and spreadsheets. When you think about it, they represent that fringe area of C# programming where you need to weigh the flexibility of C# against the development speed offered by RAD programming environments like Visual Basic. Multiple-document applications can work with more than one document at a time and could work with multiple document types simultaneously.

HTML-based applications   Work with data of some type (like single-document or multiple-document applications) but with a browser twist. Instead of a standard editor, your user will see what amounts to a web browser front end. The data normally appears formatted as a web page.

NOTE

Remember that we're talking about desktop applications in this chapter. C# is capable of creating all kinds of different code. You can use it to create DLLs, ActiveX controls, components, background executing programs like screensavers, and even extensions to C# itself.

Console

I made some statements previously that gave you an overall sense of what a console application is, but they were too sweeping to really tell you what a console application is all about. A console application has a DOS window look rather than the more familiar Windows-style appearance. It uses a monospaced font, just like you'd see in a DOS window, and you can use special input/output functions such as `Console.WriteLine()` and `Console.Read()`. However, internally, the program is a Windows application.

One of the early reasons for using console applications was to move a utility from DOS to Windows. Developers and network administrators owned a wealth of management applications that worked well at the command prompt. The high-end user didn't require a user interface and appreciated the efficiency boost that a console application could provide. Working at the command line is still a major part of the network administration experience, but many network administrators are moving from the command line to large windowed management applications such as the Microsoft Management Console (MMC).

TIP

Interestingly enough, some developers are still moving their DOS utilities to Windows. It's safe to assume that you'll be able to move the "business logic" of your DOS application to Windows using a console application. You may also be able to move some of the display and printing elements. However, it's never safe to assume that you'll be able to maintain one set of code for both DOS and Windows by using a console application—the two environments are different enough that you'll always have to make changes in the move from DOS to Windows.

Today, console applications serve a different purpose. Network administrators commonly look to console applications as a means to automate maintenance tasks. A console application is a perfect solution for scripting and task scheduling. Because a console application doesn't require a GUI interface, a network administrator can use it across a network connection from a command prompt. Console applications also support pipes and other means of redirecting output to a file. In fact, the console application is so important in this role that Microsoft actually added more command-line tools to Windows XP for the sole purpose of network and system management.

Console applications serve other purposes as well. For example, many user-level utilities either support a command-line interface or use a console interface. Many developers use console applications for experimentation. Console applications offer a clarity of coding that's often obscured by the GUI code in a Windows application.

Standard Windows

The standard Windows format is still the main method for creating desktop applications. Windows applications typically come in three styles: dialog-based, SDI, and MDI. Each of these styles serves a different purpose. A developer won't want to suffer the encumbrance of an MDI application when a dialog-based application will do. On the other hand, a dialog-based application is ill suited to present large quantities of textual or graphic information. You need an SDI or MDI application to perform most types of large-scale data manipulation.

Many programming languages differentiate between the various Windows application types. For example, Visual C++ has separate wizard settings for each type of application. C# doesn't provide a real differentiation between the three types of Windows application—every application begins as a dialog-based application. The presentation of the information and use of controls changes the application type. The following sections describe the uses for the various Windows application types, as well as presentation concerns that you need to consider as you develop the application.

Dialog-Based Applications

Many people associate dialogs with configuration screens, About boxes, and other adjuncts to a full-fledged application. Dialog-based applications have a place, too. They're extremely useful for utility-type applications where you need to display a fairly minimal amount of data and you require minimal user input. The main advantages of using a dialog-based application include:

- ▶ Quick prototyping
- ▶ Short development cycle
- ▶ Small memory footprint

TIP

When deciding whether to build a dialog-based or window-based application, think utility. If your application fits into the utility category, it's probably a good candidate for a dialog-based interface. On the other hand, if you're thinking about adding a lot of features or allowing the user to interact with the application heavily, you may want to look at an SDI or MDI application. Make sure you take future expansion into account when making your decision—a bad choice today could cost you a lot in rework time tomorrow.

So, what makes a dialog-based application better than a full-fledged window-based application? One of the more important factors is size. You can create two versions of the same application, one that uses a dialog front end and another that depends on a window. The dialog version will be smaller every time. In addition to conserving resources, you may find that the dialog version loads faster. A dialog-based application is simply more efficient than its window-based counterpart.

You may find that building a dialog-based application is faster as well. Dialog-based applications are meant to be small and efficient. If you find that you're adding a lot of bells and whistles to this kind of application, perhaps you've used the wrong kind of application to start with. Dialog-based applications normally eschew menus and other paraphernalia that a window-based application requires in order to provide a user-friendly front end. Fewer bells and whistles spell reduced development and debugging time for the programmer. Obviously, anything that speeds the programmer along is worth looking at.

The only real problem with dialog-based applications is that some programmers feel they can stuff one to the point of breaking. I've seen some dialog-based applications that are so filled with gizmos that you really can't tell what they're supposed to do. While a dialog-based application may look a little more cramped than its SDI or MDI counterpart, you shouldn't have it so crammed that no one can use it.

TIP

You can reduce clutter on a dialog-based application by using tabbed pages, just like a property dialog box used by Windows for configuration purposes. Each tab should have a specific purpose, and you should limit the number of tabs to those that can fit comfortably in the default dialog frame.

Single Document Interface (SDI)

A single-document application is one like Notepad or Microsoft Paint. It's designed to handle one document at a time, which reduces programming complexity and the amount of resources required for running the application. You'd use this kind of windowed application for something small, like a text editor or perhaps a small graphics editor. A single-document application allows users to interact fully with the document that you want them to create, but it's usually less robust than an application designed to work with multiple documents. In addition, the single-document application usually has a minimum of one less menu than a multiple-document application would—the Window menu that's used to select the document you want to edit.

SDI applications also use controls that tend to support Object Linking and Embedding (OLE). For example, the RichTextEdit control offers modes that support use of the control as an OLE container. An OLE container can act as a receptacle for data from other applications. For example, OLE enables a user to place a graphic image within a text document. Unlike some Visual Studio languages, you'll find that you need to develop OLE server capabilities in C# through manual programming techniques—none of the wizards offer to set this feature up for you.

Unfortunately, single-document window-based applications can suffer from the same problem as a dialog-based application—too much complexity. I still remember problems trying to use older versions of CorelDRAW. Every time I wanted to look at a drawing, I had to close the currently open document before doing so. This limitation made CorelDRAW a little harder to use than it needed to be. For example, I wasted a lot of time trying to compare one drawing against another. (Fortunately, Corel Corporation has corrected this oversight in current versions of CorelDRAW.)

TIP

The single-document, window-based application works surprisingly well when it comes to database management systems. The reason is fairly simple. Very few (if any) of your users will need to open more than one database at a time. Even if they do, the rules for working with databases would make it less desirable to allow the user to access multiple databases by themselves. You'll normally want to control all access to the various database elements programmatically and display the results to the user.

Multiple Document Interface (MDI)

Now we're down to the multiple-document application. You'd use this kind of window-based application to create something like a word processor or spreadsheet application. If you think about it for a second, a text editor has a limited appeal simply because it can only open one document at a time. People need to be able to compare one document to another; that's why multiple-document applications aren't only nice, but are required in so many situations.

Multiple-document applications also tend to be feature rich. (You can still go overboard; just look at all the people complaining about the bloated feature sets of major products produced by vendors today.) A text editor may provide a very simple find function and not offer any means for replacing occurrences of text. A full-fledged word processor provides both search and replace as standard features.

The failings of a multiple-document application begin with the fact that it can handle multiple documents. The capability of handling more than one document at a time means a lot of additional programming. You don't just have to keep track of all the open documents. There's the Window menu to manage, and special program features like split-screen to consider as well. You'll also need to decide whether the user will be allowed to display more than one document at once. Things like minimizing one document while keeping another maximized also require additional code. In sum, you'll need to be prepared for some major programming time before you even start a multiple-document application.

Of course, multiple-document applications have plenty of other disadvantages as well. For example, if you've ever tried to use Word for an OLE server, you know all about the frustration of waiting for this behemoth application to open every time you click on a link in another application. You've probably experienced the serious consequences of running out of memory as well. Until recently, every time you wanted to use OLE, you had to have enough memory to run both applications (the client and the server). Fortunately, Microsoft has reduced this requirement somewhat by allowing the server to take over the client's window; now the server only has to worry about working with the document itself. The client window provides a framework for the server's menus and toolbar, so there isn't any extra memory wasted.

Web-Based Applications

Web-based applications are becoming more popular as more companies require distributed application support. Combining a web page front end with data delivered using SOAP or some other XML technology makes sense in a world where developers don't even know what platform will run the application. However, before you begin thinking that a browser is the only way to create a web-based application, consider the fact that Visual Studio supports other types of web-based application development, some of which are completely invisible to the end user. For example, the help files provided with Visual Studio .NET rely on web technology, but the interface looks like a typical desktop application. The first clue that Visual Studio .NET is using an HTML-based front end is when you need something found on Microsoft's website and the application looks for an Internet connection.

TIP

You'll find Microsoft Help URLs placed throughout the book. All of these URLs begin with ms-help://. You can enter the URL in the Address Bar for Visual Studio Help, or you can open a copy of Internet Explorer and enter the URL there. One of the benefits of using Internet Explorer is that you can see an unencumbered view of the information. Of course, you lose the ability to search the rest of Visual Studio .NET Help when using Internet Explorer as your browser. However, you'll find the loss of search capability minimal when viewing lists of information, such as the list of WMI hardware classes discussed in the "Script-Based Example for Batch Jobs" section later in this chapter.

From a development perspective, you can divide web-based applications into two categories: those that rely on a browser and those that use an HTML-based front end. The browser application is more flexible because you can place it on any machine with a compatible browser. For example, it's possible to develop SOAP applications on your desktop machine that will ultimately run on a PDA using the browser application. The HTML-based front end has the advantage of functionality. You can combine standard desktop elements with HTML elements to create a type of hybrid application.

So, what good is an HTML-based document application? Think about the advantages of creating your own custom web browser. You could set it to view the company website automatically and restrict users from viewing non-business-oriented sites on the Web. Since a custom browser need not carry all of the generic features of a full-fledged browser, it would consume less memory and less disk space as well. In other words, you could create an environment that provides all of the functionality of a browser with none of the problems (at least from a company website access perspective).

However, this new application type is more valuable than you may initially think. For example, you could add HTML-enabled components to an existing application to allow it to access a web server–based help desk. Instead of creating a standard help file and adding it to your application, you can create a very specialized web browser and add it instead. (This is precisely the route that Microsoft took with Visual Studio .NET.)

The advantages of HTML-based help are clear. Using the older help files meant that you couldn't easily update the help files for your application once you sent the application to a customer or distributed it throughout the company. Updating HTML help is as easy as changing a file on your web server. In addition, working with Microsoft Help Workshop isn't easy—many developers found deciphering the arcane language used in help files akin to learning a new programming language. HTML-based help requires no compiler or special tools, just a text editor. (Theoretically, you'll want an editor designed to work with HTML before writing a huge help file.)

There are disadvantages to HTML help as well. For one thing, it's a lot of more difficult to build adequate search capability into HTML-based help. Since finding the information the user wants is just as important as creating it in the first place, HTML-based help may not be the answer of choice for novice users. In addition, HTML-based help necessitates an Internet (or, at least, an intranet) connection. If your company has many users on the road, trying to find an Internet connection may not be practical. Of course, you could always create a local copy of the required HTML files, but that would create the same problem as you had before—out-of-date help files.

WRITING CONSOLE APPLICATIONS

As previously mentioned, console applications are useful for a number of tasks, so knowing how to create a console application is important. Most of the applications so far have relied on a dialog-based presentation because the dialog presentation is good for shorter example code. The following sections show how to create two examples that you could use to work with your machine from the command prompt. The goal is to create applications that can execute in the foreground, as part of a script, as a scheduled task, or even as part of another application.

Simple Example

You can create new console applications by selecting the Console Application project in the New Project dialog box shown in Figure 9.1. The resulting project is bare. It includes only a namespace and class declaration with an empty Main() method. As previously mentioned, console applications are designed to provide their functionality with a minimum of memory and resource usage.

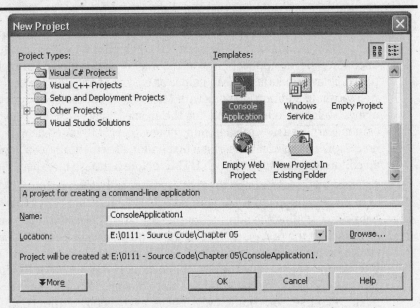

FIGURE 9.1:   The New Project dialog box contains a special icon for console applications.

Console applications generally eschew graphics of any kind. In fact, console applications can access the System.Console class for all input and output requirements. For example, if you want to output some text to the command prompt display, you could use either of these two methods:

```
Console.WriteLine("Method 1");
Console.Out.WriteLine("Method 2");
```

The first method will always output the string to the screen. The output destination of the second method depends on where you set the application output. While the default setting uses the console screen, you can use the Console.SetOut() method to select another location, such as a file, or the Windows event logs. This is a favorite technique for console applications designed to run as part of a script or of the Task Scheduler on a server.

Part of writing a console application is knowing how to process the environmental data. You don't worry about this information in a standard Windows application as much because the application isn't running at the command line. Listing 9.1 shows a simple example of reading all of the environment variables on the current machine and sending them to the console display.

NOTE   You can download all the source files for the programs featured in this chapter from the **Sybex** website at http://www.sybex.com. Search for this chapter's source book by its ISBN number, 4047, or its title, *Visual C# .NET Developer's Handbook*, and look for the Download link on the right. Once you've downloaded the files, you can follow along with the examples without having to type in the program listings.

Listing 9.1: Processing the Environment Variables

```csharp
using System;
using System.Diagnostics;

namespace SimpleConsole
{
    class CheckEnvironment
    {
        [STAThread]
        static void Main(string[] args)
        {
            int    Counter;            // Loop counter.
            // Should the application pause?
            bool  NoPause = false;
            // Determine if the user asked for help.
            if (args.Length > 0)
                for (Counter = 0; Counter < args.Length;
                    Counter++)
                    if (args[Counter] == "/?")
                    {
                        Console.WriteLine(
                            "Displays system environment " +
                            "variables.");
```

```
                    Console.WriteLine(
                        "Use the /NoPause switch to " +
                        "display without a pause.");
                    return;
                }

            // Create an instance of the process information.
            ProcessStartInfo  MyInfo = new ProcessStartInfo();

            // Process each environment variable.
            foreach(String Key in
                MyInfo.EnvironmentVariables.Keys)
            {
                // Write the current key and key value.
                Console.WriteLine(
                    "The current key is: {0}", Key);
                Console.WriteLine(
                    MyInfo.EnvironmentVariables[Key]);
                Console.WriteLine();
            }

            // Determine if we need to pause.
            if (args.Length > 0)
                for (Counter = 0; Counter < args.Length;
                    Counter++)
                    if (args[Counter].ToUpper() == "/NOPAUSE")
                        NoPause = true;

            // Only needed so application pauses.
            if (!NoPause)
            {
                Console.Write("Press any key when ready...");
                Console.ReadLine();
            }
        }
    }
}
```

The code begins by checking for the /? command-line switch. Any
console application you write should include at least a modicum of help
for those who want to use it. Generally, you'll want to include a short
description of application function and any command-line switches.

After checking for the /? command-line switch, the code creates a new ProcessStartInfo object, MyInfo object. This object contains a wealth of information about the application's starting environment, including the environment variables. You access the environment variables using MyInfo.EnvironmentVariables[]. The index is a string containing the name of the key.

The only problem with using the MyInfo.EnvironmentVariables[] index is that you don't know the key names when the application starts because every machine can have a different set of environment variables. That's where the foreach loop comes in handy. This loop accesses the MyInfo.EnvironmentVariables.Keys collection, which contains the name of every key defined on the user's machine. C# excels at working with collections using the technique shown in Listing 9.1.

The application ends by checking for the /NoPause command-line switch. Notice the use of the ToUpper() method to ensure that the code finds the switch in the args list no matter how the user capitalizes the switch. The NoPause variable determines if the application exits directly or pauses for user input. The addition of a pause enables the user to access the application from within Windows or from the command prompt with equal ease.

This is actually a handy maintenance utility to have around because you can use the Task Scheduler to output the user's environment to a known location on the server using redirection like this:

```
SimpleConsole /NoPause >> Temp.txt
```

Some applications insist on adding environment variables to the system and then don't remove them later. As the system gets more clogged with weird environment entries, it can slow. In some cases, a bad environment string can also cause some applications to fail (or, at least, not behave very well). It's also helpful to have an application parse the environment variables looking for development needs. For example, a simple script could detect the presence of path entries for the .NET environment and provide you with a simple "Ready" or "Not Ready" indicator of system setup.

Script-Based Example for Batch Jobs

Many console applications begin and end their existence at the command line because the developer doesn't need them for any other purpose. However, as network administrators begin to write more script applications, the need for console applications that can perform some type of generic low-level work increases. The console application becomes a "black box" that accepts some input from the network administrator and then provides a single output in the form of a return value. Often, the return value indicates only success or failure, but it can offer more.

The example in this section accepts a Windows Management Instrumentation (WMI) query and a text filename as input. The application outputs selected data about the query to a text file. The return value of the application is the number of devices of the requested type. If the application returns 0, then none of the requested devices exists and the text file is blank. Listing 9.2 shows the source code for this example.

Listing 9.2: WMI Provides an Interesting Basis for a Console Application

```csharp
static int Main(string[] args)
{
    // Loop Counter
    int                      Counter;

    // WMI Query Object
    ManagementObjectSearcher   MOS;

    // Query Result Collection.
    ManagementObjectCollection MOCollect;

    // Query Request String
    string                     Query;

    // Output File Object.
    TextWriter                 SendOut;

    // Output to file and screen.
    bool                       Verbose;

    // Clear the old output file.
    bool                       Clear;

    // Output Filename
    string                     OutFile;

    // Verify the user has provided input.
    if (args.Length == 0)
    {
```

```
            Console.WriteLine("You must supply a query or request" +
                "help using the /? switch.");
            return 1;
        }

        // Handle help requests.
        if (args.Length > 0)
            for (Counter = 0; Counter < args.Length; Counter++)
                if (args[Counter] == "/?")
                {
                    Console.WriteLine(
                        "Displays system information " +
                        "using Windows Management Instrumentation (WMI).");
                    Console.WriteLine();
                    Console.WriteLine("Command Line:");
                    Console.WriteLine(
                        "\tConsoleScript /Query:<Query> " +
                        "/Out:<Filename> [/V] [/Clear]");
                    Console.WriteLine();
                    Console.WriteLine(
                        "/Query:<Query>\tProvide a query " +
                        "string as input.");
                    Console.WriteLine(
                        "\t\tAn example query would be, \"" +
                        "SELECT * FROM Win32_LogicalDisk\"");
                    Console.WriteLine(
                        "/Out:<Filename>\tName of the " +
                        "file you want to use for output.");
                    Console.WriteLine(
                        "/V\t\tDisplays the output on " +
                        "screen as well as outputting to
                            the\r\n\t\tfile.");
                    Console.WriteLine(
                        "/Clear\t\tClear the output file " +
                        "before writing to it.\r\n\r\n");
                    Console.WriteLine("Return values:");
                    Console.WriteLine("\t0 - Success");
                    Console.WriteLine("\t1 - No Input Provided");
                    Console.WriteLine("\t2 - No Query Found");
                    Console.WriteLine("\t3 - Device Access Error");
                    return 0;
                }
```

```
// Locate the query.
for (Counter = 0; Counter < args.Length; Counter++)
   if (args[Counter].Length > 7)
   {
      if (args[Counter].Substring(0, 7).ToUpper()
        == "/QUERY:")
         break;
   }
   else
      if (Counter == args.Length - 1)
      {
         Console.WriteLine("No Query Found");
         return 2;
      }

// Place the query in a string.
Query = args[Counter].Substring(7) + " ";
Counter++;
while (args[Counter].Substring(0 , 1) != "/")
{
   Query = Query + args[Counter] + " ";
   Counter++;
   if (Counter == args.Length)
      break;
}

// Locate the output filename.
OutFile = "";
for (Counter = 0; Counter < args.Length; Counter++)
   if (args[Counter].Length > 5)
      if (args[Counter].Substring(0, 5).ToUpper()
        == "/OUT:")
      {
         OutFile = args[Counter].Substring(5);
         break;
      }
      else
         if (Counter == args.Length - 1)
         {
            Console.WriteLine("Using Default Filename");
            OutFile = "Temp.TXT";
         }
```

```
// Create the output file.
Clear = false;
for (Counter = 0; Counter < args.Length; Counter++)
   if (args[Counter].ToUpper() == "/CLEAR")
      Clear = true;
if (Clear)
   SendOut = new StreamWriter(OutFile, false);
else
   SendOut = new StreamWriter(OutFile, true);

// Determine if we need console output.
Verbose = false;
for (Counter = 0; Counter < args.Length; Counter++)
   if (args[Counter].ToUpper() == "/V")
      Verbose = true;

try
{
   // Create a WMI query based on user input.
   MOS = new ManagementObjectSearcher(Query);

   // Get the query results and place
   // them in a collection.
   MOCollect = MOS.Get();

   // Output the data.
   foreach( ManagementObject MO in MOCollect )
   {
      SendOut.Write("Caption: {0} Description: {1}\r\n",
        MO["Caption"], MO["Description"]);
      if (Verbose)
         Console.WriteLine(
           "Caption: {0} Description: {1}\r\n",
            MO["Caption"], MO["Description"]);
   }

   // Close the output file.
   SendOut.Close();
}
catch (System.Management.ManagementException e)
{
   // Output error information as needed.
   Console.WriteLine("Error Accessing Device");
```

```
            Console.WriteLine(e.ErrorCode);
            Console.WriteLine(e.ErrorInformation);
            Console.WriteLine(e.Message);
            Console.WriteLine(e.Source);
            return 3;
        }

        // No errors, so standard return.
        return 0;
    }
```

As you can see, this console application is a little more complex than the previous example. The first thing you should notice is that the return value of Main() has changed from void to int to allow a return value. The batch file used to test this example relies on the return value to print a message.

The code begins by ensuring that the user has provided command-line input. At the very least, the application requires a query to perform any function at all. The user can also request help using the /? command-line switch. The help for this example is more extensive because the console application can perform more work.

The next two sections of code work with the query string, *Query*. First, the code needs to locate the /Query switch within the command-line arguments. Second, the code builds the query string. The application continues processing the arguments until it runs into another switch or comes to the end of the command line. The content of *Query* looks much like a SQL statement and follows some of the same logic. A simple query always includes four elements: Select <*What to Select*> From <*WMI class name*>. For example, if you wanted to query the logical disks on your system, you'd use a string similar to, "Select * From Win32_Logical-Disk." The ManagementObjectSearcher object also allows you to filter the output using a WHERE clause such as "WHERE DriveType = 3." In this case, we'd be looking for all local drives and filtering out the network drives.

TIP

You can find a list of WMI classes in the Computer System Hardware Classes help topic (ms-help://MS.VSCC/MS.MSDNVS/wmisdk/r_32hard1_9v77.htm). Each class lists the types of information you can retrieve about the hardware in question. Some types of information, such as Description, are generic for any hardware class. Other pieces of information, such as the Compressed Value for Win32_LogicalDisk, are specific to the hardware class in question.

After it creates a query string, the code locates the output filename. Even though the help lists the /Out switch as required, it can recover from input errors by creating a default filename. The application does output a message stating that it's using a default filename instead of using one provided by the user. The code checks for the /Clear switch and then creates the file using the StreamWriter() constructor. The second argument of this constructor is true if you want to append data to the existing file. The resulting object assumes you want to use the local directory if you don't supply a path as part of the filename.

At this point, the code enters a try block. Error handling is nice in other areas of the application, but it's required here. Otherwise, the application will fail on a number of WMI supported devices, even if the device is installed and functional. The problem is one of recognition. Depending on the BIOS provided with the machine, the method used to support WMI, and Windows' ability to see the device, some devices might not appear on the list.

It's time to obtain the WMI information from the system. The code performs three steps to complete this process.

1. The code creates the query. The query will normally succeed unless the input string is malformed.

2. The code executes the query and places the result in a collection. If this step fails, the collection will contain a null value, but it won't fail.

3. The code uses a foreach loop to view each collection member. This step always fails if the device is inoperative, unrecognized, or unavailable. The example provides two forms of output. The first is to a file, while the second is an optional screen output.

Before you can compile this application, you need to add the usual using statements to the beginning of the file. You also need to add a reference to the System.Management component by selecting the Project ➢ Add Reference command. You'll see an Add Reference dialog box similar to the one shown in Figure 9.2. Highlight the System .Management entry, click Select, then click OK to add the reference to your project.

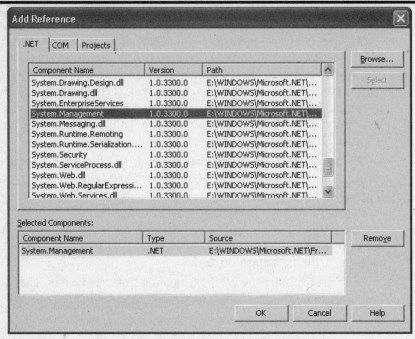

FIGURE 9.2:   Use the Add Reference dialog box to add the System.Management
component to your application.

In the following code, a simple query is accepted as input, and output
is provided based on the `ConsoleScript` invocation results:

```
ECHO OFF

REM Run the application.
ConsoleScript %1 %2 %3 %4 %5 %6 %7

REM Test the output.
If ErrorLevel 3 Goto DeviceErr
If ErrorLevel 2 Goto NoQuery
If ErrorLevel 1 Goto NoInput

REM If no error, exit.
Goto Success

REM Error Message Output.
:NoInput
ECHO No Input Provided
GOTO END
```

```
:NoQuery
ECHO Always provide an /Query input.
GOTO END
:DeviceErr
ECHO Device error - is it installed?
GOTO END

:Success
ECHO Task Completed Successfully!

:END
ECHO ON
```

Of course, you could easily use the ConsoleScript application with a script file or as part of a Task Scheduler entry. The point is that console applications help you automate many tasks and perform others in the background or at a command prompt. A console application isn't a good choice when you need to provide a large amount of user interaction, but it does fill a needed gap in the network administrator's Toolkit.

RESOURCE ESSENTIALS

You won't write many applications that can function without resources of some type. Resources include menus, accelerators, bitmaps, special controls, accessibility features, and web-access support. Resources also include fonts, brushes, and pens—the drawing tools we've used in other areas of the book. Your code interacts with the resources to present information to the user in a helpful manner.

The following sections will discuss many of the resources we haven't yet covered fully or at all. We'll work with these resources extensively as the book progresses. For example, you'll find some graphics examples later in the chapter. This chapter will also show one way to use timers in your applications.

Accelerators and Menus

Menus come in a variety of shapes and sizes. All SDI and MDI applications require a main menu. This menu normally contains a File entry, as well as some form of Help. However, Visual Studio .NET provides you with a clean slate when you create a menu, so the contents are completely up to you. Following the pattern used by existing applications is good practice because using a standard menu template makes it easier for others to learn your application.

Another typical menu type is the context menu. Most Windows objects provide a context menu so the user knows how to interact with that object. Dialog applications use context menus frequently, and you'll also find context menus in SDI and MDI applications. The menu you see in an application that resides in the Taskbar tray is a context menu, as is the menu you see when you click within the work area of an SDI or MDI application.

The main and context menus for an application are different controls: MainMenu and ContextMenu. An application can have multiple context menus, but it can contain only one main menu. The main menu attaches itself to the form where you create it and normally remains visible. In most cases, you can hide the main menu by setting the Menu property of the form to a null (blank) value. Here's an example of two context menu commands that will hide and show the main menu.

```
private void HideMainMenu_Click(
   object sender, System.EventArgs e)
{
   // Hide the main menu.
   Menu = null;
}

private void ShowMainMenu_Click(
   object sender, System.EventArgs e)
{
   // Show the main menu.
   Menu = mainMenu1;
}
```

It's interesting to note that you can use this same technique for changing between predefined main menus, rather than build each main menu by scratch. Many applications disable the menu entries the user can't access given the current environment, but sometimes it pays to create multiple main menus during design time for a quick swap during runtime. Of course, you can only use one main menu at a time.

You need to attach a context menu to an object using the object ContextMenu property to make it accessible. The context menu is only visible when the user right-clicks the object or you make the menu visible in some other way. Unlike a main menu, context menus contain only one main entry. However, you can create as many submenus as needed to complete a given task.

Despite their differences, creating a main menu and a context menu is essentially the same. You'll begin with a blank menu where you type the various menu entries, as shown in Figure 9.3. Notice the use of the ampersand to create underlines. A user can type the underlined character to access the menu entry, so you need to make the entries unique for a given menu level.

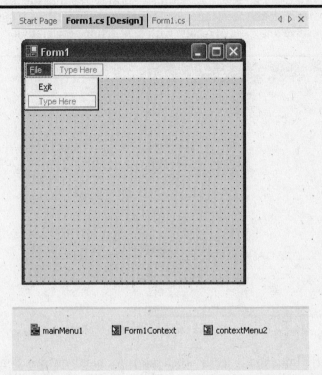

FIGURE 9.3:   Main and context menus follow essentially the same design process.

Visual Studio .NET uses a nondescript naming technique for menus—menuItem followed by a number. Most developers use a naming scheme that follows the menu hierarchy. For example, a developer might name the Exit option of the File menu mnuFileExit for easy identification.

This brings us to the topic of accelerators or shortcut keys (the term you use likely depends on the environment in which you started working). You assign an accelerator to an object using the *Shortcut* property. An accelerator enables a user to access a menu or other command using a key combination, rather than the menu hierarchy. Like menu setups, most applications use specific accelerators for the same task. For example, you can usually access the print feature of an application by pressing Ctrl+P.

One of the interesting characteristics of the C# IDE is that you can't see the accelerator you assign to a menu entry until the application is running. This means you have to assign the accelerator judiciously. Otherwise, the same accelerator could appear on two different menu entries, as shown in Figure 9.4. Experimentation shows that the first menu item to receive the accelerator key will normally use it, which means you might receive unexpected results with conflicting accelerators.

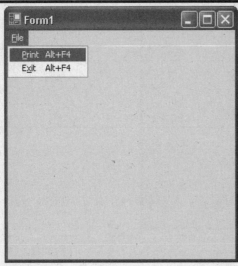

FIGURE 9.4:   Always use accelerators carefully to avoid conflicts.

C# doesn't limit you to using accelerators for menu entries. Some controls such as the DataGrid come with built-in accelerators. You can also create accelerators with labels to access the associated control faster. Type an ampersand next to the letter in the label that you want to use for access. When you press Alt+<*Letter*>, the application automatically selects the control (normally a text box) associated with the label. Some controls, such as the pushbutton, allow you to add the accelerator directly by typing the ampersand as part of the control text.

Accessibility Features

The best way to make your application friendly is to use a sensible layout, add plenty of help, and use features such as accelerators. These features help a lot; but, in some cases, they aren't enough. That's where the accessibility features come into play. Visual Studio .NET provides the means to add accessibility cues to your applications. For example, these cues could help someone who might not be able to see the application to make more sense out of what they hear about the application.

The three accessibility cues are associated with control properties. The following list tells you about each property and tells how you'd use it to increase the information about your application.

AccessibleDescription   This property provides a better description of the use of an application control than might be apparent from the control itself. For example, if you use a picture button, someone with normal vision might understand that a stop-sign symbol enables them to stop the current operation. However, you'd also want to provide an `AccessibleDescription` that tells how to use the button.

AccessibleName   This property contains the short name for a control. You'd use it when you need to provide a more descriptive name for the control than space will allow on a form but don't require a complete description. For example, this property might contain a value of "OK Button," so someone with a screen reader would know that it's a button with the word OK on it.

AccessibleRole   This property to is used to define the type of control interface. For example, you can define the role of a button or button-like control as a `PushButton`. Visual Studio appears to use the Default setting for all controls, even when it's easy to determine the type of control. All screen readers will use this property, even the readers that come with the various versions of Windows. Telling the user that they're working with a push button is helpful, especially when the push button has a unique shape or other feature. (Think about the odd buttons on the skin for the Windows Media Player.)

In addition to filling out the accessibility properties for all of the controls in your application, you can also support some accessibility features directly. For example, one of the accessibility features that many users need is high contrast. This feature is indispensable when working on some laptops, because it provides the extra information needed to see the screen in sunlight. While some people use this feature all of the time, others use it at the end of the day to reduce eyestrain.

Your application can detect when the system goes into high contrast mode by monitoring the `SystemInformation.HighContrast` property.

Of course, you'll still need to select high contrast color combinations (with black and white providing the best contrast). The point is that some screens that look great in color look terrible when put into high contrast mode. If you don't detect this property, the high contrast mode that should help the user might end up causing problems.

Graphics

In some respects, graphics haven't changed for Windows developers since the days of Window 3.x. Visual Studio still provides access to the same three graphic resources: icons (ICO), bitmaps (BMP), and cursors (CUR). The only change for Visual Studio .NET is an increase in the number of colors you can use. Unlike previous versions, you can now create your graphics in something more than 256 colors. You'll also find that icons and cursors now come in a 96 × 96–bit size.

Adding a new graphic image has changed in Visual Studio .NET. The fastest way to add a new graphic is to right-click the project entry in Solution Explorer and choose Add ➢ Add New Item from the context menu. Select the Resources category and you'll see a list of resources similar to the one shown in Figure 9.5.

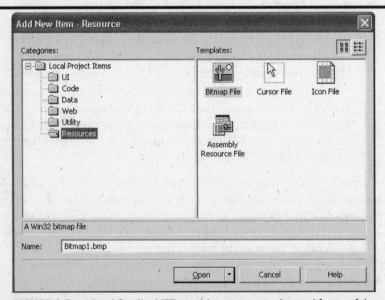

FIGURE 9.5: Visual Studio .NET provides access to enhanced forms of the graphics files you've always used.

Once you create the new graphic, you'll see a typical bit level drawing area that includes a color selection toolbar and a second toolbar with drawing tools. Anyone who's used Paint in the past will feel comfortable with the tools in Visual Studio .NET.

Bitmap files contain only one image, so if you need different resolutions of the same bitmap, you'll need to create individual bitmap files. However, cursor and icon files can both contain multiple images that vary by resolution and color depth. In fact, you'll need to define multiple images when working with icons to obtain the best display because Windows will select the best image automatically. This is especially important in Windows XP, because this new operating system uses 64×64–bit icons and greater color depth. To add a new image to the list for an icon, right-click the drawing area and choose New Image Type from the context menu. You'll see a New Icon Image Type dialog box from which you can choose a new type. Context menu options also enable you to select from an existing image type or delete one that you no longer need.

Graphic resources aren't limited to the three you can access directly in Visual Studio .NET. We'll see later that you can use the Bitmap object to import graphics that Visual Studio never supported in the past. This includes using resources such as GIFs in your applications. Anyone who's designed a web page knows the value of animated GIFs in dressing up a display so that it looks attractive to visitors. In fact, we'll create a desktop application that makes use of an animated GIF later in the "SDI Example" section of this chapter.

Timers

Timers help you keep track of time. A timer is actually one of the easiest controls to use in Windows. All you need to do is set the Interval property for the number of milliseconds between each Tick event. You create an event handler for the tick that tracks events or performs other tasks based on the time. Look in the "Dialog-Based Example" section later in this chapter for an example of an application that uses timers to keep track of your typing time.

Toolbars

Toolbars are a required resource for SDI and MDI applications because they provide a shortcut to essential application functionality. For example, users have become very dependent on the three icons used to manage documents in most SDI and MDI applications: New, Open, and Save.

In the past, developers would drop a toolbar on their application, then drop buttons on the toolbar. Visual Studio .NET takes a slightly different approach, with a vastly improved ToolBar control. Unlike previous versions, the buttons are now part of a collection that resides with the toolbar. However, how to add a button isn't quite as obvious as it might be, so some people are still using the old approach of dropping buttons on the toolbar.

Click the Buttons property on the ToolBar control and you'll see the word Collection. Click the ellipsis button and you'll see a ToolBarButton Collection Editor dialog box similar to the one shown in Figure 9.6. (Note that the figure shows a toolbar with buttons already defined—your toolbar will start out buttonless.) This dialog box is the only method for defining the properties for the buttons.

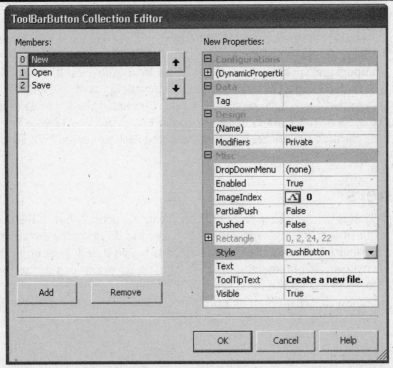

FIGURE 9.6:   Use the ToolBarButton Collection Editor to modify the appearance of the ToolBar control.

NOTE

If you want to create picture buttons for your ToolBar control, you'll want to create an ImageList control first and fill it with the images that you'll need. Associate the ImageList with the ToolBar using the ImageList property. The ImageIndex property found in the ToolBar Collection Editor dialog box enables you to choose a specific icon from the ImageList for the current ToolBarButton.

This brings us to the problem of working with a ToolBar that has embedded ToolBarButtons, rather than standard buttons placed over the ToolBar. When you use standard buttons, you can access the individual button events. However, when working with embedded ToolBarButtons, you only have access to the ToolBar events.

One of the ToolBar events is ButtonClicked. When you create an event handler for this event, the application passes you a copy of the information for the button. Unfortunately, this information doesn't include the button name. To make it possible to identify the button, you must assign the button a Tag property value. Once you have the Tag property value, you can pass the ToolBar button handling onto the associated menu event handler as shown in the following code.

```
private void mnuFileNew_Click(
   object sender, System.EventArgs e)
{
   // Display a helpful message.
   MessageBox.Show("Clicked File | New");
}

private void toolBar1_ButtonClick(object sender,
   System.Windows.Forms.ToolBarButtonClickEventArgs e)
{
   // Display a message for the button.
   MessageBox.Show("Clicked the " +
                   e.Button.Tag.ToString() +
                   " button.");

   // Do something special for the New button.
   if (e.Button.Tag.ToString() == "New")
      mnuFileNew_Click(this, e);
}
```

WRITING WINDOWS APPLICATIONS

Most of the applications you'll create with C# will likely have a GUI. Windows applications use a GUI to make the user experience better, reduce training time, and enable the user to work more efficiently. As previously mentioned, the standard Windows application types include dialog-based, SDI, and MDI. Within those three categories are an infinite array of subtypes. For example, a dialog-based application can act as a training aid or as a utility application.

The following sections examine several types of Windows applications. For example, the dialog-based example shows you how to create a utility that appears within the Taskbar Tray (Notification Area) instead of the Taskbar. This example also serves to demonstrate some of the ways in which Microsoft has improved Visual Studio .NET. Creating such an application in the previous version of Visual Studio would have required substantially more work.

Dialog-Based Example

One type of dialog-based example that we haven't discussed is the use of the Taskbar Tray for keeping utility applications active and out of the way. Previous versions of Visual Studio tended to make it difficult to create such an application. Visual Studio .NET provides several new components and controls, plus some additional form settings, that make the task almost trivial. This example is a basic timer application. It displays a message at specific intervals that remind you to take a break from typing.

This example's name is Typing Buddy. It appears in the Taskbar Tray until the predefined interval elapses. At that moment, the program displays a message box advising the user that it's time for a break. You'll need to use three special controls to make this application work properly:

- ▶ NotifyIcon
- ▶ ContextMenu
- ▶ Timer

In addition to adding new components and controls to the application, you'll also need to configure the main form differently from other projects. Make sure you set the ShowInTaskbar property to false so the application moves to the Taskbar Tray when minimized. You'll also want to start the application minimized using the WindowState property so it waits in the background without bothering the user. Figure 9.7 shows the form configuration for this example.

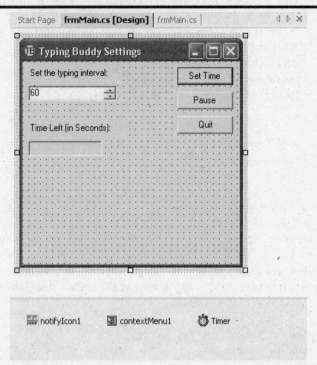

FIGURE 9.7: The Typing Buddy example includes some basic configuration controls.

This type of application relies on a certain level of automation. You want the application to start automatically when the machine starts and continue operation until the user shuts the machine down. Of course, you also need to be sure that the user configures the application properly for use. The solution is to check for an existing set of configuration options, and then create them if they are needed. Listing 9.3 shows the frmMain_Load(), which is responsible for getting the application running.

Listing 9.3: Creating the Initial Application Configuration

```
private void frmMain_Load(object sender, System.EventArgs e)
{
    // See if the user has worked with this program before.
    if (!InRegistry())
    {
```

```
            // If not, display a welcome message
            // and the configuration screen.
            MessageBox.Show("Welcome to Typing Buddy!\r\n" +
                "You need to set an initial typing value by " +
                "entering a time interval and clicking Set.",
                "Welcome Message",
                MessageBoxButtons.OK,
                MessageBoxIcon.Information);
            WindowState = FormWindowState.Normal;
        }
        else
            // Start the timer.
            Timer.Start();
    }

    private bool InRegistry()
    {
        RegistryKey oSub;              // Typing Buddy storage key.

        // Check for the application key; null if not available.
        oSub = Microsoft.Win32.Registry.LocalMachine.OpenSubKey(
            "Software\\TypingBuddy");

        // Check to see if the key exists.
        if (oSub != null)
        {
            // Set the timer value.
            TimeLeft = (int)oSub.GetValue("TimeSet");

            // Close the registry keys.
            oSub.Close();

            // Return a success value.
            return true;
        }

        // Return a failure value.
        return false;
    }
```

The main job of frmMain_Load() is to ensure that the application has
settings to use when it begins running. The choice is one of displaying the

configuration screen if this is the first use of the application or starting the timer so that the application begins running in the background without user interaction. The means for making this determination is the InRegistry() method.

The InRegistry() uses the simple technique of opening the application's registry entry. If *oSub* is null, then the registry key doesn't exist and the application isn't configured for use. On the other hand, if the registry key does exist, InRegistry() reads the contents of the *TimeSet* value and places them in *TimeLeft*.

You might wonder why InRegistry() doesn't start the timer as well. The current coding enables the application to use InRegistry() from various locations to check the configuration state of the application. We'll also use this method when configuring the application.

It's time to look at the code for the three buttons shown in Figure 9.7. The Pause context menu option also relies on this code. All three buttons and the context menu control that state of the application. Listing 9.4 shows you how.

Listing 9.4: The Set Time, Pause, and Quit Buttons Control Application State

```
private void btnSet_Click(object sender, System.EventArgs e)
{
    RegistryKey oReg; // Hive Registry Key
    RegistryKey oSub; // Company storage key.

    // Set the controls.
    TimeLeft = (Int32)TimerValue.Value * 60;
    Timer.Start();

    // Add the information to the registry.

    if (!InRegistry())
    {
        // Open the HKEY_LOCAL_MACHINE\Software
        // key for writing.
        oReg =
          Microsoft.Win32.Registry.LocalMachine.OpenSubKey(
          "Software", true);

        // Write the company subkey.
        oReg.CreateSubKey("TypingBuddy");
```

```
            // Close the registry key.
            oReg.Close();
        }

        // Write the default value.
        oSub = Microsoft.Win32.Registry.LocalMachine.OpenSubKey(
            "Software\\TypingBuddy",
            true);
        oSub.SetValue("TimeSet", TimeLeft);

        // Close the registry keys.
        oSub.Close();
    }

    bool  IsPaused;    // Is the timer paused?

    private void btnPause_Click(
      object sender, System.EventArgs e)
    {
        if (IsPaused)
        {
            // Start the timer.
            IsPaused = false;
            Timer.Start();

            // Display status information.
            btnPause.Text = "Pause";
            mnuPause.Text = "Pause";
        }
        else
        {
            // Stop the timer.
            IsPaused = true;
            Timer.Stop();

            // Display status information.
            btnPause.Text = "Restart";
            mnuPause.Text = "Restart";
            notifyIcon1.Text = "Timer is Paused";
        }
    }
```

```
private void btnQuit_Click(object sender, System.EventArgs e)
{
    DialogResult   RetValue;   // Users selection.

    // Display an exit message.
    RetValue = MessageBox.Show(
       "Are you sure you want to exit?" +
       "\r\n(Program will minimize if you select No.)",
       "Exit Application",
       MessageBoxButtons.YesNo,
       MessageBoxIcon.Question,
       MessageBoxDefaultButton.Button2);

    if (RetValue == DialogResult.Yes)
       // Exit the application.
       Close();
    else
       // Minimize the form.
       WindowState = FormWindowState.Minimized;
}
```

The `btnSet_Click()` begins by setting the control values for the application and starting the timer. This ensures that the user will see changes immediately and won't need to wait for registry operations to complete.

The next task is to determine if the registry already contains settings for the control. If the registry doesn't contain the required entries, the application makes them, and then closes the registry key. The final step is to write the new timer value into the registry so that it's ready the next time the user starts the application.

The `btnPause_Click()` method toggles the application between two operational states. The paused state sets the timer off and changes the buttons and notification icon balloon help to reflect the change. Likewise, when the application starts again, the timer state is changed and so are the buttons. The notification icon balloon help changes automatically as part of the timer functionality, so there's no need to change it here. The *IsPaused* field keeps track of the current state.

Normally, when the user selects Quit, the application exits. However, some users don't realize that minimizing the application removes the dialog display from view. Because of this problem, you'll want to write a special routine for the `btnQuit_Click()` method. Notice that this is one of the first times we've used the return value from the `MessageBox.Show()` method to control application flow. In addition, the example shows how to create a default button for the dialog box associated with the `MessageBox.Show()` call.

The return value determines if the application ends or merely minimizes. Notice the use of various built-in values for this example. You'll use the special `DialogResult` type to hold the user selection and compare it to values in the `DialogResult` class. The `FormWindowState` enumeration also enables you to set the `WindowState` property of the form with ease. Note that we use the `FormWindowState` enumeration for the `notifyIcon1_DoubleClick()` method as well.

The "heartbeat" of this application is the system clock referenced by the Timer control. This control has a single event associated with it, `Tick`. Listing 9.5 shows the code for the `Timer_Tick()` method.

Listing 9.5: The *Timer_Tick()* Method Is Central to Typing Buddy Operation

```
private void Timer_Tick(object sender, System.EventArgs e)
{
    DialogResult   RetVal;  // Return value from dialog.

    // Set the timer value.
    TimeLeft--;

    // See if the timer has expired.
    if (TimeLeft == 0)
    {
        // Reset the controls.
        TimeLeft = (Int32)TimerValue.Value * 60;
        Timer.Stop();

        // Display the stop typing message.
        RetVal = MessageBox.Show(
            "Time to stop typing! Relax!" +
            "\r\nPress OK to Restart" +
            "\r\nor Cancel to exit program.",
            "TypingBuddy Alert",
            MessageBoxButtons.OKCancel,
            MessageBoxIcon.Hand);

        if (RetVal == DialogResult.OK)
```

```
            // Restart the timer.
            Timer.Start();
        else
            // Exit the application.
            Close();
    }
    else
    {
        // Update the time left indicator.
        TypingTime.Text = TimeLeft.ToString();
        notifyIcon1.Text = "Time Left in Seconds: " +
                            TimeLeft.ToString();
    }
}
```

As you can see, the operation isn't complex. During a normal update cycle, the Timer_Tick() method decrements the TimeLeft field and performs a comparison to see if TimeLeft is at 0. Normally, the comparison will fail, so the Timer_Tick() method will update the text values for the TypingTime text box (shown in Figure 9.7) and notifyIcon1. Updating the notifyIcon1.Text property changes the value of the balloon help, so the user can hover their mouse over the icon to see how much time they have until their next break.

When TimeLeft does make it to 0, Timer_Tick() resets the TimeLeft field and turns off the timer. It displays a "break" message to the user. When the user clicks OK, the whole timing process begins again. Of course, the user can always select Cancel to end the application.

SDI Example

At one time, it was sufficient for an application to provide an appealing display of data located on either the user's hard drive or the company network. In fact, many users were happy if they could understand the display and use it to do something useful. Today, a user wants more in the way of presentation and feedback. Many applications today use simple animation to get a point across to the user.

Microsoft is at the forefront of the changes to the user interface—at least in some areas. For example, Windows Explorer uses animations to show a file moving from one location to another. The presence of action gives the user a feeling of comfort about the application, even when it doesn't do anything other than display the animated sequence.

Unfortunately, creating animations is difficult in Windows if you use the traditional methods. Fortunately, some solutions make it easy to add animation to websites and now those animations can appear on the desktop as well. One of many ways to create animations is to use an animated GIF file. Animated GIFs have been around for quite some time. You see them all the time on the Internet. All of those little animations you see on websites are very likely animated GIFs. An animated GIF file works by placing multiple images in a single file. Timing and presentation commands separate the images. Each command tells the displaying application how to present the next frame of the animation and how long to present it.

Most developers know that Visual Studio doesn't support the GIF file format as a standard graphic—at least, Visual Studio didn't provide GIF support in the past. If you tried loading an animated GIF to your project, you'd receive an error message saying the GIF was damaged or simply incorrect. The Visual Studio .NET IDE still doesn't support GIF files directly. Even if you can view the GIF inside Internet Explorer, Visual Studio .NET will steadfastly refuse to load it.

TIP

You'll find many applications you can use to create an animated GIF for your application. I designed the animated GIF for the example using the GIF Construction Set from Alchemy Mind Works. You can download this product from several places. The best place is from the vendor at http://www .mindworkshop.com/alchemy/gifcon.html. Another good alternative is Paint Shop Pro 7 from Jasc (http://www.jasc.com). Note that earlier versions of the product don't include this feature and that the current product isn't quite as capable as the GIF Construction Set.

The good news is that you can combine the new Bitmap object with the Animator object to load and support animated GIFs within your application—even desktop applications. The Bitmap object acts as a container for the graphic, while the Animator provides the means to page through each image and presents it in turn. When you combine the two objects, you see the animation sequence on screen without resorting to the odd programming techniques of the past. Listing 9.6 shows the code you'll need to make this application work.

Listing 9.6: Adding Animation to the Desktop Isn't Hard in Visual Studio .NET

```
private  String   File2Open;  // Selected Filename
private  Bitmap   AniGIF;     // Animated GIF to Display
private  int   ·  DrawSelect; // Drawing mode.
private  bool     Animated;   // Animation active.

private void mnuFileOpen_Click(
  object sender, System.EventArgs e)
{
   OpenFileDialog Dlg =
     new OpenFileDialog();   // File Open Dialog

   // Set up the File Open Dialog
   Dlg.Filter =
     "Graphics Interchange Format File (*.gif)|*.gif";
   Dlg.DefaultExt = ".gif";
   Dlg.Title = "Open File Dialog";

   // Display the File Open Dialog
   // and obtain the name of a file and
   // the file information.
   if (Dlg.ShowDialog() == DialogResult.OK)
   {
      File2Open = Dlg.FileName;
   }
   else
   {
      // If the user didn't select anything, return.
      return;
   }

   // Open the document.
   AniGIF = new Bitmap(File2Open);

   // Set the drawing mode.
   DrawSelect = 2;
   Animated = false;

   // Change the title bar.
   Form1.ActiveForm.Text =
     "GIF Animation Example - " + File2Open;
```

```
        // Force a redraw of the display area.
        DisplayArea.Invalidate();
    }

    private void DisplayArea_Paint(object sender,
        System.Windows.Forms.PaintEventArgs e)
    {
        // Can't draw the image if the bitmap is null.
        if (AniGIF != null)
        {
            switch (DrawSelect)
            {
                case 1:
                    // Animate the GIF file.
                    ImageAnimator.UpdateFrames();
                    e.Graphics.DrawImage(AniGIF,
                                         4,
                                         4,
                                         AniGIF.Width,
                                         AniGIF.Height);
                    break;

                case 2:
                    // Draw a graphic normally.
                    e.Graphics.DrawImage(AniGIF,
                                         4,
                                         4,
                                         AniGIF.Width,
                                         AniGIF.Height);
                    break;
            }
        }
    }

    private void mnuAnimationStart_Click(
        object sender, System.EventArgs e)
    {
        // Initialize the animating the
        // first time the user selects it.
        if (!Animated)
        {
            ImageAnimator.Animate(AniGIF,
                                  new EventHandler(NextFrame));
```

```
        Animated = true;
    }

    // Select a drawing mode.
    DrawSelect = 1;
}

private void mnuAnimationStop_Click(
    object sender, System.EventArgs e)
{
    // Select a drawing mode that stops the animation.
    DrawSelect = 2;
}

private void NextFrame(object sender, System.EventArgs e)
{
    // Force OnPaint() to redraw the animation.
    DisplayArea.Invalidate();
}
```

The application requires the use of four fields, as shown in the listing. It's important to make the bitmap resources universally available within the class to ensure that you can perform all of the required timing for the animation. However, nothing outside the class should require access to the bitmap. If so, you should use properties to ensure that you can track everything that affects the bitmap and animation.

When the user opens the application, they'll see a typical SDI display. The first task is to open a file. Near the end of the mnuFileOpen_Click() method, you'll see five lines of code that load the bitmap into the drawing area. The four fields now contain the values needed to present the bitmap on screen. The DisplayArea.Invalidate() call forces a redraw of the DisplayArea panel so that you can see the bitmap loaded.

The DisplayArea_Paint() method can present the bitmap in two ways. The method of choice when the bitmap first loads is as a static image. As you can see from the case 2 code, System.Windows.Forms .PaintEventArgs provides the application with a drawing area that it uses to display the bitmap on screen. All the code has to specify is the Bitmap object (AniGIF) and the drawing rectangle. (We'll discuss the case 1 code in a moment.)

The mnuAnimationStart_Click() method starts the animation process. Notice that we haven't created anything to animate the image yet and we won't—it comes as part of your application. The code verifies the animation status of the bitmap before it adds the NextFrame event handler to the existing ImageAnimator object.

Note in this example how you can continue to add new event handlers to a delegate. The delegate simply calls them each in turn. If you continue adding the same event handler to the ImageAnimator, the animation will continue to speed up until you can no longer see the animation—each event handler will advance the frame by one. Instead of seeing one frame per interval, you might begin seeing three or four. That's why the animated state check is so important. The ImageAnimator will call NextFrame() each time the command inside the animated GIF states that it's time to display another image.

The interesting thing about the NextFrame() method is that the only task it performs is invalidating the display area. This action invokes the OnPaint() method. However, in this case, the OnPaint() method will use the case 1 code. The ImageAnimator appears in this code as well. In this case, you're asking the ImageAnimator to access the next frame in the animation. When OnPaint() draws the image, it will actually draw the current image in the animated series, rather than the first image contained in the file as normal.

Stopping the animation is relatively easy. All you need to do is select the case 2 image drawing routine in OnPaint(). The animation will stop at the current point in its execution. Theoretically, you could work with this example to slow the animation down so that you could view it one frame at a time. Figure 9.8 shows the AniDisplay application with the AnimatedTime.GIF file loaded.

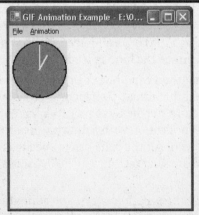

FIGURE 9.8:   Animated GIFs can provide extra pizzazz in a desktop application.

APPLICATION DEBUGGING

The debugger is the most important tool in your arsenal for ensuring that the code works as you intended after the application is released. The problem for some developers is that the debugger is also one of the most misunderstood parts of the IDE. The following sections provide a quick tutorial on using the debugger to your advantage while working on the examples in this book.

Using the Debugger

The most common way to use the debugger is to set a breakpoint on your code and start the debugger using the Start ➢ Debug command. Of course, you can also start the debugger and simply wait for your code to fail the first time.

Breakpoints come in two forms. The first is an unconditional breakpoint you set by clicking the left margin of the line of code. You can also right-click the line of code and choose Insert Breakpoint from the context menu. An unconditional breakpoint always stops execution.

The second breakpoint is conditional. It relies on a specific set of circumstances to stop execution. To set a conditional breakpoint, right-click the line of code and choose New Breakpoint from the context menu. You'll see a New Breakpoint dialog box similar to the one shown in Figure 9.9.

As you can see, this dialog box enables you to set a variety of conditional breakpoints, including breakpoints based on the value of a variable or even the breakpoint hit count. The *hit count* is the number of times the application has reached the breakpoint during normal execution. Notice the Address tab of the New Breakpoint dialog box. You can use this tab to enter the address where an application failed. The Address field will access a value in decimal or hexadecimal. Preface any hexadecimal numbers with a "0x" to ensure that the debugger sees them correctly.

TIP

The Debug ➢ Start Without Debugging command enables you to run an application from the Visual Studio .NET IDE without using the debugger. This is a useful feature if you want to check for timing errors or problems that could occur when the application runs outside the debugger. Not every problem shows up when you run the application with the debugger. In fact, some resource problems only show up when you create a release version of the application. Consequently, using the Start Without Debugging command is an essential part of checking your application execution.

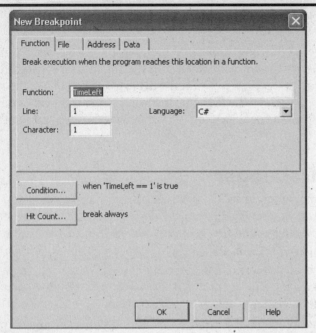

FIGURE 9.9:   You can set conditional breakpoints using the New Breakpoint dialog box.

Once the application is running under the debugger, you have a number of choices for following the execution path. All of these actions appear on the Debug toolbar shown in Figure 9.10. These buttons (in order of appearance) are: Continue, Break All, Stop Debugging, Restart, Show Next Statement, Step Into, Step Over, and Step Out (we'll cover the other two buttons later).

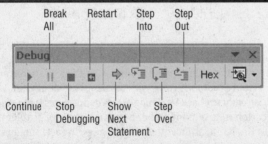

FIGURE 9.10:   The Debug toolbar contains all of the buttons you'll need to perform most debugging tasks.

The three buttons Step Into, Step Over, and Step Out enable you to follow the execution path one step at a time. If you step into a command, you'll follow the execution path one level lower. For example, if the instruction pointer rests on a function call, you'll step into that function. Stepping over a command means that you remain at the same level. The code still executes the function call, but you only see the results of the function call, not the intermediate steps. Finally, stepping out of a function means rising one level higher. The debugger will finish executing the code at the current level and stop at the next statement of the previous (higher) level. The problem is that stepping out doesn't always work if an errant instruction at the current level prevents the code from executing.

After you've learned all you can at the current breakpoint, you can choose one of three actions. Click Continue if you want the application to execute normally until it hits the next breakpoint. Click Stop Debugging if you've finished the current debugging session. Finally, click Restart if you want to start the debugging session over again. Clicking Break All will stop application execution at the current instruction, no matter what the application might be doing at the time.

Performing Remote Debugging

Not every debugging session happens with an application loaded in the debugger or even with a local application. Sometimes you'll want to debug a running process. In some cases, this process might appear on another machine. For example, you need to perform remote debugging to check the operation of a component on a server that a local client is using. If you're using a distributed application technology such as SOAP, there's no direct connection between client and server, so you need to create a separate debugging session for the remote component.

The Debug ➢ Processes command displays the Processes dialog box shown in Figure 9.11. This dialog box enables you to perform remote debugging of an existing process such as a server-side component. All you need to do is attach to the server by supplying a Transport (Default normally works fine) and a Name value. When the debugger attaches to the server, you'll see a list of the processes on that server.

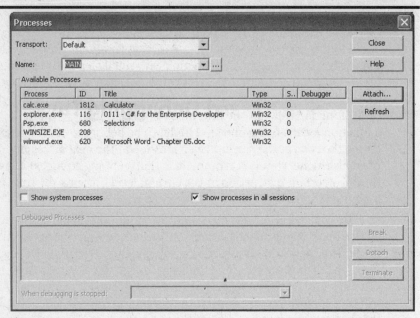

FIGURE 9.11: Use the Processes dialog box to attach to a remote server in order to debug existing processes.

NOTE

You must be part of the Debugger Users group on the remote machine in order to use the remote debugging features of Visual Studio .NET. In most cases, being a member of the Administrators group doesn't automatically extend rights to the Debugger Users group. Microsoft chose to make this security election specific in an effort to reduce the risks of security breaches on the remote machine.

Notice that the Processes dialog box includes check boxes that show the processes in all sessions and the system processes. Choosing the correct set of viewing options makes it easier to locate the process you want to view. When you find the process you want to view, click Attach. You'll see an Attach to Process dialog box that contains application debug types. This dialog box will always have the Common Language Runtime and Native options checked. If you want to debug another application type, you'll need to check the correct option. Click OK and you'll attach to the process.

At this point, you can click Break, in the Processes dialog box, to start the debugging session. You can use the same controls as you would with any application to start and stop application execution. In short, except for the attachment process, debugging a remote application is much the same as debugging a local application. Of course, you can't see any visual elements of the application unless they appear through the client on the local machine. Remote debugging is limited to work with the remote code.

Performing Standard Debugging Tasks

When you start your application, the debugger normally creates a series of seven windows along the bottom of the display area. Each of these windows serves a different purpose in helping you work with your application. The following list tells you about each window.

Autos   Some applications can get quite complex and generate more than a few variables, which can make the windows become cluttered. The Autos window contains a list of variables associated with the current and the preceding statement. This view enables you to focus on just the current task and clears up the clutter you might otherwise have to view. The window shows the variable name, value, and type.

Locals   This window contains a list of all the variables associated with the current function. It doesn't show variables outside the current function. For example, if you have a global variable, it won't appear in this window, even if the current function performs some task with the variable. You'll see the values of any arguments used to call the function. The Locals window shows the variable name, value, and type.

Watch   You'll place variables and functions that you want to watch in this window. The easiest way to do this is to highlight the code in question and drag it to the window. The Watch window also allows you to type variables and functions by hand. You can create multiple Watch windows for a given debugging session. The Watch window shows the variable name, value, and type.

Call Stack   This window answers the question of how the application got to the current point of execution. Every time the application makes a call, the call gets added to the call stack. When the call returns, Visual Studio removes it from the call stack. In short, the Call Stack window shows you a list of pending calls, which tells you how the application accessed the current function.

Breakpoints   The Breakpoints window contains a list of breakpoints for your application. It also tells you the break conditions.

You can use this window to manage breakpoints, which includes adding new breakpoints and deleting existing breakpoints. The Clear All Breakpoints button enables you to remove all of the breakpoints from your application without looking for them individually. You can also disable the breakpoints by clearing the check next to the entry. The Disable All Breakpoints button will disable all of the breakpoints in an application at once, which means the application will run as if you hadn't set any breakpoints.

Command Window You'll use the Command Window to perform queries on your application as you debug it. For example, if you typed **? <Variable Name>** in the Command Window, Visual Studio would return the current value of the Command Window. You can also perform limited "what if" analysis by trying out various permutations of function calls within the window. The reason this option is limited is that you have to avoid certain types of calls. For example, you wouldn't want to call an event handler from within the Command Window.

Output The Output window contains a list of the current debugger actions and any debug statements you place within the code. For example, this window tells you the names of all the DLLs loaded to service your application when it starts. The Output window also reports any return code from your application.

Generally, you'll find that the windows in this list provide everything you need in the way of information. You can learn the values of any variables in your application, interact with the application in various ways, and perform certain types of management tasks. However, there are times when you need to view an application in intense detail, and the debugger displays can help you there as well. For example, you can view the IL code for your application by selecting Disassembly from the View drop-down list on the Debug menu (the last button in Figure 9.10). Figure 9.12 shows a typical disassembly of the Typing Buddy application we discussed earlier. The C# statements appear in bold type, while the disassembly appears in a lighter type.

Notice the if (TimeLeft == 0) statement in Figure 9.12. The disassembly of this code is cmp dword ptr [esi+00000114h], 0. It's clear that the code is performing a DWORD (double word or 16-bit) comparison of the value pointed to by the ESI register offset by 0x00000114 with 0. However, you don't believe that the code is correct. How do you validate it? The first thing you need to know is that this value supposedly points to TimeLeft, which has a value of 3,600 according to the Autos window. So, if [esi+00000114h] actually points to a value of 3,600, there's a good chance that this code is correct.

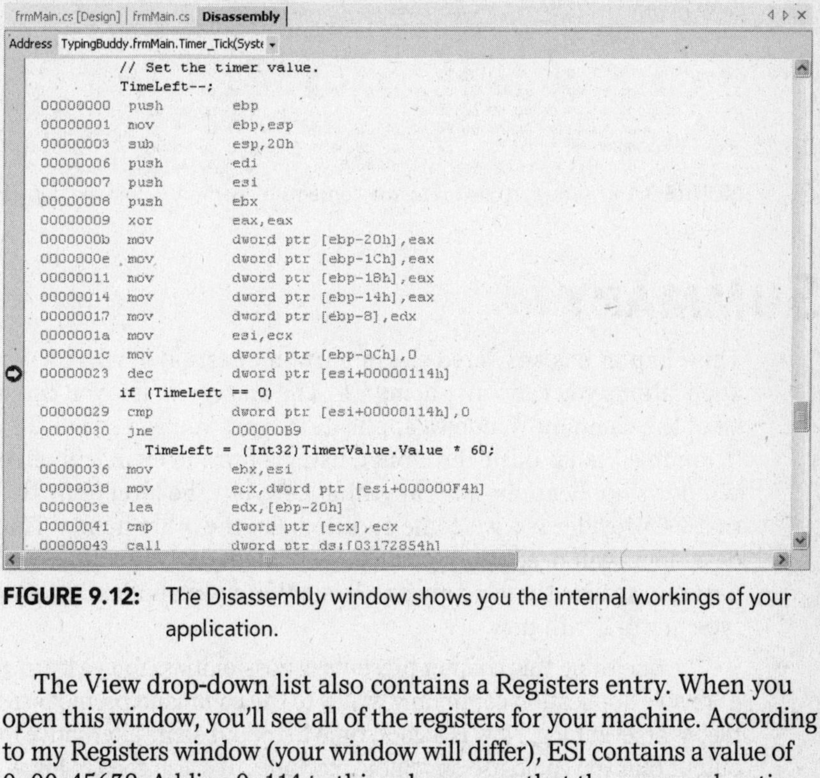

FIGURE 9.12: The Disassembly window shows you the internal workings of your application.

The View drop-down list also contains a Registers entry. When you open this window, you'll see all of the registers for your machine. According to my Registers window (your window will differ), ESI contains a value of 0x00c45638. Adding 0x114 to this value means that the memory location should point to 0x00c4574c. Open the Memory 1 window using the options in the View drop-down list, enter the address, and you'll see a display similar to the one in Figure 9.13. If you look at the value in the Memory window, you'll see that a hex value of 0x0e10 is equal to 3,600 decimal (remember that Intel processors use a little endian storage technique).

The point of this section isn't to demonstrate that you can become hopelessly mired in debugger functionality in Visual Studio .NET; it demonstrates that you can get as much detail about your application as you need. Application development boils down to knowing the details. Knowing how to use the debugger enables you to check the details, even the details of library code. In short, you might not look at the IL code for your applications every day, but it's good to know what to do if you need that level of detail somewhere along the way.

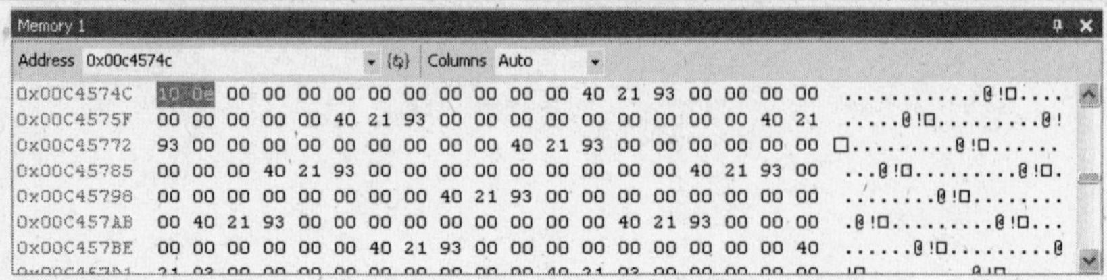

FIGURE 9.13: You can even view the contents of memory within the debugger.

Summary

This chapter has answered the important question of what type of applications you can write using C#. The answer is that you can write all of the common Windows application types you've used in the past. If you're a Visual Basic developer, using a form to create all of your Windows applications isn't anything new, but the level of flexibility that C# provides is a welcome addition. On the other hand, Visual C++ developers will need to get past the document/view architecture of the past and realize there's only one basic Windows application project type to work with now.

The one thing this chapter presents is possibilities. You've learned that a console application commonly writes to the command prompt screen, a file, or an event log. Now is a good time to try out some alternative forms of output that you could use on remote machines. It's also good to know how to work with standard C# resources so you can create feature-rich applications with a minimum of code in a minimum of time. Spend time learning the different Windows application types so you can create them as needed. Finally, learning to debug applications is a skill that's important for every kind of application. If you gain nothing else from this chapter, learning how to use the debugger is critical.

What's Next

Chapter 10 demonstrates the use of threads and threading in your application programs, so that you can take advantage of the multi-threaded nature of Windows by running tasks at the same time.

Chapter 10

WORKING WITH THREADS

Threads are a performance-enhancing feature of an application when they're developed correctly and used under the right circumstances. On the other hand, working with threads can become a mind-numbing exercise in application bugs, wasted developer time, and wasted resources. A thread (short for *thread of execution*) is a series of instructions executed independently of any other instructions within an application. An application always has at least one thread of execution, but may have many more.

This chapter provides you with a wealth of information about how threads work and how you can use them in your applications to make things run more efficiently. It's important to understand how threads get used in various types of projects. We'll also explore safety considerations for using threads. For example, we'll consider how critical sections ensure that two calling processes don't try to use the same portion of code at the same

Adapted from *Visual C# .NET Developer's Handbook* by John Paul Mueller
ISBN 0-7821-4047-5

time. This chapter also explores the things you need to consider to ensure thread safety when working with local libraries. We'll spend time working through several example programs that demonstrate how threads work in different environments.

An Overview of Threads

Developers are constantly looking for ways to use machine resources more efficiently without spending more time developing applications. One way to do this is to write an application so that it can perform more than one task at a time. Windows provides this ability using threads. A thread is essentially a single subject of execution within an application. For example, using threads, an application could print and spell check a document in the background, while the user is typing in the foreground.

Threads don't perform any kind of magic. They won't make the user's machine any faster and the processor still won't be able to perform more than one task at a time. In other words, threads don't allow a machine to perform more than one task simultaneously unless that machine has the resources (i.e., multiple processors) to do so. However, threads can make use of resources that would otherwise go unused. A background thread can continue working while a foreground thread waits for user input. Another way to look at the issue is that the background thread frees the user interface so that the user can get back to work more quickly.

NOTE
You actually need to be aware of two entities when talking about threads. The term *thread* describes one set of contiguous instructions for performing a single task. A *process*, on the other hand, describes the application as a whole. Every executing application has at least one thread and one process. There's never more than one process for an application, but applications can always produce more than one thread. The distinction between processes and threads will become clear as the chapter progresses.

In some cases, an application requires threads for purposes other than efficiency. For example, a server application might need to service more than one user at a time. In this case, each thread would contain a separate user request. The threads enable the main application thread to continue accepting requests while pending requests are serviced in the background. The use of threads, in this case, ensures server availability but might not affect server performance.

Sometimes threads are simply inappropriate. For example, if an application spawns two threads, both of which require constant user interaction, the application will tend to run more slowly because the users have to divide their attention between the two threads. Likewise, adding a disk-intensive thread to an application that's already disk intensive is unlikely to increase system performance. The new thread will compete for resources with existing threads. Finally, adding threads to an overburdened server is unlikely to enhance server availability—quite the contrary—the server might cease to work at all.

Now that you have a little more information about threads, let's look at them in more detail. The following sections will help you understand how to use threads, what types of threads you can create, and how to use threads safely.

Uses for Threads

Theoretically, you can use threads in any C# application, including something as small as a component or control. Using threads in the managed environment is similar to working in the unmanaged environment in that you have the same thread types to consider and the underlying process is the same. In short, threads are a nearly universal solution to some types of problems.

Threads don't necessarily need to be large or complex to make an application more efficient and responsive to user needs. In fact, you can use threads to perform small maintenance tasks in the background at regular intervals—something that you may not want to interrupt your main application to do. A thread can also replace timer-related tasks in some cases. In other words, threads aren't limited to performing any particular task.

TIP

One of the easiest ways to add a timed thread to your application is to use the Timer control. The Timer continues to execute in the background while your main application continues to work. Of course, this type of thread only works for tasks that execute at a regular interval, such as updating a clock or checking the status of the application environment.

However, you do need to consider some issues before you start using threads for every small task that your application may need to perform. It's important to use threads correctly in order to avoid some common problems that developers seem to face with them. The following list provides you with some guidelines on what you should think about before using threads.

Debugging   The biggest consideration from a developer perspective is that threads greatly increase the difficulty of debugging an application. A thread can actually hide bugs, or, at least, make them more difficult to find, since you'd now have to watch more than one thread of execution at a time.

Development Time   Most developers are used to thinking about application programming in a linear fashion. In other words, given a specific event, the application will perform a series of steps to handle it. Using a multiple thread approach forces the programmer to think about application processes in parallel, rather than in a linear fashion.

True Efficiency   While it's true that placing some tasks into background threads can make use of idle time in the application, there are situations when there isn't any idle time to exploit. In this situation, you'll find that the application is actually less efficient than before, because there's a certain amount of overhead and housekeeping associated with using multiple threads. In other words, only use threads in situations when you anticipate that there will be some amount of idle time to exploit.

Reliability   Multiple threads of execution don't necessarily make an application failure prone, but there are more failure points to consider. Any time you add more failure points to anything, it becomes less reliable. There's a greater probability that the application will break simply because there are more things that can go wrong with it.

Unexpected Side Effects   No matter how carefully you craft a multithreaded application, there are going to be side effects that you have to deal with, especially if the threads in the application interact. Even if you make your application thread safe and use critical sections, there's a chance that two threads will try to access the same variable at the same time in an unanticipated way. Not only do these unexpected side effects increase development and debugging time, but they make it more likely that a user will come across a problem that you can't duplicate with your setup. In other words, multithreaded applications will more than likely increase application support costs.

Now that you have a good overview of the way in which you can use threads in general, let's look at some specific multithreaded usage types. The following sections will explore the four most common ways that you'll see multiple threads in use: applications, DLLs, system services, and server applications. Each of these areas represents a major application type. We'll explore some of these multithreaded usage examples later in the chapter.

Applications

We've already explored this topic to some extent. Applications can benefit from multiple threads of execution in a number of ways. In fact, some of those ways will seem quite natural from a programming perspective, because the tasks in question can be broken from the main thread of execution quite easily. The following list will give you some ideas on how you can use multiple threads with applications.

Printing   This one major task can always benefit from multiple threads in any application. Queuing a print job takes time, which means that the user is sitting at their desk, staring at the screen, doing nothing at all. In fact, some print jobs could take enough time that the user will give up trying to use the computer at all and do something else while waiting. Printing in the background in a separate thread is always an efficient way to handle this task.

As the User Types   There are many tasks that fall into the "as the user types" category, but the two most common are spelling and grammar checks. Many applications offer the ability to check the user's spelling and grammar as they type, which reduces the need to check the whole document later. Of course, there are a lot of less common tasks that fall into this category as well. For example, you could check the validity of an equation as the user types it or make sure that a database entry is correct. For that matter, you could even suggest (as some applications do) a completed entry for the user, based on past input.

Repetition   Repagination and other repetitive tasks can always occur as background threads. There isn't any need to take up the foreground task's time with things like updating the application clock. Most repetitive, continuous tasks can be relegated to background threads.

Data Saves   Most applications now include an automatic save feature simply because many users are very poor at saving data themselves. It's not hard to figure out why—the user is engrossed in completing their document and simply forgets to perform the data save. An automatic data saving feature can allow the user to complete a document without worrying about power failures or other computer glitches that can cause data to disappear.

Updates   Streamlining the update process has become increasingly important, especially with more users relying on remote computing. Updates, in this case, aren't necessarily limited to data. For example, a user might check in with the company each morning for updated pricing schedules. A system administrator could use this habit to their advantage by also including a background thread that downloads any system updates the user may require. In other words, the user would receive both a data update and an application update at the same time. Of course, automatic data updates are a nice feature as well. The application could update pricing tables or other forms of application-specific information in the background at regular intervals, provided the machine has the capability of creating a remote connection to the company.

TIP

You can combine multiple threads and system updates in other ways. For example, you might want to include a virus-checking thread that runs in the background and checks all of the incoming data before it actually is placed on the client machine. Another use of background threads includes running diagnostics in the background, as the user works, to ensure that their machine is fully functional. An alarm would tell the user that their machine required service and that they should save any data before it's too late. As you can see, there are a lot of ways that you can use threads to protect the user, their data, and the client machine from damage.

Calculations   Math operations are notorious for consuming vast amounts of processor cycles. In some cases, you have to accept the heavy penalty of a calculation because the user requires an answer immediately. However, there are other situations when the application could complete the calculation just as easily in the background as a separate thread. In fact, many spreadsheet and graphics applications use this technique now to make foreground features more responsive to user input.

There are a few things you should consider not adding to background threads, simply because it's not feasible to do so. The one rule of thumb is that you should probably handle anything that requires direct user interaction on a constant basis as part of the main thread. On the other hand, anything the user can set once, then allow the computer to complete, is a good candidate for a separate thread. Any time you create a thread, make sure the application will realize an efficiency gain and the user an increased responsiveness. A thread that causes the entire machine to slow is somewhat counterproductive, and you should consider running the task as quickly as possible to reduce system down time.

DLLs

Dynamic link libraries (DLLs) have been around since Microsoft first introduced Windows. In fact, DLLs are actually the successors of the libraries used by DOS applications. For the most part, DLLs allow for the same uses of threads that applications do. The main difference is that you'd want to place common thread types in DLLs—threads that perform work that you may need to do in more than one application. However, developers do place some thread categories in DLLs, simply because they're major components of an application that the developer does not want to recompile every time the application is updated. Examples would include

- Spelling and grammar checkers
- Print routines
- Non-automated data formatting
- Data processing routines
- Report builders

You could potentially add other items to the list, but this list should provide you with enough ideas to get started. The reason that these items could appear in a DLL is that the developer normally creates and debugs them separately from the main part of the application. It pays to keep these elements in a DLL to reduce debugging time for the main application and to reduce application compile time.

System Services

For the most part, users never interact with system services. System services sit in the background and perform tasks such as enabling the hardware to operate or creating network connections. Consequently, there are some specialized uses for threads within a system service. The following list will provide you with a few ideas.

Service Priority Upgrade   Some system services execute as low-priority background tasks. You normally don't want them to consume valuable processor cycles unless the machine is idle or there's some type of priority task to perform. When you use a service in the second capacity, high-priority threads come into play. Rather than change the priority of the entire service, you can simply launch a single thread to perform the high-priority task.

Discovery   Most system services are low-level applications that need to discover a great deal about the system to ensure that it's working properly. Sometimes this discovery phase can occur once during service initialization; but in other cases, it's an ongoing process. Consider the network driver that has to keep track of the current system configuration, including the status of remote resources. A good use of threads, in this case, would be to allow the service to perform multiple levels of discovery at the same time without reducing its availability to the system as a whole.

Multiple Copies of the Same Task   Some services, such as the Indexing Service, perform a single task. However, they might need to perform this single task on multiple data streams or objects. In the case of the Indexing Service, each thread handles a separate catalog, ensuring that each catalog receives the same amount of processing power. It's important to handle some tasks like this to ensure that each data stream is handled in a timely manner.

Server Applications

Threads are generally a requirement for server applications. In fact, server applications are one place where you can use threads with impunity, if for no other reason than the need to fulfill multiple user requests simultaneously. Threads on a server are grouped into the following categories.

Availability   If several users will share the same process on a server, then you need threads to keep the user requests separated. For example, when working with an Internet Server Application Programming Interface (ISAPI) Extension, the DLL is passed a user context. The context identifies that user to the current thread of execution. Database applications represent another situation where threading is important; there's only one database management system (DBMS) process running, but multiple threads containing user requests exist.

Maintenance   Servers often run maintenance tasks on threads. For example, compacting a database will likely occur on a thread because you don't want to disturb the foreground processes. Likewise, tasks such as defragmenting the drive or checking drive status will likely occur in the background using threads monitored by a main process.

Reliability   Most companies want servers that run 24/7. This means running background tasks that check for reliability concerns before they become a problem. Diagnostic software often uses threads to meet the needs of redundant hardware. For example, fan-monitoring software could use a separate thread to monitor each fan on the system.

Security   Some applications use separate threads to monitor system security. The thread is outside the mainstream of other work occurring within the application and will react independently when a security breach occurs. Of course, each level of the system will have separate security checks. For example, the operation system uses threads to monitor the security of each application.

Performance   Interestingly enough, performance is one of the more uncommon uses of threads on a server. A server generally has few free resources that a thread can use to increase performance. In addition, the network administrator is likely to configure the system to favor background and service routine tasks anyway, making resources even less available. The one time when a thread will work for performance reasons is when the server supports a single application and the application is prone to use one resource over another. For example, a compute-intensive thread might work well on a server that supports a disk-intensive database application.

It isn't safe to assume that every application you write for a server will require threads. For example, components don't require threads, in most cases, because each user will create a new copy of the component. Only if more than one user will use the object at a time do you need to consider threads. Using COM+ is another example of when you need to look at the environment before you create a thread. In this case, the environment will manage threads for you, so long as you use single-threaded apartment (STA) components, making development easier.

Generally, it isn't safe to assume that a server can spawn endless threads and continue running. While the number of threads on the desktop is necessarily limited by the needs of the user, a server doesn't have any such limitation. Users will continue to make requests until there are no more resources. The need to monitor resources makes thread development for server applications more complicated than for the desktop. In most cases, you'll want to add monitoring software to thread-generating applications for servers to ensure that the thread will have enough resources to run without potential performance penalties.

Types of Threads

From a Windows perspective, you have threads and the processes that contain them and nothing else. In fact, the .NET Framework provides a single class that all threads use, so there's little difference between threads, even from a thread-specific coding perspective. However, from an application concept perspective, there are actually two kinds of threads: worker and user interface (UI).

Worker and UI threads both perform a single sequence of execution within the application. The difference comes in the way that you implement and use these two kinds of threads. A UI thread normally interacts with the user in some way, while a worker thread executes in the background where the user might not even be aware of it. The following sections talk about these two thread types and show how they're used.

TIP

You can use the Win32 CreateThread() function to create a thread that doesn't rely on the .NET Framework. The advantage of doing so is that you eliminate some overhead normally encountered using the .NET Framework. In addition, this method conserves memory (unfortunately, you have to manage that memory manually). The down side, of course, is that you can't use any of the capabilities that the .NET Framework provides and you do have to consider managed-to-unmanaged boundary conversions. In most cases, you'll find that the .NET Framework Thread class works best for threads that perform simple repetitive tasks.

Worker Threads

Worker threads are normally used for background tasks that require no user interaction. A worker thread normally performs its work and quietly exits. If an error occurs, the worker thread must throw a ThreadException event. The application should include a thread exception handler to determine if the error is critical, is something the user needs to decide about, could resolve itself through a retry to the call, or is a non-critical error that the application doesn't need to worry about. Thread exception handlers are of the `ThreadExceptionEventHandler()` type.

Another way to end a worker thread and generate an exit code is to use the `Abort()` method of the `Thread` class. Using this function will stop thread execution and perform any required cleanup before exiting to the calling application. The `Abort()` method doesn't guarantee data integrity or that the application will remain in a stable state. Calling `Abort()` automatically generates a `ThreadAbortException`. This exception is separate from the `ThreadException`, and you need a separate handler for it.

The .NET Framework won't allow you to pass parameters to the thread method when you start it. The best way to pass data to a worker thread is through the constructor. In other words, when you create the worker thread, you also set the parameters needed to make it run. Another way to pass data to the worker thread is to use properties. This enables you to provide optional variable support without creating a lot of constructor overrides. The only other way to pass data to a worker thread is by using shared fields or variables.

If you need to pass data to a worker thread using a shared resource, be sure to protect the data using an `Interlocked` class object. The `Interlocked` class ensures that changes made by one thread complete before access by another thread is allowed. See the "Understanding Critical Sections" and "Understanding Thread Safety" discussions later in this chapter for more details.

UI Threads

As the name suggests, you normally create UI threads to provide some type of user interface functionality within an application. Generally, this means creating a separate dialog box using a separate class. The UI thread can perform work once it accepts the user input, but the initial focus is on gaining any required input. In addition, a UI thread can provide user output in the form of status and completion messages. Of course, this means that UI threads are limited to applications that deal with the desktop, since there's little chance that someone would use the server console often enough to make a UI thread worthwhile.

The differentiation between a UI thread and a worker thread goes much further than the user interface element. A good example of a UI thread application is a file copy or a printing routine. The thread acquires user input, provides status messages, and then provides some type of completion message. None of these functions require support from the main thread. In short, the UI thread tends to provide self-contained support.

One of the major considerations for a UI thread is providing a user interface element that doesn't get in the way of other needs. The UI thread should only interrupt the user as necessary—when it makes sense to interrupt the user. For example, a print routine would need to interrupt the user long enough to get printer setup and document output information. Because the user expects this interaction, the UI thread isn't considered obtrusive. Likewise, most readers will want to know when the print job is done, but in this case, you should provide an option to turn off the completion message because the user might sit next to the printer and know when the job is complete by simply listening to the printer.

UI threads are different enough that some languages provide a separate class to handle them. For example, Visual C++ developers have access to the CWinThread class when working with UI threads. C# and the .NET Framework provide one class, Thread, to handle all threading requirements. The lack of a separate class doesn't make C# harder to use—actually, it means you have less to remember. However, it's important to keep the philosophy behind a UI thread in mind as you develop a C# application.

WORKING WITH THREADS

As previously mentioned, you'll generally use threads in specific environments for purposes suited to those environments. Threads also appear in both worker and UI varieties, with the UI variety limited to user application needs in general. (Server applications won't benefit from a UI thread, because no one is working at the server console to see the thread output.)

With these criteria in mind, the following sections present three example applications. The first uses a worker thread to create output for a desktop application. The application and thread code appear in the same file. The second application uses a UI thread, but the thread appears in a separate DLL file. Finally, the third application shows how you'd create a DLL for a server application. (Make sure you look at the example in the "Understanding Critical Sections" section later in this chapter for an example on sharing resources.)

Desktop Application Example

The worker thread is the most common type of thread you'll create for an application, because this type works in the background without user intervention. A worker thread enables you to perform work in the background while the user works in the foreground.

Creating the Thread Class

The example application discussed in this chapter consists of a worker thread that sleeps for a given number of milliseconds, then fires an event to show that it has completed its work. The use of events in this example shows just one way of interacting with threads. You can always use other techniques. The event mechanism does have the advantage of freeing the main thread and enabling the application to react to thread events as needed. Listing 10.1 shows the thread-related portion of the application source code.

NOTE

You can download all the source files for the programs featured in this chapter from the Sybex website at http://www.sybex.com. Search for this chapter's source book by its ISBN number, 4047, or its title, *Visual C# .NET Developer's Handbook,* and look for the Download link on the right. Once you've downloaded the files, you can follow along with the examples without having to type in the program listings.

Listing 10.1: This Worker Thread Example Relies on Events for Communication

```csharp
public class MyThread
{
    #region Private Variable Declarations
    private int    _Interval;      // Time to wait for event.
    private bool   _CreateError;   // Create an error event?
    private string _StandardMsg;   // Standard event message.
    private string _ErrorMsg;      // Event error message.
    #endregion

    public MyThread(int Interval)
    {
        // Perform a range check and
        // assign an appropriate value.
        if (Interval >= 100)
            _Interval = Interval;
```

```
        else
           _Interval = 1000;

        // Initialize private variables.
        _CreateError = false;
        _StandardMsg = "Hello World";
        _ErrorMsg = "An Error Occurred";
}

#region Public Methods
public void DoWait()
{
        // WorkerThread Arguments.
        MyEventArgs                    e;

        // Failure Arguments.
        ThreadExceptionEventArgs    fe;

        // System Exception Value.
        System.Exception            se;

        // Wait for some interval.
        Thread.Sleep(_Interval);

        // Create and fill out the event arguments.
        e = new MyEventArgs();
        e.Message = _StandardMsg;
        e.ErrorMsg = _ErrorMsg;

        // Determine if we need to throw an error.
        if (_CreateError)
        {

            // If so, create an error.
            se = new System.Exception(_ErrorMsg);
            se.Source = this.ToString();
            fe = new ThreadExceptionEventArgs(se);
            ThreadFail(this, fe);
        }

            // Otherwise, there is no error.
        else
```

```csharp
      // Fire the WorkerThread event.
      WorkerThread(this, e);
   }
   #endregion

   #region Public Properties
   public bool CreateError
   {
      get { return _CreateError; }
      set { _CreateError = value; }
   }

   public string StandardMsg
   {
      get { return _StandardMsg; }
      set { _StandardMsg = value; }
   }

   public string ErrorMsg
   {
      get { return _ErrorMsg; }
      set { _ErrorMsg = value; }
   }
   #endregion

   #region Public Event Declarations

   /// <summary>
   /// Standard event handler for successful completion.
   /// </summary>
   public event MyEventHandler WorkerThread;

   /// <summary>
   /// Error event handler for unsuccessful completion.
   /// </summary>
   public event ThreadExceptionEventHandler ThreadFail;
   #endregion
};
```

When you work with a thread, you need to decide which input is required and which is optional. Use the constructor to force input of mandatory inputs and properties to enable input of the optional arguments. Notice that the MyThread() constructor requires a wait interval as input. Instead of raising an error for inappropriate input, the constructor assigns a minimum value to the _Interval variable. The _CreateError, _StandardMsg, and _ErrorMsg variables receive standard values to ensure that the thread won't fail due to a lack of optional input.

The only method within the worker thread class is DoWait(). This method begins by sleeping for the number of milliseconds specified by _Interval. After the method wakes up, it checks for an error condition indicator simulated by _CreateError in this case. If the error condition is in place, the DoWait() method creates a System.Exception object that contains an error message and an error source. Complete implementations will also fill in the TargetSite and StackTrace properties for this object. The System.Exception object is turned into a ThreadExceptionEvent-Args object and finally passed along to the client when DoWait() fires the first of two events, ThreadFail().

The DoWait() non-error condition is a little easier to follow. All the method does is fire the second of two events, WorkerThread(). The WorkerThread() event is actually more complex than ThreadFail() because it requires the use of a custom event message handler and delegate. You can see both event declarations near the end of Listing 10.1. Notice that ThreadFail() relies upon the standard ThreadExceptionEvent-Handler, but WorkerThread() relies upon MyEventHandler. Listing 10.2 shows the specialized event delegate and event message class used for WorkerThread().

Listing 10.2: *WorkerThread()* Relies on a Specialized Delegate and Message Class

```
/// <summary>
/// The example requires a custom delegate for firing an
/// event message.
/// </summary>
public delegate void MyEventHandler(
  object Sender, MyEventArgs e);

/// <summary>
/// The System.EventArgs class doesn't
/// provide the means to pass data to the
/// event handler, so we need a custom class.
/// </summary>
public class MyEventArgs : EventArgs
{
```

```
   #region Private Variable Declarations
   // Message the user wants to dipslay.
   private string _Message;

   // Error message for event handler.
   private string _ErrorMsg;
   #endregion

   public MyEventArgs()
   {
      _Message = "No Message Supplied";
      _ErrorMsg = "An Event Error Occurred";
   }

   #region Public Properties
   public string Message
   {
      get { return _Message; }
      set { _Message = value; }
   }

   public string ErrorMsg
   {
      get { return _ErrorMsg; }
      set { _ErrorMsg = value; }
   }
   #endregion
};
```

As you can see, MyEventHandler() is a standard delegate declaration that the compiler turns into a class for you. One of the arguments for this event handler is MyEventArgs—a special class that inherits from System .EventArgs. The only additions to this class are two properties: one for the standard message and a second for the custom error message.

Creating the Test Code

Now that you understand the thread, let's look at the code for the main form. The main form contains textboxes that enable the user to input the standard and error messages, and the interval the worker thread should wait. The Test pushbutton creates a normal thread, while the Throw Error pushbutton enables the error condition and throws an error. Listing 10.3 shows the code for this portion of the example.

**Listing 10.3: The Pushbutton and Thread Event Handlers
for the Example Application**

```csharp
private void btnTest_Click(
  object sender, System.EventArgs e)
{
  // Create a new worker thread object.
  MyThread NewThread = new MyThread(
    Int32.Parse(txtInterval.Text));

  // Add the event handlers.
  NewThread.WorkerThread +=
    new MyEventHandler(WorkerThreadEvent);
  NewThread.ThreadFail +=
    new ThreadExceptionEventHandler(
    MyThreadExceptionHandler);

  // Add the messages.
  NewThread.StandardMsg = txtStandardMsg.Text;
  NewThread.ErrorMsg = txtErrorMsg.Text;

  // Create and execute the thread.
  Thread   DoThread =
    new Thread(new ThreadStart(NewThread.DoWait));
  DoThread.Start();

  // Get rid of the thread.
  DoThread = null;
  NewThread = null;
}

private void btnThrowError_Click(
  object sender, System.EventArgs e)
{
  // Create a new worker thread object.
  MyThread NewThread =
    new MyThread(Int32.Parse(txtInterval.Text));

  // Add the event handlers.
  NewThread.WorkerThread +=
    new MyEventHandler(WorkerThreadEvent);
  NewThread.ThreadFail +=
    new ThreadExceptionEventHandler(
    MyThreadExceptionHandler);
```

```csharp
   // Add the messages.
   NewThread.StandardMsg = txtStandardMsg.Text;
   NewThread.ErrorMsg = txtErrorMsg.Text;

   // Set the thread to throw an error.
   NewThread.CreateError = true;

   // Create and execute the thread.
   Thread    DoThread =
     new Thread(new ThreadStart(NewThread.DoWait));
   DoThread.Start();

   // Get rid of the thread.
   DoThread = null;
   NewThread = null;
}
#endregion

#region Thread Event Handlers
private void WorkerThreadEvent(object sender, MyEventArgs e)
{
   // Display the worker thread message.
   MessageBox.Show(
     "This is the thread message:\r\n" + e.Message,
     "Thread Success Message",
     MessageBoxButtons.OK,
     MessageBoxIcon.Information);
}

private void MyThreadExceptionHandler(object sender,
   ThreadExceptionEventArgs e)
{
   // Get user input on the error.
   DialogResult Result = new DialogResult();

   // Display the error message.
   Result = MessageBox.Show(
     "The thread error information:\r\n\tMessage:\t" +
     e.Exception.Message + "\r\n\tSource:\t" +
     e.Exception.Source + "\r\n\tStack Trace:\t" +
     e.Exception.StackTrace + "\r\n\tTarget Site:\t" +
     e.Exception.TargetSite,
     "Thread Error",
```

```
        MessageBoxButtons.AbortRetryIgnore,
        MessageBoxIcon.Error);

    // Do something based on the result.
    if (Result == DialogResult.Abort)
        Application.Exit();
    else if (Result == DialogResult.Retry)
        btnThrowError_Click(this, new System.EventArgs());
}
#endregion
```

As you can see, the btnTest_Click() and btnThrowError_Click() button event handlers follow the same process for creating the thread and starting it. Notice the use of the Int32.Parse() method for converting text input to a number for the MyThread() constructor.

Once we have a thread object to use, it's time to configure it. You must configure the thread before you start it. As previously mentioned, the MyThread class provides two event handlers, so the next step is to assign local methods to handle both. Both button event handlers assign values to the StandardMsg and ErrorMsg properties. Only the btnThrowError_Click() button event handler needs to set the CreateError property so the thread will fail.

The final three lines of code create the actual thread, start it, and assign a null value to the thread and thread object. Starting the thread isn't nearly as much work as setting it up.

Both thread event handlers display messages. The MyThreadException-Handler() event handler provides the most complete information based on the contents of the Thread-ExceptionEventArgs object. Notice the use of the *DialogResult* variable, *Result*, to handle user input. This event handler assumes that the user might want to terminate the application due to the error, but it gives the user other options as well.

Performing a Worker Thread Test

The example application helps you learn about several worker thread features. For one thing, you'd never know the worker thread even existed were it not for the event handler code. Any application can hide threads this way. The threads work in the background unnoticed unless an error or some other event occurs. Theoretically, the application could perform tasks on the user's behalf without the user's knowledge.

When you start the application, you'll see a dialog similar to the one shown in Figure 10.1. Try using different message and timing values. As you increase the thread sleep time, you'll see a longer interval before the event message appears. Using a long interval also enables you to start several threads at once by clicking either Test or Throw Error several times in succession. Changing the messages before each pushbutton press shows that the threads are truly independent and that no data corruption occurs due to shared data.

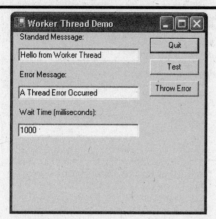

FIGURE 10.1:   The Worker Thread Demo enables you to test both success and error conditions.

One other test you'll want to try is viewing the application using the Spy++ utility found in the \Program Files\Microsoft Visual Studio .NET\Common7\Tools folder. You must set the Wait Time field to a high value to make this part of the test process work. I found that 12 seconds (12,000 milliseconds) works best, but your results will vary.

Start Spy++ and look for the WORKERTHREAD entry shown in Figure 10.2. The example begins by creating three threads. The first thread is the main window and it has all of the controls within it. The second and third threads are application-specific and you don't need to worry about them at this point.

Click the Test button on the application, then quickly press F5 in Spy++ to refresh the window. You'll see another thread added to the list. This thread won't have any display elements because it's the worker thread. In fact, you'll see one new thread generated each time you click Test or Throw Error. If you create multiple threads, you'll see multiple entries added to Spy++. After the time elapses and the event message dialog box appears, press F5 in Spy++ again. This time you'll see a new thread that does include display elements—the thread for our worker thread will be gone. Close the Success or Error Message dialog boxes and the number of threads will return to the same number you started with in Figure 10.2.

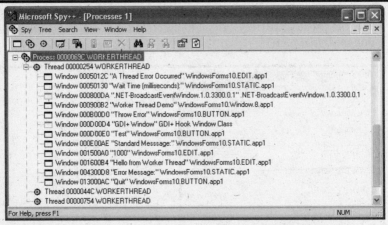

FIGURE 10.2:   Use Spy++ to see the threads in your application.

Local DLL Example

This example shows how to place the threading logic for your application in a separate file—a DLL. The reason you want to know how to use this technique is that placing the thread in a DLL enables you to use it with more than one application. This principle is at the center of the common dialogs that most developers use to create applications. A single DLL can serve many generic needs, so long as you include enough configuration features to ensure complete customization, if desired.

The example in this section contains two user interface elements. The first is the main thread—a dialog-based test application. The second element is the UI thread contained within a DLL. The test application will enable you to create multiple copies of the UI thread, with each UI thread providing independent operation for the user.

Configuring the Project

This example requires a little special configuration, due to the use of multiple UI elements. You'll begin creating the DLL portion of this example using the Class Library project. The example uses a project name of DLLThread. Add to this project a Windows Application with a name of DLLThreadTest.

NOTE

Make sure you set DLLThreadTest as your startup project to ensure that the example runs in debug mode. The Visual Studio .NET IDE will assume you want to use DLLThread as the startup project because it's the first project created. To set DLLThreadTest as the startup project, right-click DLLThreadTest in Solution Explorer and select Set as Startup Project from the context menu.

The Class Library project provides you with an empty shell. It doesn't even include a dialog box as part of the project. You'll need to add a dialog box by right-clicking DLLThread in Solution Explorer and choosing Add ➤ Add New Item from the context menu. Select Local Project Items\UI and you'll see a list of items similar to the one shown in Figure 10.3. You'll need to add the Windows Form option to the project. The example uses a name of ThreadForm.CS for the resulting file.

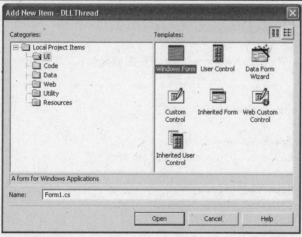

FIGURE 10.3: Visual Studio .NET allows you to add UI items to DLLs using this dialog box.

As part of the configuration process, you need to create a connection between the DLL and the test application. Right-click DLLThreadTest\References in Solution Explorer and choose Add Reference from the context menu. Select the Projects tab in the Add Reference dialog. Highlight the DLLThread project and click Select. Click OK to add the reference to the DLLThreadTest project.

Creating the DLL

The DLL code falls into two parts. First, you need to design a dialog box. The example uses a simple dialog box with a Quit button. The Quit button closes the form when you're done viewing it. You can find the code for the form in the ThreadForm.CS file. Second, you need to create code within the DLL to manage the form. The DLLThread class code appears in Listing 10.4.

Listing 10.4: The *DLLThread* Class Manages Access to the *ThreadForm*

```
public class DLLThread
{
    // Create a dialog name variable.
    private string _ThreadDlgName;

    public DLLThread(string ThreadDlgName)
    {
        // Store a dialog name value.
        if (ThreadDlgName != null)
            _ThreadDlgName = ThreadDlgName;
        else
            _ThreadDlgName = "Sample Dialog";
    }

    public void CreateUIThread()
    {
        // Create a new form.
        ThreadForm  Dlg = new ThreadForm();

        // Name the dialog.
        Dlg.Text = _ThreadDlgName;

        // Display the form.
        Dlg.ShowDialog();
    }
}
```

As you can see, the code for the DLL is relatively simple. Notice the private variable *_ThreadDlgName*. In an updated version of this program in the "Understanding Critical Sections" section of this chapter, you'll see that this variable isn't thread safe. We need a critical section in order to keep this variable safe. For now, with the current program construction, this variable will work as anticipated. However, it's important to think about potential problems in your application variables before you use the code in a multithreaded scenario.

The DLL constructor assigns a value to *_ThreadDlgName*. The check for a *null* value is important because you want to be sure the dialog has a name later. Note that you'd probably initialize other dialog construction variables as part of the constructor or use properties as we did in the worker thread example.

The CreateUIThread() method creates a new instance of the ThreadForm class, which contains the Thread dialog box. Notice that this method also assigns the name of the dialog box using the *_ThreadDlgName* variable. It's the time delay between the constructor and this assignment that causes problems in a multithreaded scenario. CreateUIThread() finishes by calling the ShowDialog() method of the ThreadForm class. It's important to use ShowDialog() rather than Show(), so you can obtain the modal result of the dialog box if necessary.

Creating the Test Program

The test program form consists of three pushbuttons and a textbox. The Quit button allows the user to exit the application. The New Dialog button will demonstrate the DLLThread class as a single-threaded application. The New Thread button will demonstrate the DLLThread class as a multithreaded application. It's important to the understanding of threads to realize that any DLL you create for multithreaded use can also be used in a single-threaded scenario. Listing 10.5 shows the test application code.

Listing 10.5: The Test Application Works in Both Single-Threaded and Multithreaded Modes

```
private void btnNewDialog_Click(
  object sender, System.EventArgs e)
{
    // Create a new thread object.
    DLLThread.DLLThread   MyThread =
        new DLLThread.DLLThread(txtDlgName.Text);
```

```
        // Display the dialog.
        MyThread.CreateUIThread();
    }

    private void btnNewThread_Click(
        object sender, System.EventArgs e)
    {
        // Create a new thread object.
        DLLThread.DLLThread   MyThread =
            new DLLThread.DLLThread(txtDlgName.Text);

        // Create and start the new thread.
        Thread   DoThread =
            new Thread(new ThreadStart(MyThread.CreateUIThread));
        DoThread.Start();

        // Get rid of the variables.
        DoThread = null;
        MyThread = null;
    }
```

The btnNewDialog_Click() method begins by creating an instance
of the DLLThread class. Notice the inclusion of the text from the application textbox as part of the call to the constructor. The method calls
CreateUIThread() to create a standard single-threaded application call
to the DLL.

The btnNewThread_Click() method begins essentially the same way
as btnNewDialog_Click(). However, in this case, the method creates a
separate thread for the dialog box. Notice that there's no difference between
this call and the one we used for the worker thread example earlier in
the chapter. The only difference is in the implementation of the thread
within the thread class.

When you run this application you'll notice that both buttons will
produce a copy of the thread form when clicked the first time. However,
if you try to click New Dialog a second time while the thread form is still
present, the application will beep. That's because the application is waiting for the modal result from the thread form. However, you can create
multiple copies of the thread form by clicking the New Thread button
because each dialog resides in a separate thread. Of course, you can only
continue clicking New Thread so long as you don't click New Dialog. The

moment you click New Dialog, the main application thread stops and waits for the thread form to complete.

Server-Based DLL Example

Threading is used for more than a few server needs. For example, when a user accesses a website and requests service from an ISAPI Extension, the DLL must track the user identification as well as operate in a thread-safe manner. The same can be said for many server services. One or more users can send information to the service, either directly or as part of another request.

The following sections show how to create a Windows service. In this case, the service monitors user access, updates an internal variable showing the last service, and provides a command for writing the number of accesses to an event log entry. The client application generates stop, start, access, and access log requests.

Creating the Windows Service

The initial part of creating a Windows service is configuration of the Windows Service project. In fact, the wizard performs a large part of the setup for you. All you really need to worry about is the service functionality—at least if you're creating a basic service that doesn't require low-level system access such as device driver interfaces. The following steps show how to create the service.

1. Create a new Windows Service project. The example uses a name of Server Thread. You'll see an initial Designer where you can place controls for the service to use. This example won't use any special controls.

2. Select the Designer window. Note that the entries in the Properties window (shown in Figure 10.4) help you configure your service. The figure shows the settings for the example service. The main property you need to set is ServiceName. Notice the Add Installer link at the bottom of the Properties window—you must add an installer after completing the service configuration.

3. Perform any required configuration of class, file, and service names. It's better to finish the service configuration before you add an installer. Otherwise, you'll need to configure both the service and the installer manually.

FIGURE 10.4: The Service properties enable you to configure general service features.

4. Create an installer by clicking the Add Installer link at the bottom of the Properties window shown in Figure 10.4. Notice that the wizard creates another Designer window for you. However, in this case, the Designer window contains two controls used to manage the service installation.

5. Select the serviceProcessInstaller1 control. Modify the Password, Username, and Account properties as needed for your service. In most cases, you'll want to leave the Password and Username properties blank, and set the Account property to **LocalSystem**.

6. Select the serviceInstaller1 control. Modify the Display-Name and StartType properties as needed for your service. The example uses a value of **Track Number of User Accesses** for the DisplayName property. Generally, you'll want to set the StartType to Automatic for services that will run all of the time.

At this point, you should have a generic Windows service project. If you compiled and installed the service, at this point, you could start, stop, and pause it. However, the service wouldn't do much more than waste CPU cycles, because you haven't added any commands to it. Listing 10.6 shows one of several techniques you can use to support commands in a Windows service.

Listing 10.6: The Windows Service Performs Much of the Work

```csharp
protected override void OnStart(string[] args)
{
    // Set the number of accesses to 0.
    _NumberOfAccesses = 0;
}

public void DoAccess()
{
    // Increment the number of accesses.
    _NumberOfAccesses++;
}

public void GetAccess()
{
    // Write an event log entry that
    // shows how many accesses occurred.
    this.EventLog.WriteEntry(
      "The number of user accesses is: "
      + _NumberOfAccesses.ToString(),
      EventLogEntryType.Information,
      1200,
      99);
}

protected override void OnCustomCommand(int Command)
{
    // Execute the default command.
    if (Command < 128)
        base.OnCustomCommand(Command);

    // Increment the number of accesses.
    if (Command == 128)
        DoAccess();

    // Write an event long entry.
    if (Command == 129)
        GetAccess();
}
```

The two commands, DoAccess() and GetAccess() work with a private variable named *NumberOfAccesses*. The only purpose for this variable is to record the number of times someone accesses the service since it was last started. To ensure that the variable always starts at a known value, the OnStart() method sets it to 0. The OnStart() method is one of several methods the wizard assumes you'll need to override, so it provides this method by default.

The user still can't access your service. We'll see later that accessing a service is a bit cryptic in C#, most likely because of the way Windows services work in general. You must override the OnCustomCommand() method if you expect the user to interact with the service directly. Notice that this method transfers any commands below 127 to the base class. It also supports two other commands, 128 and 129, which call the appropriate command. The service ignores any other command input number.

Compile the example and you'll end up with an EXE file. The EXE file won't run from the command prompt and you can't install it in a project. You must install the service using the InstallUtil ServerThread.EXE command. If you want to uninstall the service, simply add the -u switch to the command line. After you install the service, open the Services console found in the Administrative Tools folder of the Control Panel. Figure 10.5 shows the service installed.

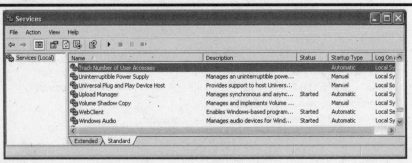

FIGURE 10.5:   The InstallUtil utility will install the Windows service on any machine that will support it.

Creating the Test Application

The client application uses a standard dialog form containing buttons to exit the application, start the service, stop the service, register a service access, and display the number of service accesses since the last service start. To access the service, locate it in the Server Explorer dialog shown in Figure 10.6. Drag the service to the form in the Designer. This action will create a new ServiceController entry in the Designer that you can use to access the service.

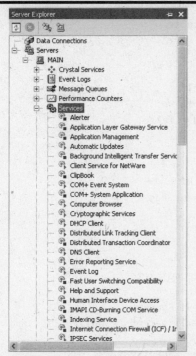

FIGURE 10.6: Use the Server Explorer to locate services on the local or any remote machine.

Now that you have access to the service, let's look at some code to interact with it. Listing 10.7 shows the code you'll use to work with a `ServiceController` named `TrackAccess`. Notice that some of the code enables and disables buttons as needed to ensure that they're accessible only when valid. This is a big concern for the developer because attempting to perform some actions with the service in an unknown state can have unfortunate side effects, such as data loss. At the very least, the application will generate an exception.

Listing 10.7: The Windows Service Client Can Stop, Start, and Access Service Commands

```
private void MainForm_Activated(
   object sender, System.EventArgs e)
{

   // Validate current service status.
   if (TrackAccess.Status == ServiceControllerStatus.Running)
```

```
        {
            btnStart.Enabled = false;
        }
        else
        {
            btnStop.Enabled = false;
            btnAccess.Enabled = false;
            btnGetAccess.Enabled = false;
        }
    }

    private void bntStart_Click(
      object sender, System.EventArgs e)
    {
        // Start the service.
        TrackAccess.Start();

        // Wait for the start to complete.
        TrackAccess.WaitForStatus(
          ServiceControllerStatus.Running,
          System.TimeSpan.FromMilliseconds(2000));

        // Change the button configuration
        // to match service status.
        btnStart.Enabled = false;
        btnStop.Enabled = true;
        btnAccess.Enabled = true;
        btnGetAccess.Enabled = true;
    }

    private void btnStop_Click(
      object sender, System.EventArgs e)
    {
        // Stop the service.
        if (TrackAccess.CanStop)
            TrackAccess.Stop();
        else
        {
            // We can't stop the service, so exit.
            MessageBox.Show("Service doesn't support stopping.",
                        "Service Stop Error",
                        MessageBoxButtons.OK,
                        MessageBoxIcon.Error);
```

```
        return;
    }

    // Wait for the start to complete.
    TrackAccess.WaitForStatus(
      ServiceControllerStatus.Stopped,
      System.TimeSpan.FromMilliseconds(2000));

    // Change the button configuration
    // to match service status.
    btnStart.Enabled = true;
    btnStop.Enabled = false;
    btnAccess.Enabled = false;
    btnGetAccess.Enabled = false;
}

private void btnAccess_Click(
  object sender, System.EventArgs e)
{
    // Access the service to increment the counter.
    TrackAccess.ExecuteCommand(128);
}

private void btnGetAccess_Click(
  object sender, System.EventArgs e)
{
    // Event log containing service entries.
    EventLog MyEvents;
    //Accesss the service to report the number of accesses.
    TrackAccess.ExecuteCommand(129);

    // Open the event log.
    MyEvents = new EventLog("Application");

    // Look at each event log entry for the correct message.
    foreach (EventLogEntry ThisEvent in MyEvents.Entries)
    {
        // The message will contain a category number of 99
        // and an event ID of 1200.
        if (ThisEvent.CategoryNumber == 99 &&
            ThisEvent.EventID == 1200)
```

```
                    // Display the message.
                    MessageBox.Show(ThisEvent.Message);
            }
    }
```

The application starts by validating the current service status in the MainForm_Activated() method. Any application that provides access to a service needs to make this check. Otherwise, you have no idea of what state the service is in and whether it's safe to work with it. Multiple users could attempt to access the service at the same time. If User A stops the service at the same time User B wants to access it, one or both calls could fail.

The bntStart_Click() and btnStop_Click() methods control the service status. You can always attempt to start a service, but some services won't allow you to stop them. The btnStop_Click() contains additional code that verifies that the service can stop before it attempts to stop the service. Notice that both methods contain a call to WaitForStatus(). This call ensures that the user is unable to do anything more with the application until the service reaches a stable state. The ServiceControllerStatus enumeration contains a number of standard service states. You must also use one of the members from the TimeSpan class to specify how long to wait for the service to change states. The example uses the From-Milliseconds() method, but any of the methods will work. Never use the infinite wait version of WaitForStatus() because the application could freeze. If the service hasn't changed states in the time provided, your application should display an error message and offer the user some options to overcome the problem.

The btnAccess_Click() method is the first to use the arcane command system used by Windows services. Notice that there's nothing to indicate the purpose of the command. You must simply know that executing command number 128 will update the number of accesses count in the service.

The ExecuteCommand() returns type void. You have no idea if the service executed the command successfully unless you look in the event log to see if there's an entry in either the System or Application logs. The ExecuteCommand() method also provides no means for returning data from the service, so you need to provide your own method.

The btnGetAccess_Click() enables the user to learn how many times the service has been accessed since it started. As you can see from Listing 10.7, the application must go to some trouble to gain access to the required information. In this case, it uses the event log as a medium for exchange. The CategoryNumber and EventID property combination is unique and unlikely to cause problems with any other entry in the event log. (Even so, you could perform additional checks on the event entry before you process it.) Figure 10.7 shows typical event log entries from the service when accessed by the client.

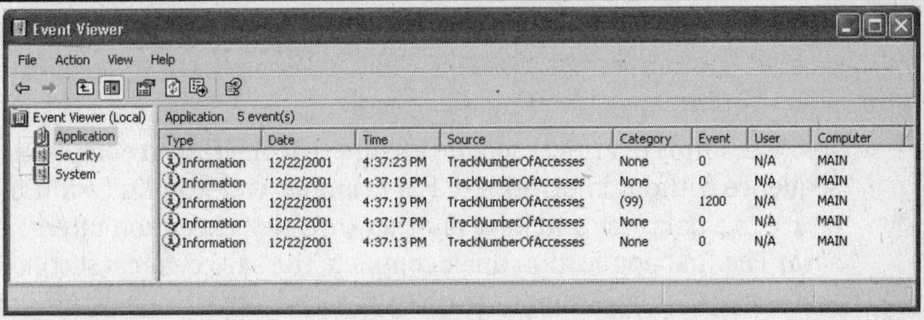

Type	Date	Time	Source	Category	Event	User	Computer
Information	12/22/2001	4:37:23 PM	TrackNumberOfAccesses	None	0	N/A	MAIN
Information	12/22/2001	4:37:19 PM	TrackNumberOfAccesses	None	0	N/A	MAIN
Information	12/22/2001	4:37:19 PM	TrackNumberOfAccesses	(99)	1200	N/A	MAIN
Information	12/22/2001	4:37:17 PM	TrackNumberOfAccesses	None	0	N/A	MAIN
Information	12/22/2001	4:37:13 PM	TrackNumberOfAccesses	None	0	N/A	MAIN

FIGURE 10.7: The client and service rely on the event log for communication.

Spending time looking through the series of event log entries in both the System and Application logs will help you better understand the way services function. Notice the special event with the Category value of (99). Figure 10.8 shows the message associated with this entry. Notice that the service provided the number of accesses in an easy to read form.

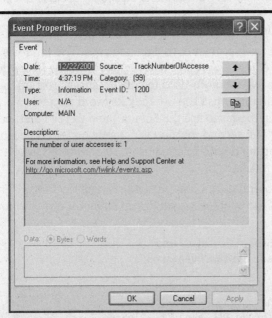

FIGURE 10.8: Event log messages must be easy to understand because they're the sole source of service communication.

UNDERSTANDING CRITICAL SECTIONS

A *critical section* is a piece of code or a variable that application threads can only access one thread at one time. If two applications require access to the same critical section, the first to make the request will obtain access. The second application will wait until the first application completes its task. In short, critical sections create bottlenecks in your code and can affect performance if you're not careful.

Some forms of critical section ensure that the thread completes code sequence without interruption. For example, you wouldn't want to begin a save to a database and have another thread of execution interrupt that save. The first application must complete the save before a second thread starts in order to ensure data integrity. The .NET Framework doesn't provide special calls to perform magic in this case; you must develop the thread in such a way that it saves the data safely. In short, the critical section helps ensure database integrity.

You may want to create a critical section for many different reasons; the most important of which is application data integrity. An application changes the contents of variables and the status of objects to meet the needs of a particular user. If another user suddenly decides to execute the same code, the lack of a critical section to protect the variable and object content would ruin the application for both parties.

A critical section must protect both data and code. The variables used in the thread are of equal importance to executing the code in the desired sequence. There are two methods used to create a critical section for use with threads. The first is to use the C# lock keyword to create a critical block. The second method is to use the Enter() and Exit() methods of the Monitor class. The second method is actually preferred because it provides you with greater flexibility and it isn't C#-specific because it relies on a .NET Framework class.

Let's look at a potential problem involving critical sections. Here's a modified version of the btnNewThread_Click() method we discussed earlier in Listing 10.5.

```
private void btnNewThread_Click(
  object sender, System.EventArgs e)
{
   // Create a new thread object.
   DLLThread.DLLThread   MyThread =
      new DLLThread.DLLThread(txtDlgName.Text);
```

```
    // Set the interval.
    MyThread.Interval = 5000;

    // Create and start the new thread.
    Thread   DoThread =
       new Thread(new ThreadStart(MyThread.CreateUIThread));
    DoThread.Start();

    // Change the interval.
    MyThread.Interval = 1000;

    // Create and start a new thread.
    Thread   DoThread2 =
       new Thread(new ThreadStart(MyThread.CreateUIThread));
    DoThread2.Start();

    // Get rid of the variables.
    DoThread2 = null;
    DoThread = null;
    MyThread = null;
}
```

When you run this code, you're using the same object for two threads. There's a possibility of the two threads creating a collision if they access the same variable at the same time. Here's a slightly modified version of the CreateUIThread() from Listing 10.4. Notice that it adds a *Counter* variable that makes collisions apparent.

```
public void CreateUIThread()
{
    // Create a new form.
    ThreadForm  Dlg = new ThreadForm();

    // Wait before assigning the dialog name.
    Thread.Sleep(_Interval);

    // Name the dialog.
    Dlg.Text = _ThreadDlgName + " " + Counter.ToString();

    // Increment the counter.
    Counter++;

    // Display the form.
    Dlg.ShowDialog();
}
```

Run this application without adding a critical section and you're likely to see the results of a collision. The two Thread Form dialog boxes will have the same number appended to the dialog box names. In some cases, you'll see the anticipated result; in others, you'll see that the second thread actually has a 1 attached to its name and the first thread has a value of 2. That's because both threads access the CreateUIThread() in a haphazard manner. The fix for this problem is as follows:

```
public void CreateUIThread()
{
    // Begin the critical section.
    Monitor.Enter(this);

    // Create a new form.
    ThreadForm  Dlg = new ThreadForm();

    // Wait before assigning the dialog name.
    Thread.Sleep(_Interval);

    // Name the dialog.
    Dlg.Text = _ThreadDlgName + " " + Counter.ToString();

    // Increment the counter.
    Counter++;

    // Exit the critical section.
    Monitor.Exit(this);

    // Display the form.
    Dlg.ShowDialog();
}
```

Notice the addition of the Monitor.Enter(this) and Monitor .Exit(this) calls. These calls ensure that the first thread always finishes before the second thread gains access to the method. As a result, the first dialog always contains a 1 and the second dialog always contains a 2.

You should also note the placement of the critical section. If you place the Monitor.Exit(this) call after Dlg.ShowDialog(), the application will stop after the first dialog appears. It will wait for you to close the first dialog before it displays the second dialog. The point is that you need to place critical sections carefully or the performance hit on your system could be substantial.

UNDERSTANDING THREAD SAFETY

One of the benefits of using libraries is code reuse. Once a developer writes and tests the code, they can place it in a library and forget about it. The functionality you'll need will be available without a lot of additional work. All you need to do is access the DLL. Windows uses this technique for all of the APIs that it supports.

Unfortunately, the black box functionality of libraries can be a double-edged sword. One of the biggest problems when using libraries with threads is that the library isn't thread safe. In other words, if two threads attempt to access the same object or function at the same time, there could be a collision, resulting in a frozen application, lost data, or other unanticipated results.

Fortunately, you can protect your libraries in a number of ways. One way is to use critical sections as needed to ensure that a sequence of events takes place without interruption. A second way is to allocate variables and objects on the stack. Finally, it's extremely important to reduce the risk of collisions by not allowing more than one thread to access the same variable—use techniques that ensure that each thread will have its own set of variables to use.

Even Microsoft's libraries aren't totally thread safe. For the most part, any object provided by the .NET Framework is thread safe at the class level but not at the object level. In other words, two threads could access different objects derived from the same class but not the same object. Fortunately, Microsoft has made thread safety a major issue in the help files that accompany Visual Studio .NET. Most of the help topics will tell you if the .NET Framework object you want to use is thread safe, so you'll want to verify thread safety each time you work with a new .NET Framework namespace or class.

However, this still doesn't guarantee thread safety for your code. You need to make your code thread safe as well. We discussed some of the techniques you can use to perform this task in the "Understanding Critical Sections" section of the chapter. Even if you don't plan to use a DLL you create today in a distributed application tomorrow, adding thread safety is insurance that the application you create tomorrow will work as anticipated.

Using Your Knowledge

Working with multiple threads can make your workstation more efficient and your server more available. However, misuse of threading techniques can easily run counter to these goals. You need to know when threads will do the job for you and when it's better to use a single-threaded approach. This chapter has provided a good understanding of how threads work and provided a good overview of when it's best to use them. You've also seen several threading examples. Now it's time to work with threading examples of your own design. Look for places that might cause conflicts and add a critical section to them. Try various access scenarios to ensure that your applications, components, and services are thread safe.

What's Next

The next four chapters of the book explain the development of database-driven software. They will show you how to read and write database data in both Windows and web-based applications.

Chapter 11

OVERVIEW OF THE ADO.NET CLASSES

ADO.NET allows you to interact with a database directly using objects of the *managed provider* classes. These objects allow you to connect to the database and execute SQL statements while directly connected to the database. Objects like the DataReader allow you to connect to a database directly and read the rows from a table in a forward-only direction.

ADO.NET also allows you to work in a *disconnected* manner. When doing this, you store information from a database locally in the memory of the computer on which your program is running. You store that information using objects of the *data set* classes. Once you have that information in the memory, you can then read and manipulate that information. For example, you can display the columns for the rows, add new rows, modify rows, and delete rows. Periodically, you'll reconnect to the database to synchronize your changes you've made locally with the database. This disconnected model allows you to write applications that run on the Internet, as well as for devices that aren't always connected to the database—PDAs such as the Palm and the Pocket PC, for example.

Adapted from *Mastering C# Database Programming*
by Jason Price
ISBN 0-7821-4183-8

This chapter provides descriptions of the ADO.NET classes. It also gives you a complete C# program that connects to a database, stores the rows locally, disconnects from the database, and then reads the contents of those local rows while disconnected from the database. This capability to store a local copy of rows retrieved from the database is one of the main strengths of ADO.NET. The example program illustrates the basic ideas of using the ADO.NET disconnected model to read rows from the database and store them locally in memory. In later chapters, you'll see how to modify data locally and then synchronize those changes with the database.

THE MANAGED PROVIDER AND GENERIC DATA SET CLASSES

To provide both connected and disconnected database access, ADO.NET defines two sets of classes: managed provider and generic data.

You use objects of the managed provider classes to directly connect to a database and to synchronize your locally stored data with the database. You can use the managed provider classes to read rows from the database in a forward-only direction. You use a different set of managed provider classes depending on the database you use.

You use objects of the generic data classes to store a local copy of the information retrieved from the database. This copy is stored in the memory of the computer where the C# program is running. The main generic data class is the System.Data.DataSet class. The generic data classes, as their name suggests, are not specific to any database, and you always use the same classes regardless of the database you use. The generic data classes represent information retrieved from the database as XML.

The Managed Provider Classes

The managed provider objects allow you to directly access a database, and you'll be introduced to the classes that allow you to create these objects in this section. You use the managed provider objects to connect to the database and read and write information to and from the database.

Figure 11.1 illustrates some of the managed provider objects and how they relate to each other.

Managed Provider Objects

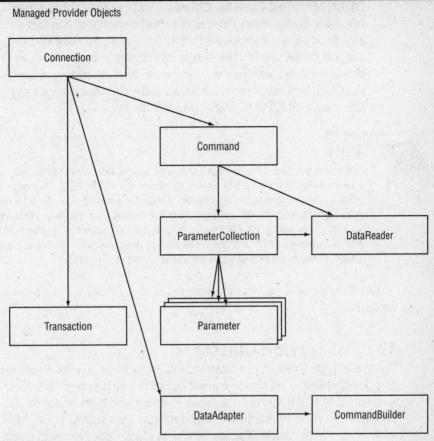

FIGURE 11.1: Some of the managed provider objects

There are currently three sets of managed provider classes, and each set is designed to work with different database standards. These three sets of classes all implement the same basic functionality.

SQL Server Managed Provider Classes   You use the SQL Server managed provider classes to connect to a SQL Server database.

OLE DB Managed Provider Classes   You use the OLE DB (Object Linking and Embedding for Databases) managed provider classes to connect to any database that supports OLE DB, such as Access or Oracle.

ODBC Managed Provider Classes   You use the ODBC (Open Database Connectivity) managed provider classes to connect to any database that supports ODBC. All the major databases support ODBC, but ODBC is typically slower than the previous two sets of classes when working with .NET. You should use the ODBC managed provider classes only when there aren't any alternative OLE DB managed provider classes.

NOTE

Whenever you see Sql at the start of a managed provider class name, you know that class is used with a SQL Server database. For example, SqlConnection allows you to connect to a SQL Server database. Similarly, OleDb is for databases that support OLE DB. For example, OleDbConnection allows you to connect to a database using OLE DB. Finally, Odbc is for databases that support ODBC. For example, OdbcConnection allows you to connect to a database using ODBC. I refer to all of these classes as the Connection classes.

You'll see some of the various managed-provider classes in the following sections.

The *Connection* Classes

There are three Connection classes: SqlConnection, OleDbConnection, and OdbcConnection. You use an object of the SqlConnection class to connect to a SQL Server database. You use an object of the OleDbConnection class to connect to any database that supports OLE DB, such as Access or Oracle. You use an object of the OdbcConnection class to connect to any database that supports ODBC. Ultimately, all communication with a database is done through a Connection object.

The *Command* Classes

There are three Command classes: SqlCommand, OleDbCommand, and OdbcCommand. You use a Command object to run a SQL statement, such as a SELECT, INSERT, UPDATE, or DELETE statement. You can also use a Command object to call a stored procedure or retrieve rows from a specific table. You run the command stored in a Command object using a Connection object.

The *Parameter* Classes

There are three Parameter classes: SqlParameter, OleDbParameter, and OdbcParameter. You use a Parameter object to pass a parameter to a Command object. You can use a Parameter to pass a value to a SQL statement or a stored procedure call. You can store multiple Parameter objects in a Command object through a ParameterCollection object.

The *ParameterCollection* Classes

There are three ParameterCollection classes: SqlParameterCollection, OleDbParameterCollection, and OdbcParameterCollection. You use a ParameterCollection object to store multiple Parameter objects for a Command object.

The *DataReader* Classes

There are three DataReader classes: SqlDataReader, OleDbDataReader, and OdbcDataReader. You use a DataReader object to read rows retrieved from the database using a Command object.

DataReader objects can only be used to read rows in a forward direction. DataReader objects act as an alternative to a DataSet object. You cannot use a DataReader to modify rows in the database.

TIP

Reading rows using a DataReader object is typically faster than reading from a DataSet.

The *DataAdapter* Classes

There are three DataAdapter classes: SqlDataAdapter, OleDbDataAdapter, and OdbcDataAdapter. You use a DataAdapter object to move rows between a DataSet object and a database. You use a DataAdapter object to synchronize your locally stored rows with the database. This synchronization is performed through a Connection object. For example, you can read rows from the database into a DataSet through a DataAdapter, modify those rows in your DataSet, and then push those changes to the database through a Connection object.

The *CommandBuilder* Classes

There are three CommandBuilder classes: SqlCommandBuilder, OleDbCommandBuilder, and OdbcCommandBuilder. You use a CommandBuilder object to automatically generate single-table INSERT, UPDATE, and DELETE commands that synchronize any changes you make to a DataSet object with the database. This synchronization is performed through a DataAdapter object.

The *Transaction* Classes

There are three Transaction classes: SqlTransaction, OleDbTransaction, and OdbcTransaction. You use a Transaction object to represent a *database transaction*. A database transaction is a group of statements that modify the rows in the database. These statements are considered a logical unit of work. For example, in the case of a banking transaction, you might want to withdraw money from one account and deposit it into another. You would then commit both of these changes as one unit, or if there's a problem, roll back both changes.

Namespaces for the Managed Provider Classes

The managed provider classes for SQL Server (SqlConnection and so on) are declared in the System.Data.SqlClient namespace. The classes for OLE DB–compliant databases (SqlDbConnection and so on) are declared in the System.Data.OleDb namespace. The classes for ODBC-compliant databases (OdbcConnection and so on) are declared in the System.Data.Odbc namespace.

In the following section, you'll learn about the generic data classes.

The Generic Data Classes

As discussed in the previous section, you can use the managed data provider objects to connect to the database through a Connection object, issue a SQL statement through a Command object, and read retrieved rows using a DataReader object; however, you can read rows only in a forward-only direction and you must be connected to the database.

The generic data objects allow you to store a local copy of the information stored in the database. This allows you to work the information while disconnected from the database. You can read the rows in any order, and you can search, sort, and filter those rows in a flexible manner. You can even make changes to those rows and then synchronize those changes with the database.

Figure 11.2 illustrates some of the generic data set objects and how they relate to each other. The bridge between the managed provider and generic data set objects is the DataAdapter, which you use to synchronize changes between your DataSet and the database.

Generic Data Set Objects

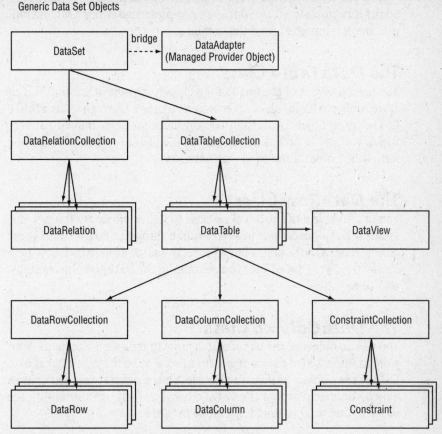

FIGURE 11.2:   Some of the generic data set objects

The following sections outline some of the generic data classes.

The *DataSet* Class

You use an object of the DataSet class to represent a local copy of the information stored in the database. You can make changes to that local copy in your DataSet and then later synchronize those changes with the database through a managed provider DataAdapter object. A DataSet object can represent database structures such as tables, rows, and columns. You can even add constraints to your locally stored tables to enforce unique and foreign key constraints.

You can also use a DataSet object to represent XML data. In fact, all information stored in a DataSet is represented using XML, including information retrieved from the database.

The *DataTable* Class

You use an object of the DataTable class to represent a table. You can store multiple DataTable objects in a DataSet through a DataTable-Collection object. A DataSet object has a property named Tables, which you use to access the DataTableCollection containing the DataTable objects stored in that DataSet.

The *DataRow* Class

You use an object of the DataRow class to represent a row. You can store multiple DataRow objects in a DataTable through a DataRowCollection object. A DataTable object has a property named Rows, which you use to access the DataRowCollection containing the DataRow objects stored in that DataTable.

The *DataColumn* Class

You use an object of the DataColumn class to represent a column. You can store multiple DataColumn objects in a DataTable through a DataColumn-Collection object. A DataTable object has a property named Columns, which you use to access the DataColumnCollection containing the DataColumn objects stored in that DataTable.

The *Constraint* Class

You use an object of the Constraint class to represent a database constraint that is to be enforced on one or more DataColumn objects of a DataTable. You can store multiple Constraint objects in a DataTable through a ConstraintCollection object. A DataTable object has a property named Constraints, which you use to access the Constraint-Collection containing the Constraint objects stored in that DataTable.

The *DataView* Class

You use an object of the DataView class to view only specific rows in a DataTable object using a filter, which specifies the criteria to restrict the rows.

The *DataRelation* Class

You use an object of the DataRelation class to represent a relationship between two DataTable objects. You can use a DataRelation object to model parent-child relationships between two database tables. You can store multiple DataRelation objects in a DataSet through a DataRelation-Collection object. A DataSet object has a property named Relations, which you use to access the DataRelationCollection containing the DataRelation objects stored in that DataSet.

The *UniqueConstraint* Class

You use an object of the UniqueConstraint class to represent a database constraint that enforces that the value stored in a DataColumn object is unique. The UniqueConstraint class is derived from the Constraint class. You can store multiple UniqueConstraint objects in a DataTable through a ConstraintCollection object.

The *ForeignKeyConstraint* Class

You use an object of the ForeignKeyConstraint class to specify the action performed when the column values in the parent table are updated or deleted.

The ForeignKeyConstraint class is derived from the Constraint class. You can either have the child rows deleted (cascading action), set the child columns to null, or set the child columns to a default value. You can store multiple ForeignKeyConstraint objects in a DataTable through a ConstraintCollection object.

Namespaces for the Generic Data Classes

The DataSet, DataTable, DataRow, DataColumn, DataRelation, Constraint, and DataView classes are all declared in the System.Data namespace. This namespace contains other classes that you can use in your programs. You can view the full set of classes declared in the System.Data namespace using the .NET documentation.

In the next section, you'll see a simple example that illustrates how to issue a SQL SELECT statement that retrieve rows from the Customers table, and then stores the returned rows in a DataSet object. This program will give you a basic understanding on how to use some of the managed provider and generic data classes previously outlined.

PERFORMING A SQL *SELECT* STATEMENT AND STORING THE ROWS LOCALLY

In the example featured in this section, you'll see how to connect to the SQL Server Northwind database and perform a SQL SELECT statement to retrieve the CustomerID, CompanyName, ContactName, and Address columns for the first 10 rows from the Customers table. These rows are stored in a DataSet object.

NOTE
Since I'll be using a SQL Server database, I'll use the SQL Server managed provider classes in the example.

Outlining the Procedure

You can use the following steps to retrieve the rows into a DataSet object:

1. Formulate a string containing the details of the database connection.

2. Create a SqlConnection object to connect to the database, passing the connection string to the constructor.

3. Formulate a string containing a SELECT statement to retrieve the columns for the rows from the Customers table.

4. Create a SqlCommand object to hold the SELECT statement.

5. Set the CommandText property of the SqlCommand object to the SELECT string.

6. Create a SqlDataAdapter object.

7. Set the SelectCommand property of the SqlAdapter object to the SqlCommand object.

8. Create a DataSet object to store the results of the SELECT statement.

9. Open the database connection using the Open() method of the SqlConnection object.

10. Call the `Fill()` method of the `SqlDataAdapter` object to retrieve the rows from the table, storing the rows locally in a `DataTable` of the `DataSet` object.

11. Close the database connection, using the `Close()` method of the `SqlConnection` object created in step 1.

12. Get the `DataTable` object from the `DataSet` object.

13. Display the columns for each row in the `DataTable`, using a `DataRow` object to access each row in the `DataTable`.

In the following sections, you'll learn the details of these steps and see example code.

Step 1: Formulate a String Containing the Details of the Database Connection

When connecting to a SQL Server database, your string must specify the following:

▶ The name of the computer on which SQL Server is running. You set this in the `server` part of the string. If SQL Server is running on your local computer, you can use `localhost` as the server name. For example, `server=localhost`.

▶ The name of the database. You set this in the `database` part of the string. For example, `database=Northwind`.

▶ The name of the user that is to connect to the database. You set this in the `uid` part of the string. For example, `uid=sa`.

▶ The password for the database user. You set this in the `pwd` part of the string. For example, `pwd=sa`.

NOTE
Typically, your organization's DBA (database administrator) will provide you with the appropriate values for the connection string. The DBA is responsible for administering the database.

The following example creates a string named `connectionString` and sets it to an appropriate string to connect to the Northwind database running on the local computer, using the `sa` user (with a password of `sa`) to connect to that database:

```
string connectionString =
    "server=localhost;database=Northwind;uid=sa;pwd=sa";
```

Your connection string will differ based on how you connect to your Northwind database.

Step 2: Create a *SqlConnection* Object to Connect to the Database

Create a SqlConnection object to connect to the database, passing the connection string created in the previous step to the constructor. You use an object of the SqlConnection class to connect to a SQL Server database.

The following example creates a SqlConnection object named mySqlConnection, passing connectionString (created in step 1) to the constructor:

```
SqlConnection mySqlConnection =
    new SqlConnection(connectionString);
```

Step 3: Formulate a String Containing the *SELECT* Statement

Formulate a string containing the SELECT statement to retrieve the CustomerID, CompanyName, ContactName, and Address columns for the first 10 rows from the Customers table. For example,

```
string selectString =
    "SELECT TOP 10 CustomerID, CompanyName,"
    +"ContactName, Address " +
    "FROM Customers " +
    "ORDER BY CustomerID";
```

NOTE

You use the TOP keyword in combination with an ORDER BY clause to retrieve the top *N* rows from a SELECT statement.

Step 4: Create a *SqlCommand* Object to Hold the *SELECT* Statement

You can call the CreateCommand() method of mySqlConnection to create a new SqlCommand object for that connection. The CreateCommand() method returns a new SqlCommand object for the SqlConnection object.

In the following example, a new SqlCommand object named mySqlCommand is set to the SqlCommand object returned by calling the CreateCommand() method of mySqlConnection:

```
SqlCommand mySqlCommand = mySqlConnection.CreateCommand();
```

Step 5: Set the *CommandText* Property of the *SqlCommand* Object to the *SELECT* String

Set the CommandText property of your SqlCommand object to the SELECT string created in step 4. The CommandText property contains the SQL statement you want to perform. In the following example, the CommandText property of mySqlCommand is set to selectString:

```
mySqlCommand.CommandText = selectString;
```

Step 6: Create a *SqlDataAdapter* Object

You use a SqlDataAdapter object to move information between your DataSet object and the database. You'll see how to create a DataSet object in step 8. The following example creates a SqlDataAdapter object named mySqlDataAdapter:

```
SqlDataAdapter mySqlDataAdapter = new SqlDataAdapter();
```

Step 7: Set the *SelectCommand* Property of the *SqlAdapter* Object to the *SqlCommand* Object

The SelectCommand property contains the SELECT statement you want to run. In the following example, the SelectCommand property of mySqlDataAdapter is set to mySqlCommand:

```
mySqlDataAdapter.SelectCommand = mySqlCommand;
```

This enables you to perform the SELECT statement defined in mySqlCommand. Step 10 actually performs the SELECT statement to retrieve rows from the database.

Step 8: Create a *DataSet* Object to Store the Results of the *SELECT* Statement

You use a DataSet object to store a local copy of information retrieved from the database. The following example creates a DataSet object named myDataSet:

```
DataSet myDataSet = new DataSet();
```

Step 9: Open the Database Connection Using the *Open()* Method of the *SqlConnection* Object

The following example calls the Open() method for mySqlConnection:

```
mySqlConnection.Open();
```

Once you've opened the database connection, you can access the database.

Step 10: Call the *Fill()* Method of the *SqlDataAdapter* Object to Retrieve the Rows from the Table

Call the Fill() method of your SqlDataAdapter object to retrieve the rows from the database, storing these rows locally in a DataTable of your DataSet object.

The Fill() method is overloaded, and the version you'll see in the example accepts two parameters:

▶ A DataSet object

▶ A string containing the name of the DataTable object to create in the specified DataSet

The Fill() method then creates a DataTable in the DataSet with the specified name and runs the SELECT statement. The DataTable created in your DataSet is then populated with the rows retrieved by the SELECT statement.

The following example calls the Fill() method of mySqlDataAdapter, passing myDataSet and "Customers" to the Fill() method:

```
mySqlDataAdapter.Fill(myDataSet, "Customers");
```

The Fill() method creates a DataTable object named Customers in myDataSet and populates it with the rows retrieved by the SELECT statement. You can access these rows, even when disconnected from the database.

Step 11: Close the Database Connection

Close the database connection using the Close() method of the SqlConnection object created in the first step. For example,

```
mySqlConnection.Close();
```

NOTE

Of course, you don't have to immediately close the database connection before reading locally stored rows from your DataSet. I close the connection at this point in the example to show that you can indeed read the locally stored rows — even when disconnected from the database.

Step 12: Get the *DataTable* Object from the *DataSet* Object

Get the DataTable object created in step 10 from the DataSet object.

You get a DataTable from your DataSet using the Tables property, which returns a DataTableCollection object. To get an individual Data-Table from your DataSet, you pass the name of your DataTable in brackets ("Customers", for example) to the Tables property. The Tables property will then return your requested DataTable, which you can store in a new DataTable object that you declare. In the following example, myDataSet .Tables["Customers"] returns the Customers DataTable created in myDataSet in step 10, and stores the returned DataTable in myDataTable:

```
DataTable myDataTable = myDataSet.Tables["Customers"];
```

NOTE

You can also specify the DataTable you want to get by passing a numeric value to the Tables property. For example, myDataSet.Tables[0] also returns the Customers DataTable.

Step 13: Display the Columns for Each Row in the *DataTable*

Display the columns for each row in the DataTable, using a DataRow object to access each row in the DataTable. The DataTable class defines a property named Rows that returns a DataRowCollection object containing the DataRow objects stored in that DataTable. You can use the Rows property in a foreach loop to iterate over the DataRow objects. For example,

```
foreach (DataRow myDataRow in myDataTable.Rows)
{
    // ... access the myDataRow object
}
```

Each DataRow object stores DataColumn objects that contain the values retrieved from the columns of the database table. You can access these column values by passing the name of the column in brackets to the

DataRow object. For example, myDataRow["CustomerID"] returns the value of the CustomerID column.

In the following example, a foreach loop iterates over the DataRow objects in myDataTable, and the column values are displayed for each row:

```
foreach (DataRow myDataRow in myDataTable.Rows)
{
  Console.WriteLine("CustomerID = " +
    myDataRow["CustomerID"]);
  Console.WriteLine("CompanyName = " +
    myDataRow["CompanyName"]);
  Console.WriteLine("ContactName = " +
    myDataRow["ContactName"]);
  Console.WriteLine("Address = " + myDataRow["Address"]);
}
```

As you can see, the name of each column is passed in brackets to each DataRow object, which then returns the column value.

NOTE
You can also specify the column you want to get by passing a numeric value in brackets. For example, myDataRow[0] also returns the CustomerID column value.

Putting It All Together

Listing 11.1 shows a complete program that uses these steps.

Listing 11.1: *SelectIntoDataSet.cs*

```
/*
  SelectIntoDataSet.cs illustrates
  how to perform a SELECT statement
  and store the returned rows in a DataSet object
*/

using System;
using System.Data;
using System.Data.SqlClient;

class SelectIntoDataSet
{
  public static void Main()
  {
    // step 1: formulate a string containing
    // the details of the database connection
```

```
string connectionString =
  "server=localhost;database=Northwind;uid=sa;pwd=sa";

// step 2: create a SqlConnection object
// to connect to the database,
// passing the connection string to
// the constructor
SqlConnection mySqlConnection =
  new SqlConnection(connectionString);

// step 3: formulate a SELECT statement to retrieve the
// CustomerID, CompanyName, ContactName, and Address
// columns for the first ten rows
// from the Customers table
string selectString =
  "SELECT TOP 10 CustomerID, CompanyName,"+
  "ContactName, Address " +
  "FROM Customers " +
  "ORDER BY CustomerID";

// step 4: create a SqlCommand object
// to hold the SELECT statement
SqlCommand mySqlCommand =
  mySqlConnection.CreateCommand();

// step 5: set the CommandText property
// of the SqlCommand object to
// the SELECT string
mySqlCommand.CommandText = selectString;

// step 6: create a SqlDataAdapter object
SqlDataAdapter mySqlDataAdapter = new SqlDataAdapter();

// step 7: set the SelectCommand property
// of the SqlAdapter object
// to the SqlCommand object
mySqlDataAdapter.SelectCommand = mySqlCommand;

// step 8: create a DataSet object to store the results of
// the SELECT statement
DataSet myDataSet = new DataSet();

// step 9: open the database connection using the
// Open() method of the SqlConnection object
mySqlConnection.Open();
```

```
          // step 10: use the Fill() method
          // of the SqlDataAdapter object to
          // retrieve the rows from the table,
          // storing the rows locally
          // in a DataTable of the DataSet object
          Console.WriteLine(
            "Retrieving rows from the Customers table");
          mySqlDataAdapter.Fill(myDataSet, "Customers");

          // step 11: close the database connection
          // using the Close() method
          // of the SqlConnection object created in Step 1
          mySqlConnection.Close();

          // step 12: get the DataTable object
          // from the DataSet object
          DataTable myDataTable = myDataSet.Tables["Customers"];

          // step 13: display the columns for
          // each row in the DataTable,
          // using a DataRow object to access
          // each row in the DataTable
          foreach (DataRow myDataRow in myDataTable.Rows)
          {
            Console.WriteLine(
              "CustomerID = " +
              myDataRow["CustomerID"]);
            Console.WriteLine(
              "CompanyName = " +
              myDataRow["CompanyName"]);
            Console.WriteLine(
              "ContactName = " +
              myDataRow["ContactName"]);
            Console.WriteLine("Address = " + myDataRow["Address"]);
          }
        }
      }
    }
```

The output from this program is as follows:

```
Retrieving rows from the Customers table
CustomerID = ALFKI
CompanyName = Alfreds Futterkiste
ContactName = Maria Anders
```

```
Address = Obere Str. 57
CustomerID = ANATR
CompanyName = Ana Trujillo Emparedados y helados
ContactName = Ana Trujillo
Address = Avda. de la Constitución 2222
CustomerID = ANTON
CompanyName = Antonio Moreno Taquería
ContactName = Antonio Moreno
Address = Mataderos  2312
CustomerID = AROUT
CompanyName = Around the Horn
ContactName = Thomas Hardy
Address = 120 Hanover Sq.
CustomerID = BERGS
CompanyName = Berglunds snabbköp
ContactName = Christina Berglund
Address = Berguvsvägen  8
CustomerID = BLAUS
CompanyName = Blauer See Delikatessen
ContactName = Hanna Moos
Address = Forsterstr. 57
CustomerID = BLONP
CompanyName = Blondesddsl père et fils
ContactName = Frédérique Citeaux
Address = 24, place Kléber
CustomerID = BOLID
CompanyName = Bólido Comidas preparadas
ContactName = Martín Sommer
Address = C/ Araquil, 67
CustomerID = BONAP
CompanyName = Bon app'
ContactName = Laurence Lebihan
Address = 12, rue des Bouchers
CustomerID = BOTTM
CompanyName = Bottom-Dollar Markets
ContactName = Elizabeth Lincoln
Address = 23 Tsawassen Blvd.
```

SUMMARY

In this chapter, you got an overview of the ADO.NET classes, and you examined a complete program that connected to a database, stored the rows locally, disconnected from the database, and then read the contents of those local rows while disconnected from the database.

ADO.NET allows you to interact with a database directly using objects of the managed provider classes. These objects allow you to connect to the database and execute SQL statements while directly connected. You use different sets of managed provider classes, depending on the database you are using.

ADO.NET also allows you to work in a disconnected manner. When doing this, you store information from a database locally in the memory of the computer on which your program is running. You store that information using objects of the *data set* classes.

Some of the SQL Server managed provider classes include SqlConnection, SqlCommand, SqlDataReader, SqlDataAdapter, and SqlTransaction. You use an object of the SqlConnection class to connect to a SQL Server database. You use an object of the SqlCommand class to represent a SQL statement or stored procedure call that you then execute. You use an object of the SqlDataReader class to read rows retrieved from a SQL Server database. You use an object of the SqlDataAdapter class to move rows between a DataSet object and a SQL Server database. You use an object of the SqlTransaction class to represent a database transaction in a SQL Server database.

You use an object of the DataSet class to represent a local copy of the information stored in a database. You can also use a DataSet object to represent XML data. Some of the objects you can store in a DataSet include DataTable, DataRow, DataColumn, DataRelation, and DataView objects.

You use an object of the DataTable class to represent a table. You use an object of the DataRow class to represent a row. You use an object of the DataColumn class to represent a column. You use an object of the Data-Relation class to represent a relationship between two DataTable objects. You use a DataRelation object to model parent-child relationships between two database tables. You use an object of the DataView class to view only specific rows in a DataTable object using a filter.

WHAT'S NEXT

In Chapter 12, you'll learn how to put these ADO.NET classes to work in your applications.

Chapter 12
ADO.NET APPLICATION DEVELOPMENT

Microsoft's database connectivity libraries have gone though numerous iterations (and abbreviations) over the years. We've seen Object Linking and Embedding Database (OLE-DB), Open Database Connectivity (ODBC), Remote Data Objects (RDO), and ActiveX Data Objects (ADO). Now it's time to look at the most recent way to connect applications to database data—ADO.NET, Microsoft's latest and greatest database access offering. Unlike previous Microsoft database technologies, however, ADO.NET isn't designed to provide an all-inclusive solution to every database need; ADO.NET is designed with distributed application requirements exclusively in mind.

This chapter tells you about ADO.NET and shows you several ways to use this new technology. Of course, the big news for ADO.NET is the disconnected application scenario, where a user on the road downloads the data they need for a particular purpose and then disconnects from the company Internet connection while continuing to work. However, ADO.NET

Adapted from *Visual C# .NET Developer's Handbook*
by John Paul Mueller
ISBN 0-7821-4047-5

makes just about every type of distributed application programming easier, because it supports the latest connection technologies. We'll also look at what passes for a live connection in ADO.NET. (Of course, you won't see any server-side cursor support with this technology.)

As part of the distributed and disconnected application scenarios, we'll also begin to look at technologies that might make your online communication events easier. Most notably, this chapter examines techniques for working with XML data. XML is the current solution for distributed application program connectivity because it enables an application to communicate with a web server through a firewall.

TIP

Microsoft is making a concerted effort to XML-enable all of their products, which includes the XML support found in SQL Server 2000. A large part of this effort is directed toward making it easier to create web services using Microsoft products. In fact, Microsoft recently released a Web Services Toolkit (http://msdn.microsoft.com/downloads/sample.asp?url=/MSDN-FILES/027/001/872/msdncompositedoc.xml) for SQL Server 2000 that makes it easier to create web service applications. The Web Services Toolkit site includes a link for the toolkit, white papers, webcasts, demonstrations, and the SQL Server–related newsgroups. Coupled with the SQL Server offering is an offering for BizTalk Server that links it with .NET. The Microsoft BizTalk Server 2002 Toolkit for Microsoft .NET includes a wealth of examples in addition to the required assemblies. You can find this toolkit at http://msdn.microsoft.com/downloads/default.asp?url=/downloads/sample.asp?url=%20/msdn-files/027/001/870/msdncompositedoc.xml.

COMPARING ADO TO ADO.NET

ADO.NET has had a rough childhood in some respects. It began as ADO+— the new and improved form of ADO—but Microsoft quickly changed the name when it became obvious that ADO.NET was going to become something different. In fact, ADO and ADO.NET are very different technologies, despite the similarities in names. Of course, this begs the question of why Microsoft used the term at all if the technologies are so different. The answer lies in the few similarities between the two technologies and not in their differences.

Both ADO and ADO.NET are high-level database access technologies. This means you do less work to accomplish any given task than you would with a low-level technology such as OLE-DB, but you also lose some flexibility and control. In addition, both of these technologies rely on OLE-DB as the low-level technology that performs most of the behind-the-scenes work. The final point of similarity between these two technologies is that they both rely on similar access techniques, such as the use of cursors and an in-memory data representation. This feature is hardly surprising considering both technologies come from the same company.

If you're familiar with ADO, the previous method of accessing database data, then you know that the basic in-memory representation for ADO is the `Recordset` object. This object contains a single table that can come from a query, individual table, stored procedure, or any other source of a single table of information. In some respects, this representation is limited, because you can only work with one set of information per `Recordset` object. However, nothing prevents you from creating more than one `Recordset` object, so in reality, the limit is more of perception than anything else. In fact, some developers state that using recordsets makes their code more readable than the ADO.NET alternative.

The ADO.NET alternative is to use a `Dataset` object. This is the same object that OLE-DB uses under .NET. A `Dataset` can contain multiple tables, which means you don't need exotic queries to gain access to precisely the information you need. The `DataTable` objects within the `Dataset` can have relations, just as they would within the database. The result is that you can create complex database setups within your application. Of course, this assumes you have so much data that you require such a complex setup for a single application. Some companies do have that much data, which is why this approach is so valuable. We'll see how to use the multiple table and relations feature of the `DataSet` object later in the chapter.

The simple, single-table `Recordset` object used by ADO means that it can also use simple commands to move between records. The `Recordset` object contains methods named `Move()`, `MoveFirst()`, `MovePrevious()`, `MoveNext()`, and `MoveLast()` that do all the work required to move from one record to another. In addition, you can easily determine the EOF and BOF conditions using the associated *Recordset* property values. This means that moving to the beginning or end of a table is easy and you can always determine your current position within the table. The record pointer associated with all of this movement is called a *cursor*. ADO supports cursors that reside on both the server and the client, which means that an application can track the current record position wherever it makes sense within a LAN application environment.

ADO.NET makes use of collections within the `Dataset`. Actually, there are groups of collections, and collections-within-collections. The advantage of this technique is that you can examine records using a foreach statement—the same technique you'd use to enumerate any other collection. Using collections also makes it easier to transfer data to display elements such as the DataGrid object. (Although, the Recordset object is actually easier to use with detail forms.) The use of collections means that it's easier to read a Dataset object from end-to-end than it is to address an individual record or to move backward within the collection. For example, let's say you want to address a single record field within the Dataset; you'd probably require code similar to the code shown here:

```
MyString = MyData.Tables[0].Rows[0].ItemArray.
    GetValue(1).ToString();
```

The equivalent code for ADO is simpler and easier to understand. Here's an example:

```
MyString = DBRecordset.get_Collect("Name").ToString()
```

As you can see, a Recordset object does have an advantage in requiring less code to access an individual value because it isn't buried in multiple layers. In addition, notice that you can access the field by name when using a Recordset object—the Dataset object offers you an integer value that you must derive from the field's position within the data result. Still, there are significant advantages to using ADO.NET, as we'll see in the sections that follow.

This brings us to the DataReader object, which uses a read-only, forward-only cursor. The main purpose of the DataReader object is to enable disconnected mode operation for applications. A user can download data from the company database while connecting using an Internet (or other) connection. The data is then available for viewing offline (but not for modification because the connection to the database is lost).

While both ADO and ADO.NET rely on OLE-DB as their connectivity technology, they each use different techniques to accomplish their goal. Both database technologies do rely on a connection. However, ADO provides little flexibility in the way data updates occur once the connection is established. ADO.NET, on the other hand, relies on a DataAdapter object, which allows you much more flexibility in performing updates.

The final point for consideration, now, is the issue of connectivity. ADO does provide remote connectivity features, but like all other COM-based technologies, it uses DCOM as the basis for data exchange across a remote network. This means the connection port number changes often and the data itself is in binary form. The benefit of this approach is that few crackers have the knowledge required to peer at your data. The disadvantage is a conflict with firewall protection—most firewalls are designed to keep ports closed and to restrict binary data.

ADO.NET gets around the firewall problems by using XML to transfer the data using HTTP or some other appropriate data transfer technology. The point is that the data is in pure ASCII and relies on a single port for data transfers. Unfortunately, many people criticize XML as a security risk and vendors have done little to make it more secure. Any attempt to encrypt the data would open the Pandora's box of binary data transfer again, making the use of XML questionable. In short, XML is a good, but not perfect, solution to the problem of remote connectivity.

USING *OLEDBDATAADAPTER* FOR DATA TRANSFER TO ADO.NET

As previously mentioned, ADO.NET relies on OLE-DB to perform low-level database connectivity chores. You're already familiar with the two objects that ADO.NET uses for this task, the OleDbConnection and the OleDbDataAdapter. The OleDbConnection object creates the actual connection between the application and the database management system (DBMS). The OleDbDataAdapter performs tasks like inserting new records, updating existing records, and deleting old records.

NOTE

The OleDbDataAdapter comes in more than one flavor. Visual Studio .NET comes with a form of this object that's optimized for SQL Server—the SqlDataAdapter. The difference between the two objects is that the SQL Server version is optimized for use with SQL Server, which means your application gains a performance benefit. Microsoft anticipates that other vendors will eventually create specialized connection and data-adapter objects for .NET. In fact, the first add-on for this technology is the ODBC.NET technology, which is readily available from Microsoft's website as a download. The performance you receive from a custom object will normally be better than the performance you obtain from the standard objects. However, the only thing you gain, in some cases, is some additional flexibility in accessing the data.

Once the data appears within the data adapter, you can access it in a number of ways. For example, it's possible to fill a Dataset object with information from the data adapter using the Fill() or the FillSchema() command. A Dataset object can contain more than one table, so it's possible to create relations and perform other tasks normally performed by a DBMS.

The Dataset object contains the whole table found in the data adapter in a raw form that you can manipulate as needed. Sometimes you don't need the raw data; you need something that's sorted, filtered, or otherwise manipulated in some way. That's where the DataView object comes into play. The DataView object can present a particular view of the information found in the data adapter. For example, you can choose to ignore specific fields or rows with certain attributes (such as deleted rows). Two DataViews that use the same data adapter can contain vastly different information, which makes the DataView somewhat limiting but also adds a level of automation to the database application.

WRITING A *DATAREADER* APPLICATION

Previous examples in the book have discussed the use of the Dataset object because it provides the type of connectivity that most developers are used to using in an application. You'll also find a new DataReader object with Visual Studio .NET that enables you to create a read-only, forward-only stream of data from a database. The main benefit of using a DataReader object is that the application saves memory (only a single record resides in memory) and the technique can help enhance application performance.

The DataReader object is useful for a number of purposes. For example, you can use it to create fast print routines and display lists. A DataReader also enables you to download data to a laptop or PDA for later use. Because the DataReader doesn't need a connection to the database once you complete the download, you can use it to create disconnected applications.

The following sections describe one use for the DataReader. We'll build a list view and a print routine based on the DataReader for a MovieGuide database. You'll also find a new type of construct in this section, the StringBuilder object. The "Using StringBuilder to Improve Performance" section describes when and where you'll use this object.

Creating the Application Shell

The application we'll create in this section uses a standard dialog box. You'll need to add a SqlConnection named MovieConnect and a SqlCommand named GetMovie. The easiest way to create the SqlConnection is to drag the ExistingMovies database from Server Explorer to the form.

To configure `GetMovie`, you'll need to select `MovieConnect` in the `Connection` property. Click the ellipses in the `CommandText` property for the `GetMovie` command and you'll see a Query Builder dialog box. Figure 12.1 shows how to format the query for this example. The graphical display at the top of the dialog box enables you to create relations and choose fields. The next section contains options for sort order and criteria. You'll see the current query listed in the third section. The fourth section of the dialog box contains parameters for the command. You should end up with a `CommandText` property value of SELECT `Name, Rating, Description, LeadActor, LeadActress` FROM `ExistingMovies` ORDER BY `Name`.

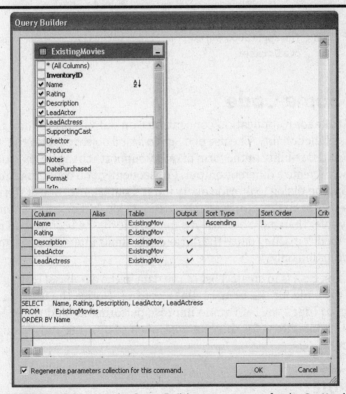

FIGURE 12.1: Use the Query Builder to create text for the `GetMovie` command.

The application also includes three buttons: Quit, List Data, and Print Data. A textbox (`txtOutput`) will hold the data that the application produces when the user clicks List Data. Figure 12.2 shows typical application output.

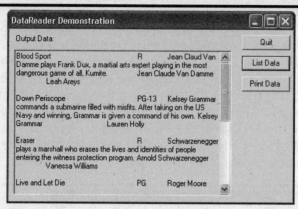

FIGURE 12.2:   The application will list or print data using a `DataReader` instead of a `Dataset`.

Adding Some Code

The `DataReader` application concentrates on output rather than full database functionality. The use of a `SqlCommand` object enables the developer to add flexibility in the form of query support—changing the query will always create a different output. Consequently, you could easily use a configuration dialog to provide query input. For instance, one of the uses for this type of application is an informational kiosk. The application is actually safer than most because it's impossible for the user to send new data or modify existing data—the `DataReader` limits interaction to requests for information only.

The first task is to create a list of the data in the database. Listing 12.1 shows the code for the `btnListData` control. Notice the use of a `StringBuilder` (`MovieList`) to improve performance and the special control requirements for this example, such as opening and closing the connection.

NOTE

You can download all the source files for the programs featured in this chapter from the Sybex website at http://www.sybex.com. Search for this chapter's source book by its ISBN number, 4047, or its title, *Visual C# .NET Developer's Handbook*, and look for the Download link on the right. Once you've downloaded the files, you can follow along with the examples without having to type in the program listings.

Listing 12.1: Use a *DataReader* When Application Security Is Paramount

```
private void btnListData_Click(object sender,
  System.EventArgs e)
{
    // Open the connection.
    MovieConnect.Open();

    // Create and initialize the DataReader.
    SqlDataReader  MovieGuide = GetMovie.ExecuteReader();

    // Create and initialize the StringBuilder.
    StringBuilder  MovieList = new StringBuilder();

    // Build the display string.
    while (MovieGuide.Read())
    {
        MovieList.Append(MovieGuide.GetString(0));
        MovieList.AppendFormat("\t{0}",
          MovieGuide.GetString(1));
        MovieList.AppendFormat("\t{0}",
          MovieGuide.GetString(2));
        MovieList.AppendFormat("\t{0}",
          MovieGuide.GetString(3));
        MovieList.AppendFormat("\t{0}\r\n\r\n",
          MovieGuide.GetString(4));
    }

    // Display the data in the textbox.
    txtOutput.Text = MovieList.ToString();

    // Close the data objects.
    MovieGuide.Close();
    MovieConnect.Close();
}
```

The first task the code performs is creating the DataReader. The easiest and most flexible way to do this is to call upon the ExecuteReader() method of the command we created earlier.

As you can see, you use a DataReader in a loop. Each call to Read() brings in another row of data. Remember that MovieGuide will contain only one row of data at a time and that you can't go back to a previous record. Therefore, you must perform any data processing on the current row while the row is in MovieGuide or store the information for future use. The DataReader object uses a 0-based index for storing the data fields in the order they appear in the query string for the SqlCommand. After you process all of the rows of data the query can provide, Read() will return false, which ends the processing loop and displays the data on screen.

Print routines follow a specific pattern in .NET. What you really need is a PrintPageEventHandler. The other basics of printing remain the same in all but a few instances. Consequently, Listing 12.2 shows the PrintPageEventHandler for the example.

Listing 12.2: The *PrintPageEventHandler PD_PrintPage()* Uses a *StringBuilder* for Output

```
void PD_PrintPage(Object sender, PrintPageEventArgs ev)
{
    Font            docFont;    // Document Font
    Font            headFont;   // Heading Font
    float           yPos = 20;  // Position of text on page.
    StringFormat    Format;     // Drawing format for details.
    Rectangle       PrintArea;  // Printing area.

    // Create the font.
    docFont = new Font("Courier New", 10, FontStyle.Bold);
    headFont = new Font("Arial", 15);

    // Create the StringFormat.
    Format = new StringFormat();
    Format.FormatFlags = StringFormatFlags.NoClip;
    Format.Trimming = StringTrimming.None;

    // Determine a print area.
    PrintArea = new Rectangle(0,
        (Int32)yPos,
        (Int32)ev.Graphics.VisibleClipBounds.Width,
        (Int32)docFont.GetHeight() * 4);

    // Print the heading.
    ev.Graphics.DrawString("Movie Guide Output",
                           headFont,
                           Brushes.Black,
                           0,
                           yPos);
    yPos = yPos + headFont.GetHeight() + 20;
```

```
// Open the connection.
MovieConnect.Open();

// Create and initialize the DataReader.
SqlDataReader  MovieGuide = GetMovie.ExecuteReader();

// Create and initialize the StringBuilder.
StringBuilder  MovieList = new StringBuilder();

// Continue printing as long as
// there is space on the page and
// we don't run out of things to write.
while (MovieGuide.Read())
{
   // Build the display string.
   MovieList.AppendFormat("{0, -51}",
      MovieGuide.GetString(0));
   MovieList.AppendFormat("{0, -6}",
      MovieGuide.GetString(1));
   MovieList.AppendFormat("{0, -1001}",
      MovieGuide.GetString(2));
   MovieList.AppendFormat("{0, -41}",
      MovieGuide.GetString(3));
   MovieList.AppendFormat("{0, -41}",
      MovieGuide.GetString(4));

   // Set the Y position.
   PrintArea.Y = (Int32)yPos;

   // Output the data.
   ev.Graphics.DrawString(MovieList.ToString(),
                          docFont,
                          Brushes.Black,
                          PrintArea,
                          Format);

   // Determine the next print position.
   yPos = yPos + (docFont.GetHeight() * 4) + 10;

   // Clear the StringBuilder object.
   MovieList =  new StringBuilder();
}
```

```
    // Close the data objects.
    MovieGuide.Close();
    MovieConnect.Close();

    // Tell the application there are no more pages to print.
    ev.HasMorePages = false;
}
```

The process of creating various fonts and using `DrawString()` to create a header is the same as before. However, this is where the similarity to other print output routines we've studied ends. The first thing you should notice is that the detail lines rely on a rectangle, not a single point, as a means for determining the output range. The upper-left corner is determined by the preferred x and y values (0 and yPos for the example). We have no way to determine the width of the page because each printer is different. Fortunately, you can retrieve this value at runtime using the `ev.Graphics.VisibleClipBounds.Width` property. It's also necessary to determine a print height based on the font used by the print routine. The example allocates four lines of text for each database entry, so the rectangle height is `docFont.GetHeight() * 4`.

Because each entry in the report can contain multiple lines of data, it's also important to create a `StringFormat` object. This object determines the formatting characteristics of the output. The example tells the CLR not to clip the output text and not to use any string trimming. These two entries are essential or the CLR will attempt to clean up your output in some cases—an undesirable trait if you want to preserve the formatting of your text.

The detail portion of the output routine looks very similar to the routine we used for the textbox on screen. However, notice the complete lack of formatting (escape) characters in the text. The example also uses the second parameter of the formatting string to force each string to occupy one more character than its maximum length, which ensures the printed entries will line up. The use of a `StringBuilder` object isn't only a performance enhancement, in this case; it's a necessary part of the print routine and we'd need a lot more code to duplicate what this object does automatically.

There are some additional pieces of code you need to consider. `StringBuilder` objects have no `Clear()` method, so you need to create a new object after each line of printed text. The `StringBuilder` object is still more efficient than using a string alternative, but not quite as efficient as the textbox portion of the example.

Note, also, that you need to change the Y property of `PrintArea` after each row of text, or the data won't print in the right area. The need to keep track of two row variables is a nuisance and could lead to errors in a complex print routines, but it's a necessity in this situation. In short, you must update both yPos and PrintArea to position the text on the printer.

Testing Using NUnit

As you create more application code and the code becomes more complex, it becomes important to have a good testing tool. Microsoft does provide some rudimentary testing tools with Visual Studio .NET, but most of these tools appear with the Enterprise Architect Edition and don't provide much in the way of automation. Consequently, third-party developers have filled in the gaps by creating automated tools for the developer. NUnit represents one of the tools that fill this gap. You can find the free NUnit tool at http://sourceforge.net/projects/nunit.

NUnit provides two forms of testing application. The GUI version is accessible from the NUnit folder of the Start menu. The GUI version enables you to run the application test immediately after adding new code and provides a neater presentation of the logged errors. You'll also find a command-line version of the program called NUnitConsole in the \Program Files\NUnit\ folder of your hard drive. The console version lets you place several testing scenarios in a single batch file and perform automated testing on more than one application at a time. You can also schedule testing using the Task Scheduler.

The product works by examining test cases that you create for your application. A test case is essentially a script that compares the result from your code to an anticipated result (what you expected the code to do). The test case can also check the truth-value of a return value. The software author, Philip Craig, recommends creating a section of code, and then creating a test case for that code. For example, you'll want to create a minimum of one test case for each method within a class. In this way, you build layers of code and tests that help locate problems quickly and tell you when a piece of code that previously worked is broken by a new addition to the application.

NUnit provides the means to perform individual tests based on a single test case or to create a test suite based on multiple test cases. The use of a special function, Assert() or AssertEquals() enables NUnit to test for the required condition. When NUnit sees a failure condition, it logs the event so you can see it at the end of the test. The point is that you don't have to create test conditions yourself—each test is performed automatically. Of course, the test cases still need to address every failure condition to provide complete application testing.

Let's look at a simple example. The example code performs simple math operations, but the code could perform any task. The DoAdd() and DoMultiply() methods both work as written. However, there's an error in the DoSubtract() method, as shown here:

```
public static string DoSubtract(string Input1, string Input2)
{
    int    Value1;
    int    Value2;
    int    Result;

    // Convert the strings.
    Value1 = Int32.Parse(Input1);
    Value2 = Int32.Parse(Input2);

    // Perform the addition.
    Result = Value2 - Value1;

    // Output the result.
    return Result.ToString();
}
```

Obviously, most developers would catch this error just by looking at the code, but it isn't always easy to find this type of error in complex code. That's why it's important to write a test routine as part of your application (or in a separate DLL). Creating the test routine consists of five steps:

1. Include the NUnitCore.DLL (located in the \Program Files\ NUnit\bin folder) as a reference to your application.

2. Create a class that relies on the NUnit.Framework.TestCase class as a base class.

3. Add a constructor that includes a string input and passes the string to the base class such as: public MathCheckTest (String name) : base(name).

4. Add a test suite property to your code formatted as: public static ITest Suite.

5. Create one or more public test scenarios.

There are a number of ways to create the test suite for your application. The two main methods are dynamic and static, with the dynamic method presenting the fewest problems for the developer. Here's an example of the dynamic test suite declaration:

```
// You must define a suite of tests to perform.
public static ITest Suite
```

```
{
    get
    {
        return new TestSuite(typeof (MathCheckTest));
    }
}
```

As you can see, it's a simple read-only property. The property returns the type of the test. In this case, it's the `MathCheckTest` class. The example actually includes two classes, so you can see how the classes appear in the test engine. If you don't include this property, the test engine will claim that there aren't any tests—even if you've defined everything else correctly.

The test can be as complex or simple as you need in order to verify the functionality of the application. The simpler you can make the test, the better. You don't want errors in the test suite to hide errors in your code (or worse yet, tell you there are errors when its obvious the code is working as anticipated). Here's an example of a simple test method.

```
// Test the add function using a simple example.
public void TestAdd()
{
    string    Expected = "5";
    string    Result = MathCheck.DoAdd("2", "3");
    Assert(Expected.Equals(Result));
}
```

Sometimes you need two or more test methods to fully examine a method. For example, the `DoDivide()` method requires two tests as a minimum. First, you must examine the code for proper operation. Second, you must verify that the code can handle divide-by-zero scenarios. It's never a good idea to include both tests in one test method—use a single method for each test as shown in the example code.

Now that you know what the code looks like, let's see the code in action. When you first start the NUnitGUI application, you'll see a dialog containing fields for the Assembly File and the Test Fixture. Select an assembly file using the Browse button and you'll see the test suites the assembly contains in the Test Fixture field. Each test suite is a separate class and the name of the class appears in the field, as shown in Figure 12.3.

If you select a test suite and click Run, NUnitGUI will run all of the tests in that suite. However, you might only want to run one test in the suite. In this case, use the NUnit ➢ Show Test Browser command to display the Show Tests dialog box shown in Figure 12.4. Highlight the individual test you want to run and click Run. The results of the individual test will appear in the main window as usual.

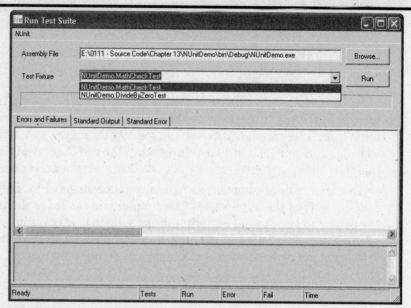

FIGURE 12.3:   An application can contain more than one test suite, but each suite must appear in a separate class.

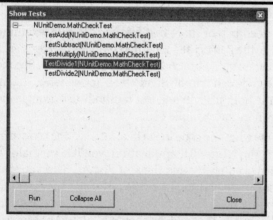

FIGURE 12.4:   Use the Show Tests dialog box to select individual tests from a suite.

So, what happens when you run the tests? As the tests run, a bar will move across the window to show the test progress. If the tests run without error, you'll see a green bar on the main window; a red bar appears when the application has errors. Figure 12.5 shows a typical example of an application with errors.

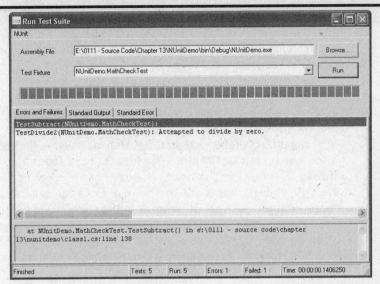

FIGURE 12.5: This application contains two errors that the test suite found with ease using simple tests.

As you can see, the test found two errors. The first is the subtraction error that I mentioned earlier in the section. Notice that the lower pane of the main window provides you with enough information to locate the error in the source code. The second error is one of omission. The DoDivide() method lacks any means for detecting a divide-by-zero error. This second error points out that NUnit can help you find errors of commission, as well as errors of omission, given a good test suite.

OTHER DEVELOPMENT TOOLS TO CONSIDER

Visual Studio .NET, like versions of Visual Studio before it, will rely heavily on third-party tools to enable the developer to perform certain tasks. For example, some developers find the profiling support in Visual Studio .NET lacking. Fortunately, DevPartner Profiler from Compuware Corporation enables you to perform a line-by-line analysis of your code. The best news is that this product is fully integrated with the Visual Studio .NET IDE, and you can download it free. You'll find DevPartner Profiler at the Compuware website (http://www.compuware.com/products/numega/dps/profiler/).

CONTINUED ➡

Another developer of performance testing tools is Mercury Interactive. LoadRunner (http://www-svca.mercuryinteractive.com/products/loadrunner/) enables the developer to place various types of loads on a system. For example, you could simulate 1,000 network users and 200 Internet users to create a mixed execution environment. You receive feedback about the effects of the load on the system as a whole through performance monitors. Astra LoadTest (http://astratryandbuy.mercuryinteractive.com/cgi-bin/portal/trynbuy/index.jsp) is one of a suite of tools you can use to perform website testing. Other tools in the suite include Astra QuickTest (automated web testing), Astra FastTrack (defect management), and Astra SiteManager (an application management tool). You can download demonstration versions of all four of these tools.

If the four database technologies we've studied so far have left you with more questions than answers, you might consider looking at Dataphor from Alphora (http://www.alphora.com/tiern.asp?ID=DATAPHOR). Dataphor is a data access alternative to the solutions that come with .NET. You'd use this technology in place of a technology such as OLE-DB or ADO.NET. The website currently includes a series of white papers explaining the product. Dataphor solves problems common in .NET data classes such as non-updateable queries, lack of navigational access, join information loss, static data types, schema duplication, and three-valued logic.

Finding information in a large application can be difficult, to say the least. For example, you might remember that you defined a variable, but finding the definition can prove challenging. FMS provides a series of .NET–related tools, such as Total .NET XRef (http://www.fmsinc.com/dotnet/default.asp) that make it easier to manage your applications. The Total .NET series includes XRef (cross-reference variables and objects in your code), SourceBook (an extensive collection of source code examples), Analyzer (automated error and performance problem detection), and Renamer (a smart alternative to find and replace).

WRITING A DATASET APPLICATION

The Dataset object enables you to store data from a variety of sources, including DataAdapters and DataTables. The point is that it doesn't really care where the data comes from, as long as it can store the data in a DataTable. Every Dataset contains zero or more DataTables. One of the main points of the example in this chapter is that the source of the data is unimportant. This example relies on a SQL Server database.

TIP

Many developers want to incorporate controls other than the standard string or check box into their DataGrid. The only problem is that Microsoft doesn't provide any additional controls as part of Visual Studio .NET. If you want to create other input forms, such as a drop-down list, then you need to create a custom class that implements the DataGridColumnStyle. Fortunately, some third-party developers are already working on this problem. For example, Axxias.ColumnStyles (http://www.columnstyles.com/) provides several types of controls you can incorporate into your DataGrid without a lot of additional programming.

Coding the Grid View

The first step in the grid example is adding the proper using statements to the beginning of the FrmGridView.CS file. The example draws from the SQL Server provider, so we need to use namespaces for that provider. Unlike OLE-DB, you actually need two namespaces to gain full functionality to SQL Server 2000 features:

```
using System.Data.SqlClient;
using System.Data.SqlTypes;
```

The SqlClient namespace takes the place of the System.Data.OleDb namespace used in Listing 12.1. You'll find all of the same functionality that the OLE-DB provider included, plus some additional functionality unique for SQL Server (not to mention the enhanced performance you'll receive). The SqlTypes namespace contains special data types you can use when working with SQL Server 2000 (previous versions of the product might not support all of the types shown in the namespace).

You'll also need to change some of the object names. For example, instead of an OleDbException, you'll need to check for a SqlException.

The actual functioning of the exception object is the same—it still produces the same error and for the same reason. You'll still receive the same information and you'll use it in the same way. The only thing that's changed is the exception object name.

Now that we have the preliminaries completed, let's look at some ways to augment the Grid view in the following sections.

TIP

It's interesting to note that you can't always create project names and namespaces that are conflict-free on the first try. For example, as an experiment for the example in this chapter, I tried naming the project "DataSet." The name should have worked given Microsoft's documentation, but it caused all kinds of odd conflicts, including a disappearing DataSet object problem. However, renaming the project files and changing the namespace entry to namespace MyDataSet didn't fix the problem. It seems the automatic code generation features of the Visual Studio IDE will continue to use the old namespace value until you change two values in the project Property Pages dialog. To view these properties, right-click the project name in Solution Explorer and choose Properties from the context menu. Open the \Common Properties\General folder and you'll see two properties: Assembly Name and Default Namespace. You must change both of these property values to the new namespace name in order to ensure that the automatic code generation features of the IDE work as intended.

Moving the Cursor on Screen

One of the first changes you'll see for the Grid view portion of this example is a new method for selecting rows. Some developers want something easier to see than the row pointer used for the first example. The most common way to make the row selection more visible is to highlight the entire row as shown here:

```
private void DoNext()
{
    // Move to the next record.
    if (AddrDataGrid.CurrentRowIndex !=
        addressDataset1.Tables[0].Rows.Count - 1)
    {
        AddrDataGrid.UnSelect(AddrDataGrid.CurrentRowIndex);
        AddrDataGrid.CurrentRowIndex++;
        AddrDataGrid.Select(AddrDataGrid.CurrentRowIndex);
    }
    else
```

```
            // Display an error message.
            MessageBox.Show("Already at last record!",
                            "Data Grid Pointer",
                            MessageBoxButtons.OK,
                            MessageBoxIcon.Exclamation);
        }
```

Notice that this version of DoNext() relies heavily on the CurrentRow-Index property to ensure proper row selection. The UnSelect() method removes the highlight from the current row, the CurrentRowIndex value is incremented, and then the Select() method is called with the new CurrentRowIndex. It's possible to expand this process to enable the user to select more than one row—simply leave the UnSelect() method call out and the *DataGrid* will continue highlighting rows as needed.

Of course, you might not want to select an entire row. Perhaps you just want to select the current cell. You can perform this task in a number of ways, but this code will provide you with some general ideas:

```
    private void DoLast()
    {
        DataGridColumnStyle  DGCS; // The column we want to view.

        // Move to the last record.
        AddrDataGrid.UnSelect(AddrDataGrid.CurrentRowIndex);
        AddrDataGrid.CurrentRowIndex =
            addressDataset1.Tables[0].Rows.Count - 1;

        // Select the cell we want to highlight.
        AddrDataGrid.CurrentCell =
            new DataGridCell(AddrDataGrid.CurrentRowIndex, 0);
        DGCS = AddrDataGrid.TableStyles[0].GridColumnStyles[0];

        // Begin an edit to highlight the cell.
        AddrDataGrid.BeginEdit(DGCS,
            AddrDataGrid.CurrentRowIndex);
    }
```

The first thing you should notice is that the code uses UnSelect() to remove the highlight from the current row, but it doesn't rely on Select() to add a highlight to the next row. The code initially selects a new cell by creating a new value for the CurrentCell property using a DataGridCell object. The example assumes the user will want to select the first column in the DataGrid, but you can use the code to select any column, including the current column.

Simply selecting the cell won't highlight it. You could press Tab, at this point, and see the next cell highlighted, but it won't highlight the current cell, which is what we want the code to do. When the user clicks Tab, the DataGrid goes into edit mode, so that's what the example code will need to do as well. This means creating a DataGridColumnStyle object and then using it as input to the BeginEdit() method. Notice that the code doesn't call EndEdit() because the user hasn't made any changes to the data yet—the edit has only begun. At this point, you have two more ways to move the cursor around on the DataGrid.

Adding and Removing Records

The Grid view comes with the capability to add and remove records due to the connectivity between the DataGrid and the DataAdapter. However, the functionality is difficult to access outside of the DataGrid and assumes the user actually understands the results of pressing the control keys. For example, pressing Del will remove a record without one note of caution from the DataGrid, which opens the database to accidental data loss.

The example includes both menu entries and toolbar buttons for adding and removing records. One special note for the Record ≻ Delete menu entry is that you also need to add the Del key as a shortcut to ensure the user can't delete a record without using the proper routine. As with many other parts of this example, the menu and toolbar event handlers merely reroute the call to a centralized routine we can use for multiple purposes (not the least of which is adding the same support to the Detail view). Listing 12.3 shows the code you'll need to add for adding and removing records.

Listing 12.3: Adding and Removing Records from the Grid View

```
private void mnuRecordAdd_Click(
   object sender, System.EventArgs e)
{
   // Add a record.
   DoAddRecord();
}

private void mnuRecordDelete_Click(
   object sender, System.EventArgs e)
{
   // Delete a record.
   DoDeleteRecord();
}
```

```
private void DoAddRecord()
{
    // The column we want to view.
    DataGridColumnStyle  DGCS;

    // Create a new data row.
    DataRow  NewRow = addressDataset1.Tables[0].NewRow();

    // Fill required fields with default information.
    NewRow["LAST_NAME"] = "";
    NewRow["FIRST_NAME"] = "";
    NewRow["COMPANY"] = "";
    NewRow["BUSINESS"] = true;
    NewRow["CONTACTED"] = DateTime.Today.ToString();

    // Begin the editing process.
    NewRow.BeginEdit();

    // Place the cursor in the data add row.
    addressDataset1.Tables[0].Rows.Add(NewRow);

    // Select the new row and prepare to edit it.
    DoLast();
}

private void DoDeleteRecord()
{
    DialogResult  Result = DialogResult.No;
    DataRow       RemoveRow;

    // Display a message asking the user
    // if they really want to delete the record.
    Result =
      MessageBox.Show(
      "Are you sure you want to remove the record?",
      "Permanent Record Deletion Warning",
      MessageBoxButtons.YesNo,
      MessageBoxIcon.Warning);

    // If the user is sure about the
    // record deletion, remove it.
    if (Result == DialogResult.Yes)
```

```
        {
            // Get the current data row.
            RemoveRow =
              addressDataset1.Tables[0].
              Rows[AddrDataGrid.CurrentRowIndex];

            // Mark the row as deleted.
            RemoveRow.Delete();

            // Update the data adapter.
            AddressDA.Update(addressDataset1);
        }
    }
```

Adding a row to the database isn't a one step process—you need to modify the dataset first. To add a row to the dataset, you need to create a new DataRow object (NewRow in this case) based on the current table schema using the addressDataset1.Tables[0].NewRow() method. Note that you must select the proper table to ensure the schema of the new row is correct.

NewRow is blank when you create it, which means that even the primary key fields are empty. If you insert the new row into the dataset immediately, the application will raise an error. Consequently, the code assigns values to the new DataRow. In this case, it also assigns a value to the BUSINESS field because the database won't allow null values and the CONTACTED field for the convenience of the user. The Add() method completes the process of adding a new record to the dataset. The code calls DoLast() to position the cursor and open the first field of the DataGrid for editing.

Notice the call to BeginEdit(). The record addition will still work even without this call. However, the user won't see the familiar blinking cursor on the first entry in the new record if you don't provide this call. The call to DoLast() won't accomplish the same purpose in this case.

The code doesn't call AddressDA.Update() when adding a record. The act of creating the record automatically calls AddrDataGrid_CurrentCellChanged(). This method contains the required AddressDA.Update() call.

Deleting a record is a three-step process. The code still uses the dataset to perform the task. As with the record addition, the code creates a DataRow object that holds the record to delete. It marks the record for deletion using the Delete() method. The call to AddressDA.Update() completes the process. The code must call the AddressDA.Update() method, in this case, because the user isn't editing the record.

Notice that the DoDeleteRecord() method includes a MessageBox .Show() call that gives the user a chance to change their mind about deleting the record. This is an important addition, because it helps keeps the database intact by reducing the chance of an accidental deletion.

There's a potential problem with all of the modifications the code performs—it's possible that a change could occur and not get recorded. Even though this event is unlikely, it's important to consider it anyway. The following event handler reduces the likelihood that a database-damaging event will occur when the application closes.

```
private void GridView_Closing(object sender,
    System.ComponentModel.CancelEventArgs e)
{
    // Create a series of data check objects.
    DataSet DeletedData =
        addressDataset1.GetChanges(DataRowState.Deleted);
    DataSet AddedData =
        addressDataset1.GetChanges(DataRowState.Added);
    DataSet ModifiedData =
        addressDataset1.GetChanges(DataRowState.Modified);

    // Check for pending updates and
    // update the database as required.
    if (DeletedData != null ||
        AddedData != null ||
        ModifiedData != null)
        AddressDA.Update(addressDataset1);
}
```

The GridView_Closing() event occurs before the main application form closes and any of the data sources close. The code checks for DataSet conditions that could cause data loss, including the existence of modified, added, or deleted records. If the DataSet contains any records of this type, the code calls AddressDA.Update() to ensure the change is recorded.

Adding Copy, Cut, and Paste

The Copy, Cut, and Paste commands are somewhat tricky to add to a database application. The default setup for the DataGrid object enables you to cut, copy, or paste single cells. However, a row can only be copied. The reason you can't cut a row is that would delete the row and the DataGrid already provides a method for accomplishing that task. Likewise, pasting a row is akin to adding a new row to the database, which is handled by another method. Unfortunately, the only way to use Copy, Cut, and Paste in a DataGrid is to rely on the control key combinations of Ctrl+C, Ctrl+X, and Ctrl+V. If you want the convenience of using menus or toolbars, then you need to add the commands separately. Listing 12.4 adds this functionality to both the menus and toolbar.

Listing 12.4: Adding Copy, Cut, and Paste to the Example Program

```
private void mnuEditCut_Click(
  object sender, System.EventArgs e)
{
   // Perform the cut function.
   DoCut();
}

private void mnuEditCopy_Click(
  object sender, System.EventArgs e)
{
   // Perform the copy function.
   DoCopy();
}

private void mnuEditPaste_Click(
  object sender, System.EventArgs e)
{
   // Perform the paste function.
   DoPaste();
}

private void DoCut()
{
   // The column we want to view.
   DataGridColumnStyle  DGCS;

   // Data grid column.
   int                  Column;

   // Place the current data on the clipboard.
   Clipboard.SetDataObject(
     AddrDataGrid[AddrDataGrid.CurrentCell]);

   // Place a blank value in the data grid.
   AddrDataGrid[AddrDataGrid.CurrentCell] = "";
```

```
    // Begin the editing process.
    Column = AddrDataGrid.CurrentCell.ColumnNumber;
    DGCS = AddrDataGrid.TableStyles[0].
       GridColumnStyles[Column];
    AddrDataGrid.BeginEdit(DGCS,
       AddrDataGrid.CurrentRowIndex);
}


private void DoCopy()
{
    StringBuilder  SelectedText = new StringBuilder();
    int            Row;
    int            Column;

    // Get the current row.
    Row = AddrDataGrid.CurrentCell.RowNumber;

    // If true, copy the entire row.
    if (AddrDataGrid.IsSelected(Row))
    {
        // Set the column value to 0.
        Column = 0;

        // Copy every entry in the row to the SelectedText
        // string.
        for(Column = 0;
           Column < AddrDataGrid.TableStyles[0].
           GridColumnStyles.Count;
           Column++)
        {
            SelectedText.Append(
               AddrDataGrid[Row, Column].ToString());

            // If this isn't the last entry, then add a tab.
            if (Column <
               AddrDataGrid.TableStyles[0].
               GridColumnStyles.Count - 1)
               SelectedText.Append("\t");
        }

        // Copy the composite string to the clipboard.
        Clipboard.SetDataObject(SelectedText.ToString());
    }
```

```
                    // If only a single cell is selected, copy just
                    // that cell.
                else
                {
                    // Set the column value to the current cell.
                    Column = AddrDataGrid.CurrentCell.ColumnNumber;

                    // Place the data on the clipboard.
                    Clipboard.SetDataObject(AddrDataGrid[Row, Column]);
                }
        }

        private void DoPaste()
        {
            // Contents of the clipboard.
            IDataObject         ClipboardData;

            // Data to paste.
            string              PasteData;

            // The column we want to view.
            DataGridColumnStyle DGCS;

            // Data grid column.
            int                 Column;

            // Verify the data is text.
            ClipboardData = Clipboard.GetDataObject();
            if (ClipboardData.GetDataPresent(DataFormats.Text))
            {
                // Get the data and place it in a string.
                PasteData =
                  ClipboardData.GetData(DataFormats.Text).ToString();

                // Paste it in the current data grid cell.
                AddrDataGrid[AddrDataGrid.CurrentCell] = PasteData;

                // Begin the editing process.
                Column = AddrDataGrid.CurrentCell.ColumnNumber;
                DGCS = AddrDataGrid.TableStyles[0].
                  GridColumnStyles[Column];
                AddrDataGrid.BeginEdit(DGCS,
```

```
                    AddrDataGrid.CurrentRowIndex);
        }
}


private void AddrDataGrid_CursorChanged(object sender,
                                       System.EventArgs e)
{
    int        Row;           // Current data grid row
    IDataObject ClipboardData; // Contents of the clipboard.

    // Get the current row.
    Row = AddrDataGrid.CurrentCell.RowNumber;

    // Ensure everything is enabled to start.
    mnuEditCut.Enabled = true;
    mnuEditCopy.Enabled = true;
    mnuEditPaste.Enabled = true;
    GridViewToolbar.Buttons[11].Enabled = true;
    GridViewToolbar.Buttons[12].Enabled = true;
    GridViewToolbar.Buttons[13].Enabled = true;

    // Determine if the row is selected.
    // If so, then turn off the cut
    // and paste buttons since we can't
    // perform either task on a row.
    if (AddrDataGrid.IsSelected(Row))
    {
        mnuEditPaste.Enabled = false;
        mnuEditCut.Enabled = false;
        GridViewToolbar.Buttons[11].Enabled = false;
        GridViewToolbar.Buttons[13].Enabled = false;
    }

    // We also need to check for an empty clipboard.
    // An empty clipboard means we can't paste
    // anything. It's also possible the clipboard
    // contains an incompatible data type,
    // so we need to check that as well.
    ClipboardData = Clipboard.GetDataObject();
    if (ClipboardData == null ||
        !ClipboardData.GetDataPresent(DataFormats.Text))
```

```
    {
        mnuEditPaste.Enabled = false;
        GridViewToolbar.Buttons[13].Enabled = false;
    }
}
```

The DoCut() method only works with a single cell. It uses the Clipboard.SetDataObject() method call to place the current text on the clipboard. Notice how this example uses a cell, rather than individual row and column references for the AddrDataGrid indexer. After it saves the contents of the cell to the clipboard, DoCut() places a null string in the current cell. However, placing the value in the cell doesn't make it permanent—an update must occur before that happens. The final three lines of code place the current cell in the editing mode. These steps ensure that the user notices a change in the appearance of AddrDataGrid. At this point, if the user presses Escape, the change on AddrDataGrid is reversed. However, the clipboard will still retain the new string value.

Because the DoCopy() method has to work for both single cells and entire rows, the code is actually a little more complex than DoCut(). The code initially determines if the user has selected an entire row or a single cell. The selection of a single cell means the DoCopy() method can simply place the value of the current cell on the clipboard without further processing. However, when working with a row of data, you must create a string containing all of the column values first. The default copy function places a tab between each field entry, but you can alter this technique to suit any requirements your application might have.

This is another situation where you can improve the performance of your application using a StringBuilder object in place of a standard string. The code appends each column value to SelectedText. If the code detects that this isn't the last column, it also adds a tab to Selected-Text. The processing continues until all of the columns have been processed and DoCopy() places the value in SelectedText on the clipboard.

Creating the DoPaste() method is the most difficult part of the coding process. Placing data on the clipboard isn't hard because you don't have to worry about problems such as data type—the clipboard takes care of the issue for you. However, when you're pasting data from the clipboard, you need to know that the data is the correct type. The first task the DoPaste() method performs is checking the data type of the clipboard data. If the data type isn't text, then the method exits without doing anything else.

NOTE

Notice that `ClipboardData` is of the `IDataObject` type. Most developers who have worked with COM know that this is a common COM interface. However, the `IDataObject` in the .NET Framework isn't a substitute for the COM interface. It does work in this situation, but probably won't work if you're creating a DLL to interact with COM in some way.

The `DoPaste()` method obtains the current clipboard contents using the `GetData()` method. Notice that you must specify a data format using the `DataFormats` enumeration. `DoPaste()` follows a process similar to `DoCut()` at this point. It makes the current cell value equal to the `PasteData` value obtained from the clipboard, and then places the cell in edit mode. If the user presses Escape, `AddrDataGrid` will reverse the change.

There's one last problem to consider for this scenario. The user depends on visual cues from the menu and toolbar to determine when it's possible to cut, copy, or paste data. This user assumption means you need some way to enable and disable both the toolbar buttons and the menu commands. You could select a number of ways to detect changes in the settings, but I chose to attach the code to the `AddrDataGrid` `CursorChanged()` event.

The code begins by enabling all of the affected buttons and menu entries. This step ensures the menu command and toolbar buttons are accessible. The code then checks for a selected row. If the user has selected a row, the code disables the cut and paste options because they only work with a single cell. Finally, the code checks the data type of the clipboard data. If the clipboard is empty or it contains data of the wrong type, then the code disables the paste function. The application can only accept text as input.

Coding the Detail View

This section of the chapter discusses a few enhancements you can add to the Detail view to make it more functional. We'll discuss what you need to do in order to add and remove records. You'll also learn about a single-record print routine that's based on data in the Detail view, instead of the data found in the Grid view. These customizations move the Detail view from barely functional to quite practical.

Adding and Removing Records in Detail View

As with other database operations for the Detail view, the Grid view already has the required code. What you really need is a means of accessing that code through the Detail view controls. Of course, the first task is to add the required controls to the form so that the user can click them as needed. Make sure you change the Modifiers property to Public so the button's Click() event is accessible from the Grid view.

All of the code for btnAdd and btnDelete appear in FrmGridView.cs file, not the FrmDetail-View.cs file as you might expect. The first task is to create a connection to the Detail view buttons by adding event handlers. The following code appears in the AddrDataGrid_Double-Click() method to ensure the event handlers aren't created unless actually needed.

```
// Create event handlers for adding and removing records.
DetailDlg.btnAdd.Click += new EventHandler(DoDetailAdd);
DetailDlg.btnDelete.Click +=
  new EventHandler(DoDetailDelete);
```

The event handlers have to do more than their Grid view counterparts. In addition to synchronization issues, you also need to consider data update issues. The event handler must ensure that the data that the Detail view sees is the same as the data in the Grid view. Here's the code for the two event handlers.

```
private void DoDetailAdd(object sender, System.EventArgs e)
{
    // Add a new record.
    DoAddRecord();

    // Ensure the record is recorded.
    AddressDA.Update(addressDataset1);

    // Fill the AddrDataGrid variables.
    ExchangeFill();

    // Fire the DataChanged event.
    DataChanged();
}

private void DoDetailDelete(
  object sender, System.EventArgs e)
{
    // Remove the current record.
    DoDeleteRecord();
```

```
        // Ensure the record is recorded.
        AddressDA.Update(addressDataset1);

        // Fill the AddrDataGrid variables.
        ExchangeFill();

        // Fire the DataChanged event.
        DataChanged();
    }
```

As you can see, the code calls upon the same DoAddRecord() or
DoDeleteRecord() methods used by the Grid view to add or remove a
record. The code then calls AddressDA.Update() to ensure the dataset
contains the correct information. This might seem like overkill, but the
need is real. The last two steps place data in a location where the Detail
view can see it and then fires an event that will force the Detail view to
perform an update.

Printing in Detail View

In terms of printing techniques, it's important to realize that users will
anticipate certain types of print jobs when looking at specific views of
their data. For example, when looking at the Detail view, users are likely
to want an individual record printout, rather than a list of contacts in the
database. The example code contains such a report. We'll discuss some of
the highlights of that report in this section.

Individual report records are somewhat easier to print than multiple
record reports because you don't need to consider any complex looping
structures. All you need is the data for a single record. Of course, the user
is likely to want complete information for that single record, so you'll need
to address the full range of data input. The formatting is going to be different as well. Using a structure similar to the Detail view for this example
works well in most cases.

One of the first changes that you'll notice in this version of the print
routine is that the heading is smaller and relies on both bold and italic font
attributes. It's easy to combine font attributes by or-ing them together.
Here's an example of multiple attribute use:

```
        headFont =
            new Font("Arial", 14, FontStyle.Bold | FontStyle.Italic);
```

Another problem with individual record reports is that you need to print
items on single lines. This change from the tabular view used in the Grid
view portion of the application means you'll calculate the yPos value more

often. Rather than incur the cost of constant recalculation of the incremental difference between lines, you should calculate it once as shown here:

```
// Determine the yIncrement value.
yIncrement = columnFont.GetHeight() + 10;
```

Users will also expect friendly text in the report. For example, you wouldn't want to place a check box on the printed report for the BUSINESS field. Likewise, a value of true or false is unattractive. You can solve the problem by using a simple comparison and printing out the desired text as shown here:

```
ev.Graphics.DrawString("Business Contact?",
                       columnFont,
                       Brushes.Black,
                       20,
                       yPos);
if (cbBusiness.Checked)
    ev.Graphics.DrawString("Yes",
                       docFont,
                       Brushes.Black,
                       180,
                       yPos);
else
    ev.Graphics.DrawString("No",
                       docFont,
                       Brushes.Black,
                       180,
                       yPos);
yPos = yPos + yIncrement;
```

Finally, you'll need some large text areas to contain notes and other memo fields in your database. The way to perform this task is to specify a rectangular area as part of the DrawString() call as shown here:

```
ev.Graphics.DrawString("Notes:",
    columnFont, Brushes.Black, 20, yPos);
ev.Graphics.DrawString(txtNotes.Text,
    docFont, Brushes.Black, new Rectangle(
    180, (Int32)yPos,
    (Int32)ev.Graphics.VisibleClipBounds.Width - 180,
    (Int32)ev.Graphics.VisibleClipBounds.Height -
    (Int32)yPos));
yPos = yPos + yIncrement;
```

Because the print routine only needs the rectangle one time, the code declares the rectangle directly, rather than as a separate object. This technique tends to reduce resource usage and the time before the CLR frees the rectangle. Notice how the various rectangle boundaries are calculated. Make sure you take any offsets into consideration when designing your print routine.

IMPORTING AND EXPORTING XML EXAMPLE

As applications develop into distributed systems, the need for some method of data exchange becomes more important. Microsoft has become convinced that various forms of XML are the answer, so they're making every effort to make their applications and application development platforms XML-enabled. This XML development extends Visual Studio .NET and the .NET Framework. You'll find a gold mine of XML development capabilities that you can easily access using C#.

This section provides a quick overview of one XML capability—the ability to import and export data in XML format using a dataset. This section is important because it creates the first link between the world of distributed applications and the world of the desktop. This section provides you with a glimpse of the possibilities for applications that you wouldn't normally associate with the Internet.

Writing the Code

The example performs two tasks. First, it enables the user to export the data found in the Movie database used earlier in the chapter to an XML file. Second, it enables the user to import data from a second XML file named SampleData.XML. Listing 12.5 shows the code we'll use in this case.

Listing 12.5: Importing and Exporting XML Is Easy in .NET

```
private void btnImport_Click(
   object sender, System.EventArgs e)
{
   // Create a data stream.
   StreamReader   SR = new StreamReader("SampleData.xml");

   // Create a dataset and associated table.
   DataTable   DT = new DataTable("NewDataElement");
   DataSet     DS = new DataSet("NewData");
```

```
          // Configure the table.
          DT.Columns.Add(new DataColumn("Data1", typeof(string)));
          DT.Columns.Add(new DataColumn("Data2", typeof(string)));
          DT.Columns.Add(new DataColumn("Data3", typeof(string)));

          // Configure the dataset.
          DS.Tables.Add(DT);

          // Import the data.
          DS.ReadXml(SR);

          // Display the new data.
          dataGrid1.DataSource = DS;
          dataGrid1.DataMember = "NewDataElement";
          dataGrid1.Update();

          // Close the stream.
          SR.Close();
      }

      private void btnExport_Click(
        object sender, System.EventArgs e)
      {
          // Create a data stream.
          StreamWriter  SW = new StreamWriter("MovieExport.xml");

          // Output the data.
          movieDS1.WriteXml(SW);

          // Close the stream.
          SW.Close();

          // Create a second data stream.
          SW = new StreamWriter("MovieExportSchema.xml");

          // Output the schema.
          movieDS1.WriteXmlSchema(SW);

          // Close the second stream.
          SW.Close();
      }
```

The btnImport_Click() method begins by creating a StreamReader object (SR). SR will open the XML file for reading. The code then creates the DataTable (DT) and the DataSet (DS) objects used to cache the data locally. Configuring the table consists of adding three columns, one of each of the columns in the sample XML file. Once DT is configured, the code adds it to DS. Reading the data is as easy as calling the ReadXml() method.

As we'll see later, the name of the DataTable must match the name of the XML elements within the sample file. Likewise, the column names must match the names of the XML child elements used to store the data. Otherwise, you'll find that the reading process works as anticipated, but you won't see any data on screen.

The final part of the process is to modify the DataSource and DataMember properties of dataGrid1. The call to Update() ensures that the new data appears on screen, as shown in Figure 12.6.

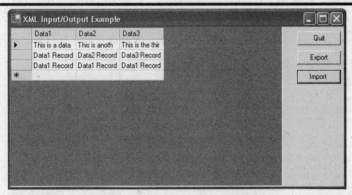

FIGURE 12.6: Modifying the DataSource and DataMember properties enables dataGrid1 to display the imported data.

The btnExport_Click() method begins by creating a StreamWriter object (SW). The WriteXml() method of movieDS1 outputs the data in XML format to the file opened by SW. Note that all you need to change to output the dataset schema instead of the data is call WriteXmlSchema().

Using the Microsoft XML Notepad

XML is almost, but not quite, readable by the average human. Reading simple files is almost trivial, but once the data gets nested a few layers deep, reading it can become tiresome. That's why you should have a tool for reading XML in your developer toolkit. The only problem is that some of these tools cost quite a bit for the occasional user. Microsoft has remedied this problem a little with the introduction of XML Notepad (`http://msdn.microsoft.com/library/default.asp?url=/library/en-us/dnxml/html/xmlpaddownload.asp`). This utility is free for the price of a download and does a reasonable job of reading most XML files. (Microsoft hasn't bothered to update the date for this site, but be assured that XML Notepad runs fine under both Windows 2000 and Windows XP.)

When you start XML Notepad, you'll see a blank project. Use the File ➤ Open command to display an Open dialog that allows you to open XML files from a local drive or from a website. All you need is a filename (and path) or a URL to get started.

Figure 12.7 shows the output of the sample XML application. Notice that the name of the elements matches the name of the table for the movie database. Likewise, each of the child elements matches the name of one of the fields within the table. The right pane shows the data contained within each one of the child elements.

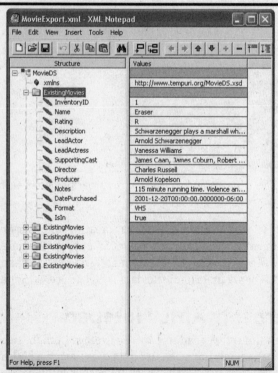

FIGURE 12.7:   The names of the elements are important when working with exported data in XML format.

Creating new data for testing purposes is relatively painless once you see the exported data from an existing database. Create a blank project using the File ➤ New command. Type the name of the dataset in the Root object. Rename the first element to reflect the new table. Add a new child element using the options on the Insert menu. You'll notice that the first element changes into a folder. Type the name of the first data column in this element. Add additional columns as needed until you complete one record's worth of entries. Finally, type values for each of the child elements.

Now that you have one complete record, you can use the Duplicate command to create copies of it. Each copy will become one record within the XML database. Figure 12.8 shows the structure and contents of the SampleData.XML file.

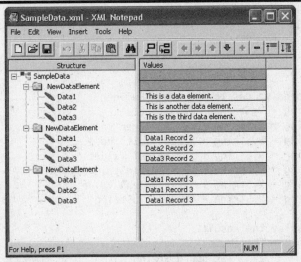

FIGURE 12.8:   Creating an XML database using XML Notepad is relatively easy as long as you follow a few rules.

As you can see, XML Notepad doesn't have some of the bells and whistles of high-end products such as xmlspy (http://www.xmlspy.com/), but it's a good alternative if you only use an XML editor occasionally and don't want to spend a lot of money. The important consideration is that you have an XML editor that you can use to view the output from your applications.

Using *StringBuilder* to Improve Performance

Strings are unusual objects in C# in that they're immutable—you can't change them. Whenever you assign a new value to a string, C# deletes the old string and creates a new one. This includes any additions to the string. For example, the following event handler actually contains eight unique copies of MyString, even though all of the strings have the same name and you can't access them individually.

```
private void btnTest1_Click(
    object sender, System.EventArgs e)
{
    // Create some objects and values.
    string    MyString = "Hello";
    string    NewString = " World";
    int       NewInt = 3;
    float     NewFloat = 4.5F;
    bool      NewBool = true;

    // Append values to the StringBuilder.
    MyString = MyString + NewString;
    MyString = MyString + "\r\nInteger Value: ";
    MyString = MyString + NewInt.ToString();
    MyString = MyString + "\r\nFloat Value: ";
    MyString = MyString + NewFloat.ToString();
    MyString = MyString + "\r\nBoolean Value: ";
    MyString = MyString + NewBool.ToString();

    // Display the result.
    MessageBox.Show(MyString.ToString(),
                    "Standard String Output",
                    MessageBoxButtons.OK,
                    MessageBoxIcon.Information);
}
```

C# will destroy the copy of MyString on the right side of the equation before it creates the new copy of MyString on the left side in each case. Your code only sees one MyString, but eight copies actually exist at different times, which makes this form of the code relatively resource intensive. In short, making string assignments could become costly if you perform this task more than a few times in your code. While the Garbage Collector will automatically recover the memory used by the old versions of a string, creating, deleting, and managing the strings does incur a performance penalty.

It's unlikely that you'll ever see the performance penalty of using strings in a desktop application (unless you literally handle hundreds of strings in the application), but the performance cost is real enough that you can notice the penalty in a server application. A StringBuilder object helps you get around this performance problem by enabling your application to use a single object to handle string manipulations. For example, the following code uses one copy of MyString in place of the eight that we used earlier.

```
private void btnTest2_Click(
    object sender, System.EventArgs e)
{
    // Create some objects and values.
    StringBuilder  MyString = new StringBuilder("Hello");
    string         NewString = " World";
    int            NewInt = 3;
    float          NewFloat = 4.5F;
    bool           NewBool = true;

    // Append values to the StringBuilder.
    MyString.Append(NewString);
    MyString.Append("\r\nInteger Value: ");
    MyString.Append(NewInt);
    MyString.Append("\r\nFloat Value: ");
    MyString.Append(NewFloat);
    MyString.Append("\r\nBoolean Value: ");
    MyString.Append(NewBool);

    // Display the result.
    MessageBox.Show(MyString.ToString(),
                    "StringBuilder Output",
                    MessageBoxButtons.OK,
                    MessageBoxIcon.Information);
}
```

It's interesting to note that a StringBuilder object also has greater flexibility than a standard string. You must convert all other objects to a string before you can add them to a standard string. Notice that the StringBuilder example has no such requirement, you can Append() any of data types that StringBuilder supports directly (which includes most value types). StringBuilder supports the AppendFormat() method that enables you to add other object types to the string without prior conversion. For example, the following code adds a number in several formats to a StringBuilder object.

```
private void btnTest3_Click(
    object sender, System.EventArgs e)
```

```csharp
{
    // Create a StringBuilder object and a value.
    StringBuilder   MyString =
      new StringBuilder("Number Formats:\r\n");
    float           NewFloat = 1004.5F;
    int             NewInt = 1005;

    // Append float values to the StringBuilder.
    MyString.Append("\r\nFrom Float:\r\n");
    MyString.AppendFormat(
      "Custom Format: {0:#,###.0000}\r\n",
      NewFloat);
    MyString.AppendFormat(
      "Currency Format: {0:C}\r\n", NewFloat);
    MyString.AppendFormat(
      "Exponential Format 1: {0:E}<End>\r\n",
      NewFloat);
    MyString.AppendFormat(
      "Exponential Format 2: {0, 20:E}<End>\r\n",
      NewFloat);
    MyString.AppendFormat(
      "Exponential Format 3: {0, -20:E}<End>\r\n",
      NewFloat);
    MyString.AppendFormat(
      "Fixed Point Format: {0:F}\r\n", NewFloat);
    MyString.AppendFormat(
      "General Format: {0:G}\r\n", NewFloat);
    MyString.AppendFormat(
      "Numeric Format: {0:N}\r\n", NewFloat);
    MyString.AppendFormat(
      "Percentage Format: {0:P}\r\n", NewFloat);

    // Append int values to the StringBuilder.
    MyString.Append("\r\nFrom Int:\r\n");
    MyString.AppendFormat(
      "Custom Format: {0:#,###.0000}\r\n", NewInt);
    MyString.AppendFormat(
      "Decimal Format: {0:D}\r\n", NewInt);
    MyString.AppendFormat(
      "Hexadecimal Format: {0:X}\r\n", NewInt);

    // Display the result.
    MessageBox.Show(MyString.ToString(),
                    "AppendFormat() Output",
                    MessageBoxButtons.OK,
                    MessageBoxIcon.Information);
}
```

This is just a small sampling of the formatting methods you can use with `StringBuilder`. The custom format is especially useful and you can perform some tricks with the standard formatting methods. Figure 12.9 shows the output from this example. Notice how the various output values look.

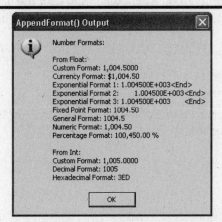

FIGURE 12.9:   The `StringBuilder` object provides more than a few methods for formatting data output.

One of the more important techniques you can learn is defining the number of digits an entry will consume. Look at the three Exponential Format entries in Figure 12.9. The first entry shows what happens if you use the E format by itself. The second entry shows the effects of right justification—the entry will consume 20 digits worth of space, but the padding appears on the left side. Likewise, the third entry shows the effects of left justification. In this case, the padding appears on the right side of the number.

SUMMARY

Database technology is an essential part of every business today. In fact, database technology is an essential part of many home installations too. We've looked at the essential database technologies that you'll use with .NET. More database technologies will likely appear on the horizon as technology changes, but for now, you've seen what Microsoft has to offer.

This chapter showed you how to use ADO.Net in your applications. You've learned the difference between a `Dataset` and a `DataReader` and how each object can help you create applications. You've also learned about the DataView object and how it can make the job of displaying data easier. Obviously, we've only scratched the surface of this topic. You'll definitely want to visit the websites listed in various places in the chapter, as well as try some of the performance techniques in your own code. Make sure you spend plenty of time experimenting with the new database features that the .NET Framework has to offer before you begin your first project.

WHAT'S NEXT

Chapters 13 and 14 further focus on one of the most important parts of the new Microsoft database structure—the Dataset.

Chapter 13

USING *DATASET* OBJECTS TO STORE DATA

In this chapter, you'll learn the details of using `DataSet` objects to store results returned from the database. `DataSet` objects allow you to store a copy of the information from the database, and you can work with that local copy while disconnected from the database. Unlike managed provider objects such as the `SqlDataReader`, a `DataSet` is generic and therefore works with any database. A `DataSet` object also allows you to read rows in any order and modify rows—unlike a `SqlDataReader`, which allows you to read rows only in a sequential forward direction. That's not to say `SqlDataReader` objects are bad: as you learned in Chapter 11, they offer very fast access to data.

You'll also learn the details of using a `DataAdapter` object to read rows from the database into a `DataSet`. The `DataAdapter` is part of the managed provider classes, and there are three `DataAdapter` classes: `SqlDataAdapter`, `OleDbDataAdapter`, and `OdbcDataAdapter`.

Adapted from *Mastering C# Database Programming*
by Jason Price
ISBN 0-7821-4183-8

You use a DataAdapter to copy rows from the database to your DataSet and also to push any changes you make to the rows in your DataSet to the database. You'll see how to make changes to the rows in a DataSet and push those changes to the database in Chapter 14, "Using DataSet Objects to Modify Data." In this chapter, you'll focus on copying rows from the database and storing them in a DataSet.

THE *SQLDATAADAPTER* CLASS

You use an object of the SqlDataAdapter class to synchronize data stored in a DataSet object with a SQL Server database. You use an object of the OleDbDataAdapter class to synchronize data with a database that supports OLE DB, such as Oracle or Access. You use an object of the OdbcData-Adapter class to synchronize data with a database that supports ODBC.

NOTE

Although the SqlDataAdapter class is specific to SQL Server, many of the properties and methods in this class are the same as those for the OleDbDataAdapter and OdbcDataAdapter classes.

Table 13.1 shows some of the SqlDataAdapter properties.

TABLE 13.1: SqlDataAdapter Properties

PROPERTY	TYPE	DESCRIPTION
AcceptChanges-DuringFill	Bool	Gets or sets a bool that indicates whether the AcceptChanges() method is called after a Data-Row object has been added, modified, or removed in a DataTable object. The default is true.
Continue-UpdateOnError	Bool	Gets or sets a bool that indicates whether to continue updating the database when an error occurs.
		When set to true, no exception is thrown when an error occurs during the update of a row. The update of the row is skipped and the error infor-mation is placed in the RowError property of the DataRow that caused the error. The DataAdapter continues to update subsequent rows.
		When set to false, an exception is thrown when an error occurs. The default is false.
DeleteCommand	SqlCommand	Gets or sets a command containing a SQL DELETE statement or stored procedure call to remove rows from the database.

TABLE 13.1 continued: SqlDataAdapter Properties

PROPERTY	TYPE	DESCRIPTION
InsertCommand	SqlCommand	Gets or sets a command containing a SQL INSERT statement or stored procedure call to add rows to the database.
Missing-MappingAction	MissingMapping-Action	Gets or sets the action to take when the incoming table or column doesn't have a matching table or column in the TableMappings collection.
		The values for this action come from the System.Data.MissingMappingAction enumeration with the members Error, Ignore, and Passthrough:
		- Error means a SystemException is thrown.
		- Ignore means the table or column is ignored and not read.
		- Passthrough means the table or column is added to the DataSet with its original name.
		The default is Passthrough.
Missing-SchemaAction	MissingSchema-Action	Gets or sets the action to take when the incoming column doesn't have a matching column in the DataTable object's Column collection.
		The values for this action come from the System.Data.MissingSchemaAction enumeration with the members Add, AddWithKey, Error, and Ignore:
		- Add means the column is added to the DataTable.
		- AddWithKey means the column and primary key information is added to the DataTable.
		- Error means a SystemException is thrown.
		- Ignore means the column is ignored and not read.
		The default is Add.
SelectCommand	SqlCommand	Gets or sets a command containing a SQL SELECT statement or stored procedure call to retrieve rows from the database.
TableMappings	DataTableMapping-Collection	Gets a DataTableMappingCollection that contains the mapping between a database table and a DataTable object in the DataSet.
UpdateCommand	SqlCommand	Gets or sets a command containing a SQL UPDATE statement or stored procedure call to modify rows in the database.

Table 13.2 shows some of the `SqlDataAdapter` methods.

TABLE 13.2: SqlDataAdapter Methods

Method	Return Type	Description
Fill()	int	Overloaded. Synchronizes the rows in the DataSet object to match those in the database. The int returned by this method is the number of rows synchronized in the DataSet with the database.
FillSchema()	DataTable DataTable[]	Overloaded. Adds a DataTable to a DataSet object and configures the schema to match the database.
GetFill-Parameters()	IDataParameter[]	Returns an array of any parameters set for the SQL SELECT statement.
Update()	int	Overloaded. Calls the respective SQL INSERT, UPDATE, or DELETE statements or stored procedure call (stored in the InsertCommand, UpdateCommand, and DeleteCommand properties, respectively) for each row that has been added, modified, or removed from a DataTable object. The int returned by this method is the number of rows updated.

Table 13.3 shows some of the `SqlDataAdapter` events.

TABLE 13.3: SqlDataAdapter Events

Event	Event Handler	Description
FillError	FillError-EventHandler	Fires when an error occurs during a fill operation.
RowUpdating	RowUpdating-EventHandler	Fires *before* a row is added, modified, or deleted in the database.
RowUpdated	RowUpdated-EventHandler	Fires *after* a row is added, modified, or deleted in the database.

You'll learn how to use some of these properties and methods to store data in DataSet objects in this chapter. You'll see how to use the other properties, methods, and the events in Chapter 14, in which you'll learn how to modify data in DataSet objects, and then push those modifications to the database.

Creating a *SqlDataAdapter* Object

You create a SqlDataAdapter object using one of the following SqlDataAdapter constructors:

```
SqlDataAdapter()
SqlDataAdapter(SqlCommand mySqlCommand)
SqlDataAdapter(string selectCommandString,
   SqlConnection mySqlConnection)
SqlDataAdapter(string selectCommandString,
   string connectionString)
```

where

> ***mySqlCommand***   Specifies your SqlCommand object.
>
> ***selectCommandString***   Specifies your SELECT statement or stored procedure call.
>
> ***mySqlConnection***   Specifies your SqlConnection object.
>
> ***connectionString***   Specifies your connection string to connect to the database.

The following example uses the SqlDataAdapter() constructor to create a SqlDataAdapter object:

```
SqlDataAdapter mySqlDataAdapter = new SqlDataAdapter();
```

Before using mySqlDataAdapter to populate a DataSet, you must set its SelectCommand property to a SqlCommand that contains a SELECT command or stored procedure call. The following example creates a SqlCommand object with its CommandText property set to a SELECT statement that will retrieve the top five rows from the Products table, and sets the CommandText property of mySqlDataAdapter to that SqlCommand object:

```
SqlCommand mySqlCommand = mySqlConnection.CreateCommand();
mySqlCommand.CommandText =
   "SELECT TOP 5 ProductID, ProductName, UnitPrice " +
   "FROM Products " +
   "ORDER BY ProductID";
mySqlDataAdapter.SelectCommand = mySqlCommand;
```

The next example uses the SqlDataAdapter(SqlCommand *mySqlCommand*) constructor:

```
SqlDataAdapter mySqlDataAdapter = new
   SqlDataAdapter(mySqlCommand);
```

The next example uses the SqlDataAdapter(string *selectCommand-String*, SqlConnection *mySqlConnection*) constructor:

```
SqlConnection mySqlConnection =
  new SqlConnection(
    "server=localhost;database=Northwind;uid=sa;pwd=sa"
  );
string selectCommandString =
  "SELECT TOP 10 ProductID, ProductName, UnitPrice " +
  "FROM Products " +
  "ORDER BY ProductID";
SqlDataAdapter mySqlDataAdapter =
  new SqlDataAdapter(selectCommandString, mySqlConnection);
```

The final example uses the SqlDataAdapter(string *selectCommand-String*, string *connectionString*) constructor:

```
string selectCommandString =
  "server=localhost;database=Northwind;uid=sa;pwd=sa";
string connectionString =
  "SELECT TOP 10 ProductID, ProductName, UnitPrice " +
  "FROM Products " +
  "ORDER BY ProductID";
SqlDataAdapter mySqlDataAdapter =
  new SqlDataAdapter(selectCommandString, connectionString);
```

WARNING

This constructor causes the SqlDataAdapter object to create a separate SqlConnection object. This is typically undesirable from a performance perspective because opening a connection to the database using a SqlConnection object takes a relatively long time. You should therefore avoid using the SqlDataAdapter(string *selectCommandString*, string *connectionString*) constructor. Instead, you should use an existing SqlConnection object with your SqlDataAdapter object.

A DataAdapter object doesn't store rows: it merely acts as a conduit between the database and an object of the DataSet class. In the next section, you'll learn about the DataSet class.

THE *DATASET* CLASS

You use an object of the DataSet class to represent a local copy of the information stored in the database. You can make changes to that local copy in your `DataSet` and then later synchronize those changes with the database through a `DataAdapter`. A `DataSet` can represent database structures such as tables, rows, and columns. You can even add constraints to your locally stored tables to enforce unique and foreign key constraints.

Figure 13.1 shows the `DataSet` and its relationship to some of the objects you can store within it. As you can see from this figure, you can store multiple `DataTable` objects in a `DataSet`, and so on.

Generic Data Set Objects

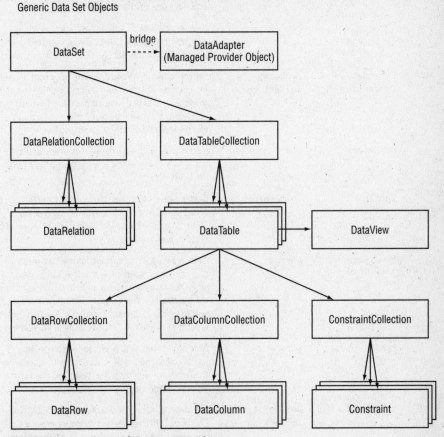

FIGURE 13.1:   Some of the `DataSet` objects

Table 13.4 shows some of the `DataSet` properties.

TABLE 13.4:   DataSet Properties

Property	Type	Description
CaseSensitive	bool	Gets or sets a bool value that indicates whether string comparisons within DataTable objects are case-sensitive.
DataSetName	string	Gets or sets the name of the current DataSet object.
DefaultView-Manager	DataViewManager	Gets a custom view of the data stored in the DataSet object. You use a view to filter, search, and navigate the DataSet.
Enforce-Constraints	bool	Gets or sets a bool value that indicates whether constraint rules are followed when updating information in the DataSet object.
Extended-Properties	Property-Collection	Gets a collection (PropertyCollection) of user information. You can use the PropertyCollection to store strings with any additional information you want. You use the Add() method through ExtendedProperties to add a string.
HasErrors	bool	Gets a bool value that indicates whether there are errors in any of the rows in the tables of the DataSet object.
Locale	CultureInfo	Gets or sets a CultureInfo object for the DataSet. A CultureInfo object contains information about a specific culture including its name, writing system, and calendar.
Namespace	string	Gets or sets the namespace for the DataSet object. The namespace is a string that is used when reading and writing an XML document using the ReadXml(), WriteXml(), ReadXmlSchema(), and WriteXmlSchema() methods. The namespace is used to scope the XML attributes and elements.
Prefix	string	Gets or sets the XML prefix for the DataSet namespace. The prefix is used in an XML document to identify the elements that belong to the DataSet object's namespace.
Relations	DataRelation-Collection	Gets the collection of relations (DataRelation-Collection) that allows navigation from a parent table to a child table. A DataRelation-Collection consists of DataRelation objects.
Tables	DataTable-Collection	Gets the collection of tables (DataTable-Collection) that contains the DataTable objects stored in the DataSet.

Table 13.5 shows some of the DataSet methods.

TABLE 13.5: DataSet Methods

METHOD	RETURN TYPE	DESCRIPTION
AcceptChanges()	void	Commits all the changes made to the DataSet object since it was loaded or since the last time the AcceptChanges() method was called.
BeginInit()	void	Used by the Visual Studio .NET designer to initialize a DataSet used in a form or component.
Clear()	void	Removes all rows from all tables in the DataSet object.
Clone()	DataSet	Clones the structure of the DataSet object and returns that clone. The clone contains all the schemas, relations, and constraints.
Copy()	DataSet	Copies the structure and data of the DataSet object and returns that copy. The copy contains all the schemas, relations, constraints, and data.
EndInit()	void	Used by the Visual Studio .NET designer to end initialization of a DataSet used in a form or component.
GetChanges()	DataSet	Overloaded. Gets a copy of all the changes made to the DataSet object since it was last loaded or since the last time the AcceptChanges() method was called.
GetXml()	string	Returns the XML representation of the data stored in the DataSet object.
GetXmlSchema()	string	Returns the XML representation of the schema for the DataSet object.
HasChanges()	bool	Overloaded. Returns a bool value that indicates whether the DataSet object has changes that haven't been committed.
Merge()	void	Overloaded. Merges this DataSet with another specified DataSet object.
ReadXml()	XmlReadMode	Overloaded. Loads the data from an XML file into the DataSet object.
ReadXmlSchema()	void	Overloaded. Loads a schema from an XML file into the DataSet object.
RejectChanges()	void	Undoes all the changes made to the DataSet object since it was created or since the last time the AcceptChanges() method was called.

TABLE 13.5 continued: DataSet Methods

METHOD	RETURN TYPE	DESCRIPTION
Reset()	void	Resets the DataSet object to its original state.
WriteXml()	void	Overloaded. Writes out the data from the DataSet object to an XML file.
WriteXmlSchema()	void	Overloaded. Writes out the schema of the DataSet object to an XML file.

Table 13.6 shows one of the DataSet events.

TABLE 13.6: DataSet Event

EVENT	EVENT HANDLER	DESCRIPTION
MergeFailed	MergeFailed- EventHandler	Fires when an attempt is made to add a DataRow to a DataSet when a DataRow with the same primary key value already exists in that DataSet.

In the next section, you'll learn how to create a DataSet object.

Creating a *DataSet* Object

You create a DataSet object using one of the following DataSet constructors:

```
DataSet()
DataSet(string dataSetNameString)
```

where *dataSetNameString* is the string assigned to the DataSetName property of your DataSet object. The setting of the DataSetName property is optional.

The following example uses the DataSet() constructor to create a DataSet object:

```
DataSet myDataSet = new DataSet();
```

The next example uses the DataSet(string *dataSetNameString*) constructor to create a DataSet object:

```
DataSet myDataSet = new DataSet("myDataSet");
```

Populating a *DataSet* Object

In this section, you'll learn how to populate a DataSet using the Fill() method of a DataAdapter. Specifically, you'll see how to populate a DataSet using

- A SELECT statement
- A range of rows
- A stored procedure

Using a *SELECT* Statement

Before you populate a DataSet you first need a Connection, a Command, and a DataAdapter:

```
SqlConnection mySqlConnection =
  new SqlConnection(
    "server=localhost;database=Northwind;uid=sa;pwd=sa"
  );
SqlCommand mySqlCommand = mySqlConnection.CreateCommand();
mySqlCommand.CommandText =
  "SELECT TOP 5 ProductID, ProductName, UnitPrice " +
  "FROM Products " +
  "ORDER BY ProductID";
SqlDataAdapter mySqlDataAdapter = new SqlDataAdapter();
mySqlDataAdapter.SelectCommand = mySqlCommand;
DataSet myDataSet = new DataSet();
mySqlConnection.Open();
```

Notice that the mySqlCommand object contains a SELECT statement that retrieves the ProductID, ProductName, and UnitPrice columns of the top five rows from the Products table.

RETRIEVING FROM MULTIPLE TABLES

Of course, you're not limited to a SELECT statement that retrieves from a single table. You can use a SELECT statement that retrieves from multiple tables using a join, however, you should typically avoid doing that because a DataTable is meant to be used to store rows from a *single* database table.

Next, to populate myDataSet with the rows from the Products table, you call the Fill() method of mySqlDataAdapter. For example,

```
int numberOfRows = mySqlDataAdapter.Fill(myDataSet,
    "Products");
```

The int returned by the Fill() method is the number of rows synchronized between the DataSet and the database via the DataAdapter. In the previous example, the int is the number of rows copied from the Products table to myDataSet and is set to 5—the number of rows retrieved by the SELECT statement shown earlier.

The first parameter to the Fill() method is your DataSet, and the second parameter is a string containing the name you want to assign to the DataTable created in your DataSet.

NOTE

The name you assign to your DataTable doesn't have to be the same as the name of the database table. You can use any string of text, though typically you should still use the same name, since it will help you keep track of what database table was used to populate the DataTable.

When you call the Fill() method for the first time, the following steps are performed by ADO.NET:

1. The SELECT statement in your SqlCommand is executed.

2. A new DataTable object is created in your DataSet.

3. Your DataTable is populated with the result set returned by the SELECT statement.

If you're finished with the database after calling the Fill() method, you should close your Connection object using the Close() method:

```
mySqlConnection.Close();
```

NOTE

The Fill() method will actually open and close the Connection for you if you don't open it first, however, it is better to explicitly open and close the Connection because that way it is clearer what your program is doing. Also, if you're calling the Fill() method repeatedly over a short span of code, you'll want to keep the database connection open and close it only when you're finished.

The DataSet is now populated with a DataTable named Products. You can read the Products DataTable from myDataSet using the following example:

```
DataTable myDataTable = myDataSet.Tables["Products"];
```

You can also read the Products DataTable using an int value:

```
DataTable myDataTable = myDataSet.Tables[0];
```

You can display the column values for each row in myDataTable using the following foreach loop that iterates over the DataRow objects stored in myDataTable; notice the use of the myDataTable object's Rows property:

```
foreach (DataRow myDataRow in myDataTable.Rows)
{
  Console.WriteLine("ProductID = " + myDataRow["ProductID"]);
  Console.WriteLine("ProductName = " +
    myDataRow["ProductName"]);
  Console.WriteLine("UnitPrice = " + myDataRow["UnitPrice"]);
}
```

The Rows property returns a DataRowCollection object that allows you to access all the DataRow objects stored in myDataTable. You can read each column value in a DataRow using the name of the column; for example, to read the ProductID column value, you use myDataRow["ProductID"]. You can also use the numeric position of the column; for example, myDataRow[0] returns the value for the first column. This is the ProductID column.

You can also use the following code to iterate over all the DataTable, DataRow, and DataColumn objects stored in myDataSet:

```
foreach (DataTable myDataTable in myDataSet.Tables)
{
  foreach (DataRow myDataRow in myDataTable.Rows)
  {
    foreach (DataColumn myDataColumn in myDataTable.Columns)
    {
      Console.WriteLine(myDataColumn + " = " +
        myDataRow[myDataColumn]);
    }
  }
}
```

Notice that you don't need to know the names of the DataTable or DataColumn objects to display them. The call to the WriteLine() method displays myDataColumn, which returns the name of the column, and myDataRow[myDataColumn], which returns the column value for the current row.

NOTE

You'll see the details of the DataTable, DataRow, and DataColumn classes
in Chapter 14.

Listing 13.1 shows a program that uses the code examples shown in
this section.

Listing 13.1: *PopulateDataSetUsingSelect.cs*

```
/*
    PopulateDataSetUsingSelect.cs illustrates
    how to populate a DataSet object using a
    SELECT statement
*/

using System;
using System.Data;
using System.Data.SqlClient;

class PopulateDataSetUsingSelect
{
  public static void Main()
  {
    SqlConnection mySqlConnection =
      new SqlConnection(
        "server=localhost;database=Northwind;uid=sa;pwd=sa"
      );

    // create a SqlCommand object
    // and set its CommandText property
    // to a SELECT statement that retrieves
    // the top 5 rows from the Products table
    SqlCommand mySqlCommand =
      mySqlConnection.CreateCommand();
    mySqlCommand.CommandText =
      "SELECT TOP 5 ProductID, ProductName, UnitPrice " +
      "FROM Products " +
      "ORDER BY ProductID";

    // create a SqlDataAdapter object
    // and set its SelectCommand
```

```
      // property to the SqlCommand object
      SqlDataAdapter mySqlDataAdapter = new SqlDataAdapter();
      mySqlDataAdapter.SelectCommand = mySqlCommand;

      // create a DataSet object
      DataSet myDataSet = new DataSet();

      // open the database connection
      mySqlConnection.Open();

      // use the Fill() method of the SqlDataAdapter
      // object to retrieve the rows from the table,
      // storing the rows locally in a DataTable
      // of the DataSet object
      Console.WriteLine(
        "Retrieving rows from the Products table");
      int numberOfRows =
        mySqlDataAdapter.Fill(myDataSet, "Products");
      Console.WriteLine("numberOfRows = " + numberOfRows);

      // close the database connection
      mySqlConnection.Close();

      // get the DataTable object from the DataSet object
      DataTable myDataTable = myDataSet.Tables["Products"];

      // display the column values for
      // each row in the DataTable,
      // using a DataRow object to access
      // each row in the DataTable
      foreach (DataRow myDataRow in myDataTable.Rows)
      {
        Console.WriteLine(
          "ProductID = " + myDataRow["ProductID"]);
        Console.WriteLine(
          "ProductName = " + myDataRow["ProductName"]);
        Console.WriteLine(
          "UnitPrice = " + myDataRow["UnitPrice"]);
      }
    }
  }
}
```

The output from this program is as follows:

```
Retrieving rows from the Products table
numberOfRows = 5
ProductID = 1
ProductName = Chai
UnitPrice = 18
ProductID = 2
ProductName = Chang
UnitPrice = 19
ProductID = 3
ProductName = Aniseed Syrup
UnitPrice = 10
ProductID = 4
ProductName = Chef Anton's Cajun Seasoning
UnitPrice = 22
ProductID = 5
ProductName = Chef Anton's Gumbo Mix
UnitPrice = 21.35
```

Using a Range of Rows

In this section, you'll learn how to populate a DataSet with a range of rows. Now, the Fill() method is overloaded and a partial list of Fill() methods is as follows:

```
int Fill(DataSet myDataSet)
int Fill(DataTable myDataTable)
int Fill(DataSet myDataSet, string dataTableName)
int Fill(DataSet myDataSet, int startRow, int numOfRows,
  string dataTableName)
```

where

dataTableName   Specifies a string containing the name of the DataTable to fill.

startRow   Is an int that specifies the position of the row in the result set to read (starting at 0).

NumOfRows   Is an int that specifies the number rows to read.

The range of rows from *startRow* to *startRow* + *numOfRows* is then stored in the DataTable. The int returned by the Fill() method is the number of rows retrieved from the database.

As you can see, the final Fill() method allows you to populate a DataSet with a range of rows. The following example shows the use of this Fill() method to store a range of rows. It retrieves the top five rows from the Products table, but stores only three rows in the Products DataTable, starting at position 1 (because rows are numbered starting at 0, position 1 corresponds to the *second* row in the result set returned by the SELECT statement):

```
SqlCommand mySqlCommand = mySqlConnection.CreateCommand();
mySqlCommand.CommandText =
  "SELECT TOP 5 ProductID, ProductName, UnitPrice " +
  "FROM Products " +
  "ORDER BY ProductID";
SqlDataAdapter mySqlDataAdapter = new SqlDataAdapter();
mySqlDataAdapter.SelectCommand = mySqlCommand;
DataSet myDataSet = new DataSet();
int numberOfRows =
  mySqlDataAdapter.Fill(myDataSet, 1, 3, "Products");
```

The numberOfRows variable is set to 3—the number of rows myDataSet was populated with. One thing to remember is that the DataAdapter still retrieves all five rows from the Products table, but only three are actually used to populate the DataSet: the other two are thrown away.

Listing 13.2 shows a program that uses the code examples shown in this section.

Listing 13.2: *PopulateDataSetUsingRange.cs*

```
/*
   PopulateDataSetUsingRange.cs illustrates
   how to populate a DataSet
   object with a range of rows from a
   SELECT statement
*/

using System;
using System.Data;
using System.Data.SqlClient;

class PopulateDataSetUsingRange
{
  public static void Main()
  {
    SqlConnection mySqlConnection =
      new SqlConnection(
        "server=localhost;database=Northwind;uid=sa;pwd=sa"
      );
```

```
        // create a SqlCommand object
        // and set its CommandText property
        // to a SELECT statement that retrieves
        // the top 5 rows from the Products table
        SqlCommand mySqlCommand = mySqlConnection.CreateCommand();
        mySqlCommand.CommandText =
          "SELECT TOP 5 ProductID, ProductName, UnitPrice " +
          "FROM Products " +
          "ORDER BY ProductID";
        SqlDataAdapter mySqlDataAdapter = new SqlDataAdapter();
        mySqlDataAdapter.SelectCommand = mySqlCommand;
        DataSet myDataSet = new DataSet();
        mySqlConnection.Open();

        // use the Fill() method of the SqlDataAdapter
        // object to retrieve the rows from the table,
        // storing a range of rows in a DataTable of
        // the DataSet object
        Console.WriteLine(
          "Retrieving rows from the Products table");
        int numberOfRows =
          mySqlDataAdapter.Fill(myDataSet, 1, 3, "Products");
        Console.WriteLine("numberOfRows = " + numberOfRows);

        mySqlConnection.Close();

        DataTable myDataTable = myDataSet.Tables["Products"];

        foreach (DataRow myDataRow in myDataTable.Rows)
        {
          Console.WriteLine(
            "ProductID = " + myDataRow["ProductID"]);
          Console.WriteLine(
            "ProductName = " + myDataRow["ProductName"]);
          Console.WriteLine(
            "UnitPrice = " + myDataRow["UnitPrice"]);
        }
      }
    }
```

The output from this program is as follows:

```
Retrieving rows from the Products table
numberOfRows = 3
ProductID = 2
```

```
ProductName = Chang
UnitPrice = 19
ProductID = 3
ProductName = Aniseed Syrup
UnitPrice = 10
ProductID = 4
ProductName = Chef Anton's Cajun Seasoning
UnitPrice = 22
```

Using a Stored Procedure

You can also populate a DataSet object using a stored procedure that returns a result set. For example, the SQL Server Northwind database contains a stored procedure called CustOrderHist() that returns the products and total number of the products ordered by a customer. The customer's CustomerID is passed as a parameter to CustOrderHist().

Listing 13.3 shows the definition of the CustOrderHist() stored procedure.

Listing 13.3: *CustOrderHist()* stored procedure

```
CREATE PROCEDURE CustOrderHist @CustomerID nchar(5)
AS
SELECT ProductName, Total=SUM(Quantity)
FROM Products P, [Order Details] OD, Orders O, Customers C
WHERE C.CustomerID = @CustomerID
AND C.CustomerID = O.CustomerID
AND O.OrderID = OD.OrderID
AND OD.ProductID = P.ProductID
GROUP BY ProductName
```

NOTE

You don't have to create the CustOrderHist() procedure yourself. It's already defined in the Northwind database.

Calling CustOrderHist() and populating a DataSet with the returned result set is straightforward. For example, the following code creates a SqlCommand object, sets its CommandText object to an EXECUTE statement that calls CustOrderHist(), and sets the @CustomerID parameter to ALFKI:

```
SqlCommand mySqlCommand = mySqlConnection.CreateCommand();
mySqlCommand.CommandText =
  "EXECUTE CustOrderHist @CustomerID";
```

```
mySqlCommand.Parameters.Add(
  "@CustomerID", SqlDbType.NVarChar, 5).Value = "ALFKI";
```

You then use code similar to that shown in the previous section to populate a DataSet with the result set returned by CustOrderHist():

```
SqlDataAdapter mySqlDataAdapter = new SqlDataAdapter();
mySqlDataAdapter.SelectCommand = mySqlCommand;
DataSet myDataSet = new DataSet();
mySqlConnection.Open();
int numberOfRows =
  mySqlDataAdapter.Fill(myDataSet, "CustOrderHist");
mySqlConnection.Close();
```

The CustOrderHist DataTable contained within myDataSet is populated with the result set returned by the CustOrderHist() procedure.

Listing 13.4 shows a program that uses the code examples shown in this section.

Listing 13.4: *PopulateDataSetUsingProcedure.cs*

```
/*
  PopulateDataSetUsingProcedure.cs
  illustrates how to populate a
  DataSet object using a stored procedure
*/

using System;
using System.Data;
using System.Data.SqlClient;

class PopulateDataSetUsingProcedure
{
  public static void Main()
  {
    SqlConnection mySqlConnection =
      new SqlConnection(
        "server=localhost;database=Northwind;uid=sa;pwd=sa"
      );

    // create a SqlCommand object
    // and set its CommandText property
    // to call the CustOrderHist() stored procedure
    SqlCommand mySqlCommand
      = mySqlConnection.CreateCommand();
```

```
mySqlCommand.CommandText =
  "EXECUTE CustOrderHist @CustomerID";
mySqlCommand.Parameters.Add(
  "@CustomerID", SqlDbType.NVarChar, 5).Value = "ALFKI";

SqlDataAdapter mySqlDataAdapter = new SqlDataAdapter();
mySqlDataAdapter.SelectCommand = mySqlCommand;
DataSet myDataSet = new DataSet();
mySqlConnection.Open();
Console.WriteLine(
  "Retrieving rows from the CustOrderHist() Procedure");
int numberOfRows =
  mySqlDataAdapter.Fill(myDataSet, "CustOrderHist");
Console.WriteLine("numberOfRows = " + numberOfRows);
mySqlConnection.Close();

DataTable myDataTable =
  myDataSet.Tables["CustOrderHist"];
foreach (DataRow myDataRow in myDataTable.Rows)
{
  Console.WriteLine(
    "ProductName = " + myDataRow["ProductName"]);
  Console.WriteLine("Total = " + myDataRow["Total"]);
}
  }
}
```

The output from this program is as follows:

```
Retrieving rows from the CustOrderHist() Procedure
numberOfRows = 11
ProductName = Aniseed Syrup
Total = 6
ProductName = Chartreuse verte
Total = 21
ProductName = Escargots de Bourgogne
Total = 40
ProductName = Flotemysost
Total = 20
ProductName = Grandma's Boysenberry Spread
Total = 16
ProductName = Lakkalikööri
Total = 15
ProductName = Original Frankfurter grüne Soße
Total = 2
```

```
ProductName = Raclette Courdavault
Total = 15
ProductName = Rössle Sauerkraut
Total = 17
ProductName = Spegesild
Total = 2
ProductName = Vegie-spread
Total = 20
```

Populating a *DataSet* with Multiple *DataTable* Objects

You can populate a DataSet with multiple DataTable objects. You might want to do this when you need to access the information stored in multiple tables in the database.

You may use any of the following techniques to populate a DataSet with multiple DataTable objects:

▶ Use multiple SELECT statements in the same SelectCommand.

▶ Change the CommandText property of the SelectCommand before each call to the Fill() method.

▶ Use multiple DataAdapter objects to populate the same DataSet.

Let's take a look at each of these techniques.

Using Multiple *SELECT* Statements in the Same *SelectCommand*

The following example sets the CommandText property of a SqlCommand object to two separate SELECT statements:

```
SqlCommand mySqlCommand = mySqlConnection.CreateCommand();
mySqlCommand.CommandText =
  "SELECT TOP 2 ProductID, ProductName, UnitPrice " +
  "FROM Products " +
  "ORDER BY ProductID;" +
  "SELECT CustomerID, CompanyName " +
  "FROM Customers " +
  "WHERE CustomerID = 'ALFKI';";
```

Notice that each SELECT statement is separated by a semicolon (;). When these SELECT statements are run, two result sets are returned: one containing the two rows from the Products table, the second containing the one row from the Customers table. These two result sets are stored in separate DataTable objects by the following code:

```
SqlDataAdapter mySqlDataAdapter = new SqlDataAdapter();
mySqlDataAdapter.SelectCommand = mySqlCommand;
DataSet myDataSet = new DataSet();
mySqlConnection.Open();
int numberOfRows = mySqlDataAdapter.Fill(myDataSet);
mySqlConnection.Close();
```

Notice the use of the Fill(myDataSet) method, which doesn't specify the name of the DataTable to be created. Instead, the names of the two DataTable objects used to store the result sets are automatically set to the default of Table and Table1. Table stores the result set from the Products table, and Table1 stores the result set from the Customers table.

The name of a DataTable object is stored in its TableName property, which you can change. For example, the following code changes the name of the Table DataSet to Products and the Table1 DataSet to Customers:

```
myDataSet.Tables["Table"].TableName = "Products";
myDataSet.Tables["Table1"].TableName = "Customers";
```

Listing 13.5 shows a program that uses the code examples shown in this section.

Listing 13.5: *MultipleDataTables.cs*

```
/*
   MutlipleDataTables.cs illustrates how to
   populate a DataSet with multiple DataTable
   objects using multiple SELECT statements
*/

using System;
using System.Data;
using System.Data.SqlClient;

class MultipleDataTables
{
  public static void Main()
  {
    SqlConnection mySqlConnection =
      new SqlConnection(
        "server=localhost;database=Northwind;uid=sa;pwd=sa"
      );
```

```
                    // create a SqlCommand object
                    // and set its CommandText property
                    // to mutliple SELECT statements
                    SqlCommand mySqlCommand =
                      mySqlConnection.CreateCommand();
                    mySqlCommand.CommandText =
                      "SELECT TOP 2 ProductID, ProductName, UnitPrice " +
                      "FROM Products " +
                      "ORDER BY ProductID;" +
                      "SELECT CustomerID, CompanyName " +
                      "FROM Customers " +
                      "WHERE CustomerID = 'ALFKI';";

                    SqlDataAdapter mySqlDataAdapter = new SqlDataAdapter();
                    mySqlDataAdapter.SelectCommand = mySqlCommand;
                    DataSet myDataSet = new DataSet();
                    mySqlConnection.Open();
                    int numberOfRows = mySqlDataAdapter.Fill(myDataSet);
                    Console.WriteLine("numberOfRows = " + numberOfRows);
                    mySqlConnection.Close();

                    // change the TableName property of the DataTable objects
                    myDataSet.Tables["Table"].TableName = "Products";
                    myDataSet.Tables["Table1"].TableName = "Customers";

                    foreach (DataTable myDataTable in myDataSet.Tables) {
                      Console.WriteLine("\nReading from the " +
                        myDataTable.TableName + " DataTable");
                      foreach (DataRow myDataRow in myDataTable.Rows)
                      {
                        foreach (DataColumn myDataColumn
                          in myDataTable.Columns)
                        {
                          Console.WriteLine(myDataColumn + " = " +
                            myDataRow[myDataColumn]);
                        }
                      }
                    }
                  }
                }
```

The output from this program is as follows:

```
numberOfRows = 3
```

```
Reading from the Products DataTable
ProductID = 1
ProductName = Chai
UnitPrice = 18
ProductID = 2
ProductName = Chang
UnitPrice = 19

Reading from the Customers DataTable
CustomerID = ALFKI
CompanyName = Alfreds Futterkiste
```

Changing the *CommandText* Property of the *SelectCommand*

You can also populate a DataSet with multiple DataTable objects by changing the CommandText property of the SelectCommand for your DataAdapter object before each call to the Fill() method. First, the following code populates a DataSet with a DataTable containing two rows from the Products table:

```
SqlCommand mySqlCommand = mySqlConnection.CreateCommand();
mySqlCommand.CommandText =
  "SELECT TOP 2 ProductID, ProductName, UnitPrice " +
  "FROM Products " +
  "ORDER BY ProductID";
SqlDataAdapter mySqlDataAdapter = new SqlDataAdapter();
mySqlDataAdapter.SelectCommand = mySqlCommand;
DataSet myDataSet = new DataSet();
mySqlConnection.Open();
int numberOfRows =
  mySqlDataAdapter.Fill(myDataSet, "Products");
```

The myDataSet object now contains a DataTable named Products.

Next, the CommandText property for the SelectCommand of mySqlData-Adapter is changed to a SELECT statement that retrieves rows from the Customers table, and the Fill() method is called again:

```
mySqlDataAdapter.SelectCommand.CommandText =
  "SELECT CustomerID, CompanyName " +
  "FROM Customers " +
  "WHERE CustomerID = 'ALFKI'";
numberOfRows = mySqlDataAdapter.Fill(myDataSet, "Customers");
mySqlConnection.Close();
```

The myDataSet object now contains an additional DataTable named Customers.

Listing 13.6 shows a program that uses the code examples shown in this section.

Listing 13.6: *MultipleDataTables2.cs*

```
/*
  MutlipleDataTables2.cs illustrates how
  to populate a DataSet object with multiple
  DataTable objects by changing the
  CommandText property of a DataAdapter
  object's SelectCommand
*/

using System;
using System.Data;
using System.Data.SqlClient;

class MultipleDataTables2
{
  public static void Main()
  {
    SqlConnection mySqlConnection =
      new SqlConnection(
        "server=localhost;database=Northwind;uid=sa;pwd=sa"
      );

    SqlCommand mySqlCommand =
      mySqlConnection.CreateCommand();
    mySqlCommand.CommandText =
      "SELECT TOP 2 ProductID, ProductName, UnitPrice " +
      "FROM Products " +
      "ORDER BY ProductID";
    SqlDataAdapter mySqlDataAdapter = new SqlDataAdapter();
    mySqlDataAdapter.SelectCommand = mySqlCommand;
    DataSet myDataSet = new DataSet();
    mySqlConnection.Open();
    int numberOfRows =
      mySqlDataAdapter.Fill(myDataSet, "Products");
    Console.WriteLine("numberOfRows = " + numberOfRows);

    // change the CommandText property of the SelectCommand
    mySqlDataAdapter.SelectCommand.CommandText =
      "SELECT CustomerID, CompanyName " +
      "FROM Customers " +
```

```
              "WHERE CustomerID = 'ALFKI'";
          numberOfRows =
              mySqlDataAdapter.Fill(myDataSet, "Customers");
          Console.WriteLine("numberOfRows = " + numberOfRows);

          mySqlConnection.Close();

          foreach (DataTable myDataTable in myDataSet.Tables) {
            Console.WriteLine("\nReading from the " +
              myDataTable.TableName + " DataTable");
            foreach (DataRow myDataRow in myDataTable.Rows)
            {
              foreach (DataColumn myDataColumn in
                myDataTable.Columns)
              {
              Console.WriteLine(myDataColumn + " = " +
                myDataRow[myDataColumn]);
              }
            }
          }
        }
      }
```

The output from this program is as follows:

```
numberOfRows = 2
numberOfRows = 1

Reading from the Products DataTable
ProductID = 1
ProductName = Chai
UnitPrice = 18
ProductID = 2
ProductName = Chang
UnitPrice = 19

Reading from the Customers DataTable
CustomerID = ALFKI
CompanyName = Alfreds Futterkiste
```

Using Multiple *DataAdapter* Objects to Populate the Same *DataSet* Object

You can also populate the same DataSet with multiple DataTable objects using different DataAdapter objects. For example, assume you already have a DataSet named myDataSet that was populated using a SqlData-Adapter named mySqlDataAdapter, and that myDataSet currently contains a DataTable named Products. The following example creates another SqlDataAdapter and uses it to populate myDataSet with another DataTable named Customers:

```
SqlDataAdapter mySqlDataAdapter2 = new SqlDataAdapter();
mySqlDataAdapter2.SelectCommand = mySqlCommand;
mySqlDataAdapter2.SelectCommand.CommandText =
  "SELECT CustomerID, CompanyName " +
  "FROM Customers " +
  "WHERE CustomerID = 'ALFKI'";
numberOfRows =
  mySqlDataAdapter2.Fill(myDataSet, "Customers");
```

Listing 13.7 shows a program that uses the code examples shown in this section.

Listing 13.7: *MultipleDataTables3.cs*

```
/*
    MutlipleDataTables3.cs illustrates how
    to populate a DataSet object with multiple
    DataTable objects using multiple
    DataAdapter objects to populate the same
    DataSet object
*/

using System;
using System.Data;
using System.Data.SqlClient;

class MultipleDataTables3
{
  public static void Main()
  {
    SqlConnection mySqlConnection =
      new SqlConnection(
        "server=localhost;database=Northwind;uid=sa;pwd=sa"
      );

    SqlCommand mySqlCommand =
      mySqlConnection.CreateCommand();
```

```
mySqlCommand.CommandText =
  "SELECT TOP 2 ProductID, ProductName, UnitPrice " +
  "FROM Products " +
  "ORDER BY ProductID";
SqlDataAdapter mySqlDataAdapter1 = new SqlDataAdapter();
mySqlDataAdapter1.SelectCommand = mySqlCommand;
DataSet myDataSet = new DataSet();
mySqlConnection.Open();
int numberOfRows =
  mySqlDataAdapter1.Fill(myDataSet, "Products");
Console.WriteLine("numberOfRows = " + numberOfRows);

// create another DataAdapter object
SqlDataAdapter mySqlDataAdapter2 = new SqlDataAdapter();
mySqlDataAdapter2.SelectCommand = mySqlCommand;
mySqlDataAdapter2.SelectCommand.CommandText =
  "SELECT CustomerID, CompanyName " +
  "FROM Customers " +
  "WHERE CustomerID = 'ALFKI'";
numberOfRows =
  mySqlDataAdapter2.Fill(myDataSet, "Customers");
Console.WriteLine("numberOfRows = " + numberOfRows);
mySqlConnection.Close();

foreach (DataTable myDataTable in myDataSet.Tables) {
  Console.WriteLine("\nReading from the " +
    myDataTable.TableName + " DataTable");
  foreach (DataRow myDataRow in myDataTable.Rows)
  {
    foreach (DataColumn myDataColumn
      in myDataTable.Columns)
    {
      Console.WriteLine(myDataColumn + " = " +
        myDataRow[myDataColumn]);
    }
  }
}
}
```

The output from this program is as follows:

```
numberOfRows = 2
numberOfRows = 1
```

```
Reading from the Products DataTable
ProductID = 1
ProductName = Chai
UnitPrice = 18
ProductID = 2
ProductName = Chang
UnitPrice = 19

Reading from the Customers DataTable
CustomerID = ALFKI
CompanyName = Alfreds Futterkiste
```

Merging *DataRow*, *DataSet*, and *DataTable* Objects into Another *DataSet*

In this section, you'll learn how to use the Merge() method to merge DataRow, DataSet, and DataTable objects into another DataSet. You might want to do this when you have multiple sources of data; for example, you might get data from many regional offices that is sent to headquarters, and you need to merge all that data into one DataSet.

The Merge() method is overloaded as follows:

```
void Merge(DataRow[] myDataRows)
void Merge(DataSet myDataSet)
void Merge(DataTable myDataTable)
void Merge(DataSet myDataSet, bool preserveChanges)
void Merge(DataRow[] myDataRows, bool preserveChanges,
  MissingSchemaAction myMissingSchemaAction)
void Merge(DataSet myDataSet, bool preserveChanges,
  MissingSchemaAction myMissingSchemaAction)
void Merge(DataTable myDataTable, bool preserveChanges,
  MissingSchemaAction myMissingSchemaAction)
```

where

> **PreserveChanges**   Specifies whether changes in the current DataSet (the DataSet with the Merge() method that is called) are to be kept.

> **MyMissingSchemaAction**   Specifies the action to take when the current DataSet doesn't have the same tables or columns as the DataRow, DataSet, or DataTable being merged into that DataSet.

You set *myMissingSchemaAction* to one of the constants defined in the System.Data.MissingSchemaAction enumeration. Table 13.7 shows the constants defined in the MissingSchemaAction enumeration.

TABLE 13.7: MissingSchemaAction Enumeration Members

CONSTANT	DESCRIPTION
Add	The column or table is added to the current DataSet. Add is the default.
AddWithKey	The column and primary key information is added to the current DataSet.
Error	A SystemException is thrown.
Ignore	The column or table is ignored and not read.

Listing 13.8 illustrates the use of the Merge() method.

Listing 13.8: *Merge.cs*

```
/*
  Merge.cs illustrates how to use the Merge() method
*/

using System;
using System.Data;
using System.Data.SqlClient;

class Merge
{
  public static void Main()
  {
    SqlConnection mySqlConnection =
      new SqlConnection(
        "server=localhost;database=Northwind;uid=sa;pwd=sa"
      );

    SqlCommand mySqlCommand =
      mySqlConnection.CreateCommand();

    // populate myDataSet with three rows
    // from the Customers table
    mySqlCommand.CommandText =
      "SELECT CustomerID, CompanyName, ContactName, " +
      " Address FROM Customers " +
      "WHERE CustomerID IN ('ALFKI', 'ANATR', 'ANTON')";
    SqlDataAdapter mySqlDataAdapter = new SqlDataAdapter();
    mySqlDataAdapter.SelectCommand = mySqlCommand;
```

```
DataSet myDataSet = new DataSet();
mySqlConnection.Open();
mySqlDataAdapter.Fill(myDataSet, "Customers");

// populate myDataSet2 with two rows
// from the Customers table
mySqlCommand.CommandText =
  "SELECT CustomerID, CompanyName, ContactName, " +
  " Address FROM Customers " +
  "WHERE CustomerID IN ('AROUT', 'BERGS')";
DataSet myDataSet2 = new DataSet();
mySqlDataAdapter.Fill(myDataSet2, "Customers2");


// populate myDataSet3 with five rows
// from the Products table
mySqlCommand.CommandText =
  "SELECT TOP 5 ProductID, ProductName, UnitPrice " +
  "FROM Products " +
  "ORDER BY ProductID";
DataSet myDataSet3 = new DataSet();
mySqlDataAdapter.Fill(myDataSet3, "Products");

mySqlConnection.Close();

// merge myDataSet2 into myDataSet
myDataSet.Merge(myDataSet2);

// merge myDataSet3 into myDataSet
myDataSet.Merge(myDataSet3, true,
  MissingSchemaAction.Add);

// display the rows in myDataSet
foreach (DataTable myDataTable in myDataSet.Tables)
{
  Console.WriteLine(
    "\nReading from the " + myDataTable + " DataTable");
  foreach (DataRow myDataRow in myDataTable.Rows)
  {
    foreach (DataColumn myDataColumn
      in myDataTable.Columns)
    {
```

```
            Console.WriteLine(myDataColumn + " = " +
              myDataRow[myDataColumn]);
          }
        }
      }
    }
  }
```

The output from this program is as follows:

```
Reading from the Customers DataTable
CustomerID = ALFKI
CompanyName = Alfreds Futterkiste
ContactName = Maria Anders
Address = Obere Str. 57
CustomerID = ANATR
CompanyName = Ana Trujillo3 Emparedados y helados
ContactName = Ana Trujillo
Address = Avda. de la Constitución 2222
CustomerID = ANTON
CompanyName = Antonio Moreno Taquería
ContactName = Antonio Moreno
Address = Mataderos  2312

Reading from the Customers2 DataTable
CustomerID = AROUT
CompanyName = Around the Horn
ContactName = Thomas Hardy
Address = 120 Hanover Sq.
CustomerID = BERGS
CompanyName = Berglunds snabbköp
ContactName = Christina Berglund
Address = Berguvsvägen  8

Reading from the Products DataTable
ProductID = 1
ProductName = Chai
UnitPrice = 18
ProductID = 2
ProductName = Chang
UnitPrice = 19
ProductID = 3
ProductName = Aniseed Syrup
UnitPrice = 10
ProductID = 4
ProductName = Chef Anton's Cajun Seasoning
```

```
UnitPrice = 22
ProductID = 5
ProductName = Chef Anton's Gumbo Mix
UnitPrice = 21.35
```

WRITING AND READING XML USING A *DATASET* OBJECT

XML is a convenient format for moving information around. You can write out the contents of the DataTable objects contained in a DataSet to an XML file using the WriteXml() method. The XML file written by this method contains the DataTable name and column names and values.

You can write out the schema of a DataSet object to an XML file using the WriteXmlSchema() method. The XML file written by this method contains the structure of the DataTable objects contained in the DataSet. You can also get the XML in a DataSet using the GetXml() method, which returns the XML in a string.

You can read the contents of the DataTable objects in an XML file into a DataSet using the ReadXml() method. You can also read the schema contained in an XML file using the ReadXmlSchema() method.

NOTE

SQL Server also contains extensive built-in XML functionality, which you can learn more about in the SQL Server Books Online.

Using the *WriteXml()* Method

Let's say you have a DataSet object named myDataSet. Assume that myDataSet has a DataTable that contains the CustomerID, CompanyName, ContactName, and Address columns for the top two rows from the Customers table. The following code shows this:

```
SqlCommand mySqlCommand = mySqlConnection.CreateCommand();
mySqlCommand.CommandText =
  "SELECT TOP 2 CustomerID, CompanyName, ContactName, " +
  " Address FROM Customers " +
  "ORDER BY CustomerID";
SqlDataAdapter mySqlDataAdapter = new SqlDataAdapter();
mySqlDataAdapter.SelectCommand = mySqlCommand;
DataSet myDataSet = new DataSet();
```

```
mySqlConnection.Open();
Console.WriteLine(
    "Retrieving rows from the Customers table");
mySqlDataAdapter.Fill(myDataSet, "Customers");
mySqlConnection.Close();
```

You can write out the contents of myDataSet to an XML file using the WriteXml() method. For example,

```
myDataSet.WriteXml("myXmlFile.xml");
```

This writes an XML file named myXmlFile.xml, as shown in Listing 13.9.

Listing 13.9: *myXmlFile.xml*

```
<?xml version="1.0" standalone="yes"?>
<NewDataSet>
  <Customers>
    <CustomerID>ALFKI</CustomerID>
    <CompanyName>Alfreds Futterkiste</CompanyName>
    <ContactName>Maria Anders</ContactName>
    <Address>Obere Str. 57</Address>
  </Customers>
  <Customers>
    <CustomerID>ANATR</CustomerID>
    <CompanyName>
       Ana Trujillo Emparedados y helados
    </CompanyName>
    <ContactName>Ana Trujillo</ContactName>
    <Address>Avda. de la Constitución 2222</Address>
  </Customers>
</NewDataSet>
```

As you can see, this file contains the columns for the rows retrieved from the Customers table.

The WriteXml() method is overloaded as follows:

```
void WriteXml(Stream myStream);
void WriteXml(string fileName);
void WriteXml(TextWriter myTextWriter);
void WriteXml(XmlWriter myXmlWriter);
void WriteXml(stream myStream, XmlWriteMode myXmlWriteMode);
void WriteXml(string fileName, XmlWriteMode myXmlWriteMode);
void WriteXml(TextWriter myTextWriter,
    XmlWriteMode myXmlWriteMode);
void WriteXml(XmlWriter myXmlWriter,
    XmlWriteMode myXmlWriteMode);
```

where *myXmlWriteMode* is a constant from the System.Data.XmlWrite-Mode enumeration that specifies how to write XML data and the schema. Table 13.8 shows the constants defined in the XmlWriteMode enumeration.

TABLE 13.8: XmlWriteMode Enumeration Members

CONSTANT	DESCRIPTION
DiffGram	Writes out the DataSet as a DiffGram, which contains the original values and the changes to those values to make them current. You can generate a DiffGram that contains only the changes by calling the GetChanges() method of your DataSet and then call WriteXml().
IgnoreSchema	Writes out only the data in the DataSet without writing the schema. IgnoreSchema is the default.
WriteSchema	Writes out the schema in the DataSet.

The following example shows the use of the XmlWriteMode.WriteSchema constant:

```
myDataSet.WriteXml("myXmlFile2.xml",
  XmlWriteMode.WriteSchema);
```

This writes an XML file named myXmlFile2.xml, as shown in Listing 13.10.

Listing 13.10: *myXmlFile2.xml*

```
<?xml version="1.0" standalone="yes"?>
<NewDataSet>
  <xsd:schema id="NewDataSet" targetNamespace="" xmlns=""
   xmlns:xsd="http://www.w3.org/2001/XMLSchema"
   xmlns:msdata="urn:schemas-microsoft-com:xml-msdata">
    <xsd:element name="NewDataSet" msdata:IsDataSet="true">
      <xsd:complexType>
        <xsd:choice maxOccurs="unbounded">
          <xsd:element name="Customers">
            <xsd:complexType>
              <xsd:sequence>
                <xsd:element name="CustomerID"
                  type="xsd:string" minOccurs="0" />
                <xsd:element name="CompanyName"
                  type="xsd:string" minOccurs="0" />
                <xsd:element name="ContactName"
                  type="xsd:string" minOccurs="0" />
```

```
                      <xsd:element name="Address"
                         type="xsd:string" minOccurs="0" />
                  </xsd:sequence>
                </xsd:complexType>
              </xsd:element>
            </xsd:choice>
          </xsd:complexType>
        </xsd:element>
      </xsd:schema>
      <Customers>
        <CustomerID>ALFKI</CustomerID>
        <CompanyName>Alfreds Futterkiste</CompanyName>
        <ContactName>Maria Anders</ContactName>
        <Address>Obere Str. 57</Address>
      </Customers>
      <Customers>
        <CustomerID>ANATR</CustomerID>
        <CompanyName>
          Ana Trujillo3 Emparedados y helados
        </CompanyName>
        <ContactName>Ana Trujillo</ContactName>
        <Address>Avda. de la Constitución 2222</Address>
      </Customers>
    </NewDataSet>
```

As you can see, this file contains the schema definition for the columns used in the original SELECT statement as well as the column values for the rows retrieved.

Using the *WriteXmlSchema()* Method

You can write out the schema of myDataSet to an XML file using the WriteXmlSchema() method. For example,

```
myDataSet.WriteXmlSchema("myXmlSchemaFile.xml");
```

This writes an XML file named myXmlSchemaFile.xml, as shown in Listing 13.11.

Listing 13.11: *myXmlSchemaFile.xml*

```
<?xml version="1.0" standalone="yes"?>
<xsd:schema id="NewDataSet" targetNamespace="" xmlns=""
  xmlns:xsd="http://www.w3.org/2001/XMLSchema"
  xmlns:msdata="urn:schemas-microsoft-com:xml-msdata">
```

```
<xsd:element name="NewDataSet" msdata:IsDataSet="true">
  <xsd:complexType>
    <xsd:choice maxOccurs="unbounded">
      <xsd:element name="Customers">
        <xsd:complexType>
          <xsd:sequence>
            <xsd:element name="CustomerID"
              type="xsd:string" minOccurs="0" />
            <xsd:element name="CompanyName"
              type="xsd:string" minOccurs="0" />
            <xsd:element name="ContactName"
              type="xsd:string" minOccurs="0" />
            <xsd:element name="Address"
              type="xsd:string" minOccurs="0" />
          </xsd:sequence>
        </xsd:complexType>
      </xsd:element>
    </xsd:choice>
  </xsd:complexType>
</xsd:element>
</xsd:schema>
```

As you can see, this file contains the schema definition for the columns retrieved from the Customers table by the original SELECT statement.

Using the *ReadXml()* Method

You can read the contents of an XML file into a DataSet object using the ReadXml() method. This method reads the rows and columns from the XML file into DataTable objects of the DataSet. For example, the following statement uses the ReadXml() method to read the XML file myXmlFile.xml previously written by the WriteXml() method:

```
myDataSet.ReadXml("myXmlFile.xml");
```

The ReadXml() method is overloaded as follows:

```
void ReadXml(Stream myStream);
void ReadXml(string fileName);
void ReadXml(TextReader myTextReader);
void ReadXml(XmlReader myXmlReader);
void ReadXml(stream myStream, XmlReadMode myXmlReadMode);
void ReadXml(string fileName, XmlReadMode myXmlReadMode);
void ReadXml(TextReader myTextReader,
  XmlReadMode myXmlReadMode);
```

```
void ReadXml(XmlReader myXmlReader,
    XmlReadMode myXmlReadMode);
```

where *myXmlReadMode* is a constant from the System.Data.XmlReadMode enumeration that specifies how to read XML data and the schema. Table 13.9 shows the constants defined in the XmlReadMode enumeration.

TABLE 13.9:   XmlReadMode Enumeration Members

CONSTANT	DESCRIPTION
Auto	Reads the XML file in an appropriate manner: - If the XML file contains a DiffGram, then XmlReadMode is set to DiffGram. - If the DataSet already contains a schema or the XML file contains a schema, then XmlReadMode is set to ReadSchema. - If the DataSet doesn't contain a schema and the XML file doesn't contain a schema, then XmlReadMode is set to InferSchema. Auto is the default.
DiffGram	Reads the XML file as a DiffGram, which contains the original values and the changes to those values to make them current. The changes are then applied to your DataSet. This is similar to calling the Merge() method of a DataSet in that changes from one DataSet are merged with another.
Fragment	Reads an XML file that contains inline XDR schema fragments such as those generated by executing SELECT statements containing FOR XML clauses.
IgnoreSchema	Reads out only the data in the DataSet, without reading the schema.
InferSchema	Infers the schema of the XML file by examining the data stored in it.
ReadSchema	Reads the schema from the XML file into the DataSet.

The following example shows the use of the XmlReadMode.ReadSchema constant:

```
myDataSet.ReadXml("myXmlFile2.xml", XmlReadMode.ReadSchema);
```

Listing 13.12 illustrates how to write and read XML files using ADO.NET.

Listing 13.12: *WriteAndReadXML.cs*

```
/*
    WriteAndReadXml.cs illustrates how to write
    and read XML files
*/
```

```
using System;
using System.Data;
using System.Data.SqlClient;

class WriteAndReadXML
{
  public static void Main()
  {
    SqlConnection mySqlConnection =
      new SqlConnection(
        "server=localhost;database=Northwind;uid=sa;pwd=sa"
      );

    SqlCommand mySqlCommand =
      mySqlConnection.CreateCommand();
    mySqlCommand.CommandText =
      "SELECT TOP 2 CustomerID, CompanyName, ContactName, " +
      "Address " +
      "FROM Customers " +
      "ORDER BY CustomerID";
    SqlDataAdapter mySqlDataAdapter = new SqlDataAdapter();
    mySqlDataAdapter.SelectCommand = mySqlCommand;
    DataSet myDataSet = new DataSet();
    mySqlConnection.Open();
    Console.WriteLine(
      "Retrieving rows from the Customers table");
    mySqlDataAdapter.Fill(myDataSet, "Customers");
    mySqlConnection.Close();

    // use the WriteXml() method to
    // write the DataSet out to an XML file
    Console.WriteLine(
      "Writing rows out to an XML file named " +
      "myXmlFile.xml using the WriteXml() method");
    myDataSet.WriteXml("myXmlFile.xml");

    Console.WriteLine(
      "Writing schema out to an XML file named " +
      "myXmlFile2.xml using the WriteXml() method");
    myDataSet.WriteXml("myXmlFile2.xml",
      XmlWriteMode.WriteSchema);
```

```
        // use the WriteXmlSchema() method to
        // write the schema of the
        // DataSet out to an XML file
        Console.WriteLine(
          "Writing schema out to an XML file named " +
          "myXmlSchemaFile.xml using the WriteXmlSchema() method");
        myDataSet.WriteXmlSchema("myXmlSchemaFile.xml");

        // use the Clear() method to clear
        // the current rows in the DataSet
        myDataSet.Clear();

        // use the ReadXml() method to read
        // the contents of the XML file into the DataSet
        Console.WriteLine("Reading rows from myXmlFile.xml " +
          "using the ReadXml() method");
        myDataSet.ReadXml("myXmlFile.xml");

        DataTable myDataTable =
          myDataSet.Tables["Customers"];
        foreach (DataRow myDataRow in myDataTable.Rows)
        {
          Console.WriteLine("CustomerID = " +
            myDataRow["CustomerID"]);
          Console.WriteLine("CompanyName = " +
            myDataRow["CompanyName"]);
          Console.WriteLine("ContactName = " +
            myDataRow["ContactName"]);
          Console.WriteLine("Address = " + myDataRow["Address"]);
        }
      }
    }
```

The output from this program is as follows:

```
Retrieving rows from the Customers table
Writing rows out to an XML file named myXmlFile.xml using
  the WriteXml() method
Writing schema out to an XML file named myXmlFile2.xml
  using the WriteXml() method
Writing schema out to an XML file named myXmlSchemaFile.xml
  using the WriteXmlSchema() method
Reading rows from myXmlFile.xml using the ReadXml() method
```

```
CustomerID = ALFKI
CompanyName = Alfreds Futterkiste
ContactName = Maria Anders
Address = Obere Str. 57
CustomerID = ANATR
CompanyName = Ana Trujillo3 Emparedados y helados
ContactName = Ana Trujillo
Address = Avda. de la Constitución 2222
```

MAPPING TABLES AND COLUMNS

The AS keyword in SQL specifies an alias for a table or column. The following example uses the AS keyword to alias the `CustomerID` column as `MyCustomer` and also alias the `Customers` table as `Cust`:

```
SELECT CustomerID AS MyCustomer, CompanyName, Address
FROM Customers AS Cust
WHERE CustomerID = 'ALFKI';
```

Figure 13.2 shows the results of this SELECT statement.

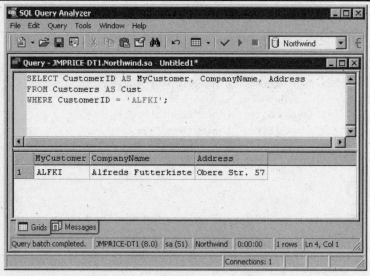

FIGURE 13.2:   Using the AS keyword

The following code uses this SELECT statement to populate a `DataSet` object named `myDataSet`:

```
SqlCommand mySqlCommand = mySqlConnection.CreateCommand();
```

```
mySqlCommand.CommandText =
  "SELECT CustomerID AS MyCustomer, CompanyName, Address " +
  "FROM Customers AS Cust " +
  "WHERE CustomerID = 'ALFKI'";
SqlDataAdapter mySqlDataAdapter = new SqlDataAdapter();
mySqlDataAdapter.SelectCommand = mySqlCommand;
DataSet myDataSet = new DataSet();
mySqlConnection.Open();
mySqlDataAdapter.Fill(myDataSet, "Customers");
mySqlConnection.Close();
```

Notice that the Fill() method specifies the name of the DataTable as Customers, which is known as the source DataTable name.

To map a DataTable in your DataSet, you create an object of the DataTableMapping class using the Add() method; this class belongs to the System.Data.Common namespace, which you should import into your program. The following example creates a DataTableMapping object named myDataTableMapping, passing Customers and Cust to the Add() method:

```
DataTableMapping myDataTableMapping =
  mySqlDataAdapter.TableMappings.Add("Customers", "Cust");
```

Notice that the Add() method is called through the TableMappings property. The TableMappings property returns an object of the Table-MappingCollection class. This object is a collection of TableMapping objects, and you use a TableMapping object to map the source name to a different DataTable name, therefore, the previous example maps the source name of Customers to Cust.

You can read this mapping using the SourceTable and DataSetTable properties of myDataTableMapping. For example,

```
Console.WriteLine(
  "myDataTableMapping.SourceTable = " +
  myDataTableMapping.SourceTable);
Console.WriteLine(
  "myDataTableMapping.DataSetTable = " +
  myDataTableMapping.DataSetTable);
```

This example displays the following:

```
myDataTableMapping.DataSetTable = Cust
myDataTableMapping.SourceTable = Customers
```

You should also change the TableName property of the DataTable object in your DataSet to keep the names consistent:

```
myDataSet.Tables["Customers"].TableName = "Cust";
```

TIP

It is important that you change the `TableName` since it will otherwise keep the original name of `Customers`, which is a little confusing when you've already specified the mapping from `Customers` to `Cust` earlier.

Next, to alias the `CustomerID` column as `MyCustomer`, you call the `Add()` method through the `ColumnMappings` property of `myDataTableMapping`:

```
myDataTableMapping.ColumnMappings.Add(
   "CustomerID", "MyCustomer");
```

The `ColumnMappings` property returns an object of the `DataColumn-MappingCollection` class. This object is a collection of `DataColumnMapping` objects. You use a `DataColumnMapping` object to map a column name from the database to a different `DataColumn` name, therefore, the previous example maps the `CustomerID` column name from the database to the `DataColumn` name `MyCustomer`.

Listing 13.13 illustrates how to map table and column names using the code shown in this section.

Listing 13.13: *Mappings.cs*

```
/*
   Mappings.cs illustrates how to map table and column names
*/

using System;
using System.Data;
using System.Data.SqlClient;
using System.Data.Common;

class Mappings
{
   public static void Main()
   {
      SqlConnection mySqlConnection =
         new SqlConnection(
            "server=localhost;database=Northwind;uid=sa;pwd=sa"
         );

      SqlCommand mySqlCommand
         = mySqlConnection.CreateCommand();
```

```
mySqlCommand.CommandText =
  "SELECT CustomerID AS MyCustomer, CompanyName, " +
  " Address FROM Customers AS Cust " +
  "WHERE CustomerID = 'ALFKI'";
SqlDataAdapter mySqlDataAdapter = new SqlDataAdapter();
mySqlDataAdapter.SelectCommand = mySqlCommand;
DataSet myDataSet = new DataSet();
mySqlConnection.Open();
mySqlDataAdapter.Fill(myDataSet, "Customers");
mySqlConnection.Close();

// create a DataTableMapping object
DataTableMapping myDataTableMapping =
  mySqlDataAdapter.TableMappings.Add(
  "Customers", "Cust");

// change the TableName property of the DataTable object
myDataSet.Tables["Customers"].TableName = "Cust";

// display the DataSetTable and SourceTable properties
Console.WriteLine("myDataTableMapping.DataSetTable = " +
  myDataTableMapping.DataSetTable);
Console.WriteLine("myDataTableMapping.SourceTable = " +
  myDataTableMapping.SourceTable);

// map the CustomerID column to MyCustomer
myDataTableMapping.ColumnMappings.Add(
  "CustomerID", "MyCustomer");

DataTable myDataTable = myDataSet.Tables["Cust"];
foreach (DataRow myDataRow in myDataTable.Rows)
{
  Console.WriteLine("CustomerID = " +
    myDataRow["MyCustomer"]);
  Console.WriteLine("CompanyName = " +
    myDataRow["CompanyName"]);
  Console.WriteLine("Address = " + myDataRow["Address"]);
}
}
}
```

The output from this program is as follows:

```
myDataTableMapping.DataSetTable = Cust
myDataTableMapping.SourceTable = Customers
CustomerID = ALFKI
CompanyName = Alfreds Futterkiste
Address = Obere Str. 57
```

READING A COLUMN VALUE USING STRONGLY TYPED *DATASET* CLASSES

A strongly typed `DataSet` object allows you read a column value using a property with the same name as the column. For example, to read the `CustomerID` of a column, you can use `myDataRow.CustomerID` rather than `myDataRow["CustomerID"]`. This is a nice feature because the compiler can then catch any errors in column spellings at compile time rather than at run time. For example, if you incorrectly spelled `CustomerID` as `CustimerID`, then the mistake would be caught by the compiler.

Another feature of a strongly typed `DataSet` is that when you work with it in VS .NET, IntelliSense automatically pops up the properties and methods of the `DataSet` when you are typing. You can then pick the property or method from the list, rather than type it all in.

The downside to using a strongly typed `DataSet` is that you must do some initial work to generate it before you can use it. If the columns in your database tables don't change very often, then you should consider using strongly typed `DataSet` objects. On the other hand, if your database tables change a lot, you should probably avoid them because you'll need to regenerate the strongly typed `DataSet` to keep it synchronized with the definition of the database table.

NOTE

You'll find a completed VS .NET example project for this section in the `Strongly-TypedDataSet` directory. You can open this project in VS .NET by selecting File ➢ Open ➢ Project and opening the `WindowsApplication4.csproj` file. You'll need to change the `ConnectionString` property of the `sqlConnection1` object to connect to your SQL Server Northwind database. You can also follow along with the instructions in this section by copying the `DataReader` directory to another directory and using that project as your starting point.

Creating a Strongly Typed *DataSet* Class

In this section, you'll create a strongly typed DataSet class that is used to access the Customers table. If you're following along with these instructions, open the DataReader project in VS .NET and double-click Form1.cs in the Solution Explorer window. You open the Solution Explorer window by selecting View ➢ Solution Explorer.

Next, select File ➢ Add New Item. Select DataSet from the Templates area and enter MyDataSet.xsd, as shown in Figure 13.3. Click the Open button to continue. VS .NET will add MyDataSet.xsd to your project, as shown in Figure 13.4.

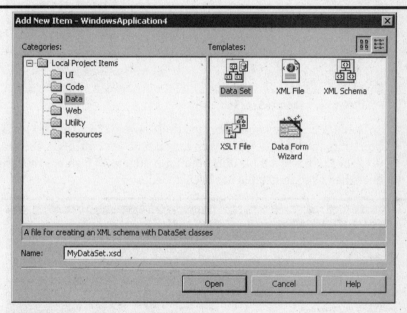

FIGURE 13.3:   Adding a new DataSet

At the bottom left of Figure 13.4, you'll notice two tabs: DataSet and XML. The DataSet tab is displayed by default and you use it to see the visual view of your DataSet. The XML tab allows you to see the XML file of your DataSet.

Next, make sure you've opened the Server Explorer window; to open the window, select View ➢ Server Explorer. Open the Data Connections node and either use an existing connection to your Northwind database or create a new one by right-clicking the Data Connections node and selecting Add Connection from the pop-up menu.

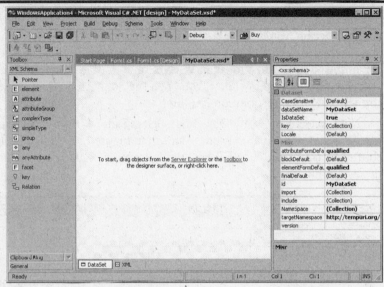

FIGURE 13.4:   `MyDataSet.xsd`

Double-click your connection and drill down to the table, view, or stored procedure you want use, and then drag it onto your form. Go ahead and drag the Customers table onto your form. Figure 13.5 shows the form once the Customers table has been added.

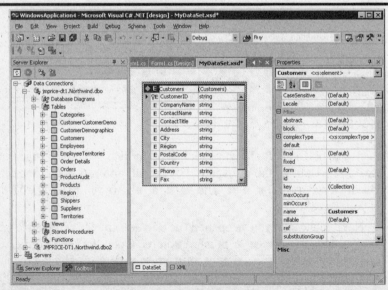

FIGURE 13.5:   Customers table added to the form

NOTE
You can add multiple tables to your form and define relations between them.

Next, save your work by selecting File ➢ Save All or by pressing Ctrl+S on your keyboard.

Your project now contains an XSD file named MyDataSet.xsd, as shown in Listing 13.14. You can view this file by clicking the XML tab at the bottom of the XML Designer window.

Listing 13.14: *MyDataSet.xsd*

```xml
<?xml version="1.0" encoding="utf-8" ?>
<xs:schema id="MyDataSet"
 targetNamespace="http://tempuri.org/MyDataSet.xsd"
   elementFormDefault="qualified"
 attributeFormDefault="qualified"
 xmlns="http://tempuri.org/MyDataSet.xsd"
 xmlns:mstns="http://tempuri.org/MyDataSet.xsd"
 xmlns:xs="http://www.w3.org/2001/XMLSchema"
 xmlns:msdata="urn:schemas-microsoft-com:xml-msdata">
  <xs:element name="MyDataSet" msdata:IsDataSet="true">
    <xs:complexType>
      <xs:choice maxOccurs="unbounded">
        <xs:element name="Customers">
          <xs:complexType>
            <xs:sequence>
              <xs:element name="CustomerID"
                type="xs:string" />
              <xs:element name="CompanyName"
                type="xs:string" />
              <xs:element name="ContactName"
                 type="xs:string" minOccurs="0" />
              <xs:element name="ContactTitle"
                 type="xs:string" minOccurs="0" />
              <xs:element name="Address"
                 type="xs:string" minOccurs="0" />
              <xs:element name="City"
                 type="xs:string" minOccurs="0" />
              <xs:element name="Region"
                 type="xs:string" minOccurs="0" />
```

```
                    <xs:element name="PostalCode"
                         type="xs:string" minOccurs="0" />
                    <xs:element name="Country"
                         type="xs:string" minOccurs="0" />
                    <xs:element name="Phone"
                         type="xs:string" minOccurs="0" />
                    <xs:element name="Fax"
                         type="xs:string" minOccurs="0" />
                  </xs:sequence>
                </xs:complexType>
              </xs:element>
            </xs:choice>
          </xs:complexType>
          <xs:unique name="MyDataSetKey1" msdata:PrimaryKey="true">
            <xs:selector xpath=".//mstns:Customers" />
            <xs:field xpath="mstns:CustomerID" />
          </xs:unique>
        </xs:element>
      </xs:schema>
```

Notice that this file contains the details of the columns in the Customers table.

Your project also contains a new class file named MyDataSet.cs, which contains your strongly typed DataSet class. You can view the contents of this file using the Solution Explorer window. You open the Solution Explorer window by selecting View ➢ Solution Explorer.

NOTE

To view the MyDataSet.cs file, click the Show All Files button in the Solution Explorer window.

Next, expand the node beneath MyDataSet.xsd. You'll see MyDataSet.cs, as shown in Figure 13.6, and a file named MyDataSet.xsx, which contains layout information for the visual view of your DataSet.

Go ahead and open MyDataSet.cs by double-clicking it in the Solution Explorer window. View the code for this form by selecting View ➢ Code. One of the classes declared in that file is MyDataSet. This class is derived from the DataSet class. You'll use it in the next section to create a strongly typed DataSet object to access the Customers table.

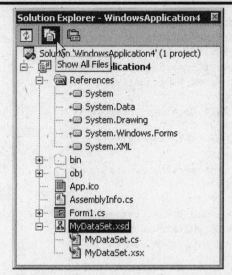

FIGURE 13.6:   Viewing all the files using the Solution Explorer window

Using a Strongly Typed *DataSet* Class

Once you have your strongly typed MyDataSet class, you can create an object of that class using the following code:

```
MyDataSet myDataSet = new MyDataSet();
```

You can also create a strongly typed DataTable table object using the MyDataSet.CustomersDataTable class, and you can populate it with rows from the Customers table. For example, you can set the Form1_Load() method of your form to retrieve the CustomerID, CompanyName, and Address column values from the Customers table and then you can add them to a ListView control named listView1. To do this, double-click Form1.cs in the Solution Explorer window, view the code, and set the Form1_Load() method as follows:

```
private void Form1_Load(object sender, System.EventArgs e)
{
    System.Data.SqlClient.SqlCommand mySqlCommand =
    sqlConnection1.CreateCommand();
    mySqlCommand.CommandText =
    "SELECT CustomerID, CompanyName, Address " +
```

```
                "FROM Customers " +
                "WHERE CustomerID = 'ALFKI'";
        System.Data.SqlClient.SqlDataAdapter mySqlDataAdapter =
                new System.Data.SqlClient.SqlDataAdapter();
        mySqlDataAdapter.SelectCommand = mySqlCommand;
        MyDataSet myDataSet = new MyDataSet();
        sqlConnection1.Open();
        mySqlDataAdapter.Fill(myDataSet, "Customers");
        sqlConnection1.Close();
        MyDataSet.CustomersDataTable myDataTable =
                myDataSet.Customers;
        foreach (MyDataSet.CustomersRow myDataRow
                in myDataTable.Rows)
        {
            listView1.Items.Add(myDataRow.CustomerID);
            listView1.Items.Add(myDataRow.CompanyName);
            listView1.Items.Add(myDataRow.Address);
        }
    }
```

The myDataRow.CustomerID property returns the value for the CustomerID column, and so on. Compile and run your form in one step by selecting Debug ➤ Start Without Debugging. Figure 13.7 shows the running form.

FIGURE 13.7:   The running form

NOTE

The MyDataSet class contains a number of methods that allow you to modify the rows stored in a MyDataSet object. These methods include NewCustomersRow(), AddCustomersRow(), FindByCustomerID(), and RemoveCustomersRow(). You can also check if a column value contains a null value using methods such as IsContactNameNull(), and you can set a column to null using methods such as SetContactNameNull(). You'll learn how to use these methods in Chapter 14.

CREATING A *DATAADAPTER* OBJECT USING VISUAL STUDIO .NET

In this section, you'll learn how to create a DataAdapter using Visual Studio .NET.

NOTE

You'll find a completed VS .NET project for this section in the DataAdapter directory. You can open this project in VS .NET by selecting File ➤ Open ➤ Project and opening the WindowsApplication4.csproj file. You'll need to change the ConnectionString property of the sqlConnection1 object to connect to your database. You can also follow along with the instructions in this section by copying the DataReader directory to another directory and using that project as your starting point.

Open your form by double-clicking Form1.cs in the Solution Explorer window. Next, create a SqlDataAdapter object by dragging a SqlDataAdapter object from the Data tab of the Toolbox to your form. When you drag a SqlDataAdapter object to your form, you start the Data Adapter Configuration Wizard, as shown in Figure 13.8. Click the Next button to continue.

You now select the database connection you want to use, or you can create a new one. Pick your connection to the Northwind database (or create a new connection if you don't have an existing one), as shown in Figure 13.9. Click the Next button to continue.

FIGURE 13.8: The Data Adapter Configuration Wizard

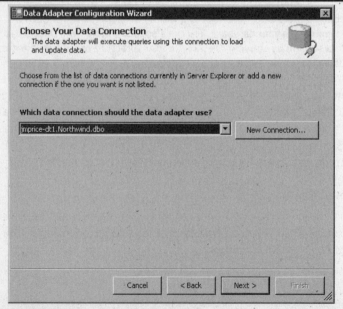

FIGURE 13.9: Choosing your data connection

Next, you set your query type to Use SQL statements. As you can see from Figure 13.10, you can set your query type to use SQL statements, create new stored procedures, or use existing stored procedures. The SQL statements or stored procedures are then used in the SelectCommand, InsertCommand, UpdateCommand, and DeleteCommand properties of your SqlDataAdapter object. You'll learn about the latter three properties in Chapter 14; they are used to insert, update, and delete rows.

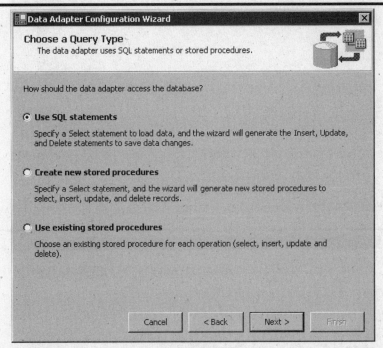

FIGURE 13.10:   Choosing your query type

Make sure you've picked Use SQL Statements, and click the Next button to continue.

You now generate the SQL statements for your SqlDataAdapter. You can enter a SELECT statement directly by typing it, or you can press the Query Builder button to build your SELECT statement visually. Enter the SELECT statement, as shown in Figure 13.11, and click the Next button to continue.

The SELECT statement you entered is now used to generate the INSERT, UPDATE, and DELETE statements along with the table mappings. Figure 13.12 shows the final dialog box of the Data Adapter Configuration Wizard.

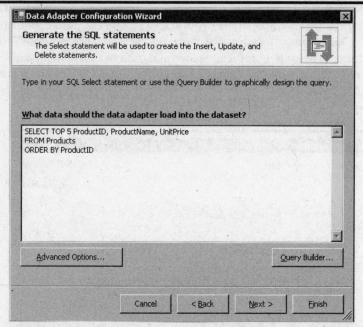

FIGURE 13.11:   Generating the SQL statements

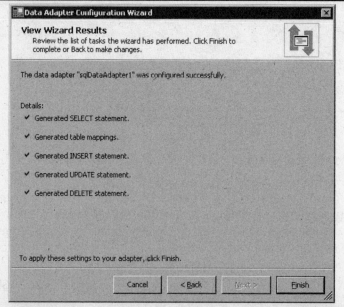

FIGURE 13.12:   Final dialog box for the Data Adapter Configuration Wizard

Click the Finish button to complete the wizard. A `SqlDataAdapter` object named `sqlDataAdapter1` is now added to the tray beneath your form, as shown in Figure 13.13.

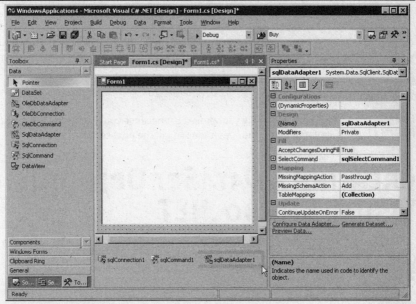

FIGURE 13.13: The new `SqlDataAdapter` object in the tray

WARNING

You need to set the `Connection` property of the `SelectCommand` in your `sqlDataAdapter1` object to your `Connection` object before the `DataAdapter` can access the database. You do this using the Properties window by drilling down from `SelectCommand` to `Connection`. You then click the drop-down list, select Existing, and select your `SqlConnection` object, which should be named `sqlConnection1`. Also check the `ConnectionString` property of your `SqlConnection` object to make sure it is set to connect to your Northwind database. If you don't do this step, you'll get an error stating that your `SqlDataAdapter` object hasn't been configured properly.

Notice the three links at the bottom of the Properties window for `sqlDataAdapter1`:

Configure Data Adapter   This link allows you to re-enter the wizard to configure your `DataAdapter`.

Generate Dataset   This link allows you to generate a `DataSet` object using the information set for your `DataAdapter`. You'll use this link in the next section to generate a new `DataSet`.

Preview Data   This link allows you to preview the data returned by the `SelectCommand` of your `DataAdapter`.

Feel free to examine the code generated by the wizard in your form for the `sqlDataAdapter1` object. When you're ready, select File ➢ Save All.

> **NOTE**
>
> Don't bother running your project yet because you'll add a `DataSet` that will be populated using your `DataAdapter` in the next section.

CREATING A *DATASET* OBJECT USING VISUAL STUDIO .NET

In this section, you'll learn how to create a DataSet using Visual Studio .NET.

> **NOTE**
>
> You'll find a completed VS .NET example project for this section in the `DataSet` directory. You can open this project in VS .NET by selecting File ➢ Open ➢ Project and opening the `WindowsApplication4.csproj` file. You can also follow along with the instructions in this section by continuing to modify the copy of the `DataReader` project you used in the previous section.

If you're following along with these instructions, open the copy of the `DataReader` project you modified in the previous section, and then open `Form1.cs` by double-clicking it in the Solution Explorer window. To create a `DataSet` object, you can perform either one of the following:

▶ Drag a `DataSet` object from the Data tab of the Toolbox to your form, and add code to your form to fill it using the `Fill()` method of a `DataAdapter` object.

▶ Click the Generate Dataset link at the bottom of the Properties window of your `DataAdapter`. You can see this link in Figure 13.13.

You'll use the second step, so go ahead and click the Generate Dataset link. The Generate Dataset dialog box is then displayed, as shown in Figure 13.14.

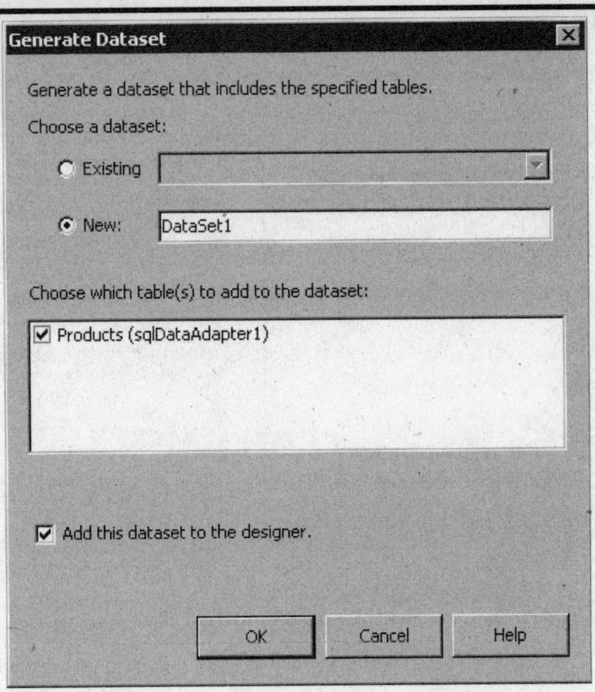

FIGURE 13.14:   The Generate Dataset dialog box

Click the OK button to continue. The new `DataSet` object named
`dataSet11` is added to the tray beneath your form, as shown in
Figure 13.15.

Your next step is to set the `Form1_Load()` method of your form as
follows:

```
private void Form1_Load(object sender, System.EventArgs e)
{
  sqlConnection1.Open();
  sqlDataAdapter1.Fill(dataSet11, "Products");
  sqlConnection1.Close();
  System.Data.DataTable myDataTable =
    dataSet11.Tables["Products"];
  foreach (System.Data.DataRow myDataRow in myDataTable.Rows)
  {
    listView1.Items.Add(myDataRow["ProductID"].ToString());
    listView1.Items.Add(myDataRow["ProductName"].ToString());
    listView1.Items.Add(myDataRow["UnitPrice"].ToString());
  }
}
```

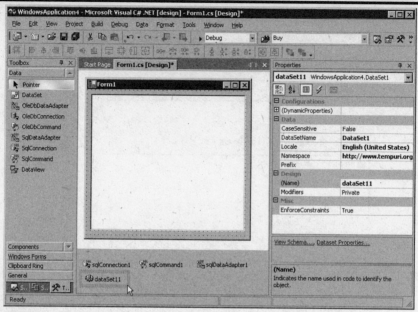

FIGURE 13.15:   The new `DataSet` object in the tray

NOTE

Remember, to view the code of your form, you select View ➤ Code. You then replace the `Form1_Load()` method with the previous code.

You can then compile and run your form. Figure 13.16 shows the running form.

FIGURE 13.16:   The running form

SUMMARY

In this chapter, you learned the details of using DataSet objects to store results returned from the database. DataSet objects allow you to store a copy of the tables and rows from the database, and you can work with that local copy while disconnected from the database. Unlike managed provider objects such as SqlDataReader objects, DataSet objects are generic and therefore work with any database. DataSet objects also allow you to read rows in any order and modify them.

You also learned the details of using a DataAdapter object to read rows from the database into a DataSet object. The DataAdapter is part of the managed provider classes, and there are three DataAdapter classes: SqlDataAdapter, OleDbDataAdapter, and OdbcDataAdapter.

You use a DataAdapter object to move rows between your DataSet object and the database and to synchronize any changes you make to your locally stored rows with the database. For example, you can read rows from the database into a DataSet through a DataAdapter, modify those rows in your DataSet, and then push those changes to the database through your DataAdapter object.

WHAT'S NEXT

In Chapter 14, you'll see how to make changes to the rows in a DataSet and then push those changes to the database.

Chapter 14

USING *DATASET* OBJECTS TO MODIFY DATA

In Chapter 13, "Using *DataSet* Objects to Store Data," you saw how to use a DataSet to store a copy of the rows retrieved from the database. In this chapter, you'll learn how to modify the rows in a DataSet, and then push those changes to the database via a DataAdapter.

Adapted from *Mastering C# Database Programming*
by Jason Price
ISBN 0-7821-4183-8

THE *DATATABLE* CLASS

You use an object of the DataTable class to represent a table. You can also store multiple DataTable objects in a DataSet. Table 14.1 shows some of the DataTable properties.

TABLE 14.1: DataTable Properties

PROPERTY	TYPE	DESCRIPTION
CaseSensitive	Bool	Gets or sets a bool value that indicates whether string comparisons within DataTable objects are case-sensitive.
ChildRelations	DataRelation-Collection	Gets the collection of relations (DataRelationCollection) that allows navigation from a parent table to a child table. A DataRelationCollection consists of DataRelation objects.
Columns	DataColumnCollection	Gets the collection of columns (DataColumnCollection) that contains DataColumn objects that represent the columns in the DataTable object.
Constraints	ConstraintCollection	Gets the collection of constraints (ConstraintCollection) that contains Constraint objects that represent primary key (UniqueConstraint) or foreign key constraints (ForeignKey-Constraint) in the DataTable object.
DataSet	DataSet	Gets the DataSet to which the DataTable belongs.
HasErrors	Bool	Returns a bool value that indicates whether any of the rows in the DataTable have errors.
PrimaryKey	DataColumn[]	Gets or sets an array of DataColumn objects that are the primary keys for the DataTable.
Rows	DataRowCollection	Gets the collection of rows (DataRow-Collection) that contains the DataRow objects stored in the DataTable.
TableName	string	Gets or sets the name of the DataTable object.

Table 14.2 shows some of the DataTable methods.

TABLE 14.2: DataTable Methods

Method	Return Type	Description
AcceptChanges()	void	Commits all the changes made to the DataTable object since it was loaded or since the last time the AcceptChanges() method was called.
Clear()	void	Removes all rows from the DataTable object.
Clone()	DataTable	Clones the structure of the DataTable object and returns that clone.
Compute()	object	Computes the given expression on the current rows that pass the filter criteria.
GetChanges()	DataTable	Overloaded. Returns a copy of the Data-Table object since it was last loaded or since the last time the AcceptChanges() method was called.
GetErrors()	DataRow[]	Overloaded. Gets a copy of all the DataRow objects that have errors.
LoadDataRow()	DataRow	Finds and updates a specified DataRow object. If no matching DataRow object is found, a new row is created using the specified values.
NewRow()	DataRow	Creates a new DataRow object in the DataTable.
RejectChanges()	void	Undoes all the changes made to the DataTable object since it was created or since the last time the AcceptChanges() method was called.
Select()	DataRow[]	Overloaded. Returns the array of DataRow objects stored in the DataTable that match the specified filter string. You can also pass a string containing details on how to sort the DataRow objects.

Table 14.3 shows some of the DataTable events.

TABLE 14.3:   DataTable Events

Event	Event Handler	Description
ColumnChanging	DataColumnChange-EventHandler	Fires *before* a changed DataColumn value is committed in a DataRow.
ColumnChanged	DataColumnChange-EventHandler	Fires *after* a changed DataColumn value is committed in a DataRow.
RowChanging	DataRowChange-EventHandler	Fires *before* a changed DataRow is committed in a DataTable.
RowChanged	DataRowChange-EventHandler	Fires *after* a changed DataRow is committed in a DataTable.
RowDeleting	DataRowChange-EventHandler	Fires *before* a DataRow is deleted from a DataTable.
RowDeleted	DataRowChange-EventHandler	Fires *after* a DataRow is deleted from a DataTable.

THE *DATAROW* CLASS

You use an object of the DataRow class to represent a row. You can also store multiple DataRow objects in a DataTable. Table 14.4 shows some of the DataRow properties.

TABLE 14.4:   DataRow Properties

Property	Type	Description
HasErrors	bool	Returns a bool value that indicates whether any of the DataColumn objects in the DataRow have errors.
ItemArray	object[]	Gets or sets all the DataColumn objects in the DataRow.
RowState	DataRowState	Gets the current state of the DataRow. The state can be Added, Deleted, Detached*, Modified, or Unchanged. The state depends on the operation performed on the DataRow and whether the Accept-Changes() method has been called to commit the changes.
Table	DataTable	Gets the DataTable object to which the DataRow belongs.

*The row has been created but isn't part of a DataRowCollection object; a DataRow is in this state immediately after it has been created and before it is added to a collection, or if it has been removed from a collection.

Table 14.5 shows some of the DataRow methods.

TABLE 14.5: DataRow Methods

Method	Return Type	Description
AcceptChanges()	void	Commits all the changes made to the DataRow object since it was loaded or since the last time the AcceptChanges() method was called.
BeginEdit()	void	Starts an edit for the DataRow object.
CancelEdit()	void	Cancels an edit for the DataRow object and restores it to the original state.
ClearErrors()	void	Clears any errors for the DataRow object.
Delete()	void	Deletes the DataRow object.
EndEdit()	void	Stops an edit for the DataRow object and commits the change.
GetChildRows()	DataRow[]	Overloaded. Returns an array of DataRow objects that contain the child rows using the specified DataRelation object.
GetColumnError()	string	Overloaded. Returns the description of the error for the specified DataColumn object.
GetColumnsInError()	DataColumn[]	Returns an array of DataColumn objects that have errors.
GetParentRow()	DataRow	Overloaded. Returns a DataRow object that contains the parent row using the specified DataRelation object.
GetParentRows()	DataRow[]	Overloaded. Returns an array of DataRow objects that contain the parent rows using the specified DataRelation object.
IsNull()	bool	Overloaded. Returns a bool value that indicates whether the specified DataColumn object contains a null value.
RejectChanges()	void	Undoes all changes made to the DataRow object since the AcceptChanges() method was called.
SetNull()	void	Sets the specified DataColumn object to a null value.
SetParentRow()	void	Overloaded. Sets the parent row to the specified DataRow object.

THE *DATACOLUMN* CLASS

You use an object of the DataColumn class to represent a column. You can also store multiple DataColumn objects in a DataRow. Table 14.6 shows some of the DataColumn properties.

TABLE 14.6:   DataColumn Properties

PROPERTY	TYPE	DESCRIPTION
AllowDBNull	bool	Gets or sets a bool value that indicates whether null values are allowed in this DataColumn object. The default is true.
AutoIncrement	bool	Gets or sets a bool value that indicates whether the DataColumn object automatically increments the value of the column for new rows. The default is false.
AutoIncrementSeed	long	Gets or sets the starting value for the DataColumn object. Applies only when the AutoIncrement property is set to true. The default is 0.
AutoIncrementStep	long	Gets or sets the increment used. Applies only when the AutoIncrement property is set to true. The default is 1.
Caption	string	Gets or sets the caption for the column. The caption for the column is shown in Windows forms. The default is null.
ColumnName	string	Gets or sets the name of the DataColumn object.
ColumnMapping	MappingType	Gets or sets the MappingType of the DataColumn object. This determines how a DataColumn is saved in an XML document using the WriteXml() method.
DataType	Type	Gets or sets the .NET data type used to represent the column value stored in the DataColumn object. This can be Boolean, Byte, Char, DateTime, Decimal, Double, Int16, Int32, Int64, SByte, Single, String, TimeSpan, UInt16, or UInt64.
DefaultValue	object	Gets or sets the default value for the DataColumn when new rows are created. When AutoIncrement is set to true, DefaultValue is not used.

TABLE 14.6 continued: DataColumn Properties

PROPERTY	TYPE	DESCRIPTION
MaxLength	int	Gets or sets the maximum length of text that may be stored in a DataColumn object. The default is –1.
Ordinal	int	Gets the numeric position of the DataColumn object (0 is the first object).
ReadOnly	bool	Gets or sets a bool value that indicates whether the DataColumn object can be changed once it has been added to a DataRow. The default is false.
Table	DataTable	Gets the DataTable to which the DataColumn object belongs.
Unique	bool	Gets or sets a bool value that indicates whether the DataColumn values in each DataRow object must be unique. The default is false.

You'll see the use of some of these properties, methods, and events later in this chapter.

ADDING RESTRICTIONS TO *DATATABLE* AND *DATACOLUMN* OBJECTS

As you know, a DataSet object is used to store a copy of a subset of the database. For example, you can store a copy of the rows from database tables into a DataSet, with each table represented by a DataTable object. A DataTable stores columns in DataColumn objects.

In addition to storing rows retrieved from a database table, you can also add restrictions to a DataTable and its DataColumn objects. This allows you to model the same restrictions placed on the database tables and columns in your DataTable and DataColumn objects. For example, you can add the following constraints to a DataTable:

► Unique

► Primary key

► Foreign key

In addition, you can add the following restrictions to a DataColumn:

▶ Whether the column can accept a null value—which you store in the AllowDBNull property of the DataColumn.

▶ Any auto-increment information—which you store in the Auto-Increment, AutoIncrementSeed, and AutoIncrementStep properties of the DataColumn. You set these properties when adding rows to a DataTable with a corresponding database table that contains an identity column. The ProductID column of the Products table is an example of an identity column.

NOTE

ADO.NET will *not* automatically generate values for identity columns in a new row. Only the database can do that. You must read the generated identity value for the column from the database. You'll see how to do that later in the sections "Retrieving New Identity Column Values" and "Using Stored Procedures to Add, Modify, and Remove Rows from the Database." Also, if your database table contains columns that are assigned a default value, you should read that value from the database. This is better than setting the DefaultValue property of a DataColumn because if the default value set in the database table definition changes, you can pick up the new value from the database rather than having to change your code.

▶ The maximum length of a string or character column value—which you store in the MaxLength property of the DataColumn.

▶ Whether the column is read-only—which you store in the ReadOnly property of the DataColumn.

▶ Whether the column is unique—which you store in the Unique property of the DataColumn.

By adding these restrictions up front, you prevent bad data from being added to your DataSet to begin with. This helps reduce the errors when you are attempting to push changes in your DataSet to the database. If a user of your program attempts to add data that violates a restriction, they'll cause an exception to be thrown. You can then catch the exception in your program and display a message with the details. The user can then change the data they were trying to add and fix the problem.

You also need to define a primary key before you can find, filter, and sort DataRow objects in a DataTable. You'll learn how to do that later in the section "Finding, Filtering, and Sorting Rows in a DataTable."

TIP

Adding constraints causes a performance degradation when you call the Fill() method of a DataAdapter. This is because the retrieved rows are checked against your constraints before they are added to your DataSet. You should therefore set the EnforceConstraints property of your DataSet to false before calling the Fill() method. You then set EnforceConstraints back to the default of true after the call to Fill().

You can use one of following ways to add restrictions to DataTable and DataColumn objects:

▶ Add the restrictions yourself by setting the properties of your DataTable and DataColumn objects. This results in the fastest executing code.

▶ Call the FillSchema() method of your DataAdapter to copy the schema information from the database to your DataSet. This populates the properties of the DataTable objects and their DataColumn objects automatically. Although simple to call, the FillSchema() method takes a relatively long time to read the schema information from the database and you should avoid using it.

You'll learn the details of both these techniques in the following sections.

Adding the Restrictions Yourself

You can add restrictions to your DataTable and DataColumn objects yourself using the properties of the DataTable and DataColumn objects.

For example, assume you have a DataSet object named myDataSet that contains three DataTable objects named Products, Orders, and Order Details that have been populated using the following code:

```
SqlCommand mySqlCommand = mySqlConnection.CreateCommand();
mySqlCommand.CommandText =
  "SELECT ProductID, ProductName " +
  "FROM Products;" +
  "SELECT OrderID " +
  "FROM Orders;" +
  "SELECT OrderID, ProductID, UnitPrice " +
  "FROM [Order Details];";
SqlDataAdapter mySqlDataAdapter = new SqlDataAdapter();
mySqlDataAdapter.SelectCommand = mySqlCommand;
```

```
DataSet myDataSet = new DataSet();
mySqlConnection.Open();
mySqlDataAdapter.Fill(myDataSet);
mySqlConnection.Close();
myDataSet.Tables["Table"].TableName = "Products";
myDataSet.Tables["Table1"].TableName = "Orders";
myDataSet.Tables["Table2"].TableName = "Order Details";
```

The primary key for the `Products` table is the `ProductID` column; the primary key for the `Orders` table is the `OrderID` column; and the primary key for the `Order Details` table is made up of both the `OrderID` and `ProductID` columns.

NOTE

You must include all the columns of a database table's primary key in your query if you want to define a primary key on those columns in your `DataTable`.

In the following sections, you'll see how to

▶ Add constraints to the `Products`, `Orders`, and `Order Details` `DataTable` objects.

▶ Restrict the values placed in the `DataColumn` objects of the `Products` `DataTable`.

Adding Constraints to *DataTable* Objects

In this section, you'll see how to add constraints to `DataTable` objects. Specifically, you'll see how to add primary key constraints to the `Products`, `Orders`, and `Order Details` `DataTable` objects. A primary key constraint is actually implemented as a unique constraint. You'll also see how to add foreign key constraints from the `Order Details` to the `Products` and `Orders` `DataTable` objects.

Constraints are stored in a `ConstraintCollection` object that stores `Constraint` objects. You access the `ConstraintCollection` using the `DataTable` object's `Constraints` property. To add a new `Constraint` object to `ConstraintCollection`, you call the `Add()` method through the `Constraints` property. The `Add()` method allows you to add unique constraints and foreign key constraints to a `DataTable`. Since a primary key constraint is implemented as a unique constraint, you can also use the `Add()` method to add a primary constraint to a `DataTable`. You'll see how to use the `Add()` method shortly.

You can also add a primary key constraint to a DataTable object by setting its PrimaryKey property, which you set to an array of DataColumn objects that make up the primary key. An array is required because the primary key of a database table can be made up of multiple columns. As you'll see in the examples, this is simpler than using the Add() method to add a primary key constraint.

CALLING THE *FILL()* METHOD OF A *DATAADAPTER* MORE THAN ONCE

The Fill() method retrieves *all* of the rows from the database table, as specified in your DataAdapter object's SelectCommand property. If you add a primary key to your DataTable, then calling the Fill() method more than once will put the retrieved rows in your DataTable and throw away any existing rows with matching primary key column values already in your DataTable.

If you don't add a primary key to your DataTable, then calling the Fill() method more than once will simply add all the retrieved rows to your DataTable again, duplicating the rows already there.

This is another reason for adding a primary key constraint to your DataTable because you don't want duplicate rows.

Adding a Primary Key to the *Products DataTable*   Let's take a look at adding a primary key to the Products DataTable. First, the following example creates a DataTable object named productsDataTable and sets it to the Products DataTable retrieved from myDataSet:

```
DataTable productsDataTable = myDataSet.Tables["Products"];
```

Now, the primary key for the Products database table is the ProductID column, therefore, you need to set the PrimaryKey property of products-DataTable to an array containing the ProductID DataColumn object. The following example shows how you do this. It creates an array of DataColumn objects named productsPrimaryKey and initializes it to the ProductID column of productsDataTable, then it sets the PrimaryKey property of productsDataTable to the array:

```
DataColumn[] productsPrimaryKey =
  new DataColumn[]
  {
```

```
        productsDataTable.Columns["ProductID"]
   };
productsDataTable.PrimaryKey = productsPrimaryKey;
```

When you set the `PrimaryKey` property of a `DataTable`, the `AllowDB-Null` and `Unique` properties of the `DataColumn` object are automatically changed as follows:

▶ The `AllowDBNull` property is changed to `false` and indicates that the `DataColumn` cannot accept a null value.

▶ The `Unique` property is changed to `true` and indicates that the `DataColumn` value in each `DataRow` must be unique.

Therefore, in the previous example, the `AllowDBNull` and `Unique` properties of the `ProductID DataColumn` are automatically changed to `false` and `true`, respectively.

Adding a Primary Key to the *Orders* DataTable   The following example sets the `PrimaryKey` property of the `Orders DataTable` to the `OrderID DataColumn`:

```
myDataSet.Tables["Orders"].PrimaryKey =
  new DataColumn[]
  {
    myDataSet.Tables["Orders"].Columns["OrderID"]
  };
```

Notice I've used just one statement in this example to make it more concise than the previous example.

You can also use the `Add()` method to add a unique, primary key, or foreign key constraint to a `DataTable`. The `Add()` method is overloaded as follows:

```
void Add(Constraint myConstraint)  // adds any constraint

// adds a primary key or unique constraint
void Add(string constraintName, DataColumn myDataColumn,
  bool isPrimaryKey)
void Add(string constraintName, DataColumn parentColumn,
  DataColumn childColumn)  // adds a foreign key constraint

// adds a primary key or unique constraint
void Add(string constraintName, DataColumn[] myDataColumn,
  bool isPrimaryKey)
```

```
// adds a foreign key constraint
void Add(string cosntraintName, DataColumn[] parentColumns,
  DataColumn[] childColumns)
```

where

> **constraintName**   Is the name you want to assign to your constraint.

> **isPrimaryKey**   Indicates whether the constraint is a primary key constraint or just a regular unique constraint.

The following example uses the Add() method to add a primary key constraint to the Products DataTable:

```
myDataSet.Tables["Orders"].Constraints.Add(
  "Primary key constraint",
  myDataSet.Tables["Orders"].Columns["OrderID"],
  true
);
```

This example does the same thing as the previous example that added the primary key constraint using the PrimaryKey property. Notice the last parameter to the Add() method is set to true, which indicates that the constraint is for a primary key.

Just as an aside, if you have a column that isn't a primary key but is unique, you can add a UniqueConstraint object to the Constraints-Collection. For example,

```
UniqueConstraint myUC =
  new UniqueConstraint(myDataTable.Columns["myColumn"]);
myDataTable.Constraints.Add(myUC);
```

Adding a Primary Key to the *OrderDetails DataTable*   Let's

consider an example of setting the PrimaryKey property for the Order Details DataTable. The primary for the Order Details table is made up of the OrderID and ProductID columns, and the following example sets the PrimaryKey property of the Order Details DataTable to these two columns:

```
myDataSet.Tables["Order Details"].PrimaryKey =
  new DataColumn[]
  {
    myDataSet.Tables["Order Details"].Columns["OrderID"],
    myDataSet.Tables["Order Details"].Columns["ProductID"]
  };
```

The following example uses the Add() method to do the same thing:

```
myDataSet.Tables["Order Details"].Constraints.Add(
  "Primary key constraint",
  new DataColumn[]
  {
    myDataSet.Tables["Order Details"].Columns["OrderID"],
    myDataSet.Tables["Order Details"].Columns["ProductID"]
  },
  true
);
```

One thing to keep in mind when adding constraints to a DataTable is that it knows only about the rows you store in it; it doesn't know about any other rows stored in the actual database table. To see why this is an issue, consider the following scenario that involves primary keys:

1. You add a primary key constraint to a DataTable.

2. You retrieve a *subset* of the rows from a database table and store them in your DataTable.

3. You add a new DataRow to your DataTable with a primary key value not used in the subset of rows retrieved into your DataTable in the previous step—but that primary key value *is* already used in a row in the database table. Your new DataRow is added without any problem to the DataTable even though you added a primary key constraint to your DataTable in step 1. Your new DataRow is added successfully because the DataTable knows *only* about the rows stored in it, *not* the other rows stored in the database table that were not retrieved in step 2.

4. You attempt to push the new DataRow to the database, but you get a SqlException that states you've violated the primary key constraint in the database table. This is because a row in the database table already uses the primary key value.

You need to keep this issue in mind when adding rows to a DataTable, which you'll see how to do shortly.

That wraps up adding the primary key constraints to the DataTable objects. Next, you'll see how to add foreign key constraints.

Adding Foreign Key Constraints to the *Order Details DataTable*

In this section, you'll see how to add a foreign key constraint to the

Order Details DataTable. To do this, you use the Add() method through the Constraints property of the DataTable.

The following example adds a foreign key constraint from the OrderID DataColumn of the Order Details DataTable to the OrderID DataColumn of the Orders DataTable:

```
ForeignKeyConstraint myFKC = new ForeignKeyConstraint(
    myDataSet.Tables["Orders"].Columns["OrderID"],
    myDataSet.Tables["Order Details"].Columns["OrderID"]
);
myDataSet.Tables["Order Details"].Constraints.Add(myFKC);
```

NOTE

Notice that the parent DataColumn (OrderID of Orders) is specified before the child DataColumn (OrderID of Order Details).

The next example adds a foreign key constraint from the ProductID DataColumn of the Order Details DataTable to the ProductID Data-Column of the Products DataTable:

```
myDataSet.Tables["Order Details"].Constraints.Add(
    "Foreign key constraint to ProductID DataColumn of the " +
    "Products DataTable",
    myDataSet.Tables["Order Details"].Columns["ProductID"],
    myDataSet.Tables["Products"].Columns["ProductID"]
);
```

That wraps up adding constraints to the DataTable objects. Next, you'll see how to add restrictions to DataColumn objects.

Adding Restrictions to *DataColumn* Objects

In this section, you'll see how to add restrictions to the DataColumn objects stored in a DataTable. Specifically, you'll see how to set the AllowDBNull, AutoIncrement, AutoIncrementSeed, AutoIncrementStep, ReadOnly, and Unique properties of the ProductID DataColumn of the Products DataTable. You'll also see how to set the MaxLength property of the ProductName DataColumn of the Products DataTable.

The ProductID column of the Products database table is an identity column. The seed is the initial value and the step is the increment added to the last number and they are both set to 1 for ProductID. The ProductID identity values are therefore 1, 2, 3, and so on.

TIP

When you set the AutoIncrementSeed and AutoIncrementStep properties for a DataColumn that corresponds to a database identity column, you should always set them both to −1. That way, when you call the Fill() method, ADO.NET will automatically figure out what values to set the AutoIncrementSeed and AutoIncrementStep to, based on the values retrieved from the database, so you don't have to figure out these values yourself.

The following code sets the properties of the ProductID DataColumn:

```
DataColumn productIDDataColumn =
    myDataSet.Tables["Products"].Columns["ProductID"];
productIDDataColumn.AllowDBNull = false;
productIDDataColumn.AutoIncrement = true;
productIDDataColumn.AutoIncrementSeed = -1;
productIDDataColumn.AutoIncrementStep = -1;
productIDDataColumn.ReadOnly = true;
productIDDataColumn.Unique = true;
```

The next example sets the MaxLength property of the ProductName DataColumn to 40. This stops you from setting the column value for ProductName to a string greater than 40 characters in length:

```
myDataSet.Tables["Products"].
    Columns["ProductName"].MaxLength = 40;
```

Listing 14.1 uses the code examples shown in this section and the previous one. Notice this program also displays the ColumnName and DataType properties of the DataColumn objects in each DataTable. The ColumnName property contains the name of the DataColumn, and the DataType contains the .NET data type used to represent the column value stored in the DataColumn.

Listing 14.1: *AddRestrictions.cs*

```
/*
    AddRestrictions.cs illustrates how to add constraints to
    DataTable objects and add restrictions to
    DataColumn objects
*/

using System;
using System.Data;
using System.Data.SqlClient;
```

```
class AddRestrictions
{
  public static void Main()
  {
    SqlConnection mySqlConnection =
      new SqlConnection(
        "server=localhost;database=Northwind;uid=sa;pwd=sa"
      );

    SqlCommand mySqlCommand =
      mySqlConnection.CreateCommand();
    mySqlCommand.CommandText =
      "SELECT ProductID, ProductName " +
      "FROM Products;" +
      "SELECT OrderID " +
      "FROM Orders;" +
      "SELECT OrderID, ProductID, UnitPrice " +
      "FROM [Order Details];";
    SqlDataAdapter mySqlDataAdapter = new SqlDataAdapter();
    mySqlDataAdapter.SelectCommand = mySqlCommand;
    DataSet myDataSet = new DataSet();
    mySqlConnection.Open();
    mySqlDataAdapter.Fill(myDataSet);
    mySqlConnection.Close();
    myDataSet.Tables["Table"].TableName = "Products";
    myDataSet.Tables["Table1"].TableName = "Orders";
    myDataSet.Tables["Table2"].TableName = "Order Details";

    // set the PrimaryKey property for
    // the Products DataTable
    // to the ProductID column
    DataTable productsDataTable =
      myDataSet.Tables["Products"];
    DataColumn[] productsPrimaryKey =
      new DataColumn[]
      {
        productsDataTable.Columns["ProductID"]
      };
    productsDataTable.PrimaryKey = productsPrimaryKey;

    // set the PrimaryKey property for the Orders DataTable
    // to the OrderID column
```

```
myDataSet.Tables["Orders"].PrimaryKey =
  new DataColumn[]
  {
    myDataSet.Tables["Orders"].Columns["OrderID"]
  };

// set the PrimaryKey property
// for the Order Details DataTable
// to the OrderID and ProductID columns
myDataSet.Tables["Order Details"].Constraints.Add(
  "Primary key constraint on the" +
    "OrderID and ProductID columns",
  new DataColumn[]
  {
    myDataSet.Tables["Order Details"].
      Columns["OrderID"],
    myDataSet.Tables["Order Details"].
      Columns["ProductID"]
  },
  true
);

// add a foreign key constraint on the OrderID column
// of Order Details to the OrderID column of Orders
ForeignKeyConstraint myFKC = new ForeignKeyConstraint(
  myDataSet.Tables["Orders"].Columns["OrderID"],
  myDataSet.Tables["Order Details"].Columns["OrderID"]
);
myDataSet.Tables["Order Details"].
  Constraints.Add(myFKC);

// add a foreign key constraint on the ProductID column
// of Order Details to the ProductID column of Products
myDataSet.Tables["Order Details"].Constraints.Add(
  "Foreign key constraint to ProductID " +
  " DataColumn of the Products DataTable",
  myDataSet.Tables["Products"].Columns["ProductID"],
  myDataSet.Tables["Order Details"].Columns["ProductID"]
);

// set the AllowDBNull, AutoIncrement,
// AutoIncrementSeed, AutoIncrementStep,
// ReadOnly, and Unique properties for
```

```
// the ProductID DataColumn of the Products DataTable
DataColumn productIDDataColumn =
  myDataSet.Tables["Products"].Columns["ProductID"];
productIDDataColumn.AllowDBNull = false;
productIDDataColumn.AutoIncrement = true;
productIDDataColumn.AutoIncrementSeed = -1;
productIDDataColumn.AutoIncrementStep = -1;
productIDDataColumn.ReadOnly = true;
productIDDataColumn.Unique = true;

// set the MaxLength property for
// the ProductName DataColumn
// of the Products DataTable
myDataSet.Tables["Products"].
  Columns["ProductName"].MaxLength = 40;

// display the details of the DataColumn objects for
// the DataTable objects
foreach (DataTable myDataTable in myDataSet.Tables)
{
  Console.WriteLine("\n\nReading from the " +
    myDataTable + " DataTable:\n");

  // display the primary key
  foreach (DataColumn myPrimaryKey
    in myDataTable.PrimaryKey)
  {
    Console.WriteLine("myPrimaryKey = " + myPrimaryKey);
  }

  // display some of the details for each column
  foreach (DataColumn myDataColumn
    in myDataTable.Columns)
  {
    Console.WriteLine("\nmyDataColumn.ColumnName = " +
      myDataColumn.ColumnName);
    Console.WriteLine("myDataColumn.DataType = " +
      myDataColumn.DataType);

    Console.WriteLine("myDataColumn.AllowDBNull = " +
      myDataColumn.AllowDBNull);
    Console.WriteLine("myDataColumn.AutoIncrement = " +
      myDataColumn.AutoIncrement);
```

```
                    Console.WriteLine(
                       "myDataColumn.AutoIncrementSeed = " +
                       myDataColumn.AutoIncrementSeed);
                    Console.WriteLine(
                       "myDataColumn.AutoIncrementStep = " +
                       myDataColumn.AutoIncrementStep);
                    Console.WriteLine("myDataColumn.MaxLength = " +
                       myDataColumn.MaxLength);
                    Console.WriteLine("myDataColumn.ReadOnly = " +
                       myDataColumn.ReadOnly);
                    Console.WriteLine("myDataColumn.Unique = " +
                       myDataColumn.Unique);
                }
            }
        }
    }
```

The output from this program is as follows:

```
Reading from the Products DataTable:

myPrimaryKey = ProductID

myDataColumn.ColumnName = ProductID
myDataColumn.DataType = System.Int32
myDataColumn.AllowDBNull = False
myDataColumn.AutoIncrement = True
myDataColumn.AutoIncrementSeed = -1
myDataColumn.AutoIncrementStep = -1
myDataColumn.MaxLength = -1
myDataColumn.ReadOnly = True
myDataColumn.Unique = True

myDataColumn.ColumnName = ProductName
myDataColumn.DataType = System.String
myDataColumn.AllowDBNull = True
myDataColumn.AutoIncrement = False
myDataColumn.AutoIncrementSeed = 0
myDataColumn.AutoIncrementStep = 1
myDataColumn.MaxLength = 40
myDataColumn.ReadOnly = False
myDataColumn.Unique = False


Reading from the Orders DataTable:

myPrimaryKey = OrderID
```

```
myDataColumn.ColumnName = OrderID
myDataColumn.DataType = System.Int32
myDataColumn.AllowDBNull = False
myDataColumn.AutoIncrement = False
myDataColumn.AutoIncrementSeed = 0
myDataColumn.AutoIncrementStep = 1
myDataColumn.MaxLength = -1
myDataColumn.ReadOnly = False
myDataColumn.Unique = True


Reading from the Order Details DataTable:

myPrimaryKey = OrderID
myPrimaryKey = ProductID

myDataColumn.ColumnName = OrderID
myDataColumn.DataType = System.Int32
myDataColumn.AllowDBNull = False
myDataColumn.AutoIncrement = False
myDataColumn.AutoIncrementSeed = 0
myDataColumn.AutoIncrementStep = 1
myDataColumn.MaxLength = -1
myDataColumn.ReadOnly = False
myDataColumn.Unique = False

myDataColumn.ColumnName = ProductID
myDataColumn.DataType = System.Int32
myDataColumn.AllowDBNull = False
myDataColumn.AutoIncrement = False
myDataColumn.AutoIncrementSeed = 0
myDataColumn.AutoIncrementStep = 1
myDataColumn.MaxLength = -1
myDataColumn.ReadOnly = False
myDataColumn.Unique = False

myDataColumn.ColumnName = UnitPrice
myDataColumn.DataType = System.Decimal
myDataColumn.AllowDBNull = True
myDataColumn.AutoIncrement = False
myDataColumn.AutoIncrementSeed = 0
myDataColumn.AutoIncrementStep = 1
myDataColumn.MaxLength = -1
myDataColumn.ReadOnly = False
myDataColumn.Unique = False
```

Adding Restrictions by Calling the *DataAdapter* Object's *FillSchema()* Method

Instead of adding restrictions yourself, you can add then by calling the FillSchema() method of your DataAdapter. The FillSchema() method does the following:

- ▶ Copies the schema information from the database.

- ▶ Creates DataTable objects in your DataSet if they don't already exist.

- ▶ Adds the constraints to the DataTable objects.

- ▶ Sets the properties of the DataColumn objects appropriately.

The properties of the DataColumn objects set by FillSchema() include the following:

- ▶ The DataColumn name—which is stored in the ColumnName property.

- ▶ The DataColumn .NET data type—which is stored in the DataType property.

- ▶ The maximum length of a variable length data type—which is stored in the MaxLength property.

- ▶ Whether the DataColumn can accept a null value—which is stored in the AllowDBNull property.

- ▶ Whether the DataColumn value must be unique—which is stored in the Unique property.

- ▶ Any auto-increment information—which is stored in the Auto-Increment, AutoIncrementSeed, and AutoIncrementStep properties.

The FillSchema() method will also determine whether the DataColumn is part of a primary key and store that information in the PrimaryKey property of the DataTable.

WARNING

FillSchema() does *not* automatically add ForeignKeyConstraint objects to the DataTable objects, nor does it retrieve the actual rows from the database; it retrieves only the schema information.

The FillSchema() method is overloaded, with the most commonly used version of this method being the following:

```
DataTable[] FillSchema(DataSet myDataSet,
    SchemaType mySchemaType)
```

where *mySchemaType* specifies how you want to handle any existing schema mappings.

You set *mySchemaType* to one of the constants defined in the System.Data.SchemaType enumeration. Table 14.7 shows the constants defined in the SchemaType enumeration.

TABLE 14.7: SchemaType Enumeration Members

CONSTANT	DESCRIPTION
Mapped	Apply any existing table mappings to the incoming schema and configure the DataSet with the transformed schema. This is the constant you should typically use.
Source	Ignore any table mappings and configure the DataSet without any transformations.

Let's take a look at an example that contains a call to the FillSchema() method. Notice the call uses the SchemaType.Mapped constant to apply any existing table mappings:

```
SqlCommand mySqlCommand = mySqlConnection.CreateCommand();
mySqlCommand.CommandText =
    "SELECT ProductID, ProductName " +
    "FROM Products;" +
    "SELECT OrderID " +
    "FROM Orders;" +
    "SELECT OrderID, ProductID, UnitPrice " +
    "FROM [Order Details];";
SqlDataAdapter mySqlDataAdapter = new SqlDataAdapter();
mySqlDataAdapter.SelectCommand = mySqlCommand;
DataSet myDataSet = new DataSet();
mySqlConnection.Open();
mySqlDataAdapter.FillSchema(myDataSet, SchemaType.Mapped);
mySqlConnection.Close();
myDataSet.Tables["Table"].TableName = "Products";
myDataSet.Tables["Table1"].TableName = "Orders";
myDataSet.Tables["Table2"].TableName = "Order Details";
```

The call to FillSchema() copies the schema information from the Products, Orders, and Order Details tables to myDataSet, setting the PrimaryKey property of each DataTable and the properties of the DataColumn objects appropriately.

Listing 14.2 shows the use of the FillSchema() method.

Listing 14.2: *FillSchema.cs*

```
/*
   FillSchema.cs illustrates how to read schema information
   using the FillSchema() method of a DataAdapter object
*/

using System;
using System.Data;
using System.Data.SqlClient;

class FillSchema
{
  public static void Main()
  {
    SqlConnection mySqlConnection =
      new SqlConnection(
        "server=localhost;database=Northwind;uid=sa;pwd=sa"
      );

    SqlCommand mySqlCommand =
      mySqlConnection.CreateCommand();
    mySqlCommand.CommandText =
      "SELECT ProductID, ProductName " +
      "FROM Products;" +
      "SELECT OrderID " +
      "FROM Orders;" +
      "SELECT OrderID, ProductID, UnitPrice " +
      "FROM [Order Details];";
    SqlDataAdapter mySqlDataAdapter = new SqlDataAdapter();
    mySqlDataAdapter.SelectCommand = mySqlCommand;
    DataSet myDataSet = new DataSet();
    mySqlConnection.Open();
    mySqlDataAdapter.FillSchema(myDataSet,
      SchemaType.Mapped);
    mySqlConnection.Close();
```

```
myDataSet.Tables["Table"].TableName = "Products";
myDataSet.Tables["Table1"].TableName = "Orders";
myDataSet.Tables["Table2"].TableName = "Order Details";

// display the details of the DataColumn objects for
// the DataTable objects
foreach (DataTable myDataTable in myDataSet.Tables)
{
  Console.WriteLine("\n\nReading from the " +
    myDataTable + " DataTable:\n");

  // display the primary key
  foreach (DataColumn myPrimaryKey
    in myDataTable.PrimaryKey)
  {
    Console.WriteLine("myPrimaryKey = " + myPrimaryKey);
  }

  // display the constraints
  foreach (Constraint myConstraint in
    myDataTable.Constraints)
  {
    Console.WriteLine(
      "myConstraint.IsPrimaryKey = " +
      ((UniqueConstraint) myConstraint).IsPrimaryKey);
    foreach (DataColumn myDataColumn
      in ((UniqueConstraint) myConstraint).Columns)
    {
      Console.WriteLine(
        "myDataColumn.ColumnName = " +
        myDataColumn.ColumnName);
    }
  }

  // display some of the details for each column
  foreach (DataColumn myDataColumn
    in myDataTable.Columns)
  {
    Console.WriteLine("\nmyDataColumn.ColumnName = " +
      myDataColumn.ColumnName);
    Console.WriteLine("myDataColumn.DataType = " +
      myDataColumn.DataType);
```

```
                    Console.WriteLine("myDataColumn.AllowDBNull = " +
                        myDataColumn.AllowDBNull);
                    Console.WriteLine("myDataColumn.AutoIncrement = " +
                        myDataColumn.AutoIncrement);
                    Console.WriteLine(
                        "myDataColumn.AutoIncrementSeed = " +
                        myDataColumn.AutoIncrementSeed);
                    Console.WriteLine(
                        "myDataColumn.AutoIncrementStep = " +
                        myDataColumn.AutoIncrementStep);
                    Console.WriteLine("myDataColumn.MaxLength = " +
                        myDataColumn.MaxLength);
                    Console.WriteLine("myDataColumn.ReadOnly = " +
                        myDataColumn.ReadOnly);
                    Console.WriteLine("myDataColumn.Unique = " +
                        myDataColumn.Unique);
                }
            }
        }
    }
```

The output from this program is as follows:

```
Reading from the Products DataTable:

myPrimaryKey = ProductID
myConstraint.IsPrimaryKey = True
myDataColumn.ColumnName = ProductID

myDataColumn.ColumnName = ProductID
myDataColumn.DataType = System.Int32
myDataColumn.AllowDBNull = False
myDataColumn.AutoIncrement = True
myDataColumn.AutoIncrementSeed = 0
myDataColumn.AutoIncrementStep = 1
myDataColumn.MaxLength = -1
myDataColumn.ReadOnly = True
myDataColumn.Unique = True

myDataColumn.ColumnName = ProductName
myDataColumn.DataType = System.String
myDataColumn.AllowDBNull = False
myDataColumn.AutoIncrement = False
myDataColumn.AutoIncrementSeed = 0
myDataColumn.AutoIncrementStep = 1
```

```
myDataColumn.MaxLength = 40
myDataColumn.ReadOnly = False
myDataColumn.Unique = False


Reading from the Orders DataTable:

myPrimaryKey = OrderID
myConstraint.IsPrimaryKey = True
myDataColumn.ColumnName = OrderID

myDataColumn.ColumnName = OrderID
myDataColumn.DataType = System.Int32
myDataColumn.AllowDBNull = False
myDataColumn.AutoIncrement = True
myDataColumn.AutoIncrementSeed = 0
myDataColumn.AutoIncrementStep = 1
myDataColumn.MaxLength = -1
myDataColumn.ReadOnly = True
myDataColumn.Unique = True


Reading from the Order Details DataTable:

myPrimaryKey = OrderID
myPrimaryKey = ProductID
myConstraint.IsPrimaryKey = True
myDataColumn.ColumnName = OrderID
myDataColumn.ColumnName = ProductID

myDataColumn.ColumnName = OrderID
myDataColumn.DataType = System.Int32
myDataColumn.AllowDBNull = False
myDataColumn.AutoIncrement = False
myDataColumn.AutoIncrementSeed = 0
myDataColumn.AutoIncrementStep = 1
myDataColumn.MaxLength = -1
myDataColumn.ReadOnly = False
myDataColumn.Unique = False

myDataColumn.ColumnName = ProductID
myDataColumn.DataType = System.Int32
myDataColumn.AllowDBNull = False
myDataColumn.AutoIncrement = False
myDataColumn.AutoIncrementSeed = 0
myDataColumn.AutoIncrementStep = 1
```

```
myDataColumn.MaxLength = -1
myDataColumn.ReadOnly = False
myDataColumn.Unique = False

myDataColumn.ColumnName = UnitPrice
myDataColumn.DataType = System.Decimal
myDataColumn.AllowDBNull = False
myDataColumn.AutoIncrement = False
myDataColumn.AutoIncrementSeed = 0
myDataColumn.AutoIncrementStep = 1
myDataColumn.MaxLength = -1
myDataColumn.ReadOnly = False
myDataColumn.Unique = False
```

FINDING, FILTERING, AND SORTING ROWS IN A *DATATABLE*

Each row in a DataTable is stored in a DataRow object, and in this section, you'll learn how to find, filter, and sort the DataRow objects in a DataTable.

Finding a *DataRow* in a *DataTable*

To find a DataRow in a DataTable, you follow these steps:

1. Retrieve the rows from the database into your DataTable.

2. Set the PrimaryKey property of your DataTable.

3. Call the Find() method of your DataTable, passing the primary key column value of the DataRow you want.

For example, the following code performs steps 1 and 2 in this list, retrieving the top 10 rows from the Products table and setting the PrimaryKey property to the ProductID DataColumn:

```
SqlCommand mySqlCommand = mySqlConnection.CreateCommand();
mySqlCommand.CommandText =
  "SELECT TOP 10 ProductID, ProductName " +
  "FROM Products " +
  "ORDER BY ProductID";
SqlDataAdapter mySqlDataAdapter = new SqlDataAdapter();
mySqlDataAdapter.SelectCommand = mySqlCommand;
DataSet myDataSet = new DataSet();
mySqlConnection.Open();
```

```
mySqlDataAdapter.Fill(myDataSet, "Products");
mySqlConnection.Close();
DataTable productsDataTable = myDataSet.Tables["Products"];
productsDataTable.PrimaryKey =
  new DataColumn[]
  {
    productsDataTable.Columns["ProductID"]
  };
```

Next, the following example performs step 3, calling the Find() method to retrieve the DataRow from productsDataTable that has a ProductID of 3:

```
DataRow productDataRow = productsDataTable.Rows.Find("3");
```

Notice that the Find() method is called through the Rows property of productsDataTable. The Rows property returns an object of the DataRowCollection class.

If the primary key for the database table consists of more than one column, then you can pass an array of objects to the Find() method. For example, the Order Details table's primary key is made up of the OrderID and ProductID columns. Assuming you've already performed steps 1 and 2 and retrieved the rows from the Order Details table into a DataTable object named orderDetailsDataTable, then the following example retrieves the DataRow with an OrderID and ProductID of 10248 and 11, respectively:

```
object[] orderDetails =
  new object[]
  {
    10248,
    11
  };
DataRow orderDetailDataRow =
  orderDetailsDataTable.Rows.Find(orderDetails);
```

Filtering and Sorting *DataRow* Objects in a *DataTable*

To filter and sort the DataRow objects in a DataTable, you use the Select() method of your DataTable. The Select() method is over-loaded as follows:

```
DataRow[] Select()
DataRow[] Select(string filterExpression)
```

```
DataRow[] Select(string filterExpression,
   string sortExpression)
DataRow[] Select(string filterExpression,
   string sortExpression,
   DataViewRowState myDataViewRowState)
```

where

filterExpression   Specifies the rows to select.

sortExpression   Specifies how the selected rows are to be ordered.

myDataViewRowState   Specifies the state of the rows to select. You set *myDataViewRowState* to one of the constants defined in the System.Data.DataViewRowState enumeration. Table 14.8 shows these constants.

TABLE 14.8:   DataViewRowState Enumeration Members

CONSTANT	DESCRIPTION
Added	A new row.
CurrentRows	The current rows, which include Unchanged, Added, and ModifiedCurrent.
Deleted	A deleted row.
ModifiedCurrent	A current row that has been modified.
ModifiedOriginal	The original row before it was modified.
None	Doesn't match any of the rows in the DataTable.
OriginalRows	The original rows, which include Unchanged and Deleted.
Unchanged	A row that hasn't been changed.

Let's take a look at some examples that use the Select() method.

The following example calls the Select() method with no parameters, which returns all rows in the DataTable without any filtering or sorting:

```
DataRow[] productDataRows = productsDataTable.Select();
```

The next example supplies a filter expression to Sort(), which returns only the DataRow objects with ProductID DataColumn values that are less than or equal to 5:

```
DataRow[] productDataRows =
   productsDataTable.Select("ProductID <= 5");
```

The following example supplies both a filter expression and a sort expression that orders the `DataRow` objects by descending `ProductID` values:

```
DataRow[] productDataRows =
    productsDataTable.Select("ProductID <= 5", "ProductID DESC");
```

The next example supplies a `DataViewRowState` of `OriginalRows` to the previous `Select()` call:

```
DataRow[] productDataRows =
    productsDataTable.Select("ProductID <= 5",
    "ProductID DESC",
    DataViewRowState.OriginalRows);
```

As you can see from the previous examples, the filter and sort expressions are similar to `WHERE` and `ORDER BY` clauses in a `SELECT` statement. You can therefore use very powerful expressions in your calls to the `Sort()` method. For example, you can use `AND`, `OR`, `NOT`, `IN`, `LIKE`, comparison operators, arithmetic operators, wildcard characters, and aggregate functions in your filter expressions.

NOTE

For full details on how to use such filter expressions, refer to the `DataColumn` `.Expression` property in the .NET online documentation.

The following example uses the `LIKE` operator and the percent wildcard character (%)—which matches any number of characters—to filter rows with a `ProductName` that start with Cha. The example also sorts the rows by descending `ProductID` and ascending `ProductName` values:

```
productDataRows =
    productsDataTable.Select("ProductName LIKE 'Cha%'",
        "ProductID DESC, ProductName ASC");
```

Notice that the string Cha% is placed in single quotes, which you must do for all string literals.

NOTE

You can also use a `DataView` object to filter and sort rows. See Chapter 12, "ADO.NET Application Development," for more information on the `DataView`.

Listing 14.3 shows a program that finds, filters, and sorts `DataRow` objects.

Listing 14.3: *FindFilterAndSortDataRows.cs*

```
/*
  FindFilterAndSortDataRows.cs illustrates how
  to find, filter, and sort DataRow objects
*/

using System;
using System.Data;
using System.Data.SqlClient;

class FindFilterAndSortDataRows
{
  public static void Main()
  {
    SqlConnection mySqlConnection =
      new SqlConnection(
        "server=localhost;database=Northwind;uid=sa;pwd=sa"
      );

    SqlCommand mySqlCommand =
      mySqlConnection.CreateCommand();
    mySqlCommand.CommandText =
      "SELECT TOP 10 ProductID, ProductName " +
      "FROM Products " +
      "ORDER BY ProductID;" +
      "SELECT TOP 10 OrderID, ProductID, UnitPrice, " +
      " Quantity FROM [Order Details] " +
      "ORDER BY OrderID";
    SqlDataAdapter mySqlDataAdapter = new SqlDataAdapter();
    mySqlDataAdapter.SelectCommand = mySqlCommand;
    DataSet myDataSet = new DataSet();
    mySqlConnection.Open();
    mySqlDataAdapter.Fill(myDataSet);
    mySqlConnection.Close();
    myDataSet.Tables["Table"].TableName = "Products";
    myDataSet.Tables["Table1"].TableName = "Order Details";

    // set the PrimaryKey property for the
    // Products DataTable to the ProductID column
    DataTable productsDataTable =
      myDataSet.Tables["Products"];
```

```csharp
productsDataTable.PrimaryKey =
  new DataColumn[]
  {
    productsDataTable.Columns["ProductID"]
  };

// set the PrimaryKey property for the
// Order Details DataTable
// to the OrderID and ProductID columns
DataTable orderDetailsDataTable =
  myDataSet.Tables["Order Details"];
orderDetailsDataTable.Constraints.Add(
  "Primary key constraint on the OrderID" +
  "and ProductID columns",
  new DataColumn[]
  {
    orderDetailsDataTable.Columns["OrderID"],
    orderDetailsDataTable.Columns["ProductID"]
  },
  true
);

// find product with ProductID of 3 using
// the Find() method to locate the DataRow
// using its primary key value
Console.WriteLine(
  "Using the Find() method to locate DataRow object " +
  "with a ProductID of 3");
DataRow productDataRow =
  productsDataTable.Rows.Find("3");
foreach (DataColumn myDataColumn in
  productsDataTable.Columns)
{
  Console.WriteLine(
    myDataColumn + " = " +
    productDataRow[myDataColumn]);
}

// find order with OrderID of 10248 and
// ProductID of 11 using the Find() method
Console.WriteLine(
  "Using the Find() method to locate DataRow object " +
  "with an OrderID of 10248 and a ProductID of 11");
```

```
object[] orderDetails =
  new object[]
  {
    10248,
    11
  };
DataRow orderDetailDataRow =
  orderDetailsDataTable.Rows.Find(orderDetails);
foreach (DataColumn myDataColumn in
  orderDetailsDataTable.Columns)
{
  Console.WriteLine(
    myDataColumn + " = " +
    orderDetailDataRow[myDataColumn]);
}

// filter and sort the DataRow objects
// in productsDataTable
// using the Select() method
Console.WriteLine(
"Using the Select() method to filter " +
"and sort DataRow objects");
DataRow[] productDataRows =
  productsDataTable.Select(
  "ProductID <= 5", "ProductID DESC",
  DataViewRowState.OriginalRows);
foreach (DataRow myDataRow in productDataRows)
{
  foreach (DataColumn myDataColumn in
    productsDataTable.Columns)
  {
    Console.WriteLine(
      myDataColumn + " = " + myDataRow[myDataColumn]);
  }
}

// filter and sort the DataRow objects
// in productsDataTable
// using the Select() method
Console.WriteLine(
  "Using the Select() method to filter " +
  "and sort DataRow objects");
```

```
        productDataRows =
          productsDataTable.Select("ProductName LIKE 'Cha*'",
            "ProductID ASC, ProductName DESC");
        foreach (DataRow myDataRow in productDataRows)
        {
          foreach (DataColumn myDataColumn in
            productsDataTable.Columns)
          {
            Console.WriteLine(myDataColumn + " = " +
              myDataRow[myDataColumn]);
          }
        }
      }
    }
}
```

The output from this program is as follows:

```
Using the Find() method to locate DataRow object
  with a ProductID of 3
ProductID = 3
ProductName = Aniseed Syrup
Using the Find() method to locate DataRow object
  with an OrderID of 10248 and a
ProductID of 11
OrderID = 10248
ProductID = 11
UnitPrice = 14
Quantity = 12
Using the Select() method to filter and sort DataRow objects
ProductID = 5
ProductName = Chef Anton's Gumbo Mix
ProductID = 4
ProductName = Chef Anton's Cajun Seasoning
ProductID = 3
ProductName = Aniseed Syrup
ProductID = 2
ProductName = Chang
ProductID = 1
ProductName = Chai
Using the Select() method to filter and sort DataRow objects
ProductID = 1
ProductName = Chai
ProductID = 2
ProductName = Chang
```

MODIFYING ROWS IN A *DATATABLE*

In this section, you'll see the steps required to add, modify, and remove DataRow objects from a DataTable and then push those changes to the database. The examples in this section show how to add, modify, and delete rows in the Customers database table.

NOTE

You'll find a complete program named AddModifyAndRemoveDataRows.cs in the ch11 directory of the source code for this book, available at www.sybex.com. This program illustrates the use of the methods shown in this section. This program listing is omitted from this book for brevity.

Setting Up a *DataAdapter* to Push Changes to the Database

In Chapter 13, you saw that before you call the Fill() method of your DataAdapter to read rows from the database, you first need to set the SelectCommand property of your DataAdapter. For example,

```
SqlCommand mySelectCommand -
    mySqlConnection.CreateCommand();
mySelectCommand.CommandText =
    "SELECT CustomerID, CompanyName, Address " +
    "FROM Customers " +
    "ORDER BY CustomerID";
SqlDataAdapter mySqlDataAdapter = new SqlDataAdapter();
mySqlDataAdapter.SelectCommand = mySelectCommand;
```

The SELECT statement is then run when you call the mySqlDataAdapter object's Fill() method to retrieve rows from the Customers table into a DataSet.

Similarly, before you can push changes to the database, you must first set up your DataAdapter with Command objects containing appropriate SQL INSERT, UPDATE, and DELETE statements. You store these Command objects in your DataAdapter object's InsertCommand, UpdateCommand, and DeleteCommand properties.

You push changes from your DataSet to the database using the Update() method of your DataAdapter. When you add, modify, or remove DataRow objects from your DataSet and then call the Update() method of your DataAdapter, the appropriate InsertCommand, UpdateCommand, or DeleteCommand is run to push your changes to the database.

Let's take a look at how to set the InsertCommand, UpdateCommand, and DeleteCommand properties of a DataAdapter.

Setting the *InsertCommand* Property of a *DataAdapter*

The following example creates a SqlCommand object named myInsert-Command that contains an INSERT statement:

```
SqlCommand myInsertCommand =
  mySqlConnection.CreateCommand();
myInsertCommand.CommandText =
  "INSERT INTO Customers (" +
  "  CustomerID, CompanyName, Address" +
  ") VALUES (" +
  "  @CustomerID, @CompanyName, @Address" +
  ")";
myInsertCommand.Parameters.Add(
  "@CustomerID", SqlDbType.NChar,
  5, "CustomerID");
myInsertCommand.Parameters.Add(
  "@CompanyName", SqlDbType.NVarChar,
  40, "CompanyName");
myInsertCommand.Parameters.Add(
  "@Address", SqlDbType.NVarChar,
  60, "Address");
```

The four parameters to the Add() method are as follows:

▶ The name of the parameter

▶ The .NET type of the parameter

▶ The maximum length of the string that may be assigned to the parameter's value

▶ The name of the corresponding database column that the parameter is bound to

NOTE
Commands and parameters are covered in Chapter 12.

As you can see from the previous code, the @CustomerID, @Company-Name, and @Address parameters are bound to the CustomerID, CompanyName, and Address columns in the database.

Next, the following example sets the InsertCommand property of mySqlDataAdapter to myInsertCommand:

```
mySqlDataAdapter.InsertCommand = myInsertCommand;
```

Setting the *UpdateCommand* Property of a *DataAdapter*

The following example creates a SqlCommand object named myUpdate-Command that contains an UPDATE statement and sets the UpdateCommand property of mySqlDataAdapter to myUpdateCommand:

```
myUpdateCommand.CommandText =
  "UPDATE Customers " +
  "SET " +
  "  CompanyName = @NewCompanyName, " +
  "  Address = @NewAddress " +
  "WHERE CustomerID = @OldCustomerID " +
  "AND CompanyName = @OldCompanyName " +
  "AND Address = @OldAddress";
myUpdateCommand.Parameters.Add(
  "@NewCompanyName", SqlDbType.NVarChar,
  40, "CompanyName");
myUpdateCommand.Parameters.Add(
  "@NewAddress", SqlDbType.NVarChar,
  60, "Address");
myUpdateCommand.Parameters.Add(
  "@OldCustomerID", SqlDbType.NChar,
  5, "CustomerID");
myUpdateCommand.Parameters.Add(
  "@OldCompanyName", SqlDbType.NVarChar,
  40, "CompanyName");
myUpdateCommand.Parameters.Add(
  "@OldAddress", SqlDbType.NVarChar,
  60, "Address");
myUpdateCommand.Parameters["@OldCustomerID"].SourceVersion =
  DataRowVersion.Original;
myUpdateCommand.Parameters[
  "@OldCompanyName"].SourceVersion =
  DataRowVersion.Original;
myUpdateCommand.Parameters["@OldAddress"].SourceVersion =
  DataRowVersion.Original;
mySqlDataAdapter.UpdateCommand = myUpdateCommand;
```

There are two things to notice about this code:

▶ The UPDATE statement's WHERE clause specifies parameters for CompanyID, CompanyName, and Address columns. This uses optimistic concurrency, which you'll learn about shortly.

▶ A property named SourceVersion for the @OldCustomerID, @OldCompanyName and @OldAddress parameters is set to DataRowVersion.Original. This causes the values for these parameters to be set to the original DataRow column values before you change them.

These items determine the concurrency of the UPDATE, which you'll now learn about.

Concurrency   *Concurrency* determines how multiple users' modifications to the same row are handled. There are two types of concurrency that apply to a DataSet:

Optimistic Currency   With *optimistic concurrency,* you can modify a row in a database table only if no one else has modified that same row since you loaded it into your DataSet. This is typically the best type of concurrency to use because you don't want to overwrite someone else's changes.

"Last One Wins" Concurrency   With *"last one wins"* concurrency, you can always modify a row—and your changes overwrite anyone else's changes. You typically want to avoid using "last one wins" concurrency.

To use optimistic currency, you have to do the following in your UPDATE or DELETE statement's WHERE clause:

1. Include all the columns used in the original SELECT.

2. Set these column values to original values retrieved from the row in the table before you changed the values.

When you do these two things in your UPDATE or DELETE statement's WHERE clause, your statement first checks that the original row still exists before updating or deleting the row. That way, you can be sure your changes don't overwrite anyone else's changes. Of course, if the original row has been deleted by another user, then your UPDATE or DELETE statement will fail.

To use "last one wins" concurrency, you just include the primary key and its value in the WHERE clause of your UPDATE or DELETE statement.

Since your UPDATE statement doesn't check the original values, it simply overwrites anyone else's changes if the row still exists. Also, a DELETE statement simply deletes the row—even if another user has modified the row.

If you return to the previous code example that set the UpdateCommand property of mySqlDataAdapter, you can see that all the columns are included in the WHERE clause of the UPDATE. That satisfies the first requirement of using optimistic concurrency shown earlier.

The second requirement is that you set the column in the WHERE clause to the original row values. You do this by setting the SourceVersion property of the @OldCustomerID, @OldCompanyName, and @OldAddress parameters to DataRowVersion.Original. At runtime, this pulls the original values from the DataColumn objects in the DataRow before you changed them and puts them in the UPDATE statement's WHERE clause.

Original is just one of the members of the System.Data.DataRowVersion enumeration; the others are shown in Table 14.9.

TABLE 14.9: DataRowVersion Enumeration Members

CONSTANT	DESCRIPTION
Current	The current column value
Default	The default column value
Original	The original column value
Proposed	The proposed column value, which is set when you edit a DataRow using the BeginEdit() method

Setting the *DeleteCommand* Property of a *DataAdapter*

The following example creates a SqlCommand object named myDeleteCommand that contains a DELETE statement and sets the DeleteCommand property of mySqlDataAdapter to myDeleteCommand:

```
SqlCommand myDeleteCommand =
  mySqlConnection.CreateCommand();
myDeleteCommand.CommandText =
  "DELETE FROM Customers " +
```

```
    "WHERE CustomerID = @OldCustomerID " +
    "AND CompanyName = @OldCompanyName " +
    "AND Address = @OldAddress";
myDeleteCommand.Parameters.Add(
    "@OldCustomerID", SqlDbType.NChar,
    5, "CustomerID");
myDeleteCommand.Parameters.Add(
    "@OldCompanyName", SqlDbType.NVarChar,
    40, "CompanyName");
myDeleteCommand.Parameters.Add(
    "@OldAddress", SqlDbType.NVarChar,
    60, "Address");
myDeleteCommand.Parameters["@OldCustomerID"].SourceVersion =
    DataRowVersion.Original;
myDeleteCommand.Parameters[
    "@OldCompanyName"].SourceVersion =
    DataRowVersion.Original;
myDeleteCommand.Parameters["@OldAddress"].SourceVersion =
    DataRowVersion.Original;
mySqlDataAdapter.DeleteCommand = myDeleteCommand;
```

Notice that the DELETE statement also uses optimistic concurrency.

This completes the setup of the DataAdapter object.

Adding a *DataRow* to a *DataTable*

In this section, you'll learn how to add a DataRow to a DataTable. Before you see this, let's populate a DataSet with the rows from the Customers table. The following code creates a DataSet object named myDataSet and populates it by calling mySqlDataAdapter.Fill():

```
DataSet myDataSet = new DataSet();
mySqlConnection.Open();
int numOfRows =
    mySqlDataAdapter.Fill(myDataSet, "Customers");
mySqlConnection.Close();
```

The int returned by the Fill() method is the number of rows retrieved from the database. The myDataSet object now contains a DataTable named Customers, which contains the rows retrieved by the following SELECT statement set earlier in the SelectCommand property of mySqlDataAdapter:

```
SELECT CustomerID, CompanyName, Address
FROM Customers
ORDER BY CustomerID
```

To add a new row to a DataTable object, you use the following steps:

1. Use the NewRow() method of your DataTable to create a new DataRow.

2. Set the values for the DataColumn objects of your new DataRow. Note that you can set a DataColumn value to null using the SetNull() method of a DataRow. You can also check if a DataColumn contains null using the IsNull() method of a DataRow.

3. Use the Add() method through the Rows property of your DataTable to add your new DataRow to the DataTable.

4. Use the Update() method of your DataAdapter to push the new row to the database.

The following method, named AddDataRow(), uses these steps to add a new row to a DataTable:

```
public static void AddDataRow(
  DataTable myDataTable,
  SqlDataAdapter mySqlDataAdapter,
  SqlConnection mySqlConnection
)
{
  Console.WriteLine("\nIn AddDataRow()");

  // step 1: use the NewRow() method of the DataTable to
  // create a new DataRow
  Console.WriteLine("Calling myDataTable.NewRow()");
  DataRow myNewDataRow = myDataTable.NewRow();
  Console.WriteLine("myNewDataRow.RowState = " +
    myNewDataRow.RowState);

  // step 2: set the values for the DataColumn objects of
  // the new DataRow
  myNewDataRow["CustomerID"] = "J5COM";
  myNewDataRow["CompanyName"] = "J5 Company";
  myNewDataRow["Address"] = "1 Main Street";

  // step 3: use the Add() method through the Rows property
  // to add the new DataRow to the DataTable
  Console.WriteLine("Calling myDataTable.Rows.Add()");
  myDataTable.Rows.Add(myNewDataRow);
  Console.WriteLine("myNewDataRow.RowState = " +
    myNewDataRow.RowState);
```

```
// step 4: use the Update() method to push the new
// row to the database
Console.WriteLine("Calling mySqlDataAdapter.Update()");
mySqlConnection.Open();
int numOfRows = mySqlDataAdapter.Update(myDataTable);
mySqlConnection.Close();
Console.WriteLine("numOfRows = " + numOfRows);
Console.WriteLine("myNewDataRow.RowState = " +
  myNewDataRow.RowState);

DisplayDataRow(myNewDataRow, myDataTable);
}
```

You'll notice I call the Open() and Close() methods of mySql-
Connection around the call to the Update() method. You don't have to
do this because the Update() method—like the Fill() method—will
automatically open and then close mySqlConnection if it is currently
closed. It is good programming practice, however, to explicitly include the
Open() and Close() calls so that you can see exactly what is going on.

NOTE

In the ADO.NET disconnected model of data access, you should typically keep
the connection to the database open for as short a period as possible. Of
course, if you're making a lot of calls to the Update() or the Fill() method
over a short time, you could keep the connection open and then close it when
you're finished. That way, your code will perform better. You might need to
experiment with your own programs to find the right balance.

The Update() method is overloaded as follows:

```
int Update(DataRow[] myDataRows)
int Update(DataSet myDataSet)
int Update(DataTable myDataTable)
int Update(DataRow[] myDataRows,
  DataTableMapping myDataTableMapping)
int Update(DataSet myDataSet, string dataTableName)
```

where *dataTableName* is a string containing the name of the DataTable
to update. The int returned by the Update() method is the number of
rows successfully updated in the database.

Going back to the previous AddDataRow() method, you'll also notice
the inclusion of Console.WriteLine() calls that display the RowState
property of myNewDataRow. The RowState property is set to one of

the constants defined in the System.Data.DataViewRowState enumeration. Table 14.10 shows the constants defined in the DataRowState enumeration.

TABLE 14.10:   DataRowState Enumeration Members

CONSTANT	DESCRIPTION
Added	The DataRow has been added to the DataRowCollection of the DataTable.
Deleted	The DataRow has been removed from the DataTable.
Detached	The DataRow isn't part of the DataTable.
Modified	The DataRow has been modified.
Unchanged	The DataRow hasn't been modified.

AddDataRow() calls a method named DisplayDataRow(), which displays the DataColumn values for the DataRow passed as the first parameter. DisplayDataRow() is defined as follows:

```
public static void DisplayDataRow(
  DataRow myDataRow,
  DataTable myDataTable)
{
  Console.WriteLine("\nIn DisplayDataRow()");
  foreach (DataColumn myDataColumn in myDataTable.Columns)
  {
    Console.WriteLine(myDataColumn + " = " +
      myDataRow[myDataColumn]);
  }
}
```

In the previous AddDataRow() method, you saw that it displays the RowState property of myNewDataRow at various points. The output from AddDataRow() and its call to DisplayDataRow() is as follows:

```
In AddDataRow()
Calling myDataTable.NewRow()
myNewDataRow.RowState = Detached
Calling myDataTable.Rows.Add()
myNewDataRow.RowState = Added
Calling mySqlDataAdapter.Update()
numOfRows = 1
myNewDataRow.RowState = Unchanged
```

```
In DisplayDataRow()
CustomerID = J5COM
CompanyName = J5 Company
Address = 1 Main Street
```

Let's examine this run in detail:

▶ After myDataTable.NewRow() is called to create myNewDataRow, its RowState is Detached, which indicates myNewDataRow isn't yet part of myDataTable.

▶ Next, myDataTable.Rows.Add() is called to add myNewDataRow to myDataTable. This causes the RowState of myNewDataRow to change to Added, which indicates myNewDataRow is now part of myDataTable.

▶ Finally, mySqlDataAdapter.Update() is called to push the new row to the database. This causes the RowState of myNewDataRow to change to Unchanged.

Behind the scenes, the Update() method runs the INSERT statement in the mySqlDataAdapter.InsertCommand property to add the new row to the Customers table. The int returned by the Update() statement is the number of rows affected by the method call. In this example, one is returned since one row was added.

Modifying a *DataRow* in a *DataTable*

To modify a DataRow in a DataTable, you use the following steps:

1. Set the PrimaryKey property of your DataTable. You need to set this to find the DataRow in the next step.

2. Use the Find() method to locate the DataRow that you want to modify in your DataTable. You locate the DataRow using the value of its primary key column.

3. Change the DataColumn values for your DataRow.

4. Use the Update() method of your DataAdapter object to push the modified row to the database.

The following method, named ModifyDataRow(), uses these steps to modify the row that was previously added by the AddDataRow() method:

```
public static void ModifyDataRow(
  DataTable myDataTable,
```

```
    SqlDataAdapter mySqlDataAdapter,
    SqlConnection mySqlConnection
  )
  {
    Console.WriteLine("\nIn ModifyDataRow()");

    // step 1: set the PrimaryKey property of the DataTable
    myDataTable.PrimaryKey =
      new DataColumn[]
      {
        myDataTable.Columns["CustomerID"]
      };

    // step 2: use the Find() method to locate the DataRow
    // in the DataTable using the primary key value
    DataRow myEditDataRow = myDataTable.Rows.Find("J5COM");

    // step 3: change the DataColumn values of the DataRow
    myEditDataRow["CompanyName"] = "Widgets Inc.";
    myEditDataRow["Address"] = "1 Any Street";
    Console.WriteLine("myEditDataRow.RowState = " +
      myEditDataRow.RowState);
    Console.WriteLine("myEditDataRow[\"CustomerID\", " +
      "DataRowVersion.Original] = " +
      myEditDataRow["CustomerID", DataRowVersion.Original]);
    Console.WriteLine("myEditDataRow[\"CompanyName\", " +
      "DataRowVersion.Original] = " +
      myEditDataRow["CompanyName", DataRowVersion.Original]);
    Console.WriteLine("myEditDataRow[\"Address\", " +
      "DataRowVersion.Original] = " +
      myEditDataRow["Address", DataRowVersion.Original]);
    Console.WriteLine("myEditDataRow[\"CompanyName\", " +
      "DataRowVersion.Current] = " +
      myEditDataRow["CompanyName", DataRowVersion.Current]);
    Console.WriteLine("myEditDataRow[\"Address\", " +
      "DataRowVersion.Current] = " +
      myEditDataRow["Address", DataRowVersion.Current]);

    // step 4: use the Update() method to push the modified
    // row to the database
    Console.WriteLine("Calling mySqlDataAdapter.Update()");
    mySqlConnection.Open();
    int numOfRows = mySqlDataAdapter.Update(myDataTable);
    mySqlConnection.Close();
    Console.WriteLine("numOfRows = " + numOfRows);
```

```
    Console.WriteLine("myEditDataRow.RowState = " +
      myEditDataRow.RowState);

    DisplayDataRow(myEditDataRow, myDataTable);
  }
```

Setting the primary key in step 1 doesn't have to be done inside the ModifyDataRow() method. You could, for example, set the primary key immediately after calling the Fill() method in the Main() method of the AddModifyAndRemoveDataRows.cs program. The reason I set the primary key in ModifyDataRow() is that you can see all the steps together in this method.

In step 3 of this method, notice that the original values for the CustomerID, CompanyName, and Address DataColumn objects are displayed using the DataRowVersion.Original constant. These are the DataColumn values before they are changed. The current values for the CompanyName and Address DataColumn objects are also displayed using the DataRowVersion.Current constant. These are the DataColumn values after they are changed.

The output from ModifyDataRow() and its call to DisplayDataRow() is as follows:

```
In ModifyDataRow()
myEditDataRow.RowState = Modified
myEditDataRow["CustomerID", DataRowVersion.Original] = J5COM
myEditDataRow["CompanyName",
  DataRowVersion.Original] = J5 Company
myEditDataRow["Address",
  DataRowVersion.Original] = 1 Main Street
myEditDataRow["CompanyName",
  DataRowVersion.Current] = Widgets Inc.
myEditDataRow["Address",
  DataRowVersion.Current] = 1 Any Street
Calling mySqlDataAdapter.Update()
numOfRows = 1
myEditDataRow.RowState = Unchanged

In DisplayDataRow()
CustomerID = J5COM
CompanyName = Widgets Inc.
Address = 1 Any Street
```

Notice that the CompanyName and Address DataColumn objects of myEditDataRow are changed. The RowState property of myEditDataRow changes to Modified after its CompanyName and Address are changed, and then to Unchanged after mySqlDataAdapter.Update() is called.

Marking Your Modifications

You can use the BeginEdit() method to mark the beginning of a modification to a DataRow. For example,

```
myEditDataRow.BeginEdit();
myEditDataRow["CompanyName"] = "Widgets Inc.";
myEditDataRow["Address"] = "1 Any Street";
```

You then use either the EndEdit() or CancelEdit() methods to mark the end of the modification to the DataRow. EndEdit() commits the modification; CancelEdit() rejects the modification and restores the DataRow to its original state before the edit began.

The following example calls the EndEdit() method of myEditDataRow to commit the changes made in the previous example:

```
myEditDataRow.EndEdit();
```

Removing a *DataRow* from a *DataTable*

To remove a DataRow from a DataTable, you use the following steps:

1. Set the PrimaryKey property for your DataTable object.

2. Use the Find() method to locate your DataRow.

3. Use the Delete() method to remove your DataRow.

4. Use the Update() method to push the delete to the database.

The following method, named RemoveDataRow(), uses these steps to remove the DataRow that was previously modified by the ModifyDataRow() method:

```
public static void RemoveDataRow(
  DataTable myDataTable,
  SqlDataAdapter mySqlDataAdapter,
  SqlConnection mySqlConnection
)
{
  Console.WriteLine("\nIn RemoveDataRow()");

  // step 1: set the PrimaryKey property of the DataTable
  myDataTable.PrimaryKey =
    new DataColumn[]
```

```
      {
        myDataTable.Columns["CustomerID"]
      };

      // step 2: use the Find() method to locate the DataRow
      DataRow myRemoveDataRow = myDataTable.Rows.Find("J5COM");

      // step 3: use the Delete() method to remove the DataRow
      Console.WriteLine("Calling myRemoveDataRow.Delete()");
      myRemoveDataRow.Delete();
      Console.WriteLine("myRemoveDataRow.RowState = " +
        myRemoveDataRow.RowState);

      // step 4: use the Update() method to remove the deleted
      // row from the database
      Console.WriteLine("Calling mySqlDataAdapter.Update()");
      mySqlConnection.Open();
      int numOfRows = mySqlDataAdapter.Update(myDataTable);
      mySqlConnection.Close();
      Console.WriteLine("numOfRows = " + numOfRows);
      Console.WriteLine("myRemoveDataRow.RowState = " +
        myRemoveDataRow.RowState);
    }
```

The output from RemoveDataRow() is as follows:

```
In RemoveDataRow()
Calling myRemoveDataRow.Delete()
myRemoveDataRow.RowState = Deleted
Calling mySqlDataAdapter.Update()
numOfRows = 1
myRemoveDataRow.RowState = Detached
```

Notice that the RowState property of myRemoveDataRow is set to
Deleted after myRemoveData.Delete() is called, and then to Detached
after mySqlDataAdapter.Update() is called—meaning that myRemove-
DataRow is no longer part of the DataTable.

NOTE

Within the source files for this book, available at www.sybex.com, you'll find a
complete program named AddModifyAndRemoveDataRows.cs in the ch11
directory that illustrates the use of the AddDataRow(), ModifyDataRow(),
and RemoveDataRow() methods. This program listing is omitted from this book
for brevity.

RETRIEVING NEW IDENTITY COLUMN VALUES

The ProductID column of the Products table is an identity column. In this section, you'll see how to insert a new row into a Products table and retrieve the new value generated by the database for the ProductID identity column.

NOTE

Within the source files for this book, available at www.sybex.com, you'll find a complete program named UsingIdentityColumn.cs in the ch11 directory that illustrates the use of the methods shown in this section. This program listing is omitted from this book for brevity.

In the examples, assume you have a DataTable named products-DataTable that is populated with the rows retrieved by the following SELECT statement:

```
SELECT
    ProductID, ProductName, UnitPrice
FROM Products
ORDER BY ProductID
```

The following example sets the PrimaryKey property of products-DataTable:

```
productsDataTable.PrimaryKey =
    new DataColumn[]
    {
        productsDataTable.Columns["ProductID"]
    };
```

The next example sets the AllowDBNull, AutoIncrement, Auto-IncrementSeed, AutoIncrementStep, ReadOnly, and Unique properties for the ProductID DataColumn of productsDataTable:

```
DataColumn productIDDataColumn =
    productsDataTable.Columns["ProductID"];
productIDDataColumn.AllowDBNull = false;
productIDDataColumn.AutoIncrement = true;
productIDDataColumn.AutoIncrementSeed = -1;
productIDDataColumn.AutoIncrementStep = -1;
productIDDataColumn.ReadOnly = true;
productIDDataColumn.Unique = true;
```

Because of these settings, when you add a new DataRow to
productsDataTable, the ProductID DataColumn of your new DataRow
will initially have the value −1.

As in the earlier section, "Modifying Rows in a DataTable," you need
to set your DataAdapter object's InsertCommand, UpdateCommand, and
DeleteCommand properties with appropriate Command objects. The
CommandText property of the Command object used in the UpdateCommand
property is as follows:

```
myUpdateCommand.CommandText =
  "UPDATE Products " +
  "SET " +
  "  ProductName = @NewProductName, " +
  "  UnitPrice = @NewUnitPrice " +
  "WHERE ProductID = @OldProductID " +
  "AND ProductName = @OldProductName " +
  "AND UnitPrice = @OldUnitPrice";
```

The CommandText property of the Command object used in the
DeleteCommand property is as follows:

```
myDeleteCommand.CommandText =
  "DELETE FROM Products " +
  "WHERE ProductID = @OldProductID " +
  "AND ProductName = @OldProductName " +
  "AND UnitPrice = @OldUnitPrice";
```

Notice the CommandText of these two Command objects aren't substantially different from those shown in the previous section, except that
they go against the Products table rather than the Customers table.

The real difference is in the CommandText of the Command object used
in the InsertCommand property, which must retrieve the ProductID
value generated by the database for the new row. To do this, you can use
the following code that contains an INSERT statement that adds a new
row, along with a SELECT statement that retrieves the ProductID value
using a call to the SQL Server SCOPE_IDENTITY() function:

```
myInsertCommand.CommandText =
  "INSERT INTO Products (" +
  "  ProductName, UnitPrice " +
  ") VALUES (" +
  "  @MyProductName, @MyUnitPrice" +
  ");" +
  "SELECT @MyProductID = SCOPE_IDENTITY();";
myInsertCommand.Parameters.Add(
  "@MyProductName", SqlDbType.NVarChar, 40, "ProductName");
```

```
myInsertCommand.Parameters.Add(
  "@MyUnitPrice", SqlDbType.Money, 0, "UnitPrice");
myInsertCommand.Parameters.Add(
  "@MyProductID", SqlDbType.Int,
  0, "ProductID");
myInsertCommand.Parameters["@MyProductID"].Direction =
  ParameterDirection.Output;
```

The SCOPE_IDENTITY() function returns the last inserted identity value into any table performed within the current database session *and* stored procedure, trigger, function, or batch. For example, calling SCOPE_IDENTITY() in the previous example returns the last identity value inserted into the Products table, which is the ProductID of the new row.

NOTE

For details on the SCOPE_IDENTITY() function, refer to SQL Server Books Online.

When you add a new DataRow to productsDataTable, the ProductID DataColumn of your new DataRow will initially have the value −1. When you call the Update() method of your SqlDataAdapter to push the new row to the database, the following steps occur:

1. Your new DataRow is pushed to the database using the INSERT statement set in myInsertCommand, with the ProductID column of the Products table being set to a new identity value generated by the database.

2. The ProductID identity value is retrieved by the SELECT statement set in myInsertCommand.

3. The ProductID DataColumn in your DataRow is set to the retrieved identity value.

Feel free to examine, compile, and run the UsingIdentityColumn.cs program located in the ch11 directory. This program performs the following high-level actions:

1. Retrieves rows from the Products table into a DataTable named productsDataTable.

2. Adds a DataRow to productsDataTable.

3. Modifies the new DataRow.

4. Deletes the new DataRow.

When you run this program you'll notice the change in the `ProductID` `DataColumn` value for a newly added `DataRow` from −1 to an actual value retrieved from the database.

USING STORED PROCEDURES TO ADD, MODIFY, AND REMOVE ROWS FROM THE DATABASE

You can get a `DataAdapter` object to call stored procedures to add, modify, and remove rows from the database. These procedures are called instead of the `INSERT`, `UPDATE`, and `DELETE` statements you've seen how to set in a `DataAdapter` object's `InsertCommand`, `UpdateCommand`, and `DeleteCommand` properties.

The ability to call stored procedures using a `DataAdapter` is a very powerful addition to ADO.NET. For example, you can use a stored procedure to add a row to a table containing an identity column, and then retrieve the new value for that column generated by the database. You can also do additional work in a stored procedure such as inserting a row into an audit table when a row is modified. You'll see examples of both these scenarios in this section.

TIP

Using stored procedures instead of `INSERT`, `UPDATE`, and `DELETE` statements can also improve performance. You should use stored procedures if your database supports them. SQL Server and Oracle support stored procedures. Oracle stored procedures are written in PL/SQL.

In this section, you'll see how to

▶ Create the required stored procedures in the Northwind database.

▶ Set up a `DataAdapter` to call the stored procedures.

▶ Add, modify, and remove a `DataRow` to or from a `DataTable`.

The C# methods shown in this section follow the same steps as shown in the earlier section, "Modifying Rows in a `DataTable`."

NOTE

Within the source files for this book, available at www.sybex.com, you'll find a complete program named PushChangesUsingProcedures.cs in the ch11 directory that illustrates the use of the methods shown in this section. The listing for this program is omitted from this book for brevity.

Creating the Stored Procedures in the Database

You'll create the following three stored procedures in the Northwind database:

▶ AddProduct4(), which adds a row to the Products table

▶ UpdateProduct(), which updates a row in the Products table

▶ DeleteProduct(), which deletes a row from the Products table

Let's take a look at these procedures.

The *AddProduct4()* Procedure

Listing 14.4 shows the AddProduct4.sql file that you use to create the AddProduct4() procedure. Refer to SQL Server Books Online if you need a refresher on the Transact-SQL language or if you need to find out how to run this script to create the procedure in the database.

Listing 14.4: *AddProduct4.sql*

```
/*
    AddProduct4.sql creates a procedure that adds a row to the
    Products table using values passed as parameters to the
    procedure. The procedure returns the ProductID
    of the new row using a RETURN statement
*/

CREATE PROCEDURE AddProduct4
    @MyProductName nvarchar(40),
    @MyUnitPrice money
AS

    -- declare the @MyProductID variable
    DECLARE @MyProductID int
```

```
-- insert a row into the Products table
INSERT INTO Products (
  ProductName, UnitPrice
) VALUES (
  @MyProductName, @MyUnitPrice
)

-- use the SCOPE_IDENTITY() function to get the last
-- identity value inserted into a table performed within
-- the current database session and stored procedure,
-- so SCOPE_IDENTITY returns the ProductID for the new row
-- in the Products table in this case
SET @MyProductID = SCOPE_IDENTITY()

RETURN @MyProductID
```

The *UpdateProduct()* Procedure

UpdateProduct() updates a row in the Products table. Listing 14.5
shows the UpdateProduct.sql file that you use to create the
UpdateProduct() procedure.

Listing 14.5: *UpdateProduct.sql*

```
/*
  UpdateProduct.sql creates a procedure that modifies a row
  in the Products table using values passed as parameters
  to the procedure
*/

CREATE PROCEDURE UpdateProduct
  @OldProductID int,
  @NewProductName nvarchar(40),
  @NewUnitPrice money,
  @OldProductName nvarchar(40),
  @OldUnitPrice money
AS

  -- update the row in the Products table
  UPDATE Products
  SET
    ProductName = @NewProductName,
    UnitPrice = @NewUnitPrice
```

```
WHERE ProductID = @OldProductID
AND ProductName = @OldProductName
AND UnitPrice = @OldUnitPrice
```

Because the WHERE clause contains the old column values in the UPDATE statement of this procedure, the UPDATE uses optimistic concurrency described earlier. This means that one user doesn't overwrite another user's changes.

The *DeleteProduct()* Procedure

DeleteProduct() deletes a row from the Products table. Listing 14.6 shows the DeleteProduct.sql file that you use to create the DeleteProduct() procedure.

Listing 14.6: *DeleteProduct.sql*

```
/*
    DeleteProduct.sql creates a procedure that removes a row
    from the Products table
*/

CREATE PROCEDURE DeleteProduct
    @OldProductID int,
    @OldProductName nvarchar(40),
    @OldUnitPrice money
AS

    -- delete the row from the Products table
    DELETE FROM Products
    WHERE ProductID = @OldProductID
    AND ProductName = @OldProductName
    AND UnitPrice = @OldUnitPrice
```

Using *SET NOCOUNT ON* in Stored Procedures

The SQL Server SET NOCOUNT ON command prevents Transact-SQL from returning the number of rows affected. Typically, you must avoid using this command in your stored procedures because the DataAdapter uses the returned number of rows affected to know whether the update succeeded.

There is one situation when you must use SET NOCOUNT ON: when your stored procedure performs an INSERT, UPDATE, or DELETE statement that affects another table besides the main one you are pushing a change to. For example, say the DeleteProduct() procedure also performed an

INSERT statement to add a row to the ProductAudit table to record
the attempt to delete the row from the Products table. In this example,
you must use SET NOCOUNT ON *before* performing the INSERT into the
ProductAudit table, as shown in Listing 14.7.

Listing 14.7: *DeleteProduct2.sql*

```
/*
   DeleteProduct2.sql creates a procedure that removes a row
   from the Products table
*/

CREATE PROCEDURE DeleteProduct2
  @OldProductID int,
  @OldProductName nvarchar(40),
  @OldUnitPrice money
AS

  -- delete the row from the Products table
  DELETE FROM Products
  WHERE ProductID = @OldProductID
  AND ProductName = @OldProductName
  AND UnitPrice = @OldUnitPrice

  -- use SET NOCOUNT ON to suppress the return of the
  -- number of rows affected by the INSERT statement
  SET NOCOUNT ON

  -- add a row to the Audit table
  IF @@ROWCOUNT = 1
    INSERT INTO ProductAudit (
      Action
    ) VALUES (
      'Product deleted with ProductID of ' +
      CONVERT(nvarchar, @OldProductID)
    )
  ELSE
    INSERT INTO ProductAudit (
      Action
    ) VALUES (
      'Product with ProductID of ' +
      CONVERT(nvarchar, @OldProductID) +
      ' was not deleted'
    )
```

By using SET NOCOUNT ON before the INSERT, only the number of rows affected by the DELETE statement is returned, and therefore the DataAdapter gets the correct value.

Transact-SQL also has a SET NOCOUNT ON command to turn on the number of rows affected. You can use a combination of SET NOCOUNT OFF and SET NOCOUNT ON if you need to perform an INSERT, UPDATE, or DELETE statement before the main SQL statement in your stored procedure.

Setting Up a *DataAdapter* to Call Stored Procedures

As mentioned earlier in "Modifying Rows in a DataTable," you need to create a DataAdapter object and set its SelectCommand, InsertCommand, UpdateCommand, and DeleteCommand properties with appropriate Command objects. This time, however, the InsertCommand, UpdateCommand, and DeleteCommand properties will contain Command objects that call the stored procedures shown earlier.

First, the following example creates a SqlCommand object containing a SELECT statement and sets the SelectCommand property of a SqlDataAdapter to that SqlCommand:

```
SqlCommand mySelectCommand =
  mySqlConnection.CreateCommand();
mySelectCommand.CommandText =
  "SELECT " +
  " ProductID, ProductName, UnitPrice " +
  "FROM Products " +
  "ORDER BY ProductID";
SqlDataAdapter mySqlDataAdapter = new SqlDataAdapter();
mySqlDataAdapter.SelectCommand = mySelectCommand;
```

The SELECT statement is then run when you call the mySqlDataAdapter object's Fill() method to retrieve rows from the Products table into a DataSet.

Before you can push changes to the database, you must set the Insert-Command, UpdateCommand, and DeleteCommand properties of your DataAdapter with Command objects. These Command objects will contain calls to the AddProduct4(), UpdateProduct(), and DeleteProduct() stored procedures that you created earlier. When you then add, modify, or remove DataRow objects from your DataSet, and then call the Update() method of your DataAdapter, the appropriate stored procedure is run to push your changes to the database.

Let's take a look at how to set the InsertCommand, UpdateCommand, and DeleteCommand properties of your DataAdapter.

Setting the *InsertCommand* Property of a *DataAdapter*

The following example creates a SqlCommand object named myInsert-Command that contains a call to the AddProduct4() stored procedure:

```
SqlCommand myInsertCommand =
    mySqlConnection.CreateCommand();
myInsertCommand.CommandText =
    "EXECUTE @MyProductID = AddProduct4 " +
    "@MyProductName, @MyUnitPrice";
myInsertCommand.Parameters.Add(
    "@MyProductID", SqlDbType.Int, 0, "ProductID");
myInsertCommand.Parameters["@MyProductID"].Direction =
    ParameterDirection.Output;
myInsertCommand.Parameters.Add(
    "@MyProductName", SqlDbType.NVarChar, 40, "ProductName");
myInsertCommand.Parameters.Add(
    "@MyUnitPrice", SqlDbType.Money, 0, "UnitPrice");
```

As you can see from the previous code, the direction of the @MyProductID parameter is set to ParameterDirection.Output, which indicates that this parameter is an output parameter. Also, the maximum length of the @MyProductID and @MyUnitPrice parameters is set to 0 in the third parameter to the Add() method. Setting them to 0 is fine because the maximum length doesn't apply to fixed length types such as numbers, only to types such as strings.

Next, the following example sets the InsertCommand property of mySqlDataAdapter to myInsertCommand:

```
mySqlDataAdapter.InsertCommand = myInsertCommand;
```

Setting the *UpdateCommand* Property of a *DataAdapter*

The following example creates a SqlCommand object named myUpdate-Command that contains a call to the UpdateProduct() stored procedure and sets the UpdateCommand property of mySqlDataAdapter to myUpdateCommand:

```
SqlCommand myUpdateCommand =
    mySqlConnection.CreateCommand();
```

```
myUpdateCommand.CommandText =
  "EXECUTE UpdateProduct @OldProductID, @NewProductName, " +
  "@NewUnitPrice, @OldProductName, @OldUnitPrice";
myUpdateCommand.Parameters.Add(
  "@OldProductID", SqlDbType.Int, 0, "ProductID");
myUpdateCommand.Parameters.Add(
  "@NewProductName", SqlDbType.NVarChar, 40, "ProductName");
myUpdateCommand.Parameters.Add(
  "@NewUnitPrice", SqlDbType.Money, 0, "UnitPrice");
myUpdateCommand.Parameters.Add(
  "@OldProductName", SqlDbType.NVarChar, 40, "ProductName");
myUpdateCommand.Parameters.Add(
  "@OldUnitPrice", SqlDbType.Money, 0, "UnitPrice");
myUpdateCommand.Parameters["@OldProductID"].SourceVersion =
  DataRowVersion.Original;
myUpdateCommand.Parameters[
  "@OldProductName"].SourceVersion =
  DataRowVersion.Original;
myUpdateCommand.Parameters["@OldUnitPrice"].SourceVersion =
  DataRowVersion.Original;
mySqlDataAdapter.UpdateCommand = myUpdateCommand;
```

Setting the *DeleteCommand* Property of a *DataAdapter*

The following example creates a SqlCommand object named myDelete-Command that contains a call to the DeleteProduct() stored procedure and sets the DeleteCommand property of mySqlDataAdapter to myDeleteCommand:

```
SqlCommand myDeleteCommand =
  mySqlConnection.CreateCommand();
myDeleteCommand.CommandText =
  "EXECUTE DeleteProduct @OldProductID, " +
  "@OldProductName, @OldUnitPrice";
myDeleteCommand.Parameters.Add(
  "@OldProductID", SqlDbType.Int, 0, "ProductID");
myDeleteCommand.Parameters.Add(
  "@OldProductName", SqlDbType.NVarChar, 40, "ProductName");
myDeleteCommand.Parameters.Add(
  "@OldUnitPrice", SqlDbType.Money, 0, "UnitPrice");
myDeleteCommand.Parameters["@OldProductID"].SourceVersion =
  DataRowVersion.Original;
myDeleteCommand.Parameters[
  "@OldProductName"].SourceVersion =
  DataRowVersion.Original;
```

```
myDeleteCommand.Parameters["@OldUnitPrice"].SourceVersion =
  DataRowVersion.Original;
mySqlDataAdapter.DeleteCommand = myDeleteCommand;
```

This completes the setup of the DataAdapter object.

Adding a *DataRow* to a *DataTable*

In this section, you'll learn how to add a DataRow to a DataTable. First, the following code creates a DataSet object named myDataSet and populates it by calling mySqlDataAdapter.Fill():

```
DataSet myDataSet = new DataSet();
mySqlConnection.Open();
int numOfRows =
  mySqlDataAdapter.Fill(myDataSet, "Products");
mySqlConnection.Close();
```

The int returned by the Fill() method is the number of rows retrieved from the database and copied to myDataSet. The myDataSet object now contains a DataTable named Products, which contains the rows retrieved by the following SELECT statement set earlier in the SelectCommand property of mySqlDataAdapter:

```
SELECT ProductID, ProductName, UnitPrice
FROM Products
ORDER BY ProductID
```

To add a new row to a DataTable object, you use the same four steps as shown earlier in the "Modifying a DataRow in a DataTable" section. The following method, named AddDataRow(), uses those steps to add a new row to a DataTable:

```
public static int AddDataRow(
  DataTable myDataTable,
  SqlDataAdapter mySqlDataAdapter,
  SqlConnection mySqlConnection
)
{
  Console.WriteLine("\nIn AddDataRow()");

  // step 1: use the NewRow() method of the DataTable to
  // create a new DataRow
  Console.WriteLine("Calling myDataTable.NewRow()");
  DataRow myNewDataRow = myDataTable.NewRow();
  Console.WriteLine("myNewDataRow.RowState = " +
    myNewDataRow.RowState);
```

```
// step 2: set the values for the DataColumn objects of
// the new DataRow
myNewDataRow["ProductName"] = "Widget";
myNewDataRow["UnitPrice"] = 10.99;

// step 3: use the Add() method through the Rows property
// to add the new DataRow to the DataTable
Console.WriteLine("Calling myDataTable.Rows.Add()");
myDataTable.Rows.Add(myNewDataRow);
Console.WriteLine("myNewDataRow.RowState = " +
  myNewDataRow.RowState);

// step 4: use the Update() method to push the new
// row to the database
Console.WriteLine("Calling mySqlDataAdapter.Update()");
mySqlConnection.Open();
int numOfRows = mySqlDataAdapter.Update(myDataTable);
mySqlConnection.Close();
Console.WriteLine("numOfRows = " + numOfRows);
Console.WriteLine("myNewDataRow.RowState = " +
  myNewDataRow.RowState);

DisplayDataRow(myNewDataRow, myDataTable);

// return the ProductID of the new DataRow
return (int) myNewDataRow["ProductID"];
}
```

Notice that no value for the ProductID DataColumn is set in step 2. This is because the ProductID is automatically generated by the database when the new row is pushed to the database by the Update() method in step 4.

When the Update() method is called, the AddProduct4() stored procedure is run to add the new row to the Products table. The database then generates a new ProductID for the row, which is then returned by the AddProduct4() stored procedure. You can then read the new ProductID using myNewDataRow["ProductID"], which now contains the new ProductID. This ProductID is then returned at the end of the AddDataRow() method.

The output from AddDataRow() and its call to DisplayDataRow() are as follows:

```
In AddDataRow()
Calling myDataTable.NewRow()
myNewDataRow.RowState = Detached
```

```
Calling myDataTable.Rows.Add()
myNewDataRow.RowState = Added
Calling mySqlDataAdapter.Update()
numOfRows = 1
myNewDataRow.RowState = Unchanged

In DisplayDataRow()
ProductID = 180
ProductName = Widget
UnitPrice = 10.99
```

As you can see, after myDataTable.NewRow() is called to create myNew-
DataRow its RowState is Detached, which indicates myNewDataRow isn't
yet part of myDataTable.

Next, myDataTable.Rows.Add() is called to add myNewDataRow to
myDataTable. This causes the RowState of myNewDataRow to change to
Added, which indicates myNewDataRow has been added to myDataTable.

Finally, mySqlDataAdapter.Update() is called to push the new row
to the database. The AddProduct4() stored procedure is run to add the
new row to the Products table, and the RowState of myNewDataRow
changes to Unchanged.

Modifying a *DataRow* in a *DataTable*

The following method, named ModifyDataRow(), uses four steps to modify
a DataRow in a DataTable object. Notice that the ProductID to modify is
passed as a parameter:

```
public static void ModifyDataRow(
    DataTable myDataTable,
    int productID,
    SqlDataAdapter mySqlDataAdapter,
    SqlConnection mySqlConnection
)
{
    Console.WriteLine("\nIn ModifyDataRow()");

    // step 1: set the PrimaryKey property of the DataTable
    myDataTable.PrimaryKey =
        new DataColumn[]
        {
            myDataTable.Columns["ProductID"]
        };
```

```
// step 2: use the Find() method to locate the DataRow
// in the DataTable using the primary key value
DataRow myEditDataRow = myDataTable.Rows.Find(productID);

// step 3: change the DataColumn values of the DataRow
myEditDataRow["ProductName"] = "Advanced Widget";
myEditDataRow["UnitPrice"] = 24.99;
Console.WriteLine("myEditDataRow.RowState = " +
  myEditDataRow.RowState);
Console.WriteLine("myEditDataRow[\"ProductID\", " +
  "DataRowVersion.Original] = " +
  myEditDataRow["ProductID", DataRowVersion.Original]);
Console.WriteLine("myEditDataRow[\"ProductName\", " +
  "DataRowVersion.Original] = " +
  myEditDataRow["ProductName", DataRowVersion.Original]);
Console.WriteLine("myEditDataRow[\"UnitPrice\", " +
  "DataRowVersion.Original] = " +
  myEditDataRow["UnitPrice", DataRowVersion.Original]);
Console.WriteLine("myEditDataRow[\"ProductName\", " +
  "DataRowVersion.Current] = " +
  myEditDataRow["ProductName", DataRowVersion.Current]);
Console.WriteLine("myEditDataRow[\"UnitPrice\", " +
  "DataRowVersion.Current] = " +
  myEditDataRow["UnitPrice", DataRowVersion.Current]);

// step 4: use the Update() method to push the update
// to the database
Console.WriteLine("Calling mySqlDataAdapter.Update()");
mySqlConnection.Open();
int numOfRows = mySqlDataAdapter.Update(myDataTable);
mySqlConnection.Close();
Console.WriteLine("numOfRows = " + numOfRows);
Console.WriteLine("myEditDataRow.RowState = " +
  myEditDataRow.RowState);

DisplayDataRow(myEditDataRow, myDataTable);
}
```

Notice this method displays the original values for the ProductID, ProductName, and UnitPrice DataColumn objects using the DataRowVersion.Original constant. These are the DataColumn values before they are changed. The method also displays the current values for the ProductName and UnitPrice DataColumn objects using the DataRowVersion.Current constant. These are the DataColumn values after they are changed. When the Update() method is called in step 4, the UpdateProduct() stored procedure is run behind the scenes to perform the update.

The output from ModifyDataRow() and its call to DisplayDataRow() is as follows:

```
In ModifyDataRow()
myEditDataRow.RowState = Modified
myEditDataRow["ProductID", DataRowVersion.Original] = 180
myEditDataRow["ProductName",
  DataRowVersion.Original] = Widget
myEditDataRow["UnitPrice", DataRowVersion.Original] = 10.99
myEditDataRow["ProductName",
  DataRowVersion.Current] = Advanced Widget
myEditDataRow["UnitPrice", DataRowVersion.Current] = 24.99
Calling mySqlDataAdapter.Update()
numOfRows = 1
myEditDataRow.RowState = Unchanged

In DisplayDataRow()
ProductID = 180
ProductName = Advanced Widget
UnitPrice = 24.99
```

Notice that the RowState property of myEditDataRow changes to Modified after it is changed, and then to Unchanged after mySqlData-Adapter.Update() is called.

Removing a *DataRow* from a *DataTable*

The following method, named RemoveDataRow(), uses four steps to remove a DataRow from a DataTable. Notice that the ProductID to modify is passed as a parameter:

```
public static void RemoveDataRow(
  DataTable myDataTable,
  int productID,
  SqlDataAdapter mySqlDataAdapter,
  SqlConnection mySqlConnection
)
{
  Console.WriteLine("\nIn RemoveDataRow()");

  // step 1: set the PrimaryKey property of the DataTable
  myDataTable.PrimaryKey =
    new DataColumn[]
    {
      myDataTable.Columns["ProductID"]
    };
```

```
// step 2: use the Find() method to locate the DataRow
DataRow myRemoveDataRow =
  myDataTable.Rows.Find(productID);

// step 3: use the Delete() method to remove the DataRow
Console.WriteLine("Calling myRemoveDataRow.Delete()");
myRemoveDataRow.Delete();
Console.WriteLine("myRemoveDataRow.RowState = " +
  myRemoveDataRow.RowState);

// step 4: use the Update() method to push the delete
// to the database
Console.WriteLine("Calling mySqlDataAdapter.Update()");
mySqlConnection.Open();
int numOfRows = mySqlDataAdapter.Update(myDataTable);
mySqlConnection.Close();
Console.WriteLine("numOfRows = " + numOfRows);
Console.WriteLine("myRemoveDataRow.RowState = " +
  myRemoveDataRow.RowState);
}
```

The output from RemoveDataRow() is as follows:

```
In RemoveDataRow()
Calling myRemoveDataRow.Delete()
myRemoveDataRow.RowState = Deleted
Calling mySqlDataAdapter.Update()
numOfRows = 1
myRemoveDataRow.RowState = Detached
```

Notice that the RowState property of myRemoveDataRow is set to Deleted after myRemoveData.Delete() is called, and then to Detached after mySqlDataAdapter.Update() is called. When the Update() method is called in step 4, the DeleteProduct() stored procedure is run behind the scenes to perform the delete.

NOTE

Within the source files for this book, available at www.sybex.com, you'll find a complete program named PushChangesUsingProcedures.cs in the ch11 directory that illustrates the use of the AddDataRow(), ModifyDataRow(), and RemoveDataRow() methods. This listing is omitted from this book for brevity.

AUTOMATICALLY GENERATING SQL STATEMENTS

As you've seen in the previous sections, supplying your own INSERT, UPDATE, and DELETE statements or stored procedures to push changes from your DataSet to the database means you have to write a lot of code. You can avoid writing this code by using a CommandBuilder object, which can automatically generate single-table INSERT, UPDATE, and DELETE commands that push the changes you make to a DataSet object to the database. These commands are then set in the InsertCommand, UpdateCommand, and DeleteCommand properties of your DataAdapter object. When you then make changes to your DataSet and call the Update() method of your DataAdapter, the automatically generated command is run to push the changes to the database.

Although you can save writing some code using a CommandBuilder, you must remember the following limitations:

▶ The SelectCommand property of your DataAdapter can retrieve rows from only a single table.

▶ The database table used in your SelectCommand must contain a primary key.

▶ The primary key of the table must be included in your Select-Command.

▶ The CommandBuilder takes a certain amount of time to generate the commands because it has to examine the database.

WARNING

Because a CommandBuilder lowers the performance of your program, you should try to avoid using them. They are intended for use by developers who aren't familiar with SQL or stored procedures. For best performance, use stored procedures.

There are three CommandBuilder managed provider classes: Sql-CommandBuilder, OleDbCommandBuilder, and OdbcCommandBuilder. You'll see the use of a SqlCommandBuilder object in this section that works with a SQL Server database. The other types of objects work in the same way.

First, you need to set the `SelectCommand` property of a `SqlDataAdapter` object. The `SELECT` statement used in this command can retrieve rows from only a single table, and in the following example the `Customers` table is used:

```
SqlCommand mySelectCommand =
  mySqlConnection.CreateCommand();
mySelectCommand.CommandText =
  "SELECT CustomerID, CompanyName, Address " +
  "FROM Customers " +
  "ORDER BY CustomerID";
SqlDataAdapter mySqlDataAdapter = new SqlDataAdapter();
mySqlDataAdapter.SelectCommand = mySelectCommand;
```

Next, the following example creates a `SqlCommandBuilder` object, passing `mySqlDataAdapter` to the constructor:

```
SqlCommandBuilder mySqlCommandBuilder =
  new SqlCommandBuilder(mySqlDataAdapter);
```

The `SqlCommandBuilder` will generate the commands containing `INSERT`, `UPDATE`, and `DELETE` statements based on the `SELECT` statement previously set in the `mySqlDataAdapter` object's `SelectCommand` property.

You can obtain the generated commands using the `GetInsert-Command()`, `GetUpdateCommand()`, and `GetDeleteCommand()` methods of `mySqlCommandBuilder`:

```
Console.WriteLine(
  "mySqlCommandBuilder.GetInsertCommand().CommandText =\n" +
  mySqlCommandBuilder.GetInsertCommand().CommandText
);
Console.WriteLine(
  "mySqlCommandBuilder.GetUpdateCommand().CommandText =\n" +
  mySqlCommandBuilder.GetUpdateCommand().CommandText
);
Console.WriteLine(
  "mySqlCommandBuilder.GetDeleteCommand().CommandText =\n" +
  mySqlCommandBuilder.GetDeleteCommand().CommandText
);
```

This code displays the following output (I've added some white space to make it easier to read):

```
mySqlCommandBuilder.GetInsertCommand().CommandText =
  INSERT INTO Customers( CustomerID , CompanyName ,
  Address ) VALUES ( @p1 , @p2 , @p3 )
```

```
mySqlCommandBuilder.GetUpdateCommand().CommandText =
  UPDATE Customers
  SET CustomerID = @p1 , CompanyName = @p2 , Address = @p3
  WHERE ( CustomerID = @p4 AND CompanyName = @p5
    AND Address = @p6 )
mySqlCommandBuilder.GetDeleteCommand().CommandText =
  DELETE FROM Customers
  WHERE ( CustomerID = @p1 AND CompanyName = @p2
    AND Address = @p3 )
```

As you can see, these commands are similar to those shown earlier in the section "Modifying Rows in a DataTable." The SQL statements used in these commands use optimistic concurrency.

You can now populate and make changes to a DataTable containing rows from the Customers table, and then push those changes to the database using the Update() method. You can use the same AddDataRow(), ModifyDataRow(), and RemoveDataRow() methods as shown in the earlier section, "Modifying Rows in a DataTable."

NOTE

Within the source files for this book, available at www.sybex.com, you'll find a complete program named UsingCommandBuilder.cs in the ch11 directory that illustrates the use of the CommandBuilder object shown in this section. This listing is omitted from this book for brevity.

EXPLORING THE *DATAADAPTER* AND *DATATABLE* EVENTS

You'll find all the code examples shown in this section in the program UsingEvents.cs located in the ch11 directory of the source files for this book, available at www.sybex.com. The listing for this program is omitted from this book for brevity. If you compile and run that program, you'll see the order in which the events fire when you add, modify, and remove a row from a DataTable that contains rows retrieved from the Customers table.

The *DataAdapter* Events

The events exposed by a SqlDataAdapter object are shown in Table 14.11.

TABLE 14.11: SqlDataAdapter Events

EVENT	EVENT HANDLER	DESCRIPTION
FillError	FillErrorEventHandler	Fires when an error occurs during a call to the Fill() method.
RowUpdating	RowUpdatingEventHandler	Fires *before* a row is added, modified, or deleted in the database as a result of calling the Update() method.
RowUpdated	RowUpdatedEventHandler	Fires *after* a row is added, modified, or deleted in the database as a result of calling the Update() method.

The *FillError* Event

The FillError event fires when you call the Fill() method and an error occurs. The following are a couple of scenarios that would cause an error:

▶ An attempt is made to add a number from the database to a DataColumn that couldn't be converted to the .NET type of that DataColumn without losing precision.

▶ An attempt is made to add a row from the database to a DataTable that violates a constraint in that DataTable.

The following example event handler, named FillErrorEvent-Handler(), checks for the precision conversion error:

```
public static void FillErrorEventHandler(
  object sender, FillErrorEventArgs myFEEA
)
{
  if (myFEEA.Errors.GetType() ==
    typeof(System.OverflowException))
  {
    Console.WriteLine("A loss of precision occurred");
    myFEEA.Continue = true;
  }
}
```

The first parameter is an object of the System.Object class, and it represents the object that raises the event. The second parameter is an object of the FillErrorEventArgs class, which like all the EventArgs classes, is derived from the System.EventArgs class. The EventArgs class is the base class for event data and represents the details of the event. Table 14.12 shows the `FillErrorEventArgs` properties.

TABLE 14.12:   `FillErrorEventArgs` Properties

PROPERTY	TYPE	DESCRIPTION
Continue	bool	Gets or sets a `bool` that indicates whether you want to continue filling your `DataSet` even though an error has occurred. The default is `false`.
DataTable	DataTable	Gets the `DataTable` that was being filled when the error occurred.
Errors	Exception	Gets the `Exception` containing the error that occurred.
Values	object[]	Gets the `DataColumn` values of the `DataRow` in which the error occurred. These values are returned in an `object` array.

You indicate that `mySqlDataAdapter` is to call the `FillErrorEvent-Handler()` method when the `FillError` event fires using the following code:

```
mySqlDataAdapter.FillError +=
    new FillErrorEventHandler(FillErrorEventHandler);
```

The *RowUpdating* Event

The RowUpdating event fires before a row is updated in the database as a result of you calling the `Update()` method of your `DataAdapter`. This event fires once for each `DataRow` you've added, modified, or deleted in a `DataTable`.

The following actions are performed behind the scenes for each `DataRow` when you call the `Update()` method of your `DataAdapter`:

1. The values in your `DataRow` are copied to the parameter values of the appropriate `Command` in the `InsertCommand`, `Update-Command`, or `DeleteCommand` property of your `DataAdapter`.

2. The `RowUpdating` event of your `DataAdapter` fires.

3. The `Command` is run to push the change to the database.

4. Any output parameters from the `Command` are returned.

5. The `RowUpdated` event of your `DataAdapter` fires.

6. The `AcceptChanges()` method of your `DataRow` is called.

The second parameter of any event handler method you write to handle the RowUpdating event of a SqlDataAdapter object is of the SqlRowUpdating-EventArgs class, and Table 14.13 shows the properties of this class.

TABLE 14.13:   SqlRowUpdatingEventArgs Properties

PROPERTY	TYPE	DESCRIPTION
Command	SqlCommand	Gets or sets the SqlCommand that is run when the Update() method is called.
Errors	Exception	Gets the Exception for any error that occurred.
Row	DataRow	Gets the DataRow to send to the database through the Update() method.
StatementType	StatementType	Gets the type of the SQL statement that is to be run. StatementType is an enumeration in the System.Data namespace that contains the following members: - Delete - Insert - Select - Update
Status	UpdateStatus	Gets or sets the UpdateStatus of the Command object. UpdateStatus is an enumeration in the System.Data namespace that contains the following members: - Continue, which indicates that the Data-Adapter is to continue processing rows. - ErrorsOccurred, which indicates that the update is to be treated as an error. - SkipAllRemainingRows, which indicates that the current row and *all* remaining rows are to be skipped and not updated. - SkipCurrentRow, which indicates that the current row is to be skipped and not updated. The default is Continue.
TableMapping	DataTable-Mapping	Gets the DataTableMapping object that is sent to the Update() method. A DataTableMapping object contains a description of a mapped relationship between a source table and a DataTable (see Chapter 13, "Using DataSet Objects to Store Data").

The following example event handler, named RowUpdatingEvent-Handler(), prevents any new rows from being added to the database with a CustomerID of J5COM:

```
public static void RowUpdatingEventHandler(
  object sender, SqlRowUpdatingEventArgs mySRUEA
)
{
  Console.WriteLine("\nIn RowUpdatingEventHandler()");
  if ((mySRUEA.StatementType == StatementType.Insert) &&
    (mySRUEA.Row["CustomerID"] == "J5COM"))
  {
    Console.WriteLine("Skipping current row");
    mySRUEA.Status = UpdateStatus.SkipCurrentRow;
  }
}
```

You indicate that mySqlDataAdapter is to call the RowUpdatingEvent-Handler() method when the RowUpdating event fires using the following code:

```
mySqlDataAdapter.RowUpdating +=
  new SqlRowUpdatingEventHandler(RowUpdatingEventHandler);
```

If you then call the AddDataRow() method shown earlier to attempt to add a row to the Customers table, the RowUpdating event will fire and call the RowUpdatingEventHandler() method. This method causes the new row to be skipped and prevents it from being added to the Customers database table.

The *RowUpdated* Event

The RowUpdated event fires after a row is updated in the database as a result of you calling the Update() method of your DataAdapter. This event fires once for each DataRow you've added, modified, or deleted in a DataTable.

The second parameter of any method you write to handle the RowUpdated event of a SqlDataAdapter object is of the SqlRow-UpdatedEventArgs class. The properties of this class are the same as those shown earlier in Table 14.13, plus one additional property shown in Table 14.14.

TABLE 14.14:   Additional SqlRowUpdatedEventArgs Property

PROPERTY	TYPE	DESCRIPTION
RecordsAffected	int	Gets an int containing the number of rows added, modified, or removed when the appropriate Command is run by the Update() method.

The following example event handler, named RowUpdatedEvent-Handler(), displays the number of records affected by the following Command:

```
public static void RowUpdatedEventHandler(
  object sender, SqlRowUpdatedEventArgs mySRUEA
)
{
  Console.WriteLine("\nIn RowUpdatedEventHandler()");
  Console.WriteLine("mySRUEA.RecordsAffected = " +
    mySRUEA.RecordsAffected);
}
```

You indicate that mySqlDataAdapter is to call the RowUpdated-EventHandler() method when the RowUpdated event fires using the following code:

```
mySqlDataAdapter.RowUpdated +=
  new SqlRowUpdatedEventHandler(RowUpdatedEventHandler);
```

The *DataTable* Events

The events exposed by a DataTable object are shown in Table 14.15.

TABLE 14.15:   DataTable Events

EVENT	EVENT HANDLER	DESCRIPTION
ColumnChanging	DataColumnChange-EventHandler	Fires *before* a changed DataColumn value is committed in a DataRow.
ColumnChanged	DataColumnChange-EventHandler	Fires *after* a changed DataColumn value is committed in a DataRow.
RowChanging	DataRowChange-EventHandler	Fires *before* a changed DataRow is committed in a DataTable.
RowChanged	DataRowChange-EventHandler	Fires *after* a changed DataRow is committed in a DataTable.

TABLE 14.15 continued: DataTable Events

Event	Event Handler	Description
RowDeleting	DataRowChange-EventHandler	Fires *before* a DataRow is deleted from a DataTable.
RowDeleted	DataRowChange-EventHandler	Fires *after* a DataRow is deleted from a DataTable.

The *ColumnChanging* and *ColumnChanged* Events

The ColumnChanging event fires before a change to a DataColumn value is committed in a DataRow. Similarly, the ColumnChanged event fires after a change to a DataColumn value is committed in a DataRow. These two events are always fired before the RowChanging and RowChanged events.

What is meant by "commit" in this context? If you simply set a new value for a DataColumn, then the change is automatically committed in the DataRow. However, if you start the change to the DataRow using the BeginEdit() method, then the change is committed only when you call the EndEdit() method of that DataRow. You can also reject the change to the DataRow using the CancelEdit() method.

The second parameter to any event handler you write to handle the ColumnChanging or ColumnChanged events of a DataTable object is of the DataColumnChangeEventArgs class. Table 14.16 shows the properties of this class.

TABLE 14.16: DataColumnChangeEventArgs Properties

Property	Type	Description
Column	DataColumn	Gets the DataColumn with the value that is changing.
ProposedValue	object	Gets or sets the new value for the DataColumn.
Row	DataRow	Gets the DataRow that contains the DataColumn with the value that is changing.

The following example method handlers, named ColumnChanging-EventHandler() and ColumnChangedEventHandler(), display the

Column and ProposedValue properties:

```
public static void ColumnChangingEventHandler(
  object sender,
  DataColumnChangeEventArgs myDCCEA
)
{
  Console.WriteLine("\nIn ColumnChangingEventHandler()");
  Console.WriteLine("myDCCEA.Column = " + myDCCEA.Column);
  Console.WriteLine("myDCCEA.ProposedValue = " +
    myDCCEA.ProposedValue);
}

public static void ColumnChangedEventHandler(
  object sender,
  DataColumnChangeEventArgs myDCCEA
)
{
  Console.WriteLine("\nIn ColumnChangedEventHandler()");
  Console.WriteLine("myDCCEA.Column = " + myDCCEA.Column);
  Console.WriteLine("myDCCEA.ProposedValue = " +
    myDCCEA.ProposedValue);
}
```

The next example creates a DataTable named customersDataTable
and adds the previous two methods to the ColumnChanging and Column-
Changed events of customersDataTable:

```
DataTable customersDataTable =
  myDataSet.Tables["Customers"];

customersDataTable.ColumnChanging +=
  new DataColumnChangeEventHandler(
  ColumnChangingEventHandler);

customersDataTable.ColumnChanged +=
  new DataColumnChangeEventHandler(
  ColumnChangedEventHandler);
```

The *RowChanging* and *RowChanged* Events

The RowChanging event fires before a change to a DataRow is committed
in a DataTable. Similarly, the RowChanged event fires after a change to a
DataRow value is committed in a DataTable.

The second parameter of any event handler you write to handle the
RowChanging or RowChanged events of a DataTable object is of the

DataRowChangeEventArgs class. Table 14.17 shows the properties of this class.

TABLE 14.17:   DataRowChangeEventArgs Properties

PROPERTY	TYPE	DESCRIPTION
Action	DataRowAction	Gets the DataRowAction that has occurred for the DataRow. The DataRowAction enumeration is defined in the System.Data namespace and contains the following members: - Add, which indicates the DataRow has been added to the DataTable. - Change, which indicates the DataRow has been modified. - Commit, which indicates the DataRow has been committed in the DataTable. - Delete, which indicates the DataRow has been removed from the DataTable. - Nothing, which indicates the DataRow has not changed. - Rollback, which indicates the change to the DataRow has been rolled back.
Row	DataRow	Gets the DataRow that contains the Data-Column with the value that is changing.

The following example event handlers, named RowChangingEvent-Handler() and RowChangedEventHandler(), display the Action property:

```
public static void RowChangingEventHandler(
  object sender,
  DataRowChangeEventArgs myDRCEA
)
{
  Console.WriteLine("\nIn RowChangingEventHandler()");
  Console.WriteLine("myDRCEA.Action = " + myDRCEA.Action);
}

public static void RowChangedEventHandler(
  object sender,
  DataRowChangeEventArgs myDRCEA
)
{
```

```
    Console.WriteLine("\nIn RowChangedEventHandler()");
    Console.WriteLine("myDRCEA.Action = " + myDRCEA.Action);
}
```

The next example adds the previous two methods to the RowChanging and RowChanged events of customersDataTable:

```
customersDataTable.RowChanging +=
    new DataRowChangeEventHandler(RowChangingEventHandler);

customersDataTable.RowChanged +=
    new DataRowChangeEventHandler(RowChangedEventHandler);
```

The *RowDeleting* and *RowDeleted* Events

The RowDeleting event fires before a DataRow is deleted from a DataTable. Similarly, the RowDeleted event fires after a DataRow is deleted from a DataTable.

The second parameter of any event handler you write to handle the RowDeleting or RowDeleted events of a DataTable is of the DataRow-ChangeEventArgs class, and Table 14.17, shown earlier, shows the properties of this class.

The following example method handlers, named RowDeletingEvent-Handler() and RowDeletedEventHandler(), display the Action property:

```
public static void RowDeletingEventHandler(
    object sender,
    DataRowChangeEventArgs myDRCEA
)
{
    Console.WriteLine("\nIn RowDeletingEventHandler()");
    Console.WriteLine("myDRCEA.Action = " + myDRCEA.Action);
}

public static void RowDeletedEventHandler(
    object sender,
    DataRowChangeEventArgs myDRCEA
)
{
    Console.WriteLine("\nIn RowDeletedEventHandler()");
    Console.WriteLine("myDRCEA.Action = " + myDRCEA.Action);
}
```

The next example adds the previous two methods to the RowDeleting and RowDeleted events of customersDataTable:

```
customersDataTable.RowDeleting +=
    new DataRowChangeEventHandler(RowDeletingEventHandler);
```

```
customersDataTable.RowDeleted +=
  new DataRowChangeEventHandler(RowDeletedEventHandler);
```

NOTE

Within the source files for this book, available at www.sybex.com, you'll find all the code examples shown in this section in the program UsingEvents.cs located in the ch11 directory. This program listing is omitted from this book for brevity.

DEALING WITH UPDATE FAILURES

So far, the examples you've seen have assumed that the updates pushed to the database by the Update() have succeeded. In this section, you see what happens when updates fail—and what you can do about it.

NOTE

Within the source files for this book, available at www.sybex.com, you'll find all the code examples shown in this section in the HandlingUpdate-Failures.cs file located in the ch11 directory. This program listing is omitted from this book for brevity.

In the examples in this section, assume that the CommandText property of a SqlDataAdapter object's UpdateCommand is set as follows:

```
UPDATE Customers
SET
  CompanyName = @NewCompanyName,
  Address = @NewAddress
WHERE CustomerID = @OldCustomerID
AND CompanyName = @OldCompanyName
AND Address = @OldAddress
```

This UPDATE statement uses optimistic concurrency because the updated columns are included in the WHERE clause.

An Update Failure Scenario

Consider the following scenario that shows an update failure:

1. User 1 retrieves the rows from the Customers table into a DataTable named customersDataTable.

2. User 2 retrieves the same rows.

3. User 1 updates the `CustomerName` DataColumn of the DataRow with the `CustomerID` DataColumn of J5COM and pushes the change to the database. Let's say User 1 changes the `CustomerName` from J5 Company to Updated Company.

4. User 2 updates the same DataRow and changes the Company-Name from J5 Company to `Widgets Inc.` and attempts to push the change to the database. User 2 then causes a `DBConcurrecyException` object to be thrown and their update fails. (The same exception occurs if User 2 tries to update or delete a row that has already been deleted by User 1.)

Why does the update fail in step 4? The reason is that with optimistic concurrency, the `CompanyName` column is used in the `WHERE` clause of the `UPDATE` statement. Because of this, the original row loaded by User 2 cannot be found anymore—and therefore the `UPDATE` statement fails. The row cannot be found because User 1 has already changed the `CompanyName` column from J5 Company to Updated Company in step 2.

That's the problem with optimistic concurrency, but what can you as a developer do about it? You can report the problem to User 2, refresh their rows using the `Fill()` method, and they can make their change again—however, if User 2 has already made a large number of changes and they can't save any of them, they'll probably be very annoyed at your program.

Fortunately, you can set the `ContinueUpdateOnError` property of your `DataAdapter` to `true` to continue updating any `DataRow` objects even if an error occurs. That way, when User 2 saves their changes they can at least save the rows that don't cause any errors. Let's take a look at how to set the `ContinueUpdateOnError` property.

Setting the *ContinueUpdateOnError* Property

The following example sets the `ContinueUpdateOnError` property to `true` for `mySqlDataAdapter`:

```
mySqlDataAdapter.ContinueUpdateOnError = true;
```

When you call `mySqlDataAdapter.Update()`, it will push all the changes that don't cause errors to the database. You can then check for errors afterwards using the `HasErrors` property of a `DataSet` or the `HasErrors` property of individual `DataTable` objects, which you'll see how to do shortly in the section "Checking for Errors."

Programming a Failed Update Example

Let's program an example of a failed update. This example will simulate the updates made by User 1 and User 2 described earlier. I'll use the following method, named ModifyRowsUsingUPDATE(), to simulate the update made by User 1 in step 3 described earlier:

```
public static void ModifyRowUsingUPDATE(
  SqlConnection mySqlConnection
)
{
  Console.WriteLine("\nIn ModifyDataRowUsingUPDATE()");
  Console.WriteLine(
    "Updating CompanyName to 'Updated Company' " +
    "for J5COM");

  SqlCommand mySqlCommand = mySqlConnection.CreateCommand();
  mySqlCommand.CommandText =
    "UPDATE Customers " +
    "SET CompanyName = 'Updated Company' " +
    "WHERE CustomerID = 'J5COM'";

  mySqlConnection.Open();
  int numberOfRows = mySqlCommand.ExecuteNonQuery();
  Console.WriteLine("Number of rows updated = " +
    numberOfRows);
  mySqlConnection.Close();
}
```

Notice that the CompanyName is set to Updated Company for the row with the CustomerID of J5COM.

I'll use the following ModifyDataRow() method to simulate the update made by User 2 in step 4. This is similar to the other ModifyDataRow() methods you've seen earlier in this chapter. Notice that the CompanyName is set to Widgets Inc. for the row with the CustomerID of J5COM:

```
public static void ModifyDataRow(
  DataTable myDataTable,
  SqlDataAdapter mySqlDataAdapter,
  SqlConnection mySqlConnection
)
{
  Console.WriteLine("\nIn ModifyDataRow()");

  // step 1: set the PrimaryKey property of the DataTable
  myDataTable.PrimaryKey =
    new DataColumn[]
```

```
{
  myDataTable.Columns["CustomerID"]
};

    // step 2: use the Find() method to locate the DataRow
    // in the DataTable using the primary key value
    DataRow myDataRow = myDataTable.Rows.Find("J5COM");

    // step 3: change the DataColumn values of the DataRow
    myDataRow["CompanyName"] = "Widgets Inc.";
    Console.WriteLine("myDataRow.RowState = " +
      myDataRow.RowState);

    // step 4: use the Update() method to push the modified
    // row to the database
    Console.WriteLine("Calling mySqlDataAdapter.Update()");
    mySqlConnection.Open();
    int numOfRows = mySqlDataAdapter.Update(myDataTable);
    mySqlConnection.Close();
    Console.WriteLine("numOfRows = " + numOfRows);
    Console.WriteLine("myDataRow.RowState = " +
      myDataRow.RowState);

    DisplayDataRow(myDataRow, myDataTable);
}
```

The next example calls ModifyRowUsingUPDATE() to perform the first update of the row with the CustomerID of J5COM:

```
ModifyRowUsingUPDATE(mySqlConnection);
```

Next, the ContinueUpdateOnError property of mySqlDataAdapter is set to true to continue updating any DataRow objects even if an error occurs:

```
mySqlDataAdapter.ContinueUpdateOnError = true;
```

Next, ModifyDataRow() is called to attempt to modify the same row as ModifyRowsUsingUPDATE():

```
ModifyDataRow(customersDataTable, mySqlDataAdapter,
  mySqlConnection);
```

Normally, this will throw an exception since the row cannot be found, but since the ContinueUpdateOnError property of mySqlDataAdapter has been set to true, no exception will be thrown. That way, if myData-Table had other updated rows, they would still be pushed to the database by the call to the Update() method.

Checking for Errors

Having set the ContinueUpdateOnError property of mySqlDataAdapter to true, no exception will be thrown when an error occurs. Instead, you can check for errors in a DataSet or individual DataTable or DataRow using the HasErrors property. You can then show the user the details of the error using the RowError property of the DataRow, along with the original and current values for the DataColumn objects in that DataRow. For example,

```
if (myDataSet.HasErrors)
{
  Console.WriteLine("\nDataSet has errors!");
  foreach (DataTable myDataTable in myDataSet.Tables)
  {
    // check the HasErrors property of myDataTable
    if (myDataTable.HasErrors)
    {
      foreach (DataRow myDataRow in myDataTable.Rows)
      {
        // check the HasErrors property of myDataRow
        if (myDataRow.HasErrors)
        {
          Console.WriteLine("Here is the row error:");
          Console.WriteLine(myDataRow.RowError);
          Console.WriteLine(
            "Here are the column details in the DataSet:");
          foreach (DataColumn myDataColumn in
            myDataTable.Columns)
          {
            Console.WriteLine(
              myDataColumn + " original value = " +
              myDataRow[myDataColumn,
              DataRowVersion.Original]);
            Console.WriteLine(
              myDataColumn + " current value = " +
              myDataRow[myDataColumn, DataRowVersion.Current]);
          }
        }
      }
    }
  }
}
```

Fixing the Error

Showing the user the error is only half the story. What can you do to fix the problem? One solution is to call the Fill() method again to synchronize the rows in your DataSet with the database. That way, the row updated by ModifyRowsUsingUPDATE() in the Customers table will be pulled from the Customers table and replace the original J5COM row in the DataSet:

```
mySqlConnection.Open();
numOfRows =
    mySqlDataAdapter.Fill(myDataSet, "Customers");
mySqlConnection.Close();
```

You might expect numOfRows to be 1 because you're replacing only one row, right? Wrong: numOfRows will contain the *total* number of rows in the Customers table. The reason for this is that the Fill() method actually pulls all of the rows from the Customers table and puts them in the Customers DataTable of myDataSet, throwing away any existing rows with matching primary key column values already in the Customers DataTable.

WARNING

If you didn't add a primary key to your Customers DataTable, then the call to the Fill() method would simply add all the rows from the Customers table to the Customers DataTable again—duplicating the rows already there.

Next, you call ModifyDataRow() again to modify the J5COM row:

```
ModifyDataRow(customersDataTable, mySqlDataAdapter,
    mySqlConnection);
```

This time the update succeeds because ModifyDataRow() finds the J5COM row in customersDataTable that was just pulled from the Customers table.

NOTE

If a user tries to update a row that has already been deleted from the database table, the only thing you can do is refresh the rows and ask the user to enter their row again.

USING TRANSACTIONS WITH A *DATASET*

Most database engines support SQL statements that can be grouped together into transactions. The transaction is then committed or rolled back as one unit. For example, in the case of a banking transaction, you might want to withdraw money from one account and deposit it into another account. You would then commit both of these changes as one unit, or if there's a problem, rollback both changes. In Chapter 11, "Overview of the ADO.NET Classes," you saw how to use a Transaction object to represent a transaction.

As you know, a DataSet doesn't have a direct connection to the database. Instead, you use the Fill() and Update() methods of a DataAdapter to pull and push rows from and to the database to your DataSet respectively. In fact, a DataSet has no "knowledge" of the database at all. A DataSet simply stores a disconnected copy of the data. Because of this, a DataSet doesn't have any built-in functionality to handle transactions.

How then do you use transactions with a DataSet? The answer is you must use the Transaction property of the Command objects stored in a DataAdapter.

Using the *DataAdapter Command* Object's *Transaction* Property

A DataAdapter stores four Command objects that you access using the SelectCommand, InsertCommand, UpdateCommand, and DeleteCommand properties. When you call the Update() method of a DataAdapter, it runs the appropriate InsertCommand, UpdateCommand, or DeleteCommand.

You can create a Transaction object and set the Transaction property of the Command objects in your DataAdapter to this Transaction object. When you then modify your DataSet and push the changes to the database using the Update() method of your DataAdapter, the changes will use the same Transaction.

The following example creates a SqlTransaction object named mySqlTransaction and sets the Transaction property of each of the

Command objects in mySqlDataAdapter to mySqlTransaction:

```
SqlTransaction mySqlTransaction =
  mySqlConnection.BeginTransaction();
mySqlDataAdapter.SelectCommand.Transaction =
  mySqlTransaction;
mySqlDataAdapter.InsertCommand.Transaction =
  mySqlTransaction;
mySqlDataAdapter.UpdateCommand.Transaction =
  mySqlTransaction;
mySqlDataAdapter.DeleteCommand.Transaction =
  mySqlTransaction;
```

Each of the Command objects in mySqlDataAdapter will now use mySqlTransaction.

Let's say you added, modified, and removed some rows from a DataTable contained in a DataSet named myDataSet. You can push these changes to the database using the following example:

```
mySqlDataAdapter.Update(myDataSet);
```

All your changes to myDataSet are pushed to the database as part of the transaction in mySqlTransaction. You can commit those changes using the Commit() method of mySqlTransaction:

```
mySqlTransaction.Commit();
```

You could also roll back those changes using the Rollback() method of mySqlTransaction.

NOTE

A transaction is rolled back by default, therefore, you should always explicitly commit or roll back your transaction using Commit() or Rollback() to make it clear what your program is intended to do.

MODIFYING DATA USING A STRONGLY TYPED *DATASET*

In Chapter 13, you saw how to create and use a strongly typed DataSet class named MyDataSet. You can use objects of this class to represent the Customers table and rows from that table. In this section, you'll see how to modify data using a strongly typed object of the MyDataSet class.

NOTE

One of the features of a strongly typed DataSet object allows you to read a column value using a property with the same name as the column. For example, to read the CustomerID of a column you can use myDataRow.CustomerID rather than myDataRow["CustomerID"]. See Chapter 13 for more details on reading column values.

The following methods in the MyDataSet class allow you to modify the rows stored in a MyDataSet object: NewCustomersRow(), AddCustomers-Row(), and RemoveCustomersRow(). You can find a row using the FindByCustomerID() method. You can check if a column value contains a null value using methods such as IsContactNameNull(), and you can set a column to null using methods such as SetContactNameNull(). You'll see these methods used shortly.

NOTE

You'll find a completed VS.NET example project for this section in the StronglyTypedDataSet2 directory. You can open this project in VS.NET by selecting File ➢ Open ➢ Project and opening the WindowsApplication4 .csproj file. You'll need to change the ConnectionString property of the sqlConnection1 object to connect to your Northwind database.

The Form1_Load() method of the form in the example project shows how to add, modify, and remove a row to a strongly typed DataSet object named myDataSet1. You can see the steps that accomplish these tasks in the following Form1_Load() method:

```
private void Form1_Load(object sender, System.EventArgs e)
{
    // populate the DataSet with the CustomerID, CompanyName,
    // and Address columns from the Customers table
    sqlConnection1.Open();
    sqlDataAdapter1.Fill(myDataSet1, "Customers");

    // get the Customers DataTable
    MyDataSet.CustomersDataTable myDataTable =
      myDataSet1.Customers;

    // create a new DataRow in myDataTable using the
    // NewCustomersRow() method of myDataTable
    MyDataSet.CustomersRow myDataRow =
      myDataTable.NewCustomersRow();
```

```
// set the CustomerID, CompanyName,
// and Address of myDataRow
myDataRow.CustomerID = "J5COM";
myDataRow.CompanyName = "J5 Company";
myDataRow.Address = "1 Main Street";

// add the new row to myDataTable using the
// AddCustomersRow() method
myDataTable.AddCustomersRow(myDataRow);

// push the new row to the database using
// the Update() method of sqlDataAdapter1
sqlDataAdapter1.Update(myDataTable);

// find the row using the FindByCustomerID()
// method of myDataTable
myDataRow = myDataTable.FindByCustomerID("J5COM");

// modify the CompanyName and Address of myDataRow
myDataRow.CompanyName = "Widgets Inc.";
myDataRow.Address = "1 Any Street";

// push the modification to the database
sqlDataAdapter1.Update(myDataTable);

// display the DataRow objects in myDataTable
// in the listView1 object
foreach (MyDataSet.CustomersRow myDataRow2
  in myDataTable.Rows)
{
  listView1.Items.Add(myDataRow2.CustomerID);
  listView1.Items.Add(myDataRow2.CompanyName);

  // if the Address is null, set Address to "Unknown"
  if (myDataRow2.IsAddressNull() == true)
  {
    myDataRow2.Address = "Unknown";
  }
  listView1.Items.Add(myDataRow2.Address);
}

// find and remove the new row using the
// FindByCustomerID() and RemoveCustomersRow() methods
// of myDataTable
myDataRow = myDataTable.FindByCustomerID("J5COM");
myDataTable.RemoveCustomersRow(myDataRow);
```

```
    // push the delete to the database
    sqlDataAdapter1.Update(myDataTable);

    sqlConnection1.Close();
}
```

Feel free to compile and run the example form.

SUMMARY

In this chapter, you learned how to modify the rows in a DataSet and then push those changes to the database via a DataAdapter.

You saw how to add restrictions to a DataTable and its DataColumn objects. This allows you to model the same restrictions placed on the database tables and columns in your DataTable and DataColumn objects. By adding restrictions up front, you prevent bad data from being added to your DataSet to begin with, and this helps reduce the errors when attempting to push changes in your DataSet to the database.

Each row in a DataTable is stored in a DataRow object, and you saw how to find, filter, and sort the DataRow objects in a DataTable using the Find() method of a DataTable. You also learned how to filter and sort the DataRow objects in a DataTable using the Select() method.

You saw the steps required to add, modify, and remove DataRow objects from a DataTable and then push those changes to the database. To do this, you must first set up your DataAdapter with Command objects containing appropriate SQL INSERT, UPDATE, and DELETE statements. You store these Command objects in your DataAdapter object's InsertCommand, UpdateCommand, and DeleteCommand properties. You push changes from your DataSet to the database using the Update() method of your DataAdapter. When you add, modify, or remove DataRow objects from your DataSet and then call the Update() method of your DataAdapter, the appropriate InsertCommand, UpdateCommand, or DeleteCommand is run to push your changes to the database.

Concurrency determines how multiple users' modifications to the same row are handled. With *optimistic concurrency*, you can modify a row in a database table only if no one else has modified that same row since you loaded it into your DataSet. This is typically the best type of concurrency to use because you don't want to overwrite someone else's changes. With *"last one wins"* concurrency, you can always modify a row—and your changes overwrite anyone else's changes. You typically want to avoid using "last one wins" concurrency.

You can get a DataAdapter object to call stored procedures to add, modify, and remove rows from the database. These procedures are called instead of the INSERT, UPDATE, and DELETE statements you've seen how to set in a DataAdapter object's InsertCommand, UpdateCommand, and DeleteCommand properties.

Supplying your own INSERT, UPDATE, and DELETE statements or stored procedures to push changes from your DataSet to the database means you have to write a lot of code. You can avoid writing this code by using a CommandBuilder object, which can automatically generate single-table INSERT, UPDATE, and DELETE commands that push the changes you make to a DataSet object to the database. These commands are then set in the InsertCommand, UpdateCommand, and DeleteCommand properties of your DataAdapter object. When you then make changes to your DataSet and call the Update() method of your DataAdapter, the automatically generated command is run to push the changes to the database.

You also saw how to handle update failures and use transactions with a DataSet, and in the final section of this chapter, you saw how to update the rows stored in a strongly typed data set.

What's Next

Chapter 15 begins the discussion on intranet topics such as ASP.NET development and web services.

Chapter 15

INTRODUCTION TO C# WEB APPLICATIONS

As you may already know, web applications are distinct from websites because they have a defined purpose: Most websites are informational, whereas most web applications are not. IIS makes that difference explicit. In this chapter, you'll see how to set up a web application in IIS, and you'll explore configuration files in detail.

Adapted From *Mastering ASP.NET with C#*
by A. Russell Jones
ISBN 0-7821-2989-7

APPLICATIONS VERSUS WEBSITES

A website is nothing more than a virtual directory associated with a specific server. The simplest way to see that is to create one yourself. Don't use Visual Studio, FrontPage, or your favorite integrated editor; do it by hand, at least this once. Start the Internet Information Services applet on your server. In Windows 2000, click Start ➢ Programs ➢ Administrative Tools ➢ Internet Services Manager to launch the applet. The Internet Services Manager (ISM) applet runs as part of the Microsoft Management Console (MMC).

You'll see the dialog in Figure 15.1 (the dialog and items vary in different Windows versions).

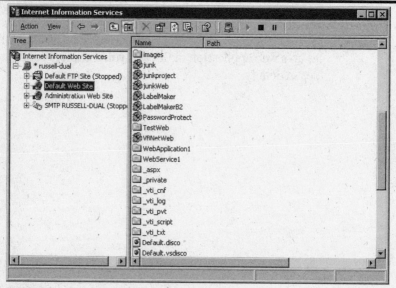

FIGURE 15.1:   Internet Services Manager applet

Select the Default Web Site (again, depending on your setup, this item may have a different title; it's configurable, but in my experience, most people leave the name set to the default). Right-click and select New ➢ Virtual Directory from the pop-up menu. You'll see the Virtual Directory Creation Wizard screen (see Figure 15.2).

Click the Next button to continue. You'll see the Virtual Directory Alias screen (see Figure 15.3).

FIGURE 15.2: Virtual Directory Creation Wizard

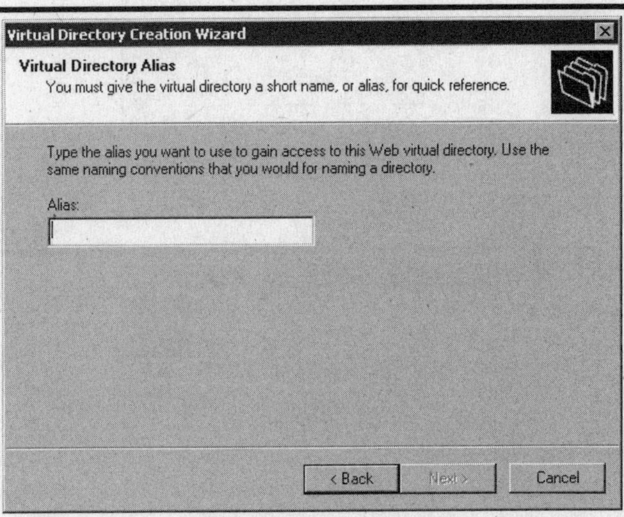

FIGURE 15.3: Virtual Directory Creation Wizard, Virtual Directory Alias screen

A virtual directory is an *alias* name for a physical directory. Enter the name **CSharpASPTest** into the Alias field and then click Next. You'll see the Web Site Content Directory screen. You need to enter the physical path of the root folder for the new virtual directory. Unfortunately, I usually get this far and *then* decide that I want to create a new directory. No problem. Launch Windows Explorer and create a new directory somewhere named

CSharpASPTest. After you've created the new directory, return to the Web Site Content Directory screen and enter the path to the new directory into the Directory field. For example, I created the new directory as c:\inetpub\wwwroot\CSharpASPTest and entered that path into the Directory field (see Figure 15.4). Click the Next button to continue.

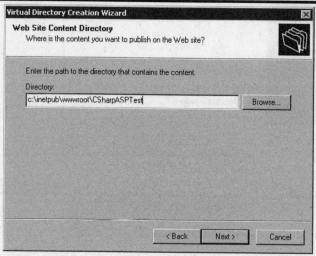

FIGURE 15.4:   Virtual Directory Creation Wizard, Web Site Content Directory screen

You'll see the Access Permissions screen (see Figure 15.5).

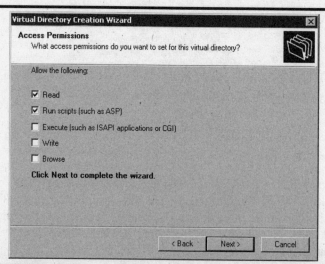

FIGURE 15.5:   Virtual Directory Creation Wizard, Access Permissions screen

The Access Permissions screen provides a first level of security protection. By default, IIS applies the Read and Run Scripts (such as ASP and ASP.NET pages) permissions to the new virtual directory. You have options (unselected by default) to let the application run executable content, let the application write to the directory, and let users browse the content.

WARNING

Normally, you should not select the Execute, Write, or Browse permissions check boxes. All these options have security ramifications. The only one you need with any regularity is the Write capability, which you should apply only to specific protected files or subfolders. You can do that with the file and directory security options in Windows Explorer at any time. Leave the three options unchecked.

Click Next to complete the wizard and then Finish to close it. The ISM creates the new virtual directory and applies the selected permissions, but it does something else, too. Look at the icon for the new virtual directory (see Figure 15.6). Of course, your virtual directory list will look different than mine. The important thing is that you see the new CSharpASPTest virtual directory in the list. The open box icon denotes an IIS *application* rather than a simple virtual directory.

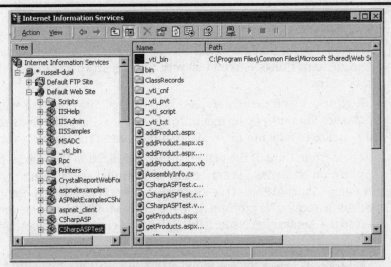

FIGURE 15.6:   Internet Information Services applet after creating the CSharpASPTest virtual directory

TIP

If the ISM didn't automatically create an application for you, the icon will not look like a box; it will look like a folder with a globe in one corner, denoting a `World Wide Web` folder. Don't worry about it. You'll see how to create the application manually in this section.

To understand the difference between an IIS application and a simple virtual directory, you have to go backward in time a little to COM+ technology, or even further back, when the name was Microsoft Transaction Server (MTS). A COM+ application runs in a virtual space, isolating it from other applications running on the same server. It's much more difficult for a COM+ application to bring down the entire server if it fails. That's the reason the default virtual directory creation settings for IIS create an IIS application rather than a simple virtual directory.

NOTE

If you don't check the Run Scripts option on the Access Permissions screen, IIS creates a plain virtual directory rather than an IIS application.

NOTE

Creating a virtual directory in IIS3 on NT4 does not create an IIS application by default.

It's worth your time to explore this topic just a little further because there are some things you can't do with the property dialogs for ASP.NET applications.

Right-click your new `CSharpASPTest` virtual directory and select Properties from the pop-up menu. You'll see the CSharpASPTest Properties dialog (see Figure 15.7). Make sure you're on the Directory tab.

The bottom third of the dialog is titled Application Settings. If the Application Name field is grayed out on your dialog or doesn't contain the name `CSharpASPTest`, the ISM applet didn't create the application for you automatically. No problem. If that's the case, click the Create button next to the Application Name field. (If ISM did create the application, the button caption reads "Remove" rather than "Create.")

Set Execute Permissions to Scripts Only and set Application Protection to Medium (Pooled). Next, click the Configuration button. You'll see the Application Configuration dialog (see Figure 15.8).

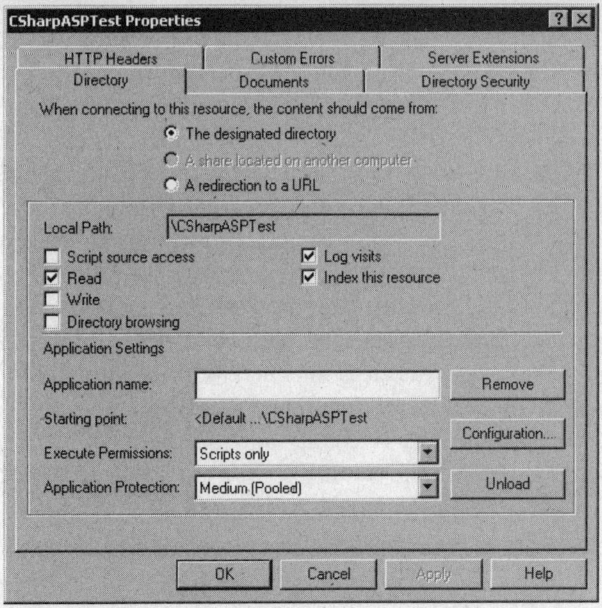

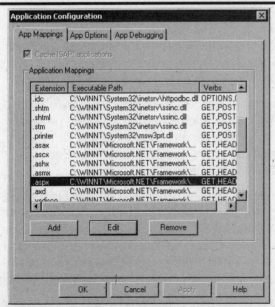

FIGURE 15.7:   CSharpASPTest Properties dialog

FIGURE 15.8:   CSharpASPTest Properties, Application Configuration dialog

This dialog has three tabs: App Mappings, App Options, and App Debugging. The App Mappings tab controls how the server treats various types of requests. Scroll down until you see the `.aspx` entry. Click the Edit button (but don't change anything; you're just exploring). You'll see the path in the Executable field, the `.aspx` extension in the Extension field, and the four "verbs" GET, HEAD, POST, and DEBUG in the Limit To field. The Script Engine check box lets the executable run in a virtual directory without Execute permissions (one marked Run Scripts in the Virtual Directory wizard or via the Virtual Directory Properties dialog). The Check That File Exists setting tells IIS to return an error message for scripting engines that don't automatically return messages for missing scripts or for requests in which the user doesn't have permission to access the requested file. If you want to add or change application mappings for a specific IIS application, you change them in this dialog. To change application mappings for the entire site, change them in the Default Web Site application properties.

Next, click the App Options tab. While it may look as though you can control some aspects of your application via this dialog, none of the options applies to ASP.NET. The options on this page apply only to classic ASP applications. The options on the last tab, App Debugging, don't apply to ASP.NET either. You configure ASP.NET application settings exclusively through the `web.config` and `machine.config` files and through page-level directives or code.

Click Cancel to close the dialogs. Look at the bottom of the `CSharpASPTest` Properties dialog again. The Application Protection setting should read Medium (Pooled). Click the arrow to drop down the options; with IIS 5 and Windows 2000, there are three of them:

Low (IIS Process)   Runs in the same address space as the server itself. Web applications that run in the IIS process address space can crash the server completely; however, web applications running in this space are faster than those that run as Pooled or Isolated applications.

Medium (Pooled)   Runs as part of a group of pooled applications. This setting provides server protection, but one errant application can bring down the entire group. However, the setting provides a good compromise. Although web applications in this space don't run as fast as those in the IIS process, they can be restarted automatically if they crash. This is the default setting.

High (Isolated)   Your application gets its own address space. This setting is the slowest but provides the greatest protection for other applications that may be running on the same server. With classic ASP applications, I recommend that people change the setting to High, but ASP.NET applications seem to be quite stable. When you're worried about the effect of installing a new application on your server, you don't have a dedicated development server, or you're building web applications that must interoperate with COM components, you should consider changing the setting from Medium to High.

Leave the dialog open for now; you'll change the setting in a minute. If you've never worked with COM+ applications, it's useful to see what effect the setting has.

Click Start ➢ Programs ➢ Administrative Tools ➢ Component Services. That launches the Component Services applet, which runs in the MMC just as the Internet Information Services applet does. In the list in the Tree pane, expand the Component Services item and the Computers item and then expand My Computer. Finally, expand the COM+ Applications item. Exactly what you'll see in the expanded list depends on the installed set of COM+ applications on your server, but one of the items is called IIS In-Process Applications (see Figure 15.9). That's where your application runs when you set the Application Protection property to Low (IIS Process).

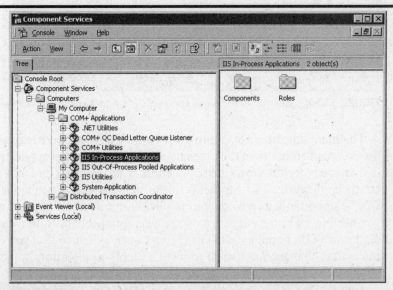

FIGURE 15.9:   Component Services applet, COM+ Applications

When you run your web application with the Medium (Pooled) setting, it runs as part of the next item, called IIS Out-Of-Process Pooled Applications. However, when you run your web application with the High (Isolated) setting, it runs as a separate application. To see that, go back to the `CSharpASPTest` Properties dialog and change the setting to High (Isolated). Click the Apply button and then close the dialog by clicking OK.

Now switch back to the Component Services applet and shut it down. Reopen it and you'll see an item named IIS-{`Default Web Site//Root/CSharpASPTest`} in the list (see Figure 15.10).

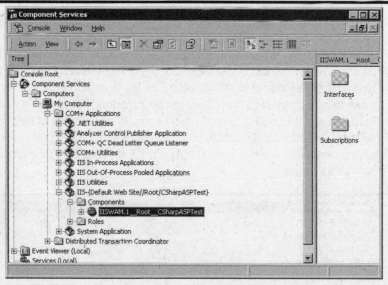

FIGURE 15.10: Component Services applet, COM+ Applications pop-up menu

The main advantage of running your application separately during development—other than the protection it provides for other applications—is that you can shut down the application, thus releasing all DLLs used by the application. This capability doesn't matter unless you're using COM components as part of your application, but when you are, and you need to make a change to a component, you probably don't want to shut down other applications—or the web server—just so that you can make that change. You can shut down a COM+ application by right-clicking the application in the list and selecting Shut Down from the pop-up menu.

NOTE

Before continuing, go back to the CSharpASPTest Properties dialog and change the setting back to Medium (Pooled).

THE *WEB.CONFIG* AND *MACHINE.CONFIG* FILES

Two files, named web.config and machine.config, allow you to control various aspects of your application. While learning about these files, you'll continue to use the CSharpASPTest application you created in the preceding section.

Is the *web.config* File Required?

So now, you have a virtual directory but no application. The question is this: Do you need a web.config file to run ASPX files? Let's see.

Launch Visual Studio and select New Project. Select Visual Basic Projects in the Project Types window, and select the ASP.NET web template. Name the application CSharpASPTest. If the location doesn't reference the root directory of the server where you created the CSharpASPTest virtual directory (http://localhost if you're running on a stand-alone development machine), change it to the correct server. Click OK. Visual Studio creates the application, but it recognizes that the virtual directory already exists, so it attaches the new application to the existing virtual directory. When you create files, that's where the "real" files reside.

The new CSharpASPTest project has a web.config file. Rename the file web_config.txt.

Next, add a new Web Form. It doesn't matter what you call it. Write a line into the Page_Load event or drag some controls onto the Web Form designer so that you'll be able to tell if the page finished properly. Compile the project, and then launch a browser instance and type in the URL of the Web Form you just created. If the project compiled, the Web Form should run fine. Obviously, you don't *have* to have a web.config file to run

Web Forms. However, if you switch back to Visual Studio, set the new Web Form as the start page for the project, and then run the project, you'll get an error. It turns out that although you can *run* Web Forms without a web.config file, you can't *debug* them without a web.config file. You can launch the project by selecting the Start Without Debugging option from the Debug menu (or pressing Ctrl+F5).

But the application has to get its configuration settings from somewhere, and you've already seen that it doesn't get them from the IIS Application Configuration settings. It turns out that ASP.NET and Visual Studio install several configuration files in the machine configuration directory. You can find the location with a little code. Create a Web Form in the CSharpASPTest application—it doesn't matter what you call it—and write the following code into the Page_Load method for the Web Form.

```
Response.Write(
    HttpRuntime.MachineConfigurationDirectory.ToString());
```

On my computer, that code produces the following output, where *n.n.nnnn* is the installed version number of the .NET Framework:

```
c:\winnt\microsoft net\framework\v.n.n.nnnn\Config
```

If you look in that directory, you'll see a file called machine.config, which contains the default application configuration settings. If you ever forget where the machine.config file resides, or if it's in a different location for a particular server, you can use the HttpRuntime.MachineConfiguration-Directory property to find it.

The *.config* File Hierarchy

You should explore the machine.config file thoroughly because it defines the default settings and behavior for your ASP.NET web applications. Unless you have a good reason, don't change the machine.config file. Some good reasons exist to change it, though. For example, the file contains default timeout (90 seconds), security, compilation, and language settings that you might want to change, default assemblies added to new projects, handlers for various file extensions, and browser definitions (used to set the HttpRequest.Browser property) that you will want to update periodically.

The most important thing at this time, though, is that you look through the file and see that a portion of it defines the same settings as the web.config file. That's because the CONFIG files form a hierarchy, where the lowest-level setting (the one closest to the executing code) has the greatest effect. When the .NET runtime looks for a setting, it starts in the currently executing file's directory and works its way up the directory hierarchy. For example, suppose you have the following hierarchical structure, where the Web Forms in the ClassRecords folder access the ClassRecords database and the Web Forms in the Northwind folder access the Northwind database:

```
c:\inetpub\wwwroot\CSharpASPTest
    ClassRecords
      Northwind
```

You could place a different web.config file in the ClassRecords folder, the Northwind folder, or both. It's important to remember that configuration files at *lower* levels take precedence over those at *higher* levels, which is perfectly logical but is exactly the opposite of what some people might expect. Unfortunately, despite the hierarchical nature of CONFIG files, simply copying the web.config file from your application's root directory and placing it in a subdirectory doesn't work, because it turns out that some of the sections aren't allowed at lower levels.

NOTE
You can work around this problem using the <location> tag, which lets you specify settings that apply to only a specific location in your application. See the section "Configuration File Location and Lock Settings" at the end of this chapter for an example.

To explore the problem, you'll need to place a web.config file at each level. In the preceding section, you renamed the web.config file web_config.txt. Rename it again, back to web.config. Create the Northwind and ClassRecords subfolders as shown earlier. Next, copy the file into both the ClassRecords folder and the Northwind folder.

By writing a small test Web Form for each folder, you can find out how the web.config files interact and which sections are not allowed in application subfolders. Create a test.aspx file in each folder, write code in each to display the current folder name, and then use the Server.Transfer command to transfer execution to the next file (see Listing 15.1).

A WORKAROUND FOR WEB FORMS WITH THE SAME NAME

Creating a Web Form in a C# web project automatically creates the code-behind file, which contains a class definition. But class names must be unique in a namespace; therefore, trying to create two Web Forms with the same name causes problems. Visual Studio lets you create the two Web Forms without an error, but the code won't compile. Here's a solution:

1. The top line of each ASPX file contains an `inherits` attribute. Switch to HTML mode in the designer to change the `inherits` attribute value.

2. Change the value of the attribute. For example, in the `test.aspx` file in the ClassRecords directory, change the attribute from `inherits=CSharpASPTest.test` to `inherits=CSharpASPTest.ClassRecords.test`, or some other name unique to your project.

3. Next, change the namespace of the class. For example, change the namespace line in the `test.aspx.cs` class in the Class-Records folder to namespace `CSharpASPTest.ClassRecords`.

After doing that, your code will compile without problems.

Listing 15.1: Testing Hierarchical Unmodified *web.config* Files

```
// in CSharpASPTest\test.aspx.cs
namespace CSharpASPTest
{
    // autogenerated code omitted

    public class test : System.Web.UI.Page
    {
        // autogenerated code omitted
        private void Page_Load(
          object sender, System.EventArgs e)
        {
            Response.Write("In ClassRecords folder<br>");
            Server.Transfer("ClassRecords/Northwind/test.aspx");
```

```
        }
      }
    }
    // in CSharpASPTest\ClassRecords\test.aspx.cs
    namespace CSharpASPTest.ClassRecords
    {
        // autogenerated code omitted

        public class test : System.Web.UI.Page
        {
            private void Page_Load(
              object sender, System.EventArgs e)
            {
                Response.Write("In ClassRecords folder<br>");
                Server.Transfer("Northwind/test.aspx");
            }
        }
    }


    // in CSharpASPTest\Northwind\test.aspx.cs
    namespace CSharpASPTest.ClassRecords.Northwind
    {
        // autogenerated code omitted

        public class test : System.Web.UI.Page
        {
            private void Page_Load(
              object sender, System.EventArgs e)
            {
                Response.Write("In Northwind folder<br>");
                Response.End();
            }
        }
    }
```

Compile the project, and then request the test.aspx file in the CSharpASPTest root directory with your browser. Unfortunately, this program as written doesn't work. There are several reasons. First, an error message appears, alerting you that an error occurred while processing a configuration file (see Figure 15.11).

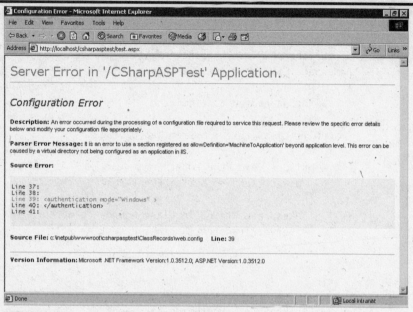

FIGURE 15.11: Nested configuration file error

The error occurs because you can't set application-level settings within `web.config` files in subdirectories.

So while `web.config` files may be hierarchical, there are some stated but well-hidden rules. The error occurs in the first-level subdirectory of the `CSharpASPTest` root—the `ClassRecords` directory. Remove the application-level settings. Here are the sections you must remove from `web.config` files in your application's subdirectories:

▶ `<authentication>`

▶ `<sessionState>`

After you remove these sections, run the application again. This time, you get a different error when you try to use the `Server.Transfer` method to switch execution to the `Northwind/test.aspx` file. Now the server can't find the file. The reason is that while the executing file is in the `ClassRecords` folder, the *context* under which the application is running is still that of the original request—the `test.aspx` file in the root folder.

If you're going to use the `ServerTransfer`, it's important to understand that it does not work quite the same way as the `Response.Redirect` method. Response.Redirect forces the *browser* to request the file; therefore, the context for the next file is appropriate to that file. In contrast, the browser is completely unaware of any Server.Transfer command, because when the Transfer method occurs, the browser still hasn't received a response.

The other settings in the web.config file may not have any effect, but they don't cause errors.

Add this key to the <appSettings> section of the web.config file in the root directory. Create the <appSettings> section if it doesn't already exist.

```
<add key="test" value="root"/>
```

Similarly, add "test" keys to the <appSettings> section for the web.config files in the ClassRecords and Northwind folders.

```
<add key="test" value="ClassRecords"/>
<add key="test" value="Northwind"/>
```

Create three new Web Forms, one in each subdirectory of the application, and call each of them test2.aspx. These files are identical to the test.aspx Web Forms except that each has an additional line to retrieve and display the value of the "test" key in its web.config file (see Listing 15.2).

Listing 15.2: Reading Application Settings from Hierarchical *web.config* **Files**

```
// in CSharpASPTest\test2.aspx.cs
namespace CSharpASPTest
{
    // autogenerated code omitted

    public class test2 : System.Web.UI.Page
    {
        private void Page_Load(
          object sender, System.EventArgs e)
        {
          Response.Write("In CSharpASPTest folder<br>");
          Response.Write("Application setting \"test\"=" +
              System.Configuration.ConfigurationSettings.
              AppSettings.Get("test") + "<br>");
          Server.Transfer("ClassRecords/test2.aspx");
        }
```

```csharp
        }
    }

    // in CSharpASPTest\ClassRecords\test2.aspx.cs
    namespace CSharpASPTest.ClassRecords
    {
        // autogenerated code omitted
        public class test2 : System.Web.UI.Page
        {
            private void Page_Load(
              object sender, System.EventArgs e)
            {
              Response.Write("In ClassRecords folder<br>");
              Response.Write("Application setting \"test\"=" +
                  System.Configuration.ConfigurationSettings.
                  AppSettings.Get("test") + "<br>");
              Server.Transfer(
                  "ClassRecords/Northwind/test2.aspx");
            }
        }
    }


    // in CSharpASPTest\Northwind\test2.aspx.cs
    namespace CSharpASPTest.ClassRecords.Northwind
    {
        // autogenerated code omitted
        public class test2 : System.Web.UI.Page
        {
            private void Page_Load(
              object sender, System.EventArgs e)
            {
              Response.Write("In Northwind folder<br>");
              Response.Write("Application setting \"test\"=" +
                  System.Configuration.ConfigurationSettings.
                  AppSettings.Get("test") + "<br>");
              Response.End();
            }

        }
    }
```

Compile the project again and then request the test2.aspx file in the CSharpASPTest root directory with your browser. This time, you'll see the output in Figure 15.12.

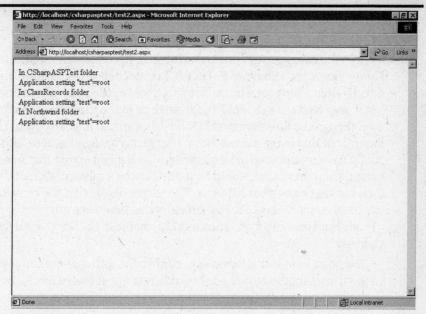

FIGURE 15.12:   Test hierarchical web.config files—display application settings.

Not exactly what you might expect, but again, the point of this exercise is that you must take into account the context in which a page executes. Despite the fact that the code transfers execution to the ClassRecords/test.aspx Web Form and then to the ClassRecords/Northwind/test.aspx Web Form, the context for application-level settings is the web.config file in the root CSharpASPTest folder—that's why you see the output Application setting test="root" regardless of which file executes.

At this point, you might think that the web.config files in the application subdirectories aren't really valid. If you read the documentation carefully, it seems that web.config files apply only to *virtual* directories. However, that's not entirely true. Change the test2.aspx.cs file in the ClassRecords directory so the Page_Load event reads this way:

```
private void Page_Load(object sender, System.EventArgs e)
{
    Response.Write("In ClassRecords folder<br>");
    Response.Write("Application setting \"test\"=" +
        System.Configuration.ConfigurationSettings.
```

```
                AppSettings.Get("test") + "<br>");
        Server.Transfer("Northwind/test2.aspx");
}
```

Note the changed `Server.Transfer` line. Recompile the application. Now, request the `CSharpASP-Test/ClassRecords/test2.aspx` file directly from a browser. Hmm. Not only does the file run without errors, but it *does* read the `web.config` file settings in the `ClassRecords` folder, even though the directory is not marked as a virtual directory (you'll see more about that in the next section). That seems unusual because, although config files are supposed to be hierarchical, you might expect that a section named `<appSettings>` would be limited to the application's root directory, but that's not what happens. The output shows that the context, as expected, is the `ClassRecords` directory this time, even after the `Server.Transfer` takes effect and the `test2.aspx` file in the `Northwind` folder executes.

The point here is that *some* `web.config` file settings—even in plain (non-virtual) subdirectories—*do* override settings at higher levels, exactly as the documentation (sort of) states.

 NOTE

One quick aside: If you change the `Server.Transfer` line in the `ClassRecords.test2.aspx.cs` file to `Server.Transfer("../test2 .aspx")`, transferring execution "up" to the application's root directory, you get a recursion error. In other words, you cannot transfer to another file and then transfer back. In fact, you can't use `Server.Execute(../test2.aspx)` to do that either, because the root `test2.aspx.cs` file transfers execution back—and you still get the recursion error. If you comment out the `Server.Transfer` line in the root `test2.aspx.cs` file, the code works fine, and the context remains that of the `ClassRecords/test2.aspx` file, so there's no problem with transferring execution from a lower to a higher point in the application folder hierarchy.

Although I haven't yet tested every standard section and setting in the `web.config` file, the only ones that seem to have *any* effect at subdirectory levels are those that deal with application settings, security, and data stored in custom sections. I'll show you how to create custom settings in the "Creating Custom Configuration Sections" section later in this chapter.

SITE HIERARCHY VERSUS DIRECTORY HIERARCHY

Go back and look at the error message in Figure 15.11. The message says that this error *can* be caused by forgetting to configure a directory as a virtual directory. In other words, you *can* nest virtual directories.

There's a difference between nesting directories and nesting *virtual* directories. When you create a virtual directory with IIS5, it automatically creates an IIS application, as you've seen. Each application gets its own set of ASP.NET objects, such as `Session`, `Application`, `Request`, `Response`, and `Server`. Unfortunately, that can lead to problems. It's worth exploring briefly, just so that you'll recognize the problems, should they occur in your application.

Launch the Internet Information Services applet, right-click the Default Web Site item in the Tree pane, and select New ➤ Virtual Directory from the pop-up menu. The Virtual Directory Creation Wizard appears. Click Next to begin, and then enter the name **ClassRecords** for the virtual directory alias name on the Virtual Directory Alias screen. Click the Next button and enter the path to the `CSharpASPTest\ClassRecords` subdirectory—normally `c:\Inetpub\wwwroot\CSharpASPTest\ ClassRecords`—into the Directory field. Click the Next button and then click Finish to close the wizard.

One more time, change the `test2.aspx.cs` file in the `ClassRecords` folder so that the `Server.Transfer` line looks like this:

```
Server.Transfer("ClassRecords/Northwind/test2.aspx");
```

Compile the application and request the `test2.aspx` file in the `CSharpASPTest` root directory with your browser. It will run. Clearly, creating an IIS application nested inside another IIS application runs without problems when you request files from the top-level application. Next, without changing anything, request the `test2.aspx` file directly from the new virtual `ClassRecords` directory: for example, `http:// localhost/ClassRecords/test2.aspx`. The request fails with the following error:

```
The resource cannot be found.
```

That makes sense. When you run the `test2.aspx` Web Form in the `ClassRecords` application directly, it can't find a file that's in the

CSharpASPTest application namespace—and the code-behind class (CSharpASPTest.ClassRecords.test2) is part of the CSharpASPTest application. Unfortunately, I know of no way to solve the problem entirely. I suspect the lesson to be learned here is that it's perfectly OK to nest directories, but that you should avoid nesting IIS applications.

INSIDE CONFIGURATION FILES

A configuration file consists primarily of sections, each of which must be declared at some level within the hierarchy of configuration files. Declaring a section involves creating a section group, within which you declare each section and associate the section with a particular type of *handler*, which provides specific programmatic access to that section.

The machine.config file contains the declarations for the standard section groups and sections.

A configuration file begins with the standard XML processing instruction. The configuration file's root element is required and must be called <configuration>.

```
<?xml version="1.0" encoding="UTF-8"?>
<configuration>
</configuration>
```

The <configuration> element may contain zero or more <configSections> elements, each of which may contain zero or more <sectionGroup> or <section> elements. The <section> elements are *not* the sections themselves—they're the *declaration* for the section. For example,

```
<?xml version="1.0" encoding="UTF-8"?>
<configuration>

    <configSections>
        <!-- tell .NET Framework to ignore CLR sections -->
        <section name="runtime"
            type="System.Configuration.IgnoreSectionHandler,
            System, Version=1.0.3300.0, Culture=neutral,
            PublicKeyToken=b77a5c561934e089"
            allowLocation="false"/>
        <section name="mscorlib"
            type="System.Configuration.IgnoreSectionHandler,
```

```
            System, Version=1.0.3300.0, Culture=neutral,
            PublicKeyToken=b77a5c561934e089"
            allowLocation="false"/>
        <section name="startup"
            type="System.Configuration.IgnoreSectionHandler,
            System, Version=1.0.3300.0, Culture=neutral,
            PublicKeyToken=b77a5c561934e089"
            allowLocation="false"/>
        <section name="system.runtime.remoting"
            type="System.Configuration.IgnoreSectionHandler,
            System, Version=1.0.3300.0, Culture=neutral,
            PublicKeyToken=b77a5c561934e089"
            allowLocation="false"/>
    <!--more section declarations-->
    </configSections>
</configuration>
```

NOTE

The version number in the machine.config entries may differ on your system, but the information should be essentially the same.

The <section> declaration attributes define the section name, the type, the version, the culture, a PublicKeyToken string, and whether the section can contain a location attribute (more on that in a second).

The type attribute is particularly interesting. In the three section declarations shown previously, the type attribute value shows the section handler type (System.Configuration.IgnoreSectionHandler); the namespace from which to load the handler (System); and the version, the culture, and a PublicKeyToken value. However, further down, the file contains section declarations for several standard section handlers. For example, each of the sections below uses a different handler type, most of which are defined in the System.Configuration namespace.

```
    <section name="system.diagnostics"
        type="System.Diagnostics.DiagnosticsConfigurationHandler,
        System, Version=1.0.3300.0, Culture=neutral,
        PublicKeyToken=b77a5c561934e089"/>
    <section name="appSettings"
        type="System.Configuration.NameValueFileSectionHandler,
        System, Version=1.0.3300.0, Culture=neutral,
        PublicKeyToken=b77a5c561934e089"/>
    <sectionGroup name="system.net">
        <section name="authenticationModules"
```

```
        type="System.Net.Configuration.
            NetAuthenticationModuleHandler,
            System, Version=1.0.3300.0, Culture=neutral,
            PublicKeyToken=b77a5c561934e089"/>
        <section name="defaultProxy"
            type="System.Net.Configuration.DefaultProxyHandler,
                System,
            Version=1.0.3300.0, Culture=neutral,
            PublicKeyToken=b77a5c561934e089"/>
        <section name="connectionManagement"
            type="System.Net.Configuration.
            ConnectionManagementHandler,
            System, Version=1.0.3300.0, Culture=neutral,
            PublicKeyToken=b77a5c561934e089"/>
        <section name="webRequestModules"
            type="System.Net.Configuration.WebRequestModuleHandler,
            System, Version=1.0.3300.0, Culture=neutral,
            PublicKeyToken=b77a5c561934e089"/>
    </sectionGroup>
```

Creating Custom Configuration Sections

The defined handlers are available for you to use for your own custom sections. You need to define a section only once—section definitions are inherited.

For example, suppose you wanted to define a set of product groups containing individual products. You could add a `<productGroups>` section and define a `<product>` section, perhaps using a `System.Configuration.NameValueFileSectionHandler` to handle returning individual product values. To see how this works, add a new section definition to the top of the `web.config` file in the root directory of your CSharpASPTest project, just after the `<configuration>` element:

```
<configuration>
    <configSections>
        <section name="product"
            type="System.Configuration.NameValueSectionHandler,
            System" />
    </configSections>
    <!-- rest of the web.config file -->
</configuration>
```

Next, add a <product> element at the end of the file, just before the </configuration> element.

```
<!-- existing web.config file content-->
<product>
<add key="Flashlights" value="Flashlights description" />
<add key="Key Rings" value="Key Rings description" />
</product>
```

The NameValueSectionHandler type implements a getConfig method that returns a NameValueCollection of product element values. The Web Form getProducts.aspx retrieves the products and loops through them, displaying the keys and values (see Listing 15.3).

Unfortunately, when you run this code, you get an error stating the following:

```
File or assembly name System, or one
  of its dependencies, was not found.
```

Although the documentation states that you can create custom configuration sections that use the NameValueSectionHandler type, you can use it only if you take one of the following steps:

▶ Create a custom configuration handler class.

▶ Add the <section> tag to your machine.config file rather than to your web.config file.

▶ Copy the system.dll file from your Winnt.Microsoft.NET\Framework\<version> folder to the bin folder of your project—in this case, the CSharpASPTest\bin folder. While I don't recommend this option, it may be the only way to get your section to work if you don't have access to the machine.config file.

The first option is the most flexible because by writing your own class, you can handle anything you like; however, it's also the most trouble. See the section "Creating a Custom Configuration Handler" later in this chapter for more information. However, if you can use one of the existing system handlers, it's much easier to use the first option. For simple key/value pairs such as the <product> example, use one of the first two options. Avoid the last option—copying the system.dll—unless you have no other choice.

Add the <section> tag to your machine.config file, and run the Web Form getProducts.aspx in the CSharpASPTest root folder, which retrieves and displays the information in the <product> tag in your web.config file. Listing 15.3 shows the code.

Listing 15.3: Retrieving Custom Configuration Settings (getProducts.aspx.cs)

```
using System.Collections.Specialized
// autogenerated code omitted

private void Page_Load(object sender, System.EventArgs e) {
    NameValueCollection nvc = null;

    nvc = (NameValueCollection) Context.GetConfig("product");
    if (nvc == null) {
        Response.Write("No products defined<br>");
    }
    else {
        foreach (String aKey in nvc.Keys) {
            Response.Write(aKey + "=" + nvc.Get(aKey) + "<br>");
        }
    }
}
```

The output from the code in Listing 15.3 looks like Figure 15.13.

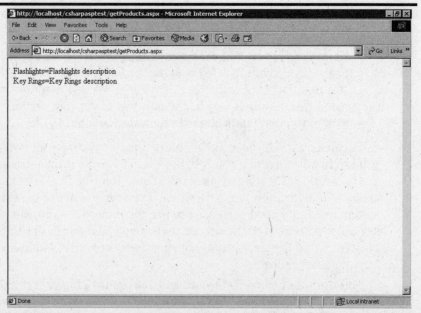

FIGURE 15.13:   Output from the Web Form CSharpASPTest.getProducts.aspx

When you are using the built-in configuration handlers, settings are read-only, so you can't use them to add new settings at runtime. It's not clear why Microsoft chose to make the handlers act in read-only mode, because there's a simple workaround. You *can* add new settings programmatically if you open the file and use the methods in System.XML to add nodes. The procedure is as follows:

1. Create an XmlDocument.

2. Load the web.config file.

3. Retrieve the section node that contains the values you want.

4. Create a new node and add attributes as needed.

5. Append the new node to the section node.

6. Save your changes.

The ASP.NET engine watches the .config file hierarchy and reloads the files if they change, so any changes you make in this manner take effect immediately. For example, the Web Form addProduct.aspx still in the CSharpASPTest application adds a new key and value to the <product> section and displays it immediately (see Listing 15.4).

Listing 15.4: Adding a Custom Configuration Setting Dynamically *(addProduct.aspx.cs)*

```
using System.Collections.Specialized;
using System.Xml;

// autogenerated code omitted
private void Page_Load(object sender, System.EventArgs e) {
   NameValueCollection nvc = null;
   XmlDocument xml = new XmlDocument();
   XmlNode node = null, product = null, keys = null;
   xml.Load(Server.MapPath(".") + "\\web.config");
   keys =
   xml.SelectSingleNode(
      "configuration/product/add[@key='Keys']");
   if (keys == null) {
      Response.Write("Adding key<br>");
      product = xml.SelectSingleNode(
         "configuration/product");
      node = xml.CreateNode(XmlNodeType.Element, "add", "");
      node.Attributes.Append(xml.CreateAttribute("key"));
```

```
            node.Attributes[0].Value = "Keys";
            node.Attributes.Append(xml.CreateAttribute("value"));
            node.Attributes[1].Value = "Keys description";
            product.AppendChild(node);
            xml.Save(Server.MapPath(".") + "\\web.config");
        }

        nvc = (NameValueCollection) Context.GetConfig("product");
        if (nvc == null) {
            Response.Write("No products defined<br>");
        }
        else {
            foreach(String aKey in nvc.Keys) {
                Response.Write(aKey + "=" + nvc.Get(aKey) + "<br>");
            }
        }
    }
```

When you run the Web Form, the output looks like Figure 15.14.

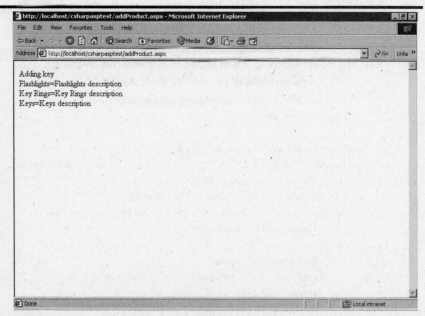

FIGURE 15.14:   Output from the Web Form CSharpASPTest.addProduct.aspx
after adding a custom setting

Creating a Custom Configuration Handler

The most flexible option for defining custom configuration sections is to create your own handler. To do that, you need to create a new project containing a class that implements the `IConfigurationSectionHandler` interface. The custom handler will read a custom section containing the same product information that you already created in the previous section and added to the `web.config` file in the CSharpASPTest project root folder; however, this time, you can use descriptive names for the tags and attributes rather than the `"key"` and `"value"` attributes required for the `System.Configuration.NameValueCollectionHandler` class. Add the following section to the CSharpASPTest project's `web.config` file:

```
<products>
    <product name="Tents"
        description="Tents description" />
    <product name="Lanterns"
        description="Lanterns description" />
</products>
```

For this example, create a new Class Library project named CSharpASP-Custom. Rename the default `Class1.cs` file `ProductsNameValueHandler.cs`, and place the code in Listing 15.5 into the file.

Listing 15.5: The ProductsNameValueHandler Custom Configuration Handler Code (*ProductₐNameValueHandler.cₐ*)

```csharp
using System;
using System.Collections;
using System.Collections.Specialized;
using System.Xml;
using System.Configuration;

namespace CSharpASPCustom
{
    public class ProductsNameValueHandler :
        IConfigurationSectionHandler {

        public virtual object Create(Object parent,
            Object context, XmlNode node) {
            NameValueCollection products = null;
            int i;
            string key;
```

```
        string val;
        products = new NameValueCollection();
        for (i=0; i < node.ChildNodes.Count; i++) {
            key = node.ChildNodes.Item(i).Attributes.
                GetNamedItem("name").Value;
            val = node.ChildNodes.Item(i).Attributes.
                GetNamedItem("description").Value;
            products.Add(key,val);
        }
        return products;
    }
  }
}
```

The class has a single function named Create that implements the System.Configuration.IConfigurationSectionHandler interface's Create method. The function receives three parameters:

▶ A parent object, which can be an object corresponding to the configuration settings for a parent tag in the config file. You can ignore that parameter for this example.

▶ An HttpConfigurationContext object. You can ignore that object for this example as well.

▶ An XmlNode object, which represents the configuration XML node itself—in this case, the <product> tag.

The code is simple. It creates a NameValueCollection object and populates it by looping through each <product> tag in the <products> section, reading the name and description attributes from each tag. Because the Create method's return value is an Object, you still need to cast the value to the appropriate type from your Web Form—just as you had to cast it when you used the System NameValueCollectionHandler.

To test the new handler, add this code to the web.config file in your CSharpASPTest root folder, just after the <configuration> tag:

```
<configuration>
  <configSections>
    <section name="products"
      type="CSharpASPCustom.ProductsNameValueHandler,
      CSharpASPCustom" />
  </configSections>
  <!-- rest of the web.config file -->
</configuration>
```

Note that the tag is identical to the `<configSections>` tag shown in the preceding section except that it references the `CSharpASPCustom` namespace and the `ProductsNameValueHandler` class rather than the `System.Configuration` namespace and the `NameValueSectionHandler` class. Build the `CSharpASPCustom` project. Save your changes to the `web.config` file.

Add a reference to the `ProductsNameValueHandler.dll` file. Right-click the References item in the Solution Explorer and select Add Reference. Click the .NET tab, and then click the `Browse` button. You'll find the `CSharpASPCustom.dll` file in the `CSharpASPCustom` project's `bin` folder.

Finally, change the line that retrieves the `"product"` configuration in the `getProducts.aspx` Web Form so that it retrieves the `"products"` (note the plural) configuration instead:

```
nvc = (NameValueCollection) Context.GetConfig("products");
```

When you run the `getProducts.aspx` Web Form now, you'll see the values from the new `<products>` section.

Configuration File Location and Lock Settings

Earlier in this chapter, you saw how to nest configuration files in sub-directories. For many purposes, a simpler and more powerful method is to apply a `<location>` tag to values that you want to make available to Web Forms in a particular location. In addition, you can prevent lower-level configuration files from overriding a setting by adding an `allowOverride` attribute to the `<location>` tag.

For example, add the following XML to the `web.config` file in the `CSharpASPTest` directory and then save the file.

```
<location path="ClassRecords">
   <product>
      <add key="Backpacks" value="Backpacks description
   ClassRecords"
   </product>
</location>
```

The Backpacks product is now only available to Web Forms placed in the `ClassRecords` folder. The file `getProductsClassRecords.aspx` in the `CSharpASPTest/ClassRecords` folder is—except for its name—identical to the getProducts.aspx file in the root CSharpASPTest folder. I simply copied the file and renamed it.

When you run the original getProducts.aspx Web Form (http://localhost/CSharpASP/getProducts.aspx), you'll see the products defined at the root level, but not the Backpacks product. But when you run the Web Form http://localhost/CSharpASP/ClassRecords/getProducts.aspx, you'll see all the products—including the Backpacks product.

Location-Specific Tags Override Higher-Level Settings

You can also use the <location> tag to override higher-level settings. For example, add a Flashlights product to the ClassRecords product location. Change the value attribute so it differs from the Flashlights value already defined. Here's how your ClassRecords product location settings might look (I added "ClassRecords" to the value attribute):

```
<location path="ClassRecords">
  <product>
    <add key="Backpacks" value="Backpacks description" />
    <add key="Flashlights"
        value="Flashlights description ClassRecords" />
  </product>
</location>
```

Now, when you run the getProducts.aspx file in the ClassRecords folder, you'll see the altered, ClassRecords-specific description for the Flashlights key rather than the original description. Using the <location> tag, you can make a section or set of sections apply to a specific file as well as an entire directory. It's important that you understand the difference between the <location> tag and nested web.config files. Using the <location> technique, you can change the settings that you cannot nest.

You just saw how easy it is to override higher-level settings using the <location> tag. That's a potential problem; a lower-level setting might inadvertently change a setting that you *want* to apply to an entire site or set of subdirectories. To solve the problem, add the allowOverride attribute to a <location> tag. The attribute takes a Boolean value of either false or true. For example, to prevent a web.config file in a subdirectory of the CSharpASPTest folder from overriding higher-level settings, add the following <location> tag around the products defined for the `CSharpASPTest` root level. The highlighted lines in the following snippet show the added code:

```
<location path="CSharpASPTest" allowOverride="false">
    <product>
        <add key="Flashlights"
         value="Flashlights description" />
        <add key="Key Rings" value="Key Rings description" />
    </product>
</location>

<location path="ClassRecords">
    <product>
        <add key="Backpacks" value="Backpacks description" />
        <add key="Flashlights"
            value="Flashlights description ClassRecords" />
    </product>
</location>
```

To test it, run the `getProductsClassRecords.aspx` Web Form. You may recall that you changed the `Flashlights` description in the preceding example, and you saw the changed description when you ran the `getProductsClassRecords.aspx` Web Form. However, after adding the `<location>` tag as shown, you will see *only* the `ClassRecords`-specific settings, which seems odd because if you're not supposed to be able to override the settings, you should *not* see the `ClassRecords`-specific `"Flashlights"` item. However, some experimentation shows that if you change the location path for the root items from `"CSharpASPTest"` to a single period (`"."`) or a blank string (`""`), it seems to work as advertised:

```
<location path="." allowOverride="false">
    <product>
        <add key="Flashlights"
            value="Flashlights description" />
        <add key="Key Rings" value="Key Rings description" />
    </product>
</location>
```

Changing the path attribute value to `"."` and running the `getProducts-ClassRecords.aspx` Web Form causes an error stating:

```
Parser Error Message: This configuration section
cannot be used at this path. This happens when
the site administrator has locked access to this
section using <location allowOverride="false"> from
an inherited configuration file.
```

As you might expect (although I didn't anticipate that exact result), the error occurs when the page tries to access the `<location path="ClassRecords">` products because they have been marked as non-overrideable. I could not force the error to occur with any path setting other than `"."`. Note that this is a *parse* error—you can't access the values with the root `getClassRecords.aspx` Web Form either using both `<location>` tags.

WARNING

The capability to prevent overrides gives administrators the power to control what behavior programmers can and can't override at lower levels. However, if programmers have access to the `Web.config` file in a higher-level directory, they can modify it using straight XML techniques as shown in the preceding example. If you use the `allowOverride` attribute, you should be sure to restrict the change permissions on the `web.config` file.

Be careful with the sequence! There's an ordering problem as well. If you change the sequence of the entries in the `web.config` file so that the `<location path="ClassRecords">` tag appears before the `<location path=""allowOverride="false">` tag, the restriction *will not take effect*. To test the problem, reverse the order of the entries as follows:

```
<location path="ClassRecords">
    <product>
        <add key="Backpacks" value="Backpacks description" />
        <add key="Flashlights"
            value="Flashlights description ClassRecords" />
    </product>
</location>

<location allowOverride="false">
    <product>
        <add key="Flashlights"
            value="Flashlights description" />
        <add key="Key Rings" value="Key Rings description" />
    </product>
</location>
```

This time, when you run the `getProductsClassRecords.aspx` Web Form, you'll see three products, and you won't get any errors.

WARNING

The order of <location> tags for which you want to disable overrides in lower-level sections is critical. Be sure that the higher-level tags containing the allowOverride attribute appear first.

One more note. If you move the ClassRecords-specific <product> section into the ClassRecords/Web.config file instead and remove the <location> tag, you no longer need the path attribute in the root folder, either. In other words, the whole thing is simpler if the files use this configuration:

In CSharpASPTest/Web.config:

```
<location allowOverride="false">
    <product>
        <add key="Flashlights"
            value="Flashlights description" />
        <add key="Key Rings" value="Key Rings description" />
    </product>
</location>
```

In CSharpASPTest/ClassRecords/Web.config:

```
<product>
    <add key="Backpacks" value="Backpacks description" />
    <add key="Flashlights"
        value="Flashlights description ClassRecords" />
</product>
```

Now you get the error only if you attempt to access the items using the getProductsClassRecords.aspx Web Form—the getProducts.aspx file still works.

WHAT'S NEXT

In this chapter, you've seen how IIS settings determine which virtual directories run as applications and how to create IIS applications manually. You've seen how to use the base machine.config file in conjunction with web.config files in the various folders of your application to control how that application responds. In Chapter 16 coming up, you'll learn about the role that XML plays in web applications.

Chapter 16

USING XML IN WEB APPLICATIONS

Despite the relative youth of the XML specification, it has rapidly become a major focus of web programming. XML is the underpinning for the newest version of HTML, called XHTML; it's the basis of web services, and in combination with the XSLT and XPath recommendations, it's one of the most effective ways to ensure the separation of your data from the interface that displays the data. XML is a crucial part of .NET, so it's not surprising that the framework provides some sophisticated, powerful, and flexible methods for reading, writing, and transforming XML data. You'll find the classes you need to manipulate XML in the System.Xml namespace.

Adapted from *Mastering ASP.NET with C#*
by A. Russell Jones
ISBN 0-7821-2989-7

CREATING THE WEB APPLICATION USED IN THIS CHAPTER

In Chapters 16, 17, and 18 of this book you'll work with a project named CSharpASP. This project was used as the source web project throughout *Mastering ASP.NET with C#*, from which Chapters 16 and 17 were adapted. The code from each chapter of that book is stored in a specific folder under the master project. The following instructions have been taken from Chapter 4 of *Mastering ASP.NET with C#*; they tell you how to create this root web application and the subfolders for the CSharpASP application.

You can find the source code from *Mastering APS.NET with C#* at www.sybex.com.

1. Launch VS.NET. Click File ➢ New ➢ Project and select the item Visual C# Projects in the left pane of the New Project dialog. In the right pane, select the Web Application icon (you may need to scroll to see the icon).

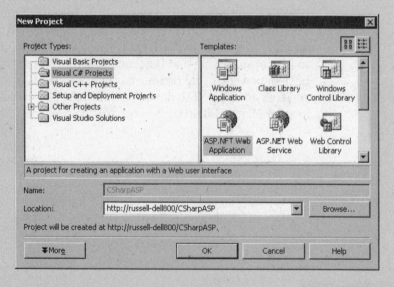

2. By default, C# names your Web Application projects Web-Application with an appended number—for example, WebApplication1—but you should always enter a specific name. Click in the Name field and enter **CSharpASP**. Check the Location field; it should contain the name of the web server you

CONTINUED ➡

want to host this application. Typically, this will read `http://localhost`. However, you may create a project on any web server for which you have sufficient permissions to create a virtual directory and write files. Make sure the information you entered is correct, and then click OK. VS.NET will create the new project.

3. You should now see the Solution Explorer pane. If the Solution Explorer is not visible, select View ➢ Solution Explorer from the menu bar.

4. Create a new folder under CSharpASP, named ch4 (or whatever name you choose). Creating subfolders works exactly like creating subfolders in a website: you simply add the name of the folder to the root URL to view a page in that folder. To create the subfolder, right-click the CSharpASP virtual root in the Solution Explorer, click Add, and then click New Folder. Finally, type **ch4** (or whatever name you choose) for the folder name.

5. Select the WebForm1.aspx file and drop it on top of your new ch4 folder. When you drop the file, VS.NET will move the ASPX file (and any associated files) into the ch4 folder. If the file is already open, close it first, and then move it. Your Solution Explorer pane should look similar to the one just above.

INTRODUCTION TO THE *SYSTEM.XML* NAMESPACE

The System.Xml namespace contains all the classes you need to work with XML in .NET. At the most basic level, the XmlDocument class lets you load and save XML documents from disk files or from strings. If you've worked with XML in other systems such as Microsoft's own msxml.dll, you'll recognize XmlDocument as similar to the root object in those systems. An XmlDocument object uses a *parser* to read the XML document and create a node tree—a hierarchical representation of the elements, attributes, and text in the document. For example, to initiate the parsing process for an XML document, you create an XmlDocument instance and pass the file you want to parse to its Load method:

```
XmlDocument xml = new XmlDocument();
Xml.Load(physical filename of XML document);
Response.Write(xml.InnerXml);
```

The code fragment loads an XML document and sends the XML string contents to the client.

What Can You Do with XML?

XML documents, by themselves, are easy for humans to read but aren't that useful to the computer. By themselves, they aren't much better than any other sequential file format—just a wordier, if easier to parse, text file format. To make them useful, you need to add some functionality. In addition to the basic XmlDocument, the System.Xml namespace contains "helper" classes that provide the capability to

▶ Find nodes and values

▶ Define the structure and data for an XML document

▶ Let you traverse a document sequentially without caching the data in memory

▶ Transform a document into another form

▶ Move seamlessly between XML and relational data

▶ Read and write XML files

Retrieve Individual Nodes or Groups of Nodes—*System.Xml.XPath*

An XML file consists of a tree of *nodes*. Each node may be an element, an attribute, a comment, a processing instruction, or a character data (CDATA) section, or any of several less common node types. An XML document contains markup that conforms to strict rules. Therefore, you can teach the parser to separate the markup from content easily, but you need to be able to retrieve individual nodes or collections of nodes to find data quickly. You do that using System.Xml.XPath. The XPath specification describes a vocabulary for navigating through the node tree.

Define the Structure and Data Types in an XML Document—*System.Xml.Schema*

Over the years, the computer industry has standardized on many file formats for various types of information. For example, each of the many types of image formats (.gif, .bmp, .jpg, and so on) has a specific file format. Only by rigidly adhering to this file format can you create a GIF file and have applications display it correctly. There's no room for customization—the file format is fixed. For those of you who have worked with Windows since version 3 days, another common example is INI (application initialization) files, which—before the Windows Registry—were the premier way to store application-specific information. An INI file had three customizable levels—a set of *sections* enclosed in square brackets, each of which could contain *keys* and *values* separated by an equal (=) sign. You can think of these three items as hierarchical levels, where level one is the sections, which had two child levels—the keys and the values. For example,

```
[section1]
key1=value1
[section2]
key1=value1
key2=value2
```

Unfortunately, without performing customized manipulations on the key or value string, there was no way to go beyond the three fixed items. The equivalent XML document could look like Listing 16.1.

Listing 16.1: A Simple XML File That Holds INI File Type Information *(XML-INI.xml)*

```
<?xml version="1.0"?>
<sections>
```

```
<section name="Section1">
  <key name"key1" value="value1" />
</section>
<section name="Section">
  <key name"key1" value="value1" />
  <key name"key2" value="value2" />
<section>
</sections>
```

In this form, the section name for each section, along with the keys and values, has become an *attribute*. Attributes are fast and easy to read but not as flexible as elements. However, you aren't constrained to using attributes. Listing 16.2 shows an extended version that uses elements rather than attributes. You can extend the number of levels or the number of items associated with a particular key very easily.

Listing 16.2: The XML Document Extends the INI File Format (XML_INI2.xml)

```
<?xml version="1.0" encoding="utf-8"?>
<sections xmlns="http://tempuri.org/XML-INI2.xsd">
  <section>
    <name>Section1</name>
    <keys>
      <key>
        <name>key1</name>
        <value>value1</value>
      </key>
    </keys>
  </section>
  <section>
    <name>Section2</name>
    <keys>
      <key>
        <name>key1</name>
        <value>value1</value>
      </key>
      <key>
        <name>key2</name>
        <value>value2</value>
      </key>
    </keys>
```

```
    </section>
  </sections>
```

Because XML data can appear in so many forms, you need to be able to describe exactly what any specific XML document can contain. A *schema* lets you do this. I'm not going to go into much depth about schemas because you don't need to know much about them to use XML efficiently. However, it's useful to know what a schema *does*. For each element and attribute, the schema defines the name and the value type. Elements can be simple (they contain only a value) or complex (they may contain a combination of other elements and attributes and a value). For example, in the first XML INI file example, the element <sections> is a complex element that contains one child element—<section>. In turn, each <section> element is a complex element that contains one attribute called name and one complex element named key. Here's a portion of the schema for the XML-INI.xml document that shows the <section> element definition:

```
<xsd:element name="section">
  <xsd:complexType>
    <xsd:sequence>
      <xsd:element name="key" minOccurs="0"
        maxOccurs="unbounded">
        <xsd:complexType>
          <xsd:attribute name="name" form="unqualified"
            type="xsd:string" />
          <xsd:attribute name="value" form="unqualified"
            type="xsd:string" />
          <xsd:attribute name="section_Id" type="xsd:int"
            use="prohibited" />
        </xsd:complexType>
      </xsd:element>
    </xsd:sequence>
    <xsd:attribute name="section_Id"
      msdata:AutoIncrement="true"
      type="xsd:int" msdata:AllowDBNull="false"
      use="prohibited" />
    <xsd:attribute name="name" form="unqualified"
      type="xsd:string"/>
  </xsd:complexType>
</xsd:element>
```

You can see that the <section> element is a complex element. Look carefully at the attributes for the key element. There are three, even though I only used two: name and value. The VS XML editor defined the section_Id element automatically. In fact, the VS XML editor defined the entire schema automatically by looking at the XML document elements and making a guess as to the types. Letting the IDE generate the schema is extremely convenient. In addition, you can use the schema it creates to define the data in a DataSet. By creating such a schema, you can load your XML directly into a DataSet and then bind it to controls.

Transform XML Documents—*System.Xml.Xsl*

XML data is *mutable*—you can change it from one form of XML into another form, using an XML vocabulary called XSL (Extensible Stylesheet Language) or XSLT (Extensible Stylesheet Language Transformations). The most popular use of XSLT has been to transform it into HTML or, more precisely, XHTML, which is simply HTML cleaned up so that it conforms to the XML specification. The advantage of transforms is that you cleanly separate the data from the markup, because the data is in the XML file, while the markup is in an XSLT file called a *stylesheet*. Using Internet Explorer (IE), you can view the results of a transform simply by loading an XML file. That's because IE contains a *default stylesheet* that it applies to XML documents that don't define their own stylesheets. Listing 16.3 shows a simple XML document called `flexible.xml`.

Listing 16.3: The *flexible.xml* XML File

```
<?xml version="1.0" encoding="utf-8" ?>
<!--<?xml-stylesheet
  type="text/xsl" href="flexible.xsl" ?>-->
<items>
  <item>XML </item>
  <item>is </item>
  <item>an </item>
  <item>extremely </item>
  <item>flexible </item>
  <item>data </item>
  <item>format </item>
</items>
```

If you request the file `flexible.xml` in IE, it looks like Figure 16.1.

Note that the default stylesheet color codes the various parts of the document and clearly shows the tree structure. It even lets you expand and collapse tags that contain child elements. That's nice, but fortunately, you're not limited to using the default stylesheet. By including a tag that references an XSL or XSLT stylesheet, IE will perform the transform for you and display the results.

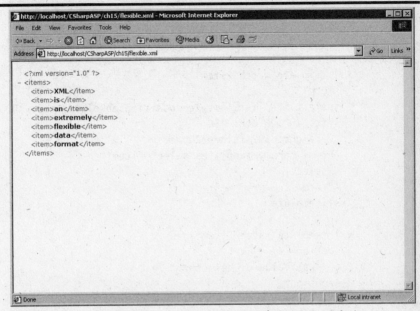

FIGURE 16.1:   The `flexible.xml` file in IE, displayed with the default stylesheet

For example, the following stylesheet displays the items in an HTML `ListBox` control (see Listing 16.4).

Listing 16.4: The *flexible.xsl* File Creates an HTML *ListBox* Containing the Items from the *flexible.xml* File (*flexible.xsl*)

```
<?xml version='1.0'?>
<xsl:stylesheet version="1.0"
    xmlns:xsl="http://www.w3.org/1999/XSL/Transform">

<xsl:output method="html" />

<xsl:template match="/">
    <html>
    <head>
    <title>Simple XSLT Stylesheet</title>
```

```
        </head>
        <body>
            <xsl:apply-templates select="items"/>
        </body>
        </html>
    </xsl:template>

    <xsl:template match="items">
        <form>
        <select id="list1" style="position:absolute; top: 100;
        left: 100; width: 150;
            height: 300" size="20">
            <xsl:apply-templates select="item" />
        </select>
        </form>
    </xsl:template>

    <xsl:template match="item">
        <option>
            <xsl:value-of select="." />
        </option>
    </xsl:template>
</xsl:stylesheet>
```

Performing Client-Side Transforms Using IE5x   Client-side
(in-browser) XSLT transforms work only with IE5 and higher; at the time
of this writing, no other browser supports XSLT transforms on the client
side. In addition, to take maximum advantage of XSLT on the client, you
must have the msxml3.dll or msxml4.dll parser installed on the client
computer. Finally, if you're using msxml3.dll, you must download and
run the xmlinst.exe file for IE to recognize the XSLT namespace. IE6
ships with msxml3, so you don't need to install the updated parser if you're
running IE6 or later.

Uncomment the following highlighted line in the flexible.xml file:

```
<?xml version="1.0" ?>
<?xml-stylesheet type="text/xsl" href="flexible.xsl" ?>
<items>
    <item>XML </item>
    <item>is </item>
    <item>an </item>
    <item>extremely </item>
```

```
        <item>flexible </item>
        <item>data </item>
        <item>format </item>
    </items>
```

When you load the file `flexible.xml` into IE, it recognizes the file type and parses the document. The processing instruction you just uncommented instructs the browser to load the stylesheet `flexible.xsl`, perform the transform, and display the results of the transform rather than the XML document itself.

If you're not familiar with XSLT, this chapter won't help you much, but I will briefly walk you through the `flexible.xsl` stylesheet.

```
<?xml version='1.0'?>
<xsl:stylesheet version="1.0"
     xmlns:xsl="http://www.w3.org/1999/XSL/Transform">
```

You can see from the first line that XSLT is an XML vocabulary, not a separate language. You can manipulate XSLT files by loading them into an `XmlDocument` just as you can any other XML file.

The second line of code references the XSLT *namespace* schema URI (Universal Resource Identifier). A URI is different from a URL in that it only needs to be unique. It doesn't need to reference a real file (although it can); it only needs to be a unique identifier. For example, if you enter the XSLT namespace into a browser, you'll see a page that shows the W3C logo and the text, "This is an XML namespace defined in the XSL Transformations (XSLT) Version 1.0 specification" along with some W3C links. You won't see the XSLT namespace schema itself because it isn't there. Instead, IE has an internal reference to the schema—you created that reference when you installed the `msxml3.dll` and ran the `xmlinst.exe` file.

The next line determines the type of output from the transform. Valid values are `html`, `xml`, and `text`. The default output type is `xml`.

```
<xsl:output method="html" />
```

The remainder of the file consists of three templates. A *template* is a block of code that handles a specific tag or group of tags. The `match` attribute in the template definition determines which tags a particular template will handle. For example, the first template matches the root node of the XML document. XSLT works from the concept of a *context node*. Until you select a node, there is no context. In this stylesheet, the root template creates <html>, <head>, <title>, and <body> tags and then tells the stylesheet to select the <items> node and apply a template to it.

```
<xsl:template match="/">
    <html>
    <head>
    <title>Simple XSLT Stylesheet</title>
    </head>
    <body>
        <xsl:apply-templates select="items"/>
    </body>
    </html>
</xsl:template>
```

The stylesheet searches for a template that matches the name items (see the next code fragment). When the stylesheet begins processing the items template, the `<items>` node becomes the context node, not the root node. Select queries within the items template work from the `<items>` node by default; in other words, changing templates is one way to change the context.

The template outputs a `<form>` tag and a `<select>` tag, then calls `xsl:apply-templates` again, this time selecting the item nodes first. Note that the `select="item"` attribute selects *all* the `<item>` elements, and the `xsl:apply-templates` method applies the matching item template once for each node in the list of item nodes.

```
<xsl:template match="items">
    <form>
    <select id="list1" style="position:absolute; top: 100;
    left: 100; width: 150;
        height: 300" size="20">
        <xsl:apply-templates select="item" />
    </select>
    </form>
</xsl:template>
```

The item template itself (see the following) writes an `<option>` tag and outputs the value of the context node—in this case, an `<item>` element. The highlighted line in the template uses a shortcut notation to select the current node, `select="."`. The value of a node is the text it contains. Each `<item>` node in the `flexible.xml` file contains a single word and a space.

```
<xsl:template match="item">
    <option>
        <xsl:value-of select="." />
    </option>
</xsl:template>
</xsl:stylesheet>
```

The stylesheet "walks the tree" from the root node to the lowest-level node, applying a template at each level. Figure 16.2 shows the result.

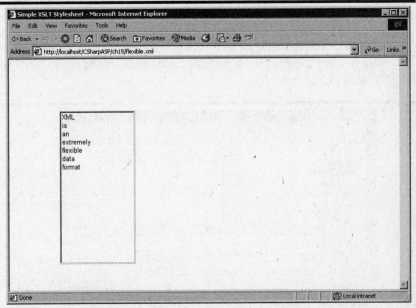

FIGURE 16.2:   Result from transforming `flexible.xml` using the XSLT stylesheet `flexible.xsl`

Interestingly, if you view the source in the browser, you'll see only the XML document. You won't see the HTML for the transform results, and you won't see the XSLT stylesheet code.

Performing Server-Side Transforms   As I mentioned at the start of the previous section, client-side automatic transforms are useful only if all your clients use IE. Future browser versions and other client types will no doubt support more XML/XSLT operations, but right now, the only cross-client solution is to perform the transform on the server and send the XHTML result to the client.

NOTE

Before you continue, comment out or delete the line that defines the stylesheet reference in the `flexible.xml` file in the ch15 folder of the CSharpASP project found at www.sybex.com. Remember that XML comments are the same as HTML comments (`<!-- -->`). Save the changes, then continue.

There are several ways to perform XSLT transforms in .NET, but the *easiest* way is to drag an XML web server control onto your Web Form's design surface. For example, create a new Web Form named ch15-1.aspx in the ch15 folder. Add an XML Server control and click the Custom Property button in the Properties dialog for the DocumentSource property. In the resulting dialog, select the ch15 folder in the Projects pane and then select the flexible.xml file from the Contents pane. You'll see the dialog in Figure 16.3.

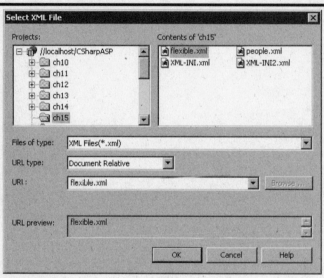

FIGURE 16.3:   The Select XML File dialog

Accept the default settings and click OK to close the dialog. Repeat the process to set the Transform-Source property to the flexible.xsl file. Now run the Web Form. The result looks identical to performing the client-side transform, but it isn't. You can prove that to yourself by viewing the browser source. This time, rather than the XML file contents, you'll see the HTML resulting from the transform. In other words, the server performed the transform for you and automatically sent the result to the browser.

The Xml web server control is extremely convenient, but what if you need to process an XML document in some other way, such as extracting only some individual data items, saving all or a selected portion of a document to a database, or performing a transform and then modifying the results using C#? To do that, you need to learn a little more about how

XML works in .NET and about the classes available in the System.Xml namespace.

READING XML DOCUMENTS

As you've seen, the XmlDocument object provides a Read method that reads an XML document and initiates parsing, but underneath, the Read method creates an XmlReader object and uses that to read the document. Of course, underneath the XmlTextReader is a TextReader object. The XmlTextReader wraps the TextReader and implements rules for accessing the content that apply specifically to the process of reading XML. Beyond the physical process of reading the file, there are several different ways of approaching the parse problem.

DOM versus SAX

Until .NET, there were two primary ways to access data in an XML document. The XmlDocument object implements the node tree, as I've already explained. Using an XmlDocument is very efficient when you need to update or extract data from a document multiple times and you don't know in advance *where* the data lies within the document. For example, suppose you have an XML document containing 50,000 usernames and passwords. You can load the document once and then check it repeatedly to search for matches to usernames and addresses. The big advantage of an XmlDocument is that, once loaded, it remains in memory; therefore, operations on loaded documents, especially XPath operations such as finding a matching node, are very efficient. The set of classes implemented to build an in-memory representation of an XML document is called the Document Object Model (DOM).

Unfortunately, the XmlDocument's greatest advantage is also its greatest liability. First, it takes much longer to parse an XML document into a DOM tree than it does to simply scroll through the file contents looking for a specific data item. Therefore, when you only need to make a single pass through the file, looking for specific content, it's much faster *not* to use the DOM model. An alternate way of extracting data from XML documents, called the Simple API for XML (SAX), reads an XML document sequentially, raising events as it encounters the elements and attributes in the file. By handling only the events you need, you can find specific nodes or values very quickly. Second, as you can imagine, building a large DOM in memory takes significant amounts of memory. A rough rule of thumb is that building a DOM requires about three to five times the memory that the XML file requires on disk. In contrast, reading the document with SAX requires very little memory—just the SAX parser and a buffer space.

The SAX model is a push model—SAX always starts at the beginning of the document and reads forward, pushing out events to your application as it encounters nodes and content. In contrast, .NET introduces a new model for reading XML document content—the pull model, implemented by the XmlReader abstract classes and the various XmlNavigator objects. The difference lies in where you put the logic. A SAX parser doesn't know whether your application needs to respond to the content available during any individual event, so it makes the data available in string form for every event. In other words, when a SAX parser encounters an element, it reads the element, determines its type, and raises an event, passing the string representation of the element as data to the event handler. In contrast, using an XmlReader, you can tell the parser in advance which elements you want to handle, and the reader can skip over all other types of content, making the XmlReader pull model much more efficient.

Using *XmlReader* Classes

Although the XmlReader class is an abstract class, the System.Xml namespace contains three fully implemented versions: the XmlTextReader, XmlNodeReader, and XmlValidatingReader classes. The XmlTextReader and XmlValidatingReader are similar, but the XmlValidatingReader supports document validation from a schema or DTD, whereas the XmlTextReader does not. Note that the XmlValidatingReader's validation capabilities also give it the capability to expand entities and read typed data, which can be a big advantage.

NOTE

The term entities as used in the preceding sentence isn't the same as the character entities already discussed. Using a DTD, you can define a substitute name for a larger block of XML data. It's the same idea as creating a named macro in a word processor that inserts a predefined block of text. Validating parsers must be able to read the DTD and expand or resolve entities whenever they find an entity name in the body of the document. Entity definitions are available only when you use a DTD—the current W3C schema specification does not support entity definitions.

But don't fall into the habit of using the XmlValidatingReader just because it covers all the bases—it's not nearly as efficient as the XmlTextReader.

You use the XmlNodeReader class to iterate through the nodes of a document that has already been loaded and parsed with an XmlDocument or XslTransform object—either a complete document, the DOM itself, or just a portion of the document, called a *DOM subtree*, or *document fragment*. The XmlNodeReader has no validation capabilities, but it can expand entities. Because this reader works directly in memory only with well-formed and possibly prevalidated nodes, it doesn't have to handle I/O or perform schema/DTD comparisons; therefore, it's extremely fast.

Using the *XmlTextReader* Class

As you might expect after having seen the set of Stream objects available for reading files, XmlTextReader can read from a file, a string, or an input stream. You provide the input type when you create an XmlTextReader instance, so it has several overloaded constructors. At the simplest level, you can pass the constructor a filename. After constructing the XmlText-Reader object, you call the Read method repeatedly. The Read method reads the next sequential node. It returns true if the read is successful and false if it reaches the end of the data. Be careful. The XmlTextReader object isn't a validating parser—it doesn't ensure that a document conforms to a schema—but it does check for well-formedness. In other words, if the XML document violates the XML syntax rules, the reader raises an error. Therefore, you should treat XML documents like any other external resource and trap for potential errors as you're reading them.

The Web Form ch15-2 shows how to read the flexible.xml file and gives you some examples of the type of information available from the XmlTextReader for each element it encounters. When the Web Form loads, it creates a new XmlTextReader object by passing it the physical path of the flexible.xml file, then it calls Read until it reaches the end, writing various available node properties and values to the browser in a table for each node the reader encountered. The properties and methods used in the Web Form ch15-2 are as follows:

NodeType Property   An enumeration value specifying the *function* of the node in the document. By applying the ToString method, you can see a human-friendly version of the NodeType property.

IsName(name) Method   Returns true if the name is a valid XML name—meaning that it conforms to the XML naming specifications, not that the name necessarily even exists in the document. The method returns true only for named nodes. For example, Element nodes are named nodes, whereas WhiteSpace nodes are not.

Name Property   The full string name of the node, including any namespace prefix. This is called the *qualified name*. For example, for the node <xsl:apply-templates>, the Name property would return xsl:apply-templates.

LocalName Property   When a node has a namespace prefix, such as <xsl:apply-templates>, the local name is the portion of the name after the prefix (apply-templates). If the node does not have a namespace prefix, the LocalName property returns the same value as the Name property.

HasAttributes Property   Returns true if the node has attributes; otherwise, it returns false.

AttributeCount Property   The number of attribute nodes in the current node. If the node has no attributes, the property returns 0.

MoveToAttribute (Overloaded)   You can supply a string name, a local name and a namespace URI, or an integer value (an index into the list of nodes). The XmlReader reads the specified node. Attribute nodes have a Name and a Value.

ReadString   Reads the text contents of the current node. The text content consists of the text, all white space, and the contents of any child CDATA section nodes concatenated together, with no delimiting characters or white space between the values.

Listing 16.5 shows the code to read the XML file and return the properties for node type, name, attributes, and value.

Listing 16.5: The Web Form *ch15-2.aspx* Uses an *XmlTextReader* to Read the *flexible.xml* File (ch15-2.aspx.vb)

```
using System.Xml;
private void Page_Load(object sender, System.EventArgs e) {
    XmlTextReader xr = new XmlTextReader(Server.MapPath(".") +
        "\\flexible.xml");
```

```
Response.Write(
  "Reading file: " + xr.BaseURI + "<br>");
Response.Write(
  "<table border=\"1\" align=\"center\">");
Response.Write("<tr>");
Response.Write(
  "<th>NodeType String</th><th>NodeType</th>" +
  "<th>isName</th><th>Element</th><th>Name</th>" +
  "<th>LocalName</th><th>HasAttributes</th>" +
  "<th>Attributes</th><th>Text</td>");
Response.Write("</tr>");
while (xr.Read()) {
  Response.Write("<tr>");
  Response.Write(
    "<td>" + xr.NodeType.ToString() + "</td>");
  Response.Write(
    "<td>" + xr.NodeType + " </td>");
  Response.Write(
    "<td>" + XmlReader.IsName(xr.Name).ToString()
    + " </td>");
  if (XmlReader.IsName(xr.Name)) {
    Response.Write("<td>" + Server.HtmlEncode("<" +
      xr.Name + ">") + "</td>");
  }
  else {
    Response.Write("<td> </td>");
  }
  Response.Write("<td>" + xr.Name + " </td>");
  Response.Write("<td>" + xr.LocalName + " </td>");
  Response.Write("<td>" + xr.HasAttributes.ToString() +
    " </td>");
  Response.Write("<td>");
  if (xr.HasAttributes) {
    for (int i = 0; i < xr.AttributeCount; i++) {
      xr.MoveToAttribute(i);
      Response.Write(xr.Name + "=" + xr.Value);
      if (i < (xr.AttributeCount - 1)) {
        Response.Write(", ");
      }
    }
  }
  else {
```

```
            Response.Write(xr.AttributeCount.ToString());
        }
        Response.Write("</td>");
        if (xr.NodeType == XmlNodeType.Text) {
            Response.Write("<td>" +
    Server.HtmlEncode(xr.ReadString()) +
            "</td>");
        }
        else {
            Response.Write("<td> </td>");
        }
    }
    Response.Write("</table>");
}
```

Figure 16.4 shows how the Web Form ch15-2.aspx looks in the browser.

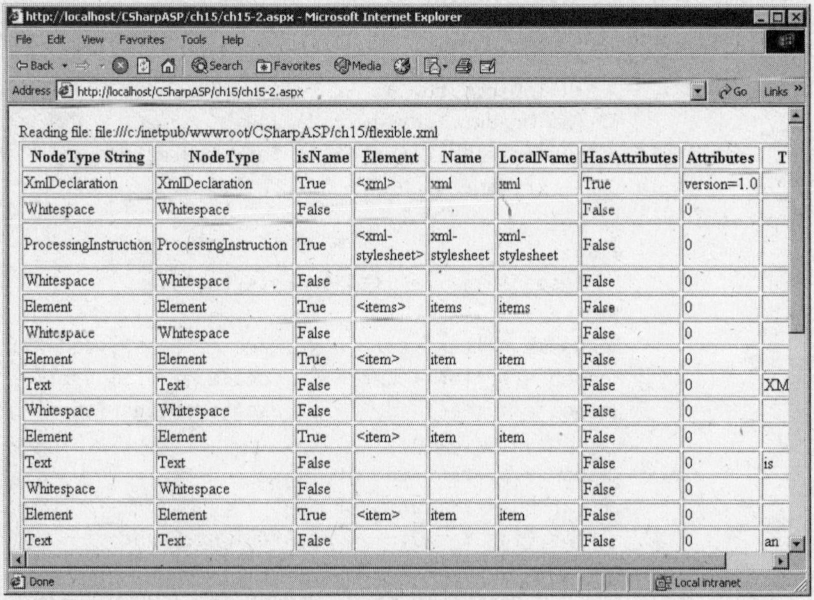

FIGURE 16.4: The Web Form ch15-2.aspx uses an XmlTextReader to display node values from the flexible.xml file

The XmlReader contains several other useful properties and methods not shown in the example Web Form ch15-2.aspx. I'm not going to list all the properties and methods because they're available in the Class

Explorer and the documentation, but I've listed the most important ones in the following section.

More *XmlTextReader* Properties   The following list shows the most important XMLTextReader properties.

Depth   Retrieves the count of ancestor nodes for the current node. Among other things, you can use this property to create indented or "pretty-print" XML output. The property returns 0 for the root node of a document.

LineNumber   Retrieves the line number of the line containing the current node. This property is useful only if the document lines have intrinsic meaning—for example, if the document is stored in human-readable form.

LinePosition   Retrieves the character position of the current node in the current line. Unlike the LineNumber property, this property value is useful even when a document is not stored in human-readable form.

NameTable   Retrieves the NameTable object used by the reader (see the section "Using the *XmlNameTable*," later in this chapter, for more information).

There are more properties than I've shown here. I urge you to use the MSDN documentation and the Object Browser to explore the XmlTextReader class thoroughly.

More *XmlTextReader* Methods   The following list shows the most commonly used XMLTextReader methods.

GetInnerXML   Retrieves the markup and content that lie between the start and end tags of the current node.

GetOuterXML   Retrieves the node markup and content, including the start and end tags of the current node.

GetRemainder   Retrieves the remainder of the XML document as a TextReader. One use for this method is to open a second XmlTextReader to read a different portion of the document while maintaining an existing XmlTextReader at a specific position.

IsStartElement   Returns true if the current node is the start tag of an element.

MoveToNextAttribute, MoveToPreviousAttribute   Causes the reader to read the attribute after or preceding the current attribute.

MoveToLastAttribute   Causes the reader to skip to the last attribute for the current node.

MoveToElement   When reading attributes, you can move the reader *back* to the parent element. You would use this if you needed to ensure that an attribute or attribute value exists in the document before dealing with the element's contents. For example, if you had the following element structure, you could test the value of the `level` attribute and output only names of the employees at level g5.

```
<employee id="em2930" level="g3">
   Bob Whitehead
</employee>
<employee id="em0830" level="g5">
   Amanda Criss
</employee>
```

MoveToContent   Moves the reader to the next node that contains text content. You can use this to skip over nodes that contain only markup.

Skip   Skips the current element. By skipping elements, you can reduce the processing time for documents that contain content you don't need.

There are more methods than I've shown here. I urge you to use the MSDN documentation and the Object Browser to explore the XmlTextReader class thoroughly.

Using the *XmlNameTable*

The XmlNameTable class is an *abstract* class. The table stores string names in a format that provides fast lookups. The implementation of the XmlNameTable class for the XmlTextReader is called NameTable, without the Xml prefix.

As the reader progresses through the document, it can check the set of names in its NameTable against the current node name. Strings are immutable in .NET; therefore, this scheme is advantageous because as the reader progresses through the document, it doesn't have to perform string comparisons for names it already has in the table; instead, it can simply compare the two strings to see if they reference the same object. The .NET documentation states that because of the difference between string comparison and reference comparison, using an XmlNameTable is faster.

You can retrieve the NameTable object from a reader and add names to it programmatically to improve the speed of node name comparisons, or you can create a new XmlNameTable object, add names to it, and then apply that XmlNameTable object to the XmlTextReader.

For example, suppose you wanted to find a single tag in a reasonably long document. By adding the tag name to the reader's NameTable, you can improve the comparison speed. I tested the theory using a loop. To eliminate the side effects that occur when you load a file from disk, the following example creates an XML string in memory using a String-Builder, then provides that string to the overloaded XmlTextReader constructor. The overloaded constructor can take a Stream object instead of a file URL, which you can provide by opening a StringReader object on the generated XML string. For example,

```
// open an XmlTextReader on a string
// (sXML) containing some XML
// using a StringReader to provide the Stream argument.
XmlTextReader xtr =
    new XmlTextReader(new StringReader(sXML));
```

Here's how you add names to the NameTable:

```
// create a new NameTable
Object itemXObj;
xnt = new NameTable();
itemXObj = xnt.Add("itemX");
```

The XML string the example constructs is a list of 1,000 <item> tags, each of which contains a different value. The last tag in the list is named <itemX>. The code searches for that tag. The generated XML file looks like this:

```
<?xml version="1.0"?>
<items>
    <item>Item1</item>
    <item>Item2</item>
    <item>Item3</item>
    ...
    <item>Item999</item>
    <itemX>Item1000</itemX>
</items>
```

The example code creates the document and then loops through it 1,000 times, hunting for the <itemX> tag. When it finds the tag, it increments a counter, proving that the code found a match for each loop iteration.

Using this test, the results are language dependent. In C#, there's no improvement for the version that uses the XmlNameTable—in fact, the version that does *not* use a NameTable is slightly faster. As each loop searches through 1,000,000 tags, you can see that for most web application XML documents, the improvement is unlikely to be noticeable.

NOTE

Interestingly, if you translate the code to VB.NET, the NameTable version consistently runs about 5 percent faster than the version that doesn't use the NameTable, even for this simple document.

You can run the comparison using the Web Form ch15-3.aspx (see Listing 16.6). This Web form constructs an XML Document in code and uses an XmlTextReader both with and without a specific NameTable to read through the document.

Listing 16.6: Using an *XmlTextReader* to Read Through a Document (*ch15-3.aspx.cs*)

```
using System.Xml;
using System.Text;
using System.IO;
// auto-generated code omitted
private void Page_Load(object sender, System.EventArgs e) {
    XmlTextReader xtr = null;
    String sXML;
    NameTable xnt = null;
    int counter;
    Object itemObj;
    Object itemXObj;
    int startTick, endTick;
    StringBuilder sb = new StringBuilder(50000);
    int tickDuration1, tickDuration2;

    sb.Append("<?xml version=\"1.0\"?>");
    sb.Append("<items>");
    for(int i = 1; i <= 1000; i++) {
        if (i == 1000) {
```

```
        sb.Append("<itemX>");
        sb.Append("Item" + i.ToString());
        sb.Append("</itemX>");
    }
    else {
        sb.Append("<item>");
        sb.Append("Item" + i.ToString());
        sb.Append("</item>");
    }
}
sb.Append("</items>");
sXML = sb.ToString();

// output the method used and the current time
startTick = System.Environment.TickCount;
Response.Write(
    "Starting reader without NameTable lookup at: "
    + System.DateTime.Now.Second + ":" +
    System.DateTime.Now.Millisecond + "<br>");
// parse the string in a loop
counter = 0;
for (int i = 1; i <= 1000; i++) {
    xtr = new XmlTextReader(new StringReader(sXML));
    while (xtr.Read()) {
        if ((xtr.NodeType == XmlNodeType.Element) &&
            (xtr.Name == "itemX")) {
            counter += 1;
        }
    }
}
endTick = System.Environment.TickCount;
// output the method used and the current time
Response.Write(
    "Ending reader without NameTable lookup at: " +
    System.DateTime.Now.Second + ":" +
    System.DateTime.Now.Millisecond + "<br>" + "Found " +
    counter.ToString() + " instances." + "<br>");
tickDuration1 = endTick - startTick;
Response.Write("Duration in milliseconds = " +
    tickDuration1.ToString());
Response.Write("<br>");
```

```csharp
// Now repeat, using a NameTable
Response.Write(
  "Starting reader with NameTable lookup at: " +
  System.DateTime.Now.Second + ":" +
  System.DateTime.Now.Millisecond + "<br>");
// parse the string in a loop
startTick = System.Environment.TickCount;
counter = 0;

// create a new NameTable
xnt = new NameTable();
itemXObj = xnt.Add("itemX");
itemObj = xnt.Add("item");
for (int i = 1; i <= 1000; i++) {
    xtr = new XmlTextReader(new StringReader(sXML), xnt);
    while (xtr.Read()) {
        if ((xtr.NodeType == XmlNodeType.Element) &&
            (xtr.Name == xnt.Get("itemX"))) {
            counter += 1;
        }
    }
}
endTick = System.Environment.TickCount;
// output the method used and the current time
Response.Write(
  "Ending reader with NameTable lookup at: " +
  System.DateTime.Now.Second + ":" +
  System.DateTime.Now.Millisecond + "<br>" + "Found " +
  counter.ToString() + " instances." + "<br>");
tickDuration2 = endTick - startTick;
Response.Write("Duration in milliseconds = " +
  tickDuration2.ToString() + "<br>");
Response.Write("<br>");
Response.Write("The NameTable version is " +
  (((tickDuration1 -
  tickDuration2) / tickDuration1)).ToString("p") +
  " faster than the " +
  "non-NameTable version.");
}
```

Based on this test, I wouldn't bother using the `NameTable` in C# applications for simple documents. However, it seems likely that as the number of elements and the complexity of the document increases, you would get a corresponding increase in the relative efficiency of NameTables. You should, of course, perform your own tests on your own documents.

Regardless of the NameTable results, if you ran the ch15-3.aspx Web Form, you can see by the timings that the XmlTextReader is extremely fast. When you need to read a document one time to extract values quickly, use an XmlTextReader. But that's not the only way to find nodes and values in a document. You saw a little about how to use XSLT and XPath in stylesheets, but you can also use XPath queries in code.

Querying XML Documents for Data

Three classes in the System.Xml namespace let you use XPath to query their contents: XmlDocument, XmlDataDocument, and XPathDocument. I'll discuss the XmlDataDocument in more detail in the upcoming section "Using the XmlDataDocument Class," but the only real difference between an XmlDataDocument and the other two DOM document types is that an XmlDataDocument can be synchronized to a DataSet rather than a file. However, regardless of the data source, after parsing the XML data into a DOM tree, the *concepts* for retrieving data from an XmlDataDocument are the same as the ones shown in the following section, although the methods differ slightly.

Using the *SelectSingleNode* and *SelectNodes* Methods

At the simplest level, all you need to do to retrieve a data item from an XML document is create an XmlDocument object, call its Load method, and then use the SelectSingleNode or SelectNodes method with the appropriate XPath query to retrieve a data-specific node or set of nodes. For example, the following code fragment writes the word extremely in the browser, as that word is the text content of the fourth <item> node from the flexible.xml file.

```
XmlDocument xml = new XmlDocument();
xml.Load(Server.MapPath(".") + "\\flexible.xml");
Response.Write(xml.SelectSingleNode(
   "/items/item[4]").InnerText);
```

Similarly, you can use the SelectNodes method to select multiple nodes from a loaded XmlDocument object. For example,

```
XmlDocument xml = new XmlDocument();
xml.Load(Server.MapPath(".") + "\\flexible.xml");
```

```
foreach (XmlNode N in xml.SelectNodes("/items/item")) {
    Response.Write(N.InnerText);
}
```

The preceding code fragment writes "XML is an extremely flexible data format" to the browser.

Using the *XPathDocument* and *XPathNavigator* Classes

When you're loading a document just to make a few queries, it doesn't matter which XmlDocument type you use, but when you need to query a document repeatedly, it's more efficient to load it into an XPathDocument object than to load and scroll through the document for each query.

The XPathDocument object maximizes the efficiency of XPath queries. Rather than using the SelectNodes and SelectSingleNode methods, you use an object called an XPathNavigator to perform XPath requests. For example,

```
XPathDocument xml = new XPathDocument(Server.MapPath(".") +
    "\\flexible.xml");
XPathNavigator xpn == xml.CreateNavigator();
XPathNodeIterator xpni;
xpni = xpn.Select("/items/item");
while (xpni.CurrentPosition < xpni.Count) {
    xpni.MoveNext();
    Response.Write(xpni.Current.Name +
        "=" + xpni.Current.Value  + "<br>");
}
```

The preceding code fragment writes the following output:

```
item=XML
item=is
item=an
item=extremely
item=flexible
item=data
item=format
```

You should explore XPath in detail to make full use of these objects. Unfortunately, a thorough discussion of XPath is beyond the scope of this book, but there are numerous online resources available to you.

USING THE *XMLDATADOCUMENT* CLASS

So far, you've worked exclusively with XML documents stored on disk or created as strings. But the XmlDataDocument class represents a third type of top-level DOM document. The main difference between an XmlData-Document object and the XmlDocument or XPathDocument object is that an XmlDataDocument is closely tied to the DataSet class, so it lets you treat loaded XML data in a relational manner. You can populate the XmlData-Document object via a DataSet. For example, the Web Form ch15-4.aspx uses a DataSet containing the Students table from the ClassRecords database. I dragged a SqlConnection and a SqlDataAdapter from the Toolbox onto the form design surface and configured the resulting Sql-DataAdapter1 instance with a SQL query that returns all the fields from the Students table. When you right-click the SqlDataAdapter1 on that Web Form, you see the option to Generate Dataset. When you do that, you'll see the Generate Dataset dialog (see Figure 16.5).

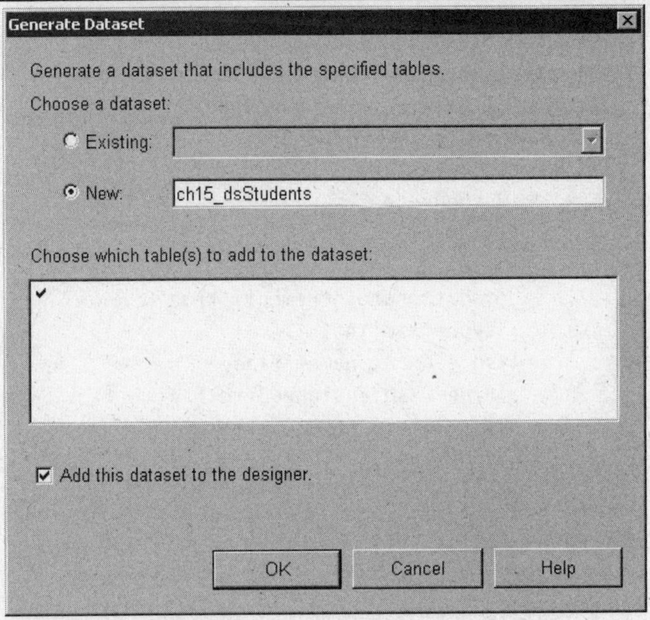

FIGURE 16.5: The Generate Dataset dialog

Click the New radio button and enter the name **ch15_dsClass-Records_Students**. Check the Add This DataSet To The Designer option. When you click OK, the designer generates a schema for the DataSet and a class and adds both to the current folder in the Solution Explorer. Double-click the Ch15_dsClassRecords_Students.xsd item in the Solution Explorer to open the schema in the designer. You'll see the schema in Listing 16.7.

Listing 16.7: Generated XSD Schema for the ClassRecords Students Table

```
<xsd:schema id="Ch15_dsClassRecords_Students"
targetNamespace=
    "http://www.tempuri.org/Ch15_dsClassRecords_Students.xsd"
    xmlns="http://www.tempuri.org/
    Ch15_dsClassRecords_Students.xsd"
    xmlns:xsd="http://www.w3.org/2001/XMLSchema"
    xmlns:msdata="urn:schemas-microsoft-com:xml-msdata"
    attributeFormDefault="qualified"
    elementFormDefault="qualified">
  <xsd:element name="Ch15_dsClassRecords_Students"
    msdata:IsDataSet="true">
  <xsd:complexType>
    <xsd:choice maxOccurs="unbounded">
      <xsd:element name="Students">
        <xsd:complexType>
          <xsd:sequence>
            <xsd:element name="StudentID"
              msdata:ReadOnly="true"
              msdata:AutoIncrement="true"
              type="xsd:int" />
            <xsd:element name="Grade"
              type="xsd:unsignedByte" />
            <xsd:element name="LastName"
              type="xsd:string" />
            <xsd:element name="FirstName"
              type="xsd:string" />
          </xsd:sequence>
        </xsd:complexType>
      </xsd:element>
    </xsd:choice>
  </xsd:complexType>
```

```
        <xsd:unique name="Constraint1" msdata:PrimaryKey="true">
          <xsd:selector xpath=".//Students" />
          <xsd:field xpath="StudentID" />
        </xsd:unique>
      </xsd:element>
    </xsd:schema>
```

The schema shows you how the XML representation of the data will look. For example, the root element will be `<Students>`; each field becomes an element in a sequence that follows the order of the fields in the SQL query for the `SqlDataAdapter`. Notice that the `StudentID` element has an attribute with the name and value `msdata:Auto-Increment="True"`, meaning that the schema understands that the `StudentID` field is marked as an `Identity` field in SQL Server. Also, look at the constraint definition toward the end of the schema. The schema also captures the fact that the `StudentID` is a primary key as well as the `XPath` query to select the `<Students>` and the name of the primary key field.

WARNING

XML is case sensitive, so be careful with your SQL and XPath query names.

The generated class is interesting as well, and I urge you to look at it, although due to its size, I won't show it here. You should *not* alter the generated code manually because the system will overwrite the code if you later regenerate or alter the `DataSet`.

You can now use the `Fill` method to fill `ch15_dsClassRecords_Students DataSet` and print the result to the browser so you can see the XML. For example, the `Form_Load` method in the `ch15-4.aspx` Web Form displays the `DataSet`'s XML document contents using very little hand-generated code. One of the reasons it uses so little code is that the `SqlDataAdapter.Fill` method opens and closes the associated `Connection` object automatically, so you don't have to do it yourself. However, as you've seen, if you write the code, you have control over what can be seen when page tracing is enabled, whereas when you rely on the designers, you don't.

```
private void Page_Load(object sender, System.EventArgs e) {
    DataSet ds = new ch15_dsClassRecords_Students();
    sqlDataAdapter1.Fill(ds);
```

```
    Response.Write(Server.HtmlEncode(ds.GetXml()));
    sqlDataAdapter1.Dispose();
    Response.End();
}
```

You can see from the result that the DataSet does indeed contain the data from the Students table in XML form, but the results aren't very satisfying. Fortunately, the GetXml method's return value already contains line breaks and indentation. If you place the results of the DataSet.GetXml call between <pre></pre> tags, you'll get a better format. Here's another version with better output (see Figure 16.6).

```
private void Page_Load(object sender, System.EventArgs e) {
    DataSet ds = new ch15_dsClassRecords_Students();
    sqlDataAdapter1.Fill(ds);
    Response.Write("<pre>" + Server.HtmlEncode(ds.GetXml()) +
    "</pre>");
    sqlDataAdapter1.Dispose();
    Response.End();
}
```

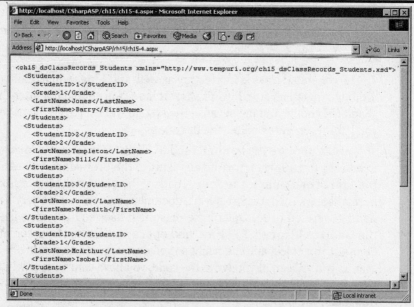

FIGURE 16.6:   Formatted contents of the Ch15_dsClassRecords_Students1 dataset

THE *XMLEXCEPTION* CLASSES

One of the biggest flaws of the msxml.dll parser was that it allowed programmers to call its Load method with a malformed XML document without raising a COM error. Instead, the Load method returned a Boolean value that programmers all too often ignored. The System.Xml classes don't suffer from that particular malady. When you attempt to load a malformed document, compile or perform an XSLT transform, or validate an invalid document against a schema, your code will throw one of the following exceptions:

- ▶ XmlException
- ▶ XmlSyntaxException
- ▶ XmlSchemaException
- ▶ XsltException
- ▶ XsltCompileException

There's nothing particularly special about any of these exceptions compared to other Exception objects, but they do provide detailed information about the cause of the error. When an error occurs while loading a document, the XmlException.LineNumber and XmlException.Line-Position properties are particularly important because they can help you pinpoint the location of the error. For Xslt-Exceptions, the SourceUri property contains the path of the stylesheet that generated the error. The XmlSchemaException object has the LineNumber, LinePosition, and SourceUri properties and adds a SourceSchemaObject property containing the XmlSchemaObject that generated the error. The XmlSyntaxException object has none of these properties, just the common Message property.

Because Exception objects may "wrap" other Exception objects, you should always check the Inner-Exception property to see if the Exception contains other, wrapped Exceptions. Particularly when dealing with third-party components, the component vendor may create a component with custom exceptions but include the underlying base exceptions in the InnerException property. Each wrapped Exception object may itself contain wrapped Exceptions. You can either traverse the list of linked exceptions using the InnerException property or use the GetBase-Exception method to obtain the original Exception directly.

PERFORMING XSLT TRANSFORMS PROGRAMMATICALLY

Early in this chapter, I promised to show you how to perform server-side transforms programmatically after you learned more about the System.Xml namespace. At this point, you should have at least a tenuous grasp on the various types of DOM objects, how to read XML data, how to find nodes, and how to extract XML from a database. You've also seen how to use the Xml web server control to perform a transform. Now it's time to use some of the objects you've seen to perform one yourself.

Here's the basic procedure:

1. Load the XML into an XmlDocument, XPathDocument, or XpathNavigator.

2. Load the stylesheet into an XslTransform instance.

3. Call the XslTransform.Transform method.

The Transform method is overloaded. It can do the following:

▶ Send the result of the transform to a TextWriter, Stream, or XmlWriter that you supply as a parameter.

▶ Write the result of the transform to a file.

▶ Return an XmlTextReader object that you can use to process the result.

TIP

The .NET documentation states that you should use an XPathDocument object when possible because it is optimized for XSLT transformations.

The Web Form ch15-5.aspx contains an example that's actually a little more complex than it needs to be at this point because it uses a client-side script, but it provides a good XSLT sorting example in addition to a simple programmatic server-side transform.

The example reads an XML document named people.xml and an XSLT stylesheet named people.xsl. The people.xml file contains a last name, first name, telephone number, and e-mail address for several fictional people. Here's a sample:

```xml
<?xml version="1.0"?>
<people>
   <person>
      <last>Jones</last>
      <first>Bob</first>
      <tel>555-666-7777</tel>
      <email>bjones@someco.com</email>
   </person>
   <person>
      <last>Jones</last>
      <first>Fred</first>
      <tel>839-298-7328</tel>
      <email>fjones@anytel.com</email>
   </person>
   <!-- more person tags here -->
</people>
```

The stylesheet transforms the document into an HTML table, creating a row for each person and putting the four data items (last, first, tel, and email) in separate columns. It also has two parameters named sortfield and sortorder that control the way the stylesheet sorts and orders the data. Initially, the sortfield parameter is set to last, and the sortorder parameter is set to ascending, so the stylesheet sorts the people by last name in ascending order.

However, the user can change the sort order by clicking on a column header, which fires a client-side function called sort that sets a hidden form field to the title of the column the user clicked and then forces the default form (Form1) to submit to the server. The Page_Load event creates a string containing the client-side code and then "registers" the script with the page using the RegisterClient-ScriptBlock method.

```csharp
private void Page_Load(object sender, System.EventArgs e) {
   String sort_script;
   sort_script = "<script type=\"text/javascript\" " +
      "language=\"javascript\">" +
      "function sort(column) {" +
      "document.getElementById(\"Form1\")" +
      ".sortfield.value=column;" +
      "document.getElementById(\"Form1\").submit();}" +
      "</script>";
   this.RegisterClientScriptBlock(
      "sort_script", sort_script);
}
```

The server retrieves the name of the clicked column and uses it to set the stylesheet's `sortfield` parameter. In this example, the server simply alternates between sorting columns in ascending or descending order.

```
if (IsPostBack) {
    mSortfield = Request.Form["sortfield"];
    mSortorder = Request.Form["sortorder"];
    Response.Write("Server sortorder=" + mSortorder +
        "<br>");
    if (mSortorder=="ascending") {
        mSortorder = "descending";
    }
    else if (mSortorder=="descending") {
        mSortorder="ascending";
    }
    else {
        Response.Write("ERROR: sortorder=" + mSortorder);
        Response.End();
    }
}
```

The hidden input fields are a simple way to get the name of the clicked column posted to the server. The hidden fields aren't hard-coded into the HTML (`.aspx`) file; instead, the server creates the controls dynamically and sets their values. So that the form will post the values, you need to place the hidden input controls into the default server form. The Page object provides an automatic way to do that with the RegisterHidden-Field method, which accepts two string arguments: the name of the hidden input and its initial value. The RegisterHiddenField method performs the equivalent of this series of steps:

```
// create a hidden input control
HtmlInputHidden hidden_field = new HtmlInputHidden();

// find the default Form control
// and add the new control to its
// Controls collection
this.FindControl("Form1").Controls.Add(hidden_field);

// set the id and value for the new hidden input control
hidden_field.ID=someIDString;
hidden_field.Value=someValueString;
```

You can perform a similar series of steps to create any type of web server or HTML control dynamically. The most common error people make while doing this is to add the control to the Page.Controls collection rather than the "Form1" form's Controls collection.

Because adding hidden input controls is such a common operation, you can accomplish the entire procedure in a single step:

```
this.RegisterHiddenField("someID", "someValue");
```

That's extremely convenient. Typically you would add controls in the Page_Load or the PreRender event. The RegisterHiddenField method renders like this:

```
<input type="hidden" name="someID" value="someValue" />
```

Listing 16.8 shows the code for the ch15-5.aspx.cs class.

Listing 16.8: Programmatic Server-Side XSLT Transform Example *(ch15-5.aspx.cs)*

```csharp
using System;
using System.Collections;
using System.ComponentModel;
using System.Data;
using System.Drawing;
using System.Web;
using System.Web.SessionState;
using System.Web.UI;
using System.Web.UI.WebControls;
using System.Web.UI.HtmlControls;
using System.Xml;
using System.Xml.Xsl;
using System.Xml.XPath;

namespace CSharpASP.ch15
{
    /// <summary>
    /// Summary description for ch15_5.
    /// </summary>
    public class ch15_5 : System.Web.UI.Page
    {

        private void Page_Load(
          object sender, System.EventArgs e) {
            String sort_script;
            XPathDocument xml = null;
            XslTransform xslt = null;
            XsltArgumentList param = null;
            String mSortfield = "last";
```

```
String mSortorder = "ascending";
try {
   if (IsPostBack) {
      mSortfield = Request.Form["sortfield"];
      mSortorder = Request.Form["sortorder"];
      if (mSortorder=="ascending") {
         mSortorder = "descending";
      }
      else if (mSortorder=="descending") {
         mSortorder="ascending";
      }
      else {
         Response.Write("ERROR: sortorder=" +
            mSortorder);
         Response.End();
      }
   }
   xml = new XPathDocument(Server.MapPath(".") +
      "\\people.xml");
   xslt = new XslTransform();
   xslt.Load(Server.MapPath(".") + "\\people.xsl");
   this.RegisterHiddenField(
      "sortorder", mSortorder);
   this.RegisterHiddenField(
      "sortfield", mSortfield);

   param = new XsltArgumentList();
   param.AddParam("sortorder", "",mSortorder);
   param.AddParam("sortfield", "",mSortfield);
   xslt.Transform(xml, param,Response.OutputStream);
}
catch (XsltException exxslt) {
   Response.Write(
      "XsltException: " + exxslt.Message);
}
catch (XmlException exxml) {
   Response.Write(
      "XmlException: " + exxml.Message);
}
catch (Exception ex) {
```

```
            Response.Write(ex.GetType().Name +
                ": " + ex.Message);
        }

        sort_script = "<script type=\"text/javascript\" " +
            "language=\"javascript\">" +
            "function sort(column) {" +
            "document.getElementById(\"Form1\")." +
            "sortfield.value=column;" +
            "document.getElementById(
                \"Form1\").submit();}" +
            "</script>";
        this.RegisterClientScriptBlock("sort_script",
    sort_script);
        }

        // autogenerated code omitted

    }
}
```

The XSLT stylesheet (see Listing 16.9, later in this chapter) has several interesting points. First, notice the two `<xsl:parameter>` tags defined near the top of the file, which have default initial values of last and ascending, respectively:

```
<xsl:param name="sortfield" select="last" />
<xsl:param name="sortorder" select="ascending" />
```

The stylesheet first selects the root node of the input XML document:

```
<xsl:template match="/">
```

So that you can see what's happening, the stylesheet then writes the current parameter values to the output:

```
Sorting by <xsl:value-of select="$sortfield"/><br/>
Order = <xsl:value-of select="$sortorder"/><br/>
```

Next, it outputs a `<table>` tag and selects all the child nodes of the `<people>` tag in the input XML document, sorting them by the named parameter values. In XSLT, you reference variables by placing a dollar ($) sign in front of the name, for example $sortfield:

```
<table border="1" align="center">
    <xsl:apply-templates select="people/child::node()[1]"
    mode="thead"/>
```

```
   <tbody>
     <xsl:apply-templates select="/people/person">
       <xsl:sort select="*[name(.) = $sortfield]"
         order="{$sortorder}"/>
       </xsl:apply-templates>
   </tbody>
</table>
```

If you were to hard-code the sort field, you could write

```
<xsl:sort select="last" />
```

The interesting point of the sort is that you can't simply substitute the parameter name:

```
<xsl:sort select="$sortfield" />
```

Instead, you have to select the nodes where the node name is equal to the sortfield parameter's value.

```
<xsl:sort select="*[name(.) = $sortfield]" />
```

The <xsl:sort> tag can accept an order attribute that can take either an ascending or descending value. The default is ascending. Again, you can't simply use the variable reference $sortorder because that references the parameter node itself, not its value. By placing the variable name in curly brackets, XSLT substitutes the text value of the node. Therefore, the complete sort tag is this:

```
<xsl:sort select="*[name(.) = $sortfield]"
   order="{$sortorder}"/>
```

Listing 16.9 shows the entire stylesheet.

Listing 16.9: XSLT Stylesheet that Sorts According to the *sortfield* and *sortorder* Parameter Values

```
<?xml version="1.0"?>
<xsl:stylesheet
  xmlns:xsl="http://www.w3.org/1999/XSL/Transform"
  version="1.0">
  <xsl:param name="sortfield" select="last" />
  <xsl:param name="sortorder" select="ascending" />
  <xsl:template match="/">
    Sorting by <xsl:value-of select="$sortfield"/><br/>
    Order = <xsl:value-of select="$sortorder"/><br/>
    <table border="1" align="center">
```

```
        <xsl:apply-templates select="people/child::node()[1]"
            mode="thead"/>
        <tbody>
            <xsl:apply-templates select="/people/person">
                <xsl:sort select="*[name(.) = $sortfield]"
                    order="{$sortorder}"/>
            </xsl:apply-templates>
        </tbody>
        </table>
    </xsl:template>

    <xsl:template match="person">
        <tr>
            <xsl:for-each select="child::node()">
            <td>
                <xsl:value-of select="."/>
            </td>
            </xsl:for-each>
        </tr>
    </xsl:template>


    <xsl:template match="person" mode="thead">
        <thead><tr>
            <xsl:for-each select="child::node()">
                <th>
                    <xsl:attribute name="onclick">
                        sort('<xsl:value-of select="local-
                        name()"/>');</xsl:attribute>
                    <xsl:attribute name="style">
                        cursor:hand</xsl:attribute>
                    <xsl:value-of select="local-name()"/>
                </th>
            </xsl:for-each>
        </tr></thead>
    </xsl:template>

</xsl:stylesheet>
```

Figure 16.7 shows the output of the ch15-5.aspx Web Form running in a browser, sorted by first name in descending order.

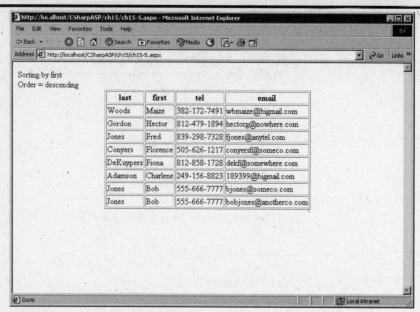

FIGURE 16.7: The Web Form ch15-5.aspx output sorted by first name in descending order

WHAT'S NEXT

In this chapter, you've seen the rudiments of how to create, modify, search, and transform XML documents using the System.Xml classes. Because XML is so important right now—not just to .NET and web applications, but to computing in general—if you haven't worked with XML before, you should practice creating XML documents and schema, creating datasets, searching documents using XPath, and writing XSLT transforms until you're comfortable with the basic operations.

If you do feel comfortable with all of the above tasks, then it's time to move on to the concept of web services, discussed in Chapter 17.

Chapter 17
WEB SERVICES

Web services are, in the simplest terms, class methods exposed via an HTTP call. In other words, just as you can call a method in a class in your application, you can call a method that exists on your own or some other server. In this chapter, you'll explore Visual Studio's built-in support for web services, and you'll create and consume a web service from several different client types.

Adapted from *Mastering ASP.NET with C#*
by A. Russell Jones
ISBN 0-7821-2989-7

INTRODUCTION TO WEB SERVICES

In C#, creating a web service is as simple as adding a few attributes to your class and to each method in the class that you want to expose to remote computers. The exposed methods are the public interface to your web service. A single web service may have many exposed methods, just as a class may have many public methods and properties. The difference is that a web service is stateless. The server instantiates an instance of the web service on demand and then destroys that instance after it finishes servicing a call—just as it does with the Web Form classes. In fact, the *only* conceptual differences between a Web Form and a web service are that a Web Form returns HTML, whereas a web service returns XML.

Remote Method Calls and XML

XML is at the heart of web services and provides several huge advantages over existing methods for calling code running on remote servers.

Standardized file format   XML has a simple syntax, readable (with some effort) by human beings. Best of all, the XML file format has been standardized by the W3C. Despite the relative newness of XML, parsers are already available for every major programming and scripting language, so you can read XML regardless of which platform or language you need to use. XML parsers check whether documents are "well-formed" and can raise errors when reading a document that contains errors. The error messages and properties tell you exactly where an error occurred, greatly reducing the number of errors that occur due to malformed data.

Self-describing   Unlike simple delimited or fixed-width field text file formats, XML files use tag markup to describe the type of data included in each field. Well-chosen tag names add to legibility in both programming code and when viewing raw XML documents.

Hierarchical   Unlike flat-file delimited or fixed-width field text file formats, XML documents can represent an arbitrary number of hierarchical relationships. The capability to model relationships also means that you can use a tag name appropriately, even if it duplicates a tag name that appears elsewhere in the document. For example, the following document uses the <name> tag to represent several different types of information: a person's name, his children's names, a book title, and the name of a country; but due to the hierarchical placement of the <name> tags, they aren't ambiguous. For example, it's easy to see that the <name> tag in the <child> element belongs to the child, and the <name> tag in the <book> element belongs to the book.

```
<?xml version="1.0"?>
<items>
    <person>
        <name>John Smith</name>
            <children>
                <child>
                    <name>Joyce</name>
                </child>
            <children>
    </person>
    <book>
        <name>Wicked</name>
    </book>
    <country>
        <name>United States</name>
    <country>
</items>
```

Can hold both structured and unstructured data   Relational databases already provide a common way to store hierarchical *structured* data, but they're not ideal for storing unstructured data because a relational database works best when you can clearly define the relationships between different items and groups of items. XML documents can model relational schema very easily, so they're eminently suited for hierarchical structured data, but because there's no *requirement* to model hierarchical relationships, XML documents work just as well for unstructured data.

Supports queries   Using a standardized grammar called XPath, you can query an XML document, finding or counting XML elements, attributes, and values. In contrast, there's no standardized way to find a data item in a text file. Databases also support queries, and they're optimized for large data sets, whereas XML is not. Using a combination of both databases and XML, you can model the relationships in a larger database within a much smaller data subset in XML. That's the idea behind ADO.NET data sets.

Passes through firewalls   XML is composed of plain text; therefore, it can easily pass through firewalls and let companies expose internal code to external clients without affecting security.

Supports schema and validation   Until recently, the only way to specify the schema of a document was to use Document Type Definitions (DTDs). However, the W3C recently released the XML schema recommendation (usually called XSD or XSDL schema, which stands for XML Schema Definition Language), which uses a second XML document to describe an XML document. Because XSD schemas are XML documents, you can read them programmatically, making machine-to-machine communications possible even when the communicating computers don't know the full protocol in advance. In addition, you can use an XML schema to *validate* the contents of a document. While parsers checking for well-formedness catches only syntax errors, validation catches *content* errors. Using a validating parser, you can check the contents of a document against a schema, ensuring that the document contains all the elements and attributes that it *should* contain; that the relative positions, and thus the hierarchy of the document, are correct; and that the values associated with validated elements and attributes are the correct types, ranges, and/or values. The advent of schema, XML, robust parsers, and of course ubiquitous HTTP connections and the Internet makes web services possible.

Interoperating Across Applications/Platforms

The common file format and the simple text base of XML documents mean that you can create, parse, and transfer XML documents very easily, not only between applications running on one platform, but also between applications running on disparate platforms. For example, it's just as easy to create an XML document in Java as it is in .NET; therefore, a Java application running on a Unix workstation can call a web service running on a Windows platform and receive a return value as long as both applications pass properly formatted XML. In other words, any server can service any client that can create and parse XML.

A web service is *not* a specific type of application—it's a way to *expose* application functionality via (usually, but not necessarily) an HTTP interface. There's no special language requirement and no special platform requirements.

Although I won't attempt to show you cross-platform web services in this book (it's a .NET book, after all), you should keep in mind that when you build a web service, you're building generic code that any application or platform can consume. Web services are the *first* true cross-platform code, because they require nothing but a parser, some string-handling capabilities, and HTTP connection capabilities on the part of the client.

When Should You Use Web Services?

In web applications, web services are particularly useful for updating specific areas of the page *without* redrawing the entire page. By doing this, you can avoid the "flash" that typically occurs when the browser requests a page.

For example, suppose you have a list of customers in a ListBox, and you want to display customer details when the user selects a customer from the list. For a small number of customers, you could download the entire set of details and handle all the display logic on the client. But that becomes less and less palatable as the number of customers increases. Eventually, you'll have to let the user select a customer, return to the server, get the details for that customer, and display the details on the client. But when the browser makes the request for the details, if you're keeping the list on the page at the same time, the server will have to resend the customer list as well as the details and any other items on the page. Not only is that inefficient and slow, but it also means that you have to add logic to maintain the selected list item. Finally, the page flashes when it redraws.

Obviously, it would be better if you could just fill the detail fields with the selected customer data. A web service is ideal for such situations because it accepts a request and returns the data in an easy-to-use form. You can use an XML parser to extract the individual data values and display them in the appropriate fields.

Another reason to use web services is when you need to provide data to clients both inside and outside your company firewall. Because the XML data traverses firewalls freely via a standard HTTP connection, you don't have to open extra ports (potential security hazards) to your servers.

By default, web services are stateless, which makes them highly scalable. You can run web services in a multiserver (server farm) environment. Clients initiate web service requests using standard HTTP GET and POST methods, so you can use the same web farm setup to handle web service requests as you do to handle ASP.NET or HTML requests. If you *must* maintain state in a web service, you can derive it from the `WebService` class, which gives you access to the .NET Framework `HttpContext` objects, so that you can use `Cookies`, `Session`, and `Application` variables just as you would in a Web Form.

How Does VS.NET Help?

To create a web service, you add class and method attributes that identify a class as a web service and identify the publicly exposed methods (called `WebMethods`). When you do that, VS.NET automatically creates XML documents that help you find and consume the web service. Using these documents, VS.NET also automatically creates a web service Description page that shows you the title of the web service as well as the set of operations it supports (see Figure 17.1).

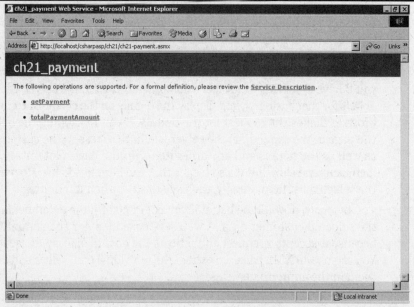

FIGURE 17.1: Web service Description page generated automatically by VS.NET

When you click the operation links, VS.NET provides a Web Form you can use to test each operation. For example, if you click the getPayment link shown in Figure 17.1, you'll see the page in Figure 17.2.

The page also shows you sample Simple Object Access Protocol (SOAP) request and response documents. (You'll see how to use SOAP with web services later in this chapter.) Finally, the Web Method Operation page shows GET and POST requests and responses for the WebMethod.

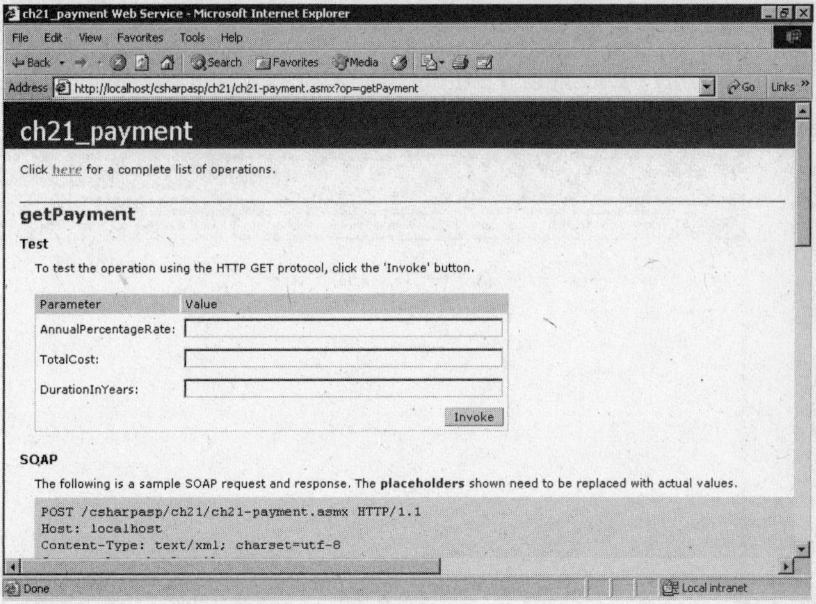

FIGURE 17.2: The Test Web Method Operation page generated automatically by VS.NET

For example, the getPayment WebMethod shown in Figure 17.2 calculates a mortgage payment. The WebMethod requires three parameters—the APR (AnnualPercentageRate), the amount of the loan (TotalCost), and the mortgage duration in years (DurationInYears). If you look at the bottom of the Web Form, you'll see that a GET request generates a simple XML document that returns a string element containing the monthly payment amount (see Figure 17.3).

HTTP GET

The following is a sample HTTP GET request and response. The **placeholders** shown need to be replaced with actual values.

```
GET /csharpasp/ch21/ch21-payment.asmx/getPayment?AnnualPercentageRate=string&TotalCost=string
Host: localhost
```

```
HTTP/1.1 200 OK
Content-Type: text/xml; charset=utf-8
Content-Length: length
```

```
<?xml version="1.0" encoding="utf-8"?>
<string xmlns="http://CSharpASP/ch21/">string</string>
```

FIGURE 17.3: VS-generated sample GET request and response for the getPayment WebMethod

The bottom half of the second box in Figure 17.3 shows the response XML. When you fill in the fields and post the form, you can quickly test the return values from your web service methods using the GET method. For example, when you send 6.5 as the annual percentage rate, $200,000 for the loan amount, and 30 as the mortgage duration, the web service calculates the monthly payment and returns the XML document shown in Figure 17.4.

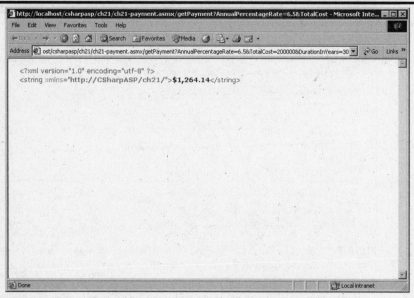

FIGURE 17.4:   XML response from the GET request for the getPayment WebMethod

In the next sections, you'll create the Mortgage Payment Calculator web service and consume it from a browser, from a Windows Forms .NET application, and from a VB6 client application.

BUILDING A WEB SERVICE

VS.NET takes care of most of the details for you. To create a web service, simply add a new web service item to your project. Web services use an .asmx extension. For this project, name the service ch21-payment.asmx. Visual Studio (VS) adds three files to your project: the ASMX file, a code-behind VB file, and a resources RESX file.

Switch to Code view. Notice that VS automatically creates the code-behind file with a reference to the System.Web.Services namespace and that the ch21_payment class inherits from the System.Web .Services.WebService class.

```
using System.Web.Services;
public class ch21_payment : System.Web.Services.WebService {
}
```

You don't *have* to inherit from this class to create a web service, but doing so makes it very easy to use the ASP.NET framework objects, such as the Request, Response, Session, and Application objects.

You should provide a WebService namespace attribute for each web service you create. Strictly speaking, this isn't necessary, but VS warns you to provide a namespace before using your web service in production mode, so you might as well get in the habit of adding the namespace at the beginning.

A namespace is nothing more than a unique identifier. It doesn't have to be globally unique—just unique for your server. A namespace doesn't have to refer to anything in particular, and it has nothing to do with the physical location of the web service itself, even though it's formatted as a URI. In other words, the namespace does *not* have to point to a physical location. Here's the WebService attribute and the namespace used in the Mortgage Payment Calculator web service class:

```
[WebService(Namespace="http://CSharpASP/ch21/")]
public class ch21_payment :
    System.Web.Services.WebService {
}
```

The WebService attribute is *part of the class definition line.* You're perfectly free to write the entire class definition line in a single code line, but you'll find that it's better to wrap the code because the length of the WebService attribute usually causes the class name to disappear off the right side of the screen, making the code difficult to read on-screen.

The Visual Studio web service template inserts the new constructor, the InitializeComponent method, and the Dispose method. I'll show that code here—once (see Listing 17.1). For subsequent listings I'll omit that code (because it's essentially the same every time) and insert a line such as ...autogenerated code omitted at the top of the listings.

NOTE
You can find the complete code for this project at www.sybex.com.

Listing 17.1: VS Autogenerated Code for the *ch21-payment* *.asmx* web service (*ch21-payment.asmx.cs*)

```
using System;
using System.Collections;
using System.ComponentModel;
using System.Data;
using System.Diagnostics;
using System.Web;
using System.Web.Services;
using Microsoft.VisualBasic;

namespace CSharpASP.ch21
{
    /// <summary>
    /// Summary description for ch21_payment.
    /// </summary>
    [WebService(Namespace="http://CSharpASP/ch21/")]
    public class ch21_payment :
      System.Web.Services.WebService
    {
        public ch21_payment()
        {
            //CODEGEN: This call is required by the ASP.NET Web
            //Services Designer
            InitializeComponent();
        }

        #region Component Designer generated code

        //Required by the web services Designer
        private IContainer components = null;

        /// <summary>
        /// Required method for Designer support -
        /// do not modify
        /// the contents of this method with the code editor.
        /// </summary>
        private void InitializeComponent()
        {
            //
            // ch21_payment
            //
```

```
        }

        /// <summary>
        /// Clean up any resources being used.
        /// </summary>
        protected override void Dispose( bool disposing )
        {
            if(disposing && components != null)
            {
                components.Dispose();
            }
            base.Dispose(disposing);
        }

        #endregion

        // custom code here
    }
}
```

Add the two methods shown in Listings 17.2 and 17.3 to the web service's code-behind class. The getPayment method accepts two doubles for the AnnualPercentageRate and TotalCost parameters, and an integer for the DurationInYears parameter. Interestingly, the Microsoft .VisualBasic namespace contains a Financial function called Pmt, which calculates a monthly payment given an annual percentage rate, the total amount financed, the future worth of the loan amount, and a constant that represents whether payments are made at the beginning or end of the payment period. You can reference the namespace, add a using line, and then use the Pmt method to calculate the payment and total amounts (see Listing 17.2).

Listing 17.2: The Mortgage Payment Calculator Web Service's *getPayment* Method *(ch21-payment.asmx.cs)*

```
[WebMethod()] public String getPayment
    (Double AnnualPercentageRate, Double TotalCost,
    int DurationInYears) {
    Double payment;

    // divide the APR by 100 to get a decimal
    // percentage, if necessary
```

```
if (AnnualPercentageRate > 1) {
    AnnualPercentageRate /= 100;
}

// and then divide by 12 for the number of months
// in a year to get the percentage interest rate
// per payment. Multiply the DurationInYears
// by 12 to get the total number of payments.
payment = Microsoft.VisualBasic.Financial.Pmt
    (AnnualPercentageRate / 12, DurationInYears * 12,
    TotalCost,0,
    Microsoft.VisualBasic.DueDate.EndOfPeriod);

// the Pmt function returns the payment as
// a negative number
payment = System.Math.Abs(payment);
return payment.ToString("$###,###,##0.00");
}
```

You need to make only *one* alteration to a Public method to expose it through a web service: just add the [WebMethod()] attribute to the front of the method declaration. However, you *must* add the [WebMethod()>] attribute to methods you want to expose or else the method won't be included in the web service's list of operations.

While it's useful to know what the monthly payment is for a proposed mortgage loan, it's also enlightening to see how altering the percentage rate, the loan amount, or the mortgage duration affects the total amount that you'll have to pay to satisfy the mortgage. The totalPaymentAmount function in Listing 17.3 lets you calculate that value.

Listing 17.3: The Mortgage Payment Calculator Web Service's *totalPaymentAmount* Method (ch21-payment .asmx.cs)

```
[WebMethod()] public String totalPaymentAmount
    (Double MonthlyPayment, int DurationInYears) {

    return (MonthlyPayment *
        (DurationInYears * 12)).ToString("C");
}
```

There are three ways to call a WebMethod function from a client:

Use a GET request. The first way is to use a special URL that identifies the web service, names the method, and includes any parameter values. The web service will attempt to cast the parameter values to the correct types, then it returns an XML-formatted message. For example, to find the monthly payment for a 30-year mortgage on a $200,000 house at an annual percentage rate of 6.5 percent, you can call the web service with the following URL:

```
http://localhost/CSharpASP/ch21/ch21-
    payment.asmx/getPayment?
    AnnualPercentageRate=6.5&
    TotalCost=200000&DurationInYears=30
```

NOTE

I've broken the URL into separate lines in the code, but you would enter it as a single line in a browser.

You can easily type the URL to call a web service from IE, which simply displays the returned data XML document (see Figure 17.4 again for the returned XML).

Use a POST request. Using a POST request, you place the individual data values into named fields in the form. By default, ASP.NET uses the GET method in the WebMethod test form that it creates automatically (see Figure 17.3). However, you can easily test the page using the POST method by saving the output from the automatically generated test page (right-click in the browser and select View Source to get the HTML), finding the <form> tag in the page, changing the METHOD attribute value to POST, and saving the page. There's no difference between the output from the GET and POST methods. The WebMethod test page shows a sample request and response using a POST method (see Figure 17.5).

HTTP POST

The following is a sample HTTP POST request and response. The **placeholders** shown need to be replaced with actual values.

```
POST /csharpasp/ch21/ch21-payment.asmx/getPayment HTTP/1.1
Host: localhost
Content-Type: application/x-www-form-urlencoded
Content-Length: length

AnnualPercentageRate=string&TotalCost=string&DurationInYears=string
```

```
HTTP/1.1 200 OK
Content-Type: text/xml; charset=utf-8
Content-Length: length

<?xml version="1.0" encoding="utf-8"?>
<string xmlns="http://CSharpASP/ch21/">string</string>
```

FIGURE 17.5: VS-generated sample POST request and response for the getPayment WebMethod

Use a SOAP request. The GET and POST methods work only for web services that use simple data types. For more complex request and return types, and for the best performance, you should use SOAP messaging to handle the requests and responses. SOAP messages are XML-formatted documents. The .NET Framework transparently handles serializing complex objects and data to and from SOAP requests and responses. Again, the WebMethod test page shows you sample SOAP request and response messages (see Figures 17.6 and 17.7). You'll see more about using SOAP messages with web services later in this chapter.

SOAP

The following is a sample SOAP request. The **placeholders** shown need to be replaced with actual values.

```
POST /csharpasp/ch21/ch21-payment.asmx HTTP/1.1
Host: localhost
Content-Type: text/xml; charset=utf-8
Content-Length: length
SOAPAction: "http://CSharpASP/ch21/getPayment"

<?xml version="1.0" encoding="utf-8"?>
<soap:Envelope xmlns:xsi="http://www.w3.org/2001/XMLSchema-instance" xmlns:xsd="http://www.w3
  <soap:Body>
    <getPayment xmlns="http://CSharpASP/ch21/">
      <AnnualPercentageRate>double</AnnualPercentageRate>
      <TotalCost>double</TotalCost>
      <DurationInYears>int</DurationInYears>
    </getPayment>
  </soap:Body>
</soap:Envelope>
```

FIGURE 17.6:   VS-generated sample SOAP request for the getPayment WebMethod

---

SOAP

The following is a sample SOAP response. The **placeholders** shown need to be replaced with actual values.

```
HTTP/1.1 200 OK
Content-Type: text/xml; charset=utf-8
Content-Length: length

<?xml version="1.0" encoding="utf-8"?>
<soap:Envelope xmlns:xsi="http://www.w3.org/2001/XMLSchema-instance" xmlns:xsd="http://www.w3
  <soap:Body>
    <getPaymentResponse xmlns="http://CSharpASP/ch21/">
      <getPaymentResult>string</getPaymentResult>
    </getPaymentResponse>
  </soap:Body>
</soap:Envelope>
```

FIGURE 17.7:   VS-generated sample SOAP response for the getPayment WebMethod

---

Testing WebMethods with IE using the auto-generated information and test pages is useful for quick-and-dirty testing, but it's not particularly useful in real-world applications. After you know that the WebMethod works, you can use client-side code to request the data, process the data, and then display it.

The Web Service Description Language (WSDL) File

You may be wondering how VS.NET generates the test pages. The answer is that the framework uses the classes in the System.Reflection namespace, which "reflects" runtime information back to the running code, to discover the web service's name, methods, and parameter types dynamically. It uses this information to create a Web Service Description Language (WSDL) file automatically. The WSDL file is—as you probably expect by now—an XML document containing a complete description of the web service. WSDL is a W3 specification that defines an XML format for describing automated network services. Internally, VS.NET uses the WSDL document to perform an XSLT transform that creates the HTML for the test pages. In other words, the WSDL document and the HTML test pages aren't static pages—they're created on demand.

You can see the WSDL file by clicking the Service Description link on the page generated when you request the ch21_payment.asmx file with no parameters (see Figure 17.8 for a partial view of the file).

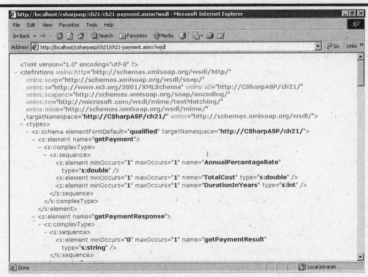

FIGURE 17.8: Partial view of the ch21_payment WSDL XML document in IE

The WSDL Document

The W3C has issued a note describing WSDL in detail at http://www .w3.org/TR/wsdl. Even a rather cursory look at the file shows that you can use a WSDL document to discover everything you need to know to call the service it describes from another program, including the name, location, methods, parameter types, supported call types (this web service supports GET, POST, and SOAP calls), and return types. Listing 17.4 contains the full WSDL document.

Listing 17.4: The WSDL Document for the Mortgage Payment Calculator Web Service (ch21_payment.asmx)

```xml
<?xml version="1.0" encoding="utf-8"?>
<definitions xmlns:s="http://www.w3.org/2001/XMLSchema"
    xmlns:http="http://schemas.xmlsoap.org/wsdl/http/"
    xmlns:mime="http://schemas.xmlsoap.org/wsdl/mime/"
    xmlns:tm="http://microsoft.com/wsdl/mime/textMatching/"
    xmlns:soap="http://schemas.xmlsoap.org/wsdl/soap/"
    xmlns:soapenc="http://schemas.xmlsoap.org/soap/encoding/"
    xmlns:s0="http://CSharpASP/ch21/"
    targetNamespace="http://CSharpASP/ch21/"
    xmlns="http://schemas.xmlsoap.org/wsdl/">
  <types>
    <s:schema attributeFormDefault="qualified"
      elementFormDefault="qualified"
      targetNamespace="http://CSharpASP/ch21/">
      <s:element name="getPayment">
        <s:complexType>
          <s:sequence>
            <s:element minOccurs="1" maxOccurs="1"
              name="AnnualPercentageRate" type="s:double" />
            <s:element minOccurs="1" maxOccurs="1"
              name="TotalCost"
              type="s:double" />
            <s:element minOccurs="1" maxOccurs="1"
              name="DurationInYears" type="s:int" />
          </s:sequence>
        </s:complexType>
      </s:element>
      <s:element name="getPaymentResponse">
        <s:complexType>
          <s:sequence>
            <s:element minOccurs="1" maxOccurs="1"
              name="getPaymentResult" type="s:string" />
          </s:sequence>
        </s:complexType>
```

```
        </s:element>
        <s:element name="totalPaymentAmount">
          <s:complexType>
            <s:sequence>
              <s:element minOccurs="1" maxOccurs="1"
                name="MonthlyPayment" type="s:double" />
              <s:element minOccurs="1" maxOccurs="1"
                name="DurationInYears" type="s:int" />
            </s:sequence>
          </s:complexType>
        </s:element>
        <s:element name="totalPaymentAmountResponse">
          <s:complexType>
            <s:sequence>
              <s:element minOccurs="1" maxOccurs="1"
                name="totalPaymentAmountResult"
                type="s:string" />
            </s:sequence>
          </s:complexType>
        </s:element>
        <s:element name="string" type="s:string" />
      </s:schema>
    </types>
    <message name="getPaymentSoapIn">
      <part name="parameters" element="s0:getPayment" />
    </message>
    <message name="getPaymentSoapOut">
      <part name="parameters"
        element="s0:getPaymentResponse" />
    </message>
    <message name="totalPaymentAmountSoapIn">
      <part name="parameters"
        element="s0:totalPaymentAmount" />
    </message>
    <message name="totalPaymentAmountSoapOut">
      <part name="parameters"
        element="s0:totalPaymentAmountResponse" />
    </message>
    <message name="getPaymentHttpGetIn">
      <part name="AnnualPercentageRate" type="s:string" />
      <part name="TotalCost" type="s:string" />
      <part name="DurationInYears" type="s:string" />
    </message>
```

```
<message name="getPaymentHttpGetOut">
  <part name="Body" element="s0:string" />
</message>
<message name="totalPaymentAmountHttpGetIn">
  <part name="MonthlyPayment" type="s:string" />
  <part name="DurationInYears" type="s:string" />
</message>
<message name="totalPaymentAmountHttpGetOut">
  <part name="Body" element="s0:string" />
</message>
<message name="getPaymentHttpPostIn">
  <part name="AnnualPercentageRate" type="s:string" />
  <part name="TotalCost" type="s:string" />
  <part name="DurationInYears" type="s:string" />
</message>
<message name="getPaymentHttpPostOut">
  <part name="Body" element="s0:string" />
</message>
<message name="totalPaymentAmountHttpPostIn">
  <part name="MonthlyPayment" type="s:string" />
  <part name="DurationInYears" type="s:string" />
</message>
<message name="totalPaymentAmountHttpPostOut">
  <part name="Body" element="s0:string" />
</message>
<portType name="ch21_paymentSoap">
  <operation name="getPayment">
    <input message="s0:getPaymentSoapIn" />
    <output message="s0:getPaymentSoapOut" />
  </operation>
  <operation name="totalPaymentAmount">
    <input message="s0:totalPaymentAmountSoapIn" />
    <output message="s0:totalPaymentAmountSoapOut" />
  </operation>
</portType>
<portType name="ch21_paymentHttpGet">
  <operation name="getPayment">
    <input message="s0:getPaymentHttpGetIn" />
    <output message="s0:getPaymentHttpGetOut" />
  </operation>
  <operation name="totalPaymentAmount">
    <input message="s0:totalPaymentAmountHttpGetIn" />
    <output message="s0:totalPaymentAmountHttpGetOut" />
```

```
        </operation>
      </portType>
      <portType name="ch21_paymentHttpPost">
        <operation name="getPayment">
          <input message="s0:getPaymentHttpPostIn" />
          <output message="s0:getPaymentHttpPostOut" />
        </operation>
        <operation name="totalPaymentAmount">
          <input message="s0:totalPaymentAmountHttpPostIn" />
          <output message="s0:totalPaymentAmountHttpPostOut" />
        </operation>
      </portType>
      <binding name="ch21_paymentSoap"
        type="s0:ch21_paymentSoap">
        <soap:binding
          transport="http://schemas.xmlsoap.org/soap/http"
          style="document" />
        <operation name="getPayment">
          <soap:operation
            soapAction="http://CSharpASP/ch21/getPayment"
            style="document" />
          <input>
            <soap:body use="literal" />
          </input>
          <output>
            <soap:body use="literal" />
          </output>
        </operation>
        <operation name="totalPaymentAmount">
          <soap:operation        soapAction=
            "http://CSharpASP/ch21/totalPaymentAmount"
            style="document" />
          <input>
            <soap:body use="literal" />
          </input>
          <output>
            <soap:body use="literal" />
          </output>
        </operation>
      </binding>
      <binding name="ch21_paymentHttpGet"
        type="s0:ch21_paymentHttpGet">
        <http:binding verb="GET" />
```

```
<operation name="getPayment">
  <http:operation location="/getPayment" />
  <input>
    <http:urlEncoded />
  </input>
  <output>
    <mime:mimeXml part="Body" />
  </output>
</operation>
<operation name="totalPaymentAmount">
  <http:operation location="/totalPaymentAmount" />
  <input>
    <http:urlEncoded />
  </input>
  <output>
    <mime:mimeXml part="Body" />
  </output>
</operation>
</binding>
<binding name="ch21_paymentHttpPost"
  type="s0:ch21_paymentHttpPost">
  <http:binding verb="POST" />
  <operation name="getPayment">
    <http:operation location="/getPayment" />
    <input>
      <mime:content
        type="application/x-www-form-urlencoded" />
    </input>
    <output>
      <mime:mimeXml part="Body" />
    </output>
  </operation>
  <operation name="totalPaymentAmount">
    <http:operation location="/totalPaymentAmount" />
    <input>
      <mime:content
        type="application/x-www-form-urlencoded" />
    </input>
    <output>
      <mime:mimeXml part="Body" />
    </output>
  </operation>
```

```
    </binding>
    <service name="ch21_payment">
      <documentation>Mortgage Payment web service
        Calculator</documentation>
      <port name="ch21_paymentSoap"
        binding="s0:ch21_paymentSoap">
        <soap:address
          location=
          "http://localhost/CSharpASP/ch21/ch21-payment.asmx"
          />
      </port>
      <port name="ch21_paymentHttpGet"
        binding="s0:ch21_paymentHttpGet">
        <http:address
          location=
          "http://localhost/CSharpASP/ch21/ch21-payment.asmx"
          />
      </port>
      <port name="ch21_paymentHttpPost"
        binding="s0:ch21_paymentHttpPost">
        <http:address
          location=
          "http://localhost/CSharpASP/ch21/ch21-payment.asmx"
          />
      </port>
    </service>
  </definitions>
```

CONSUMING A WEB SERVICE

Now that you've created and tested a web service, you can use it in your applications. In this section, you'll see how to create a Web Form that calls the Mortgage Payment web service from a browser using IE and the equivalent Windows Form application that consumes the same web service using SOAP messages.

Consuming Web Services from IE

This example uses a browser client—IE version 6—to call the Mortgage Payment web service and display the results. Because Mortgage Payment is a simple web service, this example uses the GET method to simplify the process.

The ch21-1.aspx Web Form uses the MSXML.DLL COM parser, which exposes an XMLHTTPRequest-Object object, to make a background GET request and parse the results for display in the page.

> **NOTE**
>
> You can use the XMLHTTPRequest object to make HTML requests as well as XML requests, or even to retrieve plain text or binary files; therefore, think of this example as a more-or-less generic way to retrieve information in the background from a web page in IE.

ch21-1.aspx contains a form that users can fill out. They click the Get Payment button to contact the web service and display the results in the area below the form (see Figure 17.9).

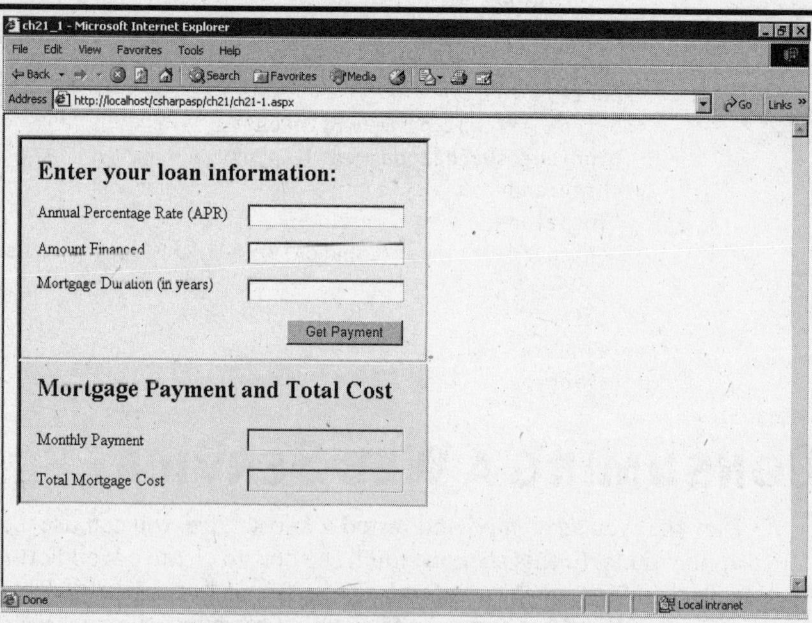

![ch21_1 - Microsoft Internet Explorer window showing a loan information form with fields for Annual Percentage Rate (APR), Amount Financed, Mortgage Duration (in years), a Get Payment button, and Mortgage Payment and Total Cost section with Monthly Payment and Total Mortgage Cost fields.]

FIGURE 17.9: The Mortgage Calculator web service interface

The form contains standard Web Server Control Label, TextBox, and Validation controls except for the Get Payment button, which is an HTML `<input type="button">` control. The reason the form uses an HTML button rather than a Web Server Control Button control is that the Web Server Button control always submits the form—and in this case, you don't *want* to submit the form. In contrast, the HTML button does only what you tell it to do. In this case, it calls a client-side JScript function called getPayment(), which makes sequential requests to the getPayment and totalPayment-Amount web service methods (see Listing 17.5).

Listing 17.5: Calling Web Service Methods and Displaying the Results (ch21-1.aspx.cs)

```
function getPayment() {
    if (!Page_ClientValidate()){
        return;
    }
    var s="";
    var apr = document.getElementById("txtAPR").value;
    var total = document.getElementById("txtTotal").value;
    var duration =
        document.getElementById("txtDuration").value;
    var doc = new ActiveXObject("MSXML2.DOMDocument.3.0");
    var xhttp = new ActiveXObject("MSXML2.XMLHTTP");
    var url =
        "http://localhost/CSharpASP/ch21/ch21-payment.asmx/" +
        "getPayment? AnnualPercentageRate=" +
        apr + "&TotalCost=" +
        total + "&DurationInYears=" + duration;
    xhttp.Open("GET", url, false);
    xhttp.Send();
    doc.load(xhttp.ResponseXML);
    s = doc.selectSingleNode("//string").text;
    document.getElementById(
        "lblPaymentResult").innerHTML = s;

    // get the total payment
    // strip the dollar sign from the monthly payment amount
    s = s.substr(1);
    url = "http://localhost/CSharpASP/ch21/ch21-payment.asmx/
        totalPaymentAmount?MonthlyPayment=" + s +
    "&DurationInYears="
        + duration;
    xhttp.Open("GET", url, false);
    xhttp.Send();
    doc.load(xhttp.ResponseXML);
    s = doc.selectSingleNode("//string").text;
    document.getElementById("lblCostResult").innerHTML = s;
}
```

Because the ch21-1.aspx Web Form contains Validation controls, ASP.NET automatically includes a reference to a JScript that performs validation. However, ASP.NET performs that validation only when you submit the form—and in this case, you're not going to submit the form. But it's useful to hook into the validation script anyway, so you can take advantage of the generic client-side validation code and the Validation Web Server controls. The first lines in the script force validation. If validation fails, the function exits without calling the web service methods. The validation process displays any validation error messages.

```
if (!Page_ClientValidate()){
    return;
}
```

TIP

Take advantage of ASP.NET's client-side validation process by calling the Page_ClientValidate() method included in the validation script.

Next, the script creates a DOMDocument object and an XMLHTTPRequest object:

```
var doc = new ActiveXObject("MSXML2.DOMDocument.3.0");
var xhttp = new ActiveXObject("MSXML2.XMLHTTP");
```

NOTE

I'm using the release version of the MSXML.DLL parser, version 3, downloadable from MSDN. To use version 3 in IE 5 or 6, you must also download and run a small program named xmlinst.exe; otherwise, you won't be able to create the DOMDocument or XMLHTTPRequest object.

The script creates the GET request by appending the user-entered values to the base web service URL.

```
var url = "http://localhost/CSharpASP/ch21/" +
    "ch21-payment.asmx/getPayment?AnnualPercentageRate="
    + apr + "&TotalCost=" + total + "&DurationInYears=" +
    duration;
```

To send the URL, use the XMLHTTPRequest object's Open method. The first parameter, GET, specifies the request method; the second parameter specifies the URL; and the third (optional) parameter specifies whether the object makes a synchronous or asynchronous call. Because the default is asynchronous, and you don't want the script to continue until it gets the values, the call explicitly passes false. For secured requests, two other optional parameters (not shown) accept a username and password. After setting up the request with the Open method, you must call the Send method to begin the request process:

```
xhttp.Open("GET", url, false);
xhttp.Send();
```

When the Send method returns, the ResponseXML property holds the return XML document. The script loads that into the DOMDocument object.

```
doc.load(xhttp.ResponseXML);
```

The returned XML for both methods looks like this (although, of course, the value of the <string> element changes based on the user input values):

```
<?xml version="1.0" encoding="utf-8" ?>
  <string xmlns="http://CSharpASP/ch21/">$1,264.14</string>
```

The script then selects the contents of the <string> element and displays the result value in the Monthly Payment field in the second half of the form.

```
s = doc.selectSingleNode("//string").text;
    document.getElementById("lblPaymentResult").innerHTML
        = s;
```

The script follows an identical process to call the getPaymentTotal method. When the user enters valid values, the result looks like Figure 17.10.

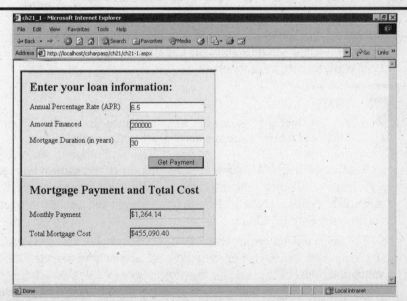

FIGURE 17.10: The Mortgage Payment response after executing successfully

There are other ways to access a web service from IE. If you're building an intranet application in which all the clients have IE 5.5 or later, you can download and use an HTML behavior (.htc) file from Microsoft at

```
http://msdn.microsoft.com/downloads/samples/internet/
default.asp?url=/downloads/samples/internet/behaviors/
library/webservice/default.asp
```

An HTML behavior is a referenced script file with an .htc extension that runs on the client. Behavior files have access to the DOM for the page, which means you can write very abstract behavior logic that works generically for almost any HTML page.

The webservice behavior lets you use SOAP requests rather than HTTP GET or POST requests to access a web service. Because the audience for pure IE 5+ applications is considerably smaller than the audience for a wider range of browsers, and because you're about to see two other ways to consume web services using SOAP messages, I haven't included an example. However, if you *do* have exclusively IE 5+ clients, HTML behaviors are extremely powerful, and I recommend that you investigate the topic thoroughly.

Consuming Web Services from a .NET Windows Forms Application

In this section, you'll create a C# Windows application that uses the Mortgage Calculator web service to display calculated payments. The code for this project is separate from the CSharpASP ASP.NET project you've been working with in other chapters.

NOTE

See the sidebar "Creating the Web Application Used in This Chapter" in Chapter 16 for instructions on working with the CSharpASP project.

First, create a new Windows Application project and name it Mortgage-Calculator. Although the interface uses Windows Form controls, it's essentially identical to the Web Form interface you just saw in the preceding section (see Figure 17.11).

The major differences are that Validation controls aren't (yet) available in the System.Windows.Forms namespace, so you have to code your own validation. Most of the code for the project does exactly that—checks the user-entered values to make sure they meet the web service requirements. For example, you must ensure that you can cast the APR and Amount

Financed to doubles and the Mortgage Duration to an integer as well as ensure that the values are within some reasonable range.

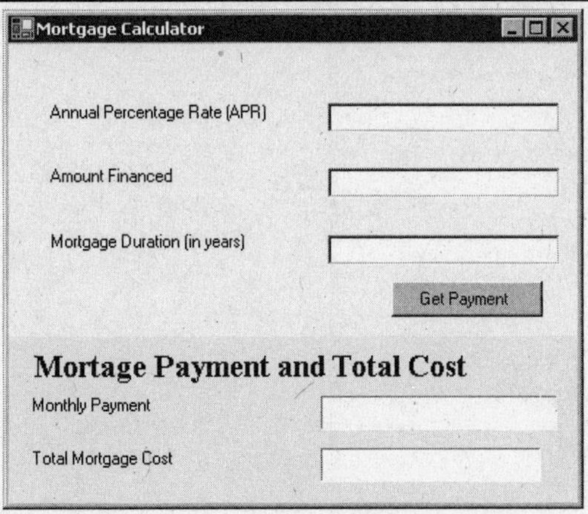

FIGURE 17.11: The Mortgage Payment Windows Form application interface

Just as with the IE-based UI, the button on the form makes two calls to the Mortgage Calculator web service: one to the getPayment method to obtain the monthly payment, and one to retrieve the total cost of the mortgage. It places the results into the two labels (that look like text boxes) in the lower panel of the form. The form acts just like the IE interface, but it communicates with the web service via SOAP messages rather than with an HTTP GET request.

Adding a Web Reference

The .NET Framework makes the process extremely simple. All you need to do is add a web service reference to the form. To do that, right-click the References item in the Solution Explorer and select the Add Web Reference menu item from the pop-up menu. You'll see the Add Web Reference dialog shown in Figure 17.12.

In my setup, the CSharpASP project is on the local web server; therefore, I was able to use the Web References on Local Web Server link at the bottom of the left panel to find the reference. If the web server containing the CSharpASP project is *not* on the same machine as your VS.NET development environment, you'll need to enter the server address in the Address field at the top of the dialog in the form http://yourServerName. The left panel is a WebBrowser, so you can navigate to the correct location if links are available to do so.

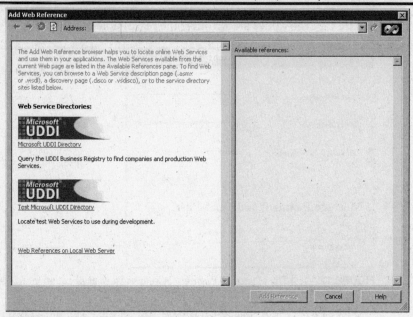

FIGURE 17.12:   The Add Web Reference wizard

If you can't find the reference, enter the following name, substituting your server name for `localhost` if you aren't using your local machine server:

```
http://localhost/CSharpASP/ch21/ch21-payment.asmx/wsdl
```

When the Add Web Reference wizard finds the server, it requests a discovery file called `default.vsdisco`, which is an XML file containing locations to look in (and to avoid looking in) for web services available on that server. The left panel of the dialog displays the results of the search, while the wizard reads the file and fills the right panel with links to the various web services available on that server. Each .NET project on the server also has a `.vsdisco` file containing a similar list of locations in which the server can find web services exposed by that project. Find the CSharpASP project and select it. You'll see the `ch21-payment.asmx` web service shown in the right panel and the `.vsdisco` file that describes the location of the web service in the left panel (see Figure 17.13).

Click the Add Reference button at the bottom of the dialog window to add the reference to your project. When you do this, VS.NET creates a proxy that your project can use to call the web service just as you call any other class methods.

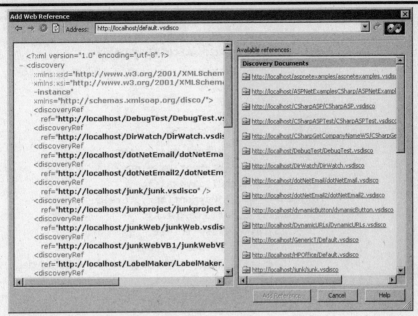

FIGURE 17.13: The CSharpASP ch21-payment.asmx web service in the Add Web Reference wizard

WARNING

If your web server is not on the same machine as your VS.NET development environment, you'll need to delete the Web Reference to the ch21-payment.asmx web service and then add it back using the correct server.

VS.NET adds a Web References item to your Solution Explorer window containing one item that has the same name as the selected server. That item, in turn, contains a WSDL file describing the web service interface (see Listing 17.4 for details), a .disco file containing location information for files related to the web service, and a Reference.map file that maps URLs to the local cached file location and contains references to the discovery (.disco) file and the WSDL files.

Using the Web Service

After adding the Web Reference, using the referenced web service is straightforward. For example, after validating the user input, the button click event for the Get Payment button on the form calls a runWebMethods method that calls the web service methods and updates the two Label controls in the bottom half of the form (see Listing 17.6).

**Listing 17.6: The MortgageCalculator Form's *runWebMethods*
Method (*MortgageCalculator
:frmMortgageCalculator.cs*)**

```
private void runWebMethods(Double apr, Double totalCost,
    int durationInYears) {
    String payment;
    String cost ;
    try {
        this.Cursor = Cursors.WaitCursor;
        localhost.ch21_payment ws = new
            localhost.ch21_payment();
        payment = ws.getPayment(apr, totalCost,
            (Int16) durationInYears);
        this.lblPaymentResult.Text = payment;
        payment = payment.Substring(1);
        cost = ws.totalPaymentAmount(Double.Parse(payment),
            (Int16) durationInYears);
        lblCostResult.Text = cost;
    }
    catch (Exception ex) {
        this.Cursor = Cursors.Default;
        MessageBox.Show("An error occurred: " + ex.Message,
            "An Error Occurred", MessageBoxButtons.OK,
            MessageBoxIcon.Error,
            MessageBoxDefaultButton.Button1,
            MessageBoxOptions.DefaultDesktopOnly);
    }
    finally {
        this.Cursor = Cursors.Default;
    }
}
```

The highlighted lines create an instance of the web service proxy and
call its methods. Use the syntax `servername.WebServiceName` to create
the proxy object. Note that after obtaining the proxy object, calling its
methods is identical to calling methods for any other class. VS.NET uses
the WSDL file to provide IntelliSense for method names and parameters.

Cross-Platform Interface Issues

Visual Studio's transparent use of the WSDL and `.disco` files makes consuming web services from a Windows client much easier than consuming

the same web services from IE, and it has two ramifications that will have a huge effect on future application development—and probably on *your* web application development tasks as well.

The first is that, until now, it's been relatively difficult to provide a rich-client UI because HTML, while it has many strengths as a data *display* markup language, has many weaknesses as an interactive GUI interface. In contrast, Windows, Mac, and other windowing client interfaces support superior GUI interfaces but lack a means for generically displaying information, lack intrinsic support for network communications, are bound to specific platforms and hardware configurations, and are often difficult to distribute and install.

Many attempts have been made to solve this problem. Initially, Java was touted as the answer to cross-platform problems. Browsers were able to host Java *applets*, small binary programs that used all or a portion of the browser window to provide capabilities that HTML was incapable of providing, such as dynamic graphics, background server communications, and complex GUI controls. As long as the host machine had a platform-specific Java runtime package installed, the browser could download and launch applet code on command. The runtime constrained the actions that applets could take by running them in a "sandbox" that prevented the applet, for example, from writing files or launching local applications. Despite an initial flurry of interest when applets first appeared, poor runtime implementations, restricted bandwidth, and the slower machines available at the time caused users to categorize applets as "slow."

Although all these problems have been solved or (in the case of bandwidth) ameliorated, the technology never recovered its initial allure. A similar, more powerful, but much more dangerous Microsoft-specific technology used COM components called ActiveX controls or ActiveX documents hosted in Internet Explorer. To avoid IE displaying default security warnings about such components, they had to be "signed," thus letting you trace the author of malevolent code (after the damage was done) before IE would let them run (although users can defeat the warnings via the security settings). Unfortunately, they also had to be installed and registered like any other COM component, with all the attendant versioning and portability problems. ActiveX controls delivered with Internet Explorer or distributed inside intranets have enjoyed widespread use, but the Internet at large eschewed and vilified the technology because of its potential for abuse.

The Java applet and ActiveX control efforts focused on improving browser interfaces and capabilities through hosted code add-ons. At the same time, a third effort, Dynamic HTML (DHTML), focused on improving the browser's intrinsic capabilities. DHTML is a good idea that has never quite managed to come to fruition because browser manufacturers' support for DHTML varies widely. In addition, because DHTML was (and is) a work in progress, developers face many problems supporting even different versions of browsers from the *same* manufacturer.

Web services help solve this problem by letting you create platform-specific rich-client interfaces that communicate relatively transparently with servers through a simple XML-based format. In other words, web services give platform-specific applications many of the networking capabilities that browsers provide—without being version specific (although it remains to be seen how robust and stable SOAP and other protocols will be); bound to individual manufacturers like IE, Netscape, and Java are; or dependent on complex, specific binary implementations, like DCOM and CORBA. In my opinion, the advent of web services is one step toward the end of the browser era. Browsers will remain important as generalized display applications but will rapidly diminish in importance as application delivery platforms, because using a robust native environment to build interactive data-driven applications provides a better user experience than general-purpose browsers can provide.

The second way web services will affect your web application development is that, because they give you a clean way to abstract program logic and data from the interface, the demand for that separation will inevitably grow. Despite all the emphasis on web development and browsers, the future reality is much broader. Browsers are *not* the only clients, and Internet/intranet development is highly likely to become even more important than it already is. HTTP-based communications are part of the new application infrastructure not because they're more efficient or easier to develop, but because they're standardized and widely available. As the number of devices increases, the pressure to develop centralized ways of delivering the same data to multiple types of devices also increases. It's just not efficient—from either the user or the business point of view—to create multiple applications that store or consume the same types of data in different ways.

For example, many applications use contact lists, but I'm sure you're well aware of the difficulties involved in transferring data from one application to another because most applications use proprietary formats to store the lists. Typically, the most popular programs buy or reverse-engineer the file formats of other popular programs so that they can "import" or "export" data. However, now XML and schema remove the necessity for programs to create proprietary binary formats for common data. That means you'll see increasing interoperability and simplified data sharing between different applications. However, the concept reaches further than that. If you can share data between the various applications, then there's no need to maintain multiple *copies* of that data other than for speed and for use when the applications can't connect to a central server.

Again, web services hold the promise of a solution. By making it easy for applications of all types to communicate with and retrieve data from a central server via common and ubiquitous network protocols, they also increase the probability that common data will be stored as "master files" in a centrally located store.

Web services also help solve the real and increasing problems within and between organizations that have incompatible hardware and software. An entire branch of programming, called Enterprise Application Integration (EAI), has grown up around writing software that enables these incompatible systems to exchange data. Because it's much easier and faster to write web services wrappers for the applications than to write custom code to translate from one format to another, EAI's future probably lies almost entirely within web services.

Finally, because any type of application can read and process XML without much effort, you can write programs that can find or "discover" and consume web services without knowing in advance where those services are or knowing the details of communicating with those services. Until such capabilities become so commonplace that they're part of the background infrastructure, it's useful to know a little bit about the technologies involved. From the .NET viewpoint, you should be aware of two public standards: the Universal Description, Discovery, and Integration (UDDI) specification, which lets programs find web services, and the Simple Object Access Protocol (SOAP), which lets them communicate. You've already seen the third piece of this puzzle, WSDL, which describes the requirements that you need to create properly formatted SOAP messages.

SOAP (SIMPLE OBJECT ACCESS PROTOCOL)

Even though XML reduces the process of remote communication to simple XML-formatted text files, for programs to interoperate, you must have a standard that specifies a request and response format. Several different formats have been proposed, but the current standard is the Simple Object Access Protocol (SOAP).

Benefits and Disadvantages of Using SOAP

To understand why SOAP is important, it's useful to compare it to existing remote access methods such as Microsoft's Distributed COM (DCOM), the Object Management Group's Common Object Request Broker Architecture (CORBA), and Java's Remote Method Invocation (RMI). All three (DCOM, CORBA, and RMI) use binary messages to communicate between the client and server. All three address security, garbage collection, activation, and state management. SOAP addresses none of these things—it's just a wire protocol. But that simplicity makes it extremely portable—each platform or machine can use different methods for state maintenance, activation, security, and garbage collection.

Unfortunately, there are some serious tradeoffs when using SOAP:

You lose the capability to maintain state easily between method calls.   Using DCOM, CORBA, or RMI, you can call servers that remember state between calls, which is a huge advantage with small numbers of clients because it simplifies development. As the number of clients increases, the stateless model becomes more and more attractive because, with stateless calls, you can route client requests to any available server. In contrast, maintaining server state means you must route clients to the specific server that maintains that specific client's state. The only way to combine the two approaches is to store state on yet another server, which is exactly what web farm applications using database tables to store state do, and it's exactly what Microsoft's State Server does, running in StateServer mode (out-of-process) or SQLServer mode (using a SQL Server database). In the end, state maintenance problems with web services are no different from the state maintenance problems you've already explored with C# web applications, and they can be solved the same way.

The SOAP messages themselves are rather bulky.   XML, while very generic, is also a "heavy" format compared to binary representations of the same data. The increased message size increases network traffic and slows the process of sending and receiving the data.

You must cast SOAP data values to the correct types.   A SOAP message contains a string representation of the data values. The cast requirements contribute to the increased size because the message must also contain a representation of each data type in the message. Using XSD schema improves the speed and reduces the message size, but it does not absolve the receiving code from casting (and checking) each data value.

SOAP doesn't have built-in security, compression, activation, or garbage collection.   Microsoft's web service implementation handles garbage collection, and efforts are well under way to provide standardized methods for handling security needs and compression.

There is no support for asynchronous processing.   Because clients don't typically run a web server, a web service has no way to initiate communications with the client; therefore, you can't invoke a web service asynchronously (or rather, you can't receive any status or completion messages from the server). However, in some situations, you can use messaging queues (such as MSMQ) to help solve the problem. Using a message queue, the client would post the request and then continue with other processing. The queue would deliver the request, and the server would queue the response message. The queue would notify the client when the response was available. Message queues have proven to be very scalable and effective. Unfortunately, there's no generic worldwide support for any specific type of message queue. Until that occurs, all solutions will be custom code.

SOAP Basics

SOAP consists of two types of messages—requests and responses—and both are XML documents. The request XML document contains the following:

- ▶ An *envelope* element that surrounds the SOAP *payload* (the message). The envelope is the root element of a SOAP XML document.

- ▶ A *header* (optional) that describes the type of SOAP message.

- ▶ A *body* (mandatory) that carries the method call name and parameter names and values. For example, suppose you have a web service that provides mortgage payment information. Given an interest rate, a total cost, and the number of years in the mortgage, the web service returns the payment amount per month.

Listing 17.7 shows a simple SOAP request message for the getPayment method of the Mortgage Calculator web service.

Listing 17.7: SOAP Request Message for the Mortgage Calculator Web Service's *getPayment* Method

```xml
<?xml version="1.0" encoding="utf-8"?>
<soap:Envelope
    xmlns:xsi="http://www.w3.org/2001/XMLSchema-instance"
    xmlns:xsd="http://www.w3.org/2001/XMLSchema"
    xmlns:soap="http://schemas.xmlsoap.org/soap/envelope/">
  <soap:Body>
    <getPayment xmlns="http://CSharpASP/ch21/">
      <AnnualPercentageRate>6.5</AnnualPercentageRate>
      <TotalCost>200000</TotalCost>
      <DurationInYears>30</DurationInYears>
    </getPayment>
  </soap:Body>
</soap:Envelope>
```

The server can parse this message and determine the data types using the WSDL schema generated by the web service on demand. After obtaining the correctly typed data values, it calls the requested method and creates a response SOAP message containing the return value from the method, which it returns to the client (see Listing 17.8).

Listing 17.8: SOAP Response Message for the Mortgage Calculator Web Service's *getPayment* Method

```xml
<?xml version="1.0" encoding="utf-8"?>
<soap:Envelope
    xmlns:xsi="http://www.w3.org/2001/XMLSchema-instance"
    xmlns:xsd="http://www.w3.org/2001/XMLSchema"
    xmlns:soap="http://schemas.xmlsoap.org/soap/envelope/">
  <soap:Body>
    <getPaymentResponse xmlns="http://CSharpASP/ch21/">
      <getPaymentResult>string</getPaymentResult>
    </getPaymentResponse>
  </soap:Body>
</soap:Envelope>
```

Notice that the <soap:Body> element return uses the name of the web service method plus the term Response: <getPaymentResponse>. That element contains a similarly named element with the postfix

Result: <getPaymentResult>. All standard .NET-generated SOAP messages follow this convention, but you're not at all constrained by the SOAP specification to follow it in your applications. By defining the element names and types yourself, you can create SOAP messages that are specific to your particular application.

Complex SOAP Messages

The simple web service envelope has a simple response body that returns a string, but you aren't limited to returning strings. For example, the following SOAP return message returns a DataSet object. Interestingly, if you look at the return type sample SOAP message, it's coded as an <xsd:schema> type. That makes sense because a DataSet serialized to XML for transport via SOAP—or any object, for that matter—consists of nothing more than a schema and some supporting XML data needed to reinstantiate the object at some other point. By default, .NET objects serialize by writing out their public properties.

For example, suppose you define a simple NameObject class that has LastName and FirstName properties:

```csharp
using System;
namespace CSharpASP.ch21 {
    /// <summary>
    /// Summary description for NameObject.
    /// </summary>
    public class NameObject {
        private String mFirstName="NA";
        private String mLastName="NA";
        public NameObject() {
        }
        public NameObject(String first, String last) {
            mFirstName=first;
            mLastName=last;
        }
        public String FirstName {
            get {
                return mFirstName;
            }
            set {
                mFirstName=value;
            }
        }
        public String LastName{
            get {
                return mLastName;
```

```
            }
            set {
                mLastName=value;
            }
        }
    }
}
```

If you were to create a `WebMethod` that returned an instance of the `NameObject` class, it would return SOAP messages similar to this:

```
<?xml version="1.0" encoding="utf-8"?>
<soap:Envelope
    xmlns:xsi="http://www.w3.org/2001/XMLSchema-instance"
    xmlns:xsd="http://www.w3.org/2001/XMLSchema"
    xmlns:soap="http://schemas.xmlsoap.org/soap/envelope/">
    <soap:Body>
        <getNameObjectResponse
            xmlns="http://CSharpASP/NameObject">
            <getNameObjectResult>
                <LastName>string</LastName>
                <FirstName>string</FirstName>
            </getNameObjectResult>
        </getNameObjectResponse>
    </soap:Body>
</soap:Envelope>
```

Note that the response carries the public properties needed to instantiate a copy of the object on the client. Also note that returning a simple object type is one way to return more than a single value. You can return arrays of values or collection objects as well. For example, you can easily alter the Mortgage Calculator so it returns both the monthly payment and the total cost of the loan, either as an object or as a two-item array. Whether you would want to do that depends on how you use the web service. In the Mortgage Calculator, creating a single method that returns both values would eliminate a round trip for the example applications, which would be much more efficient.

Secured Web Services

The examples shown in this chapter don't use the optional SOAP header element, which carries information such as versioning, security, identification IDs, and so forth. SOAP messages work fine over Secure Sockets Layer (SSL), so if you're simply interested in encrypting the content of the messages themselves, access your web services via SSL. However, if you also need to build in authentication and authorization, you have two choices: You can use ASP.NET's built-in authentication methods, or you can specify custom security options in the SOAP header.

The built-in choices are similar to those you can use with Web Forms, except that you can't use Forms authentication (because they use redirection and an HTML-based user interface to provide authentication credentials and, thus, can't be automated easily). You can use Basic encryption to pass (lightly) encrypted username and password information data between the client and the server. Except in low-security intranet environments, you should avoid Basic authentication because it transmits usernames and passwords in plain text. If you *must* use Basic authentication, combine it with SSL, which provides much better security. For Windows clients, you can also use Windows Digest, Integrated Windows, or Client certificates authentication.

FINDING WEB SERVICES (UDDI)

Unless you're exclusively building and consuming your own web services, you'll need to find and reference web services created by others. Interestingly, you can use a web service to find other web services. The Universal Description, Discovery, and Integration (UDDI) service acts as a centralized directory of available web services, and you can use it either manually or programmatically to find out what services are available at a given UDDI registry.

Discovery may seem like a rather trivial operation, but in fact it's crucial to the automatic workings of web services. For example, suppose you're a corporate buyer and you want to buy 300 laptop computers. You know exactly what model and features you want; now you're searching for the best price. Today, the only way to compare prices is to compile a list of possible vendors and then either call them or visit their websites individually. For some products, sites exist that perform such tasks for you, but there's no generally available solution. In contrast, if enough businesses register their services in UDDI registries, you can create an automated price-hunting program that would find and query laptop vendors, comparing prices until it found the best price. For some tasks, this might save days or weeks of human effort.

In version 1.0, UDDI contains four types of information; each defines part of the business:

> **businessEntity** Contains general information about the business itself. Each businessEntity contains one or more businessService descriptions.

businessService   A general description of the services available at a business.

tModel   A unique type ID that identifies a single type of service. For example, time services would be one tModel; credit card validation would be another. Multiple services may use the same tModel. A large number of generic tModel identifiers already exist, so most web services should be able to use one of the existing tModels.

bindingTemplate   A way to map web services to tModels. When you find a company that exposes services belonging to the particular tModel you're looking for, you use the binding-Template information to get an exact location for the web service detailed description. Although the description is usually a WSDL file, you should know that while a UDDI location *might* store web service descriptions as WSDL, that's not a requirement. You may find web services that are *not* described with WSDL.

There are huge advantages for businesses and individuals to being able to find and interact with exposed business services programmatically. You probably can also see that a truly useful UDDI registry must contain a huge amount of information. To gather industry support for UDDI, Microsoft, Ariba, and IBM are spearheading UDDI registries, providing online help, developer information, and integration services to combine multiple UDDI registries into a global directory for web services. You can find more information about UDDI at

```
http://uddi.microsoft.com/default.aspx
```

and

```
http://www-109.ibm.com/cgi-
    bin/dWsearch.pl?selScope=dW&UserRestriction=UDDI
```

WHAT'S NEXT

You've seen how to create and consume a simple web service from Internet Explorer and a C# Windows Forms application. However, it's important that you realize exactly how ubiquitous this way of handling application data is likely to become, and what the ramifications are for you as a developer. The next chapter focuses on building reusable controls in ASP.NET environments.

Chapter 18

BUILDING YOUR OWN WEB CONTROLS

In addition to the Web Forms Server controls and HTML controls that you get with ASP.NET, you can build your own controls that work in any of three different ways. First, User controls are essentially stand-alone Web Forms; you can design them almost exactly like a Web Form, placing controls on a form, or you can create controls at runtime. Second, you can create controls that tie two or more Server controls together as a *Composite* control. Finally, you can build Custom controls in which you can define everything about the control. This is the equivalent of creating a brand-new control.

In this chapter, you'll build a User control, a Composite control, and a Custom control and see the relative advantages and disadvantages of each type.

Adapted from *Mastering ASP.NET with C#*
by A. Russell Jones
ISBN 0-7821-2989-7

BUILDING A USER CONTROL

The simplest type of control you can build is a User control, which is essentially an ASPX page changed to have an `.ascx` extension. When you install .NET, it prevents IIS from displaying files with an `.ascx` extension directly, so users can't request your User controls by themselves.

So that you can see all the differences, it's useful to attempt to change a Web Form into a User control (that is, change an ASPX page into an ASCX page). For example, create a Web Form called `testChange.aspx`, place a Button control on it, and set the button's `Text` property to `My Button`.

Add a client-side script to display an `alert` when a user clicks the button:

```
private void Button1_Click(object sender,
    System.EventArgs e) {
    this.Page.RegisterStartupScript("msg",
    "<script language='JScript'>" +
    "alert('My Button clicked!');</script>");
}
```

Next, right-click the `testChange.aspx` file and select the `Rename` item from the pop-up menu. Change the file's extension to `.ascx`. You'll see a warning about changing file extensions. Answer Yes to accept the change. When you save your changes, the code-behind class and the RESX file also are renamed to reflect the changed extension, but just renaming the file isn't quite enough. After renaming the file, you have just four manual changes to make to change the Web Form into a User control:

1. User controls inherit from `System.Web.UI.UserControl` rather than `System.Web.UI.Page`. In the code-behind file, change the class definition

   ```
   public class testChange : System.Web.UI.Page
   ```

   to

   ```
   public class testChange : System.Web.UI.UserControl
   ```

2. Although Visual Studio changes the *name* of the associated code-behind file, it doesn't change the *reference* to it in the ASPX file. Open the `testChange.ascx` file in the HTML editor, then change the `Codebehind` attribute in the top line from

   ```
   Codebehind="testChange.aspx.cs"
   ```

   to

   ```
   Codebehind="testChange.ascx.cs"
   ```

3. Change the Page attribute in the top line to Control. Now, you no longer have a Page object; you have a Control object.

4. Remove the <form> tag but not the <asp:Button> tag. Actually, this last step is not really required—the rule is, you can't have two <form> tags in a Web Form *that run at the server*, so it's perfectly OK to leave the <form> tag in place, but you must remove the runat="server" attribute. However, for simple controls, it's easier not to deal with the added complexity of forms embedded in forms; normally you should remove the <form> tag. In this particular case, it doesn't matter.

Now test the new User control in a Web Form. Create a new Web Form in the ch23 folder and name it ch23-1.aspx. In HTML mode, change the id attribute of the <form> tag to Form1. In the code-behind file, add this line to the Form_Load method:

```
this.FindControl("Form1").Controls.Add
    ((ch23.testChange) this.LoadControl("testChange.ascx"));
```

When you compile and run the Web Form, you'll see the button from your User control in the browser window. When you click it, you'll see the JavaScript alert shown in Figure 18.1.

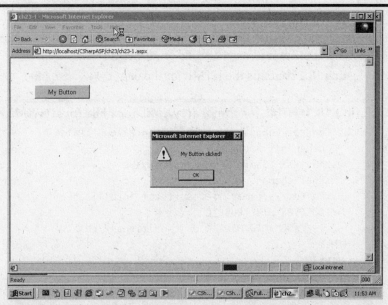

FIGURE 18.1:   The Web Form contains an instance of the User control testChange .ascx, which displays an alert when you click the button.

Creating a Web Form and then changing it to a User control is one easy way to create a User control. You may be thinking, "But there's a User control file type in the Add Item dialog!" That's true—I'll show you that in a minute. But changing a Web Form into a User control shows you how few differences there are between the two types. Also, after you've built a Web Form, you may at some point realize that it would be better implemented as a User control. Now you know how to accomplish the change.

To compare the two approaches, you should try building a User control directly. Add a new User control to your CSharpASP project. Name the control prettyXML.ascx. Note that you can't create a User control with a name like 23-1—VS.NET doesn't allow dashes in class names.

NOTE

See the sidebar "Creating the Web Application Used in This Chapter" in Chapter 16 for instructions on working with the CSharpASP project.

This time, you'll create a read-only control that can display any XML file in "pretty-print" form in a TextBox control on any Web Form. You can control the XML file URL and the size and position of the TextBox. The User control itself is very simple: It contains one TextBox Web Server control named txtXML. It doesn't matter where you place the control on the Web Control design surface because it won't appear in that position anyway—you can provide an absolute position if you wish, or use FlowLayout mode to position the TextBox as you would any other HTML control.

Listing 18.1 contains the HTML for the prettyXML.ascx file.

Listing 18.1: HTML for the *prettyXML.ascx* File *(prettyXML.ascx)*

```
<%@ Control Language="c#" AutoEventWireup="false"
   Codebehind="prettyXML.ascx.cs"
   Inherits="CSharpASP.ch23.prettyXML"
   targetSchema=
      "http://schemas.microsoft.com/intellisense/ie5"%>
<!DOCTYPE HTML PUBLIC
   "-//W3C//DTD HTML 4.0 Transitional//EN">
<HTML>
   <HEAD>
      <title>ch23_2</title>
      <meta content="Microsoft Visual Studio.NET 7.0"
name="GENERATOR">
      <meta content="Visual Basic 7.0" name="CODE_LANGUAGE">
```

```
        <meta content="JavaScript"
          name="vs_defaultClientScript">
        <meta
    content="http://schemas.microsoft.com/intellisense/ie5"
          name="vs_targetSchema">
    </HEAD>
    <body MS_POSITIONING="GridLayout">
       <form id="Form1" method="post">
          <asp:TextBox id="txtXML" TextMode="MultiLine"
             EnableViewState="False" ReadOnly="True"
             runat="server">
          </asp:TextBox>
       </form>
    </body>
  </HTML>
```

All the code in Listing 18.1 is VS generated except for the `<asp:textbox>`
Web control tag. I included it here so that you can see that the control is
absolutely plain; it has no `style` attribute and no `rows` or `cols` attributes—
no layout attributes whatsoever. The only attributes it contains are
`ReadOnly="True"`, `EnableViewState="False"`, and `TextMode="Multi-
Line"`. These three attributes enforce the control's purpose: to display
(not to provide editable) XML documents in read-only mode. When
designing a control, you should change hats: Stop thinking in Web
Form designer mode and start thinking in control author mode. As a
control author, your job is to expose as much functionality to the potential users of your control as possible. At the same time, you want to set
reasonable defaults. In this case, because you want the control to be
read-only, it's reasonable to enforce that at the control level. But the
control doesn't contain style attributes or other display settings because
it's reasonable to use the default TextBox control settings unless the user
overrides them.

When developers use your control, they need to be able to pass the
filename of an XML file to display, so you must add a property. Add a private
string variable named `mXMLFile` and a public property named `XMLFile` to
the code-behind class file.

```
// private class level member variable
private String mXMLFile="";

// public property
public String XMLFile {
```

```
        get{
            return mXMLFile;
        }
        set {
            mXMLFile = value;
        }
    }
```

When the Web Form runs, you want the control to open the XML file, read it, and format it as a string that you can place into the TextBox. The getPrettyXML method accepts an XML filename and returns the formatted string containing the document formatted with indented elements—much as you'd see the document if you loaded it into IE:

```
public String getPrettyXML(String aFilename ) {
    if (aFilename != null) {
        FileInfo aFile = new FileInfo(aFilename);
        if (aFile.Exists) {
            StringBuilder sb = new StringBuilder((int)
                aFile.Length * 2);
            XmlDocument doc = new XmlDocument();
            const int indent = 3;
            doc.Load(XMLFile);
            XmlTextWriter writer = new XmlTextWriter
                (new StringWriter(sb));
            writer.Formatting = Formatting.Indented;
            writer.Indentation=indent;
            doc.WriteContentTo(writer);
            return sb.ToString();
        }
        else {
            return null;
        }
    }
    else {
        return null;
    }
}
```

The preceding code snippet creates a StringBuilder to hold the formatted XML, creates a DOMDocument, loads the file, and then creates an XmlTextWriter object named writer that formats and writes the content. The last three lines do all the work. The first tells the XmlTextWriter to create indented XML output:

```
writer.Formatting = Formatting.Indented;
```

Next, the code uses a Microsoft-specific DOM extension called WriteContentTo that writes the XML content of an XmlDocument to an XmlTextWriter:

```
doc.WriteContentTo(writer);
```

Finally, because the XmlTextWriter object writes the content to a StringBuilder (the variable sb), the method just returns the StringBuilder's text contents:

```
return sb.ToString();
```

TIP

This code illustrates a very convenient trick because it's not as easy as you might think to format and indent an XML file with custom code.

Finally, you should override the Render method to call the getPrettyXML routine and fill the TextBox with the results. In addition, you want to "pick up" any style attributes that the control user set in the ASPX file and apply them to the TextBox control. By adding the style attributes at render time, you give the control user the capability to set the look and position of your control. When you override a control method, you should normally call the base method as well.

```
protected override void Render(System.Web.UI.HtmlTextWriter
    writer)
{
    String aValue;
    if (this.XMLFile != null) {
        txtXML.Text = getPrettyXML(XMLFile);
        // allow style attributes override
        if (this.Attributes.CssStyle != null) {
            foreach(string key in
              this.Attributes.CssStyle.Keys) {
                aValue = this.Attributes.CssStyle[key];
                txtXML.Attributes.CssStyle.Add(key, aValue);
            }
        }
    }
    base.Render(writer);
}
```

The last line calls base.Render, passing the HtmlTextWriter object received by the Render event. That's a specific decision. I decided that the TextBox control should render even if the control user doesn't set the

XMLFile property, which gives the user a visual clue (because the control renders an empty TextBox) that the XMLFile property is missing. However, it's equally valid to decide that the control shouldn't render anything. You can accomplish that by moving the base.Render method call inside the first if block, as in the following altered version:

```
protected override void Render(System.Web.UI.HtmlTextWriter
    writer)
{
    String aValue;
    if (this.XMLFile != null) {
        txtXML.Text = getPrettyXML(XMLFile);
        // allow style attributes override
        if (this.Attributes.CssStyle != null) {
            foreach(string key in
              this.Attributes.CssStyle.Keys) {
              aValue = this.Attributes.CssStyle[key];
              txtXML.Attributes.CssStyle.Add(key, aValue);
            }
        }
        base.Render(writer);
    }
}
```

Now you need to create a Web Form to test the control. Create a new Web Form named ch23-2.aspx, change the default form id attribute to Form1, and drag the prettyXML.ascx item from the Server Explorer to the design surface. It should look like Figure 18.2.

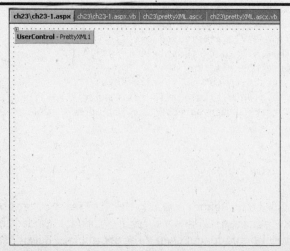

FIGURE 18.2:   Web Form designer surface with prettyXML.ascx User control

Note that you can't drag a User control and place it where you want and the representation of the User control in the Web Form doesn't *look* like the control you just built. That's a User control limitation. Don't worry about the look of the control in the designer. Click the User control and then look at the Properties box. You won't see the XMLFile property for the User control either, despite the fact that the property is public—that's another limitation. Rather than setting properties in the property browser and defining the look and position of the User control in the designer, you must work directly with the HTML. Change the designer to HTML mode. The HTML for the completed Web Form looks like Listing 18.2.

NOTE

Be sure to correct the hard-coded path in Listing 18.2 if it doesn't match that required for your server.

Listing 18.2: HTML Code for the *ch23-2.aspx* Web Form That Displays the *prettyXML* User Control (*ch23-2.aspx*)

```
<%@ Page language="c#" Codebehind="ch23-2.aspx.cs"
   AutoEventWireup="false"
      Inherits="CSharpASP.ch23.ch23_2" %>
<%@ Register TagPrefix="uc1" TagName="prettyXML"
   Src="prettyXML.ascx" %>
<!DOCTYPE HTML PUBLIC
   "-//W3C//DTD HTML 4.0 Transitional//EN" >
<HTML>
   <HEAD>
      <title>ch23-2</title>
      <meta name="GENERATOR"
         Content="Microsoft Visual Studio 7.0">
      <meta name="CODE_LANGUAGE"
         Content="C#">
      <meta name="vs_defaultClientScript"
         content="JavaScript">
      <meta name="vs_targetSchema" content=
            "http://schemas.microsoft.com/intellisense/ie5">
   </HEAD>
   <body MS_POSITIONING="GridLayout">
      <form id="Form1" method="post" runat="server">
         <uc1:prettyXML id="PrettyXML1" runat="server"
```

```
XMLFile="c:\inetpub\wwwroot\CSharpASP\ch23\people.xml">
            </ucl:prettyXML>
    </form>
  </body>
</HTML>
```

The highlighted lines define, insert, and format the `prettyXML` User control. The first highlighted line defines the tag and code location for the control:

```
<%@ Register TagPrefix="ucl" TagName="prettyXML"
    Src="prettyXML.ascx" %>
```

The `@ Register` directive defines the XML tag (`ucl:prettyXML`). `TagPrefix` controls the portion of the tag before the colon; `TagName` controls the portion of the tag after the colon. The names you see here are the default names (`ucl` stands for User control 1) inserted by VS when you drop a User control onto a Web Form, but you are free to change them to anything you like. Similarly, the `Src` attribute, in this case, contains only a filename because the control is in the same project folder as the Web Form, but the `Src` attribute accepts a relative URL for any location *in the same project*.

TIP

User controls must be in the same project as the Web Form that references them. If you want to reuse a User control, copy it into your current project.

When you run the Web Form, you'll see a small multiline text (a `<textarea>`) control containing the `people.xml` file contents. That doesn't look very nice. Try making the control bigger by creating a `style` attribute for the `<ucl:prettyXML>` tag. For example, change the tag so it looks like this:

```
<ucl:prettyXML id="PrettyXML1" runat="server"
    XMLFile="c:\inetpub\wwwroot\CSharpASP\ch23\people.xml"
    style="position: absolute; left: 50: top: 50;
    width: 500; height: 500;">
</ucl:prettyXML>
```

The highlighted code shows the added `style` attribute. Save the changes and request the Web Form again from your browser. This time, the generated `<textarea>` tag is large enough for you to see the XML contents clearly. Note that the contents are read-only as defined in the User control itself. In addition, the control doesn't maintain `ViewState` because the `EnableViewState` attribute in the `prettyXML.ascx` file is set to `false`.

Loading User Controls at Runtime

You don't have to site User controls on a Web Form at design time; you can load them dynamically. For example, suppose you wanted to load one of two User controls based on a user's identity. You *could* put them both on the Web Form and then hide one with client-side script, but that wouldn't be particularly efficient. A better way is to load the appropriate control using program logic. The Page.LoadControl method accepts a filename and returns a UserControl object or a PartialCaching-Control object (more about that later). For example, the following code shows how to load an instance of the prettyXML.ascx control, set its properties and display characteristics from code-behind code, and add the control to the default <form> tag's child controls. The code in Listing 18.3 is equivalent (other than the control size) to the preceding example, where you created the User control instance in the HTML file.

Listing 18.3: Loading a User Control Dynamically *(ch23-3.aspx.cs)*

```
private void Page_Load(object sender, System.EventArgs e)
{
   prettyXML ctl =
      (prettyXML) this.LoadControl("prettyXML.ascx");
   ctl.XMLFile =
      @"c:\inetpub\wwwroot\CSharpASP\ch23\people.xml";
   ctl.Attributes.Add("style","left: 10; top: 10; " +
      "width: 500; height: 500;");
   this.FindControl("Form1").Controls.Add(ctl);
}
```

Remember to cast the generic object returned from the LoadControl method to the correct type, add all attributes (even style attributes) for a User control via the Attributes collection property, and place the control inside the server-side form tag. To do that, use the FindControl method to obtain a reference to the control and then add the new User control instance to the form's Controls collection.

Partial Page Caching and User Controls

Even if you don't need User controls, you should seriously consider creating them for those parts of your pages that don't change often, because they let you cache a portion of a page at the server level. Most site designs have static page portions around the edges and change the center of the page to display page content. For example, navigation bars, headers, and footers are often static or contain only one or two dynamic portions, such as ad tags and counters. However, most sites also created these mostly static portions by using #INCLUDE directives, which referenced files containing the dynamic code for ads and counters. Although IIS did cache these pages in memory, the classic ASP engine still had to run the contained code to create each request for the page.

In contrast, in ASP.NET applications, you can create User controls for the dynamic parts of the page and cache them based on query string or form parameters, custom strings, file dependencies, or duration. To cache a User control, add an OutputCache directive to the page:

```
<%@ OutputCache Duration="20" VaryByParam="None" %>
```

This directive caches the User control for 20 seconds.

TIP

You can speed up pages and reduce server load dramatically by implementing partial page caching in the form of User controls.

BUILDING A COMPOSITE CONTROL

User controls are sufficient for building simple UI collections of controls, but they have several limitations that make them unsuitable for commercial products, for repeated use in multiple projects, and for handing off to HTML authors.

- ▶ User controls must reside in the same project as the Web Forms that use them. That's a serious limitation because it means you can't create a single User control and then reference it in projects; instead, you must have multiple copies of the User control files—one for each project where you want to use it.

- ▶ User control properties don't appear in the property browser; the control users must know what they are in advance and write them into the HTML tag manually or set them via code. That's OK for controls you build for your own use, but it isn't suitable for controls you build for others.

- ▶ User controls in design mode don't look like they do at runtime; therefore, from a designer's viewpoint, they can be difficult to align, size, and control.

Instead, ASP.NET supports two other types of custom controls, termed Composite controls and (confusingly) Custom Server controls. These types of controls are exactly the same as the ASP.NET intrinsic Web Server controls, except that you must define them yourself, in code.

A Composite control, unlike a User control, compiles to an assembly and has design-time support for letting control users set properties in the Properties window and move and size the control at design time. A Composite control combines controls by creating the child controls programmatically. To the control user, a Composite control, like a User control, is a single entity. The user of a Composite control adds one item to a Web Form, but that single action may create any number of controls contained *inside* the Composite control. The user may or may not have direct access to the control properties; as the control author, you can decide. The ASP.NET framework contains several examples; the data-bound controls such as Repeater, DataList, and DataGrid are Composite controls that contain child controls.

One common task when building input forms of almost any kind is the addition of paired Label and TextBox controls (see Figure 18.3). You can create the Label and the TextBox as a single composite control.

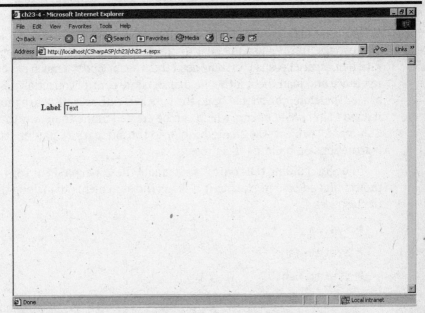

FIGURE 18.3:   The LabeledTextBox Composite control default interface

In this section, you'll build a Composite control named Labeled-TextBox. A Composite control consists of a single class in which you must do the following:

- Inherit the `Control` or `WebControl` class.
- Override the `CreateChildControls` method.
- Implement the `INamingContainer` interface.
- Optionally, override the `Render` method.

The base `Control` or `WebControl` class handles events such as rendering ASP.NET or HTML controls, manages ViewState for the child controls, and supports ASP.NET events. The `CreateChild-Controls` method fires when the framework signals the control to create its child controls. The method fires only once for any instance of the control.

The `INamingContainer` interface tells the framework to create a new naming scope, ensuring that the child controls within the naming scope have unique names. In other words, if there is already a ListBox on the Web Form, the framework encounters your control and changes the naming scope. Then when you add the child ListBoxes, the new name scope ensures that they aren't named `ListBox1` and `ListBox2`, which would otherwise be the default names.

You can build the Composite control in your Web application project namespace, but it's usually best to create generic controls in a separate namespace because you may need them again, and it's much easier to reference and load them if they're in a separate control collection namespace. Therefore, you should build the LabeledTextBox control in a project named `CSharpASPCustom`, which can be created in the same way that the `CSharpASP` project was created. Refer to the sidebar in Chapter 16 for instructions on building this project.

To begin building the control, first create the `CSharpASPCustom` project and add a new class to it. Add `using` statements to include these namespaces:

- `System`
- `System.Web`
- `System.Web.UI`
- `System.Web.UI.WebControls`

Create the class name—this is the name that will appear in the Toolbox for control consumers. In this case, name the class `LabeledTextBox`. You

can inherit from either the System.Web.UI.Control or the System.Web
.UI.WebControls.WebControl base classes. To choose, consider how
much support your control needs at design time. If you're building a visible
control, you might want to expose UI properties such as Width, Height, and
Font. In that case, inherit from WebControl; otherwise, just inherit from
the Control class. Implement the INamingContainer interface. Because the
LabeledTextBox control is a visible control that designers should be able
to size and place on the page, it inherits from the WebControl class.

The code for the LabeledTextBox control resides in the CSharpASP-
Custom project.

```
using System;
using System.Web;
using System.Web.UI;
using System.Web.UI.WebControls;
namespace CSharpASPCustom
{
    public class LabeledTextBox :
        System.Web.UI.WebControls.WebControl, INamingContainer
    {
        // more code here
    }
}
```

Although you don't have to predefine variables for the child controls,
it's convenient and prevents you from having to refer to them later using
an index into your control's child controls. In this project, there are three
controls: two Labels and one TextBox:

```
private System.Web.UI.WebControls.Label lbl = null;
private System.Web.UI.WebControls.Label lblSpacer = null;
private System.Web.UI.WebControls.TextBox tx = null;
```

The lbl control displays the label text for the control. The lblSpacer
control acts as a spacer between the Label containing the text and
the TextBox. The TextBox lets users input data. You override the
CreateChildControls method to create the controls:

```
protected override void CreateChildControls() {
    lblSpacer = new Label();
    lblSpacer.Height = Unit.Pixel(25);
    lbl = new Label();
    lbl.Height = Unit.Pixel(25);
    tx = new TextBox();
    tx.Height = Unit.Pixel(25);
    Controls.Add(lbl);
```

```
        lblSpacer.Text = "";
        Controls.Add(lblSpacer);
        Controls.Add(tx);
    }
```

You can expose custom properties by adding public properties to
your control. Public control properties appear in the Properties window by default. For example, the LabeledTextBox control exposes five
public properties. Their names are self-explanatory: Text, LabelText,
LabelWidth, TextWidth, and SpaceBetweenControls. The call to the
EnsureChildControls method in each property setting ensures that
the child controls exist—if you forget this call, you'll get an error stating
that the control doesn't exist when it tries to site itself.

```
public String Text {
    get {
        EnsureChildControls();
        return tx.Text;
    }
    set {
        EnsureChildControls();
        tx.Text = value;
    }
}
public String LabelText {
    get {
        EnsureChildControls();
        return lbl.Text;
    }
    set {
        EnsureChildControls();
        lbl.Text = value;
    }
}
public Unit TextBoxWidth {
    get {
        EnsureChildControls();
        return tx.Width;
    }
    set {
        EnsureChildControls();
        tx.Width = value;
    }
}
public Unit LabelWidth {
    get {
```

```
            EnsureChildControls();
            return lbl.Width;
        }
        set {
            EnsureChildControls();
            lbl.Width = value;
        }
    }
    public Unit SpaceBetweenControls {
        get {
            EnsureChildControls();
            return lblSpacer.Width;
        }
        set {
            EnsureChildControls();
            lblSpacer.Width = value;
        }
    }
}
```

Exposing the LabelWidth, TextBoxWidth, and SpaceBetweenControls properties as the type System.Unit lets users enter any of several specific unit types for that property. The ASP.NET engine translates the string representation to the appropriate value. For example, 30px, 1in, and 10pt are all valid Unit measurements. Because the control inherits from System.Web.UI.WebControls.WebControl, it also inherits several public properties such as Width, Height, Font, BackColor, ForeColor, BorderStyle, and a few others. Listing 18.4 shows the full code.

Listing 18.4: The LabeledTextBox Composite Control Code (*CSharpASPCustom.LabeledTextBox.cs*)

```
using System;
using System.Web;
using System.Web.UI;
using System.Web.UI.WebControls;

namespace CSharpASPCustom
{
    [ToolboxData("<{0}:LabeledTextBox runat='server'
        style='position:absolute; width:300px; height: 30px'
        Text='Text' LabelText='<b>Label</b>:'
        SpaceBetweenControls='5px'/>")]
    public class LabeledTextBox :
        System.Web.UI.WebControls.WebControl, INamingContainer
```

```
{
    private System.Web.UI.WebControls.Label lbl = null;
    private System.Web.UI.WebControls.Label
      lblSpacer = null;
    private System.Web.UI.WebControls.TextBox tx = null;
    public LabeledTextBox() {
    }
    public String Text {
        get {
            EnsureChildControls();
            return tx.Text;
        }
        set {
            EnsureChildControls();
            tx.Text = value;
        }
    }
    public String LabelText {
        get {
            EnsureChildControls();
            return lbl.Text;
        }
        set {
            EnsureChildControls();
            lbl.Text = value;
        }
    }
    public Unit TextBoxWidth {
        get {
            EnsureChildControls();
            return tx.Width;
        }
        set {
            EnsureChildControls();
            tx.Width = value;
        }
    }
    public Unit LabelWidth {
        get {
            EnsureChildControls();
            return lbl.Width;
        }
```

```
            set {
                EnsureChildControls();
                lbl.Width = value;
            }
        }
        public Unit SpaceBetweenControls {
            get {
                EnsureChildControls();
                return lblSpacer.Width;
            }
            set {
                EnsureChildControls();
                lblSpacer.Width = value;
            }
        }
        protected override void CreateChildControls() {
            tx = new TextBox();
            lbl = new Label();
            lblSpacer = new Label();
            lbl.Height = Unit.Pixel(25);
            lbl.Text = "Label";
            tx.Height = Unit.Pixel(25);
            tx.Width = Unit.Pixel(200);
            tx.Text = "Text";
            Controls.Add(lbl);
            lblSpacer.Text = "";
            Controls.Add(lblSpacer);
            Controls.Add(tx);
        }
    }
}
```

The full code listing contains one item I haven't yet explained—the
ToolboxData attribute.

```
[ToolboxData("<{0}:LabeledTextBox runat='server'
        style='position:absolute; width:300px; height: 30px'
        Text='Text' LabelText='<b>Label</b>:'
        SpaceBetweenControls='5px'/>")]
```

By default, when you drag and drop a control from the Toolbox to
the design surface, VS.NET inserts a "blank" tag—in other words, the
default control tag won't have the properties you might want. You'll find
that even setting the properties in code won't help because those properties

won't appear in the designer, but the properties you set in the Tool-boxData attribute will appear. The value of the ToolboxData attribute is the full tag that you want the control to have. VS.NET replaces the {0} placeholder at the front of the tag with the tag prefix for the control class. The ToolboxData attribute for the LabeledTextBox control sets every custom property to a default value. Build the control and save it. Be sure to compile the project before attempting to add an instance of the control to the project.

Customizing the Toolbox

One of the advantages of Composite and Custom controls is that you can add them to the Toolbox where they then act just like any other ASP.NET Server control. To add the controls, right-click the Toolbox and select the Customize Toolbox item. Note that you can add both COM components and components that reside within .NET assemblies to the Toolbox (see Figure 18.4).

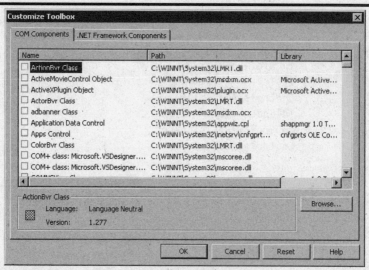

FIGURE 18.4: The Customize Toolbox dialog

Click the .NET Framework Components tab. You won't find custom assemblies in the list. Click the Browse button, find the CSharpASPCustom folder (if you don't know where the project resides, you can find it in the Project Properties dialog), navigate to the bin subfolder, and select the compiled CSharpASPCustom.dll file.

Selecting the file adds all the public classes in the file to the .NET Framework Components tab. Find the LabeledTextBox item and make sure it's checked, and then click OK to close the dialog.

NOTE

If you have multiple public classes in an assembly, VS adds them all to the list visible from the .NET Framework Components tab in the Customize Toolbox dialog.

Any components you add to the Toolbox appear at the bottom of the Toolbox. You may have to scroll down to see your added item(s).

How to Add a Custom Toolbox Bitmap for Your Control

By default, VS.NET uses a "gear" bitmap for your custom controls. You can assign a specific bitmap using the ToolboxBitmap attribute. The bitmap should be 16×16 pixels in size. You need to add a using System.Drawing statement to the top of your class to use the attribute. The attribute has an overloaded constructor that can load an image from a file or from a resource in the same or a different assembly. Add the ToolboxBitmap attribute above the class declaration.

Test the LabeledTextBox Composite Control

Add a Web Form named ch23-4.aspx to test the LabeledTextBox Composite control. Change the default form tag ID to Form1. Find the LabeledTextBox component in the Toolbox and drag it onto the design surface. VS.NET adds a new instance of the control to the designer. You should immediately see that it's much easier to work with Composite controls than with User controls. Click the added LabeledTextBox item and look at the Properties window. You will find the control's properties (Text, LabelText, LabelWidth, TextBoxWidth, and SpaceBetweenControls) under the Misc. category (sort the Properties window entries by category using the leftmost button on the Properties window toolbar to see this).

For example, if you set the control's BackColor, BorderStyle, and BorderWidth properties and add some LabelText and Text values, the control might look similar to Figure 18.5.

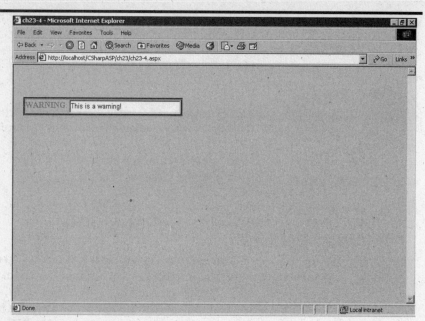

FIGURE 18.5: LabeledTextBox Composite control with custom property settings

NOTE

The control's properties change at design time, just like any other ASP.NET Server control.

BUILDING A CUSTOM SERVER CONTROL

In this section, you'll build a basic control called DateTable and see how you can use it in multiple projects. The difference between a Custom Server control and a Composite control is that with a Custom Server control, you handle drawing the interface yourself by overriding the Render method rather than creating controls during the CreateChildControls method. The control displays a date within a table tag. You can control all the UI features—colors, the border, font characteristics, and the date itself from the Web Form that hosts the control.

Creating the DateTable Custom Control

The DateTable Custom control displays a date of your choice in an HTML table cell. By default, the control looks like Figure 18.6 in the designer. I took this screenshot after double-clicking in the ToolBox to add the control without sizing it or setting any properties.

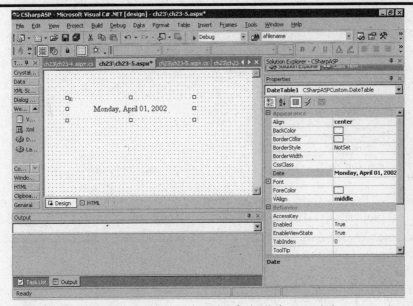

FIGURE 18.6:   DateTable Custom control default UI characteristics

Not too exciting, is it? But it's a powerful concept. Even with this plain example, you can immediately see that a major difference between a Custom control and a User control is that you can provide a customizable design-time user interface for a Custom control, but you can't for a User control. The control displays the current date by default. For this example, the control *always* displays the date in LongDateTime format—that's easy enough to change if you want to extend the control.

Next, here's the Properties window for the DateTable control (see Figure 18.7).

The default property for the control is called Date, and it has a default date value (the current date) as soon as you add the control. Custom controls inherit a reasonable set of properties from the System.Web.UI.WebControl class—most of the properties shown are inherited. You control which properties you want to display in the Properties window via Property attributes.

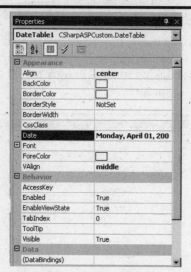

FIGURE 18.7:   DateTable Custom Control Properties window

Because the control supports design-time properties, by setting those properties, you can radically alter the look of the control (see Figure 18.8).

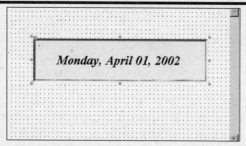

FIGURE 18.8:   DateTable Custom control after setting design-time properties

Despite the fact that Custom controls inherit some default design-time features, such as BackColor, BorderColor, BorderWidth, Font, CssClass, and so forth, you do have to write some other common properties. Listing 18.5 shows the code for the DateTable class.

Listing 18.5: Code for the DateTable Custom Control (*CSharpASPCustom.DateTable.cs*)

```
using System;
using System.Web.UI;
```

```csharp
using System.Web.UI.HtmlControls;
using System.ComponentModel;
using System.Drawing;

namespace CSharpASPCustom
{
    /// <summary>
    /// Summary description for DateTable.
    /// </summary>
    public enum TextAlign {
        left = 1,
        right = 2,
        center = 3,
        justify = 4
    }
    public enum TextVAlign {
        top = 1,
        middle = 2,
        bottom = 3,
        baseline = 4,
        subscript = 5,
        superscript = 6,
        text_top = 7,
        text_bottom = 8
    }

    [ Description("Exposes a Date in an HTML Table tag")]
    [ DefaultProperty("Date"),
      ToolboxData("<{0}:DateTable " +
      "runat=server style='position: absolute; width:300: " +
      "height: 100;' />")]
    public class DateTable :
      System.Web.UI.WebControls.WebControl,
        INamingContainer {
        private DateTime mDate = new DateTime();
        private String mNow = DateTime.Now.ToLongDateString();
        private TextAlign mAlign = TextAlign.center;
        private TextVAlign mVAlign = TextVAlign.middle;

        [Bindable(true), Category("Appearance"),
            DefaultValue("Monday, January 1, 0001")]
        public String Date {
            get {
```

```
            if (mDate.Year == 1) {
                return DateTime.Now.ToLongDateString();
            }
            else {
                return mDate.ToLongDateString();
            }
        }
        set {
            mDate = DateTime.Parse(value);
        }
    }
    [Bindable(true), Category("Appearance"),
DefaultValue("center")]


    public TextAlign Align {
        get {
            return mAlign;
        }
        set {
            mAlign = value;
        }
    }


    private String AlignText {
        get {
            return TextAlign.GetName(mAlign.GetType(),
                mAlign);
        }
    }


    [Bindable(true), Category("Appearance"),
DefaultValue("middle")]
    public TextVAlign VAlign {
        get {
            return mVAlign;
        }
        set {
            mVAlign = value;
        }
    }
```

```
    private String VAlignText {
        get {
            if (mVAlign == TextVAlign.subscript) {
                return "sub";
            }
            else if (mVAlign == TextVAlign.superscript) {
                return "super";
            }
            else {
                return TextVAlign.GetName(mVAlign.GetType(),
                    mVAlign);
            }

        }
    }


    protected override void Render
        (System.Web.UI.HtmlTextWriter output) {
        HtmlTable tbl = new HtmlTable();
        HtmlTableRow row = new HtmlTableRow();
        HtmlTableCell cell = new HtmlTableCell();
        String aValue;
        tbl.Style.Add(" color",
System.Drawing.ColorTranslator.ToHtml(this.ForeColor));
        tbl.Style.Add(" background-color",
System.Drawing.ColorTranslator.ToHtml(this.BackColor));
        tbl.Style.Add(" border-color",
System.Drawing.ColorTranslator.ToHtml(this.BorderColor));
        tbl.Style.Add(" border-style",
this.BorderStyle.ToString());
        tbl.Style.Add(" border-width",
this.BorderWidth.ToString());
        tbl.Style.Add(" width", this.Width.ToString());
        tbl.Style.Add(" height", this.Height.ToString());
        tbl.Style.Add(" text-align", this.AlignText);
        cell.Style.Add(" vertical-align", this.VAlignText);
        if (this.Font != null) {
            if (this.Font.Names.Length > 0) {
                tbl.Style.Add(" font-family",
                    ArrayJoin.Join(this.Font.Names));
```

```
            }
            tbl.Style.Add(" font-size",
                this.Font.Size.ToString());
            if (this.Font.Bold) {
                tbl.Style.Add(" font-weight", "bold");
            }
            if (this.Font.Italic) {
                tbl.Style.Add(" font-style", "italic");
            }
            if (this.Font.Overline) {
                tbl.Style.Add(
                  " font-decoration", "overline");
            }
            if (this.Font.Strikeout) {
                tbl.Style.Add(
                  " font-decoration", "line-through");
            }
            if (this.Font.Underline) {
                tbl.Style.Add(
                  " font-decoration", "underline");
            }
        }
        if (this.Attributes.CssStyle != null) {
          foreach (String key in
            this.Attributes.CssStyle.Keys) {
              aValue = this.Attributes.CssStyle[key];
              tbl.Attributes.CssStyle.Add(
                " " + key, aValue);
          }
        }
        cell.InnerText = this.Date;
        tbl.Rows.Add(row);
        row.Cells.Add(cell);
        tbl.RenderControl(output);
      }
    }
  }
```

You can see that the class implements only three public properties: Date, Align, and VAlign. It defines text Align and text VAlign enumerations and uses those as the property type values for the private Align and VAlign properties, respectively.

Note that (other than the `Property` attributes) there's no special code to support design-time properties or any Property Window special code or types; all that is built into the .NET Framework. For string properties, all you need to do is make sure the properties you want to expose to the designer are defined as public properties.

TIP

The default designer handles simple types such as strings, but for more complex property types such as arrays of strings or custom property types, you'll need to set the `Designer` attribute to the proper type or create a custom designer class or interface—see the MSDN help for more information on custom `Designer` classes.

In fact, most of the code is in the overridden `Render` method. The `Render` method creates `HtmlTable`, `HtmlRow`, and `HtmlCell` objects and then assigns style attributes and values based on the properties the user set in the HTML tag in the Web Form, or using the Properties window to render the HTML for the control. After setting up the table, the method writes the table using the `RenderControl` method, passing the `Html-TextWriter` received by the overridden `Render` method as the only parameter.

The `RenderControl` method writes an HTML string containing a single-row/single-column HTML `<table>` tag.

More About Attributes

Attributes are classes in .NET. Each of the built-in attribute class names ends with the word "Attribute," but in the shorthand version shown, you don't have to include the *Attribute* portion. For example, as shown in Listing 18.5, the class attribute list looks like this:

```
[DefaultProperty("Date"), ToolboxData("<{0}:DateTable " +
    "runat=server
    style= position: absolute; width:300: " +
    "height: 100;' />")]
```

TIP

To search for an attribute in Help or the Object Browser, remember to append the word "Attribute" to the end of the class name.

If you used the full attribute class names rather than the default short-hand version, you could write this:

```
[DefaultPropertyAttribute("Date"),
    ToolboxDataAttribute("<{0}:DateTable " +
    "runat=server style='position: absolute; width:300: " +
    "height: 100;' />")]
```

The DefaultProperty attribute declares that the class DateTable has a default property called Text. Just as in the LabeledTextBox control code you saw earlier in the chapter, the ToolboxData attribute controls the initial tag that the designer places into the Web Form HTML when you drop a control onto the design surface.

NOTE

If you have a VB background, the DefaultProperty attribute replaces the rather quirky (and well-hidden) method used in classic VB to define a default property for a class. That's true for all classes in .NET, not just classes created as web controls.

It's worth noting that attributes aren't required for Custom controls—they're all optional. You can delete all the default attributes without adverse effects.

You can add as many tag attributes as needed to the ToolboxData class attribute.

The property attributes affect both design-time and runtime aspects of the control. Design-time properties are those that appear in the Properties window when a user adds your control to a Web Form at design time. Again, the designer uses the shorthand form of the attribute class names by default. Remember that the full names of these attribute classes are BindableAttribute, CategoryAttribute, and DefaultValueAttribute.

The Bindable attribute controls whether you can bind the property to a data value. The Category attribute controls in which area or category of the Properties window a property appears. It's not always clear which area you should specify. For example, does the Date value belong in the Appearance category or the Data category? At any rate—you get to choose. Although the built-in categories usually suffice, you can create custom categories if necessary.

The DefaultValue attribute, of course, is the default value of the control. That property accepts only hard-coded values. For example, you can't call a function to set a derived value as the default control value using a property attribute. In other words, this `DefaultValue` attribute is acceptable:

```
[DefaultValue("This is some text")]
// property declaration here
```

In contrast, the following version is not acceptable and will not compile:

```
[DefaultValue(getDefaultValue())]
// property declaration here


private String getDefaultValue() {
    return "This is some text";
}
```

Despite that, you can work around it by creating an "impossible" default value and then handling that condition explicitly in code. For example, the default Date property specifies a date of "Monday, January 1, 0001".

```
[Bindable(true), Category("Appearance"),
DefaultValue("Monday, January 1, 0001")]
public String Date {
    // implementation here
}
```

However, as you can see in the figures, the default date that *appears* in the control is the current date. This is the workaround for not being able to specify a `DefaultValue` and run the `DateTime.Now.To-LongDateString` method. The `Date` property implementation explicitly checks for the condition Year == 1. When that evaluates to true, the property returns the current date. It's true that this means users wouldn't be able to use the control to set an explicit date in the year 0001—but that's an acceptable risk.

```
public String Date {
    get {
        if (mDate.Year == 1) {
            return DateTime.Now.ToLongDateString();
        }
        else {
            return mDate.ToLongDateString();
        }
    }
    set {
        mDate = DateTime.Parse(value);
    }
}
```

Attributes are an extremely powerful concept. .NET contains a large number of predefined attribute classes, which you should explore thoroughly. If the built-in attribute classes don't meet your needs, you can define your own custom attribute classes. Attributes aren't limited to classes and properties; you can apply attributes to assemblies, constructors, delegates, enums, events, fields, interfaces, parameters, return values, and structs.

There are several interesting features related to using the control in the designer. First, look at the Web Form ch23-5.aspx in the VS designer. The Web Form has a single DateTable control. Try selecting the DateTable control and then entering an invalid date for the Date property. You'll see an error message, but it doesn't stop the program. The error message (see Figure 18.9) is automatic—you get property value type-checking and conversion for free.

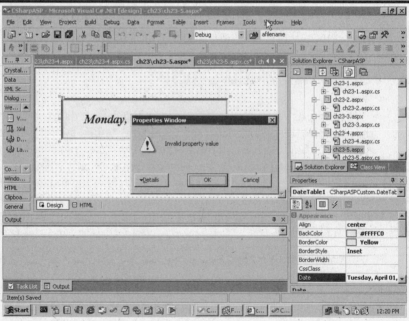

FIGURE 18.9:   Automatic property error dialog appears after an invalid date is set.

Another interesting feature is that the Properties window seamlessly accommodates the enumeration types. Click the Align or VAlign property, and you get a list of values corresponding to the appropriate enumeration names. Again, this feature is free—you don't have to add special code to make it work.

In the Render method, you access properties set by the control user by retrieving them from the class itself, using the this keyword. The .NET Framework helps a great deal by being able to transform color selections to their HTML equivalents using the ColorTranslator class's static ToHtml method. The ColorTranslator changes the colors either to common color names, such as red, or to the HTML color representation, such as #C0C0C0.

```
tbl.Style.Add(" color",
    System.Drawing.ColorTranslator.ToHtml(this.ForeColor))
```

Because the font-family CSS attribute can accept a list of font names, the Properties window lets you enter more than one font name. If a client browser can't display the first font in the list, it tries subsequent font names in sequence until it finds one it can use. If none of the named fonts are available, the browser displays the control's text content in the browser's default font. The font names the control user enters appear as a Font property called Names, which returns an array of string objects. You need to turn that array into a comma-delimited string. In classic ASP, using VBScript, you could use the Join method to accomplish that. In .NET, the Array class doesn't have a Join method, but you can write a small helper class to iterate through the array and accomplish the task:

```
If Me.Font.Names.Length > 0 Then
    tbl.Style.Add(" font-family", _
        ArrayJoin.Join(Me.Font.Names))
End If
```

The ArrayJoin class (in the CSharpASPCustom project) accepts an array and returns a comma-delimited string object containing a string representation (using the ToString() method inherited from Object class) of each element in the array (see Listing 18.6).

Listing 18.6: Code for the ArrayJoin Helper Class (*CSharpASPCustom.ArrayJoin.cs*)

```
using System;
using System.Text;
using System.Collections;

namespace CSharpASPCustom
{
    public class ArrayJoin
    {
```

```
public ArrayJoin()
{
}

public static String Join(Array arr) {
    StringBuilder sb = new StringBuilder(arr.Length *
        (arr.GetValue(0).ToString().Length + 1));
    for (int i = 0; i < arr.Length; i++) {
        if (i < arr.Length - 1) {
            sb.Append(arr.GetValue(i).ToString() + ";");
        }
        else {
            sb.Append(arr.GetValue(i).ToString());
        }
    }
    return sb.ToString();
}
}
}
```

TRANSFERRING DATA BETWEEN ASP.NET WEB FORMS AND COMPONENTS

One of the more commonly asked questions about ASP.NET is how to transfer or share data between an ASP.NET Web Form and other components, such as Custom controls and web services. The simplest answer is to set parameters for the methods you want to call that accept the data you need to share. For example, to set the text of a Custom control to the value of a TextBox entered by the user, you would post the Web Form from the browser and then, on the server, create or reference the Custom control instance and call the method you want to set.

If passing the data around between multiple objects becomes too onerous, you can cache the data at the Session or Application scope. You can also create custom classes to hold the data and cache them at Session or Application scope, which often makes using the data much easier than using raw scalar values stored in Session or Application variables.

As you've seen, any component activated during the process of running a Web Form or web service has access to the user's context, via the `System.Web.HttpContext.Current` property. In turn, the `Current` context exposes the `Response`, `Request`, `Server`, and other objects (the same objects that you have available through the Web Form itself) so that you can access `Request` data or values stored in `Application` or `Session` variables from *any* .NET component you create—not just ASP.NET specific classes, such as the Custom control, but any .NET class.

What's Next

In this chapter, you've seen how to create several types of custom controls. This capability is particularly important for ASP.NET applications because you can use the controls to cache data and HTML, which can improve the efficiency and scalability of your applications. Next, in the following chapters, we'll start our foray into some advanced C# topics.

Chapter 19

OVERCOMING HOLES IN THE .NET FRAMEWORK

There are few, if any, perfect programming platforms in the world and .NET is no exception. Developers who spend any time working in the unmanaged environment before they begin working with .NET will notice some distinct problems with functionality in the .NET environment. Some of these holes (such as those in the security area) are apparent and require an immediate fix; others (such as the lack of support for a Beep( ) function) are subtle and you might never notice them. The point is that the .NET Framework is new technology and there are bound to be some holes in coverage, and you'll notice them frequently.

This chapter provides a quick overview of some major areas of omission in the .NET Framework. I want to say at the outset that I feel the .NET Framework is a big improvement over using unmanaged code, but it's new and lacks some features that most developers will need. I'm not here to tell you that the .NET Framework is technically flawed. The goal of this chapter is to help you plan your development efforts to make the best use of

Adapted from *.NET Framework Solutions: In Search of the Lost Win32 API* by John Paul Mueller

0-7821-4134-X

existing .NET Framework functionality and to access the Win32 API when the .NET Framework proves less than perfect.

NOTE

Visual C++ represents a unique language in .NET because it provides both managed and unmanaged coding environments. Consequently, you can access the Win32 API in its entirety from Visual C++ using the same unmanaged techniques you used before .NET appeared on the scene. This unique functionality means that Visual C++ developers won't need the special techniques found in this chapter. It also means that you can use Visual C++ as a language bridge between managed and unmanaged environments.

WHY ACCESS THE WIN32 API?

Many of you have a lot of experience working with the Win32 API and are already familiar with the programming requirements for unmanaged code. The idea of working with unmanaged code presents few problems for the seasoned developer. However, the .NET Framework that Microsoft has advertised is supposed to obviate the need to work with unmanaged code, so the first question on most developer's minds is why they would even need to access the Win32 API. The short answer is that you'll find a lack of functionality in some areas, such as DirectX, the Microsoft Management Console (MMC), and direct hardware access, when working with the .NET Framework. You can only gain access to this functionality through the Win32 API.

The long answer requires a little more explanation. For example, not all .NET languages have an equal measure of missing functionality. The .NET Framework doesn't include a Beep() function, so you'll find this feature missing in C# as well. However, because Visual Basic includes a Beep() function as part of the language, it doesn't require any special programming to access this Win32 API feature. In sum, the question of missing functionality is a matter of determining if the language you're using provides the feature and then determining the best method to access the feature if it is missing.

You'll find that the question of Win32 API access becomes more complex as you move from simple functions such as Beep() to major programming projects such as creating an MMC Snap-in. The level of Win32 API access varies by language, which is why this chapter addresses both C# and Visual Basic. This chapter, for example, contains separate

C# and Visual Basic sections because the two languages provide varying levels of Win32 API access. Thus the third issue in Win32 API access is whether the target language provides support for the required feature. It might not, which means you'll need to create wrappers for the missing functionality.

Now that you have a basic overview of the question of why you'd want to access the Win32 API, let's discuss the issues in more detail. The following sections describe needs and requirements for Win32 API access in a generic manner. You can apply this material equally to any language you might want to use with .NET.

A Case of Missing Functionality

As previously mentioned, the .NET Framework lacks functionality for some basic calls such as Beep(). This means that a C# developer who needs to create a sound within an application has to find some other way to do it. There's no doubt that the functionality is missing, but the technique used to create the desired functionality varies by language capability, environment, and flexibility. For example, when working with Visual Basic, you already have access to a basic Beep() function, so no additional coding is required if you require a simple beep. However, as shown in Listing 19.1, there are actually four ways to create a beep in C# and not all of them provide the same features.

Listing 19.1: Creating a Beep in C#

```
// Import the Windows Beep() API function.
[DllImport("kernel32.dll")]
private static extern bool Beep(int freq, int dur);

// Define some constants for using the PlaySound() function.
public const int SND_FILENAME = 0x00020000;
public const int SND_ASYNC = 0x0001;

// Import the Windows PlaySound() function.
[DllImport("winmm.dll")]
public static extern bool PlaySound(string pszSound,
                                    int hmod,
                                    int fdwSound);

[STAThread]
static void Main(string[] args)
```

```
{
    // Create a sound using an escape character.
    Console.Write("\a");
    Console.WriteLine("Press Any Key When Ready...");
    Console.ReadLine();

    // Create a sound using a Windows API call.
    Beep(800, 200);
    Console.WriteLine("Press Any Key When Ready...");
    Console.ReadLine();

    // Create a sound using a Visual Basic call.
    Microsoft.VisualBasic.Interaction.Beep();
    Console.WriteLine("Press Any Key When Ready...");
    Console.ReadLine();

    // Create a sound using a WAV file.
    PlaySound("BELLS.WAV",
              0,
              SND_FILENAME | SND_ASYNC);
    Console.WriteLine("Press Any Key When Ready...");
    Console.ReadLine();
}
```

It's important to note that using an escape character to produce a sound only works for a console application—you can't use this technique in a GUI application. However, this technique does enable you to circumvent the requirement to access the Win32 API just to create a beep. The technique is important because it provides you with another choice; one that doesn't rely on unmanaged code.

The Win32 API Beep() function has the advantage of providing the greatest flexibility for the smallest cost in resources. To use this technique, you must declare the Win32 API Beep() function as a DLL import using the [DllImport] attribute. In this case, you must use unmanaged code to achieve your objective, but you don't need a wrapper DLL—C# and Visual Basic both provide all the support required. Notice that the Win32 API Beep() function enables you to choose both the tone (frequency) and duration of the beep, which is something you won't get using an escape character or Visual Basic's built-in function.

Some developers might not realize that they are able to access other language features from within the current language by relying on a .NET Framework feature called Interaction. The third method, shown in

Listing 19.1, simply calls the Visual Basic Beep() function. You need to include a reference to the Microsoft.VisualBasic.DLL to make this portion of the example work. This technique requires a little more effort than making a direct Win32 API call, but it has the advantage of using pure managed code within the C# application.

Sometimes you don't want to use a plain beep within an application, so it's helpful to know how to access WAV files. The fourth technique, shown in Listing 19.1, has the advantage of complete sound source flexibility. However, this technique also has the dubious honor of being the most complicated way to produce a sound. The function call to PlaySound() is more complicated than the Beep() Win32 API call. You also need to define constants to use it.

The point of this section is that you'll find missing functionality within the .NET Framework, but you don't always have to rely on Win32 API calls to fill the gap. In many situations, you can rely on language interoperability or built-in operating system functionality. When you do need to rely on the Win32 API, you'll find that some functions are easier to use than others. It isn't always necessary to use the most complex method when a simple one will work. In fact, in some cases, you'll find that you can't use the full-featured function because the target language won't support it.

Win32 Function Types

One of the problems in determining if a piece of functionality is missing from the .NET Framework is that the framework is relatively large—not as large as the Win32 API, but large nonetheless. (At the time of this writing, the download size for the .NET Framework was 21MB.) So it pays to know where you'll find holes in the .NET Framework most often. The following sections discuss the various places where other developers have found holes in the .NET Framework coverage of the Win32 API. You might find other areas when working with special Win32 API features, but these sections provide you with a fairly complete overview.

Hardware

Every time Microsoft releases a new technology, they find a way to add yet more layers of code between the developer and the hardware, and .NET is no exception. Any hope you entertained of direct hardware access will quickly fade as you make your way through a few programming tasks. You'll even find it difficult to access Windows driver and low-level DLL functionality—the access just isn't there. Generally, you'll find that the .NET Framework provides you with objects that indirectly relate to some type of hardware functionality, such as the use of streams for hard drive and printer access.

The lack of direct hardware access isn't always a negative, however. Once you get used to using the .NET Framework objects, you might find that direct hardware access is unnecessary or, at least, a rare event. Common hardware types, such as printers and hard drives, won't present a problem in most cases. However, some developers have complained about the level of support provided for common low-level devices like the serial ports.

You'll also run into problems when working with hardware that Microsoft didn't anticipate. For example, accessing many USB devices is a frustrating experience when working with .NET. In most cases, you'll need to use unmanaged code and a third-party library to access new devices.

Security

Microsoft's latest security craze is role-based security. It's true that role-based security is extremely easy to use and requires less effort on the part of the developer. In many cases, role-based security is also more flexible than the security that Microsoft provided in the past. However, role-based security is also less than appropriate if you need low-level control over the security features of your application.

There's a place for tokens, access control lists, and all of the other paraphernalia of Win32 API security in many applications, but you can't gain access to these features within the .NET Framework. To gain access to the low-level details of security within Windows, you still need to use the security calls provided by the Win32 API. We'll discuss security access within Chapter 20, "Overcoming Security Issues."

Operating System

It would seem that the operating system is the first thing you'd need to support as part of development platform, but this isn't necessarily true. Consider two existing types of application that don't rely very heavily on the operating system: browser-based applications and Java applications. Yes, both technologies require basic access to the operating system, but you'll find that for the most part. You can't access the operating system as an entity. These development platforms rely on runtime engines that interact with the operating system in a predefined manner.

The .NET Framework is a modern development platform that will hopefully see implementation on other platforms. Consequently, you won't see any operating system support in the core namespaces, but will see some support in the Microsoft-specific namespaces. The separation of .NET functionality from operating system functionality is understandable, given Microsoft's stated goal of platform independence. However, unlike other platforms, the .NET Framework does provide limited operating system interfaces. In fact, there are three levels of operating system support that you need to consider when working with the .NET Framework—and .NET only supports one of them.

Upper-Level Interface   This is the level of operating support that the .NET Framework does support. The support appears in several areas, but the two main namespaces are `System.Windows`. `Forms` and `Microsoft.Win32`. As the names imply, the first namespace helps you gain access to the GUI features that Windows provides, while the second namespace provides access to features like the registry. The level of support in both areas is extensive, but limited to features that Microsoft felt a developer would need to create business applications.

Low-Level Services   There are a lot of low-level services that the .NET Framework doesn't even touch. For example, if you want to learn about the capabilities of the display, you'll need to use a Win32 API call to do it. Likewise, if you want to learn the status of the services on a remote machine, you'll have to resort to the Win32 API.

Version-Specific Features   Generally, you'll find that any operating system features that the .NET Framework does support are also found in all versions of Windows since Windows NT. In some cases, you'll also find the new features originally found in the Windows 9x operating system interface. However, if you want to use the new graphical features found in Windows XP, you'll have to rely on the Win32 API.

Multimedia

Microsoft engineered the .NET Framework for business users. You won't find support for any sound capability and barely any functions for graphics. There isn't any support for devices such as joysticks. In short, if you want to work with multimedia, your only choices are using the Win32 API calls or employing DirectX. Both of these solutions currently require the use of unmanaged code. Microsoft has said they plan to create a managed version of DirectX, but it's not a high priority.

Utility

There are a number of utility applications within Windows that require special interfaces. The most prominent of these utility applications is the Microsoft Management Console (MMC), which acts as a container for special components called *snap-ins*. The MMC is a vital tool for network administrators (and even for the common user) because it enables you to perform tasks such as monitor computer performance and manage user security. Unfortunately, the .NET Framework doesn't include support for this necessary utility, despite constant requests from developers during the beta process.

DirectX

It wasn't long ago that game developers fought with Microsoft over the need to access hardware directly in a way that would keep Windows in the loop without the performance-robbing penalty of actually using Windows. The result of this conflict is DirectX—an advanced programming technology for working with a wide range of multimedia hardware. Given Microsoft's goal of making the .NET Framework business friendly, it's not too surprising they failed to include any DirectX support.

Unfortunately, some business application developers rely on DirectX to produce complex reports and perform other business-related multimedia tasks. Part of the problem may be that Microsoft viewed the behemoth that is DirectX and decided they needed to implement it at a later date to get the .NET Framework out in a timely manner. Rumors abound that Microsoft plans to release a .NET Framework friendly version of DirectX sometime in the future, but for now, you need to rely on unmanaged programming techniques to work with DirectX.

NOTE

"DirectX version 9," forthcoming at the time of this writing, is slated to contain managed .NET Framework classes for easy access from C#.

Win32 Access Requirements

It's important to know what you need to do in order to access the Win32 API once you decide that the .NET Framework doesn't provide a required level of support. Generally speaking, Win32 API access isn't difficult for general functions. If you look again at the Beep() example in Listing 19.1, you'll notice that gaining access to the required functions doesn't require a lot of code. However, you do need to know something about the function you want to access, including the fact that it exists. The following list details some of the information you need.

- A knowledge of the function and its purpose
- A complete list of all function arguments and return values
- A description of any constants used with the function
- Complete details about any structures the function requires for data transfer
- The values and order of any enumeration used with the function

Not every function requires all of this information, but you need to at least verify what information the function does require. A simple function may require nothing more than a [DLLImport] entry and a call within your code. Complex functions might require structures, which means converting the data within the structure to match the language you're using within .NET. The most complex functions may have data structure elements such as unions that are impossible to replicate properly within a managed environment, which means creating a wrapper function in an unmanaged language such as Visual C++.

Sometimes what appears to be a single function call actually requires multiple functions. For example, the .NET Framework doesn't offer any way to clear the console screen, so you need to perform this task using a Win32 API call. Unfortunately, clearing the screen means moving the cursor and performing other low-level tasks—a single call won't do. Listing 19.2 shows a typical example of a single task that required multiple function calls.

Listing 19.2: Clearing the Screen Requires Multiple Function Calls

```
// This special class contains an enumeration of
// standard handles.
class StdHandleEnum
{
    public const int STD_INPUT_HANDLE   = -10;
    public const int STD_OUTPUT_HANDLE  = -11;
    public const int STD_ERROR_HANDLE   = -12;
};

// This sructure contains a screen coordinate.
```

```csharp
[StructLayout(LayoutKind.Sequential, Pack=1)]
  internal struct COORD
{
   public short X;
   public short Y;
}

// This stucture contains information about the
// console screen buffer.
[StructLayout(LayoutKind.Sequential, Pack=1)]
   internal struct CONSOLE_SCREEN_BUFFER_INFO
{
   public COORD    Size;
   public COORD    p1;
   public short    a1;
   public short    w1;
   public short    w2;
   public short    w3;
   public short    w4;
   public COORD    m1;
}


// We need these four functions from kernel32.dll.
// The GetStdHandle() function returns a handle to any
// standard input or output.
[DllImport("kernel32.dll", SetLastError=true)]
public static extern IntPtr GetStdHandle(int nStdHandle);

// The GetConsoleScreenBufferInfo() returns information
// about the console screen buffer so we know how much to
// clear.
[DllImport("kernel32.dll", SetLastError=true)]
public static extern bool GetConsoleScreenBufferInfo(
   IntPtr hConsoleOutput,
   out CONSOLE_SCREEN_BUFFER_INFO
   lpConsoleScreenBufferInfo);

// The SetConsoleCursorPosition() places the cursor on the
// console screen.
[DllImport("kernel32.dll", SetLastError=true)]
public static extern bool SetConsoleCursorPosition(
   IntPtr hConsoleOutput,
   COORD dwCursorPosition);
```

```
// The FillConsoleOutputCharacter() allows us
// to place any character on the console screen.
// Using a space clears the display area.
[DllImport("kernel32.dll", SetLastError=true,
   CharSet=CharSet.Auto)]
public static extern bool FillConsoleOutputCharacter(
   IntPtr hConsoleOutput,
   short cCharacter,
   int nLength,
   COORD WriteCoord,
   out int lpNumberOfCharsWritten);

[STAThread]
static void Main(string[] args)
{
   // Needed ask Windows about the console screen
   // buffer settings.
   CONSOLE_SCREEN_BUFFER_INFO   CSBI;
   // Handle to the output device.
   IntPtr                       hOut;
   // Number of characters written to the screen.
   int                          CharOut;
   // Home cursor position.
   COORD                        Home;

   // Write some data to the screen.
   Console.Write("Some Text to Erase!" +
                 "\r\nPress any key...");
   Console.ReadLine();

   // Clear the screen.
   // Begin by getting a handle to the console screen.
   hOut = GetStdHandle(StdHandleEnum.STD_OUTPUT_HANDLE);

   // Get the required console screen buffer information.
   GetConsoleScreenBufferInfo(hOut, out CSBI );

   // Set the home position for the cursor
   // (upper left corner).
   Home.X = 0;
   Home.Y = 0;

   // Fill the console with spaces.
```

```
FillConsoleOutputCharacter(hOut,
                        (short) ' ',
                        CSBI.Size.X * CSBI.Size.Y,
                        Home,
                        out CharOut);

// Place the cursor in the upper left corner.
SetConsoleCursorPosition(hOut, Home);

// Show the screen is clear.
Console.ReadLine();
}
```

Notice that this example uses more of the elements typical of a Win32 API call, including an enumeration and two structures. The code requires an enumeration for standard output handles. An output handle is simply a pointer to a device such as the screen. The three standard devices are input, output, and error. We also need two structures to fulfill the needs of the Windows API calls used in the example. The code listing describes each structure's task.

The example code relies on four Windows API functions, all of which appear in the KERNEL32.DLL. All four perform some type of console screen manipulation. The code listing describes each function's task.

The short part of the code is actually demonstrating the console screen clearing process. Main() creates some output on screen. The ReadLine() call merely ensures that the code will wait until you see the text. Press Enter and the clearing process begins.

The first thing we need is a handle to the console output. The handle tells Windows what device we want to work with. Once we have a handle to the output device, we need to ask Windows about its dimensions. The dimensions are important because you want to ensure that the console screen erases completely. The FillConsoleOutputCharacter() function call fills the screen with spaces—the equivalent of erasing its content. Finally, we place the cursor in the upper-left corner—the same place the CLS command would place it.

Of course, working with Windows means more than just making simple function calls; sometimes you need to work with COM as well. Once you get past simple functions and into the COM environment, development quickly gains a level or two of complexity. For example, if you want to create a COM equivalent component, you'll also need to discover and implement the interfaces supported by the unmanaged component. Sometimes the interfaces can become complex and difficult to re-create.

WIN32 ACCESS FOR C# DEVELOPERS

C# developers have a number of advantages over other .NET languages when it comes to Win32 access. The most important is the ability to use unsafe code and pointers. Many developers find that C# is an outstanding choice for the low-level programming tasks required for Win32 access. Of course, there's no free lunch—you pay a price whenever you gain some level of flexibility in the development environment. The following sections provide you with an overview of the pros and cons of using C# as your development language.

Understanding the Effects of Unsafe Code

The term "unsafe code" is somewhat ambiguous because it doesn't really tell you anything about the code. A better way to view unsafe code is unmanaged code that appears within a managed environment. Any code that relies on the use of manual pointers (* symbol) or addresses (& symbol) is unsafe code. Whenever you write code that uses these symbols, you also need to use the unsafe keyword in the method declaration as shown below.

```
unsafe private void btnTest_Click(
  object sender, System.EventArgs e)
{
    int   Input =
      Int32.Parse(txtInput.Text); // Input string.

    // Convert the input value.
    DoTimeIt(&Input);

    // Display the result
    txtOutput.Text = Input.ToString();
}

unsafe private void DoTimeIt(int* Input)
{
    int   Output;  // Output to the caller.

    // Display the current minute.
    txtMinute.Text = System.DateTime.Now.Minute.ToString();

    // Create the output value.
    Output = *Input;
    Output = Output * System.DateTime.Now.Minute;
```

```
        // Output the result.
        *Input = Output;
    }
```

This is a simple example that we could have created using other methods, but it demonstrates a principle you'll need to create applications that rely on the Win32 API later. The btnTest_Click() accesses the input value, converts it to an *int*, and supplies the address of the *int* to the DoTimeIt() method. Because we've supplied an address, rather than the value, any change in the supplied value by DoTimeIt() will remain when the call returns.

The DoTimeIt() method accesses the current time, multiplies it by the value of the input string, and then outputs the value. Notice the use of pointers in this method to access the values contained in the Input and Output variables. The reason this code is unsafe is that the compiler can't check it for errors. For example, you could replace the last line with Input = &Output; and the compiler would never complain, but you also wouldn't see the results of the multiplication.

Besides using the unsafe keyword, you also need to set your application to use unsafe code. Right-click the project name in Solution Explorer and choose Properties from the context menu. Select the Configuration Properties\Build folder and you'll see the Allow unsafe code blocks option shown in Figure 19.1. Set this option to True to enable use of unsafe code in your application.

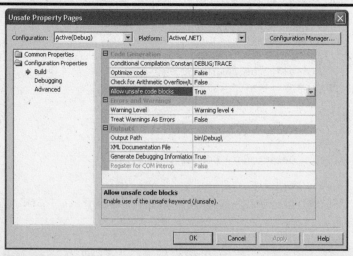

FIGURE 19.1:   Using the Allow unsafe code blocks option to enable use of unsafe code in your application.

NOTE
You can't use pointers on managed types, but you can use them on values. For example, you can't obtain the address of a `string` because a `string` is a managed type. The reason this example works in C# is that `int` is a value type. If you need to pass a string, then it's important to know other ways to mimic pointers. For example, you can pass a string using the `ref` or `out` keywords, or you can marshal it using various techniques.

Generally, you should avoid using unsafe code whenever possible, if only to get as much help as possible from the compiler. The "Understanding the Effects of Pointers" section tells you about managed alternatives that mimic pointers. In short, while unsafe code is a necessity when working with the Win32 API, you should avoid it whenever possible.

Understanding the Effects of Pointers

One of the first issues that you'll face when working with the Win32 API is the use of pointers—the Win32 API uses them by the gross. You'll find pointers as function arguments, within structures, and even nested within each other. The problem with pointers is that they aren't objects; they really aren't anything. A pointer is an abstraction, an address for something real. The pointer to your house is the street address found on letters and packages. The .NET Framework refrains from relying on pointers (from a developer's perspective) and uses the actual object whenever possible. The pointers are still there; the Common Language Runtime (CLR) simply manages them for you.

NOTE
The Common Language Runtime (CLR) is the layer of code that manages the execution of your programs. Your "compiled" code is executed by the CLR.

As mentioned in the previous section, you can use actual pointers in C# if you're also willing to deal with the problems of unsafe code. Unlike other .NET languages, C# embraces C++ type pointers, which makes it ideal for creating low-level routines and even wrapper DLLs in many situations. However, there are many ways to mimic pointers so that you can gain the benefits of the Win32 API without losing the benefits of the managed environment.

The first thing to consider is that pointers aren't always necessary. For example, the code in Listing 19.1 works fine without pointers because we're passing values to the Win32 API and not expecting anything in return. Avoid pointers whenever possible by verifying the need for them first. In many situations, you can simply pass a value to the Win32 API when a return value isn't needed by your application.

Another issue to consider is the use of pointer substitutes. Look at the FillConsoleOutputCharacter() method declaration in Listing 19.2 and you'll notice that it relies on the out keyword to return the number of characters written to the screen. An IntPtr easily handles the console output handle (essentially a pointer to a pointer). In fact, you can place this usage of an IntPtr among your rules of thumb. Generally, you can replace a handle with an IntPtr for all Win32 API calls.

Sometimes you must use a pointer—there simply isn't any way around the issue. For example, you'll often find that COM calls require pointers to pointers, such as when you want to work with an interface. In this situation, you might find it impossible to develop a substitute for pointers. When this problem occurs, try to localize the pointer code to a special function, even if it might not make sense to create a separate function from a program flow perspective. Placing the pointer in its own function makes it simpler to work with the pointer, reduces the probability of missed pointer errors, and makes it easier to debug the application later.

Advantages for the C# Developer

C# developers have certain advantages when using the Win32 API. We've already discussed some of these advantages, but the most important is support for pointers and unsafe code. However, C# has some other advantages and I'd be remiss not to mention them.

C-like language structures   Most of the information you'll need to access in Win32 API is found in the C header files that come with Visual Studio. In fact, when you research a function in the Visual Studio help files, the information is often presented using C header file entries. C# isn't C, but it does have many of the same features, making conversion a lot easier than in other languages.

Direct language conversion   It's possible to re-create most C structures using C# without much effort. There are only small changes in "old style" C declarations to account for language differences between C and C#. Because you don't have to interpret the structures, you'll find that writing the code to access the Win32 API from C# is relatively easy. The only time you'll run into problems is when you need to write code for complex COM interfaces and methods.

Less language baggage   Generally, you'll find that if the .NET Framework doesn't support a Win32 API feature, then C# doesn't support it either. Knowing this fact saves time because you don't have to research the language to discover if it provides the required support. Of course, this could also be viewed as a negative because C# will require Win32 API function calls more often than languages that do provide robust language support for Windows features.

Better Microsoft support   It may be a quirk, but every time someone from Microsoft demonstrates a low-level language example for .NET, it appears in C# before it appears in any other language. C# is also the language of choice on newsgroups and on websites in many cases. Visual Basic is next on the list. Interestingly enough, the language most capable of handling Win32 API calls is the one that is seldom used—Visual C++.

WIN32 ACCESS FOR VISUAL BASIC DEVELOPERS

In the past, Advanced Visual Basic developers were used to accessing Win32 API functions because Visual Basic has always had certain holes in its coverage of Windows features. From this perspective, nothing has changed for Visual Basic .NET developers. What has changed is that you now have the additional hurdle of working with managed code when accessing the Win32 API, and this can make a significant difference.

WARNING

Don't get the idea that you can use your old Visual Basic code directly in Visual Basic .NET. Some developers have stated that Microsoft created an entirely new language when they developed Visual Basic .NET. While this view might not be strictly true, it's true that your old code won't run as is—even the Win32 API access code. Your old code does provide a starting point, however, so make sure you use it as a reference as you develop your new Visual Basic .NET code.

Visual Basic still offers ease of use features that C# doesn't have. You can still prototype applications quickly using very little code. Unfortunately, the addition of managed code has put Visual Basic developers at a decided disadvantage in the Win32 API access arena. There are certain types of Win32 API access that you simply can't create using Visual Basic because it lacks support for unsafe code and pointers.

The following sections detail the advantages and disadvantages of using Visual Basic to access the Win32 API. At times you'll consider the disadvantages more important and may even decide to implement the Win32 API access using a wrapper DLL. However, Visual Basic does have features that make it the best language choice, in some cases, and we'll discuss them as well.

Understanding Visual Basic Limitations

The biggest limitations for Visual Basic .NET developers are lack of unsafe code and lack of pointer support. You can get around some of these limitations using the techniques in the "Understanding the Effects of Pointers" section earlier in this chapter. Essentially, you need to be able to provide the input to the Win32 API call using something other than a pointer, which often means either a compromise or not using the call at all.

Visual Basic developers also have language problems to overcome. If you want to use the Win32 API, you also need to know how the C header files work, which means having some knowledge of the C language. Many Visual Basic developers lack this knowledge, making it difficult to create a Visual Basic version of a structure, function call, or other construct originally written in C.

In most cases, Visual Basic developers will find it difficult to re-create complex COM interfaces. For example, the MMC example defies implementation in Visual Basic because it relies heavily on COM interface simulation. In fact, this particular task is barely doable in C# and you still need to create a Visual C++ wrapper for certain MMC function calls. In short, some tasks will defy every effort to complete in Visual Basic because there's no conduit for communication with the Win32 API.

Another problem with Visual Basic is that you can't re-create some of the stranger Win32 API structures. For example, some structures include unions, which is a feature that Visual Basic doesn't support. Unfortunately, there isn't any workaround for this problem other than to emulate the union in some other manner. In many cases, there isn't any way to emulate the union, making it impossible to call the Win32 API function that relies on the structure in question.

One of the advantages of Visual Basic is also a disadvantage. Developers gain a significant development speed boost by using Visual Basic. It enables a developer to prototype applications quickly. Coding and debugging are equally fast in most cases. All of these features come with a price, however, a lack of contact with the lower-level functions of the operating system. Visual Basic hides a lot of the usual operating system plumbing from the developer—a bonus when you don't require such access and a problem when you do.

Advantages for the Visual Basic Developer

Visual Basic .NET does have some limitations when it comes to Win32 API access, but it also has some advantages. Faster development time is just one advantage we've discussed so far and it's an important issue in a world where speed is everything. However, there are other factors in favor of Visual Basic and the following list tells you about them.

Existing code   Even though you can't use existing Visual Basic code to access the Win32 API, you can use it as a source of information, and that's worth quite a bit to developers on a time schedule. The existing code is well understood, debugged, and ready to use. Simple Win32 API calls present the least number of problems for the Visual Basic developer. For example, the various beep function calls examined in Listing 19.1 present few problems because they require basic input and no output.

Stronger language support   Remember that it's only necessary to call the Win32 API if the .NET Framework and the language lack support for a Windows feature. For example, C# lacks support for any type of beep function, so we need to create one. However, Visual Basic doesn't have this lack—it supplies a beep function, so you don't even need to use the Win32 API in this case. Visual Basic provides more built-in features than many other languages, making Win32 API access unnecessary in the first place.

SUMMARY

This chapter has introduced you to the needs and requirements for Win32 API access from .NET languages. We've discussed some of the potential problems of working with the Win32 API and why you need to exercise care when making a Win32 call. This chapter has also pointed out some areas where the .NET Framework lacks certain types of support, so it shows that the need to use the Win32 API is very real.

Make sure you run the examples in this chapter, because they demonstrate some important essential principles. It's also important to begin learning the rules of thumb presented throughout the chapter. For example, you should only use pointers when necessary in an application; otherwise, you might find it difficult to troubleshoot an errant pointer or figure out why an application misbehaves in some strange way.

WHAT'S NEXT

The next chapter covers the new security features that can be found in the .NET Framework.

Chapter 20
Overcoming Security Issues

Security is an increasingly important issue for most developers because the developer is being made responsible for ensuring the safety of data produced by an application. The .NET Framework comes complete with some good security features that are easier to use than security features in the past. However, the security emphasized by the .NET Framework is role based—it emphasizes the role an object or user occupies when requesting data to a system resource. Some development scenarios work well with this new technology; others don't. For example, I can't imagine trying to create a massive web application using token-based security—that type of project works best when you can define the roles that the users will fulfill.

Many developers are used to using the token-based security originally implemented in Windows NT. The token-based security uses a lock and key view of application security. In some cases, this view is actually easier to use and implement.

Adapted from *.NET Framework Solutions: In Search of the Lost Win32 API* by John Paul Mueller
ISBN 0-7821-4134-X

For example, if you want to check the locks on an individual file or the keys owned by an individual user, then you'll need to use the older style of security.

This chapter doesn't answer the question of which security strategy is best for a given situation. However, it does provide you with the techniques for accessing both strategies from within a managed application. We'll take a quick tour of the two security strategies and then look at several examples of how you can implement the older token-based security strategy in a .NET application.

NOTE

This chapter provides a quick overview of the .NET role-based security model for comparison purposes. It doesn't provide any complete role-based security examples because you can create them using standard .NET language calls. You'll find a few code snippets that demonstrate differences between token-based and role-based security. You'll find examples of the standard .NET language calls in my book *Visual C# .NET Developer's Handbook* (Sybex, 2002).

AN OVERVIEW OF WINDOWS SECURITY

The Windows security API is vast and performs many functions within the operating system and the applications it supports. Unfortunately, understanding the security portion of the Win32 API is about as easy as learning a new language while performing a handstand. It's not that the concept is so difficult to understand. The difficulty most developers have is getting the essentials they need from the vast supply of documentation that Microsoft provides—much of which is written in security speak. The most important purpose of this section of the chapter is to provide you with Win32 API–based security information without all of the mumbo jumbo.

We're going to talk about two essential topics in this portion of the chapter. The first is the security API, which we'll discuss in detail from a programmer's perspective. Although the user may be faintly aware that there's a security API, they're unlikely to use it or even care that it exists. As a programmer, you need to be very aware of this part of Windows 2000 and Windows XP and know how to use the various API calls to make your applications secure.

USING THE BIOMETRICS API TO EASE SECURITY CONCERNS

One security API to consider relies on biometrics, the use of human body parts such as the iris and fingerprints for identification purposes. The Biometrics API (BAPI) helps programmers embed biometric technology into applications. A consortium of vendors—including IBM, Compaq, IO Software, Microsoft, Sony, Toshiba, and Novell—originated BAPI. Learn more about BAPI at the IO Software website (http://www.iosoftware.com/pages/Products/SecureTec%-20SDK/BAPI/index.asp). You can download an overview, general information, technical information, and the BAPI software development kit (SDK). Lest you think that all of these APIs are vendor specific, you can also find biometrics standards at the Biometrics Consortium website (http://www.biometrics.org/). This site contains helpful information about seminars, standards progress, and public information, such as periodicals. Another interesting place to look for information is the National Institute of Standards and Technology (http://www.itl.nist.gov/div895/isis/projects/biometricsproject.html). The main interests at this site are the publications, conferences, products, and success stories.

The second important topic is the use of security functions. This section provides an overview of some of the security-related Win32 API functions you need to know about. As previously mentioned, there are many security-related functions, so knowing where to start is essential. We'll discuss some functions that will help you gain the access you need quickly. Of course, there are many esoteric functions you'll learn about as you delve more deeply into the security functions.

WHY WORRY ABOUT TOKEN-BASED SECURITY?

Some developers are under the misconception that the .NET Framework is a complete solution or that it will answer every need. The problem is that the .NET Framework is a new technology that extends what developers used in the past—you can't count on it to answer many of the old problems you have. In many cases, you'll find that a particular level of functionality is completely missing. The examples in this chapter demonstrate those lost security features.

CONTINUED ➡

However, the problem isn't limited to just missing functionality. The .NET Framework also presents situations where you could assume one level of functionality when the .NET Framework provides another. Consider the System.IO.FileStream.Lock() method. In theory, you should use this method to lock a file. In fact, it will lock the file if no one else is using it at the time.

Unfortunately, the Lock() method uses the LockFile() function found in KERNEL32.DLL, not the more functional LockFileEx() function. This means you don't have the option of asking Lock() to wait until it can lock the file—the method always returns immediately. In addition, you can't differentiate between a shared and an exclusive lock. Your only choices to get around this problem are to create a loop and continually poll the file until it locks, or use PInvoke to execute the LockFileEx() function. In short, the .NET Framework is incomplete and you'll need to know how to work with the Windows API to overcome those limitations.

A Detailed View of the Windows Security API

The security portion of the Win32 API is large and cumbersome. However, the actual theory behind Windows security is simple. Every object has a lock and every object requestor has a key. If the requestor's key fits the lock, then the requestor gains access to the object and the resources it provides. This is token-based security. The user's token is their key to resources on the local machine, the network and intranet, and even the Internet.

It's important to understand that the user's access is limited to the combination of groups and individual rights that the administrator assigns. However, most of the configuration options available to the administrator affect Windows as a whole. If you want the administrator to set user-level access for your application, then you must provide a feature to set user access for each object or task your application provides.

User-level access depends on a security ID (SID). When the user first logs into the system, Windows assigns an access token to the user and places the user's SID (stored on the domain controller or other security database) within it. The user object carries both the access token and the SID around for the duration of the session. An access token also contains both a Discretionary Access Control List (DACL) and a Security Access

Control List (SACL). The combination of access control lists (ACLs) and SIDs within the access token is a key that allows the user access to certain system resources.

A key is no good without a lock to open. The lock placed on Windows resources is called a security descriptor. In essence, a security descriptor tells what rights the user needs to access the resource. If the rights within the ACLs meet or exceed the rights in the security descriptor, then the lock opens and the resource becomes available. Figure 20.1 shows the content of the ACL and the security descriptor used for token-based security. The following sections provide more details about how token-based security actually works. We'll use Figure 20.1 as the point of discussion.

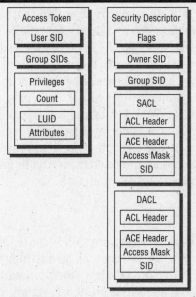

FIGURE 20.1:   Token-based security relies on ACLs and security descriptors.

Understanding Access Tokens

There are two ways of looking at a user's rights under Windows: individual access and group access. Remember that previously we talked about the user's SID—the account number that Windows assigns to the user during login. The access token that holds the SID also contains other structures that identify the groups the user belongs to and what privileges the user has. Each group entry also has a SID. This SID points to other structures that tell what rights the group has. To understand what rights the user has, you need to know both the user's individual rights and the rights of the groups to which the user belongs. You'd normally use the Local Users and Groups or the Active Directory Users and Computers Microsoft Management Console (MMC) snap-in to change the contents of this access token.

Let's talk about the "privileges" section of the access token shown in Figure 20.1. It begins with a count of the number of privileges that the user has—the number of special privilege entries in the access token. This section also contains an array of privilege entries. Each privilege entry contains a locally unique identifier (LUID)—essentially a pointer to the entry object—and an attribute mask. The attribute mask tells what rights the user has to the object. Group SID entries are essentially the same. They contain a privilege count and an array of privilege entries.

One of the things that you need to know as part of working with some kinds of objects is that object rights flow down to the lowest possible node unless overridden by another SID. For example, if you give a user read and write rights to the \Temp directory on a hard drive, those rights would also apply to the \Temp\Stuff directory unless you assigned the user specific rights to that directory. The same holds true for containers. Assigning a user rights to a container object like a Word document gives the user the right to look at everything within that container, even other files in most cases. It's important to track a user's exact rights to objects on your server through the use of security surveys because you could inadvertently give the user more rights than they need to perform a certain task.

Using Access Tokens

Let's talk briefly about the token calls in the security API because they are the first stepping-stones you'll need to know about. To do anything with a user's account—even if you want to find out who has access to a particular workstation—you need to know about tokens. As previously stated, tokens are the central part of the user side of the security equation. You'll usually begin a user account access with a call to OpenProcessToken(). Notice the name of this call—it deals with any kind of a process, user or otherwise. The purpose of this call is to get a token handle with specific rights attached to it. For example, if you want to query the user account, you need the TOKEN_QUERY privilege. (Your access token must contain the rights that you request from the system, which is why an administrator can access a token but other users can't.) Any changes to the user's account require the TOKEN_ADJUST_PRIVILEGES privilege. There are quite a few of these access rights, so we won't go through them all here.

Once you have an access token handle, you need to decide what to do with it. For example, you can change a user's privilege to do something by accessing the LUID for the privilege you want to change. All of these appear in the WINNT.H file with an SE_. For example, the SE_SYSTEM_PROFILE_NAME privilege enables the application to gather profiling information for the entire system. Some SE values don't relate to users (for example, the SE_LOCK_MEMORY_NAME privilege that allows a process to lock system memory). You get the LUID for a privilege using the LookupPrivilege-Value() call. Now you can combine the information you've gotten so far to change the privilege. In general, you'll use the AdjustTokenPrivileges() call to make the required change.

Querying the user's account (or other token information) is straightforward. You use the GetTokenInformation() call to retrieve any information you need. This call requires a token class parameter, which tells Windows the type of information required. For example, you'd use the TokenUser class to learn about a specific user. You'll also supply an appropriate structure that Windows can use for storing the information you request—which differs by token class.

Understanding Security Descriptors

At this point, you have a better idea of how the access token (the key) works. Now let's look at the security descriptor (the lock). Figure 20.1 shows that each security descriptor contains five main sections. The following list describes each section.

Flags The header consists of version information and a list of control flags. The flags tell you the descriptor status. For example, the SE_DACL_PRESENT flag indicates the presence of a DACL. If the DACL is missing or if it's NULL, then Windows allows everyone to use the object. Knowing the security descriptor status can greatly reduce the work you need to perform when determining security descriptor specifics.

Owner SID The owner SID tells who owns the object. This doesn't have to be an individual user; Windows allows you to use a group SID here as well. The limiting factor is that the group SID must appear in the token of the person changing the entry.

Group SID The group SID tells which group owns the object. This entry only contains the main group responsible for the object and won't contain a list of all groups with access to the object.

NOTE

Of the two security descriptor SIDs, the owner SID is important only under Windows. The Macintosh and POSIX security environments use the group SID. According to the Platform SDK documentation, Windows 2000 and above ignores the contents of the group SID.

SACL   This section controls the Windows auditing feature. Every time a user or group accesses an object when the auditing feature for that object is on, Windows makes an entry in the audit log. There's more than one entry in this section in most cases, so Windows stores the information in an array. The SACL is often left as a NULL value or not included in the security descriptor at all.

DACL   This section controls object use. You can assign groups and users to a specific object. There's more than one entry in this section in most cases, so Windows stores the information in an array. A DACL can contain a custom value, a default value, or a NULL value, or not appear in the security descriptor at all (this last option is rare and dangerous). You'll normally find more objects with default values than any other DACL type.

UNDERSTANDING THE SECURITY DESCRIPTOR TYPES

There are two types of security descriptors: absolute and self-relative. *Absolute* security descriptors contain a copy of each ACL within the descriptor structure. Use this type of security descriptor for objects that require special handling. For example, the root directory of a disk drive often uses an absolute security descriptor.

The *self-relative* security descriptor contains only a pointer to the SACL and DACL. This type of descriptor saves memory and reduces the time required to change rights for a group of objects. You'd use it when all objects in a particular group require the same level of security. For example, you could use this method to secure all threads within a single application.

Windows requires that you convert self-relative security descriptors to absolute format before you save them or transfer them to another process. Every descriptor you retrieve using API calls is of the self-relative type. You can convert a security descriptor from one type to another using the MakeAbsoluteSD() and MakeSelf-RelativeSD() API calls.

Understanding ACLs

As previously mentioned, a security descriptor relies on a SACL and a DACL to control the security of an object. Both of these elements use the same basic ACL data structure but for different purposes. An ACL consists of two entry types. The first is a header that lists the number of access control entries (ACEs) in the ACL. Windows uses this number to determine when it's reached the end of the ACE list. (There isn't any end-of-structure record or other way to determine the size of each ACE in the structure.) The second entry is an array of ACEs.

> **WARNING**
>
> Never directly manipulate the contents of an ACL or SID—Microsoft may change its structure in future versions of Windows. The Windows API provides functions such as `GetSecurityDescriptorDacl()` and `SetSecurityDescriptor-Dacl()` to change the contents of these structures. (Of course, you have to create the security descriptor structure using the `InitializeSecurity-Descriptor()` function—you'll learn more about security descriptor construction as the chapter progresses.) Always use an API call to perform any task with either structure type to reduce the impact of changes in structure on your application.

An ACE defines the object rights for a single user or group. Every ACE has a header that defines the type, size, and flags for the ACE. It includes an access mask that defines rights a user or group has to the object. Finally, there's an entry for the user or group SID.

There are four main ACE header types. Windows currently uses three out of the four. The following list tells you about each of these:

General Access   This header type appears in the DACL and grants object rights to a user. Use it to add to the rights a user already has to an object on an instance-by-instance basis. For example, you might want to prevent the user from changing the system time so that you can keep the machines on the network synchronized. However, there might be one situation—such as daylight savings time—when the user would need this right. You could use an access-allowed ACE to allow the user to change the time in this one instance.

NOTE

Windows divides each of the access header types into two subtypes: allowed and denied. For example, there's both an ACCESS_ALLOWED_ACE_TYPE and an ACCESS_DENIED_ACE_TYPE header type.

Object Access　This is a special header type for Windows 2000 and Windows XP. It enables you to assign specific security to software objects and subobjects. For example, you could use this type of ACE to assign security to the property of a COM object. To use this type of ACE, you need to obtain or create a globally unique identifier (GUID) for the object in question.

System Audit　This ACE header type works with the SACL. It defines which events to audit for a particular user or group. There are system audit header types for both general and object use. Only Windows 2000 and Windows XP systems can use the object-related system audit ACE header type.

System Alarm　This is the currently unused ACE type. It enables either the SACL or the DACL to set an alarm when specific events happen.

Using Security Descriptors

Understanding what a security descriptor is and how the various structures it contains interact is only one part of the picture. You also need to know how to access and use security descriptors to write a program. Windows doesn't generalize security descriptors as it does tokens. You can't use a standard set of calls to access them.

NOTE

Only NTFS provides full security, while VFAT provides it to a lesser degree. You can't assign or obtain security descriptors for either HPFS or FAT/FAT32 file systems. The FAT/FAT32 file system doesn't provide any extended attribute space, one requirement for adding security. The HPFS file system provides extended attributes, but they don't include any security features. Of all the file systems described, NTFS is the most secure. However, never assume that any file system is completely secure.

Windows includes five classes of security descriptors, each of which uses a different set of descriptor calls to access the object initially. (You

must have the SE_SECURITY_NAME privilege to use any of these functions.)
The five classes of security descriptors are as follows:

Files, Directories, Pipes, and Mail Slots Use GetFile-
Security() and SetFileSecurity().

**Processes, Threads, Access Tokens, and Synchronization
Objects** Use GetKernelObjectSecurity() and SetKernel-
ObjectSecurity(). All these objects, even access tokens, are
kernel objects. As such, they also have their own security
descriptors.

Window Stations, Desktops, Windows, and Menus Use
GetUserObjectSecurity() and SetUserObjectSecurity().
A window station is a combination of keyboard, mouse, and
screen. Desktops contain windows and menus. These four objects
inherit rights from each other in the order shown. In other words,
a desktop will inherit the rights of the window station.

System Registry Keys Use RegGetKeySecurity() and
RegSetKeySecurity(). Notice that these two calls start
with Reg, just like the other registry-specific calls Windows
supports.

TIP

You can set some types of permissions using the .NET Framework System
.Security.Permissions namespace. For example, the RegistryPermission
class provides access to the registry security values. However, you won't gain
access to the same level of information using the .NET Framework and you
might find that some functionality is lacking.

Executable Service Objects Use QueryServiceObject-
Security() and SetServiceObjectSecurity(). For some
strange reason, neither call appears with the other security calls
in the Windows API help file. An executable service is a background task such as the UPS monitoring function.

Once you do gain access to the object, you can perform a variety of
tasks using generic API calls. For example, the GetSecurityDescriptor-
DACL() retrieves a copy of the DACL from any descriptor type. The
descriptors for all of these objects follow roughly the same format—although
the lengths of most of the components differ. One reason for the

differences in size is that each object will contain a different number of ACEs. The SID's size differs as well.

The next step to query or modify security descriptor content is to disassemble the components. For example, you could view the ACEs within a DACL or a SACL using GetACE(). You could also use the owner and group SIDs for a variety of SID-related calls. In essence, any security descriptor access will always consist of the same three steps:

1. Get the descriptor.

2. Remove a specific component.

3. Modify the contents of that component.

To change the security descriptor, you reverse the process. Use a call like AddACE() to add a new ACE to an ACL, use SetSecurityDescriptorSACL() to change SACL within a descriptor, and finally, save the descriptor using a call like SetFileSecurity().

THE IMPORTANCE OF ORDER FOR SECURITY

Once you know how Windows evaluates the ACEs in the DACL, you'll discover a few problem areas — problems that the Windows utilities address automatically. Order is an important consideration when working with Windows security because Windows uses a very basic method for determining how to evaluate the security elements. You'll need to program around these problems to derive the result found in the various Windows utilities. The SACL has the same problem, but it only affects auditing, so the effect is less severe from the system security standpoint.

Windows evaluates the ACEs in an ACL in the order in which they appear. At first, this might not seem like a very big deal. However, it could become a problem in some situations. For example, what if you want to revoke all of a user's rights in one area but their list of ACEs includes membership in a group that allows access to that area? If you place the access-allowed ACE before the access-denied ACE in the list, the user would get access to the area. The bottom line is that you should place all your access-denied ACEs in the list first to prevent any potential breach in security.

CONTINUED ➡

Also, use care in the ordering of group SIDs. Rights that a user acquires from different groups are cumulative. This means a user who's part of two groups, one that has access to a file and another that doesn't, will have access to the file if the group granting the right appears first on the list. In addition, if one ACE grants read rights and another write rights to a file and the user is asking for read and write rights, Windows will grant the request.

Obviously, you could spend all your time trying to figure out the best arrangement of groups. As the number of groups and individual rights that a user possesses increases, the potential for an unintended security breach does as well. That's why it's important to create groups carefully and limit a user's individual rights.

An Overview of the Functions

Now that you have a better idea of how token-based security works, let's look at some of the functions we'll use later in the chapter to create example applications. Table 20.1 contains a list of the various API functions that you'll commonly use to change the user's access token. This list provides only an overview, not a detailed description, of each API function.

TABLE 20.1: Common User Access Token Function Overview

FUNCTION NAME	DESCRIPTION
AdjustTokenGroups	Allows you to adjust one or more group flags that control group usage within the access token. For example, you can use this function to replace the group's owner.
AdjustTokenPrivileges	Allows you to adjust one or more privileges within the access token. This function enables or disables an existing privilege; you can't add or delete privileges from the access token.
AllocateLocallyUniqueId	Creates a new locally unique identifier (LUID). The LUID is unique only for the current computer session on a particular computer. Unlike a GUID, a LUID is temporary.

TABLE 20.1 continued: Common User Access Token Function Overview

FUNCTION NAME	DESCRIPTION
BuildExplicitAccessWithName	Creates an EXPLICIT_ACCESS data structure for the named trustee. This data structure defines the trustee's ACL information. Use this data structure with API functions like SetEntriesInAcl() to define a trustee's access level to objects. The EXPLICIT_ACCESS data structure can affect either the SACL or DACL, depending on the access mode you set for it.
BuildTrusteeWithName	Creates a TRUSTEE data structure used to identify a specific trustee. You supply a trustee name and Windows fills the other data structure elements with default values. You'll need to modify the data structure before using it.
BuildTrusteeWithSid	Creates a TRUSTEE data structure that relies on a SID rather than a trustee name. Windows modifies the default data structure values appropriately.
CheckTokenMembership	Determines whether a SID appears within an access token. This can help you determine whether a user or process belongs to a particular group.
CreateRestrictedToken	Creates a duplicate of an existing token. The new token will have only a subset of the rights within the existing token. You can't use this function to add new rights to the resulting token.
DuplicateToken	Creates a copy of an existing token. Using this technique allows you to create a new token that varies from an existing token by one or two privileges.
DuplicateTokenEx	Creates a duplicate of a token. This function allows you to create either a primary or impersonation token. You can set access rights to the new token as part of the duplication call.
GetAuditedPermissionsFromAcl	Returns a list of ACL entries that result in an audit log entry for the specified trustee. This includes ACL entries that affect the trustee as well as groups to which the trustee belongs. You get a complete list of all audit-generating access events, not just those associated with the trustee. Windows returns the audited access in an ACCESS_MASK data structure.
GetEffectiveRightsFromAcl	Returns a list of ACL entries that list the effective rights for the specified trustee. Windows returns the effective rights in an ACCESS_MASK data structure.
GetExplicitEntriesFromAcl	Returns an array of EXPLICIT_ACCESS data structures that define the level of access each ACE within an ACL grants the trustee. The data structure provides information like the access mode, access rights, and inheritance setting for each ACE.

TABLE 20.1 continued: Common User Access Token Function Overview

FUNCTION NAME	DESCRIPTION
GetTokenInformation	Returns a data structure containing complete information about the access token. This includes the token's user, groups that appear within the token, the owner of the token, the impersonation level, and statistics associated with the token.
GetTrusteeForm	Returns a constant from one of the TRUSTEE_FORM enumeration values for a trustee. In most cases, the constants indicate whether the trustee is a name, SID, or object.
GetTrusteeName	Returns the name associated with a name trustee. If the TRUSTEE data structure that you provide is for a SID or object, Windows returns a NULL value.
GetTrusteeType	Returns a constant from one of the TRUSTEE_TYPE enumeration values for a trustee. In most cases, the constants indicate whether the trustee is a user, group, domain, or alias. There are also values to show deleted or invalid trustees.
IsTokenRestricted	Detects whether the access token contains one or more restricting SIDs.
LookupPrivilegeDisplayName	Converts a privilege name listed in WINNT.H to human-readable form. For example, SE_REMOTE_SHUTDOWN_NAME might convert to "Force shutdown from a remote system."
LookupPrivilegeName	Allows you to convert a privilege name specified by a LUID to one of the constant forms listed in WINNT.H.
LookupPrivilegeValue	Allows you to convert a privilege name as listed in WINNT.H to a LUID.
OpenProcessToken	Opens a token associated with a process (application). As with file tokens, you need to specify a level of access to process the token. For example, the TOKEN_ALL_ACCESS constant gives you complete access to the token.
OpenThreadToken	Opens a token that's associated with a thread within an application. As with a process token, you need to request a specific level of access when making the request.
SetEntriesInAcl	Creates a new ACL by merging new access control or audit control information into an existing ACL. You can use this function to create an entirely new ACL using the ACL creation function, BuildExplicitAccess-WithName().

TABLE 20.1 continued: Common User Access Token Function Overview

FUNCTION NAME	DESCRIPTION
SetThreadToken	Used mainly to implement impersonation within a thread. Use this function to give different rights to a single thread within an application. This allows the thread to perform tasks that the user may not have the rights to perform.
SetTokenInformation	Sets the information contained within an access token. Before you can set the information within the token, you have to have the required access rights. The three data structures associated with this function allow you to adjust owner, primary group, and DACL information.

Normally, you'll never work with SIDs directly. The reason is that you can address a user by their login name and make your code both easier to debug and understand. However, there are certain situations in which you'll want to work with SIDs. The most important of these situations is when you're dealing with common SIDs like the one for the World, which has a SID of S-1-1-0. The SID for the World always remains the same, but the name for the World could change from country to country. Always refer to common, universal SIDs by their SID rather than by a common name. With this in mind, you'll want to know about the SID-related functions, so you'll be familiar with them when you want to work with common SIDs. Table 20.2 contains a list of SID-related functions.

TABLE 20.2: Common SID-Related Function Overview

FUNCTION NAME	DESCRIPTION
AllocateAndInitializeSid	Creates and initializes a SID with up to eight subauthorities.
ConvertSidToStringSid	Converts a SID to a string in human-readable format. This format consists of values in the form *S-R-I-SA*, where *S* designates the string as a SID, *R* is the revision level, *I* is the identifier authority value, and *SA* is one or more subauthority values. Note that the dashes between SID values are always part of the SID string.
ConvertStringSidToSid	Converts a specially formatted string into a SID.
CopySid	Creates a duplicate of an existing SID.
EqualPrefixSid	Compares two SID prefixes for equality. A SID prefix is the SID value minus the last subauthority value. This test is useful for detecting two SIDs in the same domain.

TABLE 20.2 continued: Common SID-Related Function Overview

FUNCTION NAME	DESCRIPTION
EqualSid	Compares two SIDs for equality in their entirety.
FreeSid	Deallocates the memory used by a SID previously created using the AllocateAndInitializeSid() function.
GetLengthSid	Returns the length of a SID in bytes.
GetSidIdentifierAuthority	Returns a pointer to a SID_IDENTIFIER_AUTHORITY data structure. This data structure contains an array of six bytes that specify the SID's top-level authority. Predefined authorities include NULL (0), local (1), world (2), creator (3), and Windows NT/Windows 2000/Windows XP (5).
GetSidLengthRequired	Returns the length of a buffer required to hold a SID structure with a specified number of subauthorities.
GetSidSubAuthority	Returns the address of a specific subauthority within a SID structure. The subauthority is a relative identifier (RID).
GetSidSubAuthorityCount	Returns the address of a field used to hold the number of subauthorities within the SID. Use this address to determine the number of subauthorities within the SID.
InitializeSid	Sets the identifier authority of a SID structure to a known value using a SID_IDENTIFIER_AUTHORITY data structure. Subauthority values aren't set using this function. Use the AllocateAndInitializeSid() function to initialize a SID completely.
IsValidSid	Determines the validity of a SID structure's contents. This function checks the revision number and ensures that the number of sub-authorities doesn't exceed the maximum value.
LookupAccountName	Retrieves the SID (and accompanying data) for a specific account. You must supply an account and system name.
LookupAccountSid	Retrieves the name and machine associated with a given SID. It also returns the name of the SID's first domain.

Security isn't this one sided. Once Windows determines the rights a user or other object has, it must match those rights to the access requirements of the system resource. This means working with security descriptors. A *security descriptor* is a lock on the object or other system resource. Either the key (access token) fits the lock or it doesn't. Windows grants or denies access when the key fits the lock. Table 20.3 is an overview of the security descriptor API functions.

TABLE 20.3: Security Descriptor Function Overview

FUNCTION NAME	DESCRIPTION
ConvertSecurityDescriptor-ToStringSecurityDescriptor	Converts a security descriptor to string format. Flags determine the level of information returned in the string. A complete string contains the owner SID, the group SID, a DACL flag list using coded letters, a SACL flag list using coded letters, and a series of ACE entries.
ConvertStringSecurityDescriptor-ToSecurityDescriptor	Converts a specially formatted string into a security descriptor.
GetNamedSecurityInfo	Returns the security descriptor for the named object provided as input. Flags determine what kind of information to retrieve.
GetSecurityDescriptorControl	Returns the security descriptor control information and revision number for the security descriptor structure provided as input.
GetSecurityInfo	Returns the security descriptor for an object that is specified using an object handle. Windows provides flags that determine which security descriptor entries to retrieve.
SetNamedSecurityInfo	Modifies the security descriptor information for an object specified by name.
SetSecurityDescriptorControl	Modifies the control bits of a security descriptor. Functions related to this one include Set-SecurityDescriptorDacl, which allows you to set other control bits of the security descriptor.
SetSecurityInfo	Modifies the owner, group, SACL, or DACL within the security descriptor for an object. Each information type requires a separate data structure, which includes flags to tell Windows which elements to change. A handle and object type descriptor identifies the object.

By now, you should have some idea of how to work within the security portion of the Win32 API. The divisions I set up within the tables are artificial; they're for description purposes to make the functions easier to comprehend and use. In a real-world application, you'll combine elements of all three tables to create a complete security picture.

USING THE ACCESS CONTROL EDITOR

The Access Control Editor is a COM control that helps you add a standard interface to your application—this allows your administrators to set application security as needed. These are the same property pages that Microsoft uses within Windows 2000 and Windows XP to set security. The Access Control Editor uses two sets of property pages. The user will normally see the simple property page dialog shown in Figure 20.2.

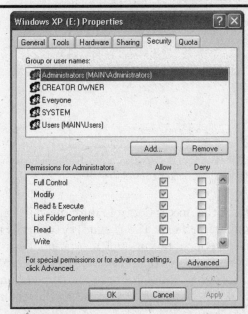

FIGURE 20.2: The Access Control Editor is a generally accessible component.

I chose this particular example so that you'd see the dialog in action. The content of the dialog changes to meet object requirements. The Administrator will normally use the advanced property page shown in Figure 20.3.

As you can see, both property pages allow the administrator to work with the security settings for an application with relative ease. Notice that the advanced dialog provides complete controls for setting every security aspect for this particular object. The Permissions tab sets the DACL, the Auditing tab the SACL, and the Owner tab the owner information. The only missing element is the group information, which isn't important at the user level in many cases.

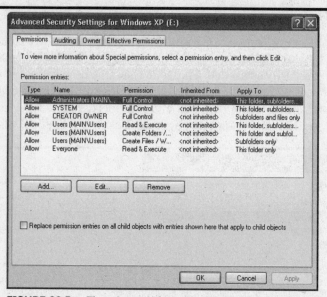

FIGURE 20.3:   The advanced features of the Access Control Editor provide the administrator with full access control.

You can easily implement the Access Control Editor in a .NET application by creating the proper interfaces. The ISecurityInformation interface is the essential component of this implementation. I won't go into the programming details in this section. However, it's important to know that you can add the Access Control Editor to your applications by adding the appropriate COM interfaces and implementing the required functions the interfaces describe.

For the Win32 API developer, the Access Control Editor fulfills another purpose. We'll use this operating system feature to verify changes made by the sample applications. Security is one of those difficult changes to verify unless you want to build a lot of test applications. The Access Control Editor is one of many tools that enable you to check the output of your application, but this particular tool is one of the easiest to use and the most reliable. In general, you'll want to use this tool before you use anything else.

It's also easy to use the Access Control Editor to set up test cases for your applications. For example, you might want to ensure that your application detects certain types of security changes. (This behavior often occurs when a virus is at work, so the ability of your application to detect odd changes is important.) The Access Control Editor enables you to make changes on a test object quickly. You can then test your application to see how the change affects its operation. Generally, your applications need to at least detect changes within certain ranges of approved behavior. For example, an application would want to detect files that have security turned off if the information they contain is sensitive.

USING THE SECURITY CONFIGURATION EDITOR

The Microsoft Security Configuration Editor is an administration tool that reduces both security management and analysis time. Initially, you'll use this tool to configure the operating system security parameters. Once these parameters are in place, you can use the Security Configuration Editor to schedule periodic tests.

THE SYSTEM CONFIGURATION MANAGER

Windows NT provides one MMC snap-in for the Security Configuration Editor; it's called the System Configuration Manager. You can use the System Configuration Manager to work with the security database (SDB) and security configuration (INF) files you create using the Security Configuration Editor. Windows 2000 and Windows XP divide the Security Configuration Editor into two parts. The Security Configuration and Analysis MMC snap-in helps you configure the security database. The Security Templates MMC snap-in helps you work with the security configuration files. All of these operating systems provide similar functionality. Windows 2000 and Windows XP do provide some advanced features. All screen shots in this section of the chapter depict the Windows XP setup.

The overall goal of the Security Configuration Editor is to provide a single place to manage all of the security concerns for a network. However, it doesn't actually replace all of the tools you used in the past—the Security Configuration Editor augments other security tools. The Security Configuration Editor also provides auditing tools that Windows has lacked in the past.

One of the unique ideas behind the Security Configuration Editor is that it's a macro-based tool. You'll create a set of instructions for the Security Configuration Editor to perform and then allow it to perform those instructions in the background. Obviously, this saves a lot of developer time because the developer doesn't have to wait for one set of instructions to complete before going to the next set. You can also group tasks, which saves input time.

At this point, you may wonder why a developer should care about this tool at all. After all, configuring network security is a network administrator task. That idea used to be true—a network administrator was responsible for all security on the network. However, as computer networks become more complex and the technologies used with them more flexible, part of the responsibility for network security has shifted to the developer. As a developer, you need to know how this tool works so that you can test the applications you create. This is especially true for token-based applications because the .NET Framework provides nothing in the way of internal checks for your application. For the Win32 API developer, this is an essential test tool.

Creating a security setup begins when you choose an existing template or create a new one using the Security Templates MMC snap-in. If you want to use an existing template as a basis for creating a new one, you can right-click the desired template and use the Save As command found on the context menu. Microsoft supplies a variety of templates designed to help you start creating this security database, as shown in Figure 20.4.

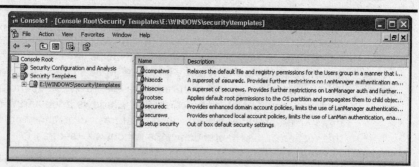

FIGURE 20.4:   The Security Configuration Editor provides a number of standard templates for creating your security setup.

Each of the security templates is designed for a different purpose (which is indicated by the name). The one I'll use in this section is the compatibility workstation template (compatws), but all of the other templates work about the same as this one. All of the templates contain the same basic elements shown in Figure 20.5.

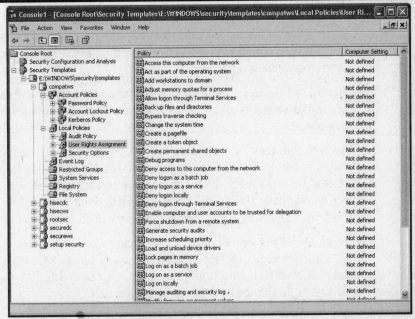

FIGURE 20.5: Each of the security templates contains the same security elements.

As you can see from the figure, each template defines a number of security elements. The following list describes each of these elements for you:

Account Policies Defines the password, account lockout, and Kerberos policies for the machine. Password policies include items like the minimum password length and the maximum time the user can use a single password. The account lockout policy includes the number of times a user can enter the wrong password without initiating a system lockout. Kerberos policies feature elements like the maximum user ticket lifetime.

Local Policies Defines the audit policy, user rights assignment, and security options. Audit policies determine the types of data you collect. For example, you could audit each failed user logon attempt. User rights assignments are of special interest because this policy affects the rights you can assign to a user (the access token).

The security options policy contains the elements that determine how the security system will react given a set of circumstances. For example, one policy will log a user off when their usage hours expire.

Event Log   Defines how the event log stores data and for how long. These policies also determine maximize event log size and event log viewing rights.

Restricted Groups   Defines groups that can't access the workstation or server at all, or restricts the amount of access they can obtain.

System Services   Displays a list of the system services on the target machine. Double-clicking a service displays a dialog that allows you to set the policy for that service and adjust its startup mode. Normally, you'll leave the icons in this policy alone. However, you can safely change any system service DLLs you create.

Registry   Contains all of the major registry hives. Double-clicking a branch displays a dialog you use to set the security for that branch. In addition, you can choose the method of security inheritance by children of this branch.

File System   Contains protected file system entries. You can add new files to the list or modify existing entries. Double-clicking a file system entry displays a dialog you use to set the security level for that file system member. In addition, you can choose the method of security inheritance by children of this file system entity (applies only to folders).

Active Directory Objects   This entry is only available if you have Active Directory enabled (which means you must have a domain controller set up). It allows you to edit the security settings for any Active Directory objects, including users and groups.

UNDERSTANDING HOW .NET ROLE-BASED SECURITY DIFFERS

Even though this chapter is about using token-based security, it's important to realize that the .NET Framework does provide a substantial set of security classes. The big difference is that the .NET Framework uses role-based, not token-based, security in most cases. This section helps you understand how role-based security compares. I've provided it as an optional overview of role-based security and you can easily skip the section if desired.

Most of the security features we'll discuss in this section appear in the System.Security namespace. However, it's important to realize that Microsoft attempted to order the .NET Framework for convenience. Despite the fact that most security features appear in the security-related name-spaces, you'll find a few in odd places. For example, if you want to lock a file, you'll use the System.IO.FileStream.Lock() method. Likewise, if you want to ensure that your web pages synchronize properly, you'll want to use the System.Web.HttpApplicationState.Lock() method. There's even a System.Drawing.Design.ToolboxItem.Lock() method you can use to lock individual properties in a toolbox item. In short, if Microsoft feels that a developer would have better access to a security method within the affected object's class, the method appears in that location.

The .NET Framework provides several levels of security. However, you can easily divide security into application and role-based security. Application security defends the code elements used to create an application. In addition, it protects the system from code elements that originate outside the system (such as code downloaded from a website) by assigning such code a lower security level. In short, the code receives a trust value based on its origin. Role-based security defines the actions a user (or other entity) is allowed to perform based on their organizational role. This differs from the older individual and group token access because a user can "change hats" (roles) based on current environmental and access conditions. Together, the two levels of security enable you to protect applications without worrying too much about low-level functionality. Of course, these features only work if you've already defined the various security elements.

NOTE

Many of the security features that the .NET Framework provides affect only managed code. If your application uses a combination of managed and unmanaged code, you'll need to implement security that works in both arenas, namely the security portion of the Win32 API we discussed earlier.

Another way to look at .NET security is to consider the method of code implementation. You can programmatically define a security feature using declarative or imperative syntax. Some security features require that you use a specific method, while others allow implementation using either method.

Declarative syntax relies on attributes. The attributes can appear at the assembly, class, or member levels and they can request, demand, or override the security options currently in place. Applications use requests to change their current security settings. A request can ask for more or less access to objects. A demand protects the object from caller access. On the other hand, an override changes the default security settings. Here's an example of declarative syntax in action:

```csharp
[System.Security.Permissions.FileIOPermission(
    SecurityAction.Deny, All="E:\\Temp.txt")]
private void btnDeny_Click(
    object sender, System.EventArgs e)
{
    Stream   FS = null;  // A test file stream.

    // Try to access the file.
    try
    {
        FS = new FileStream("E:\\Temp.txt",
                            FileMode.Open,
                            FileAccess.Read);
    }
    catch(SecurityException SE)
    {
        MessageBox.Show("Access Denied\r\n" +
                        SE.Message,
                        "File IO Error",
                        MessageBoxButtons.OK,
                        MessageBoxIcon.Error);
        return;
    }

    // Display a success message.
    MessageBox.Show("File is open!",
                    "File IO Success",
                    MessageBoxButtons.OK,
                    MessageBoxIcon.Information);

    // Close the file if opened.
    FS.Close();
}
```

The btnAllow_Click() will always fail because the FileIOPermission attribute is set to deny all access to the file. The Assert() or Demand() methods would allow access to the same file (the example uses the

Assert() method). As you can see, the result of this code is that the TEMP.TXT file is protected, even if the user would normally have access to it.

Imperative syntax relies on security objects. An application creates a security object and then uses the object to set permissions or perform other tasks. You can use imperative syntax to perform demands and over-rides, but not requests. Here's an example of imperative syntax in action:

```
private void btnDeny_Click(
    object sender, System.EventArgs e)
{
    FileIOPermission  FIOP;        // Permission object.
    Stream            FS = null;   // A test file stream.

    // Create the permission object.
    FIOP = new FileIOPermission(FileIOPermissionAccess.Read,
               "E:\\Temp.txt");

    // Deny access to the resource.
    FIOP.Deny();

    // Try to access the object.
    try
    {
        FS = new FileStream("E:\\Temp.txt",
                     FileMode.Open,
                     FileAccess.Read);
    }
    catch(SecurityException SE)
    {
        MessageBox.Show("Access Denied\r\n" +
                 SE.Message,
                 "File IO Error",
                 MessageBoxButtons.OK,
                 MessageBoxIcon.Error);
        return;
    }

    // Display a success message.
    MessageBox.Show("File is open!",
                "File IO Success",
                MessageBoxButtons.OK,
                MessageBoxIcon.Information);

    // Close the file if opened.
    FS.Close();
}
```

The btnDeny_Click() method will always fail because the imperative security call, FIOP.Deny(), denies access to the file. Notice how the code initializes the FileIOPermission object before using it. The code requires a full path to the file in question. As with the declarative syntax, you can use the Assert() or Demand() methods to allow access to an object.

LOOKING UP AN ACCOUNT SID EXAMPLE

Sometimes you know the name of a well-known account, such as Administrators, but you don't know anything else about it. The Win32 API provides an answer to this dilemma. You can create a SID for the account without knowing anything about it and then look up the information for that account. This technique proves handy for a number of uses. For example, if you know that you want to create a new user that has starting rights that are the same as those used for a well-known account, you can begin by obtaining information about the well-known account SID. Listing 20.1 shows the code you'll need for this example. (Note that the list of well-known SIDs shown in Listing 20.1 is incomplete—you'll find a complete list on the source book's page on the Sybex website.)

Listing 20.1: Converting a SID to Human-Readable Form

```
// This function returns a SID for a well-known account.
[DllImport("AdvAPI32.DLL",
   CharSet=CharSet.Auto, SetLastError=true )]
public static extern bool CreateWellKnownSid(
   WELL_KNOWN_SID_TYPE WellKnownSidType,
   IntPtr DomainSid,
   IntPtr pSid,
   ref Int32 cbSid);

// This enumeration contains a list of the well-known SIDs.
public enum WELL_KNOWN_SID_TYPE
{
   WinNullSid                                = 0,

   // Lots of other well-known
   // SIDs appear in the source code.
```

```
    WinAccountRasAndIasServersSid                = 50,
};

// This define is normally calculated by a macro, but it's
// unlikely to change for either Windows 2000 or Windows XP.
public const int SECURITY_MAX_SID_SIZE = 68;

// This function accepts a SID as input and obtains human
// readable data about it.
[DllImport("AdvAPI32.DLL",
  CharSet=CharSet.Auto, SetLastError=true )]
public static extern bool LookupAccountSid(
    String lpSystemName,
    IntPtr Sid,
    StringBuilder Name,
    ref Int32 cbName,
    StringBuilder DomainName,
    ref Int32 cbDomainName,
    ref SID_NAME_USE peUse);

// This enumeration determines the use of the account.
public enum SID_NAME_USE
{
    SidTypeUser = 1,
    SidTypeGroup,
    SidTypeDomain,
    SidTypeAlias,
    SidTypeWellKnownGroup,
    SidTypeDeletedAccount,
    SidTypeInvalid,
    SidTypeUnknown,
    SidTypeComputer
};


private void btnTest_Click(
    object sender, System.EventArgs e)
{
    Int32         SIDSize;    // Size of the returned SID.
    IntPtr        GuestSID;   // SID of the Guest account.

    // Last error produced by an API call.
    int           LastError;
```

```
Int32          NameSize;    // Size of the account name.
Int32          DomainSize;  // Size of the domain name.
StringBuilder  Name;        // Account name.
StringBuilder  Domain;      // Domain name.
SID_NAME_USE   Use;         // Account use.

// Allocate memory for the SID.
GuestSID = Marshal.AllocHGlobal(SECURITY_MAX_SID_SIZE);

// Create the SID.
SIDSize = SECURITY_MAX_SID_SIZE;
if (!CreateWellKnownSid(
  (WELL_KNOWN_SID_TYPE)cbSelect.SelectedIndex,
  IntPtr.Zero,
  GuestSID,
  ref SIDSize))
{
   // Get the last error.
   LastError = Marshal.GetLastWin32Error();

   // Display an error message
   // and exit if not successful.
   MessageBox.Show("Error creating the account SID." +
     "\r\nLast Error: " + LastError.ToString(),
     "Application Error",
     MessageBoxButtons.OK,
     MessageBoxIcon.Error);

   // Free the memory we allocated.
   Marshal.FreeHGlobal(GuestSID);

   // Exit the routine.
   return;
}

// Obtain the size of the Name and Domain strings.
NameSize = 0;
DomainSize = 0;
Use = SID_NAME_USE.SidTypeAlias;
LookupAccountSid(null,
                 GuestSID,
                 null,
                 ref NameSize,
                 null,
```

```
                            ref DomainSize,
                            ref Use);

    // Allocate memory for the strings.
    Name = new StringBuilder(NameSize);
    Domain = new StringBuilder(DomainSize);

    // Obtain the SID information.
    if (!LookupAccountSid(null,
                            GuestSID,
                            Name,
                            ref NameSize,
                            Domain,
                            ref DomainSize,
                            ref Use))
    {
        // Get the last error.
        LastError = Marshal.GetLastWin32Error();

        // Display an error message
        // and exit if not successful.
        MessageBox.Show(
            "Error obtaining the account SID data." +
            "\r\nLast Error: " + LastError.ToString(),
            "Application Error",
            MessageBoxButtons.OK,
            MessageBoxIcon.Error);
    }
    else
    {
        // Display the account information.
        MessageBox.Show("Obtained the SID Account Information" +
            "\r\nName: " + Name.ToString() +
            "\r\nDomain: " + Domain.ToString() +
            "\r\nUse: " + Use.ToString(),
            "Application Output",
            MessageBoxButtons.OK,
            MessageBoxIcon.Information);
    }

    // Free the memory we allocated.
    Marshal.FreeHGlobal(GuestSID);
}
```

Windows provides a wealth of well-known SIDs—predefined SIDs that every machine can use. The CreateWellKnownSid() function will create a SID for a well-known value such as the World. All you need to supply is an enumerated SID type, a pointer to a buffer to hold the SID, and the size of the SID buffer. The domain SID is optional. However, supplying this value will enable you to look up SIDs on other machines. There are 51 enumerated SID types to choose from and the example application lets you test them all. (Some of the well-known SIDs might not work on your machine if you don't have the required support installed.)

The LookupAccountSid() function accepts a SID as input. It doesn't matter where you get the SID as long as the SID is valid. If the call to this function fails, you can assume the SID was invalid—even if it's a well-known SID. In some cases, this function can tell you which operating system features are installed because some security accounts are only installed when you install the appropriate operating system feature. The LookupAccountSid() function returns the name and domain information for the SID along with the SID usage as indicated by the SID_NAME_USE enumeration.

One of the first tasks the code has to perform is allocating memory for the SID. In many cases, the code could allocate local memory as shown in the Platform SDK documentation. However, when working with a .NET application, it's best to use the Marshal.AllocHGlobal() function. This function returns an IntPtr to the allocated memory, which you must deallocate later using the Marshal.FreeHGlobal() function. The SECURITY_MAX_SID_SIZE constant defines the maximum size of the SID. This is yet another instance where you can convert a Visual C++ macro into a constant with the caveat that Microsoft could change the size of a SID at some later date. The alternative, in this case, is to write a small wrapper DLL to calculate the value for you. Using this technique is more expensive in development time, but it does protect you from future changes.

We've used a number of techniques for gaining access to error information. This example uses the Microsoft-recommended technique of setting the SetLastError argument of the [DllImport] attribute to True and then using the Marshal.GetLastWin32Error() function to return the error number. Note that the .NET Framework doesn't provide any means for converting this number into a human-readable form. You still need to use the Win32 API FormatMessage() function to perform the conversion.

Once the code obtains the desired SID, it uses the LookupAccountSid() function to determine the SID information. However, the code requires two calls to the LookupAccountSid() function to perform this task. The first call returns the size of the strings used to contain the account name and domain information. The code uses this information to allocate two StringBuilder variables. The second call returns the actual information. Figure 20.6 shows typical output from this example for the WinAnonymousSid enumerated value.

Application Output

Obtained the SID Account Information
Name: ANONYMOUS LOGON
Domain: NT AUTHORITY
Use: SidTypeWellKnownGroup

OK

FIGURE 20.6: The example application outputs the name, domain, and use for a well-known SID.

USING THE *GETFILESECURITY()* FUNCTION EXAMPLE

One of the problems that many developers have noted with the .NET Framework security is a lack of access to file (and other object) security information. For example, it's hard to tell who owns a file without using the Win32 API calls. That's where the GetFileSecurity() function comes into play. It enables you to retrieve file security information in the form of a security descriptor. From the theoretical discussion earlier in the chapter, you know that the security descriptor contains just about every piece of security information that Windows can supply. The example shown in Listing 20.2 shows how to obtain the owner identification for a file. However, the same techniques can help you obtain the SACL, DACL, and other security elements.

Listing 20.2: One Technique for Accessing File Security Information

```
// This function retrieves the
// security information for a file.
```

```csharp
[DllImport("AdvAPI32.DLL",
  CharSet=CharSet.Auto, SetLastError=true )]
public static extern bool GetFileSecurity(
    String lpFileName,
    SECURITY_INFORMATION RequestedInformation,
    IntPtr pSecurityDescriptor,
    Int32 nLength,
    ref Int32 lpnLengthNeeded);

// This enumeration tells what type
// of information we want to retrieve
// about the file's security.
public enum SECURITY_INFORMATION : uint
{
    OWNER_SECURITY_INFORMATION                 = 0x00000001,
    GROUP_SECURITY_INFORMATION                 = 0x00000002,
    DACL_SECURITY_INFORMATION                  = 0x00000004,
    SACL_SECURITY_INFORMATION                  = 0x00000008,
    PROTECTED_DACL_SECURITY_INFORMATION        = 0x80000000,
    PROTECTED_SACL_SECURITY_INFORMATION        = 0x40000000,
    UNPROTECTED_DACL_SECURITY_INFORMATION      = 0x20000000,
    UNPROTECTED_SACL_SECURITY_INFORMATION      = 0x10000000
};

// This function retrieves the security descriptor for the
// file owner.
[DllImport("AdvAPI32.DLL",
  CharSet=CharSet.Auto, SetLastError=true )]
public static extern bool GetSecurityDescriptorOwner(
    IntPtr pSecurityDescriptor,
    out IntPtr pOwner,
    ref Boolean lpbOwnerDefaulted);

private void btnTest_Click(
  object sender, System.EventArgs e)
{
    // File security information.
    IntPtr          SecurityDescriptor;

    // Security descriptor size.
    Int32           SDSize;
```

```csharp
// Required security desc. size.
Int32           SDSizeNeeded;

// Last Win32 API error.
int             LastError;

// SID of the owner account.
IntPtr          OwnerSID;

// Is this a defaulted account?
Boolean         IsDefault;

// Size of the account name.
Int32           NameSize;

// Size of the domain name.
Int32           DomainSize;

StringBuilder   Name;                   // Account name.
StringBuilder   Domain;                 // Domain name.
SID_NAME_USE    Use;                    // Account use.

// Determine the size of the security descriptor.
SecurityDescriptor = new IntPtr(0);
SDSizeNeeded = 0;
GetFileSecurity(@txtFile.Text,
   SECURITY_INFORMATION.OWNER_SECURITY_INFORMATION,
   SecurityDescriptor,
   0,
   ref SDSizeNeeded);

// Allocate the memory required for
// the security descriptor.
SecurityDescriptor = Marshal.AllocHGlobal(SDSizeNeeded);
SDSize = SDSizeNeeded;

// Get the security descriptor.
if (!GetFileSecurity(@txtFile.Text,
   SECURITY_INFORMATION.OWNER_SECURITY_INFORMATION,
   SecurityDescriptor,
   SDSize,
   ref SDSizeNeeded))
```

```
{
    // Get the last error.
    LastError = Marshal.GetLastWin32Error();

    // Display an error message and
    // exit if not successful.
    MessageBox.Show(
        "Error obtaining the security descriptor." +
        "\r\nLast Error: " + LastError.ToString(),
        "Application Error",
        MessageBoxButtons.OK,
        MessageBoxIcon.Error);

    // Free the memory we allocated.
    Marshal.FreeHGlobal(SecurityDescriptor);

    // Exit the routine.
    return;
}

// Obtain the owner SID for the file.
IsDefault = false;
if (!GetSecurityDescriptorOwner(SecurityDescriptor,
                                out OwnerSID,
                                ref IsDefault))
{
    // Get the last error.
    LastError = Marshal.GetLastWin32Error();

    // Display an error message and
    // exit if not successful.
    MessageBox.Show(
        "Error obtaining the owner SID." +
        "\r\nLast Error: " + LastError.ToString(),
        "Application Error",
        MessageBoxButtons.OK,
        MessageBoxIcon.Error);

    // Free the memory we allocated.
    Marshal.FreeHGlobal(SecurityDescriptor);

    // Exit the routine.
    return;
}
```

```
// Code to obtain the user information from
// the SID and some display
// code appears in this area.


}
```

The GetFileSecurity() function retrieves a security descriptor for the file requested by lpFileName. However, the function doesn't retrieve a complete security descriptor. It instead asks you to supply a SECURITY_ INFORMATION enumeration value that chooses one of several pieces of a standard security descriptor. This means that the call must match the data you want to work with later. Notice that the SECURITY_INFORMATION enumeration contains all of the elements we discussed in the theoretical portion of the chapter. You must also provide a buffer pointer and the buffer length. The GetFileSecurity() function returns the security descriptor that you requested and the amount of buffer space needed to store the information.

Remember that we discussed the fact that you should never work with the security descriptor directly, but instead use the Win32 API–supplied functions. The GetSecurityDescriptorOwner() function will retrieve owner information from a security descriptor if such information exists. There are also other functions, such as GetSecurityDescriptorDacl() and GetSecurityDescriptorGroup(), for retrieving other elements of the security descriptor. The GetSecurityDescriptorOwner() function accepts a security descriptor as input and returns a SID containing the owner information.

The code actually calls the GetFileSecurity() function twice. The first call is used to determine the size of the buffer needed to hold the security descriptor. The second call retrieves the security descriptor if the buffer is large enough to hold the data. Notice that this code uses the Marshal.AllocHGlobal() function to allocate the buffer for the Security Descriptor buffer.

Once the code obtains a security descriptor, it uses the GetSecurity-DescriptorOwner() function to retrieve the SID. Notice that this second function accepts the uninitialized OwnerSID as an out value. If you try to initialize OwnerSID and send it as we did for the GetFileSecurity() function, the function will fail with an invalid parameter error. The GetSecurityDescriptorOwner() function points out that you won't always interact with the Win32 API functions in the same way. Be prepared to send an initialized variable in one case and an uninitialized one in other cases. At this point, we have a SID and can use the

LookupAccountSid() function to retrieve the applicable information. Figure 20.7 shows the output from this example.

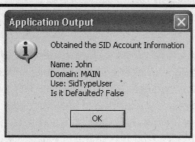

FIGURE 20.7:   The example application will tell you who owns a particular file on the hard drive.

WORKING WITH AN ACEs EXAMPLE

So far, we've looked at examples of how to work with the access token and the security descriptor and the vagaries of working with specific objects such as files. This example completes the tour of security support for the Win32 API by looking at the ACEs that make up the SACL and the DACL. Because you're most likely to work with the DACL, this example emphasizes access over auditing. However, working with the ACEs in either structure is about the same. Listing 20.3 shows how you'd access the ACEs for a file.

Listing 20.3: Gaining Access to the ACEs Means Reading the ACL

```
public const Int32 ERROR_SUCCESS = 0;

// This function uses the DACL to retrieve
// an array of explicit entries, each of which
// contains information about individual ACEs
// within the DACL.
[DllImport("AdvAPI32.DLL",
   CharSet=CharSet.Auto, SetLastError=true )]
public static extern Int32 GetExplicitEntriesFromAcl(
   IntPtr pacl,
   ref UInt32 pcCountOfExplicitEntries,
   out EXPLICIT_ACCESS []pListOfExplicitEntries);
```

```
// This data structure is used to
// create the explicit entry array.
[StructLayout(LayoutKind.Sequential, Pack=1)]
public struct EXPLICIT_ACCESS
{
    public UInt32        grfAccessPermissions;
    public ACCESS_MODE   grfAccessMode;
    public UInt32        grfInheritance;
    public TRUSTEE       Trustee;
}

// The ACCESS_MODE enumeration tells what type
// of ACE entry we're working with.
public enum ACCESS_MODE
{
    NOT_USED_ACCESS = 0,
    GRANT_ACCESS,
    SET_ACCESS,
    DENY_ACCESS,
    REVOKE_ACCESS,
    SET_AUDIT_SUCCESS,
    SET_AUDIT_FAILURE
}

// This structure contains the trustee
// information for the ACE.
[StructLayout(LayoutKind.Sequential, Pack=1)]
public struct TRUSTEE
{
    public IntPtr                     pMultipleTrustee;
    public MULTIPLE_TRUSTEE_OPERATION
      MultipleTrusteeOperation;
    public TRUSTEE_FORM               TrusteeForm;
    public TRUSTEE_TYPE               TrusteeType;
    public String                     ptstrName;
}

// The MULTIPLE_TRUSTEE_OPERATION
// enumeration determines if this is a single
// or a multiple trustee.
public enum MULTIPLE_TRUSTEE_OPERATION
{
```

```csharp
      NO_MULTIPLE_TRUSTEE,
      TRUSTEE_IS_IMPERSONATE,
}

// The TRUSTEE_FORM enumeration determines
// what form the ACE trustee takes.
public enum TRUSTEE_FORM
{
      TRUSTEE_IS_SID,
      TRUSTEE_IS_NAME,
      TRUSTEE_BAD_FORM,
      TRUSTEE_IS_OBJECTS_AND_SID,
      TRUSTEE_IS_OBJECTS_AND_NAME
}

// The TRUSTEE_TYPE enumeration determines
// the type of the trustee.
public enum TRUSTEE_TYPE
{
      TRUSTEE_IS_UNKNOWN,
      TRUSTEE_IS_USER,
      TRUSTEE_IS_GROUP,
      TRUSTEE_IS_DOMAIN,
      TRUSTEE_IS_ALIAS,
      TRUSTEE_IS_WELL_KNOWN_GROUP,
      TRUSTEE_IS_DELETED,
      TRUSTEE_IS_INVALID,
      TRUSTEE_IS_COMPUTER
}

// This function retrieves the DACL from the file's security
// descriptor.
[DllImport("AdvAPI32.DLL",
   CharSet=CharSet.Auto, SetLastError=true )]
public static extern bool GetSecurityDescriptorDacl(
      IntPtr pSecurityDescriptor,
      ref Boolean lpbDaclPresent,
      out IntPtr pDacl,
      ref Boolean lpbDaclDefaulted);

private void btnTest_Click(
   object sender, System.EventArgs e)
{
      Boolean             DACLPresent;    // Is the DACL present?
```

```
// Is the DACL defaulted?
Boolean          Defaulted;
IntPtr           DACL;          // Pointer to the DACL.
Int32            Result;        // Result of a call.

// Number of ACEs in DACL.
UInt32           ACECount;

// An array of ACE entries.
EXPLICIT_ACCESS  []ACEList;

// Obtain a security descriptor containing the DACL.
if (!GetFileSD(txtFile.Text,
   SECURITY_INFORMATION.DACL_SECURITY_INFORMATION))
   return;

// Obtain the DACL.
DACLPresent = false;
Defaulted = false;
if (!GetSecurityDescriptorDacl(SecurityDescriptor,
                               ref DACLPresent,
                               out DACL,
                               ref Defaulted))
{
   // Display an error message.
   MessageBox.Show("Unable to retrieve the DACL.",
                   "Application Error",
                   MessageBoxButtons.OK,
                   MessageBoxIcon.Error);

   // Free the memory we allocated.
   Marshal.FreeHGlobal(SecurityDescriptor);

   return;
}

// Make sure there is a DACL to display.
if (!DACLPresent)
{
   // If not, tell the user there is no DACL.
   MessageBox.Show("There is no DACL.",
                   "Processing Report",
                   MessageBoxButtons.OK,
                   MessageBoxIcon.Information);
```

```
        // Free the memory we allocated.
        Marshal.FreeHGlobal(SecurityDescriptor);

        return;
    }

    // Obtain the array of ACEs from the DACL.
    ACECount = 0;
    Result = GetExplicitEntriesFromAcl(DACL,
                                       ref ACECount,
                                       out ACEList);

    // Check the results.
    if (Result != ERROR_SUCCESS)
    {
        // Display an error message.
        MessageBox.Show("Unable to retrieve the ACEs.",
                        "Application Error",
                        MessageBoxButtons.OK,
                        MessageBoxIcon.Error);

        // Free the memory we allocated.
        Marshal.FreeHGlobal(SecurityDescriptor);

        return;
    }

    // Display the number of ACEs.
    MessageBox.Show("The file has " + ACECount.ToString() +
                    " ACEs attached to it.",
                    "Number of ACEs",
                    MessageBoxButtons.OK,
                    MessageBoxIcon.Information);

    // Free the memory we allocated.
    Marshal.FreeHGlobal(SecurityDescriptor);
}
```

The code begins with a simple define—a reminder that the various Win32 API functions return different values. In this case, the GetExplicit-EntriesFromAcl() function returns a value of ERROR_SUCCESS if successful or an error value if unsuccessful. You compare the return value with constants to determine the cause of error.

Notice that the GetExplicitEntriesFromAcl() function is also unique in that it's the only function so far that requires an array as input. You don't define a specific number of array elements—just the fact that the return value is an array. The call will still work in this case, whether you provide an IntPtr or a single EXPLICIT_ACCESS structure value. The difference is that you won't actually be able to use the return value if you don't use an array.

WARNING

Microsoft acknowledges problems with the various functions used to work with ACEs. For example, the GetExplicitEntriesFromAcl() function can return the incorrect number of ACEs in some cases. (See Microsoft Knowledge Base Article Q260307 for details.) The suggested alternatives of working with the GetAclInformation(), GetAce(), and LookupAccountSid() functions doesn't really replace the missing functionality, so you might need to get creative at times in using the Win32 API. Make sure you check for appropriate Microsoft Knowledge Base articles at http://search.support.microsoft.com/search/default.aspx when you run into problems with any of the Win32 API functions.

The EXPLICIT_ACCESS structure is relatively complex. It includes both an enumerated value and another structure, TRUSTEE. The other two values are flags, which means you have to go through the complicated comparison routine we've used in other examples to determine what the flag values mean.

While the TRUSTEE structure looks relatively simple, it can become complex because it also includes enumerated values that determine what each of the fields in the structure means. For example, the *ptstrName* variable has meaning only if the TRUSTEE_FORM enumeration value is TRUSTEE_IS_NAME. Matters are further complicated by hidden rules. The MULTIPLE_TRUSTEE_OPERATION should always equal NO_MULTIPLE_TRUSTEE because Microsoft hasn't implemented this feature yet, or at least its developers haven't documented it.

The GetSecurityDescriptorDacl() is another of the functions we talked about earlier for working with the security descriptor. Remember that you should never change the security descriptor directly because other applications might try to access it at the same time. This function has an odd return value until you consider that most parts of the security descriptor are optional. The *lpbDaclPresent* tells you if the DACL is present in the security descriptor. The call can succeed even if the security descriptor doesn't contain a DACL, so you need to know this additional information.

In general, the btnTest_Click() method doesn't contain too many surprises. Of course, the first major call is to GetSecurityDescriptorDacl() because the code has to check the security descriptor created with the GetFileSD() function for a DACL. If there's no DACL, the application hasn't actually experienced an error—it has simply found an unprotected file. Consequently, you need to handle the return as a type of legitimate return value. It simply might not be the return value you were expecting.

The next call is to GetExplicitEntriesFromAcl(). Theoretically, the *ACECount* variable could contain a 0 on return, so you should check it. Again, it's not an actual application error—the DACL could simply be empty. It's unlikely that you'll ever see this happen unless the GetExplicitEntriesFromAcl() function experiences some type of error (see the previous warning for details).

At this point, we're ready to test the code. Figure 20.8 shows that the example file contains four ACE entries. When you run the code, you'll find that it reports the same number.

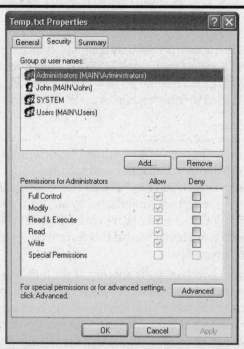

FIGURE 20.8:   The example application will output the number of ACEs associated with the test file, as shown here.

SUMMARY

This chapter has provided you with the tools you need to begin using the Win32 API token-based security calls in your code. The Win32 API is huge in this area, so we didn't cover every nuance of the security system. In addition, some tasks, such as encrypting and decrypting data, are better performed using the .NET Framework calls, so they aren't discussed at all here. However, you do know how to check the keys and locks used by the token-based security system, and that's the basis of most of the calls you'll need to make given the good security coverage provided by the .NET Framework.

You now have a decision to make. Which type of security is best for your application? It's an important question that you should answer before you write the first line of code for an application. Most security professionals know (and the crackers agree) that security has to be part of the application design, not added on at the last moment. This statement means that you need to consider what type of security to use now, not later. In some cases, you might want to combine the best elements of both role-based and token-based security to give your application an edge in an increasingly hostile application environment.

It's helpful to get as many opinions as possible when making security decisions. In many cases, security is a matter of perception—viewing things from the angle of the person who will attack your applications. The various examples in this chapter help you gain the insights needed to write great security for your application. Make sure you spend some time researching your topic and then trying out some example applications. For example, it's often helpful to build a token-based and a role-based version of the same application to see which type of security is easiest to use, fastest to develop, easiest to understand, and least likely to fail.

If you're interested in another security example, check out the Effective Rights example found in the \Extras\EffectiveRights folder on the book's page on the Sybex website. This short example demonstrates how to determine the effective rights of a specific individual or group. The example is helpful in that it suggests how you might check the credentials of a user in any application.

WHAT'S NEXT

Chapter 21 shows you how to develop mobile applications using the Microsoft Mobile Internet Toolkit.

Chapter 21

GETTING STARTED WITH THE MOBILE INTERNET TOOLKIT

This chapter introduces the basics of setting up and working with the Microsoft Mobile Internet Toolkit. By the end of the chapter, you should understand how to install and run the Mobile Internet Designer in Visual Studio. We will also create some introductory applications in the C# language and view them in our emulators.

Adapted from *.NET Wireless Programming*
by Mark Ridgeway
ISBN 0-7821-2975-7

CHECKING SYSTEM REQUIREMENTS

The system requirements for the Mobile Internet Toolkit are the same as those required for Visual Studio .NET. To run the Mobile Internet Designer (the Visual Studio component of the Mobile Internet Toolkit), you will need to run one of the following operating systems:

- ▶ Windows 2000 Professional SP2

- ▶ Windows 2000 Server SP2

- ▶ Windows 2000 Advanced Server SP2

- ▶ Windows XP

- ▶ Windows NT 4.0 Workstation (supported only for client-side development) SP6

Your computer will also need to run IIS 5.0 and Internet Explorer 6.0. Hardware requirements for Visual Studio .NET include the following:

- ▶ Minimum 450MHz Pentium II processor—anything less and it runs agonizingly slow

- ▶ Minimum 64MB RAM (128MB is *a lot* better)

- ▶ 3GB of available hard drive space (Microsoft recommendation)

- ▶ Microsoft specifies a CD-ROM (and, presumably, a monitor, keyboard, and mouse!)

Once installed, the Mobile Internet Toolkit will only take up an additional 2.5MB of hard drive space. You will also need to obtain a range of mobile emulators such as contained in the Openwave or Nokia SDKs.

INTRODUCING THE MICROSOFT MOBILE INTERNET TOOLKIT

The Microsoft Mobile Internet Toolkit is a variation of ASP.NET that has been both customized and optimized for mobile web applications. The Mobile Web Forms Designer, which provides developers with a graphical interface for building applications, is included in Microsoft Visual Studio .NET. However, developers who prefer a slightly more intrepid approach to their projects are still able to lovingly handcraft their code with only a text editor and command-line compiler as accompaniment.

I will assume that you are expecting to use Visual Studio .NET and have a copy loaded and functioning correctly upon your computer. You may also have some experience with working with ASP.NET to create web applications. If so, you will find building .NET mobile applications a very similar experience. See Figure 21.1 for a look at the Visual Studio .NET Mobile Web Forms Designer.

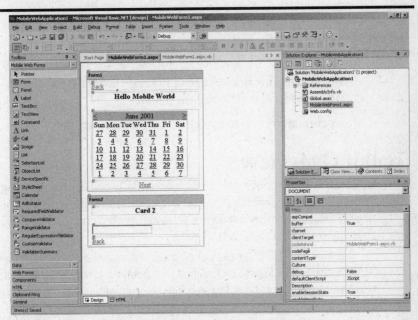

FIGURE 21.1:   Visual Studio .NET Mobile Web Forms Designer

Obtaining the Toolkit

The kit may be downloaded from the Microsoft download site at `http://msdn.microsoft.com/downloads`. The file is approximately 4.0MB and can be found in the Software Development Kit section. If the toolkit has been included with your copy of Visual Studio .NET, then open up Windows Explorer and navigate to Program Files ➤ Microsoft Visual Studio .NET ➤ Visual Studio SDKs ➤ Mobile Internet Toolkit. Installation involves double-clicking the `MobileIT.msi` file and following the prompts.

Toolkit Contents

The Microsoft Mobile Internet Toolkit contains the following:

Mobile Internet controls runtime   A set of controls that can be dropped onto a Mobile Web Form to generate appropriate content for the specific device accessing them.

Mobile Internet Designer   Development interface that integrates into Visual Studio .NET for building mobile applications.

Device capabilities   For mobile devices.

Device adaptor code   Code that enables support for new devices to be added through the extensibility model.

QuickStart tutorial   A useful tutorial provided by Microsoft that introduces how to use the toolkit.

Documentation   Language and technical reference.

Toolkit Overview

Building a .NET mobile application essentially consists of creating a Mobile Web Form, which is in fact a specialized ASP.NET Web Form page. This is a text file saved with the .aspx extension (and can be just as easily written in Notepad).

Note that ASP.NET should not be confused with the more traditional ASP (Active Server Pages) technology that many of us would be familiar with when using Microsoft products to build dynamic web pages. ASP uses the .asp extension and is very different from the newer ASP.NET. Although ASP pages cannot easily be directly converted (generally speaking) to ASP.NET, the two technologies can coexist on the same server and run side by side.

NOTE

Be aware that some key differences, such as difficulties using page-level tracing to debug mobile applications, exist between ASP.NET and Mobile Web Forms.

Using the Mobile Web Forms Designer, various mobile controls can be dragged onto this form. These controls are capable of exposing a device-independent object model containing properties, methods, and events. Double-clicking the controls in the design phase gives access to the code behind the form, which can be used to add additional functionality to the controls and to the application. This code is eventually compiled and stored in a bin directory, which is normally in the same directory as the Mobile Forms we create. We will be mainly using VB .NET for our "code behind." Figure 21.2 illustrates a directory listing for a simple Mobile application. The `Mobile.aspx` file is the Mobile Web Form, and the compiled code for the controls on this form is stored in the bin directory.

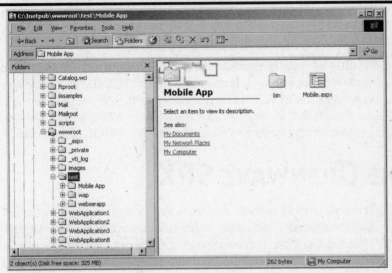

FIGURE 21.2:   Sample directory

We can also take a more distributed approach to our applications and make use of XML Web Services to provide additional functionality. These XML Web Services may be located on our own machine, the local network, or elsewhere on the Internet. We will be looking later at how to create a simple Web Service and make use of it from our mobile (or, for that matter, non-mobile) applications.

We can also use COM objects to provide access to code in a slightly less public manner than XML Web Services. These have been traditionally used in ASP programming to separate the so-called business logic from the presentation layer in a web-based application. ASP pages tended to mix the business of building the web page in with the code that carried out whatever functionality the application required. Separating this functionality out and compiling it as a COM object in its own right offered advantages across the board in terms of performance, security, reusability, upgrade ability, and general reliability. The same applies to our mobile applications.

As stated earlier, a Mobile Web Form Page may contain multiple forms, an approach that mimics the card and deck design that is popular with many mobile development platforms. The Mobile Web Form Page is a more limited design vehicle than the Web Form environment included in Visual Studio .NET. Controls can only be added one at a time down the form; the designer doesn't have the luxury of placing the control exactly where he or she expects it to appear in the live application. The order of controls on the form can also be important—for example, we will see later in this chapter how the placement of links and their order in relation to other controls determines whether they will be rendered as a list of HREFs or as Option Onpicks in the final application.

Although multiple forms and Mobile Web Pages can be used to mimic the card and deck approach favored in WAP and HDML, this design approach is not an exact fit. ASP.NET delivers each form, one at a time, to the client on request, not all together as a collection of forms from the one page as happens with a collection of cards on a single WML page or deck.

The Openwave SDK

It is best to use a range of devices to test your mobile applications. The Mobile Internet Toolkit adaptively renders an application to match the particular device that is accessing your application; however this can produce some unexpected results due to the range and variety of devices and technologies available. The wide range of devices and protocols in use means that it is not very practical to try and obtain a version of every device likely to access your application. To a certain extent, you can circumvent this by using the freely available emulators that most manufacturers provide for the purpose of development and testing. These can normally be obtained from the relevant websites.

One of the most popular emulators is provided by Openwave as part of their Software Development Kit. Along with the Nokia kit, this forms the minimum range of kits with which most developers test. Openwave- and Nokia-derived browsers are used by a large variety of cell phone manufacturers for Internet access.

For the purposes of this chapter, we will work with the Openwave emulator, which is part of the OpenWave SDK (see Figure 21.3). The full SDK can be obtained from the Openwave site at http://www.openwave.com. You will need to select the link to the Openwave Developer Site. The SDK itself is approximately a 16MB download.

You can also view your mobile pages directly in Visual Studio .NET by choosing the View In Browser option from the File menu as shown in Figure 21.4.

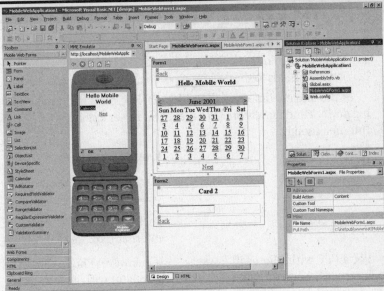

Image of Openwave SDK courtesy Openwave Systems, Inc.

FIGURE 21.3:   The Openwave SDK

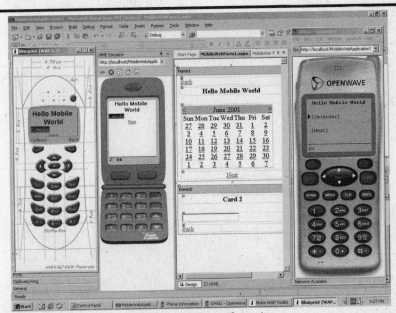

Image of UP.SDK courtesy Openwave Systems, Inc.

FIGURE 21.4:   Viewing a Mobile Web Site in Visual Studio .NET

SUPPORTED DEVICES

As new devices appear on the market, support will be made available in the toolkit on an ongoing basis. It is also possible for the developer to create his or her own extensions to the device support base within individual applications.

At the original time of writing (Beta 2), Microsoft had tested the following devices and emulators (to a greater or lesser extent) with the Mobile Internet Toolkit:

Devices	Emulators
Mitsubishi T250	Microsoft Mobile Explorer version 2.01
Nokia 7110	Pocket PC with Microsoft Pocket Internet Explorer version 4.0
Pocket PC with Microsoft Pocket Internet Explorer version 4.5	(Openwave) Phone.com UP.SDK 4.1 emulator with generic skin
Ericsson R380	(Openwave) Phone.com UP.SDK 3.2 for WML emulator with Mitsubishi T250 skin
Microsoft Internet Explorer 5.5	DoCoMo 502
Microsoft Internet Explorer 6.0	
NEC N502I	
Nokia 6210	
Palm VIIx	
Palm V	
Panasonic P502i	
RIM Blackberry 950	
RIM Blackberry 957	
Samsung 850	
Siemens S-35i	
Sprint Touchpoint phone	

This list had grown considerably by the time that the RC version of the Mobile Internet Toolkit was released. It's also worth noting that individual devices may still require some extra code massaging to render your applications correctly. Keep an eye on the Microsoft documentation for any identified problems and suggested fixes.

TIP

Microsoft recommends that, where possible, device displays should be set fit-to-screen when viewing pages rendered by the toolkit.

GETTING STARTED

Let's start with a Microsoft Mobile Internet Toolkit version of a "Hello World" type application. Open up Visual Studio .NET and click the New Project option. See Figure 21.5.

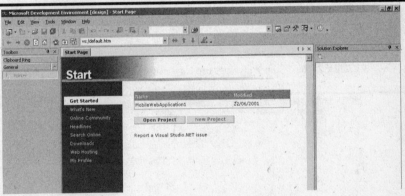

FIGURE 21.5:   Step 1 of creating a mobile web application

In the New Project dialog box, choose Visual C# Projects from the Project Type options and Mobile Web Application from the Templates options. As the name that you give the application becomes its URL, it is a good idea to choose a name other than the default MobileWeb-ApplicationN. We will call this project MobileWebApplicationCSharp1. If you wish to save your project to a location other than the default, now is the time to choose it (see Figure 21.6). I usually tend to stick with the default, particularly for small projects; I always know where to find them, and I don't have to get into any unnecessary arguments with Visual Studio .NET about where they should be!

If all went according to plan, your screen should look something like Figure 21.7. You may need to add or remove some windows with the View menu and resize others. As there is not much actual layout design involved with the toolkit and the controls are simply placed one after the other down the Mobile Web Form, I tend to keep this area fairly narrow—only as wide as the controls.

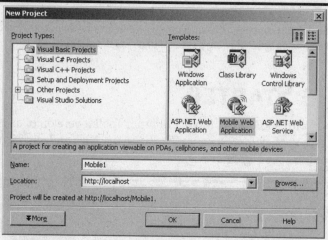

FIGURE 21.6: Step 2 involves the New Project dialog box.

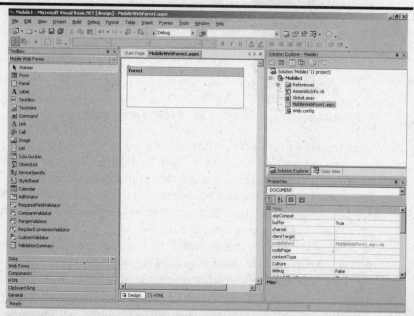

FIGURE 21.7: Step 3 involves the Mobile Web Form Designer with Toolbox, Solution Explorer, and the Properties window.

The window on the left contains the Toolbox, which includes the traditional runtime controls that we can drag and drop to our forms and some additional features such as the Clipboard Ring, which are described in the next section on the Toolbox. The middle window contains the Mobile Web Forms Designer where we define our Mobile Web Forms, add controls, and do all (well, most) of our coding. The window on the right contains the Solution Explorer, which lists the various components of our application, and the Properties window where we can define many of the properties that apply to the particular controls we are using.

The Toolbox

The Toolbox contains the runtime controls available with the toolkit. Many of these controls would be very familiar to anyone used to working with Microsoft development environments. Some controls (such as PhoneCall and DeviceSpecific) are unique to the Mobile Internet Toolkit, while others are either quite different when used as mobile controls or have experienced some changes under the shift to .NET. An example of this is the Label control, which now has a Text property in line with the TextBox control rather than the Caption property found in earlier versions of VB.

To use a control from the Toolbox, select the control and drag it to the MobileWebForm. This is a slightly different process from those used to earlier incarnations of Microsoft's IDE.

WARNING

You have to be a little careful as well that you don't accidentally click into the Web Forms controls in the Toolbox and try and start dropping non-mobile components onto your forms. A warning message will occur, but it can be a little disconcerting the first time it happens.

Data controls are grouped under the Data section of the Toolbox. It is also worth browsing the controls available under the HTML and Web Forms categories (not that we are really likely to use them for our mobile applications).

Another useful addition to the Toolbox is the Clipboard Ring, which can be used to store multiple code snippets as you work. Simply highlight what you wish to copy, drag it to the Clipboard Ring; and when you wish to reuse it, drag it from the ring back to your code. If you wish to remove it from the ring, right-click the reference and choose Delete.

The Mobile Web Form Designer

The central window contains the Mobile Web Form Designer. A new project opens by default with a single form on the Mobile Web Page and in the Design View. You can generate the card and deck approach by creating more forms on the Mobile Web Page. Controls are created on the form by clicking and dragging from the Toolbox. As mentioned earlier, controls are placed sequentially down the form and cannot be resized or located in specific parts of the form as can occur with Web Forms. To illustrate this, Figure 21.8 shows two forms with a succession of Label controls added to Form 1 and a number of Command Button controls added to Form 2.

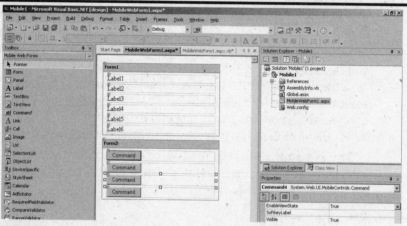

FIGURE 21.8:   Example of two forms with multiple controls

To get back to our project, drag a (single) Label control to Form 1. Double-click the control or the form itself to show the code behind. This is where we get to work with our Visual Basic (although not in this example). Above the Class and Method windows at the top of the Code Behind window, you will see a set of tabs. Choosing the MobileWebForm1.aspx tab will take us back to the Design View. Alternatively, we could click the View Designer button in the traditional View Object position at the top of the Solution Explorer window. We can return to the code by choosing the MobileWebForm1.aspx.cs* tab, double-clicking the form or controls, or clicking the View Code button next to the View Designer button. Well, we cannot say that Microsoft doesn't give us lots of options!

The other aspect of the form we need to consider is the code of the actual ASPX page itself. This is what we would be writing if we were building this project using Notepad rather than the Mobile Web Forms Designer.

Right-click the form in Design View and choose the View HTML Source option. The result is seen in Figure 21.9. We can edit this code directly from here if we wish, right-click and select View Design, or click the Design tab in the bottom left corner of the window to return to Design View. (Clicking the HTML tab will take us back to the ASPX code.) Note that the view in Figure 21.9 has Word Wrap activated from the Advanced option in the Edit menu.

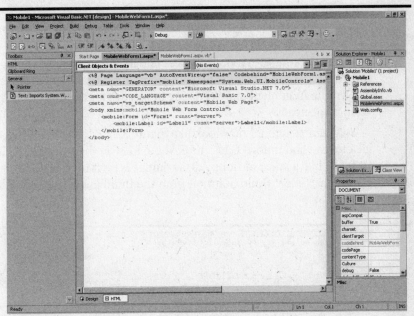

FIGURE 21.9:   HTML View of our ASPX page

The Properties Window

The Properties window is little changed except in appearance from what most Microsoft developers have become used to over the years. Its default organization is now Categories rather than Alphabetical, and it still seems to need more screen space than it actually gets.

Clicking the Label control in our Design window will bring up the properties for Label in the Properties window. Note that a number of properties carry a Not Set tag as their default value. This setting leaves the exact rendering of the control up to the individual device. In the case of our label, set the following properties in Table 21.1.

TABLE 21.1:   Property Settings for Label Control

PROPERTY	VALUE
Alignment	Left
Text	Hi There
Wrapping	Wrap
StyleReference	Title

When working with mobile devices and in doubt about wrapping, be sure to wrap! Click somewhere on the form other than the Label control and set the Alignment and Wrapping properties for the form to Left and Wrap respectively.

Your screen should now look like Figure 21.10. It's probably a good idea to save about now! Click the Save All icon on the standard toolbar. (It looks like a stack of floppy disks, and it is next to the traditional Save icon.) Select Build Solution from the Build menu to compile the application.

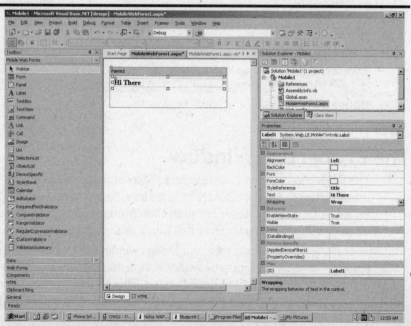

FIGURE 21.10:   Hello World application in Design View

Testing the Application with the Emulators

Now, we'll view our application in the Openwave emulator. Choose the Openwave emulator by opening Openwave SDK Wap, Edition ➤ Openwave SDK, Wap Edition from the Start ➤ Programs menu, and type `http://localhost/MobelWebApplicationCSharp1/MobileWebForm1.aspx` into the Address window and then press Enter (see Figure 21.11).

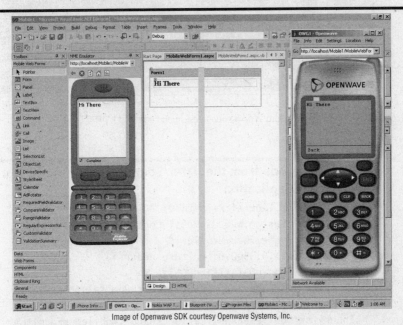

Image of Openwave SDK courtesy Openwave Systems, Inc.

FIGURE 21.11: Hello World application displayed in the Openwave emulator

Take a look at the HTTP Response window in the Openwave SDK. This will display the source code as received by the Openwave emulator (see Figure 21.12). If you are familiar with WML, you will see that it is the standard markup code for this type of application.

Return to the Visual Studio .NET IDE and right-click the form in Design View and choose View HTML Source. Have a look at the tags for the Form and Label controls within the Body section of the code. I have reproduced this code in Listing 21.1. Note that the C#-specific code discussed here in Chapter 21 is available for download from this Complete book's page at the Sybex website. The properties that we have defined for these controls are now specified within these tags. These properties can be edited directly in this window, and indeed, some properties that we will need to specify for our applications later on will have to be done here.

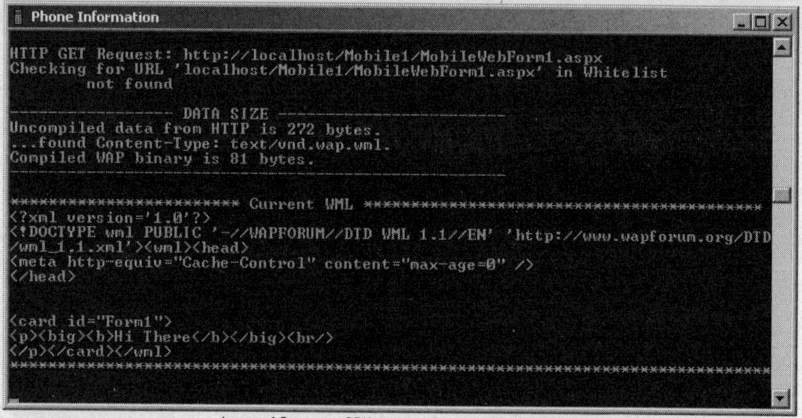

Image of Openwave SDK courtesy Openwave Systems, Inc.

FIGURE 21.12:   Hello World source code as received by the Openwave emulator

Listing 21.1: Code from the HTML Source View for Hello World Application

```
<%@ Register TagPrefix="mobile"
Namespace="System.Web.UI.MobileControls"
Assembly="System.Web.Mobile,
     Version=1.0.3300.0, Culture=neutral,
PublicKeyToken=b03f5f7f11d50a3a" %>
<%@ Page Language="c#" AutoEventWireup="false"
Codebehind="MobileWebForm1.aspx.cs"
Inherits="MobileWebApplicationCSharp1.MobileWebForm1" %>
<meta name="GENERATOR"
   content="Microsoft Visual Studio 7.0">
<meta name="CODE_LANGUAGE" content="C#">
<meta name="vs_targetSchema"
content="http://schemas.microsoft.com/Mobile/Page">
<body Xmlns:mobile=
   "http://schemas.microsoft.com/Mobile/WebForm">
   <mobile:Form id="Form1" runat="server" Wrapping="Wrap"
Alignment="Left">
     <mobile:Label id="Label1"
       runat="server" Wrapping="Wrap"
   Alignment="Left" StyleReference="title">
       Hi There
     </mobile:Label>
```

```
    </mobile:Form>
  </body>
```

It is also worth noting that the runat attributes for these control tags are normally set to Server.

BUILDING A SIMPLE TWO-CARD DECK

For our next introductory application, we will build a simple two-card deck and use it to illustrate both navigation between cards and the importance of the order of control placement in the Mobile Internet Toolkit.

Create a new mobile project (called MobileWebApplicationCSharp2) using Visual C#. Create a second form in the designer and add Label and Link controls as depicted in Figure 21.13.

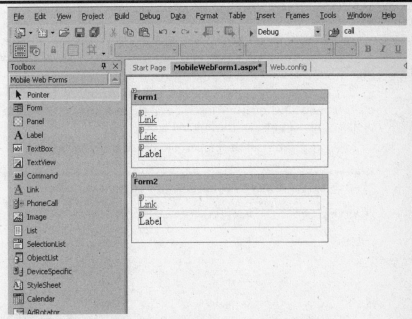

FIGURE 21.13:   Control layout for the "Simple Two-Card Deck" project

For the controls in Form1 set the following properties listed in Table 21.2.

TABLE 21.2: Property Settings for the Controls in Form1

CONTROL	PROPERTY	VALUE
Link1	Text	A Link to Somewhere
	SoftKeyLabel	\<empty\>
	Visible	True
	NavigateURL	\<empty\>
Link2	Text	Next Card
	SoftKeyLabel	\<empty\>
	Visible	True
	NavigateURL	#Form2
Label1	Alignment	Center
	StyleReference	Title
	Text	Simple Deck

By placing Link1 and Link2 above Label1 on the form, we ensure that Link1 and Link2 are rendered as HREFs rather than Option Onpicks in the Openwave browser.

Link1 is a dummy link for the purpose of the example. Later on we will make it more functional and insert a real address into the NavigateURL property. Link2 provides the link to Form2.

To set up Form2, set the property values as in Table 21.3.

TABLE 21.3: Property Settings for the Controls in Form2

CONTROL	PROPERTY	VALUE
Link3	Text	Back
	SoftKeyLabel	\<empty\>
	Visible	False
	NavigateURL	#Form1
Label2	Text	Card 2

In this Form, we have kept Link3 inactive for the moment by setting its Visible property to False, but it will eventually act as a Back softkey.

Select Build Solution from the Build menu and open the Openwave emulator. Type in the following URL:

```
http://localhost/MobileWebApplicationCSharp2/MobileWebForm1.aspx
```

Your two cards should appear as in Figure 21.14. Notice that in Form2 a Back softkey appears at the bottom of the screen.

Image of Openwave SDK courtesy Openwave Systems, Inc.

FIGURE 21.14:   The simple two-card deck as it appears in the Openwave emulator

Let's play a little further with our links in the application. Move the two links below the Label control on Form1, save everything, and refresh the Openwave emulator by clicking in the Address field and pressing the Enter key (or by simply pressing F5). The Openwave emulator should now show its links as Option Onpicks. See Figure 21.15 for the code and Figure 21.16 for the screenshot of the browser.

In the Openwave emulator, Option Onpicks are far nicer than simple HREFs. However, they are not always the best way to go, and to give the user a Back option, we have to include it as one of the URL choices. They can also be fiddly in the Nokia environment, although, thankfully, it doesn't appear as if the Mobile Internet Toolkit generates them for Nokia.

Image of UP.SDK courtesy Openwave Systems, Inc.

FIGURE 21.15:   WML generated for Openwave emulator showing links as Option Onpicks

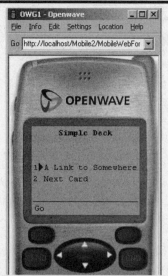

Image of Openwave SDK courtesy Openwave Systems, Inc.

FIGURE 21.16:   Screenshot showing the Openwave emulator with Option Onpicks

NOTE

Note that the Nokia has by default a Back right softkey. Our current setup with Card 2 (once the link is made active by setting the Visible property to True) contains the slightly absurd situation of the Nokia of having both right and left softkeys labeled as Back.

Return to the design environment, and select the properties for Link3 on Form2. Change the Text property from Back to Card 1, the SoftKey-Label to Back, and the Visible property to True. Save and refresh the Openwave browser (by pressing F5).

Click through to Card 2. Link 3 should now appear in the window as [Card 1]. Highlight the link to give the left softkey the label of Back that we entered into the links properties.

In Visual Studio, delete the SoftKeyLabel property for Link3, save, and return to the Openwave browser. Refresh and use the up and down arrows on the browser to deselect the link. It should now show the softkey label as simply Link.

Delete the link entirely. Save and refresh the browser. We now have the default Back softkey in the bottom left of the screen. The Nokia device (if you are using it) has only its single default Back softkey.

This might seem all rather trivial, but it demonstrates that even at this fairly basic level, there are differences in how our applications are going to present. It's worth knowing what they are in advance, and it's worth testing as much as possible to ensure that what we are building isn't going to come back to bite us in some horrible fashion in the near future. Of particular interest is that, by virtue of their placement on the form, the relative positions of the links determine whether the Openwave emulator uses HREFs or Option Onpicks to render its links.

USING CODE BEHIND

In this project we will build a simple application that illustrates the use of the code-behind feature in designing mobile applications with the Mobile Internet Toolkit.

Create a new project and name it MobileWebApplicationCSharp3. Drag a Label and Command control onto the form in Design View (see Figure 21.17).

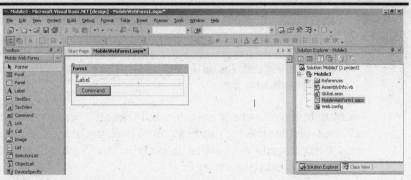

FIGURE 21.17:   Control layout for the "Simple Code Behind" project

Set the text property of the label (Label1) to Hi There! and the text property of the command button (Command1) to Click Me. Double-click the command button to enter the code behind. Add the code in Listing 21.2 to the subroutine.

Listing 21.2: Code for the *Command1_Click* subroutine in the Simple Code Behind Project

```
private void Command1_Click(
    object sender, System.EventArgs e)
        {
        Label1.Text=("Hi Mobile World!");
        }
```

This is a straightforward and very typical "Hello World" style application that sets the Text property of Label1 in response to the Click event of Command1.

TIP

Don't forget to compile your code before we leave this screen. Click the Build command under the Build menu. This is important because code behind requires a design time compile for it to be available to the project. The ASPX code can be simply saved because it is not compiled until runtime.

An Output window will appear in the bottom of your screen displaying the progress and eventual success (or otherwise!) of your build (see Figure 21.18).

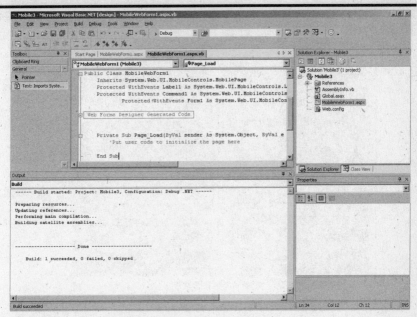

FIGURE 21.18:   Visual Studio .NET showing the Output window after a successful build

Close the Ouput window to recover some screen space, and click back to the Design View of your form (using either the View Designer button on the Solution Explorer or the `MobileWebForm1.aspx` tab at the top of the Mobile Web Page).

Save the project and open it in Internet Explorer using the URL `http://localhost/MobileWebApplicationCSharp3/MobileWebForm1.aspx`. Click the Command button to change the text message from Hi There to Hi Mobile World. See Figure 21.19 for the expected output as displayed in Internet Explorer.

Finally, it is worth noting that we could also have built this simple application using similar code but only using the HTML View window.

Open a new project as `MobileWebApplicationCSharp4` and re-create the form, the label, and the command button from `MobileWebApplicationCSharp3`. Open the Mobile Web Form in HTML View and add the code from Listing 21.3.

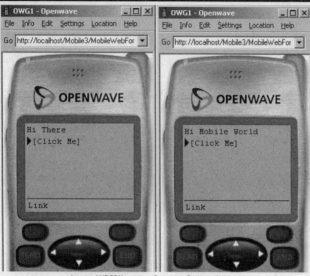

Image of UP.SDK courtesy Openwave Systems, Inc.

FIGURE 21.19: Expected output for the "Simple Code Behind" project

Listing 21.3: HTML Code for Simple Code Behind Project Running Only as an ASPX Page

```
<%@ Register TagPrefix="mobile"
Namespace="System.Web.UI.MobileControls"
Assembly="System.Web.Mobile,
        Version=1.0.3300.0, Culture=neutral,
PublicKeyToken=b03f5f7f11d50a3a" %>
<%@ Page Language="c#" AutoEventWireup="false"
Codebehind="MobileWebForm1.aspx.cs"
Inherits="MobileWebApplicationCSharp4.MobileWebForm1" %>
<meta name="GENERATOR"
  content="Microsoft Visual Studio 7.0">
<meta name="CODE_LANGUAGE" content="C#">
<meta name="vs_targetSchema"
content="http://schemas.microsoft.com/Mobile/Page">

<script runat="server" language="C#">
   protected void Command1_Click(
     Object sender, EventArgs e)
   {
      Label1.Text=("Hi Mobile World!");
```

```
    }
</script>

<body Xmlns:mobile=
    "http://schemas.microsoft.com/Mobile/WebForm">

    <mobile:Form id="Form1" runat="server">
        <mobile:Label id="Label1" runat="server">Hi
There</mobile:Label>
        <mobile:Command id="Command1" runat="server"
OnClick=" Command1_Click ">Click Me</mobile:Command>
    </mobile:Form>
</body>
```

The main difference here is the addition of the following script, which contains the code we previously used in the code behind:

```
<script runat="server" language="C#">
    protected void Command1_Click(
        Object sender, EventArgs e)
    {
        Label1.Text=("Hi Mobile World!");
    }
</script>
```

Save the project and open it using Internet Explorer. The output should be identical to that of `MobileWebApplicationCSharp3`.

SUMMARY

Although the Mobile Internet Toolkit offers clear advantages for developers, we still need to be aware of the variations introduced by the range of client devices and configurations available. We need to remember to test our applications in as many configurations as possible and be conscious that even simple applications may give unexpected results when rendered across different devices.

Despite this, the Mobile Internet Toolkit offers a fast and effective method to develop mobile applications. The Mobile Designer, coupled with Visual Studio .NET, is easy to use and can be configured to give instant feedback on the progress of a development using emulators and SDKs such as the Openwave SDK. Other emulators and devices can run in conjunction with the toolkit and can also be used for ongoing testing.

The real test for an application is an "in the wild" test on a real phone. This is relatively easy to do if your mobile phone is already set up for WAP and your computer has a dial-up or direct line to the Internet. (Those of us developing behind secure corporate firewalls need not apply!) Connect your computer to the Internet and identify its IP address. If you have a dial-up connection, type **ipconfig** in a command window (Start ➤ Run, then type **cmd**) for Windows NT and 2000 machines. From your WAP phone, access your application URL using your IP address as the first part of the URL (for example, `http://255.255.255.1/mobile3/Mobile-WebForm1.aspx`). Yes, I know it's tedious, but think of the adventure!

Finally, be aware that there are some options when developing mobile sites with the Toolkit. For smaller applications and when performance is less of an issue, it may make more sense to code everything directly onto the ASPX page, rather than using the code-behind environment.

INDEX

Note to the reader: Throughout this index **boldfaced** page numbers indicate primary discussions of a topic. *Italicized* page numbers indicate illustrations.

Symbols & Numbers

− (decrement operator), 51

& (ampersand)

    in C# unsafe code, 857

    for underlined menu characters, 407

!= (not equal to operator), overloading, 259

#INCLUDE directive, 820

% (percent) as wildcard, 631

* (manual pointer), in C# unsafe code, 857

. (period; dot operator), 6

    for .NET Framework hierarchy, 309

    to access object fields and methods, 155–156

/* and */ for comments, 4, 48

// (forward slashes), for comments, 4, 5, 48

/// (slashes), for XML documentation, 50

: (colon), for derived classes, 217, 246

?: (conditional operator), 52, 53

" (quotation marks), for string literal, 35

@Register directive, 818

+ (addition operator), overloading, 258, **260–262**

    to concatenate strings, 83

++ (increment operator), 51, 53

= (assignment operator), overloading, to copy strings, 84

== (equal to operator)

    overloading, 257–258, **258–259**

    to test for equal strings, 84–85

A

Abort() method, of Thread class, 445

absolute security descriptor, 872

absolute value of time span, **143**

abstract classes and methods, **245–248**

abstract keyword, 245

accelerators, for desktop applications, **405–408**, *409*

AcceptChanges() method

    of DataRow object, 605

    of DataSet object, 547

    of DataTable object, 603

AcceptChangesDuringFill property, of SqlDataAdapter class, 540

Access Control Editor, *883*, **883–885**

    advanced features, *884*

Access Control Entries (ACEs), 873

    example, **902–908**

    header types, 873–874

    order of, 876–877

Access Control Lists (ACLs), **873–874**

access modifiers, **192–197**

    and derived classes, **226–229**

access permissions, for virtual directory, 695

access tokens, **869–871**

accessibility features, for desktop applications, **408–410**

AccessibleDescription property, of controls, 409

AccessibleName property, of controls, 409

AccessibleRole property, of controls, 409

account lockout policy, 887

Account Policies, for security setup, 887

accounts, looking up well-known, **892–897**

ACEs (Access Control Entries), 873

    example, **902–908**

    header types, 873–874

    order of, 876–877

ACLs (Access Control Lists), **873–874**

Action property, of DataRowChangeEventArgs class, 677

Active Directory objects, security setup, 888

ActiveX controls, 799

ActiveX Data Objects (ADO), vs. ADO.NET, **496–499**

Add() method

of CheckedListBox control, 348–349

of DateTime object, 117, **123–124**

for foreign key, 615

for key constraint for DataTable, 612

of TimeSpan object, 138, **142–143**

Add New Item dialog box, *378*, 378

for DataSet, *585*

Add New Item - DLL Thread dialog box, *457*

Add New Item - Resource dialog box, *410*

Add Reference dialog box, *308*, 308–309, 336, 403, *404*

Add Web Reference dialog box, 795–796, *796*

AddDays() method of DateTime object, 117, 124–125

AddEllipse() method, of GraphicsPath object, 342

AddHours() method of DateTime object, 117, 124–125

addition operator (+), overloading, 258, **260–262**

to concatenate strings, 83

AddMilliseconds() method of DateTime object, 117

AddMinutes() method of DateTime object, 117, 124–125

AddMonths() method of DateTime object, 117, 124–125

AddRange method

of Items collection, 349

of MenuItems collection, 364

AddSeconds() method of DateTime object, 117

AddTicks() method of DateTime object, 117

AddYears() method of DateTime object, 117, 124–125

AdjustTokenGroups function, 877

AdjustTokenPrivileges function, 877

ADO.NET

vs. ActiveX Data Objects (ADO), **496–499**

classes, 475. *See also* generic data classes; managed provider classes

DataReader application development, **500–511**

adding code, **502–507**

creating shell, **500–501**

testing using NUnit, **507–511**

Dataset application, **513–529**

adding and removing records, **516–519**

coding Detail view, **525–529**

coding grid view, **513–514**

copy, cut and paste, **519–525**

cursor movement on screen, **514–516**

printing, **527–529**

development tools, **511–512**

importing and exporting XML example, **529–533**

writing code, **529–531**

OleDbDataAdapter class for data transfer, **499–500**

StringBuilder for performance improvement, **534–537**

Alchemy Mind Works, GIF Construction Set, 422

alias

in SQL, AS keyword for, 580

virtual directory as, 693–694

alias directive, 310–311

alignment of strings, **90–91**

AllocateAndInitializeSid function, 880

AllocateLocallyUniqueId function, 877

AllocHGlobal() function of Marshal class, 896

AllowDBNull property, of DataColumn object, 606, 608, 622

AllowFullOpen property, of ColorDialog control, 371

allowOverride attribute, for <location> tag, 722–725

Alphora, Dataphor, 512

ampersand (&)
  in C# unsafe code, 857
  for underlined menu characters, 407
Analyzer (FMS), 512
Anchor property, of child form, 378
AND operator, short-circuit evaluation, **53–54**
animated GIF files, 422–426
animating controls, **345–348**
animation, 421–422
Animator object, Bitmap object combined with, 422–425
AnyColor property, of ColorDialog control, 371
Append() method of StringBuilder class, 103, **104–105**
AppendFormat() method of StringBuilder class, 103, **104–105**, 535
applets in Java, 799
Application Configuration dialog box, 696, 698
  App Mappings tab, *697*
Application object, Run method, 379
application security, 889
ApplicationException class, 69, 72
applications. *See* desktop applications
arithmetic operators, 50–51
Array class of System namespace, 266
ArrayList class, 285, **295–299**
arrays, 265, **266–282**
  of arrays, 267, **277–280**
  creating, **268–270**
  foreach statement, **271–272**
  multidimensional, **275–277**
  non-zero lower bound, **280–282**
  of structs, **272–275**
AS keyword (SQL), 580
as operator, for type conversion, **44–45**
.ascx file extension, 810
ASMX file, for web service, 776, 778–780
ASP (Active Server Pages), vs. ASP.NET, 914
ASP.NET applications, 10
ASP.NET Web Form, Mobile Web Form as, 914

ASP.NET Web Services, 10
.aspx file extension, 914
assemblies, **306–312**
  manifest for, **306–307**, *307*
  namespaces and, 309, 312
  referencing, **307–309**
AssemblyInfo.cs file, 306
assignment operator (=), overloading, to copy strings, 84
assignment operators, 51–52
Astra LoadTest, 512
asynchronous processing, SOAP and, 803
Attach to Process dialog box, 430
AttributeCount property, of XmlReader class, 744
attributes
  in .NET Framework, **837–842**
  in XML, 732
audit policies, 887
authentication, 807
auto-completion feature, in Code Editor, *30*
AutoIncrement property, of DataColumn object, 606, 608
AutoIncrementSeed property, of DataColumn object, 606, 608, 616
Autos window for debugging, 431
Axxias.ColumnStyles, 513

B

background thread, 436
BAPI (Biometrics API), **867**
base class, 216
  hiding members, **230–234**
base keyword, 217
base type, for custom enumerations, 31
Basic encryption, 807
batch jobs, script-based console application for, **397–405**
Beep() function, creating in C#, **847–849**
BeginEdit() method, of DataRow object, 605, 648
BeginInit() method, of DataSet object, 547

BinarySearch method, of Array class, 266

Bindable attribute, 838

Biometrics API (BAPI), **867**

Bitmap object, combining with Animator object, 422–425

bitmaps

    access to, 410

    multiple files for different resolutions, 411

bitwise operators, 51

    overloading, 263

BizTalk Server 2002 Toolkit for Microsoft .NET, 496

BOF for Recordset, 497

bool type, 33

    and implicit conversions, 40

Boolean data type, default values, 160

Boolean operators, 51

boxing, **243–245**, 267–268

breakpoints, 427

Breakpoints window, 431–432

browsers, future importance, 800

bugs

    from case sensitivity, 25

    from conversion-related syntax errors, *38*, 38

Build menu (VS.NET), 15

    ➢ Build Solution, 16, 334

BuildExplicitAccessWithName function, 878

building project, 16

BuildTrusteeWithName function, 878

BuildTrusteeWithSid function, 878

buttons. *See* round buttons dancing

Buttons property, of ToolBar control, 412

byte type, 33

    explicit type conversion for, 43

    implicit type conversion for, 40

C

C# programming

    Beep() function, **847–849**

developer access to Win32 API, **857–861**

    advantages, **860–861**

    effects of pointers, **859–860**

    effects of unsafe code, **857–859**

    first program, **2–9**

The C Programming Language (Kernighan and Ritchie), 2

caching, partial page, **819–820**

calculations, threads for, 440

Calendar class, 111

Call Stack window for debugging, 431

calling methods, **165–167**

camel notation, for identifiers, 24

CancelEdit() method, of DataRow object, 605

Capacity property, of StringBuilder class, 102

Caption property, of DataColumn object, 606

case

    converting for string, **93**

    sensitivity of identifiers, 24, 25

    when comparing strings, 82

CaseSensitive property

    of DataSet object, 546

    of DataTable object, 602

cast operator, 42–43

cast requirements for SOAP, 803

casting objects, **251–256**

    downcasting, 251, **253–256**

    and enumerations, *32*

    upcasting, 251, **252–253**

casting operators, 52

catch statement. *See* try...catch...finally statements

Category attribute, 838

char type, 33

    explicit type conversion for, 43

    implicit type conversion for, 40

character data type, default values, 160

characters

    in string

        finding, **88–89**

        removing from beginning and end, **91–92**

removing from string, **89–90**

replacing, **90**

in StringBuilder object, **106**

CheckedListBox control, 348. *See also* ListBox control

CheckTokenMembership function, 878

child forms for MDI applications, 377

Anchor property of, 378

displaying, **380–381**

ChildRelations property, of DataTable object, 602

class keyword, 4, 153

class library

adding reference to project, 336

creating, **330–339**

adding event, 333–335

adding field, 332

adding method, 333

adding property, 333

code listing, 335

invoking members, **336–339**

instantiating object, 338

setting fields and properties, 338–339

using method, 338

wiring event, 339

thread safety, 473

Class Library project, 457

class members, 153

Class View, 14, **323–324**, *324*

classes, **152–153**

collection, **284–303**

declaration of, **153–155**, **186–188**

with indexer, **282–284**

member availability outside, 193–194

vs. structs, 59, 208–209

Clear() method

of Array class, 266

of DataSet object, 547

of DataTable object, 603

of Items collection, 354–355

ClearErrors() method, of DataRow object, 605

client space of form, 344

Clipboard, 14, 369

pasting from, 524–525

Clipboard Ring, in Mobile Web Forms Designer, 921

Clone() method

of DataSet object, 547

of DataTable object, 603

of String class, 78

Close() method, of SqlConnection class, 488–489, 643

closing Command Prompt tool, 16

CLR (Common Language Runtime), 859

"cockroach" theory, 69

code-behind file, for web service, 776

Code Editor

auto-completion feature, *30*

opening Object Browser from, **326**

collection classes, **284–303**

ArrayList class, **295–299**

dictionaries, **300–303**

interfaces, **286–287**

queues, **291–295**

stacks, **287–291**

CollectionBase class, 285

collections, 265

in ADO.NET Dataset, 497–498

for toolbar buttons, 412

Collections namespace, 284, 313

classes in, 285–286

Stack class, 287

colon (:), for derived classes, 217, 246

Color common dialog box, selecting and saving color from, **300–303**, *302*

Color dialog, *371*, **371–372**

ColorDialog control, AllowFullOpen property of, 371

Column property, of DataColumnChangeEventArgs class, 675

ColumnChanged event, of DataTable object, 604, 674, **675–676**

ColumnChanging event, of DataTable object, 604, 674, **675–676**

ColumnMapping property, of DataColumn object, 606

ColumnName property, of DataColumn object, 606, 622

Columns property, of DataTable object, 602

columns, reading value using strongly typed classes, **584–591**

COM, 856

COM+ application, 696

ComboBox control. *See* ListBox control

Command classes, **478**

command-line compiler (csc), 7

Command Prompt tool

    changing directory, 7

    closing, **16**, *17*

    for command-line compiler, 7

    for console applications, 387

    to run executable file, 8, 16

Command property, of SqlRowUpdatingEventArgs class, 672

Command Window, 432

CommandBuilder classes, **479–480**

    for generating SQL statements, **667–669**

CommandText property

    of Command object, 651

    of SqlCommand object, 543

comments, 4, **48–50**

    in XML, 739

    XML documentation, **50**

Common dialogs, **368–377**

    code listing, 376–377

    Color dialog, *371*, **371–372**

    Font dialog, **372**, *372*

    Open dialog, **373–375**, *376*

    Save As dialog, **373–375**

Common Language Runtime (CLR), 859

Common Object Rquest Broker Architecture (CORBA), 801

Compare() method

    of DateTime object, 116, 120–121

    of String class, 77, **81–82**

    of TimeSpan object, 138

CompareOrdinal() method of String class, 77

CompareTo() method

    of DateTime object, 118

    of String class, 78

    of TimeSpan object, 138

comparison operators, 51

compatibility, for casting objects, 251

compiling

    program source file, **6–8**

    troubleshooting, method overloading, 179

    in Visual Studio .NET, **16**, *17*

Composite controls, 809, **820–829**, *830*

    adding to Toolbox, **828–829**

    vs. Custom Server control, 830

    testing, **829**, *830*

Compute() method, of DataTable object, 603

computer, current date and time on, 6, **119**

Computer System Hardware Classes help topic, 402

Compuware Corporation, DevPartner Profiler, 511

Concat() method of String class, 77, **83**

concurrency, of database update, 639–640, 679–680

conditional breakpoint, 427

conditional operator (?:), 52, 53

.config file hierarchy, **702–710**

<configSections> element, 712

<configuration> element, 712

Connection classes, **478**

    closing object, 550

Connection property, of SelectCommand, 595

console applications, 10, 386, **387–388**

    example, **394–397**

        script-based for batch jobs, **397–405**

Console class, 6

Console class of System namespace, 394

console output, handle to, 856

const keyword, 28

constants, 28–29
  enumeration, **29–33**
Constraint class, **482**
ConstraintCollection object, 610
Constraints property, of DataTable object, 602, 610
constructors, 155, 197, **198–207**
  copy, **204–207**
  default, 198
  for derived classes, 217
  overloaded, **201–204**
context menus, 406
context node in XSLT, 737
ContextMenu control, 406
Continue property, of FillErrorEventArgs class, 671
ContinueUpdateOnError property
  of DataAdapter, **680**
  of SqlDataAdapter class, 540
Control Panel, System, 8
Convert class of System namespace, 45
  in Object Browser, *46*
converting case of string, **93**
ConvertSecurityDescriptorToStringSecurity-
  Descriptor function, 882
ConvertSidToStringSid function, 880
ConvertStringSecurityDescriptorToSecurity-
  Descriptor function, 882
ConvertStringSidToSid function, 880
copies of parameters, passing by value, **172–174**
copy constructors, **204–207**
copy, cut and paste, in Dataset application,
  519–525
Copy() method
  of Array class, 266
  of DataSet object, 547
  of String class, 77, **83–84**
copying structs, 210–211
CopySid function, 880
CopyTo() method
  of Array class, 266
  of String class, 78

CORBA (Common Object Rquest Broker
  Architecture), 801
CPU (Central Processing Unit), machine code
  customized for, 9
Craig, Philip, 507
CreateInstance method, of Array class, 266
CreateRestrictedToken function, 878
CreateThread() function (Win32), 444
CreateUIThread() method, 459
CreateWellKnownSid() function, 896
critical sections, 459
  for threads, **470–472**
cross-platform interface
  web services issues, **798–801**
  XML for, 772–773
.cs file extension, 3
csc (command-line compiler), 7
current date and time on computer, **119**
CurrentRowIndex property, of DataGrid, 515
Cursor property of form, for mouse pointer, 288
cursors
  access to, 410
  for ADO Recordset, 497
  moving on screen, **514–516**
custom colors, allowing user to define, 371
custom reference types, 34–35
Custom Server controls, **830–842**
  attributes, **837–842**
Customize Toolbox dialog box, *828*, **828–829**

D

DACL (Discretionary Access Control List), 868
  in security descriptor, 872
Data Adapter Configuration Wizard, 591–595, *592*
  Choose Query Type, *593*
  Generate SQL Statements, *594*
  View Wizard Results, *594*
data integrity, critical sections to protect, 470
Data namespace, 313, 483

data types, definition in XML, **731–734**

data, unstructured, XML for, 771

DataAdapter classes, **479**, 480, 539–540

    Command objects, **685–686**

    creating object with Visual Studio .NET, **591–596**

    events, **669–674**

    multiple objects to populate one DataSet, 565–568

    objects to call stored procedures, **653–666**

        setting up, **658–661**

    properties

        DeleteCommand property, 640–641, **660–661**

        InsertCommand property, 637–638, **659**

        UpdateCommand property, 638–640, **659–660**

    to push changes to database, **636–641**

    SQLDataAdapter class, **540–544**

        creating object, **543–544**

database

    stored procedures to change, **653–666**

    update failures, **679–684**

        checking for errors, **683**

        ContinueUpdateOnError property, **680**

        error fixing, **684**

        programming example, 681–682

        scenario, 679–680

database connection, string to contains details for, 485–486

database management systems, SDI application for, 390

DataColumn class, **482**, 489, **606–607**

    adding constraints, **607–608**

        by setting properties, **609–621**, **615–621**

    restrictions on, 608

DataColumnChangeEventArgs class, properties, 675

Data.DataSet class of System namespace, 476

DataGrid object, including controls in, 513

Dataphor (Alphora), 512

DataReader application, **500–511**, *502*

    adding code, **502–507**

    creating shell, **500–501**

    printing in, 504–506

    testing using NUnit, **507–511**

DataReader classes, **479**, 498

    advantage of, 500

    application development, **500–511**

        adding code, **502–507**

        creating shell, **500–501**

        testing using NUnit, **507–511**

DataRelation class, **483**

DataRow class, **482**, 489–490, **604–605**

    foreach statement to iterate through, 551

DataRow objects

    adding to DataTable object, **641–645**, **661–663**

    filtering and sorting in DataTable, **629–635**

    finding in DataTable, **628–629**

    modifying in DataTable object, **645–648**, **663–665**

    removing from DataTable object, **648–649**, **665–666**

DataRowChangeEventArgs class, properties, 677

DataRowState enumeration, 644

DataRowVersion enumeration, 640

Dataset application, **513–529**

    adding and removing records, **516–519**

    coding Detail view, **525–529**

    coding grid view, **513–514**

    copy, cut and paste, **519–525**

    cursor movement on screen, **514–516**

    printing from, **527–529**

DataSet class, **481–482**, 497, 539, **544–572**

    creating object, **548**

        with Visual Studio .NET, **596–598**

    generic objects, *545*

    mapping tables and columns, **580–584**

merging DataRow, DataSet and DataTable
objects into another, **568–572**

methods, 547–548

populating object, **549–560**

   with multiple DataTable objects,
   560–568

   with range of rows, **554–557**

   with SELECT statement, **549–554**

   with stored procedure, **557–560**

properties, 546

for storing results of SQL SELECT
statement, **484–493**

   1. string for database connection
      details, 485–486

   2. SqlConnection object creation,
      486

   3. string for SELECT statement, 486

   4. SqlCommand object for SELECT
      statement, 486–487

   5. CommandText property of
      SQLCommand object, 487

   6. SqlDataAdapter object creation, 487

   7. SelectCommand property of
      SqlAdapter object, 487

   8. DataSet object creation for holding
      results, 487

   9. opening database connection, 488

   10. Fill() method to retrieve table
       rows, 488

   11. closing database connection,
       488–489

   12. getting DataTable object from
       DataSet object, 489

   13. column display in DataTable,
       489–490

   procedure outline, **484–485**

   program code, 490–493

strongly typed

   creating, **585–588**

   to modify data, **686–689**

   to read column value, **584–591**

   using, **589–591**

transactions with, **685–686**

updating changes to database, 519

writing and reading XML, **572–580**

   with ReadXml() method, **576–580**

   with WriteXML() method, **572–575**

   with WriteXmlSchema() method,
   575–576

XmlDataDocument class and, 755

DataSet property, of DataTable object, 602

DataSetName property, of DataSet object, 546

DataTable class

   adding constraints, **607–628**

      by setting properties, **610–615**

   events, **482**, 489–490, 497, 604, **674–679**

      ColumnChanged event, **675–676**

      ColumnChanging event, **675–676**

      RowChanged event, **676–678**

      RowChanging event, **676–678**

      RowDeleted event, **678–679**

      RowDeleting event, **678–679**

   methods, 603

   primary key for, 611–614

   properties, 602

DataTable object

   adding DataRow object to, **641–645**,
   661–663

   filtering and sorting DataRow objects in,
   629–635

   finding DataRow in, **628–629**

   modifying rows in, **636–649**, **663–665**

   removing row from, **648–649**, **665–666**

   retrieving new identity column values,
   650–653

DataTable property, of FillErrorEventArgs
class, 671

DataTableMapping class, 581

DataType property, of DataColumn object,
606, 622

datatypes. *See* types

DataView class, **482**, 500

DataViewRowState enumeration, 630

Date property of DateTime object, 115, 119

dates, **110–136**

DateTable custom control

    creating, **831–842**

    default UI characteristics, *831*

    properties window, 831–832, *832*

DateTime struct of System namespace, **110–136**

    creating instances, **110–111**

    properties and methods, **115–136**

        adding to instance, 123–124

        checking equality, 121–122

        code listing, 130–136

        comparing DateTime instances, 120

        converting string to DateTime instance, **123**

        date conversion to long and short strings, 126

        Date property, 119

        DateTime conversion to string, 127

        Day property, 119

        DayOfWeek property, 119–120

        DayOfYear property, 120

        leap year determination, **122**

        Now and UtcNow properties, **119**

        obtaining number of days in month, 122

        overloading operators, 121

        subtracting from instance, 123–124

        Ticks property, 120

        time conversion to long and short strings, 126

        TimeOfDay property, 120

        Timestamp conversion, 125

    time spans, **112–115**

Day property of DateTime object, 115, 119

DayOfWeek property of DateTime object, 115, 119–120

DayOfYear property of DateTime object, 116, 120

Days property of TimeSpan class, 137, 139–140

DaysInMonth() method of DateTime object, 116, **122**

DCOM (Distributed COM), 801

Debug menu (VS.NET), 15

debugging applications, **427–433**

    performing standard tasks, **431–434**

    remote, **429–431**

    threads and, 438

    toolbar, *428*

    web.config file for, 702

decimal type, 34

    explicit type conversion for, 43

    and implicit conversions, 40

declaration

    of array of structs, 273

    of arrays, 268

    of classes, **153–155**, **186–188**

    of constants, 28

    of delegate class used with event, **185–186**

    of enumeration constants, 32–33

    of events, **184–185**

    of variable type, 26–27

declarative syntax for security feature, 889–890

decrement operator (−), 51

default constructor, 198

default stylesheet for XML, in Internet Explorer, 734, *735*

default values, for database columns, 608

DefaultProperty attribute, 838–839

DefaultValue property, of DataColumn object, 606

DefaultViewManager property, of DataSet object, 546

default.vsdisco file, 796

definite assignment, **27**, 157

delegate operators, 52

delegates, 184

    adding new event handlers to, 426

    declaration, 333–334

    declaring class used with event, **185–186**

Delete() method, of DataRow object, 605

DELETE statement (SQL)

    and SET NOCOUNT ON command, 656–657

    WHERE clause, 639–640

DeleteCommand property
    of DataAdapter, 640–641, **660–661**
    of SqlDataAdapter class, 540
deleting
    characters from string, **89–90**
    characters from StringBuilder object, **106**
    DataRow object from DataTable, **648–649**
    records from Dataset, 516–519
Depth property, of XmlTextReader class, 747
Dequeue method, of Queue class, 291, 292
derived classes
    abstract classes and methods, **245–248**
    casting objects, **251–256**
        downcasting, 251, **253–256**
        upcasting, 251, **252–253**
    hiding members, **230–234**
    inheritance, **216–221**
    member accessibility, **226–229**
    operator overloading, **257–263**
        addition operator, **260–262**
        equal operator, **258–259**
    polymorphism, **221–226**
    sealed classes and methods, **248–251**
    System.Object class as base, **238–245**
        boxing and unboxing, **243–245**
        overriding methods, **241–243**
    versioning, **234–237**
Description pane, in Object Browser, 328–329
design guidelines, of .NET Framework, **332**
design-time properties, 838
desktop applications
    console applications, 10, 386, **387–388**
        example, **394–405**
    debugging, **427–433**
    vs. distributed applications, 385
    resources, **405–413**
        accelerators and menus, **405–408**
        accessibility features, **408–410**
        graphics, **410–411**

timers, **411**
toolbars, **411–413**
standard Windows, **388–391**. *See also*
    Windows applications
threads in, **439–441**, **446–456**
    performing worker thread test,
        454–456
    test code creation, **451–454**
    Thread class creation, **447–451**
Web-based, **392–393**
destructors, **207–208**
Detail view
    adding and removing records, **526–527**
    coding, **525–529**
    printing in, **527–529**
development environment, exception handling
    in, 67–68
DevPartner Profiler (Compuware Corporation), 511
DHTML (Dynamic HTML), 800
Diagnostics namespace, 313
dialog-based applications, 386, **388–389**
    in Windows, **414–421**, *415*
dialog boxes. *See* Common dialogs
dictionaries, **300–303**
DictionaryBase class, 285
directives, namespace, **310–311**
directories
    changing in Command Prompt tool, 7
    creating virtual, 693–694
Directory class, 370
directory hierarchy for web applications, vs. site
    hierarchy, **711–712**
DirectoryInfo class, 370
DirectX, .NET Framework and, **852**
Disassembly window, 432–433, *433*
disconnected data sets, 475
discovery, threads for, 442
Discretionary Access Control List (DACL), 868
    in security descriptor, 872
Distributed COM (DCOM), 801

DivideByZeroException, 63

DLLs (Dynamic link libraries), **441**

   assemblies for, 306

   local example using threads, **456–461**

      DLL creation, **458–459**

      project configuration, **456–457**

      test program creation, **459–461**

   server-based example using threads, **461–469**

      test application creation, **464–469**

      Windows service creation, **461–464**

do while statement, 57–58

Dock property, of RichTextBox control, 369

document fragment, 743

Document Object Model (DOM), vs. SAX, **741–742**

documentation, for .NET, **17–21**

DOM subtree, 743

DOMDocument object, xmlinst.exe file for creating, 792

dot operator (.), 6

   for .NET Framework hierarchy, 309

   to access object fields and methods, 155–156

double type, 34

   explicit type conversion for, 43

   and implicit conversions, 40

downcasting, 251, **253–256**

downloading

   Mobile Internet Toolkit, **913**

   .NET Software Development Kit (SDK), 2

   source files, 3

Downloads link in Visual Studio .NET, 12

Drawing namespace, 313

DTDs (Document Type Definitions), 772

DuplicateToken function, 878

DuplicateTokenEx function, 878

Duration() method, of TimeSpan object, 138, **143**

Dynamic HTML (DHTML), 800

dynamic properties, 29

dynamic strings, **100–110**

E

EAI (Enterprise Application Integration), 801

Edit menu

   implementing, **370–371**

   in Visual Studio .NET, 14

efficiency, threads and, 438

emulators

   for mobile application testing, **925–927**

   Openwave SDK, **916–917**, *917*

   supported by Mobile Internet Toolkit, **918–919**

Enabled property, of Timer component, 345

encapsulation, 153, 194

   private fields and, 181

EndEdit() method, of DataRow object, 605

ending console application, 16

EndInit() method, of DataSet object, 547

EndsWith() method of String class, 78, **86–87**

EnforceConstraints property, of DataSet object, 546

Enqueue method, of Queue class, 291

EnsureCapacity() method of StringBuilder class, 103

Enter() method, of Monitor class, 470, 472

Enterprise Application Integration (EAI), 801

entities, 742

enumeration

   DataRowState, 644

   DataRowVersion, 640

   DataViewRowState, 630

   SchemaType, 623

   ServiceControllerStatus, 468

   XmlReadMode, 577

   XmlWriteMode, 574

enumeration constants, **29–33**

   built-in, 29–30

   custom, 31–33

   declaring, 32–33

envelope element for SOAP payload, 803

environment variables, processing, 395–397

EOF for Recordset, 497

equal to operator (==), overloading, 257–258, **258–259**

    to test for equal strings, 84–85

EqualPrefixSid function, 880

Equals() method

    of DateTime object, 116, 121–122

    of String class, 77

    of StringBuilder class, 103

    of System.Object class, 238

        overloading, 259

        to test for equal strings, **84**

    of TimeSpan object, 138

EqualSid function, 881

error handling, for Fill() method, 670–671

error messages

    CS0165: Use of unassigned local variable, 157

    "File or assembly name System, or one of its dependencies, was not found", 715

    warning: CS0114: *method* hides inherited member ..., 235

ErrorProvider component, 296, *296*

errors

    in updating

        checking for, **683**

        fixing, **684**

    in XML documents, 743

Errors property

    of FillErrorEventArgs class, 671

    of SqlRowUpdatingEventArgs class, 672

escape characters, in strings, 76

event handler, 183

    adding menu item event to existing, *361*

event log settings, for security setup, 888

Event Properties dialog box, *469*

Event Viewer, *469*

EventArgs class, 670

    of System namespace, 185

EventArgs class of System namespace, 185, 670

events, **183–192**, 339

    adding to library, 333–335

    declaration of, **184–185**

    declaring delegate class used with, **185–186**

exception handling, **61–72**

    for data entry errors, 608

    Exception objects, **71–72**

    throwing exceptions, **68–71**

    with try...catch...finally statements, **62–68**

Exception objects

    Message property, vs. ToString method, 65

    properties, 72

.exe file extension, 8

executable files, 7

    assemblies for, 306

    namespace for, 309

    Path environment variable to list directories containing, 8

ExecuteCommand() method, for Windows service, 468

Exit() method, of Monitor class, 470, 472

explicit type conversion, **41–44**

exporting XML, **529–533**

ExtendedProperties property, of DataSet object, 546

Extensible Stylesheet Language (XSL), 734

Extensible Stylesheet Language Transformation (XSLT), 734

external configuration file, for dynamic properties, 29

F

FAT/FAT32 file system, and security, 874

Fibonacci series, array creation for, 269–270

fields in classes, 4, 153

    adding to library, 332

    default values, **160–162**

    setting, 338–339

file access, in .NET Framework, **370**

File class, 370

file extension, for C# source files, 3

file formats, 731

File menu

creating for application, 365

in Visual Studio .NET, 14

➤ New ➤ Project, 12

"File or assembly name System, or one of its dependencies, was not found" error message, 715

FileInfo class, 370

files, accessing security information, **897–902**

FileStream class, 370

Fill() method

of DataAdapter, 611

of SqlDataAdapter class, 488, 542, 550

constraints on Dataset and performance, 609

overloading, 554–555

FillConsoleOutputCharacter() function, 856

FillError event, of SqlDataAdapter class, 542, **670–671**

FillErrorEventArgs class, 670–671

FillSchema() method

of DataAdapter, 609, **622–628**

of SqlDataAdapter class, 542

filter, for Save As Type drop-down list, 374

filtering DataRow objects, in DataTable object, **629–635**

Finalize() method of System.Object class, 238

finally keyword, 65–66. *See also* try...catch...finally statements

Find Symbol dialog box, *330*, 330

finding

characters in string, **88–89**

DataRow object, in DataTable object, **628–629**

substrings, **87–88**

web services, **807–808**

firewall, XML and, 772, 773

flags, in security descriptor, 871

float type, 34

explicit type conversion for, 43

implicit type conversion for, 40

flow control statements, **55–59**

do while statement, 57–58

goto statement, 55–57

with switch, 57

while statements, 57

FMS, 512

Font dialog, **372**, *372*

fonts, 841

for printing, 527

foreach statement iteration

through array of structs, 273

through arrays, **271–272**

through DataRow objects, 551

foreign key constraints, adding to DataTable object, 614–615

ForeignKeyConstraint class, **483**

Format() method of String class, 77, **85**

FormatMessage() function, 896

formatting

with StringBuilder object, 535, 537, *537*

strings converting from DateTime, 127

built-in formats, **129–130**

forms

client space of, 344

IsMDI Container property of, 378, *379*

Menu property of, 363

forward slashes (//), for comments, 4, 5, 48

FreeHGlobal() function of Marshal class, 896

FreeSid function, 881

FromDays() method of TimeSpan object, 138, 141

FromFileTime() method of DateTime object, 117, 125

FromHours() method of TimeSpan object, 138, 141

FromMilliseconds() method of TimeSpan object, 138, 141

FromMinutes() method of TimeSpan object, 138, 141

FromOADate() method of DateTime
object, 117

FromSeconds() method of TimeSpan object,
138, 141

FromTicks() method of TimeSpan object, 138, 141

G

game developers, 852

garbage collection, 157, 197

   vs. destructors, 207

General Access ACE header, 873

general catch clause, 62

Generate Dataset dialog box, 597, 755

generic data classes, 476, **480–483**, 481

   namespaces for, **483**

get methods, 181, 333

GET request, to call WebMethod function,
780–781

Get Started link in Visual Studio .NET, 11

GetAuditedPermissionsFromAcl function, 878

GetChanges() method

   of DataSet object, 547

   of DataTable object, 603

GetChildRows() method, of DataRow object, 605

GetColumnError() method, of DataRow
object, 605

GetColumnsInError() method, of DataRow
object, 605

GetDateTimeFormats() method of DateTime
object, 118

GetDeleteCommand() method, of
SqlCommandBuilder, 668

GetEffectiveRightsFromAcl function, 878

GetEnumerator() method, of String class, 78

GetErrors() method, of DataTable object, 603

GetExplicitEntriesFromAcl() function, 878,
907, 908

GetFileSecurity() function, 875, **897–902**

GetFillParameters() method, of SqlDataAdapter
class, 542

GetHashCode() method

   of DateTime object, 118

   of StringBuilder class, 103

   of System.Object class, 78, 238

   of TimeSpan object, 138

GetInnerXML() method, of XmlTextReader
class, 747

GetInsertCommand() method, of
SqlCommandBuilder, 668

GetKernelObjectSecurity() function, 875

GetLastWin32Error() function of Marshal class, 896

GetLength method, of Array class, 266

GetLengthSid function, 881

GetLowerBound method, of Array class, 266, 281

GetNamedSecurityInfo function, 882

GetOuterXML() method, of XmlTextReader
class, 747

GetParentRow() method, of DataRow object, 605

GetParentRows() method, of DataRow object, 605

GetRemainder() method, of XmlTextReader
class, 747

GetSecurityDescriptorControl function, 882

GetSecurityDescriptorDacl() function, 873, 901,
907–908

GetSecurityDescriptorGroup function, 901

GetSecurityDescriptorOwner() function, 901

GetSecurityInfo function, 882

GetSidIdentifierAuthority function, 881

GetSidLengthRequired function, 881

GetSidSubAuthority function, 881

GetSidSubAuthorityCount function, 881

GetTokenInformation function, 879

GetTrusteeForm function, 879

GetTrusteeName function, 879

GetTrusteeType function, 879

GetType() method

   of DateTime object, 118

   of StringBuilder class, 103

   of System.Object class, 78, 238

   of TimeSpan object, 139

GetTypeCode() method, of String class, 78

GetUpdateCommand() method, of
SqlCommandBuilder, 668

GetUpperBound method, of Array class, 266

GetUserObjectSecurity() function, 875

GetValue method, of Array class, 266

GetXml() method, of DataSet object, 547

GetXmlSchema() method, of DataSet object, 547

GIF files, animated, 422–426

Globalization namespace, Calendar class, 111

Globalization.Calendar class of System
namespace, 111

goto statement, 55–57

    with switch, 57

graphics, for desktop applications, **410–411**

GraphicsPath object, for form shape, 342

GregorianCalendar class, 111

group access, 869

group SID, in security descriptor, 871–872

GUI (graphical user interface)

    animation, 421–426

    HTML and, 799

    for Windows applications, 414

H

handling exceptions. *See* exception handling

hard drives, 850

hardware

    .NET Framework access, **849–850**

    for Visual Studio .NET, 912

HasAttributes property, of XmlReader class, 744

HasChanges() method, of DataSet object, 547

HasErrors property

    of DataRow object, 604

    of DataSet object, 546

    of DataTable object, 602

Hashtable class, 285

headers

    for SOAP message, 803

    types for ACEs, 873–874

Headlines link in Visual Studio .NET, 12

heap, 197

HebrewCalendar class, 111

Hello World program, 2–4

    origins, 2

help, HTML-based, 393

Help menu (VS.NET), 15

HelpLink property, of Exception object, 72

hexadecimal numbers, 427

hiding

    derived class members, **230–234**

    field, **168–170**

hierarchical relationships, in XML, 770–771

high contrast accessibility feature, 409–410

HijriCalendar class, 111

hit count for breakpoints, 427

Hour property of DateTime object, 116

Hours property of TimeSpan class, 137, 139–140

HPFS, and security, 874

.htc file extension, 794

HTML-based applications, 386

HTML-based help, 393

HTML behavior, 794

I

ICollection interface, 286

IComparer interface, 286

IConfigurationSectionHandler interface, 719

    Create method, 720

icons, access to, 410

IDataObject type, 525

identifiers, **24–26**. *See also* constants;
    methods; types; variables

identity column, retrieving new values, **650–653**

IDictionary interface, 287, 300

IDictionaryEnumerator interface, 287

IEnumerable interface, 287

IEnumerator interface, 287

if statement, statement block in, 57

IHashCodeProvider interface, 287

IList interface, 287

ImageList control, for pictures for Toolbar control, 413

ImageList property, of ToolBar control, 413

imperative syntax for security feature, 891–892

implicit type conversion, **40–41**

importing XML, **529–533**

INamingContainer interface, 822

#INCLUDE directive, 820

increment operator (++), 51, 53

index for .NET documentation, 17, *19*

Index property, of MenuItems collection, 364

indexers, **282–284**

indexes

for arrays, 267

retrieving items from ListBox by, **353**

IndexOf() method

of Array class, 266

of String class, 78, **87–88**

IndexOfAny() method of String class, 78, **88–89**

information gathering, about compiled program elements, 314, *318*

inheritance, **216–221**

sealed classes to restrict, **248–251**

INI files, 731

initialization

of array of structs, 273

of arrays, 269

Initialize method, of Array class, 266

initializer for field class value, 160

InitializeSid function, 881

initializing, variables, 26–27

Inner-Exception property, for wrapped exceptions, 759

Insert() method

of Items collection, 350

of String class, 78, **89**

of StringBuilder class, 103, **105**

INSERT statement (SQL)

CommandText property for, 651

and SET NOCOUNT ON command, 656–657

InsertCommand property

of DataAdapter, 637–638, **659**

of SqlDataAdapter class, 541

instantiation

of array of structs, 273

of arrays, 268–269

of class object, 338

of objects, 156

int type, 34

conversion to long, 41–42

explicit type conversion for, 43

implicit type conversion for, 40

Intellisense, 584

Interaction, in .NET Framework, 848–849

interfaces, for collection classes, **286–287**

Interlocked class, 445

Intern() method of String class, 78

internal access modifier for classes, 192–194

Internet Explorer

consuming web services with, **789–794**, *790*

default stylesheet for XML, 734, *735*

for Microsoft Help, 392

Internet Information Services, starting, 692

Internet Services Manager, 692, *692*

Interval property, of Timer component, 345

IntPtr, 860

Invalidate() method, of DisplayArea object, 425

IO namespace, 313

IO.Filestream class of System namespace, Lock() method, 868

"is a" relationship, 216

is operator, 52, 53

ISecurityInformation interface, 884

IsFixedSize property, of Array class, 267

IsInterned() method of String class, 78

IsLeapYear() method of DateTime object, 117

IsMDI Container property, of form, 378, *379*

IsName() method, of XmlReader class, 744

IsNull() method, of DataRow object, 605

IsReadOnly property, of Array class, 267

IsStartElement() method, of XmlTextReader class, 747

IsSynchronized property, of Array class, 267

IsTokenRestricted function, 879

IsValidSid function, 881

ItemArray property, of DataRow object, 604

Items collection

    AddRange method of, 349

    Clear method of, 354–355

    Insert() method of, 350

    Remove() method of, 355

J

jagged array, 267, **277–280**

JapaneseCalendar class, 111

Jasc, Paint Shop Pro 7, 422

Java, 799

    RMI (Remote Method Invocation), 801

JIT (Just In Time) compiler, 9

Join() method, of String class, 78, **85**

joins, in SELECT statement, for DataSet, 549

joysticks, 851

JulianCalendar class, 111

jumps, with goto statement, 55–57

Just In Time (JIT) compiler, 9

K

KERNEL32.DLL, 856

Kernighan, Brian, *The C Programming Language*, 2

keywords in C#, **25–26**

L

Label control, in Composite control, *821*, 821–828

"last one wins" concurrency, 639

LastIndexOf() method

    of Array class, 266

    of String class, 78, **87–88**

LastIndexOfAny() method of String class, 79, **88–89**

LayoutMdi method, of parent form, 383

leap year, determining, 122–123

left-alignment of strings, **91**

Length property

    of Array class, 267

    of StringBuilder class, 102

    of strings, 77, **80–81**

libraries. *See* class library; DLLs (Dynamic link libraries)

library files (.DLL), assemblies for, 306

LIKE operator, 631

LineNumber property

    of XmlException class, 759

    of XmlTextReader class, 747

LinePosition property

    of XmlException class, 759

    of XmlTextReader class, 747

ListBox control, **348–359**

    adding array, **349**, *350*

    adding integer array to, 271–272

    adding item, 348, *349*

    clearing item, **354–355**

    code listing, 357–359

    deleting items, **355**

    positioning by index, **350–351**, *351*

    retrieving by index, **353**

    retrieving multiple checked items, **353–354**

    retrieving multiple selections, **355–356**, *356*

    retrieving selected text, **352**

LoadDataRow() method, of DataTable object, 603

LoadRunner, 512

local policies, for security setup, 887–888

local variables, **165**

Locale property, of DataSet object, 546

locally unique identifier (LUID), 870

LocalName property, of XmlReader class, 744

Locals window for debugging, 431

<location> tag, in web.config file, 721, 722

lock keyword, 470

Lock() method

of FileStream class, 868

namespace locations, 889

logical errors, throwing exceptions to handle, 68

logical operators, 51

short-circuit evaluation, **53–54**

long type, 34

explicit type conversion for, 43

implicit type conversion for, 40

int type conversion to, 41–42

LookupAccountName function, 881

LookupAccountSid() function, 881, 896, 897

LookupPrivilegeDisplayName function, 879

LookupPrivilegeName function, 879

LookupPrivilegeValue function, 879

looping

with do while statement, **58–59**

with while statement, **58**

low-level services, .NET operating support, 851

lower bound for arrays, non-zero, **280–282**

LUID (locally unique identifier), 870

M

machine code, 9

machine.config file, 702

Main() method, **4–8**

adding lines, 16

generated by VS.NET, 15–16

for Startup object in MDI application, 379

MainMenu control, 359–360, *360*, 406

maintenance tasks on servers, threads for, 443

managed provider classes, 475, **476–480**, 477

Command classes, **478**

CommandBuilder classes, **479–480**

Connection classes, **478**

DataAdapter classes, **479**

DataReader classes, **479**

namespaces for, **480**

ODBC managed provider classes, 478

OLE DB managed provider classes, 477

Parameter classes, **478–479**

ParameterCollection classes, **479**

SQL Server managed provider classes, 477

Transaction classes, **480**

manifest, for assemblies, **306–307**, *307*

manual pointer (*), in C# unsafe code, 857

mapping DataTable to DataSet, 581

Marshal.AllocHGlobal() function, 896

Marshal.FreeHGlobal() function, 896

Marshal.GetLastWin32Error() function, 896

MaxCapacity property of StringBuilder class, 102

MaxLength property, of DataColumn object, 607, 608, 616, 622

MDI (multiple document interface) applications, **377–383**, *384*, 386, **391**

disadvantages, 391

displaying children, **380–381**

Startup Object setting, **379–380**, *380*

Window menu, **381–383**

measuring time for operation, 148–149

member access operator, 52

Members pane, in Object Browser, 328

MemberwiseClone() method of System.Object class, 238

memory, allocation for SID, 896

memory stack, 197

MemoryStream class, 370

Menu property, of forms, 363

menus, **359–368**, *360*

adding copy, cut, and paste to, 520–525

auto-generated code, **361–365**

coding by hand, 366–368

context, 406

for desktop applications, **405–408**

enabling and disabling commands, 525

for RichTextBox control application, 364–368

Mercury Interactive, 512

Merge() method of DataSet object, 547

overloading, **568–572**

MergeFailed event, of DataSet object, 548

Message property, of Exception object, 65, 72

MessageBox enumeration constants, 29

MessageBoxIcon enumeration, 29

messaging queues, 803

metadata, reflection and, 314, *318*

methods, 4, 153, **162–181**

adding to library, 333

availability outside class, 5

calling, **165–167**

defining, **163–165**

hiding field, **168–170**

local variables, **165**

overloading, **178–181**

parameters, 166, **171–178**

out parameters, **176–178**

passing by reference, **174–176**

passing by value, **172–174**

returning value from, **164–165**, 166

sealed, **248–251**

using from class library, 338

Microsoft BizTalk Server 2002 Toolkit for Microsoft .NET, 496

Microsoft Help URLs, 392

Microsoft Intermediate Language (MSIL), **9**

Microsoft Knowledge Base, 907

Microsoft Management Console, 852

System Configuration Manager, 885

Microsoft State Server, 802

Microsoft, support for C#, 861

Microsoft Transaction Server (MTS), 696

Microsoft XML Notepad, **531–533**, *532*

Microsoft.CSharp namespace, 313

Millisecond property, of DateTime object, 116

Milliseconds property, of TimeSpan class, 137, 139–140

Minute property, of DateTime object, 116

Minutes property, of TimeSpan class, 137, 139–140

MissingMappingAction property, of SqlDataAdapter class, 541

MissingSchemaAction property, of SqlDataAdapter class, 541

mobile applications, Openwave SDK for testing, **916–917**, *917*

Mobile Internet Toolkit

basics, **912–916**

contents, **914**

obtaining, **913**

with code behind, **931–935**, *934*

Hello World program, **919–927**

compiling, 924

design view, *924*

testing, **925–927**

Openwave SDK, **916–917**, *917*

supported devices, **918–919**

system requirements, **912**

two-card deck building, *927*, **927–931**

Mobile Web Forms Designer, 912–915, *913*, *920*, **922–923**

Properties window, **923–924**

toolbox, **921**

Monitor class, Enter() and Exit() methods, 470, 472

month, obtaining number of days in, 116, 122

Month property, of DateTime object, 116

Mortgage Payment calculator, *793*

runWebMethods method, 798

web form to call, **789–801**

as web service, **776–789**

MoveToAttribute() method, of XmlReader class, 744

MoveToContent() method, of XmlTextReader class, 748

MoveToElement() method, of XmlTextReader class, 748

MoveToLastAttribute() method, of XmlTextReader class, 748

MoveToNextAttribute() method, of XmlTextReader class, 748

MoveToPrevious Attribute() method, of XmlTextReader class, 748

MSDN Online Library, searching, 12

MSIL (Microsoft Intermediate Language), **9**

msxml3.dll parser, 736

msxml4.dll parser, 736

    Load method flaw, 759

MTS (Microsoft Transaction Server), 696

multidimensional arrays, 267, **275–277**

multimedia, .NET Framework and, **851**

Multiple Document Interface. *See* MDI (multiple document interface) applications

multiplication, overloading operators, 263

My Profile link in Visual Studio .NET, 12

N

n-dimensional arrays. *See* multidimensional arrays

Name property, of XmlReader class, 744

namespace keyword, 311

Namespace property, of DataSet object, 546

namespaces, 6, **309–312**

    in .NET Framework, **313–314**

    assemblies and, 309, 312

    creating, **311–312**

    directives, **310–311**

    for generic controls, 822

    for generic data classes, **483**

    for managed provider classes, **480**

    members, **312**

    naming for project, 514

    for SQL Server provider, 513

    for web service, 777

NameTable property, of XmlTextReader class, 747

NameValueSectionHandler type, 715

naming conventions, for identifiers, 24

National Institute of Standards and Technology, 867

Negate() method, of TimeSpan object, 139, **143–144**

nesting virtual directories, 711

.NET documentation, **17–21**, *18*

.NET Framework

    attributes in, **837–842**

    design guidelines, **332**

    file access, **370**

    garbage collection, 208

    Interaction in, 848–849

    interfaces, 286

    limitations, 845

        language variations, 846

    namespaces in, **313–314**

    Object Browser to view structure, **325–330**

    pre-built enumerations, 29

    thread creation independent of, 444

    thread safety in, 473

    XSLT transformations in, 740

.NET Framework Software Development Kit (SDK)

    documentation, accessing, **17–20**, *18*

    downloading, 2

.NET Windows forms, consuming web services from, **794–798**

network administrators, console applications for, 387

NetworkStream class, 370

New Breakpoint dialog box

    Address tab, 427

    Function tab, *428*

new operator, 52, 155, 198

    for array instantiation, 268–269

    to hide members of base class, 230

    for struct instance, 210

New Project dialog box, 13, *13*
  Class Library project, 331, *331*
  Console application, *394*, 394
  for Mobile web application, 919, *920*
NewRow() method, of DataTable object, 603, 642
Next method, of Random object, 289
nodes in XML file, 731
NodeType property, of XmlReader class, 743
non-zero lower bound for arrays, **280–282**
Northwind database, stored procedures
  creation, **654–658**
    AddProduct4(), 654–655
    DeleteProduct(), 656
    UpdateProduct(), 655–656
not equal to operator (!=), overloading, 259
Notepad, for source file editing, 3
Now property of DateTime object, 6,
  115, **119**
NTFS, and security, 874
null values
  DLL check for, 459
  for objects, **157–160**
  from as operator after unsuccessful
    conversion, 44
numeric data types, default values, 160
NUnit, **507–511**
  testing with, *510*

O

Object Access ACE header, 874
Object Browser, **325–330**
  class definition of object in, *326*
  Convert class methods in, *46*
  displaying class members in, *337*
  enumeration constant list members, *30*,
    31, *32*
  interface, *327*, **327–330**
    Description pane, 328–329
    Members pane, *328*

Object pane, 327–328, *328*
    toolbar, 329–330
  opening, **325–326**
  setting scope, **329**
  string variables in, *36*
  System.Collections namespace in, *285*
Object class of System namespace, **238–245**, 310
  boxing and unboxing, **243–245**
  methods, 238–241
  overriding methods, **241–243**
  ToString method, **47**
Object Linking and Embedding (OLE), 390
object-oriented programming languages, 152–153
Object pane, in Object Browser, 327–328, *328*
object type, 34
objects, **152–153**
  array of, 267–268
  casting, **251–256**
    downcasting, 251, **253–256**
    upcasting, 251, **252–253**
  ContextMenu property, 406
  creating, **155–162**, **197–208**
    with constructors, **198–207**
    default field values and initializers,
      160–162
    null values, **157–160**
  creating and using, **188–192**
  destructors, **207–208**
  maximum capacity for StringBuilder, 101
  removing from memory, 197
  Shortcut property, 407
  this to reference, **170–171**
  variables as, **243–245**
ODBC managed provider classes, 478
OdbcCommand class, 478
OdbcCommandBuilder class, 479–480, 667
OdbcConnection class, 478
OdbcDataAdapter class, 479
OdbcDataReader class, 479

OdbcParameter classes, 478–479

OdbcParameterCollection class, 479

OdbcTransaction class, 480

OLE (Object Linking and Embedding), 390

OLE DB managed provider classes, 477

OleDbCommand class, 478

OleDbCommandBuilder class, 479–480, 667

OleDbConnection class, 478, 499

OleDbDataAdapter class, 479

    for data transfer, **499–500**

OleDbDataReader class, 479

OleDbParameter classes, 478–479

OleDbParameterCollection class, 479

OleDbTransaction class, 480

OnCustomCommand() method, in Windows
    service, 464

one-dimensional arrays, 267

    creating, 268–269

Online Community link in Visual Studio .NET, 12

OnStart() method, in Windows service, 464

Open dialog, **373–375**, *376*

Open() method, of SqlConnection class, 488, 643

OpenFileDialog control, 375

    code to display, 315

OpenProcessToken() function, 870, 879

OpenThreadToken function, 879

Openwave SDK, **916–917**, *917*

    emulator display of application, *925*

    testing application, **925–927**

operating systems

    .NET Framework and, **850–851**

    for Mobile Internet Toolkit, 912

    XML documents on multiple, 772–773

operator keyword, 259

operators, **50–55**

    as operator, **44–45**

    precedence, 54–55

optimistic concurrency, 639, 679–680

Option Onpicks, in Openwave emulator, 929–930

OR operator, short-circuit evaluation, **53–54**

order for security, 876–877

Ordinal property, of DataColumn object, 607

out keyword, 860

out parameters, **176–178**

output, from console application, 394

output handle, 856

Output window for debugging, 432

OutputCache directive, 820

overloaded constructors, **201–204**

overloading

    methods, **178–181**

    operators, 50, **257–263**

        for DateTime addition and
            subtraction, 124

        for DateTime comparisons, 121

override keyword, 222–223

overriding methods, of System.Object class,
    241–243

OverwritePrompt property, of SaveFile
    Dialog, 375

owner SID, in security descriptor, 871

P

PadLeft() method of String class, 79, **90–91**

PadRight() method of String class, 79

Paint Shop Pro 7 (Jasc), 422

Parameter classes, **478–479**

ParameterCollection classes, **479**

parameters, **171–178**

    for methods, 163

    out parameters, **176–178**

    passing by reference, **174–176**

    passing by value, **172–174**

parent form

    IsMDI Container property for, *379*

    for MDI applications, 377

Parse() method

    of DateTime object, 117, **123**

    of TimeSpan object, 138, **141–142**

ParseExact() method of DateTime object, 117

parser, for XmlDocument, 730

Pascal notation, 24

passwords, policies, 887

Path environment variable, 8

Peek method, of Queue class, 291, 292, *293*

peeking in stack, 287

performance

CommandBuilder classes and, 667

critical sections placement and, 472

StringBuilder object and, **534–537**

performance of server, threads and, 443

PlaySound() function, 849

pointers

effects of, 859–860

and managed types, 859

manual (*), in C# unsafe code, 857

polymorphism, **221–226**

sealed classes to restrict, **248–251**

popping the stack, 287, 290

POST request, to call WebMethod function, 781

precedence of operators, 54–55

predefined C# types, 33–34

Prefix property, of DataSet object, 546

primary key

adding to DataTable object, 611–614

for DataSet vs. database, 614

for DataTable object, 610–611

in SelectCommand property of
DataAdapter, 667

PrimaryKey property, of DataTable object, 602,
611, 645

printers, 850

printing

in DataReader application, 504–506

from Dataset application, **527–529**

thread for, 439

private access modifier for classes, 192–194,
226–229

private fields, properties and, 181

Processes dialog box, 429–430, *430*

processes, vs. threads, 436

program code, 3

compiling, **6–8**

Project menu (VS.NET), 15

➤ Add Reference, 308

➤ Add Windows Form, 377

projects in Visual Studio .NET, 11

adding library reference to, 336

creating, **12–13**, *13*

renaming, 514

properties, 6

adding to library, 333

defining, **181–183**

of strings, 76

of User controls, 820

Properties window, dynamic properties, 29

ProposedValue property, of
DataColumnChangeEventArgs class, 675

protected access modifier for classes, 192–194,
226–229

pseudo-random numbers, 289

public access modifier for classes, 154,
192–194, 226–229

public keyword, 5

for fields, 332

pull model for reading XML, 742

push model for reading XML, SAX as, 742

pushing on stack, 287, 290

Q

queries, of XML documents, **753–754**, 771

Query Builder dialog box, *501*, 501

QueryServiceObjectSecurity() function, 875

Queue class, 285

queues, **291–295**

quotation marks ("), for string literal, 35

R

RAD (Rapid Application Development) tool, 9.
See also Visual Studio .NET

Random class of System namespace, 289

random numbers, 289

Rank property, of Array class, 267

reading characters in string, Length property
for, **80–81**

ReadOnly property, of DataColumn object,
607, 608

ReadString method, of XmlReader class, 744

ReadXml() method of DataSet object, 547,
576–580

    overloading, 576

ReadXmlSchema() method, of DataSet object, 547

records, adding and removing from Dataset,
516–519

RecordsAffected property, of
SqlRowUpdatedEventArgs class, 672

Recordset object, for ADO, 497

rectangle, specifying for printing, 528–529

ref keyword, **174–176**

reference, 155

    passing parameters by, **174–176**

reference types, 34

    variables, 60

ReferenceEquals() method of System.Object
class, 238

references, to assemblies, **307–309**

referencing, this keyword for objects, **170–171**

reflection, **314–322**, *318*, *322*, *323*

    code listing, 319–321

Reflection namespace, 313

Reflection.Emit namespace, 313

RegGetKeySecurity() function, 875

Region property, of form, and shape of form, 342

RegisterHiddenField method, 762

Registers window, 433

Registry, security setup, 888

RegSetKeySecurity() function, 875

RejectChanges() method
    of DataRow object, 605
    of DataSet object, 547
    of DataTable object, 603

relational operators, overloading, 263

Relations property, of DataSet object, 546

reliability, threads and, 438, 443

remote calls, and XML, **770–772**

remote debugging of applications, **429–431**

Remote Method Invocation (RMI), 801

Remove() method
    of Items collection, 355
    of String class, 79, **89–90**
    of StringBuilder class, 103, **106**

removing. *See* deleting

Renamer (FMS), 512

Render method
    accessing properties, 841
    overriding, 837

repetitive tasks, background thread for, 439

Replace() method
    of String class, 79, **90**
    of StringBuilder class, 103, **106**

reserved keywords in C#, **25–26**

Reset() method, of DataSet object, 548

resources for desktop applications, **405–413**
    accelerators and menus, **405–408**
    accessibility features, **408–410**
    graphics, **410–411**
    timers, **411**
    toolbars, **411–413**

restricted groups, for security setup, 888

RESX file, for web service, 776

return keyword, 163, 164

returned values from methods, 5

Reverse method, of Array class, 266

RichTextBox control, 390
    Dock property of, 369

RichTextBox control application
    Common dialogs for, **368–377**

Edit menu implementation, **370–371**

loading text into, **375**

menus for, 364–368

saving contents of control, 373–375

right-alignment of strings, **90–91**

Ritchie, Dennis, *The C Programming Language*, 2

RMI (Remote Method Invocation), 801

role-based security, 850, 865

.NET Framework differences, **888–892**

rollback of transactions, 685, 686

round buttons dancing, **342–348**

animating controls, **345–346**

code listing, 346–348

round button creation, **342–344**, *343*

toggling button, **344**

Row property

of DataColumnChangeEventArgs class, 675

of DataRowChangeEventArgs class, 677

of SqlRowUpdatingEventArgs class, 672

RowChanged event, of DataTable object, 604, 674, **676–678**

RowChanging event, of DataTable object, 604, 674, **676–678**

RowDeleted event, of DataTable object, 604, 675, **678–679**

RowDeleting event, of DataTable object, 604, 675, **678–679**

RowError property, of DataRow object, 683

rows in database, returning number affected, 656

rows in DataTable object, **636–649**

adding DataRow, **641–645**

DataAdapter to push changes to database, **636–641**

DeleteCommand property setting, 640–641

InsertCommand property setting, 637–638

UpdateCommand property setting, 638–640

modifying DataRow, **645–648**

removing DataRow, **648–649**

Rows property of DataTable object, 602

to call Find() method, 629

RowState property, of DataRow object, 604

RowUpdated event, of SqlDataAdapter class, 542, 670, **673–674**

RowUpdating event, of SqlDataAdapter class, 542, 670, **671–673**

Run method, of Application object, 379

run-time heap, 60

runtime, loading User controls at, **819**

S

SACL (Security Access Control List), 868–869. *See also* Access Control Entries (ACEs)

in security descriptor, 872

safety, of threads, **473**

Save As dialog, **373–375**

SaveFile Dialog, OverwritePrompt property of, 375

saving RichTextBox control contents, 373–375

SAX (Simple API for XML), vs. DOM, **741–742**

sbyte type, 33

explicit type conversion for, 43

implicit type conversion for, 40

Schema class, in System.XML namespace, **731–734**

schema in XML, 733

generating for DataSet, 756–757

SchemaType enumeration, 623

scope of Object Browser, **329**

scope of variables, local, **165**

SCOPE_IDENTITY() function (SQL Server), 651–652

screen display

displaying line of output on, 6

function calls to clear, 853–856

script-based console application for batch jobs, **397–405**

scripting, console applications for, 387

SDI (single-document interface) applications, 386, **390**

example, **421–426**

SE_ privileges, 871

sealed classes and methods, **248–251**

Search Online link in Visual Studio .NET, 12

searching. *See also* finding

    index for .NET documentation, *18*, 18

Second property of DateTime object, 116

Seconds property of TimeSpan class, 137, 139–140

<section> element, 712–713

<sectionGroup> element, 712

Secure Sockets Layer (SSL), 806

secured web services, **806–807**

security

    .NET Framework and, **850**

    .NET role-based security differences, **888–892**

    Access Control Editor, **883–885**

    ACEs (Access Control Entries) example, **902–908**

    functions for, **877–882**

    GetFileSecurity() function, **897–902**

    order for, 876–877

    overview, **865–867**

    security ID (SID), conversion to readable form, **892–897**

    threads to monitor, 443

    Windows Security API, **868–877**

Security Access Control List (SACL), 868–869

    in security descriptor, 872

Security Configuration Editor, **885–888**

security descriptors, 869, **871–872**, **874–878**, 881

    classes, 875

    functions for, 882

security ID (SID), 868

    for group, 869

    working with, 880

Security namespace, 889

Security Templates MMC snap-in, 886

Security.Permissions namespace, 875

Select Component dialog box, 336, *336*

Select() method of DataTable object, 603

    overloading, 629–630

SELECT statement (SQL)

    to populate DataSet object, **549–554**

        multiple SELECTs in one SelectCommand, 560–563

    setting Data Adapter Configuration Wizard for, 593

    storing results in DataSet object, **484–493**

        1. string for database connection details, 485–486

        2. SqlConnection object creation, 486

        3. string for SELECT statement, 486

        4. SqlCommand object for SELECT statement, 486–487

        5. CommandText property of SQLCommand object, 487

        6. SqlDataAdapter object creation, 487

        7. SelectCommand property of SqlAdapter object, 487

        8. DataSet object creation for holding results, 487

        9. opening database connection, 488

        10. Fill() method to retrieve table rows, 488

        11. closing database connection, 488–489

        12. getting DataTable object from DataSet object, 489

        13. column display in DataTable, 489–490

        procedure outline, **484–485**

        program code, 490–493

Select XML File dialog, *740*

SelectCommand property

    of DataAdapter, and CommandBuilder, 667

    of SqlDataAdapter class, 487, 541, 668

selected text, retrieving from ListBox, **352**

selecting row in Dataset, 515

SelectNodes() method, to query XML documents, 753–754

SelectSingleNode() method, to query XML documents, 753–754

self-relative security descriptor, 872

serial ports, 850

server applications, threads for, **442–444**

Server Explorer, 14, *465*

ServiceControllerStatus enumeration, 468

set methods, 181, 333

SET NOCOUNT ON command (SQL Server), **656–658**

SetEntriesInAcl function, 879

SetFileSecurity() function, 875

SetKernelObjectSecurity() function, 875

SetNamedSecurityInfo function, 882

SetNull() method, of DataRow object, 605, 642

SetParentRow() method, of DataRow object, 605

SetSecurityDescriptorDacl() function, 873

SetSecurityInfo function, 882

SetServiceObjectSecurity() function, 875

SetThreadToken function, 880

SetTokenInformation function, 880

SetUserObjectSecurity() function, 875

SetValue method, of Array class, 267

short-circuit evaluation, **53–54**

short type, 34

explicit type conversion for, 43

implicit type conversion for, 40

shortcut keys, 407–408, *409*

ShowDialog() method, of ThreadForm class, 459

ShowInTaskbar property, of form, 414

SID (security ID), 868

for group, 869

working with, 880

side effects of threads, 438

Simple API for XML (SAX), vs. DOM, **741–742**

Simple Object Access Protocol (SOAP). *See* SOAP (Simple Object Access Protocol)

single-document interface (SDI) applications, 386, **390**

example, **421–426**

single-line comments, 4, 5

site hierarchy for web applications, vs. directory hierarchy, **711–712**

sizeof operator, 52

Skip() method, of XmlTextReader class, 748

snap-ins (MMC), 852

SOAP (Simple Object Access Protocol), **801–807**

basics, **803–805**

benefits and disadvantages, **802–803**

to call WebMethod function, 782

complex messages, **805–806**

secured web services, **806–807**

Solution Explorer, 14

to allow unsafe code, *858*, 858

References node, 307, *308*

for web service, 795

sort fields, for XML document, 765–766

Sort method, of Array class, 267

SortedList class, 286, **300–303**

sorting DataRow objects

in DataTable object, **629–635**

sound

Beep() function

in C#, **847–849**

in Win32 API, 848

WAV files, 849

source files, downloading, 3

SourceBook (FMS), 512

SourceSchemaObject property, of XmlSchemaException class, 759

SourceUri property, of XsltException class, 759

spaces, removing from beginning and end of string, **91–92**

Split() method of String class, 79, **86**

Spy++ utility, 455–456, *456*

SQL Server managed provider classes, 477

SQL statements, automatic generation, **667–669**

SqlClient namespace, 513

SqlCommand class, 478, 502

CommandText property, 487

change, 563–565

multiple SELECT statements in object, 560–563

object creation to hold SELECT statement, 486–487, 658

SqlCommandBuilder class, 479–480, 667

SqlConnection class, 478

    Close() method, 488–489

    object creation for database connection, 486

    Open() method, 488

SqlDataAdapter class, 479, **540–544**

    creating object, **543–544**

    Fill() method of, 488

    FillError event of, **670–671**

    object creation, 487

    RowUpdated event, 670, **673–674**

    RowUpdating event, 670, **671–673**

    SelectCommand property of, 487

SqlDataReader class, 479

SQLException, 71

SqlParameter class, 478–479

SqlParameterCollection class, 479

SqlRowUpdatingEventArgs class, properties, 672

SqlTransaction class, 480

SqlTypes namespace, 513

SSL (Secure Sockets Layer), 806

stack, 60, **287–291**

    in memory, 197

Stack class, 286, 287

StackTrace property, of Exception object, 72

standard devices, 856

Start

    ➢ Programs

        ➢ Accessories, ➢ Command Prompt, 7

        ➢ Administrative Tools ➢ Internet Services Manager, 692

        ➢ Microsoft Visual Studio .NET, ➢ Microsoft Visual Studio, 11

        ➢ .NET Framework SDK, ➢ Overview, 17

        ➢ Administrative Tools ➢ Component Services, 699

    ➢ Settings ➢ Control Panel, 8

StartsWith() method of String class, 79, **86–87**

Startup Object setting, for MDI applications, **379–380**, *380*

startup project, setting, 457

state maintenance

    SOAP and, 801

    in web service, 774

statement block, in if statement, 57

StatementType property, of SqlRowUpdatingEventArgs class, 672

[STAThread] attribute, 379

static keyword, 5

static properties, 6

Status property, of SqlRowUpdatingEventArgs class, 672

stepping through application, 429

stored procedures

    to change database rows, **653–666**

    creating in Northwind database, **654–658**

        AddProduct4(), 654–655

        DeleteProduct(), 656

        UpdateProduct(), 655–656

    to populate DataSet object, **557–560**

    SET NOCOUNT ON command for, **656–658**

stream, for reading or writing files, 370

String class of System namespace, 36

string literals, quotation marks (") for, 35

string type, 34

string variables, **35–36**

StringBuilder object, 506

    for copy process, 524

    and performance, **534–537**

StringFormat object, 506

strings. *See also* dynamic strings

    code listing, 93–100

    concatenation operator, 51

    converting DateTime to, **127–129**

        built-in formats, **129–130**

        formatting, 127

    converting StringBuilder object to, **106**

    converting to DateTime instance, **123**

creating, **76**

default values, 160

properties and methods, **76–79**

 case conversion, **93**

 checking for equal strings, **84**

 checking start or end of string, **86–87**

 Compare() method, **81–82**

 concatenation, **83**

 copying strings, **83–84**

 finding characters, **88–89**

 finding substrings and characters, **87–88**

 formatting, **85**

 inserting substring, **89**

 joining multiple strings, **85**

 left-alignment, **91**

 Length property to read characters, **80–81**

 listing, 93–100

 removing characters, **89–90**

 replacing characters, **90**

 retrieving substrings, **92–93**

 right-alignment, **90–91**

 splitting strings, **86**

 trimming start and end, **91–92**

 removing from memory, 197

strongly typed DataSet class

 creating, **585–588**

 to modify data, **686–689**

 using, **589–591**

strongly typed language, C# as, **36–39**

structs, **59–61**, **208–212**

 arrays of, **272–275**

style attribute, for <textarea> control, 818

stylesheet in XSLT, 734, 765

subscribing to event, 334

Substring() method of String class, 79, **92–93**

substrings

 comparing, 82

 finding, **87–88**

inserting into string, **89**

replacing, **90**

retrieving from string, **92–93**

testing string beginning or end for, **86–87**

Subtract() method

 of DateTime object, 118, **123–124**

 of TimeSpan object, 139, **142–143**

switch statement, goto statement with, 57

symbolic constants, 28

SyncRoot property, of Array class, 267

System Alarm ACE header, 874

System Audit ACE header, 874

System Configuration Manager, 885

System namespace, 6, 313

 InvalidCastException, 44

system services

 for security setup, 888

 threads and, **441–442**

System.Array class, 266

System.Collections namespace, 284, 313

 classes in, 285–286

 Stack class, 287

System.Console class, 394

System.Convert class, 45

 in Object Browser, 46

System.Data namespace, 313, 483

System.Data.DataSet class, 476

System.DateTime struct, **110–136**

 creating instances, **110–111**

 properties and methods, **115–136**

  adding to instance, 123–124

  checking equality, 121–122

  code listing, 130–136

  comparing DateTime instances, 120

  converting string to DateTime instance, **123**

  date conversion to long and short strings, 126

  Date property, 119

  DateTime conversion to string, 127

Day property, 119

DayOfWeek property, 119–120

DayOfYear property, 120

leap year determination, **122**

Now and UtcNow properties, **119**

obtaining number of days in month, 122

overloading operators, 121

subtracting from instance, 123–124

Ticks property, 120

time conversion to long and short strings, 126

TimeOfDay property, 120

Timestamp conversion, 125

time spans, **112–115**

System.Diagnostics namespace, 313

System.Drawing namespace, 313

System.EventArgs class, 185, 670

SystemException class, 72

SystemException class of System namespace, 72

System.Globalization.Calendar class, 111

SystemInformation.HighContrast property, 409–410

System.IO namespace, 313

System.IO.Filestream class, Lock() method, 868

System.Object class, **238–245**, 310

boxing and unboxing, **243–245**

methods, 238–241

overriding methods, **241–243**

ToString method, **47**

System.Random class, 289

System.Reflection namespace, 313

System.Reflection.Emit namespace, 313

System.Security namespace, 889

System.Security.Permissions namespace, 875

System.String class, 36

System.Text namespace, 313

System.Text.RegularExpressions namespace, 313

System.Text.StringBuilder class, 100–101

code listing, 107–110

creating objects, **101–102**

maximum capacity for object, 101

properties and methods, **102–110**

appending to object, **104–105**

converting StringBuilder object to string, **106**

inserting string, **105**

removing characters, **106**

replacing characters, **106**

System.Timer namespace, 314

System.TimeSpan class, 112

System.Web namespace, 314

System.Web.Services namespace, 314

System.Web.UI namespace, 314

System.Web.UI.UserControl class, 810

System.Web.UI.WebControl class, custom control inheritance from, 831

System.Windows.Forms namespace, 314, 342

validation for, 794–795

System.XML namespace, 314, **730–741**

helper classes, 730

Schema class, **731–734**

XPath class, **731**

Xsl class, **734–740**

T

tabbed pages, for dialog-based application, 389

Table property

of DataColumn object, 607

of DataRow object, 604

TableMapping property, of SqlRowUpdatingEventArgs class, 672

TableMappings property, of SqlDataAdapter class, 541, 581

TableName property, of DataTable object, 581–582, 602

Tables property, of DataSet object, 546

TargetSite property, of Exception object, 72

Task Scheduler, to schedule testing, 507

Taskbar Tray, 414

templates
- classes as, 155
- for security setup, 886–887, *887*
- in XSLT stylesheet, 737

ternary operator, 53

testing
- Composite controls, **829**, *830*
- mobile applications, Openwave SDK for, **916–917**, *917*
- with NUnit, **507–511**, *510*
- User controls, 811

text files, source files as, 3

Text namespace, 313

<textarea> control, style attribute, 818

TextBox control
- in Composite control, *821*, 821–828
- User control to display XML file in, 812–816
  - HTML code, 817–818

TextBoxBase class, 371

Text.RegularExpressions namespace, 313

Text.StringBuilder class of System namespace, 100–101
- code listing, 107–110
- creating objects, **101–102**
  - maximum capacity for object, 101
- properties and methods, **102–110**
  - appending to object, **104–105**
  - converting StringBuilder object to string, **106**
  - inserting string, **105**
  - removing characters, **106**
  - replacing characters, **106**

third-party tools, for Visual Studio .NET, **511–512**

this keyword, **170–171**
- to access properties, 841

Thread class
- Abort() method of, 445
- events for interaction, 447–450

ThreadAbortException event, 445

ThreadException event, from worker thread, 444

ThreadForm class, ShowDialog() method of, 459

threads
- basics, **436–437**
- critical sections for, **470–472**
- in desktop application, **446–456**
  - performing worker thread test, **454–456**
  - test code creation, **451–454**
  - Thread class creation, **447–451**
- local DLL example, **456–461**
  - DLL creation, **458–459**
  - project configuration, **456–457**
  - test program creation, **459–461**
- safety, **473**
- server-based DLL example, **461–469**
  - test application creation, **464–469**
  - Windows service creation, **461–464**
- types, **444–446**
  - UI threads, **445–446**
  - worker threads, **444–445**
- uses, **437–444**
  - in applications, **439–441**
  - DLLs, **441**
  - server applications, **442–444**
  - system services, **441–442**

throwing exceptions, **68–71**

ticks, 111

Ticks property
- of DateTime object, 116, 120
- of TimeSpan class, 137, **140**

time spans, 75, **112–115**, **136–149**
- adding and subtracting, **123–124**
- creating instances, **136–137**
- measuring requirement for addition operation, 148–149
- properties and methods, **137–149**
  - code listing, 144–148

TimeOfDay property of DateTime object, 116, 120

Timer component, for animation, 345

Timer control, 437

Timer namespace, 314

timers, for desktop applications, **411**

times, **110–136**

TimeSpan class, 112, 468

timestamp of file, converting DateTime to, 125

ToBoolean method, of Convert class, 45

ToCharArray() method of String class, 79

Today property of DateTime object, 115

ToFileTime() method of DateTime object, 118, 125

ToInt16 method, 39

token-based security, 865–866, 867–868, *869*

TOKEN_ADJUST_PRIVILEGES privilege, 870

TOKEN_QUERY privilege, 870

ToLocalTime() method of DateTime object, 118

ToLongDateString() method of DateTime object, 118, 126

ToLongTimeString() method of DateTime object, 118, 126

ToLower() method of String class, 79, **93**

ToOADate() method of DateTime object, 118

ToolBarButton Collection Editor, 412, *412*

toolbars

    adding copy, cut, and paste to, 520–525

    Class View button, *324*

    Debugging, *428*

    for desktop applications, **411–413**

    enabling and disabling buttons, 525

    in Object Browser, 329–330

Toolbox

    customizing, **828–829**

    dragging and dropping control from, 827

ToolboxBitmap attribute, for control, 829

ToolboxData attribute, for control, 827–828

Tools menu (VS.NET), 15

ToShortDateString() method of DateTime object, 118, 126

ToShortTimeString() method of DateTime object, 118, 126

ToString() method, 39, **47–48**, *48*

    of DateTime object, 118, **127–129**

    of Exception object, 65, *65*, 72

of String class, 79

of StringBuilder class, 101, 103, **106**

of System.Object class, 238

    overriding, **241–243**

of TimeSpan object, 139

Total .NET XRef, 512

TotalDays property of TimeSpan class, 137, 140

TotalHours property of TimeSpan class, 137, 140

TotalMilliseconds property of TimeSpan class, 137, 140

TotalMinutes property of TimeSpan class, 137, 140

TotalSeconds property of TimeSpan class, 137, 140

ToUniversalTime() method of DateTime object, 118

ToUpper() method of String class, 79, **93**

Transaction classes, **480**

Transaction property, of Command object, 685

transactions, with DataSet class, **685–686**

transforming XML documents, **734–740**

    client-side using IE5x, 736–739

    server-side, 739–740

Trim() method of String class, 79, **91–92**

TrimEnd() method of String class, 79, **92**

TrimStart() method of String class, 79, **92**

troubleshooting compiling, method overloading, 179

try...catch...finally statements, exception handling with, **62–68**

type conversion, 37, **39–48**

    explicit, **41–44**

    implicit, **40–41**

    methods for, **45–46**

        ToString method, **47–48**, *48*

    as operator for, **44–45**

typeof operator, 52, 280–281

types, **33–39**

    C# as strongly typed language, **36–39**

    reference vs. value, 34

    string variables, **35–36**

typing, background thread for other activities during, 439

Typing Buddy, 414–421, *415*

    Timer_Tick() method, 420–421

U

UDDI (Universal Description, Discovery, and Integration), 801, **807–808**

UI (user interface) threads, 444, **445–446**

uint type, 34

    explicit type conversion for, 43

    implicit type conversion for, 40

ulong type, 34

    explicit type conversion for, 43

    implicit type conversion for, 40

unary operators, overloading, 263

unboxing, **243–245**, 267–268

unconditional breakpoint, 427

underlined characters, in menus, 407

Unicode character encoding system, 35, 76

Unique property, of DataColumn object, 607, 608, 622

UniqueConstraint class, **483**

Universal Description, Discovery, and Integration (UDDI), 801, **807–808**

unmanaged code, 846

unsafe code in C#, **857–859**

unstructured data, XML for, 771

upcasting, 251, **252–253**

Update() method

    of DataAdapter, 636 637, 642

        overloading, 643

    of SqlDataAdapter class, 542

UPDATE statement (SQL)

    and SET NOCOUNT ON command, 656–657

    WHERE clause, 639–640

UpdateCommand property

    of DataAdapter, 638–640, **659–660**

    of SqlDataAdapter class, 541

updates, threads and, 440

updates to database, failures, **679–684**

upper-level interface, .NET operating support, 851

URI (Universal Resource Identifier), for XSLT namespace schema, 737

USB devices, 850

User controls, **810–820**

    limitations, 820

    loading at runtime, **819**

    partial page caching and, **819–820**

    testing, *811*, 811, 816–817

user interface (UI) threads, 444, **445–446**

user-level access, 868

user requests on server, threads to keep separate, 442–443

user rights assignments, 887

ushort type, 34

    explicit type conversion for, 43

    implicit type conversion for, 40

using directive, 310

UtcNow property, of DateTime object, 115, **119**

utility, .NET Framework and, **852**

V

validation

    web form controls for, 792

    of XML documents, 772

value keyword, 182, 333

value, passing parameters by, **172–174**

value types, 34

    variables, 60

Values property, of FillErrorEventArgs class, 671

variables, **26–33**

    constants, 28–29

        enumeration, **29–33**

    debug windows to display, 431

    definite assignment, **27**

    local, **165**

    as objects, **243–245**

    removing from memory, 197

string, **35–36**

value-type vs. reference-type, 60

VB.NET, strongly typed option, 37

verbatim strings, 76

version-specific features in .NET operating support, 851

versioning, in derived classes, **234–237**

View menu (VS.NET), 14

    ➤ Class View, 323

    ➤ Other Windows, ➤ Object Browser, 325

virtual directories

    nesting, 711

    web.config file and, 709

Virtual Directory Creation Wizard, 692–695, *693, 694*, 711

virtual keyword, 222

virus-checking thread, 440

Visual Basic

    advantages, **863**

    Beep() function, calling, 849

    developer access to Win32 API, **861–863**

        limitations, **862–863**

Visual C++, 846

Visual Studio .NET, 3, **9–16**

    to access documentation, *20*, **20–21**

    and animated GIF files, 422

    compiling and running program, *16, 17*

    to create DataAdapter object, **591–596**

    to create DataSet object, **596–598**

    entering URL in Address Bar for Help, 392

    environment, **13–15**, *14*

    links, **11–12**

    mobile web site in, *917*

    modifying code generated by, **15–16**

    project creation, **12–13**, *13*

    Solution Explorer, 14

    starting, 11, *11*

    third-party tools for, **511–512**

    and web services, **774–776**

void keyword, 5

.vsdisco file, 796

W

WaitForStatus() method, 468

Watch window for debugging, 431

WAV files, accessing, 849

web application Properties dialog box, *697*, 698–699

web applications. *See also* XML

    configuration files, **712–714**

        changing settings programmatically, 717–718

        custom handler configuration, **719–721**

        custom sections, **714–721**

        location and lock settings, **721–725**

    running and shutting down, 700

    site hierarchy vs. directory hierarchy, **711–712**

    web.config file

        need for, **701–702**

        testing hierarchy, 704–707

    vs. websites, **692–700**

    for XML, creating example, **728–729**

Web-based desktop applications, **392–393**

web browsers, future importance, 800

web controls

    bitmaps for, 829

    Composite control, **820–829**, *830*

        adding to Toolbox, **828–829**

        testing, **829**

    Custom Server control, **830–842**

        attributes, **837–842**

    User control, **810–820**

        limitations, 820

        loading at runtime, **819**

        partial page caching and, **819–820**

        testing, 811, *811*, 816–817

web farms, 773

web forms

    changing to user control, 810–811

    transferring data between ASP.NET components and, **842–843**

    User control, to display XML file in TextBox control, 812–816

    workaround for those with same name, **704**

Web Hosting link in Visual Studio .NET, 12

Web namespace, 314

web resources, about Unicode, 35

web services, 769

    ASP.NET, 10

    building, **776–789**

        WSDL document, **783–789**

        WSDL (Web Service Description Language) file, **783**

    consuming, **789–801**

        from .NET Windows forms application, **794–798**

        cross-platform interface issues, **798–801**

        from Internet Explorer, **789–794**

    finding, **807–808**

    introduction, **770–776**

        operating across applications/platforms, **772–773**

        remote calls and XML, **770–772**

        uses, **773–774**

        Visual Studio .NET and, **774–776**

    SOAP (Simple Object Access Protocol), **801–807**

        basics, **803–805**

        benefits and disadvantages, **802–803**

        complex messages, **805–806**

        secured web services, **806–807**

Web Services Toolkit for SQL Server 2000, 496

web.config file

    need for, **701–702**

    testing hierarchy, 704–707

Web.Services namespace, 314

Web.UI namespace, 314

Web.UI.UserControl class of System namespace, 810

    custom control inheritance from, 831

well-known accounts, looking up, **892–897**

what if analysis, in Command Window, 432

What's New link in Visual Studio .NET, 12

while statements, 57

white space, 35

whitespace, removing spaces from string, 92

Win32 API, **846–856**

    Access Control Editor for security testing, 884–885

    access requirements, **852–856**

    Beep() function, 848

    C# developer access, **857–861**

        advantages, **860–861**

        effects of pointers, **859–860**

        effects of unsafe code, **857–859**

    function types

        DirectX, **852**

        hardware, **849–850**

        multimedia, **851**

        operating systems, **850–851**

        security, **850**

        utility, **852**

    security, **866–877**

    Visual Basic developer access, **861–863**

        advantages, **863**

        limitations, **862–863**

window interfaces

    Common dialogs, **368–377**

        code listing, 376–377

        Color dialog, *371*, **371–372**

        Font dialog, *372*, **372**

        Open dialog, **373–375**, *376*

        Save As dialog, **373–375**

    Edit menu implementation, **370–371**

    ListBox, **348–359**

        adding array, **349**, *350*

adding item, 348, *349*

clearing item, **354–355**

code listing, 357–359

deleting items, **355**

positioning by index, **350–351**, *351*

retrieving by index, **353**

retrieving multiple checked items, **353–354**

retrieving multiple selections, **355–356**, *356*

retrieving selected text, **352**

MDI applications, **377–383**, *384, 384.* *See also* MDI (multiple document interface) applications

displaying children, **380–381**

Startup Object setting, **379–380**, *380*

Window menu, **381–383**

menus, **359–368**, *360*

auto-generated code, **361–365**

coding by hand, 366–368

round buttons dancing, **342–348**

animating controls, **345–346**

code listing, 346–348

round button creation, **342–344**, *343*

toggling button, **344**

Window menu

in MDI applications, **381–383**

in Visual Studio .NET, 15

Windows

.NET version support, 851

security overview, **866–867**

Windows applications, **388–391**

dialog-based, **414–421**, *415*

SDI (single-document interface), **390**

example, **421–426**

using web service, **794–798**

from Visual Studio .NET, 10

Windows Management Instrumentation query, 398

class list, 402

Windows Security API, **868–877**

Windows Service project, **461–464**

validating current status, 468

Windows.Forms namespace, 314, 342

validation for, 794–795

WindowState property, of form, 414

worker threads, **444–445**

testing, **454–456**

WriteLine() method, 6

WriteXml() method of DataSet object, 548, **572–575**

overloading, 573–574

WriteXmlSchema() method, of DataSet object, 548, **575–576**

WSDL (Web Service Description Language), **783**

document, **783–789**

X

XHTML, 727, 734

XML, 496

capabilities, **730–741**

comments in, 739

importing and exporting, **529–533**

and security, 499

and web services, **770–772**

writing and reading, **572–580**

with ReadXml() method, **576–580**

with WriteXML() method, **572–575**

with WriteXmlSchema() method, **575–576**

XML documentation, **50**

XML documents

DOM vs. SAX, **741–742**

querying for data, **753–754**

read-only control to display in TextBox control, 812–816

HTML code, 817–818

reading, **741–754**

structure and data type definition, **731–734**

transforming, **734–740**
    client-side using IE5x, 736–739
    server-side, 739–740
    XmlReader classes, **742–753**
        XmlName class, **748–753**
        XmlTextReader class, **743–748**
XML namespace, 314, **730–741**
    helper classes, 730
    Schema class, **731–734**
    XPath class, **731**
    Xsl class, **734–740**
XML Notepad (Microsoft), **531–533**, *532*
XML Schema Definition Language (XSDL), 772
XML schema recommendation, 772
XML web server control, 740
XML Web Services link in Visual Studio
    .NET, 12
    for mobile web application, 915
XmlDataDocument class, **755–758**
XmlDocument class, 730, 741
XmlException classes, **759**
XMLHTTPRequest object, 790
    xmlinst.exe file for creating, 792
xmlinst.exe file, 736, 792
XmlName class, **748–753**
XmlNodeReader class, 742
XmlReader classes, **742–753**
XmlReadMode enumeration, 577
XmlSchemaException, 759
xmlspy, 533
XmlSyntaxException, 759

XmlTextReader class, 742, **743–748**
XmlValidatingReader class, 742
XmlWriteMode enumeration, 574
XPath class
    to query XML namespace classes, 753
    in System.XML namespace, **731**
XPathDocument class, **754**
XPathNavigator class, **754**
XRef (FMS), 512
XSD file, 587–588
XSDL (XML Schema Definition Language), 772
Xsl class, in System.XML namespace, **734–740**
XSL (Extensible Stylesheet Language), 734
XSLT (Extensible Stylesheet Language
    Transformation), 734
    stylesheet, 734, 765
XSLT namespace schema, URI (Universal
    Resource Identifier) for, 737
XSLT transforms
    in .NET Framework, 740
    performing programmatically, **760–767**
XsltCompileException, 759
XsltException, 759

Y

year, determining leap year, 122–123
Year property, of DateTime object, 116

Z

zero-based array, 269

ABOUT THE CONTRIBUTORS

Some of the best—and best-selling—Sybex authors have contributed chapters from their books to *C# Complete*.

Harold Davis is a software development consultant and writer, who has established a strong reputation for his clearly written introductory technical books. He is the author of the best-selling *Visual Basic 6: Visual QuickStart Guide* from Peachpit, as well as books on Linux, Delphi, and web development. He had a previous career as a professional photographer, so he is that rare combination of techie and artist.

Mike Gunderloy is an internationally recognized database developer, the author of *ADO and ADO.NET Programming*, and coauthor of *.NET E-Commerce Programming* and the best-selling *Access 2002 Developer's Handbook*, from Sybex. He has written many articles on Microsoft Programming topics.

A. Russell Jones, Ph.D., a confessed former zookeeper and professional musician, now composes computer applications. He is a consultant and the managing Web Development editor for the leading website for professional developers, www.devx.com. He is a regular contributor to Visual Studio magazine, and wrote Sybex's *Mastering Active Server Pages 3* and *Visual Basic Developer's Guide to ASP and IIS*.

John Paul Mueller is a freelance author and technical editor; he has written 53 books and 200 articles on various programming and networking topics. He has written articles for *Visual C++ Developer*, *Visual Basic Developer*, and *SQL Server Professional* magazines. He is currently the editor of the .NET electronic newsletter for Pinnacle Publishing.

Jason Price has more than 10 years' experience in the software industry. He is an MCSE, OCP, and has extensive experience with C#, .NET, and Java. He is the author of *Java Programming with Oracle SQLJ* (O'Reilly).

Mark Ridgeway is Head of Information Technology at Kyneton Secondary College in Victoria, Australia. Because of his remote location, he has had a compelling reason to dive into learning wireless technologies. He is a regular contributor to one of the leading wireless application development websites, www.anywhereyougo.com, and has also written for the developer website DevX.com.

Sharpen Your
C# PROGRAMMING SKILLS

Comprehensive Desktop References

Mastering™ Visual C#™.NET
by Jason Price
and Mike Gunderloy
ISBN: 0-7821-2911-0
$49.99

Mastering™ ASP.NET with C#™
by A. Russell Jones
ISBN: 0-7821-2989-7
$49.99

C# Wisdom from the Masters

Visual C#™.NET Developer's Handbook™
by John Paul Mueller
ISBN: 0-7821-4047-9
$59.99

Visual C#™.NET Programming
by Harold Davis
ISBN: 0-7821-4046-7
$39.99

SYBEX®
www.sybex.cor

Comprehensive Coverage of
.NET Programming

Meet the challenges of Visual Basic® .NET with books from Sybex. The authors and titles focus on the needs of corporate developers as they upgrade to .NET. Whether you're developing a database, building a dynamic website, or creating e-commerce applications, the lineup of new VB .NET books is aimed at getting you up to speed with the new tools as quickly as possible.

Mastering™ Visual Basic® .NET *By Evangelos Petroutsos* · ISBN: 0-7821-2877-7 · $49.99

Mastering™ ASP.NET with VB .NET *By A. Russell Jones* · ISBN: 0-7821-2875-0 · $49.99

Mastering™ Visual Basic® .NET Database Programming *By Evangelos Petroutsos and Asli Bilgin* · ISBN: 0-7821-2878-5 · $49.99

Mastering™ Visual C#™ .NET *By Jason Price and Mike Gunderloy* ISBN: 0-7821-2911-0 $49.99

SYBEX®

WWW.SYBEX.COM

TELL US WHAT YOU THINK!

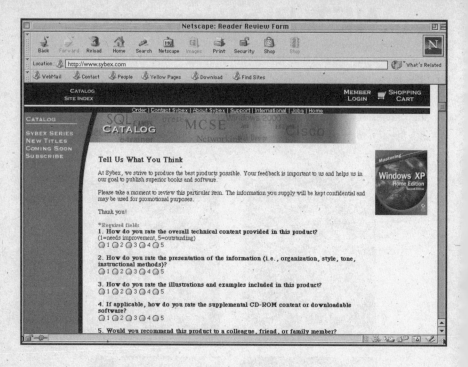

Your feedback is critical to our efforts to provide you with the best books and software on the market. Tell us what you think about the products you've purchased. It's simple:

1. Go to the Sybex website.
2. Find your book by typing the ISBN number or title into the Search field.
3. Click on the book title when it appears.
4. Click **Submit a Review.**
5. Fill out the questionnaire and comments.
6. Click **Submit.**

With your feedback, we can continue to publish the highest quality computer books and software products that today's busy IT professionals deserve.

www.sybex.com

SYBEX Inc. • 1151 Marina Village Parkway, Alameda, CA 94501 • 510-523-8233

Mastering™ Visual C#™ .NET

Jason Price, Mike Gunderloy

ISBN: 0-7821-2911-0   1,008 pages   US $49.99

Mastering Visual C# .NET is the best resource for getting everything you can out of the new C# language and the .NET Framework. You'll master C# language essentials, quickly taking advantage of the many improvements it offers over C++ and see tons of examples that show you all the ways that .NET can make your programming more efficient and your applications more powerful. You'll learn how to create stand-alone applications, as well as build Windows, web, and database applications. You'll even see how to develop web services—a technology that holds great promise for the future of distributed application.

.NET Wireless Programming

Mark Ridgeway

ISBN: 0-7821-2975-7   592 pages   US $49.99

Microsoft's .NET strategy embraces a vision for integrating diverse elements of computing technology and data services. The wireless Internet and mobile devices are core components of that strategy. Visual Studio .NET includes a powerful set of tools—the Mobile Internet Toolkit—for developing websites and applications that can be accessed from all kinds of mobile devices. *.NET Wireless Programming* provides the technical details you need to master to develop end-to-end wireless solutions based on .NET technology. You'll learn to take advantage of the Mobile Internet Toolkit's automated deployment capabilities, which enable a single site or application to work with nearly any mobile device. Work with styles and templates. Create custom controls. Read from and write to databases. And use Microsoft's Web Services in support of a distributed architecture. Five case studies, including a mobile intranet, a contacts database, and an online game, illustrate solutions to real problems and techniques for maximizing application flexibility.

MASTERING™ A1SP.NET WITH C#™
A. RUSSELL JONES

ISBN: 0-7821-2989-7   848 pages   US $49.99

In recent years, creating dynamic, server-side web applications has become the most vital part of web development. Now, thanks to ASP.NET and Visual C#, you can build cleaner, more powerful web applications, and you can do it more quickly than ever before. *Mastering ASP.NET with C#* is an essential guide to harnessing the power of the .NET Framework to develop and consume Web Services of all kinds. This book is packed with the skills you need to get started creating ASP.NET applications, including using Web Forms, connecting to databases with ADO.NET, and working with XML.

VISUAL C#™ .NET PROGRAMMING
HAROLD DAVIS

ISBN: 0-7821-4046-7   576 pages   US $39.99

The aim of *Visual C# .NET Programming* is to teach you and other experienced programmers the most effective ways to program using the C# language in the environment it was designed for, the .NET Framework. To this end, it offers plenty of strong opinions and pays special attention to one of .NET's most prominent features: web services. Right out of the chute, you'll build a simple web service and create an application that consumes it, quickly gaining a basic familiarity with the resources Microsoft has placed at your disposal. Then, with this practical introduction under your belt, you'll delve into the details of C# and its relationship with .NET—details that, by the end of the book, will enable you to tackle a wide variety of sophisticated programming challenges and accomplish many other things, as well. You'll learn how to create more effective user interfaces, first for a web service consumer and then for a traditional Windows application. You'll also get a solid grounding in the world of C# objects and classes, discovering what they make possible within the context of .NET. Then you'll explore the language itself, beginning with syntax, continuing with arrays, and concluding with the ins and outs of object-oriented programming and string manipulation.